THE SOUND OF THINGS TO COME

THE SOUND OF THINGS TO COME

AN AUDIBLE HISTORY OF THE SCIENCE FICTION FILM

• TRACE REDDELL •

University of Minnesota Press
Minneapolis
London

The University of Minnesota Press gratefully acknowledges financial support for the publication of this book from the Emergent Digital Practices program, the Department of Media, Film, and Journalism Studies, and the division of Arts, Humanities, and Social Sciences at the University of Denver.

Readers will find playlists, podcasts, and other *Sonic Science Fiction* material at https://sonicsciencefiction.com.

Material on the Vortex Concerts originally appeared in "Cyborg Ritual and Sentic Technology in the Vortex Concerts," *Sonic Acts XIII—The Poetics of Space: Spatial Explorations in Art, Science, Music, and Technology,* edited by Arie Altena and Sonic Acts (Amsterdam: Sonic Acts Press, Paradiso, 2010).

Copyright 2018 by the Regents of the University of Minnesota

All rights reserved. No part of this publication may be reproduced, stored in a retrieval system, or transmitted, in any form or by any means, electronic, mechanical, photocopying, recording, or otherwise, without the prior written permission of the publisher.

Published by the University of Minnesota Press
111 Third Avenue South, Suite 290
Minneapolis, MN 55401-2520
http://www.upress.umn.edu

The University of Minnesota is an equal-opportunity educator and employer.

Library of Congress Cataloging-in-Publication Data
Names: Reddell, Trace, author.
Title: The sound of things to come : an audible history of the science fiction film / Trace Reddell.
Description: Minneapolis : University of Minnesota Press, [2018]. | Includes bibliographical references and index. |
Identifiers: LCCN 2018001587 (print) | ISBN 978-0-8166-8312-3 (hc) | ISBN 978-0-8166-8313-0 (pb)
Subjects: LCSH: Science fiction films–History and criticism. | Sound in motion pictures.
Classification: LCC PN1995.9.S26 R435 2018 (print)| DDC 791.43/615–dc23
LC record available at https://lccn.loc.gov/2018001587

UMP LSI

I hear a new world.
Calling me . . . calling me . . . calling me.
So strange and so real,
Haunting me . . . haunting me . . . haunting me.

—Joe Meek and the Blue Men
"I Hear a New World" (1959)

CONTENTS

Introduction • New Sounds in Science Fiction • 1

1 • The Origins of Sonic Science Fiction (1924–50) • 43

2 • Ambient Novum, Alien Novum (1950–59) • 91

3 • Cosmos Philosophy and Thought Synthesizers (1959–68) • 191

4 • Sonic Alienation and Psytech at War (1971–77) • 285

5 • Sonorous Object-Oriented Ontologies (1979–89) • 361

Acknowledgments • 435

Bibliography • 437

Index • 455

• INTRODUCTION •
New Sounds in Science Fiction

ysterious and otherworldly! A tune from another world! The electrical music instrument of the future! In the final years of the 1920s, the sounds of Léon Theremin's new electronic instrument, the etherphone, prompted journalists and music critics to evoke the spacey and futuristic vocabulary of a sonic science fiction.[1] The device certainly looked futuristic. Its only visible controllers consisted of two antennae mounted on a wooden cabinet, which housed the electric components. The proximity of the performer's hands to the antennae on the right determined pitch, the one on the left amplitude. While lowering the hand toward the volume control could dampen shifts between notes for more discrete changes of pitch, the etherphone favored vibrato and sirenlike oscillations between tones rather than exact movements. The essence of its ethereal nature, the gliding electric sound set the etherphone apart from acoustic instruments even as it suggested a violin in the higher octaves, hinted at a cello in the lower, and could eerily mimic a trembling soprano voice. But never precisely. It was this fundamental difference of tonality, the wavering of electric current, that prompted early reviewers to stretch their vocabulary beyond the limits of the Earth, in flights of purple prose, as they sought to convey the instrument's unique sound on the page of newspapers and periodicals. In "Wave of a Hand Draws Music from the Air" (1928), Lawrence Gilman evokes the "mysterious

• 1

2 • INTRODUCTION

and otherworldly" voice of the electric instrument for readers of the *New York Herald Tribune*, describing "a musical quality so alembicated and enchanting, that one's imagination leaped wildly in contemplating their possibilities" (in Glinsky 2005, 78). Indeed, countless early listeners, among them popular conductor Leopold Stokowski, leapt far beyond the mundane here and now to the rarefied and refined reaches of a "cosmic resonance" as they contemplated sounds from "out of space" and speculated on the cultural impact of this new "music of the spheres" played on an instrument "of the future."[2]

Even as Theremin's apparatus evoked ideas of an ethereal cosmos of new sounds, it also pointed toward a more immediately pending era in which the invisible forces of electricity would completely transform human culture and reshape history. In this way, the etherphone sonified popular fantasies about electric fields and radio wave transmission, turning the intangible and invisible into something stylish and musical. As the etherphone preceded radio and briefly surpassed the gramophone as a sonic pastime, its early promoters thought that the device would help to modernize the home, community, and state. After a personal demonstration by Theremin in 1922, Lenin himself intended the inventor to tour the etherphone as a way of stimulating the electrification of the Soviet Union. The etherphone became more than just a novel technical extrapolation in musical instrument design; it served as a point of cultural speculation that would, over the course of a few years, move from symbolizing socialist unity to embodying new forms of capitalist investment in the convergence of popular science, emerging media, and electric home entertainment. Theremin predicted that his "invention would be in every home, like the wireless," to meet the entertainment needs of a growing class of leisure consumers in Europe and the United States (Glinsky 2005, 62–63). Five years after Lenin's private

---

1. "Mysterious and otherworldly" comes from Lawrence Gilman, "Wave of a Hand Draws Music from the Air," *New York Herald Tribune*, January 25, 1928; "A tune from another world" comes from "Magic Music Fills the Albert Hall," (London) *Daily Chronicle,* December 13, 1927; and "The electrical music instrument of the future" comes from RCA vice president Alfred N. Goldsmith, "Music Lurks in a Glass Bulb," *New York Times,* September 7, 1930. Cited in Glinsky (2005, 78, 69, 147).

2. D. K. Bradley, "Airphonic Music," *Sackbut* 10, no. 7 (February 1930), 187; Alfred Einstein, "Aetherwellen-Musik," *Dur und Moll* 6 (October 25, 1927), 5; Lemuel F. Parton, "Music to Be Created by Wave of Hand," *Oakland* (California) *Tribune,* January 20, 1928; Leopold Stokowski, "'Electric' Concerts Now Possible," *Musical Advance,* June 1929, 4. Cited in Glinsky (2005, 108, 71, 76, 111).

demo, RCA purchased the patent rights to what they simply called the theremin, and they hired the inventor to relocate to New York City to represent them. Theremin quickly morphed from an inventor-lecturer to a salesman pitching his namesake to both proper concert hall audiences and attendees of the increasingly noisy international expos and technology fairs.

As the invention of musical instruments targeted emerging consumer markets for novel electronic devices, it also accelerated a collision of aesthetic sensibilities with the emerging sound-making mechanisms that would shape popular music throughout the twentieth century. The theremin challenged presumptions about "serious music"—what constituted it, who could play it, and what role electric instrumentation might play in it. As the sounds of the theremin rippled through classical and avant-garde music alike, technological innovation became a force of musical inventiveness in its own right. But it did so by opening up divisions between the musical and the technical. Theremin introduced the etherphone as a soloist's instrument, performing the classical compositions he had learned as a young cellist—Saint-Saën's "The Swan" was a personal favorite—but he was always careful to qualify his performances as technical demonstrations presented by an engineer, not a musician. It would take a few dedicated thereminists—Clara Rockmore and Lucie Bigelow Rosen foremost among them—to introduce the device as a serious instrument and so open up new fields of virtuosity that demanded modes of performance combining traditionally revered music with novelty of sound making and a spectacle of audiovisual media production. Rockmore and Rosen, both New Yorkers who had studied with Theremin, were brilliant soloists who made a convincing case for the integration of the new electric instrument into the more conventional settings of orchestra or chamber ensemble. But new kinds of musical groups were also in the offing. By the early 1930s, Theremin had outfitted both an "Electrio" group and a Theremin Electro-Ensemble. One enthusiastic reviewer dreamed of the "titanic chorus of the electro-magnetic voices" of a whole orchestra of theremins, and although the inventor had plans for a group of forty, he settled on a more modest ensemble of sixteen, which he dubbed the Theremin Electrical Symphony Orchestra (Vuillermoz 1928). By the time this group performed in Carnegie

4 • INTRODUCTION

Hall on April 1, 1932, Theremin had significantly modified his original design, adding a keyboard with pedals and a tuning dial as well as organlike stops that could be used to emulate specific timbres on command. There was also a new fingerboard theremin, commissioned by Leopold Stokowski, which added a cellolike neck that allowed the performer to control pitch by sliding a finger along a celluloid strip. The first electric drum machine—the Russian inventor Joseph Schillinger's Rhythmicon—provided percussion for the electrical orchestra. Theremin also demonstrated a new optical device at Carnegie Hall, which used neon-filled tubes that flickered with a stroboscopic effect at a rate corresponding to a particular pitch's frequency. Theremin further modified his original device for modern dancers, resulting in the "terpsitone," an "ether wave dance stage" on which a performer's choreographed gestures controlled sound with movements of the entire body (Glinsky 2005, 143–44).

In the long run, though, few composers and fewer conductors found the theremin appealing and practical for the contemporary concert hall. By the end of the 1940s, the instrument was poised for its introduction into pop culture, first as a creepy special effect for horror and suspense radio dramas and movie soundtracks, then as a novelty device on several space-age lounge records, and finally a staple of the science fiction films of the 1950s. First heard in Kurt Neumann's *Rocketship X-M* (1950), the theremin would typify sonic science fiction for about five years. But long after the theremin had become a sonic cliché, the connection of new electric tones to tales of the ethereal and the cosmic, the alien, the otherworldly and mysterious, the menacing and unknown, persisted. By the middle of the 1950s, new electronic instruments both more stable in pitch and more familiar in method of playing had largely replaced the theremin in SF film scores. Tasked with creating unusual sounds for the SF film, composers and musicians found themselves going back to earlier generations of neglected electric keyboards and protosynthesizers such as the Ondes Martenot (1928), the Hammond Novachord (1939), the Clavioline (1947), and the ANS synthesizer (1937). With the exception of the Clavioline, these instruments had been manufactured in such small numbers and had proven quirky enough in function to have never enjoyed widespread adoption by composers and popular musicians, so they retained an ambience of the new and alien well after their initial invention. Instruments including the electric violin, the electric guitar, and the Hammond organ and other keyboards could evoke original sounds, though for years these would mimic the shimmering vibrato and glides of the theremin and would be mistaken as such. At the same time, new sound-making devices and instruments regularly appeared on a burgeoning market for electric devices, and the science fiction film would prove a routine testing ground for these sonic inventions.

The degree to which the making of new sounds for the SF film necessitates material innovation is noteworthy. The novelty of a given sound seems to depend on the development of new ways of making and processing sounds as well as on new methods of reproducing and listening to them. Music scholar Mark Brend notes that this closure of the gap between new sonic events and new sound-making methods is symptomatic of electronic music production: "The art needs an apparatus; there is a symbiotic relationship. The development of the music cannot be separated from the emergence of new technologies and the invention of new instruments and techniques" (2012, x). The sonic novelty of SF films frequently involves new electronic ways of making sound, as Brend suggests, but there are countless examples of other methods used to represent the alien, cosmic, and futuristic: cleverly modified acoustic instruments, so-called primitive or exotic devices, noninstrumental objects, transformed human voices, animal sounds, tape music, and musique concrète. Several composers for SF films have drawn on dissonant modern innovators of atonal music (the Russian composers Alexander Scriabin and Igor Stravinsky), serialism or twelve-tone music (Austrian composer Arnold Schoenberg and the Second Viennese School), and micropolyphony (Hungarian-Austrian composer György Ligeti and the Polish composer Krzysztof Penderecki).

Other pioneering work in the field has taken the form of creative sound editing and design. SF film history is replete with acts of tape music and musique concrète, including the magnetic tape manipulations with which composer Bernard Herrmann depicted "the day the earth stood still" in the 1951 film of that title; the combination of prepared instruments and recordings with which Akira Ifukube created the sounds of the monster in *Gojira* (1954); or the audio tape collages of abstract electronic tones generated by Louis and Bebe Barron for *Forbidden Planet* (1956). In the hands of the auteur filmmakers, creative sound editing fell to the directors themselves, as we hear in the strategically out-of-synch arrangements of recorded sounds in Chris Marker's *La Jetée* (1962) and Jean-Luc Godard's *Alphaville* (1965). Stanley Kubrick's use of diverse orchestral selections in *2001: A Space Odyssey* (1968) is noteworthy, as the film retained recordings from commercial album releases that the director had used while editing the film in lieu of Alexander North's original score. One of the landmarks of sound design in SF cinema is the mixture of radio chatter, public service announcements, police alerts, advertisements, Muzak, and other broadcast noise that Walter Murch created for George Lucas's first film, *THX-1138* (1971). As an incubator for the professional field of sound design, the SF film has long made the creation of diegetic soundscapes an artistic practice in its own right, as heard in films such as George Lucas's *Star Wars* (1977), Ridley Scott's *Blade Runner* (1982), and Steven Lisberger's *TRON* (1982). Each of these films assuredly mark what film sound scholar Philip Hayward calls the "new edge of accomplishment and originality for the genre" characterized by "those works that attempt to auralise the otherworldliness of outer or cyber space through the combination of music and sound design" (Hayward 2004b, 25). This otherworldliness extends into the spaces in which we view and hear films. Particularly since the late 1970s, SF films have provided research and development zones for auditory innovations that shape the aesthetic sensibilities of their audiences. By introducing noise reduction technologies, multichannel sound reproduction, theater design, loudspeaker configuration, and home entertainment media formats, SF films have profoundly changed how we listen. Whether directly or indirectly, sonic science fiction involves not only the making of sound but also the creation of the auditory experiences and expectations of film audiences.

Given how significant the role of SF cinema has been as a site of sonic innovation, it is surprisingly underexplored. The only book-length study is film scholar William Whittington's *Sound Design and Science Fiction* (2007), which contributes to our understanding of sound design as an aesthetic form in the SF film. Sound design plays an undeniably important role in meaning production and narrative as well as thematic signification. However, Whittington's book offers a highly selective and limited account of SF sound as a result of its emphasis on Hollywood films since the 1970s. This neglects not only the longer and more varied history of new sound technologies and emerging sonic sensibilities and meanings in the SF film, but also the full breadth of a cinematic form that is international in scope and independent of film industry innovations. Whittington's emphasis on the field of sound design and its reliance on emerging forms for the cinematic reproduction of sound in movie theaters overshadows the important interrelated role of instrument design and musical innovation in SF cinema, elements that throughout much of SF film history aren't yet called "sound design" and yet clearly aren't musical in any typical sense of the word. Most important, we should avoid the sense of determinism that underwrites Whittington's account of technical lineage, in which each film's sound design is treated as an advance or refinement within the entertainment industry. This has consequences for our ability to interpret and make meaning out of SF films. When Whittington tracks the ways in which new sound technologies have "reconfigured the cinematic experience" by showcasing multichannel sound systems, for instance, he fails to explore the conceptual applications and aesthetic significance beyond noting a reformulation of "the film experience into spectacle" (116). This smacks of a teleological disposition that ultimately short-circuits the audience's critical engagement with the SF film, in no small part by appropriating a visually oriented language for sonic critique. By contrast, consideration of multiple alternative histories of sound in the SF film proves crucial to our understanding of the ways in which filmmakers variously embrace, transform, and even periodically reject electronic or technological sounds as different and therefore meaningful. The popularization of new sound technologies in the science fiction film goes hand in hand with its cyclical embrace and rejection of avant-garde experiments with composition, instrumentation, performance, and cultural contextualization.

The two other edited volumes contributing specifically to a scholarship of sonic science fiction studies—Philip Hayward's *Off the Planet* (2004c) and Mathew J. Bartkowiak's *Sounds of the Future: Essays on Music in Science Fiction Film* (2010b)—focus on the musical scores and, to a lesser extent, sound design in individual films or groups of films arranged in tight historical and geographical clusters. Both of these books feature significant and informative essays from multiple disciplinary frames, including film studies, musicology, and cultural studies. While acknowledging the pioneering foundation of film sound studies that these books provide in terms of their close treatments of key films, my project ultimately claims that the overarching relevance of sound in the SF film has less to do with music per se than to our understanding of science fiction as a tool for technocultural navigation. This is the specific goal of *The Sound of Things to Come*, which discusses several complex sonic apparatuses at work across an eclectic range of films. Although offering a historically aware account of sound in science fiction cinema—through which our concept of the new is repeatedly renewed—this book does not provide a singular timeline of mounting sophistication and perfection but rather a compilation of multiple, divergent, and alternative histories of sound and technology repeatedly indicative of things strange and different. The book is also not primarily musicological in purpose but approaches sound as a mixture of cultural artifact, object, event and experience at work within SF narratives, in technologies, and in the minds and bodies of listeners. I hope that two sustained arguments regarding the nature of sonic invention will make this book valuable: first as a form of science fiction studies, which I approach through the notion of the sonic novum in order to construct audible histories of difference, and second as a media theory invested in the intersection of film sound and consciousness, which I approach through the framework of sonic psychotechnologies. In the following sections of this introduction, I define the key terms of both of these arguments and claim the necessity of their sonic turn.

NOVUMS OLD AND NEW

Science fiction studies describe the fictional novum, a concept that I apply to sound. The novum is an analogic and metaphorical device used to identify the fictive newness at the core of a SF text's narrative and thematic extrapolations. Throughout *The Sound of Things to Come*, I treat the sounds of SF films in ways that will expand the role of the novum as traditionally understood. Certainly the sonic objects of SF films are speculative constructions involved in the imaginary production of the futuristic and alien. However, science fictional sound objects are also actual, technical innovations in means, methods, and materials for creating and reproducing new sounds. I call these speculative/material hybrids sonic novums.

The novum was introduced as a science fictional trope by Darko Suvin (1979, 1988). Suvin considers the role of the fictive devices that objectify and represent newness in the narrative worlds of science fiction texts. Whether the novum is the imaginary novelty featured in a tale of invention, discovery, cosmic catastrophe, or future sociopolitical relations, it deviates from known reality to generate the fictional world. As a literary device that transposes reality through the introduction of imaginary change, the novum condenses the historical into an "analogical historicity [that] is the epistemological key logically necessary for interpreting or allotting meaning to any SF tale" (Suvin 1988, 38). As it holds up a distorted-mirror version of familiar situations, the novum provides the yardstick by which Suvin not only deems a respective SF text successful but also determines whether the work is in fact science fiction. As a formal and cognitive device that estranges its audience from present conditions, the novum must appear immanently plausible and must prove consistent with contemporary scientific epistemologies. While Suvin distinguishes the magnitude of the novum's difference from a single new gadget or device to an entirely new world, he measures the "cognitive believability of its validation" and most importantly the "degree of relevance" to its contemporary audience (1988, 77). The novum must be conceivable to such a degree that its differences register not just as a reflection but also as a critique of current historical conditions. In short, we must be prompted to imagine a world not only other than our own but also measurably better or worse.

Suvin's emphasis on logical consistency, plausibility, and scientific validation is meant to distinguish the narrative form of science fiction from tales of fantasy and the supernatural. This also seems to be an effort to legitimate science fiction as a method of deductive inquiry, a critical mode of thought, and a way of knowing the world in its own right. For Suvin, science fiction should share the hypothetical methods of experimental science and mathematics, postulating a "what if?" and then deducing from it "a universe of possibilities" (1988, 42). Once set in motion by the novum, the SF text becomes a controlled thought experiment.

10 • INTRODUCTION

Formal rules govern its methodology, while the range of "feedback oscillation between two realities" measures the scope of its cognitive consequences (37). I wish that Suvin's references to feedback and oscillation indicated that critical sonics were already at play. A cybernetic frame is more likely, however; Suvin describes the conceptual feeding back of the alternative reality, which the novum generates, into familiar reality. This feedback between virtual and actual systems allows us to perceive within SF texts their "analogy to unrealized possibilities" as well as "a parable about ourselves" (37). Science fiction's function as analogy and parable links the tropes of the genre to real-world equivalents, making the fictive novum a reflection of present conditions even as it critically represents the potential and hope for actual historical change. The measurable degree of the novum's relevance links science fiction to utopian values and situates the genre at the point where aesthetics, ethics, and politics meet extrapolation with varying intensities of plausible correspondence and authenticity. According to Suvin, the hope for a better world fires the utopian imagination, both personally and culturally, and this hope is at work in the novums of the most essential SF texts despite the evidence suggesting that science fiction may in fact have a propensity for dystopian scenarios. However, by hitching the experiment of cognitive estrangement to the utopian spectrum, Suvin's work ultimately limits the capacity of the genre's ability to suggest the radically different and unknown:

> For all its adventure, romance, science popularization or wish-fulfillment, SF can finally be written only between the utopian and the anti-utopian horizon. All imaginable intelligent life, including ours, can in the final instance only be organized more perfectly or less perfectly: there is no value-free wonder or knowledge. In that sense, utopia and anti-utopia are not only literary genres, but also horizons within which humanity and all its endeavours, including SF, is irrevocably collocated. (42)

Though invested in the forces of actual historical change, and though a believer in literature's potential to liberate the collective consciousness of humanity, Suvin constrains the concept of the novum to discussions of fictional novelty; that is, the novum analogically mirrors actual historical conditions, but it does so without participating in the forces of historical change themselves.

The dystopian turn of the novum is the defining arc of critical theorist Fredric Jameson's work. By measuring the novum according to its utopian dimensions, the trajectory of Jameson's criticism tracks the novum from its roots in the philosophy of Ernst Bloch, through its absorption by concepts of the modern, and then its suspension in the crisis state of the utopian imagination that follows modernism. In *Marxism and Form* (1972), Jameson describes the novum as that which is "utterly and unexpectedly new, the new which astonishes by its absolute and intrinsic unpredictability" (126). By *Postmodernism* (1992), Jameson asserts that modern space presents itself as a novum, "as the breakthrough onto new forms of life itself, the radically emergent, that 'air from other planets' (Stefan George) that Schoenberg . . . liked to evoke, the first telltale sign of the dawning of a new age" (163). Explicitly otherworldly, alien, and futuristic (though only implicitly sonic, given the undeveloped allusion to the cosmic final movement of Schoenberg's second string quartet of 1907), modern architecture favors an "ambiguous cultural modification" by which the novum can just as easily be read as the sign of "systematic replication as of impending change" (163). This modern novum reproduces and intensifies the logic of the system rather than engaging the forces of actual historical newness. Though operating at greater densities, the modern novum does little more than run ahead of the dominant cultural logic. Jameson turns the liberating cognitive feedback of SF's mirror of material reality into a still life, an image of a change that has not only already occurred but, merely by having already occurred, failed. This presents a crisis for the utopian imagination specifically. In *Archaeologies of the Future* (2005), the novum becomes a marker of the persistence of the utopian imagination operating in its decline and according to its own logic of systematic replication and depletion (229). With the atrophy of the "imagination of otherness and radical difference," Jameson relegates science fiction "to succeed by failure, and to serve as unwitting and even unwilling vehicles for a meditation, which, setting forth for the unknown, finds itself irrevocably mired in the all-too-familiar, and thereby becomes unexpectedly transformed into a contemplation of our own absolute limits" (289). Even the most remarkable texts become "monuments" to the "utopian vocation" that reveal our collective imprisonment by "systematic, cultural and ideological closure" (289). The closing of utopia and emptying of the novum has dire consequences for the science fiction genre, Jameson concludes, where estrangement and "the shock of otherness" reveal themselves at last to be "a mere aesthetic effect and a lie" (286). Jameson determines that science fiction can no longer be defined by "its capacity to keep the future alive, even in imagination" (288). By this account, not only is science fiction unable to access a new future, either conceptually or practically, but also its so-called futures become little more than projections of our current situation—backward shadows, moments of the past, a time of newness and renewal having already come and gone. The novum is nothing but an artifact in an archaeological dig.

Both Suvin and Jameson limit the terms of our encounter with the novum. Their insistence that it function as a historical reflection—measured by essential humanist values suspended in an existentialist crisis—culminates in a fatalistic cosmic anthropocentrism. Suvin's emphases on the integrity of SF's literary structure, the reliability of formal function, and what amounts to a twin burden of hope and logic in the face of lived history replace the desire for something new with something eternally valued. Where Suvin's novum ultimately leads to an ahistorical stalemate, Jameson's "epistemological pessimism" brings us to the utopian end game.[3] Both writers deny the fictive novum's participation in the forces of actual newness. The novum thus ends up policing SF forms from moments of self-reflexivity, ambiguity, experiment, and play for its own sake, as well as from internal critique and experiences of radical alterity.

Despite the imposition of Suvin's analogic limit and the impasse posed by Jameson's work, the novum and the cognitive estrangement that it triggers are important enough to the operations of science fiction that simply chucking the terminology entirely is not a particularly useful option. In this regard, contributions to SF studies by Istvan Csicsery-Ronay Jr., Tom Moylan, Patrick Parrinder, and Stephen Zepke are

---

3. The term comes from Freedman's (2000, 103) discussion of Stanislaw Lem's *Solaris*. Zepke (2012) associates the term with Jameson's utopian theory.

beginning to open up the novum to more critically robust functions and consequences. These writers reconsider the analogic function of science fiction and demonstrate the capacity of the novum to provide both a form for and mode of encountering futurity and alterity in their own right. For some genre theorists, the novum is the source of our engagement with science fiction's ludic, contingent, and indeterminate properties. Csicsery-Ronay argues that the most important "underlying satisfaction of the novum is not primarily critical analysis or utopian longing, but a vertiginous pleasure, more ludic than cognitive, more ecstatic than disciplinary, in accommodating new relationships under controlled and friendly conditions" (2008, 55). Conceptualizing newness as a point of contingent play, Csicsery-Ronay opens up the novum to more varied cognitive as well as affective states than the critical modes of the utopian spectrum favored by Suvin and Jameson.

Disentangling the novum "from teleological destiny-discourse, leaving any particular novum's outcome indeterminate," Csicsery-Ronay proposes a new novum that is "an open question, a problem to be solved," and which circles back on itself in order to probe "the meaning of *a given moment of newness*" (2008, 53–54). Likewise, several writers featured in Patrick Parrinder's *Learning from Other Worlds* (2001) reexamine the novum with the intent of understanding how cognitive estrangement can itself be estranged. Parrinder explains that science fiction involves an "inherently self-reflexive" process that extends to the relationship between SF theory and other modes of science fiction, so that "the experience of studying and criticism means taking up an attitude of cognitive estrangement to the cognitive estrangement found in the text" (9). In this regard, rather than analyzing the novum in ways that would resolve its estranging features in order to reveal their critical and analogic relevance to present historical conditions, SF criticism becomes a formally estranging and conceptually speculative method in its own right.

The new novum can also be chaotic, even destructive, as it suggests creative tropes antithetical to our current ideas regarding the boundaries of the Anthropocene. The novum may actually "neutralize human hopes and consciousness" altogether, as Csicsery-Ronay suggests, "by depicting their unsurpassable limits" (2008, 54). This limit significantly differs from the depletion that Jameson describes; it posits hope in some

14 • INTRODUCTION

otherwise unimaginable posthuman state. The emergence of a posthuman novum also accounts for the critical turn to the dystopian in the work of Tom Moylan and Stephen Zepke. While Moylan continues to measure the novum in terms of Suvinian sensibilities fixated on the "aesthetic/epistemological encounter with its historical conjuncture," the dystopia functions antithetically as a liberating form (2001, 66). More radically, Zepke (2012) looks to dystopian SF forms and narratives in search of "a future that has escaped its human conditions." Zepke valorizes forms of dystopian SF in which a new novum, not contingent on human epistemologies or formal methodologies, "confronts the present with the unhistorical and ontological force of becoming itself." That is, where the novum had traditionally established and regulated the limits of utopian discourse, the new novum determines the conditions for the emergence of the future and the unknown.

Foremost among the revitalizations of the novum is the shift from an emphasis on futurity to radical forms of difference. This returns us to Suvin's original definition of the novum as "a strange newness" (1979, 3), but stresses the strange over the new. Newness in this respect indicates historical time less than it does alien modes of being and alternative states of consciousness. Discarding the historical orientation of analogic novum, Zepke (2012) approaches newness in science fiction by way of Friedrich Nietzsche's concept of the untimely (that is, the Other of the historical itself), and he draws on the writings of Michel Foucault, Gilles Deleuze, and Félix Guattari to propose an "alternative future, a future undetermined by the present. This would be a future that was not simply a reflection of current modes of being, but the eruption of a becoming capable of producing something genuinely 'new.'" If science fiction is to provide sites of such alterity and become a force for radical difference, then the novum must be able to do more than oscillate between two realities. Its feedback must become generative of newness and difference. And it must do this in ways that produce ambiguity at least as often as it corresponds logically or analogically to present history in order to be validated by this correspondence. That is, challenging Suvin's evaluative criteria pushes the novum toward an engagement with its own newness, through an estrangement of its own newness, in order to generate more widely varied states of cognition, being, and becoming than analogy alone allows.

At once speculative, imaginary constructs as well as material, technical innovations, the sonic novums encountered in this book are both newer even than the conceptual fictive novums described by Csicsery-Ronay (2008) and stranger than the cinematic narrative novums that Zepke (2012) theorizes. Well before 1950, science fiction films provided a creative nexus linking practical technical innovation to a sonic aesthetic that privileges conceptual play and experimentation with the speculative and cognitive aspects of the genre. Even as early as the 1920s, the SF film played a crucial role in the unfolding histories of new instrumentalities for producing sound and technologies for processing existing sounds, and representing them to audiences in new technical formats and in changing theatrical conditions. With the advent of cinematic sound in the 1930s, the acousmatic capacities of new electronic instrument design, audio synchronization, and electroacoustic sound reproduction become an important part of science fiction cinema, and they fuel its apparent imperative to sonify technoculture. As SF film scholar Konstantin Kaminskij suggests, SF films made "electricity acoustically perceptible on the movie screen" (2013, 273), acculturating the listener to the electrified and electronic voices of both robots and computers. Ears adapted toward electronic tonalities participate within a profound, widespread popularization of musical and sonic experiences that otherwise might remain within a more insular avant-garde culture. Lisa Schmidt emphasizes the common debt that science fiction, cinema, and avant-garde music owe to the discourses of modernism. As modern forms in technoculture, written SF, cinema, and avant-garde music, occasionally together, have taken up "a grand speculation on the future of music" in which the "applications of technology" take center stage as a kind of tangible extrapolation (2010, 27). In terms of sonic newness, Schmidt meets head-on one of the most problematic limits of the novum: its inability to reflect on itself, to feed the repercussive effects of the change that it has triggered back into its own causal operations and ontological identity.

Suvin suggests that we treat the novum as a principal cause that is immune from its own effects and influence. The analogic purpose of the novum supersedes analysis of what caused the novum; the traditional novum thus knows only the language of effects, which are then fed back into itself as cause in a classic teleological move. This a priori

16 • INTRODUCTION

position shields the novum from the forces of its own newness. The novum can "be used to estrange social conditions and ideology, but not the conditions of its own operation," Csicsery-Ronay explains. He then wonders, "But what prevents the novum from altering its own mechanism" (2008, 53)? This important question puts self-reflexive, generative, and autopoietic forces into play. The new novum does more than evoke ideas of newness. It resists the normalizing forces of technoculture by defamiliarizing the role of scientific agency within its "determining myth-narrative" (53). The novum's self-reflexivity problematizes its relationship to technology and science, without which science fiction would be unable to critically reflect on the technoculture that seems to underwrite it. As we will hear repeatedly in this book, SF cinema's sonic novums defamiliarize their own myth narratives by participating in the problematic, complex, and interrelated histories of new music and noise in the twentieth century. As *New Yorker* music critic Alex Ross has characterized them, most histories of music since 1900 read as "a teleological tale, a goal-obsessed narrative full of great leaps forward and heroic battles with the philistine bourgeoisie" (2007, xviii). Key works and even specific composers are often omitted from such accounts because they move in unexpected ways, sit outside of established institutions and schools, or work within the traditions of past sonic sensibilities—frequently sensibilities that prove to have the broadest public appeal. This sets up an artificial pair of "distinct repertories," Ross writes, "one intellectual and one popular" (xviii). Not only does this pairing belie the kind of popular avant-garde of compositional experimentation and technical innovation so prominent in the history of sound in science fiction cinema, but it also promotes "the often ill-defined or imaginary border separating classical music from neighboring genres" such as jazz and rock (xvii). Rather than tracking a singular sequence of ever-mounting perfection and refinement of musical taste, along which each innovation establishes a firewall between it and what came before, Ross disperses twentieth-century music along "an unbroken continuum" of "dissimilar" sounds (xvii). Film sound theorist Michel Chion (2009) also argues against a singular, homogeneous modernism; he rather attributes the sweeping transformations of cinema after World War II to plural modernisms that resist a monolithic attribution to technologically determined causes. For Chion, these alternative modernisms are necessary to bring the development of radiophonics and cinematic sound design into dialogue with the canon of modernist musical composition. The continuum of sonic science fiction is composed of dissimilar parts that interact in nonteleological fashion, with no precise end or goal in sight, and with a high degree of contingency among its components in any given instance. Now we need to explore the capacity of electronic tonalities to construct the self-referencing noise worlds and alien sonorous objects that make up the sonic novum.

THE SONIC NOVUM

New sounds in science fiction do more than imaginatively engage audiences through film narratives. Rather, as composers, musicians, sound designers, editors, and directors take advantage of the exploratory opportunities provided by SF filmmaking, they become instrumental agents in the technical remediation of the human ear precipitated throughout modern and postmodern technoculture. Frequently borrowing from or developing in parallel to the avant-garde, the creators of sonic novums prioritize experimental transformations of the means of sound and music production and presentation through popular forms of media. Brend suggests that SF films and TV shows were the first to "smuggle" otherwise outré forms of electronic sound and music into popular culture, acting as a historical intermediary between the technical experiments of the avant-garde and the emergence of electric psychedelic rock in the 1960s (2012, ix–x). We could easily push Brend's timeline back into the 1950s, where we find the earliest forms of electronic music, space-age pop, lounge exotica, and jazz all playing in the middle ground between serious experimental music and popular idioms that new technologies made available. While science fictional motifs, images, and ideas link the histories of the experimental avant-garde and modern music with popular forms like jazz, rock, funk, and electronic music, SF films prove especially susceptible to rapid absorption by pop culture even as they retain their strangeness, giving new sounds both a safe haven, which preserves their differences from more familiar sonic experiences, and mass exposure as they proliferate throughout culture as indicators of the new and otherness. Hayward notes that the "creative space" of the science fiction genre—what he calls SF's "imaginative frame and scope"—demands sonic "representations of and reflections on the future, new technologies and/or alien worlds and life forms *within* established fictional frameworks and conventions" (2004b, 25). Despite a tendency of Hollywood films to normalize cultural values and auditory expectations, SF films provide viable sites for the introduction of unfamiliar listening experiences. Lisa Schmidt clarifies that the SF film doesn't simply popularize "some otherwise inaccessible musical style" of the avant-garde; rather, "instruments and sounds were adopted from the musical avant-garde into a popular genre and . . . *these elements remain truly avant-garde while being truly popular*" (2010, 26). The SF film is not simply a mediator of sonic activities otherwise relegated to an underground avant-garde, sneaking them into popular culture. Rather, SF cinema provides a site of avant-popular hybridity that facilitates forces of newness and difference on its own terms, while part of the appeal of such films is the unusual sonic experiences that they provide.

Science fictional sounds—or simply, sonic novums—do more than figuratively represent the new, unusual, and alien elements of narrative through new kinds of nondiegetic musical accompaniment or the strange, sonic diegetic objects, events, and creatures encountered in the imaginary world of an SF film. The sonic novum also points to the unfamiliar set of material objects, resources, and new sound-making processes and practices at the source of these sounds. The sonic novum's reliance on such a high degree of material innovation is one of its most distinct features compared to other forms of science fictional novum. That is, the development of new technologies of writing and bookmaking, and even of films (though special visual effects will prove to be another matter) plays a relatively rare role in the case of the production and presentation of novums in fictional texts and films. The sonic novum, however, oscillates rapidly between speculation about technology and formal experimentation and innovation with technology, so much so that it is almost impossible to separate the two. In this way, the unusual tonalities of sonic science fiction are often literally, rather than figuratively, a novum in the sense that Csicsery-Ronay defines it—that is, "the result of an invention or discovery, whose unexpected appearance elicits a wholesale change in the perception of reality" (2008, 6). Sonic extrapolation and speculation work very close to material resources, typically tugging those materials into the domain of speculative play through new instrument design and manufacture. Sonic novums are material forces of newness in their own right.

Each sonic novum is distinguished by its own characteristic "thingness." Throughout this book, the thingness of the sonic novum takes shape at the point of converging sonic, machinic, technical, organic, acoustic, and imaginary materials. Straddling the material and imaginary domains of speculation, the sonic novum corresponds in significant ways to the sonorous object theorized and realized through French radio engineer Pierre Schaeffer's experiments in musique concrète beginning in the 1940s. As a producer of new sounds, Schaeffer pioneered many of the techniques that would inform the field of cinematic sound design and experimental composition for SF films: reversing the direction of recordings, altering their playback speed and pitch, looping brief sounds, and manipulating the attack and decay of sounds. The sonorous object that Schaeffer describes sits somewhere among three components: the devices, processes, and procedures that captured and created the recorded object; the sound media, distinct from the original source material, that presents the audio to the listener; and the body and mind of the listening subject. A successful combination of these three resulted in a musique concrète reducible neither to the particular recorded source that produced it (a piano, a spinning top, or a train, for instance) nor to the form and method of its reproduction and presentation to a listener (for example, on magnetic tape played over loudspeakers). The challenges that the production of musique concrète presented for Schaeffer revolved around issues of sonic representation, making them highly relevant to the search for alien sounds that concerns us here.

Four characteristics identified by Schaeffer in his *Treatise on Musical Objects* (2017) essentially obstruct sonic representation and so define the emergence of the sonorous object under acousmatic conditions, which prevent our ability to recognize sound through "the identification of sound sources" (66). "Pure listening," Schaeffer defines, "takes place without the help of sight" (66). He continues:

20 • INTRODUCTION

> Often taken by surprise, sometimes uncertain, we discover that much of what we thought we could hear was in reality merely seen, and explained, by the context. This is why it is just about possible to confuse some sounds produced by instruments as different as strings and woodwind. (66)

Of course, cinema does not screen sound in the way that Schaeffer has in mind—his sonorous objects are quintessentially radiophonic in nature—but it can achieve a similar "dissociation of sight and hearing [that] encourages another way of listening" (66). The cinema could be described as an acousmatic space and experience as a result of its reliance on content played back from a recorded film or digital source over loudspeakers, and with the particular sound sources unseen. Sound presented in this way either attaches to a specific diegetic image, or it remains unattached to images—nondiegetically in the case of the musical score, or due to its diegetic source being located off the screen. In science fiction and horror films in particular, sound often hides behind and around the screen until it is called forth to attach itself to something particular in the flow of images and so emerges in the visible world of the film, which it had existed in previously as an off-screen sonorous object. Further, cinema exploits the acousmatic principles of the sonorous object as filmmakers take advantage of sound's ability to frame and direct perception, often whether we want it to or not. Sound, not solely in the case of nondiegetic music, gives the cinematic image its pace, its emotional pitch, and its rhythm, and it is generally responsible for temporalizing the film viewing experience, even as we tend not to actively think about the instrumental sources of those sounds, nor actively seek to attach them to visible sources on the screen.

The remaining three conditions that Schaeffer outlines also prove relevant to a consideration of the sonic novum in the SF film: "listening to effects," "variations in listening," and "variations in the signal." When instrumental causes of a sound object are hidden, and we "attend to the objects in their own right," attention shifts away from sound sources and toward "the physical symbol made possible by recording." This emphasis on sonic "effects" is in fact an emphasis on a new kind of cause, the sonorous object working on our perception "as a concept worth studying." The pair of variations that Schaeffer introduces bring the subjectivity of the listener to bear on the process, the first suggesting that even when we listen to a sound repeatedly "under physically identical conditions," "different perspectives or ways of hearing," whether "deliberate or unconscious," emerge to "reveal a new aspect of the object." The last variation points to the essential processes of musique concrète, our ability to "operate on sound" by controlling and altering "the physical signal fixed on the record or the tape." Myriad "divergent sound effects" can thus be rendered "from one material cause," each one its own sonorous object (66).

Schaeffer will go on to outline four additional observations concerning what the sound object is not; the alien thing, it may turn out, can only be experienced in negative. The sonorous object is not the source that made it, whether this is a violin or a creaking door. The sonorous object is not the magnetic tape, "a *sound medium* or an *acoustic signal*." An auditory difference underwrites Schaeffer's observation here: "Listened to by a dog, a child, a Martian, or a citizen of another musical civilization, this signal takes on different meanings." Similarly, the sound object is not singular. If a signal or tape is varied, these "manipulations . . . did not change *a* sound object with its own intrinsic existence. They *created others*." For all the talk of effects, each sound object is in fact causally generative according to variations detected by a single listener and among multiple listeners, and due to variations of the signal or recorded object. Finally, Schaeffer is wary of putting too much emphasis on the subjective, clarifying that "*the sound object is not a state of mind*." Encountering a sound object is not such an individual experience that its characteristics and features are "incommunicable, and practically ungraspable" (67). Schaeffer concludes by noting a telling ambiguity: the sonorous object, and likewise what I am calling the sonic novum, is an "objectivity bound to subjectivity" (69). This ambiguity "will surprise us only if we persist in seeing 'the workings of the mind' and 'external realities' as opposites" (68).

As a movie screen replaces the screen of Pythagoras that Schaeffer describes (64), unusual sounds produced and reproduced under acousmatic conditions prove highly susceptible to the visual magnetism, redirection, and misattributions typical of cinematic experience. In the context of the SF film, the countless strange objects, characters, places, and events are ideally receptive to the aura of the unusual that new sounds bring to them. Moreover, many of the sonic novums of SF cinema spring from mystery technologies, black box instruments first encountered in the austere minimalism of the theremin. Sonically, when listeners first encountered the theremin, they could not help but mistake it for something like a violin, or a cello, or a soprano voice, as it hovered somewhere between all three, not quick mimicking them, and yet not possessing its own distinct sound in the mind of the listener, who had to settle for a language of the alien, the ethereal, the otherworldly, or the futuristic. Highly technical interfaces act as acousmatic shields in their own right by removing traditional instrumental gestures from the making of music and sound. The processes of mixing and manipulating sounds recorded to magnetic tape or other forms of recording media further obfuscate the means of sonic production from traditional sound-making gestures. I sometimes use the term "technoacousmatic" to emphasize the complicated interplay of real and imaginary technological screens involved in the creation and presentation of the sonic novum. The product of at least a double screening, the sonic novum can therefore be said to splice speculative sonorous objects to both the unfamiliar devices responsible for making new sounds in material reality as well as the unfamiliar things making new sounds in the fictional world of the film.

To the extent that nonhuman sounds are inherent to both electronic instruments and the tonal range they make available, musique concrète and tape music also inform the emergence of the sonic novum as the science fiction film develops along concurrent trajectories with the sound experiments of the postwar avant-garde. There were two major schools of thought and practice: the *elektronische Musik* studios of the national broadcaster, Westdeutscher Rundfunk (WDR) in Cologne, Germany, and the Groupe de Recherche de Musique Concrète (GRMC) at the French Radio Institution in Paris (see Holmes 2016, 48–79). Both studios were founded in 1951. The former housed the work of composers Werner Meyer-Eppler, Robert Beyer, and the studio's first director, Herbert Eimert. They were joined in 1953 by Karlheinz Stockhausen and later other members of a generation of classically trained composers beginning to integrate, and ready to advance beyond, the influence of post-romantic, twelve-tone serialism and abstraction by means of electronic sound generation. The GRMC was founded by Pierre Schaeffer and was the site of his experiments in musique concrète and radiophonics. After World War II, the science fiction film became the most important zone of sonic production in popular culture to combine the practical and theoretical innovations of both branches of the avant-garde, resolving critical and aesthetic biases that otherwise pit Schaeffer's allegedly primitive and untrained musique concrète (his detractors liked to point out that he wasn't a trained musician but rather a radio engineer and technician) against the putatively purer forms of abstract electronic music coming out of the WDR studios. A number of conceptual and practical issues could be differentiated here, but it is ultimately the common concerns among composers of *elektronische Musik* and makers of musique concrète that concern me. Investigations into the formal properties of sound, interest in how and what sounds signify, and the need (or not) to determine and control sounds all strike me as relevant to a discussion of the sonic novum. Given the demand for new sound experiences in the SF film, perceptual distinctions between electronic music and musique concrète were dissolved for the listener just as they had been for the film's producers and composers, who eagerly chased new sounds by any means necessary.

As a form of sonorous object, the sonic novum involves formal innovation in the means, methods, and materials for creating and reproducing new sounds. It also requires mechanisms for channeling the imaginary contributions of the subjective listener experiencing the new sound in the unique kind of acousmatic setting that the movie theater provides. Sound's ability to change how we see by shaping the spaces in which we hear triggers new affective postures and embodiments within the soundscape of the cinema, generating original modes of auditory subjectivity bound to equally new forms of sonorous objectivity. The technoacousmatic nature of the movie theater involves something more than simply hearing musical accompaniment; it turns the cinema into a space for the electroacoustic presentation and reception of sounds that can exist only as recorded media. Where both the conceptual and material spaces of SF films rely on new production techniques, the reproduction of sound proves equally important, for it helps map out what happens to the embodied listening subject during encounters with the alien sonic novum. The science fiction film, I claim, develops specifically

24 • INTRODUCTION

in order to mediate the transformation of the ear and listening body given the changing technocultural conditions of emerging acoustic ecologies in the twentieth century.

PSYCHOTECHNOLOGY AND CINEMATIC CONSCIOUSNESS

One of the most intriguing ways in which science fiction cinema reinforces the sonorous object's ambiguous blending of the subjective, psychological workings of the mind and the objective materials of external reality is through the development of intermediary psychotechnologies, which I call sonic psytech. Here I point film studies toward a sonically oriented analysis of mediated consciousness in SF films. But first I should establish the origins of the term and make a case for its ongoing relevance. The concept of psychotechnology comes from the pioneering theory of psychologist Hugo Münsterberg, whose professional surveys of the early film industry, as well as his personal experiences as a film viewer, prompted him to publish the first book of film theory, *The Photoplay: A Psychological Study* (1916). Münsterberg's approach to film was rooted in his groundbreaking work in applied psychology for industrial efficiency, *Grundzüge der Psychotechnic* (Basics of psychotechnology, 1914), which addresses matters of mental monotony, fatigue, and attention in the workplace, outlining an interconnected dynamic between the mind and environment. Münsterberg's work maps the technical mechanisms of film not only along aesthetic registers but also in terms of psychological resonances. He describes a "general principle" of film utterly different from staged drama, one that controls "the relation between the mental mechanism and the pictures on the screen" ([1916] 2002b, 110). His analysis links subjective perception to the technologies of the motion picture camera, drilling down to specific cognitive functions and their corresponding technological subroutines. Attention, memory, imagination, and emotion map onto specific visual techniques of the close-up, the flashback, the dream sequence, and the special visual effect.

Variations of cinematic psychotechnologies echo throughout the history of film theory. Béla Balázs, for instance, describes a cinema of visual technique in which the psyche is encountered in the mechanisms that transform images rather than in the images themselves. "Our psychic apparatus," Balázs concludes in *Der Geist des Films* (The spirit of film, 1930), "reveals itself in these transformations. If fading, distorting, or copying could be executed without any specific image, that is, if the technique could be divorced from any particular object, then this 'technique as such' would represent the mind as such" (in Kittler 1999, 120). Deleuze also takes a psychotechnological approach to film: "The film does not record the filmic process . . . without projecting a cerebral process. A flickering brain, which relinks or creates loops—this is cinema" (1989, 215). In the latter half of the 1980s, media theorist Friedrich Kittler updated the term for post-McLuhan media studies, more broadly discussing the relay between "psychology and media technology under the pretext that each psychic apparatus is also a technological one, and vice versa" (1999, 160). When cataloging the decline of literary discourse in the wake of new communication and data storage media, Kittler explores not only film but also the gramophone and typewriter as forms of a complex "psychic apparatus" by which modernity in general, and the psychoanalytic field more particularly, have constituted human subjectivity in terms of information technologies (166). As he distributes media hybridization across data storage formats, Kittler devises an early type of convergence theory: "Media-technological differentiations opened up the possibility for media links. After the storage capacities for optics, acoustics, and writing had been separated, mechanized, and extensively utilized, their distinct data flows could also be reunited" by computation (170). Though Kittler's emphasis on digitization precludes analog film sound, the complex and multimodal psychotechnologies of science fiction cinema have in fact fostered conceptual and material linkages across visual, sonic, and narrative domains since the release of Fritz Lang's *Metropolis* (1927). From the start, the SF film provides a site of media hybridization of formal novum, which includes sound, and opens up new modes of sonic psychotechnology.

More contemporary studies nudge cinematic psychotechnology in the direction of the "cosmic consciousness" first described in Deleuze's cinema books. Deleuze suggests that the screen itself is a site of cosmic psychotechnology where "the internal sheets of memory and the external layers of reality will be mixed up, extended, short-circuited and will form a moving life, which is at once that of the cosmos and of the brain" (1989, 209). This vulnerable space proves susceptible to the manufactured collective gaze of cinematic spectacle and, by sonic extension, collective consciousness. Patricia Pisters discovers in Deleuze's work on cinema "a whole psycho-mechanics" of a cosmic cinema, which she further casts in the somewhat ominous language of "a spiritual automaton that can indicate the highest exercise of thought, but can also become possessed of automization of the masses" (2006, 133). A pathway between microcosm and macrocosm zigzags "from cosmos to earth (and back)," an image Pisters borrows from Deleuze. Though Pisters follows Deleuze's lead by sticking to a discussion of the image and not sound, her twinned "automizations" evoke the power of cinematic sound to work outside the limits of the visual field and impose itself beyond the conscious control and active participation of the auditor-viewer.

Pia Tikka works along similar lines, arguing that as cinema externalizes consciousness, it exposes the mind's "functional structures in its productive procedures" (2006, 140). The mechanisms by which inner and outer experience switch places ultimately disconnect consciousness from the familiar world and replace it with a "mirroring interaction between the brain and the cinematic representation" (140). For Tikka, cinematic consciousness is characterized by "recursive loops of cognition and perception" that take a narcotizing turn toward immersion: "By definition, cinema is about authored moving image representations that provoke in the viewer an experience of immersion—a conscious state that relates the emotive-cognitive experiences of the viewer to the stream of events of the film in such a manner that she momentarily can be claimed *not* to be fully conscious about the other events around her" (141). Both Pisters and Tikka conjure the possibilities of automization, distraction, redirection, disconnection, and narcotization. While such cinema seems to resolve the "brain–body–world division" and thereby entangle "both neurobiological and techno-cultural domains" (Tikka 2006, 145), it also radically immerses human subjects within a cosmic cinematic enclosure, rendering them incapable of critical reflection and engagement. By this account, cinematic consciousness is a contraction of the mind, "a 'miniature' consciousness" that reveals itself through framing structures and streaming events shared between mind and projector (141). This contraction involves a rewiring of sense ratios within the mediating environment of the cinema, and it includes the typical affective codes and postures of viewing: decreased physical movement, enhanced visual and sonic stimulation, and disassociated or desensitized experiences of touch, smell, and taste. These contractions of the bodily senses and consciousness into localized and automatic forms through cinematic immersion paint a picture of cinematic psytech at its most passive and uncritical. This can be particularly deleterious in the context of the SF film, with its propensity for flights of fancy into the cosmic beyond, its escape to other worlds, and its technological wish fulfillments. While neither Pisters nor Tikka, nor Deleuze's own cinema theory for that matter, discuss sound, undoubtedly cinematic music and sound design have a capacity for immersion that exceeds the screen, literally surrounding us in the space of the theater—a space that frequently takes an explicitly cosmic turn in SF films. It is to this sonic dimension that we now turn.

Throughout *The Sound of Things to Come*, there will be a noticeable tension between those cinematic devices that favor immersion and those that mobilize us and help us to navigate technoacousmatic spaces by expediting methodologies of critical listening. We must reexamine the nature of newness and the role of estrangement in science fiction, particularly as sonic tropes can help us recast SF genre theory in ways that better facilitate our encounters with the utterly unexpected and the otherwise unknown. As Csicsery-Ronay (2008, 11–12) anticipates, a turn toward the study of science fictional music and sound promises not only a means of better comprehending the genre as a narrative form, and of interpreting its stories and understanding how they respond to and affect culture and the human condition; it also activates SF's function as a critical apparatus. In this respect, the sonic novum will prove to resonate with another key aspect of the SF film, the special visual effect, such as those described by Scott Bukatman in his study of *Blade Runner* (1997). According to Bukatman, the special effect provides a "*space of accommodation* to an intensely technological existence," with moments of spectacle on the screen often pointing beyond diegetic spaces altogether and toward the spaces of their original production in special effects workshops or at computer graphics stations (8). Not only the narratives of SF film but also, and all the more so, special visual effects and image processing open up a conceptual space in which "the shock

28 • INTRODUCTION

of the new is aestheticised and examined" (8). A similar awareness of the relation between what we hear in a film and the special places and practices involved in sound production will prove essential to the critical examination of the sonic novum and the psychotechnological entanglement that it affords.

The privileged role of sound design in genre films, like that of special visual effects, poses a unique pitfall for theorists and fans alike, who may tend to confuse what Whittington calls an intellectual "mastery over the material means of its manufacture" with critical reflections on the same (2007, 7). Since the mid-1970s, popular media surrounding the SF, fantasy, and horror film industries consistently combine discussion of the building of new worlds and convincing narrative events with high-profile expositions of the industry's technical "secrets" behind the making of those highly illusory worlds. The expositional content of pop culture magazines like *Starlog, Cinemagic, SPFx,* and *Cinescape,* and later the special features routinely included on DVDs, Blu-ray discs, and the Web, fosters a kind of technological appreciation and even sophistication. But substituting technical insight for critical engagement is one way that a spectacular medium keeps its audiences immersed not only in its end products but also in their manufacture. It does so by dispelling precisely those states of ambiguity and wonder that Whittington and other SF scholars valorize. And it does so at the expense of thematic analysis and critical evaluation. Faced with this quite complex situation, Whittington's discussion of sound stalls as he makes unresolved and contradictory statements about artifice and the sonic spectacle. He acknowledges that cinematic artifice is "a construction to create speculation, hesitation, and doubt. Science fiction ideology thrives on this artifice and a self-reflexive awareness of it by filmgoers, and multichannel sound has contributed significantly to this project in cinema, offering us sonic spectacle that fuses wonder, speculation, and belief" (120). As Csicsery-Ronay (2010) has noted, however, Whittington never actually explains how SF films combine critical self-reflection and doubt with wonder and belief. This is a particularly significant shortcoming because sound in cinema is imposed on us and works its effects on us whether we want it to or not. Further, the entangled relationship between novel sonic content—the sonic imaginary, if you will—and the material innovation of tools that create sounds in studios, as well as of the technologies that reproduce them in state-of-the-art theaters, makes it far too easy for sound to simply contribute to "the hegemony of immersive spectacle" (Csicsery-Ronay 2010) at the expense of the genre's dependence on cognitive estrangement and difference as a means for critical engagement. This is where a more potent SF film sound theory must step up.

As SF cinema creates zones for encountering new sounds and experiencing new auditory technologies, it extends the forces of sonic experiment, innovation, and change to listening bodies. Sound brings with it potential for a critically engaged science fiction cinema that embraces theorization by causing us to listen to listening itself. But sound also threatens to mystify and control the spectators of film. It does so precisely at the point of sonic psytech entanglement. Csicsery-Ronay (2010) describes how SF film creators and sound designers "exploit the psychology of sonic perception to create their worlds, which means that the range of suggested dimensions expands far outside the focal limits of vision and the screen." Because hearing is both more vague and subtler than sight, "the possibilities for entraining the audience to the rhythm of the screen action are increased exponentially. With new sound techniques, today's films can deliver deeper intimacies and more immersive spectacles than classical cinema." At stake here is the possibility, most notable in the case of contemporary film industry productions, that cinema's "unique and powerful soundscapes . . . will make willing audiences accept any image without resistance." Sound thus becomes part of the control mechanisms of immersive spectacle. "It is an axiom of theoretical work on SF film as a distinct medium (distinct both from other kinds of film and from SF in other media)," Csicsery-Ronay concludes, "that the field is a laboratory for new technologies of consciousness-manipulation, as well as for expressing cultural ambivalence about them" (2010). Because the new sonic and auditory experiences of science fiction cinema challenge the primacy of the visual even while borrowing from the playbook of the spectacle, critical audiences must be cognizant of those techniques of production that would circumvent our capacity for doubt and ambiguity as well as for self-reflexivity and critical engagement.

The collusion of visual spectacle and immersive sound in the SF

30 • INTRODUCTION

film threatens to short-circuit those imaginative faculties that make science fiction both a useful tool for cognitive estrangement and a vehicle for encounters with radical difference. Clearly, we need a model of psychotechnological film studies that acknowledges cinema's ability to transform consciousness in ways that engage rather than preclude the critical faculties. Anna Powell (2007) provides a good model of this that pushes the encounter with alterity to the fore of cinematic experience. Powell's discussion ranges from experimental and independent films to mainstream popular cinema, which, "aided by effects technology, has expanded its parameters to include lavish spectacles of alterity. Even in conventional narratives, ecstatic and visionary sequences engineer audience participation" (12–13). Documenting a range of "affective forces" that go well beyond the entrancing disembodiments and narcotizing contractions theorized by Pisters (2006) and Tikka (2006) into more expansive forms, Powell argues for a cinema of "encounter" (2007, 3).

Though not drawing explicitly on Münsterberg's theory, Powell (2007) theorizes a cinema of altered states that broadly magnifies the scope of the relationship between film production technologies and the varying perceptual and cognitive behaviors to which they correspond. By designing a taxonomy of psytech subroutines of unusual, extreme, and rarefied correlatives between cinematic effect and unusual psychological and affective states, Powell classifies the different modes of altered states cinema: depiction of dreams, hallucinations, pharmacological states, death, trances, and ecstasies. She then categorically outlines specific cinematic techniques that work to derange the senses and thereby estrange the mind within cinematic moments that simultaneously exceed and epitomize the context of their given narratives. Treating the experience of film itself as a form of altered state pushes forward a language of "stimulus" (3) and "triggers" (4) that retrieves a consideration of causes within a field dominated by effects even as it makes an invaluable general turn toward affect. Powell explains,

> Unlike perception, which seeks to identify and quantify external stimuli, affection is qualitative, acting by the intensive vibration of a "motor tendency on a sensible nerve" (Bergson, *Matter and Memory*). Rather than being "geographically" located, affect surges in the center

of indetermination. Its pre-subjective processes engage a kind of auto-contemplation that participates in the wider flux of forces moving in duration. (2)

Powell suggests that a kind of psytech engineering is at work in film, vastly extending the scope of cinema's neurological, psychological, and philosophical registers. However, her work is also disappointingly silent beyond the description of a cinematic encounter working at the vibratory intersection of material and imaginal forces. This relatively common submerging of auditory phenomenologies within a visually dominant language demonstrates precisely the need for an explicitly sonic turn in film and media theory.

SONIC PSYCHOTECHNOLOGIES

While the contemporary turn toward the cosmic and the altered state in psychotechnological film theory may inform our understanding of the operations of cinematic affect, embodiment, and phenomenology, it fails to address sound. Therefore, the search for critical models that will open up the psytech dimension of cinematic sound necessitates consideration of scholarship concerned with the new modes of listening that experimental and electronic music introduce, entrain, and critically empower. Much of this work is explicitly framed as a recuperation of the sonic against the visual bias of film and media theory. Salomé Voegelin argues that listening entails both "actual practice" and a "conceptual sensibility," which lends to the ear a capacity for engaging the kind of "philosophical problems around subjectivity and objectivity" that are too often reserved for visual arts, with representation and signification foremost among them (2010, xiii). Voegelin pushes critical listening beyond "interpretive fantasies" and instead connects "the experience of sound with the notion of virtuality and possible worlds that are not linked to the logic and rational of a visual reality but augment that reality through the blind sight of sound within its depth" (xiii–xiv). Here, Voegelin's language already inhabits territories and explores phenomena familiar to science fiction—the virtual and possible worlds—and it does so in a way amenable to the particular needs of an audience critically engaged with the act of listening. That is, it concentrates on "sound as its 'object' of investigation" while speculating on "new ways to consider art, the world and our position within the production of art and the world through a sonic sensibility" (xiv). Electronic sound has a unique capacity for critical engagement, concludes Joanna Demers (2010). Electric technologies can produce sounds that are musically familiar or comparable to nonmusical sounds and noises from daily life. Something wilder is possible: the discovery of a sound that no one has heard before, not even the producer of the sound. Because of the expansive breadth of available timbre, electronic sound resists identification and so estranges our ears, drawing us deep into the workings of sonic psytech. "All electronic music is a meditation on the act of listening to sounds both old and new," Demers notes, and "therefore a meditation on the cognitive processes that accompany listening" (22). There could not be a clearer evocation of sonic psytech. In the SF film, critical listening to electronic sound is explicitly self-reflective while also a moment of cognitive estrangement. With the convergence of electronic sound and estranged listening, sonic psytech becomes its most cosmic.

Though no prior critical projects have made explicit the psytech imbrication that I detect within the alien sonorous objects of SF cinema, some efforts suggest that a psychotechnological study of SF film sounds is necessary. The keenest is that of Rebecca Leydon, who argues that by the middle of the 1950s, electronic sound in particular had already become a conventional "index for both Outer Space and intra-psychic space" (2004a, 61). Leydon attributes electronic sound's twofold indexical qualities to the unique listening situation presented by such sounds within cinematic contexts, where the "signifying potential" of music is greatly determined by its association with SF film imagery and narrative (61). Rooted in a theory of musical semiotics, Leydon's work prioritizes the relationship between the meaningfulness of sounds and our sense of (or at least our ability to imagine) the source that would make a particular sound, both in reality and as presented in the film world. Identifying sources accurately turns out to be less important than understanding the ways in which sonic psytech activate technocultural subroutines that open up what Leydon calls the "intangible spaces, both extraterrestrial and psychological" (64) of SF cinema. The sonorous objects heard in science fiction films require an extrapolative methodology bolstered by a taxonomic approach to sonic novums that will account for: the technocultural means of producing, processing, and reproducing sound; the specific sonic aspects of SF themes, characterization, narrative, and world building; the varieties of auditory phenomena; and the range of sound's psychological and affective resonances.

Given the absence of a general theory of sound in science fiction cinema, I have pulled together an admittedly far-out collection of resources drawn from discussions of sound in the philosophy of Gilles Deleuze and Félix Guattari, particularly their work on cosmos philosophy and thought synthesizers, as well as their work on the refrain, a way of thinking about sonic territorialization. From Guattari's solo work, I have found that his insights into subjectivity, particularly its polyphonic and hence sonic qualities, as well as the machinic unconscious facilitate working further into this intersection of thought synthesis and the explicitly sonic dimensions of the cognitive apparatus. While study of Deleuze's work on cinema has also proven useful on occasion, particularly in terms of scoping out the cosmic dimensions of film in ways that update Münsterberg's psychotechnology, I have pushed to its limits his concept of the virtual image, which I consider to be the sonorous object of cinema. Some more recent theoretical work also informs the project. This includes elements of new and post–media theory that emphasize the processes, over the objects, of mediation, including Frances Dyson's history of sonic embodiment and immersion, as well as the vital process orientation of Sarah Kember and Joanna Zylinska. At the same time, given the ongoing relevance of Schaeffer's sonorous object to my work, I draw on object-oriented ontology, particularly the complex hyperobject theory of Timothy Morton along with Ian Bogost's work on alien phenomenology, to consider how sound objects withdraw from us and can never be completely explained by our subjective experiences of them. Finally, the postcinematic and sonic affect theories of Steven Shaviro and Steve Goodman shift attention to the precognitive impact that sounds have on listening bodies. Readers should note that rather than a comprehensive introduction to any of these philosophers and their works, I adapt and adopt them in a way that may once have been described in terms of bricolage, or which others might call a tool kit,

34 • INTRODUCTION

but which I prefer to think of in terms of the modular components of my own thought synthesizer as it modulates its way toward the cosmic sounds of the science fiction film.

The demands of the SF film for new, alien, and otherworldly sounds make the genre an ideal platform for musicians, engineers, and designers to explore sound technologies in new ways. It facilitates a speculative encounter for those who seek to discover new sounds through their own practice as creators as much as express themselves (whether ideas or feelings) through existing vocabularies of sound. These sound makers thus engage the tools for musical creation at the far limits of accepted function, tonality, and process. Consequently, the music and sound designs of science fiction cinema have cultivated new aesthetic programs based on emerging sound technologies as well as new ways to perceive and be in the cosmos. Cosmic music has historically provided the more esoteric trail to planetary science and astronomy. The classic Pythagorean music of the spheres always had an element of inner harmony associated with it, whether the Platonic complementarity among the twin sciences of the eye (astronomy) and the ear (music), or Kepler's celestial mechanics, in which the spiritual and metaphysical harmonics of sacred geometry play out in both astronomical and astrological registers. The earliest and most fully developed ideas of the sonic cosmos are found in Indian classical music, where instrumental voices at once invoke, embody, and represent a universe explicitly recognized as sonic vibrations. Buddhism also articulates a vibration-based cosmology that, like Hindu and Western hermetic models, conjoins an outer cosmos and the interior spaces of mind, consciousness, spirit, or psyche. With modernity, our sonic cosmologies of outer and inner space have become increasingly technologized and entangled in self-reflexive ways and to the extent that cosmic music comes to represent a technological exploration of new modes of consciousness and being. We hear this in everything from works by the German composer Karlheinz Stockhausen or Ligeti to the space jazz of Sun Ra and his Arkestra, the psychedelic space rock of Pink Floyd and Hawkwind, the Afrofuturist glitch-hop of Flying Lotus, and countless New Age musicians and producers of techno and electronic dance music. Just as radio astronomy makes the universe audible by means of various technical instruments, allowing us to listen to the otherwise inaudible eventfulness of outer space, cosmic music has been linked, over the course of the twentieth century, to the introduction of new, mostly electronic instrumentalities. The combination of new sonic technologies with science fictional tropes makes cosmic music a speculative form in its own right. That is, such music can do what science fictional forms should do, whether literary or cinematic. It provides a space of cognitive estrangement from the familiar sounds of known reality. It provides a space of critical, self-reflective contact with technological change. It opens up the possibilities of something new. It seems to come from the future, or from some other space altogether. It is alien.

Cosmic music connects outer space, and electronic and other unusual kinds of sound, to consciousness in ways that testify to an ongoing human need not just to understand the cosmos as an object of scientific inquiry but also to experience it intuitively, affectively, and aesthetically. Discussing the technical and creative resources required in the making of a new musical instrument, synthesizer inventor Robert Moog suggests that "ideas and concepts permeate our universe and our consciousness, forming what might be called a 'cosmic network,' and some of us are adept at noticing them and drawing on them. This is not something you learn about in Engineering School" (2002, vi). Moog's cosmic network extends across all kinds of musical genres and formats of media, and certainly the SF film has provided a principal conduit for its development as a popular, at times even populist, form. For Moog it is not simply a matter of an increasingly rapid evolution of electronic technologies. Rather, "technology and our culture are constantly interacting as they themselves evolve" (viii). But Moog eagerly opens the scale of evolution to that of the sonic cosmos. For the synthesizer designer immersed in technoculture, the story of how "technical, commercial, and cultural trends shape one another" is likewise the story of how the "cosmic network . . . contributes to human creativity and innovation" (viii). As Trevor Pinch and Frank Trocco (2002) outline, this story—which largely accounts for the contemporary history of electronic instrument design and development—has to do with a cultural landscape in which outlets like SF films and television introduce and disperse new and unusual sounds throughout popular culture. A cybernetic model of the musician–instrument system maximizes the role of intuition in design: "In terms of modern information theory, the musician–instrument system contains a multiplicity of complex feedback loops" that value the designer's participation with emerging systems for making music through "a certain arrangement of materials" (Moog 2002, vi). Moog wonders why so many of the early electronic instruments have been abandoned and fallen into obscurity while more contemporary designs of sound making and modifying devices (Moog mentions the keyboard-controlled synthesizer, the phaser processor, and the fuzz box distortion effect) have proliferated throughout popular music. Considering how common innovations pop up in different places at the same time, Moog describes a morphogenetic field that exists at the fringe of modern science, technology, and engineering. He also tracks the temporal chains of intuitive design modifications that emerge as instrumentalities pass from one designer to another. However, morphogenetic synchronicities and design chains only partly account for the vast repository of not widely accepted or frequently abandoned instruments: "As electronic technology has itself advanced, the cosmic network has constantly hummed with ideas for new devices that musicians could play" (vii). Moog's intuition-driven, cosmic network is a psychotechnological structure operating on a vast scale; it has to do with sonic instrumentalities and emerging forms of listening bodies.

Moog's cosmic synthesizer design network bridges the expanding consciousness and body of the space-traveling technician to new techno-cultural modes of knowing and being. Synthesized sound provides the primary model for thinking under the influence of cosmic philosophy after modernism. The iconic value of the synthesizer is its reliance on additive waveform generation as well as subtractive filtering, which, according to Deleuze and Guattari "makes audible the sound process itself, the production of that process, and puts us in contact with still other elements beyond sound matter," as they describe in their discussion of the sonic refrain (1987, 343). As a philosophical venture, cosmic music "is like a thought synthesizer functioning to make thought travel, make it mobile, make it a force of the Cosmos (in the same way as one makes sound travel)" (343). Philosophy in this mode, Deleuze and Guattari write, "tends to elaborate a material of thought in order to capture forces that are not thinkable in themselves. This is Cosmos philosophy" (342).

This points us back to the sonic possible worlds that Voegelin described, which make available a philosophical strata not only beyond sight but also beyond the directly perceptible. Additive waveforms and subtractive filters process sound without being the prior sound object itself. We catch something of this highly mobilized thought—thought as cosmic force—throughout the history of science fiction cinema, in which new and alien sounds render the audible rather than reflect and reproduce the audibly known. Sonically, science fiction cinema is a particularly compelling site for the converging forces of technological innovation, experimental sound-making processes, and the cosmic ideas, themes, and images that we so often find there. But it also enables a philosophical encounter with forces "not thinkable in themselves" but only through their psychotechnological imbrication in the sonic novum. Both Moog's intuitive, universal sonic network and Deleuze and Guattari's cosmic thought synthesizers resonate with musicologist Adam Harper's *Infinite Music* (2011), where the author proposes an unfolding sonic cosmos within which an elusive "new music" periodically emerges. The opportunity facing creators and listeners is this, Harper asserts: "By imagining music in terms of paths of possible change running through a space of infinite possibility, we learn how the restrictions of unwitting convention and the apparent finitude of our imaginations can be detected and thus overcome" (11). New music emerges at the intersection of changing compositional practices, adventurous listening habits, and an ongoing cascade of transformative technologies. Rather than just matters of compositional practice or technical innovation, Harper's infinite music, like Moog's cosmic network, posits the making of music as a kind of cosmic practice that produces new relationships among mind, sound, technology, body, and outer space across vast historical expanses.

The cosmological imagination fosters an exploratory approach to new sound-making technologies and new ways of listening, in part to privilege itself as a vehicle for speculative thought and creative synthesis invested in philosophical ventures. Compared to sight, listening is an inherently unusual mode of philosophy. Hearing is a phenomenon that we are always catching up to cognitively, and in this sense it is an alien event by its very nature, working on our bodies just prior to our minds. While the absence of sonic predispositions and prior associations could account for a particular sound striking us as new, unusual, or alien, listening in fact precedes signification and eludes referentiality. Sonic science fiction exploits the fundamental act of estrangement that is listening. What first changed with the introduction of the theremin at the peak of modernity, and with the electrification of music and sound more broadly, is the idea that even as cosmic music facilitates a convergence of outer and inner space at the point of audition, it buffers and modulates the cognitive effect of technological changes to our "sonic epistemologies" and "aural ontologies" (Dyson 2009, 7). Sound and new media theorist Frances Dyson characterizes the intersection of thinking and being in terms of multimodal resonances that develop between mind and body through auditory practice (7). "In listening," she writes, "one is engaged in a synergy with the world and the senses, a hearing/touch that is the essence of what we mean by gut reaction—a response that is simultaneously physiological and psychological" (4). One reason why so many existing studies of cinematic consciousness may have largely neglected sound, Dyson implies, is because of the challenge that auditory phenomena present to Western metaphysical and cultural assumptions about the differentiation of the object and subject. Sound confuses epistemological and ontological boundaries, and in so doing, "it resists theorization, while also invoking . . . notions of transcendence that obscure audio media's technological and cultural origins" (4). While acknowledging sound's ambiguities, mystifications, and evasions, Dyson neatly summarizes how useful Schaeffer's practice and theories are when, in an effort to differentiate and catalog various types of sound, we navigate our relationship to sonorous objects in domains at once material and virtual. "Categorizing sound is also a process of objectifying the ephemeral and immaterial," Dyson concludes, "of giving conceptual substance to phenomena that are quasi, liminal, and virtual" (10). The object centeredness of Schaeffer's approach challenges systems of representation and ocular-centric approaches to technoculture and new media, in fact suggesting a prototypical form of object-oriented ontology that is explicitly sonic. A sonorous object-oriented ontology, in fact, turns out to be handy when considering science fiction films. By exploiting both the "representational lack and ontological ambiguity" (10) of acousmatic conditions of sonic production and reproduction, SF cinema facilitates the emergence of new materials for the speculative imagination through its promotion of sonic difference. The authenticity of new sounds, the distinction among types of sounds (how they should be classified and where they exist relative to cinematic diegesis), and most broadly the technologizing of sound all relate to broader genre concerns with estrangement, difference, and technocultural accommodation approached from the point of view—or rather at the point of audition—of the listener.

APPROACHING THE FILMS

In this book, I suggest ways to listen to the science fiction film. From the moon to Mars, Alphaville to Solaris, the *Nostromo*, cyberpunk L.A., Tatooine, Devil's Tower, or postpunk Berlin, and back to the moon— the sonic novums of the science fiction films discussed here facilitate a dense interplay of an audible history as new psychotechnologies imbue sound into the very substance of alien worlds. *The Sound of Things to Come* covers more than thirty films and over sixty years of film history. The filmography is meant to be indicative and exemplary, but it is hardly exhaustive. It emphasizes the analog years of SF film sound production, taking us right to the cusp of the widespread digitalization of sound and cinema—and hence the newest forms of sonic novum—that began in the 1990s and continues into the first two decades of the twenty-first century. Quite a few of these are familiar, even iconic films, the sonic dimensions of which have been well documented and often discussed: *Forbidden Planet* (1956), *2001: A Space Odyssey* (1968), *Star Wars* (1977), *Close Encounters of the Third Kind* (1977), *Alien* (1979), and *Blade Runner* (1982). But this book is the first to draw these films into a general theory of sound in the science fiction film. I also consider the generally neglected sonic dimensions of several classic SF films, including *Metropolis* (1927), *Things to Come* (1936), *Rocketship X-M* (1950), *The Day the Earth Stood Still* (1951), *Gojira* (1954), *This Island Earth* (1955), *Fantastic Voyage* (1966), *Barbarella* (1968), *The Andromeda Strain* (1971), and *John Carpenter's The Thing* (1982). Finally, I broaden the scope beyond mainstream, mostly American studio productions to consider art-house and independently produced international films—Chris Marker's *La Jetée* (1962), Jean-Luc Godard's *Alphaville* (1965), and Klaus Maeck's

40 • INTRODUCTION

Decoder (1984)—along with works from the borders of the genre like the planetarium Vortex Concerts of Jordan Belson and Henry Jacobs (1957–59) and Al Reinert's quasi-mystical documentary of the Apollo missions, *For All Mankind* (1989). While a couple of films considered here approach the digitalization of sound in SF—namely *TRON* and *Blade Runner,* both from 1982—the impact of digital technologies on all phases of audio production, but also on sound presentation in theaters and homes, demands its own sustained analysis.[4] Digitalization of the sonic novum and the emergence of digital sonic psychotechnologies do not manifest in a singular or unilateral fashion. Rather, the varieties of digital sonic novum are many; they are complex and contradictory, shaping our experience and understanding of SF films in ways that exceed the scope of the current project.

Although the book presents a chronology depicting the ongoing play of the new and renewal that comprises the sonic novum, the most important story concerns the strange newness that lurks beyond history and human limitation in the various forms of alternative realities and posthuman conditions accessed through the sonic novum. In this respect, the history of science fictional sound expresses the core extrapolative and speculative energies of the genre, which maintains its critical value relative to the degree that it estranges us from our personal lives and shared cultures. As much as I want readers to finish this book knowing more than they did before about sound in SF cinema, I also hope that they will end up feeling that they know less—which is another way of saying that I hope they become aware that there is more that remains

---

4. The complexity of this digitalization warrants a more substantial study beyond a chapter or two in the current project. Reserved for a future volume, then, is discussion of films including *Total Recall* (1990), *Terminator 2: Judgment Day* (1991), *Until the End of the World* (1991), *WAX, or The Discovery of Television among the Bees*(1991), *Ghost in the Shell* (1995), *Strange Days* (1995), *The Fifth Element* (1997), *eXistenZ* (1999), the Matrix trilogy (1999–2003), *The Wild Blue Yonder* (2005), *A Scanner Darkly* (2006), *Southland Tales* (2006), *WALL-E* (2008), *Avatar* (2009), *Enter the Void* (2009), *Beyond the Black Rainbow* (2010), *Dredd* (2012), *Under the Skin* (2014), *Chappie* (2015), *Arrival* (2016), *Blade Runner 2049* (2017), and *Ready Player One* (2018). This additional volume will also establish the state of sonic science fiction as a cinematic form in new media contexts. Audiovisual performance, interactive media, and immersive media have emerged as sites of postcinematic play in which science fiction continues to measure and push the boundaries of technocultural conditions, particularly where auditory experiences are concerned.

unknown because I have successfully pushed these films further on their way toward alien domains of thought and experience, toward new mysteries and the unknown. Far from claiming that all of sonic science fiction has worked toward this present moment and these conclusions, I trust that the multiple film histories contained here will demonstrate science fiction's ability to act, again and again, as a rejuvenating catalyst for creativity and a vehicle for the future of sound.

• CHAPTER 1 •

The Origins of Sonic Science Fiction (1924–50)

Science fiction first came to the silver screen in a sequence of silent exploratory missions that established the major narrative tropes of the genre before 1920. There were robots run amok in French film pioneer Georges Méliès's *Gugusse et l'Automate* (1897); lunar missions in Méliès's *Le Voyage dans la lune* (1902) and the U.K.'s first SF film, a lost adaptation of H. G. Wells's *The First Men in the Moon* (1919); comet collision in Danish director August Blom's *Verdens Undergang* (1916); postapocalyptic urban disaster in German Richard Oswald's *Die Arche* (1919); and a mission to a pacifist Martian utopia in the 1918 Danish film *Himmelskibet,* directed by Holger-Madsen. Concurrent with early cinema, several modern composers explored the sonic dimensions of emerging mechanical and technological forms, often in conjunction with the futuristic atmospheres of multimedia experiences and spectacles. The sounds of industry, the modern city, and new electronic communications technologies were all sporadically drawn into the tool kit of composers throughout Europe, Russia, and the United States. Among the earliest experiments was a production of Jean Cocteau's *Parade* by the Parisian Ballets Russes, whose previous premiere of Igor Stravinsky's *The Rite of Spring* in 1913 had triggered a war of howls between scandalized grandes dames and enthusiastic aesthetes (Ross 2007, 81–82). Cocteau's *Parade* debuted in spring 1917. The event pushed Stravinsky's

• 43

aggressive orchestration and roughly hewn, rhythmic primitivism into a spectacle of urban modernity with a delirious celebration of low culture that included American pop music played at the wrong speed on gramophones and evoked the cinema, the street, sideshows, and music halls. *Parade* acts as a who's who of modern art, including Cocteau's libretto, costumes and sets designed by Pablo Picasso, choreography by Léonide Massine (who had taken Vaslav Nijinsky's place as male lead of the Ballets Russes), program notes in which French poet Guillaume Apollinaire first coins the term "surrealism," and a strange new kind of music by pianist Erik Satie. Satie's composition draws from a wish list compiled by Cocteau that included an electromechanical dynamo, sirens, a steamship engine and an airplane motor, a Morse code machine, and typewriters. Though in actuality Saties's compositions for *Parade* may have achieved what Ross calls its "pseudo-American aesthetic" through a conceptual and metaphorical, rather than literal, evocation of machine noise, his work nonetheless precipitated an opening up of sonic practices to organized noise as well as expressive music (2007, 106–7; see also Chadabe 1997, 23). This investment in noise as a new mode of music would influence sound in the SF film throughout the century.

This chapter considers a trio of SF films—the Russian *Aelita* (1924), the German *Metropolis* (1927), and the British *Things to Come* (1936)—which feature the earliest forms of the sonic novum. Though the first two of these are technically silent films, all three feature original scores by popular composers. Though in the case of *Aelita* the original composition has been lost, its compelling sonic dimensions consist of more than the score to include a singularly significant plot detail: an intercepted radio transmission from Mars catalyzes the narrative even as it stokes contemporary Soviet fervor for outer space. In both *Metropolis* (restored with lost footage and synchronized to Gottfried Huppertz's original complete score) and *Things to Come,* moments of sonic ingenuity exceed the classical and romantic sonic motifs already established by silent era film accompaniment practices and the occasional, original score. Where early films typically associate acoustic instrumentation with humanist values, encoding more or less stock affective responses and characterization through familiar musical cues, the most fascinating

THE ORIGINS OF SONIC SCIENCE FICTION • 45

moments in *Metropolis* and *Things to Come* involve the composers approaching forms of sonic difference.

In Huppertz's score, atonality, dissonance, and mechanical rhythms evoke *Metropolis*'s themes of mechanization and dehumanization. The *Metropolis* score demonstrates what I consider a modern machinic expressionism, as Huppertz turns to musical speed and repetition as a way to convey the changing pace and scale of existence that has transformed all aspects of life for the polarized classes of the futuristic city. Huppertz evokes this transformation through the use of noisy modernist forms of composition as well as by incorporating a fox-trot. Use of both avant-garde and popular sonic forms propels the cinematic psychotechnologies of *Metropolis,* which fulfills several of the speculative elements of Münsterberg's analysis. Publishing on the photoplay in 1916, Münsterberg anticipates expressionist cinema and sound synchronization, making both essential to his speculation that the photoplay would constitute a world-building enterprise quantifiably distinct from the theatrical play. The expressionist special effects that Münsterberg imagines would soon take film to new and unexpected dimensions beyond the limits of everyday reality. Further, his proposal for innovation in cinematic sound anticipates the emergence of sonic psychotechnological entanglements that audiovisual synchronization would facilitate.

Things to Come refines the expressionist aspects of *Metropolis* by turning away from the crude mechanisms of labor toward airy, gleaming postwar industry. My analysis concentrates on the building of the futuristic Everytown. In an extended sequence depicting the extraction of building materials from raw resources to develop increasingly delicate, liquefied, translucent, and plastic textiles, Arthur Bliss's score achieves a type of industrial impressionism. Where Huppertz's music had drawn on modernist noise compositions and popular dance forms to express the mechanization of the human mind, body and spirit, Bliss develops an idealized suprahuman form that points the naturalistic impressions and abstract emotional atmospheres of Claude Debussy and Maurice Ravel toward an increasingly refined evocation of manufacturing, artificial realities, ambient media, and space age technologies. Ultimately, though, the most surprising aspect of *Things to Come*—the first SF film

46 • THE ORIGINS OF SONIC SCIENCE FICTION

to feature synchronized sound—may consist of its silencing of musical accompaniment altogether.

1924 | *AELITA*

Martian culture is the subject of Soviet director Yakov Protazanov's *Aelita*, sometimes subtitled *Queen of Mars* (1924). With striking constructivist sets and costumes, *Aelita* is one of the most impressive-looking science fiction films of the silent era. Adapting Aleksey Nikolayevich Tolstoy's 1923 novel of the same name, the film affirms the successes of the Russian civil war and valorizes the newly minted Soviet Union. Centered on the mutual infatuation of engineer Los (Nikolai Tsereteli) and Aelita (Yuliya Solntseva), the queen of Mars, the narrative peaks with Los's instigation of Martian proletariat revolt against their decadent rulers, including Aelita's father, a regent so pragmatic that he puts his workers in cold storage when they aren't needed.

Creating a fictive novum that upholds ideology rather than proposes something new proved no easy task for Protazanov. The director was a famous and prolific prerevolutionary filmmaker who now had to work in more guarded fashion with the support of the new Soviet film trust, Sovkino. The historical newness of Soviet revolution had already occurred and could not be challenged through the kind of ideological one-upmanship that had positioned the peace-loving, vegetarian Martians of Holger-Madsen's *Himmelskibet* as superior to world warring Earthlings. Rather, the revolutionary change that had occurred in actual history had to be validated by being replicated elsewhere—in this case, an extraterrestrial elsewhere, making this the first of many communist films to imagine a cosmic Soviet. This replication would, by analogy, validate the idea of spreading communism around the globe. The novum here thus imprints its ideological approval of the current state of things by providing a blueprint for future change elsewhere. While keeping the director within ideological guidelines, Sovkino did want Protazanov to do something new in the form of cinematic spectacle. The film trust hoped that the director might forge a new form of cinema capable of appealing to a mass audience already "impatient with too much moralizing politics or experimental techniques" (Stites 1992, 56). The long lost score composed for the film's Moscow premiere was clearly a gesture toward popular favor, composed as it was by Valentin Kruchinin, writer of the proletariat hit "Little Bricks." With its lavish sets and costumes and complete original score, *Aelita* was designed to be the first SF blockbuster. One of the most fascinating sonic aspects of the film was its marketing campaign, which included a series of radio spots that sounded like the broken code of interplanetary communications chatter (Broad 2010). Despite Sovkino's request for a more accessible entertainment, *Aelita* was hardly escapist; it featured many realistic depictions of Soviet hardship during the civil war period as a means of justifying the revolution in retrospect. But it proved ideologically out-of-step. While the film proved popular enough with audiences during its first run in theaters, Russian director and formalist theorist, Lev Kuleshov, argued that *Aelita* was in fact old hat, exemplifying "the blind alley of pre-revolutionary cinema," while proletarian newspaper *Kinonedelya* deemed its scriptwriters "alien to the working class." The moderate *Kino-gazeta* simply labeled the film "ideologically unprincipled" (Youngblood 1994, 112). In some ways prerevolutionary in tone, perhaps *Aelita* also went too far in the direction of cultural criticism. While the film mirrors the social impact of Lenin's new economic policy of Soviet state capitalism, it also exposes the cultural assumptions built into Tolstoy's source novel by amplifying and exacerbating the "contradictory realities of NEP life," as Asif Siddiqi explains in his study of Russian science fiction (2010, 101). For Siddiqi, *Aelita*'s apparent endorsement of the revolution is in fact "riddled with ambiguities that do not demarcate strictly along bipolar lines (capitalist–communist, benevolent–exploitative); nothing is really what it seems" (100). Perhaps nothing undermines its ideological message more than turning the story of Soviet revolution on the red planet into Los's fleeting dream, which begins after he has fallen asleep at the controls of his radio receiver. This is where the film's most exciting sonic elements come into play.

The mysterious Martian radio signals that engineer Los receives (or dreams that he receives) not only set the narrative in motion, they align the film's thematic concerns with a populist form of Russian cosmism. Siddiqi situates *Aelita* squarely within an early Soviet discourse on outer space. "From literature to film to painting to poetry to architecture to language," Siddiqi writes, "clusters of artists produced works that reflected their belief that cosmic travel was an inevitable part of their future" (2010, 97). Soviet space enthusiasts would value *Aelita* less as correct ideology and become more enamored with its various speculations on interplanetary communication, space travel, and romantic alien encounter. A spiritually inflected cosmic philosophy had long distinguished Soviet mysticism from the utopians' infatuation with modernist technologies, but space exploration provided a unifying network. *Aelita* tapped into these growing enthusiasms. Attendance of lectures sponsored by the Moscow Society for the Study of Interplanetary Communication and other space-related societies boomed after the release of the film (Siddiqi 2010, 100). Forty-five years after its release, *Aelita* still proved inspirational, most notably in the case of the Soviet Ministry for General Machine Building and rocket designer Vladimir Chelomei, who in 1969 proposed an epically scaled mission to Mars referred to as the Aelita program (Harvey 2007, 300). With its "radio signal from Mars" narrative, *Aelita* also initiates one of the most significant, recurring sonic novums of modern technoculture, particularly in Soviet-bloc SF films. The idea of first contact through alien sound artifacts becomes a defining motif of *Nebo Zovyot* (1959), *Der Schweigende Stern* (1960), *Planeta Bur* (1962), *Mechte Navstrechu* (1963), and *Solaris* (1972), all films that I will discuss in a later chapter.

1927 | *METROPOLIS*

Fritz Lang's *Metropolis* (1927), with an original score by Gottfried Huppertz, is the first futuristic film that strains toward a science fictional sound. The score amplifies the film's iconic visual and narrative novums in several sequences depicting the effects of futuristic machines, the roboticization of the workforce, and popular dance music's maintenance of the mythoerotic underpinnings of mechanized society. Huppertz's work includes brief atonal sequences along with up-tempo and repetitive motifs, including a fox-trot, which echo Lang's primary themes of modernization and dehumanization. While silent films with original scores were exceptions to the norm, Huppertz's *Metropolis* scores, one for piano and another for full orchestra, proved a notable exception—so notable, in fact, that some early reviewers of *Metropolis* were kinder to the score than the film itself. The popularity of the score prompted the German Vox label to release a pair of 78 rpm records featuring themes from *Metropolis* as well as a short promotional recording of Fritz Lang discussing the making of the film. Supplementary and cross-promotional materials, as well as commercial tie-in products like soundtrack albums, are now completely typical elements of convergence media, but for the time, Huppertz's *Metropolis* records were novel enough, already a kind of material sonic novum set loose in popular culture (Bar-Sagi, Koerber, and the 78 RPM Records Mailing List 2001). *Metropolis* has enjoyed a particularly robust and complicated life as an artifact in multiple media formats. The film has suffered from edits and censorship, first by Germany's UFA studios, then more drastically by the film's American and international distributors, and not many audiences would see the original version of the film that premiered in Berlin on January 10, 1927. Audiences would not experience anything close to Lang's original version until 2010, when a restored print was presented in its entirety with live orchestration at the 60th Berlin International Film Festival, then released along with a complete symphonic recording of Huppertz's score by Berlin's Rundfunk Symphony Orchestra, conducted by Frank Strobel, on Kino International DVD and Blu-ray as The Complete *Metropolis*. This is a significant rediscovery of a film that circulated for years on videocassette, laser disc, and DVD with horrible visual transfers and canned musical accompaniments, and which was infamously re-created, colorized, and rescored by Italian record producer Giorgio Moroder in 1984. This new soundtrack featured Moroder's own instrumental passages as well as pop songs by Pat Benatar, Freddie Mercury, Adam Ant, Loverboy, and others. While the style of patchwork compilation of popular motifs may be typical of silent film accompaniment—and here it lived on, MTV style—not much of the music heard in the Moroder version, replete as it is with synthesizers, sonically represents science fiction (though a whole lot of it represents mid-1980s-era music videos).

For that matter, not much in the original Huppertz score actually signifies science fiction either. The music is variously majestic, solemn, or tender, and it makes a prominent nod to popular dance forms, the waltz and fox-trot in particular. The latter may prove to be the film's

50 • THE ORIGINS OF SONIC SCIENCE FICTION

most significantly critical sonic event, though not necessarily science fictional, at least on first listen. I will return to this fascinating fox-trot. But some sense of the overall sonic tapestry of *Metropolis* needs to be established. After the Wagnerian prelude that accompanies the opening title sequence, Huppertz for the most part sticks to conventional compositional pastiches of Western classical and romantic traditions, suggesting nothing so much as a medley of familiar Liszt, Wagner, and Tchaikovsky passages transcribed for piano. In its day, the popularity of Huppertz's score may be due to its adherence to convention rather than any originality the work possessed. Thomas Elsaesser, in a recent reconsideration of the score, decides that this is absolutely "salon music, curiously irrelevant to the film because it is devoid of associations other than to the pomposity of first-night audiences at mid-1920s movie palace premieres" (2000, 125). Despite its life as a pop collectible for the home listener, within seven months of the premiere, much of Huppertz's score was replaced by more familiar musical elements. German reviewer Balthasar (Roland Schacht) described the new score in September 1927. Though still attributed to Huppertz, the revised version now featured "the tried and tested medley of Chopin, *Frieschütz* and *Traviata* along with popular songs from the Kinothek," a film library of sheet music composed by Giuseppe Becce (in Patalas 2000, 115). Italian composer Becce, who lived in Berlin, wrote close to fifty movie themes between 1919 and 1933, each cataloged by a reference number and with a title indicating the type of scene it was intended to accompany, such as "Kinothek 14: Tragic Moments (Andante Mosso)," "Kinothek 30: Sinister Agitato," "Kinothek 42: Dramatic Climax," and "Kinothek 47: Witchcraft (Semi Mysterious Andante)" (Wierzbicki 2009, 56). In the case of *Metropolis*, it seems that whether the score was original or not, and even in Moroder's 1980s remix, the music tends to function according to common conventions by which the familiarity of musical styles and motifs guarantee automatic emotional corollaries.

Certain familiarizing sensibilities are already in place at the start of the history of sonic science fiction, first in *Aelita*, with its choice of popular comrade-composer, and then in *Metropolis*, where the bulk of its musical composition is ultimately replaceable. But *Metropolis* also provides early examples of the sonic novum and its ability to work in critically resonant ways. The newest sounds in the score take the form of frenzied strings, martial horns, high-pitched woodwinds, pounding timpani, vertiginous glides among all the instruments, and loud, atonal climaxes. The first of these sequences comes early in the film, during the montage of abstracted industrial activity that immediately follows the opening titles. Pistons pump, wheels and gears spin, shafts churn, and a brilliant, abstract lighting effect cuts across the screen. Most of these machine parts are shot in extreme close-up. Several are mirrored in kaleidoscopic triplicate. At last the montage becomes so dense and unrealistic in its orgy of gleaming metal parts that it suggests the ideal of machinic motion. The scene cuts to a ten-hour clock, its hand ticking upward as the music becomes less dense but more insistent. A metronomic pulse then takes over with its high-pitched, strident measure. As the clock at last strikes 10, an atonal blast accompanies an image of a blowing steam whistle. The intertitle announces "Schicht" (shift change). The same blasting notes are held throughout the intertitle, then pause and repeat as we cut to a worker's tunnel, with a dour-clad line of laborers standing six abreast and separated from another group by a slowly rising iron gate. There is a beat of silence; then, as the workers shuffle forward in lockstep, heads down, the music returns with a slow, solemn procession.

This brief instance of Huppertz's machine music embraces the atonal properties of modern composition in ways that mimic the sonic landscape of the industrialized twentieth century. In contrast to the primarily romantic sensibilities heard in most of the score, this music measures the impact of technology on the human condition. It does so in other scenes as well, when the film's protagonist, Freder (Gustav Fröhlich), enters the great underground hall of the machines in search of a young woman, Maria (Brigette Helm). A refrain briefly states the earlier machine theme, now paired with images of human workers who are dwarfed by the equipment around them as they move through a stylized, choreographed routine of repetitive motions at their control panels. Pounding drums and low brass notes, above which the strings circle several times through a brief minimal phrase, accompany Freder's inspection of the boiler room. Higher tones and new instrumental voices are gradually added to the sequence as we watch a worker struggle with the controls of a machine. A temperature gauge rises steadily, and the music speeds up before an industrial accident sends several workers to the infirmary, if not their death. Freder sinks into a visionary panic in which the vast machinery transforms into a worker-devouring Moloch. In this sequence, elements of musical modernism—atonal noise, rhythmic primitivism, and minimal phrases repeated in short loops—accompany Freder's reaction to these disastrous events. This is the first of a few significant moments that link the film's dystopian futurism to the psychological atmospheres of expressionism in order to critique the mechanization of the human workforce. The first sonic novum of science fiction cinema, *Metropolis*'s machine theme marks the moment when a modernist leitmotif representing the machine becomes just as important in terms of cuing audience reactions to dramatic, and in this case specifically futuristic, events as the emotive, romantic motifs typically associated with human characters.

Surprisingly, the most science fictional scene of the film—the transferal of Maria's life force into a robot—lacks any sonic equivalent to the various devices and instruments seen inside Rotwang's (Rudolf Klein-Rogge) laboratory. Rather, this crucial scene is accompanied by an airy musical theme suggestive of mystery and wonder rather than science and technology. The work that Rotwang performs is more like alchemy, and visual elements such as the inverted pentagram painted on the wall above the robot's head suggest that black magic is involved. Where discord and thunder had evoked machinic processes earlier in the film, it seems that the electric spark of science and technology is too delicate for conveyance by something as rough as the machine theme. Certainly, the mysterious music seems intended to reinforce the sleek, gleaming, and femininely shaped refinement of what Rotwang calls "the Machine Man," an elegant and seductive form that contrasts sharply with the clunky, cylindrical agents of robotic mayhem seen in other silent SF films.

1913–37 | NOISE, MUSIC, AND TECHNOLOGY IN THE MODERN AVANT-GARDE

I will come back to *Metropolis*. First, however, I want to contextualize the more adventurous aspects of its score in terms of activities of the sonic avant-garde in the first three decades of the twentieth century. Very briefly surveying some work and theories of composers from Europe, Russia, and the United States, I jump around the chronological timeline a bit in order to emphasize an aesthetic progression from the incorporation of raw mechanical sounds to early forms of graphic sound synthesis and then to interactions between sound and film. Not only should these inform an understanding of music in *Metropolis,* the experiments and technological aesthetics of modern and avant-garde music will reemerge during the golden age of the science fiction film after World War II.

The expansion of the composer's sonic palette that had remained metaphorical in Satie's earlier contributions to *Parade* had to be actualized through real mechanical noise. American composer George Antheil's 1924 work, *Ballet Mécanique,* was originally to have accompanied the dadaist art film of the same name created by French painter and sculptor Fernand Léger, American filmmaker Dudley Murphy, and American painter and photographer Man Ray. Discrepancies between the film's running time and the lengthier composition led to the music's independent run as a concert piece. It premiered in Paris in 1926. Even on its own terms, Antheil's composition was as much a visual spectacle as a sonic event. The piece featured multiple player pianos, electric bells, sirens, numerous percussive instruments, and industrial fans sonified by wooden sticks or leather straps thrust between the blades. In some instances, the fans were aimed toward the audience. Antheil's American debut took place at Carnegie Hall in 1927. The evening's program combined jazz and ultramodern experiments in noise. When the expected riots failed to materialize, as one headline dismissively announced the day after the performance, a disappointed Antheil ended up in Hollywood, making his living writing scores for films such as Cecil B. DeMille's *The Buccaneer* (1938).

The most militant celebration of symphonic noise is found in the work of Russian composer and sound theorist Arseny Avraamov. The anniversary of the Soviet revolution in 1922 was celebrated with a performance of Avraamov's *Symphony for Factory Whistles* at the port of Baku on the Caspian Sea. Along with the factory sirens of the piece's title, the "orchestra" consisted of artillery guns and cannons, machine guns, bus and automobile horns, engines, emergency sirens, and the fog-horns of the Caspian fleet. While a military band and choir performed "The Internationale" and "La Marseillaise" anthems, a team of conductors outfitted with flags and pistols led the machine orchestra (Ross 2007, 240). Avraamov later became one of several Soviet pioneers in the art of synthesis through graphical sound design, creating musical works by drawing or photographing "ornamental" forms directly onto the magnetic band of sound filmstrips. By 1930, Avraamov founded the Multzvok Group, dedicated to the research and development of "new mictrotonal 'Ultrachromatic' music" (Smirnov 2013, 181). Members of the group rapidly produced a variety of compositional programs exploring new scales and harmonics as well as the manufacture of unheard overtones and undertones and the visual synthesis of gliding sounds, crossfades among timbres, and polyphony (181). All of this work was not just about sound but rather an original synthesis of music and graphic art. The extrapolative dimensions of such a project would guide the work of German animator Oskar Fischinger. Fischinger (1932) comes to the conclusion that visual ornaments amount to a new music of the future:

> If you look at a strip of film from my experiments with synthetic sound, you will see along one edge a thin stripe of jagged ornamental patterns. These ornaments are drawn music—they are sound: when run through a projector, these graphic sounds broadcast tones of a hitherto unheard of purity, and thus, quite obviously, fantastic possibilities open up for the composition of music in the future.

Fischinger is an early proponent of the field of optical music synthesis that would later include Daphne Oram's sound-generating film scanner process, Oramics, in 1957, as well as the ANS photoelectronic instrument developed by Yevgeny Murzin from 1937 to 1957, who used hand-drawn spectrograms on glass plates to generate electronic sounds. The ANS device in particular would become most explicitly futuristic when used by Russian composer Eduard Artemiev in his scores for the Russian science fiction films, *Mechte Navstrechu* (1963) and *Solaris* (1972). Deeply synesthetic in practice, the various systems of graphic, ornamental or optical music synthesis point to the increasingly intertwined development of early sound and film technologies. For Fischinger, such electronically synthesized sounds possess an "unheard of purity." The graphic score closes the gap between composition and performance of the tone. In this case, the representation of a tone is the tone for all practical purposes.

American composer John Cage also framed his early observations on the unexpected sound-making capacities of film in terms of a future music. However, whereas Avraamov and Fischinger explored the capacity for images drawn on film to synthesize new sounds, Cage suggested something more along the lines of musique concrète. In Cage's 1937 manifesto, "The Future of Music: Credo," he speculates that manipulation and synthesis of a new kind of music will come not just from traditional instruments but also from "any and all sounds that can be heard, photoelectric, film, and mechanical mediums" ([1937] 2004, 26). The most sustained argument in Cage's credo centers on the role of film sound effects, in which he articulates some of the ways in which these sounds might become compositional elements in their own right:

> The sound of a truck at fifty miles per hour. Static between the stations. Rain. We want to capture and control these sounds, to use them not as sound effects but as musical instruments. Every film studio has a library of "sound effects" recorded on film. With a film phonograph it is now possible to control the amplitude and frequency of any one of these sounds and to give to it rhythms within or beyond the reach of the imagination. Given four film phonographs, we can compose and perform a quartet for explosive motor, wind, heartbeat, and landslide. (25–26)

The film phonograph allowed playback of recorded sounds independent of the projected image and so provided an adjunct to the standard practices of the Foley room, where sound effects are created for addition to or replacement of sounds captured on a film set. Filmmakers could draw on this sound effect library rather than resort to creating Foley room recordings each time they shot a movie. For Cage, film phonography made possible a new way to create music by looping isolated bits of film soundtracks at unnatural speeds until they generated new sounds. Cage called this percussion music, as tempo and repetition created previously unheard rhythmic patterns out of noise. Cage's approach to library-style menus of sounds would inform his work with future SF film scorers Louis and Bebe Barron on the 1952 tape collage piece *Williams Mix*. The Barrons recorded hours of material organized into six categories of sounds: city sounds, country sounds, electronic sounds, sounds that were manually produced, sounds produced by the wind, and "small" sounds that required amplification in order to be heard. Cage's 192-page score, created with guidance from the *I Ching*, instructed the arrangement of eight layers of taped sources, indicating where and in what way the contents of an individual layer of magnetic tape should be spliced together. Cage's early ideas about "the future of music" as well as his later composition and performance practices involving the combination of sound effects, field recordings, and radio noise and signals respond to the "electric consciousness" taking shape at the intersection of cinema, the performing arts, and radio in ways traditional music could not (Cage 1990, 452).

Antheil, Avraamov, Fischinger, and Cage each pushed musical composition toward an incorporation of mechanical and electrical sounds. Informing their work is a new aesthetic regarding both the sounds of technology, which no longer needed to be faked or otherwise represented imaginatively by acoustic instruments, and actual new sound making and processing technologies such as film projectors and record or tape players. But the future of music that so many of these composers theorized would in fact depend on an eventual turn to science fiction as its primary platform. The practical and conceptual convergences around the medium of film not only informed the development of new sounds in SF cinema but also shaped the capacity for the sonic novum to accommodate, and so provide a space for reflection on, the development of organized noise as a critical activity in its own right.

Even more explicitly than in the previous set of pioneering projects, new arguments for listening to noise converged with new technologies for making sound in several vital but ultimately failed or unrealized experiments in early SF cinema. Italian futurist Luigi Russolo, initially a painter, was inspired to write his famous manifesto, "The Art of Noises" ([1916] 1986), after a 1913 performance of composer Francesco Balilla Pratella's atonal, tempo-shifting *Musica Futurista*. Unlike Pratella's attempts to expand conventional instruments through the use of new tonal and rhythmic systems, Russolo challenged the idea of music itself, and he proposed new methods and machines for making noise in controlled performances. His first invention, the *intonarumori*, were boxy, mechanical noisemakers that Russolo arranged in families of noises: thunders, explosions, hisses, puffs, whispers, grumbles, creaks, rustles, metallic and wooden percussion, and vocal sounds ranging from shouts, screams, and shrieks to death rattles and sobs. The *intonarumori* were assembled for noise concerts as early as 1914, culminating with the *Gran Concerto Futuristico* in 1917, which was met with the requisite outburst and riot, and at last culminated with the arrest of Russolo and his futurist compatriot, F. T. Marinetti (Holmes 2002, 38–41). Russolo's dissatisfaction with the devices led to a second generation of noise machines called the *rumorarmonio*, designed to create facsimiles of the sounds of nature, such as wind, running water, and wildlife, while putting to rest the bane of the symphonic tone poem and program music, which often used musical instruments to represent sounds from the real world. No more would French horns call foxhunters to the chase, timpani announce the onset of a storm, or percussion represent the clash of armies.

Russolo's *intonarumori* and *rumorarmonio* didn't imitate noise; they made noise. Noises as subtle and delicate as nature or as brutal as modern industry and mechanized warfare could be achieved with the turn of a handle. Anticipating Avraamov's Ultrachromatic music, Russolo was attracted to the density of harmonics encountered in noise, and he sought to open music up to the harmonic complexities of modern life— and modern death. Russolo's machines recuperated noise for use in art by repressing the identification of a sound by familiar instrumentation, with the boxy design obscuring the generative mechanism, other than the very modern action of turning a crankshaft to set gears in motion. Such an indifferent interface could hardly be called an instrument, separating as it did the audible event from its material sources, hiding these in a barrel or cabinet where perhaps tumbling rocks turned into thunder and spinning fans into wind. Surprisingly, the desire to liberate sound through this acousmatic approach was tempered by Russolo's efforts to tame, transform, and ultimately dominate noise. His project entailed an authoritative index of sounds, a menu by which noises were, in his own words, "mastered, servile, completely controlled, conquered and

58 • THE ORIGINS OF SONIC SCIENCE FICTION

constrained to become elements of art" ([1916] 1986, 87). Russolo sits at the head of a stern table, ruling over noisy families in a manner by which "this unstable material could be absorbed . . . through a familiar process of domestication," as sound theorist Douglas Kahn explains (1999, 81). In the end, Russolo's project failed to propose "a fundamentally different notion of auditive materiality, which would have guaranteed a degree of autonomy for his art of noises, or transform a relationship to nature to be more amenable to a new artistic aurality" (81). Instead, the categorical taxonomies of a familial ear restrained the potential newness of sounds, putting every noise in its proper place.

One of the ways in which Russolo planned to domesticate noise involved using the *rumorarmonio* as an accompaniment to silent films. One machine was briefly installed in Parisian Studio 28 before being trashed during the violence that followed a screening of Luis Buñuel's controversial film *L'Age d'Or* in 1930. However, it was not controversy so much as practicality that beat Russolo in the emerging market for sound effect design. He was simply unable to compete with the theater organs, such as the Wurlitzer, which could summon up realistic-enough sound effects such as thunder, gunshots, and stampedes as well as orchestral sounds and percussion. As early as 1913, a catalog of instruments for making noises to accompany movies was available to cinemas, with its inventory including devices that produced the sounds of weather, animals, vehicles, and more. Sound film would of course quickly make such on-site sound effect generators altogether unnecessary. Russolo makes a couple of last shadowy appearances in the prehistory of SF cinema, in lost or rumored collaborations with French filmmaker Eugene Deslaw. Russolo scored an "abstract mechanical symphony," since lost but once meant to accompany Deslaw's equally abstract, so-called pattern film of machines in motion, *La Marche des Machines* (1929). In 1930, Deslaw announced that Russolo's *rumharmonium* would accompany his short film *Vers les Robots*. By the time the film was released in 1932, it featured synchronized sound, and Russolo was not among those credited (Kahn 1999, 129). Though invested in themes of mechanization, Deslaw's works do not quite qualify as science fiction, but they do suggest that new noises need to accompany sequences of machine motion.

A technical innovator with *Napoleon* (1927)—a six-hour cinematic experience projected on three side-by-side screens—French filmmaker Abel Gance turned specifically to science fiction with an ear toward cinematic sound design in his disaster movie, *La fin du monde* (1931). About the impending collision of a comet with Earth, *La fin du monde* was to be France's first sound film. Gance worked on the film for almost two years, sapping an unheard of budget of five million francs. A good deal of this money was spent on the pioneering pseudo-stereophonic sound system that he hoped to develop. Gance designed sound playback equipment that utilized notches in the film to trigger sequenced sound effects from a set of loudspeakers situated around the theater. Gance believed this surround sound system would be crucial to the success of his space disaster, and in a brief manifesto composed for his production crew, he stressed the "considerable extent" to which the film would rely on its sound design: "The whole of the cataclysm sequence, in particular, can be orchestrated, organized in terms of sound, making it possible to achieve some extraordinary effects" (in Hayward 2004b, 5). Gance understood sound's ability to foster an audience's commitment to the speculative exercise of the science fiction film. Unfortunately, *La fin du monde* was never completed to the director's satisfaction. Finally pulled from his control by the producers, *La fin du monde* was brutally cut from more than three hours to 105 minutes and then further trimmed to fifty-four minutes for its American release (Erickson 2011, 17). In a fit of revenge for the lavish budget, the studio excised entirely an important character played by Gance himself. *La fin du monde* was both a commercial and critical flop. Despite the fact that it bears the distinction of being France's first sound film, it failed at the box office and virtually disappeared from the history of cinema, science fiction or otherwise. In a final irony, its failure was due in no small part to its contemporary reviewers finding the sounds "harsh and grating" (Hayward 2004b, 5). Though never released with Gance's desired sound system, the innovative ideas planned for his SF film suggest the technologies that would become industry standards. More importantly, Gance clearly grasped not only that sound would organize the film experience, but it would play an immersive role beyond that of large-scale visual projection. Sound gave the most appropriate scale to history and its end, and it was

60 • THE ORIGINS OF SONIC SCIENCE FICTION

an all-encompassing world of realistic noises that would best provide a cinematic mechanism for cultural memory.

Early technical experiments in sound design—its composition, production, and theatrical presentation—move toward crisis points in the creative and economic failures of Russolo and Gance even as they gravitate toward science fictional motifs of robotic laborers and space disasters. Russolo's blind box instruments, organized around classes of industrial and nature-mimicking noises, as well as the multi-speaker sound spaces that Gance designed, only hint at features that would define sound's place in science fiction cinema. The unrealized technical ambitions, undeveloped scores, and lost films of the first half of the twentieth century reveal emerging aesthetic sensibilities in their nascency as well as new technical approaches to sound creation, which embrace noise, microtonality, and synthesis as compositional devices. They also anticipate new technologies for listening that facilitate the development of sound design and immersive cinematic reproduction. At the same time, the unusual and often brutal sonic experiences encountered in early experimental music and its noise machines must wait for the science fiction film to give them broader public purchase.

1916–27 | PSYCHOTECHNOLOGY IN THE PHOTOPLAY AND *METROPOLIS*

With the modern and futurist music of the early avant-garde set on a trajectory toward the science fiction film, I want to return to Lang's *Metropolis* and consider its new sounds in terms of Hugo Münsterberg's theory of psychotechnology. Huppertz's score shares the sensibilities of Lang's striking visual effects, which alter the scale of human perception in ways consistent with the psychotechnology of German expressionist cinema. Consider the opening title montage. The sequence epitomizes Lang's approach to visual perspective as it shifts from screen-encompassing interiors of undefined moving machine parts to shots of the city exterior, also claustrophobically dense with looming skyscrapers and aerial bridges, and streets and skies alike teeming with motorized traffic. The mechanization of life pushes inner and outer experience beyond the scale of the human body. As Huppertz's machine music matches the pace of visual montage and scale of panorama, the rapid tempo and tonal densities critically engage the apparatuses of a sonic cinema, which bears its own impact on human perception. The entire score is caught up in the whir of cinematic speed. Huppertz's notes show that his score is meant to accompany the film projected at 28 fps, a figure that substantially exceeds the era's typical frame rate of 16 fps (even though the effect of normal movement is achieved at 20 fps). It even appears that a change of the film's screening frame rate may have been partly responsible for the replacement of Huppertz's score with stock selections (Erickson 2010). Changes to the frame rate of recording or playback fundamentally alter what we see and hear. The faster frame rate would give everything in the film an accelerated appearance, while the final chase scene on the last reel of the film has been undercranked to make things faster still. The rush of moving parts in the *Metropolis* score is an emblematic motif of the noisiness of its own apparatus; and not only the camera. The buzzing strings and thunderous clamor of *Metropolis*'s machine music also point to the technical apparatus underlying the cinematic experience and become an aesthetic amplification of that "whirring of the machine"—film's primal underscore—the sound of the projector itself being "the first noise of cinema" (Chion 2009, 8). With this turn toward self-audition, Lang's film epitomizes a science fictional form of sonic psytech.

That expressionist sensibilities would culminate in one of the first great science fiction films was a sure sign of the continuing impact of the German psychotechnics movement. Between the world wars, Germany was the scene of intense speculation into the psychological impact of new technologies as well as the systematic application of psychological approaches to industrialization. Psychotechnical-oriented faculty positions were added to the departments of six German colleges between 1918 and 1927, and several new institutions were founded, such as the Institute for Industrial Psychotechnology at the Technical Academy of Berlin–Charlottenburg. In the early 1920s, the German ministry of labor added a branch of government devoted to the development of rationalist psychotechnological tools for the country's reconstruction after World War I and reduction of escalating labor conflicts. These tools ranged from workplace analysis and aptitude tests to ergonomics and structural design. A new law required occupational agencies and employers to consult psychologists with hopes of quelling the industry and labor disputes that had precipitated the Bolshevik revolution in Russia. This particular branch of applied behavioral psychology is the main candidate for Lang's critique of psychotechnics in *Metropolis* (Pickren and Rutherford 2010, 196). The film's central narrative conflict revolves around the mechanization of human labor and its consequences, reflecting the mounting suspicion among German workers that psychotechnical systems in fact favored their employers. Workplace regulation was quickly coming to mean capitalist exploitation. Lang takes this on by turning psychotechnics on its head, using cinema as a complex self-reflexive mechanism for exposing psychotechnological imbrication in the rescaled bodies, minds, and spirits of the divided social classes of the Metropolis.

Just as other German expressionist films exteriorize psychological drama through their radical set design, strange lighting and shadow effects, and visual tricks such as double exposure, *Metropolis* alters the scale of perception in ways that emphasize the impact of new technologies on the psyches of human subjects. Feder's delirious visions not only create an atmosphere of expressionist strangeness but also demonstrate the cumulative challenge facing the human mind as it struggles to measure and comprehend the modern landscape. Of course, this plays out literally in the great visual imagery of the city with its towering skyscrapers, air bridges, and underground equipment, but it also appears in the corresponding interior, mental terrain of dreams and deliriums filled with primal sexual urges and religious iconography. The robot, disguised as Maria, catalyzes transformations within the hearts and minds of Metropolis's human subjects by inciting lust, murderous rage, dissent, and a workers' rebellion. Where the human Maria serves as a spiritual leader of the workers and prophesizes the coming of a messianic human "Mediator" capable of uniting the city's ruling thinkers and its workers, her mechanical duplicate is a false idol of psychotechnical autocracy that brings about precisely the kind of labor-based class warfare that the industrial systems of applied psychology were meant to defuse.

To understand how Lang's cinematic psychotechnologies provide an antidote to the out-of-control psychotechnics depicted in his film, and to appreciate his pioneering combination of expressionist technique with science fictional themes, I find it useful to turn to the film theories of Hugo Münsterberg. Beyond his prescient theories of emerging cinema, Münsterberg was a major proponent of behavioral psychology and psychotechnics, popularizing the field in the United States. In the early 1890s, William James invited Münsterberg to chair Harvard's psychology laboratory for three years, and Münsterberg later served as president of the American Psychological Association. A pair of books, *Psychology and Industrial Efficiency* (1912) and *Basics of Psychotechnology* (1914), applied cutting-edge psychological perspectives to a consideration of industrial efficiency, emphasizing the issues of mental monotony, fatigue, and attention spans in the modern workplace. Münsterberg's fieldwork in applied psychology expanded beyond industry to organizational, legal, forensic, and other domains, including film. By bringing the psychotechnological approach to the emerging "photoplay," Münsterberg set out to understand the forms of creative and technical expression newly embodied within the motion film camera and to understand the psychological consequences of this dramatic technology.

Less interested in film content per se, Münsterberg's writings are instead concerned with filmic mechanisms as these relate to mental phenomena. Cataloging those moments in which film eclipses not merely the theatrical stage but also the limited capacities of the body and face of physical actors, Münsterberg describes the ways in which emotion captured on film exceeds the expressivity of the human face and body. As the scope of his discussion expands to include the entire cinematic set, lighting, the motion of the camera, and other effects, he anticipates the most typical innovations of an expressionist cinema yet to come. In a key section of his 1916 text, Münsterberg imagines the following filmed sequence:

> If we see on the screen a man hypnotized in the doctor's office, the patient himself may lie there with closed eyes, nothing in his features expressing his emotional setting and nothing radiating to us. But if now only the doctor and the patient remain unchanged and steady, while everything in the whole room begins at first to tremble and then to wave and to change its form more and more rapidly so that a feeling of dizziness comes over us and an uncanny, ghastly unnaturalness

64 • THE ORIGINS OF SONIC SCIENCE FICTION

> overcomes the whole surrounding of the hypnotized person, we ourselves become seized by the strange emotion. ([1916] 2002b, 108)

Münsterberg acknowledges that such cinematic sequences of fancy and imagination "still belong entirely to the future," when camera workers will have grasped the uniqueness of their art form and stop trying to put stage productions on the screen (108). As expressionist directors would realize, the special visual effect becomes a privileged conduit of emotional seizure, a means of conveying hypnotized affect and of fostering bodily unease in order to transmit the extremes of vicarious psychological experience. A better example of what Münsterberg predicts can hardly be found than Robert Wiene's *The Cabinet of Dr. Caligari* (1920). This tale of mesmerism, madness, and murder plays out against a psychologically charged landscape in characteristic expressionist fashion. The unusual lighting and outrageous set designs convey the otherwise invisible drama taking place within and among the characters' minds during episodes of hypnosis, somnambulism, dream invasion, and remote viewing. Rather than convey a single, objective reality, *Caligari* takes us in and out of different realities—or rather the illusionistic constructions of "reality" that exist in characters' minds in various states of consciousness. *Caligari* is a film about the technologies of the psyche, and it evokes an examination of film itself as psychotechnology (see Andriopoulos 2008, 91–127). By reflecting the film's inquiry into the workings of the mind back onto film technology itself in the form of lighting effects and perspective-changing set designs, Wiene exploits a powerful synergy between the cinematically exteriorized consciousness of his characters and the projected points-of-view of the audience. The cinematic apparatus, including the screen, constructs a middle ground in which the dual exteriorizations of consciousness meet and entangle character and spectator.

The unusual states of consciousness that expressionism explores on screen require moments of visual excess. Münsterberg puts great store in the role of visual effects, perhaps because his first trip to the cinema was to see Herbert Brenon's 1914 mermaid fantasy, *Neptune's Daughter*, at a moment in which he was particularly susceptible to escapist fantasy. During this year, the middle-aged scholar had found himself losing the respect of his esteemed colleagues. His skepticism of spiritualist mysticism alienated him from William James, while his views against prohibition and support for Germany in World War I distanced him from other American colleagues. In this fraught atmosphere, *Neptune's Daughter* was like a retreat to childhood (Langdale 2002, 6–7). Fairy tales struck Münsterberg as particularly ripe for cinematic development and an excellent avenue by which the medium could be distinguished from the stage with the most fantastic results. "Writers who have the unlimited possibilities of trick pictures and film illusions in mind have proclaimed that the fairy tale with its magic wonders ought to be its chief domain, as no theater stage could enter into rivalry," writes Münsterberg. He continues, enthralled by film's illusions:

> How many have enjoyed *Neptune's Daughter*—the mermaids in the surf and the sudden change of the witch into the octopus on the shore and the joyful play of the watersprites! How many have been bewitched by Princess Nicotina [from the 1909 short film *Princess Nicotine, or The Smoke Fairy*] when she trips from the little cigar box along the table! No theater could dare to imitate such raptures of imagination. ([1916] 2002b, 150)

Taken completely by cinema's ability to project convincing illusions of fairy tale worlds, Münsterberg recognized that film could free itself not only of the slavish imitation of reality but also from the conventions of theatrical production. Münsterberg speculates on the potential for visual effects that would manipulate time by physically altering the film speed, reversing the direction of the film's playback, or putting the camera on unsteady supports in order to give filmed motions "an uncanny whirling character" ([1916] 2002b, 107). Such an effect, which "never occurs in nature and which could not be produced on the stage," would open up film to all sorts of "rhythms" and so create a sense that a "certain vibration goes through the world like the tremolo of the orchestra" (107). As Münsterberg proposes innovative experiments that would draw visual effects and technological illusions into the domains of a meaningful and unique critical discourse about film, he pushes the silent form to its very limit, where only a sonic metaphor can characterize this new spectacle of visual motion.

Münsterberg writes in far-reaching ways about the camera, film editing, and special visual tricks as part of cinema's unique psychological and emotional cachet. The more he considers the emerging aesthetic of cinema as something distinct from other art forms and media—those of theater in particular—the more he formulates aesthetic values that exceed the cinematic imitation of reality. In this way, he advocates for new avenues by which filmmakers and viewers can explore the connection between emerging technological processes and their corresponding psychological effects. "As soon as such abnormal visual impressions stream into our consciousness," Münsterberg writes, "our whole background of fusing bodily sensations becomes altered, and new emotions seem to take hold of us" ([1916] 2002b, 107–8). The argument that film changes human consciousness is at the heart of Münsterberg's theory of cinematic experience:

> A work of art may and must start from something which awakens in us the interests of reality and which contains traits of reality, and to that extent it cannot avoid some imitation. But *it becomes art just in so far as it overcomes reality, stops imitating and leaves the imitated reality behind it.* It is artistic just in so far as it does not imitate reality but changes the world, selects from its special features for new purposes, remodels the world, and is, through this, truly creative. (114)

Cinema thus fulfills a fundamentally cosmological function that places world building at the disposal of human consciousness through imaginative play bolstered by technological innovation. By Münsterberg's account, film appears to be waiting for the self-reflexive turn of a psychotechnological convergence that would first occur in expressionism's fantasies of horror and science fiction. But what it is really waiting for is sound. "The musical accompaniment of the photoplays is one of the most urgent questions in the realm of this new art," he asserts in a 1916 interview conducted by Paramount Pictures, eventually published in the *New York Dramatic Mirror*:

> No responsible producing company ought to send out a photoplay without making sure that music of their own selection be rendered at the performance, and this selection must not be a routine choice of

favorite melodies, but a truly musical interpretation of the play. . . . The most artistic adjustment of the music to the play is the one condition upon which everything depends. It can be done, and it has been done, but exception must become the rule; and such a change will react favorably on the total world of the film. ([1916] 2002a, 202–3)

Music—and not just any music but rather work composed specifically with the needs of the particular film in mind—is the key condition on which film depends not only as an artistic unit but also as a self-sufficient world. Münsterberg here gestures beyond the musical score to what would later become known as sound design, which involves the world building combination of music and noise. It is clear to me that the makers of *Metropolis* sought a music that was more than its nondiegetic score; they recognized the importance of crafted sonic design as a way to achieve the critically engaged, speculative world building of the science fiction film.

The sonic experience of *Metropolis* evokes changes not only to human perception but also to the living, moving human body, particularly with its inclusion of the fox-trot that accompanies scenes in the exotic nightclub, Yoshiwara. Most of the Yoshiwara material was cut for the American version of the film that, by April 1927, was being distributed internationally and even to German cinemas (Minden and Bachmann 2000, 42–43). Whether cut for being obscene or because of their critique of capitalist culture, the impact of their loss on the sonic dimensions of the film is significant. During these scenes of lavish decadence, the evil robot duplicate of the noble schoolteacher, Maria, is shown at its most licentious and depraved. The false Maria, who hides the robot form of the Machine Man under her womanly appearance, incites a crowd into a jittery and delirious fox-trot even as the city itself is on the verge of disaster. This episode would seem to confirm the suspicions of several European and Russian critics who detected in this particular, popular dance form a bourgeois embrace of the machinic transformation of life under capitalism. In the First All-Russian Conference on Music in 1929, Marxist revolutionary Anatoly Lunacharsky would condemn the fox-trot's "extreme mechanization of rhythm" (Ball 2003, 103). Lunacharsky concluded that the "bourgeois and his slave are accustomed to machines, to machine technology, to machine rhythm in which there is nothing alive, in which the main thing is an extreme metronomic precision and also a sort of lifeless originality" (103). The artificial essence of the fox-trot, with its speed, repetition, and brassy, mechanized pounding, was for Lunacharsky "the direct antithesis to music, an anti-human sound" (103). In the film, Lang's association of the fox-trot with the false Maria and decadence in general suggests similar suspicions of jazzy dance music. The irony that the fox-trot composed by Huppertz should become one of the most popular *Metropolis* themes featured on the Vox record may have been lost on the presumably pompous audience at the film's Berlin premiere, likely not much different from the crowd at the Yoshiwara.

Lang's inclusion of the fox-trot is a unique instance in *Metropolis* of diegetically represented music rather than nondiegetic accompaniment. Chion notes the surprising frequency with which silent films feature footage of dancers, singers, bands, and orchestras. It was rare, however, for actual singers and musicians in the pit to try and match the images of musical performance on the screen. Rather, the musician or ensemble would provide "a sort of simultaneous translation," often on completely different instruments than those shown on the screen (2009, 9). Certainly no one in the film's audience would be expected to believe that they were actually hearing the singers or instruments on the screen anymore than they could hear intertitle transcripts as actual dialogue. Between "pit and screen," Chion writes, "there existed a poetic distance, an irreducible gap that allowed filmgoers to continue their aural dreaming of the screen's music without ever confusing that with its stylized embodiment" by the accompanying performers (10). As far as *Metropolis* goes, this gap is most narrow when its music approaches a kind of diegetic representation of what we see on the screen: not only in the Yoshiwara but also the noise of the machines heard during the opening sequence and the boiler room disaster. These connections strike me as intentional and also occur visually; sequences of dense montage effects used nowhere else in the film link the early shots of machine frenzy with that of the Yoshiwara partiers, particularly the kaleidoscopic mesh of leering, isolated eyes and the mouths of men watching the false Maria dance. Here science fiction cinema's first sonic novum dramatizes the theme of the mechanized replacement of the human heart that by the film's end we are told must join mind and hand together. The pushing of this sonic theme from pit to screen takes the silent film to its limits in anticipation of the era of sound synchronization. This is the beginning of the end of the "poetic distance" that Chion describes—a distance removed by the closing of the gap between the inner ear with its "aural dreaming" and the outer alterity of music's "stylized embodiments." But with the removal of one gap, another appears.

The noise-music of *Metropolis* promises the mechanical synchronization that would allow all sounds to unfold not as a property inherent to the image but rather as what Chion calls "added value," which facilitates a still greater poetic distance between image and sound in postproduction (2009, 212). The closing of the gap between diegetic noise and nondiegetic music, a distance that seems to disappear when both become matters of design, assemblage and compositing during editing, is an aural illusion. Sound has to come from elsewhere, not from within, in order to bring to the image an "expressive and informative" enrichment, which is added and yet gives the impression "that this information or expression 'naturally' comes from what is seen, and is already contained in the image itself" (212). The noise that results from the atonal layering of instrumental voices and accelerated rhythms, heard in both the machine music sequences and the fox-trot scene, strains toward the status of sound effect or diegetic music—in either case, a sound that emits from the imaginary world of the film. It does so by appearing to be, paradoxically, "non-illusionist," as Chion labels it, a "more 'sublimated' evocation of noises via musical accompaniment" than music proper, and of a sound that has found its place because it never left it (7). As Huppertz realizes in his *Metropolis* score, machine music announces the end of the autonomy of earlier silent film accompaniment styles, not because it abandons the patchwork of interchangeable musical cues with familiar kinds of cinematic events and their corresponding human emotions but because it strives toward new kinds of sounds and musical styles associated specifically with special visual effects (abstracted machine parts approaching kinetic sculpture, kaleidoscopic montage, special lighting processes). The sound effect of machine music also resonates with narrative themes concerning the mechanization of the human labor force,

70 • THE ORIGINS OF SONIC SCIENCE FICTION

dystopian class stratification, the hypnotic effect of the decadent foxtrot, and the dangers posed to social justice by the artificial replicant.

This new sonic sensibility points to different kinds of events and themes within the narrative but also to imminent changes to the nature and form of sonic cinematic experience. Even as early SF films begin to embrace new sounds, conventional acoustic instrumentation and melodic sensibilities dominate the form in ways that ultimately bolster the underlying humanist messages of the films rather than valorize sonic newness on its own terms. The spectacle of the Yoshiwara sequence consists of an extended dance routine with provocative costumes, a foxtrot song, and some remarkable special visual effects. This mechanical synchronization of human motion—first in the underground tunnels of the workers, next in the fox-trots of Yoshiwara—is key to the sonic novum of *Metropolis,* which anticipates the very precision of synchronized accompaniment that would only come with sound films and mask the whirring of the projector with its own noises. Sound here, even when most adventurous, is tied to quite a conservative humanism. When inhuman rhythms and the harsh clock of machinic time signatures conquer leisure as well as work, popular music becomes an emblem of mass sensory manipulation and control, a spectacular equivalent to the lockstep rhythms of hard labor. The Yoshiwara segment of *Metropolis,* unseen for decades before its discovery in an Argentinian theater, thus suggests more than a peak of early cinematic special effects. This moment of spectacular excess stalls narrative momentum even while it remains critical of spectacle.

The Yoshiwara scene points toward the pending popularization—and popularizing excesses—of synchronized sound. Just a few years after the release of *Metropolis,* the added sonic values of cinematic spectacle were radically amplified in David Butler's film, *Just Imagine* (1930). Dismissing any hint of the irony that underscored Lang's Yoshiwara sequence, the elaborate song and dance routines of this musical take place in the futuristic setting of 1980's New York City. Images of technological innovation are played for wonder, but the narrative of "present-day boy meets the girl of the future" plays strictly for laughs. Though the comedic events, sets, and costumes support the futuristic aspects of the narrative, the song and dance routines demonstrate no sonic innovations whatsoever. As J. P. Telotte notes, the film may look like 1980, but it sounds just like 1930 (1999, 116). This particular turn toward the sonic spectacle as a familiarizing element is common to many Depression-era musicals, in which a variety show full of musical numbers may be strung together by a flimsy narrative running through them. It seems to be a part of cinema's struggle to appear live and immediate, which required, Chion notes, creation of the "illusionistic whole" of cinematic experience (2009, 231). With the advent of sound synchronization, both aesthetic design and meaning become matters of postproduction edits, the mixing down and aligning of the auditory and visual experience. This synchronized wholeness is illusory because the addition of sound to film actually inserts that new gap which I mentioned earlier, the one that takes shape between the act of filming and the reproduction of the film's narrative flow during sound editing. This gap between film and sound is quite different in synchronized works than the prior distance between the orchestral pit and screen, largely because the nonillusionistic presence of an accompanying pianist or ensemble once gave every theatrical film screening what Chion calls "the allure of a true performance" (9). Chion concludes that with silent films, sound's "real and imaginary dimensions are created in collaboration with the image, and at the same time sound is always overflowing and transgressing it" (249). In the case of *Just Imagine*, even as the choreographed song and dance numbers break out as spectacle for its own sake, in celebration of the kind of sonic overflowing typical of silent-era films, they forego any possibility of science fictional estrangement in favor of novelty and cleverness. The same is true in the 1935 serial *Phantom Empire*, which provides a vehicle for singing cowboy Gene Autry. The film pits Autry, whose character both runs a ranch and performs daily as a radio star, against visiting marauders from the underground city of Murania. The city's evil queen, Tika, threatens surface dwellers with her advanced technologies, including flamethrower-equipped robots. The *Phantom Empire* series offers plenty of sequences of Autry singing on the radio, giving viewers a solid dose of down-to-earth Americana in the form of hillbilly novelty songs and cowboy ballads that emotively counteract the technological perils in the story even while embracing new broadcast media formats. Both *Just Imagine* and the *Phantom Empire* serials approach cinema as a site of remediation, drawing from their roots in Broadway musicals and live radio broadcasts while ultimately commemorating the lost form of live cinematic experience typical of the silent era. Dance routines and song sequences ultimately prove inconsequential to the coherence of both narratives while aesthetically offsetting the films' science fictional aspects with what Hayward calls "a sense of cultural 'normality'" (2004b, 7). The familiarizing, even uplifting songs in these films respond more to Depression-era scarcity, anxiety, and malaise than to concerns over emerging technologies and other science fictional themes (see Spring 2010, 67–85). In this respect, they lack true sonic novums.

1936 | *THINGS TO COME*

The first SF film to develop the sonic novum through synchronized sound is William Cameron Menzies's *Things to Come* (1936). The film was the product of the popular British writer H. G. Wells, which variations of the title in early promotional materials often made explicitly clear, perhaps in an effort to legitimate the project by clearly associating it with the man whose scientific romances like *The Time Machine* (1895), *The Island of Doctor Moreau* (1896), and *The War of the Worlds* (1897) would certainly define the shape of science fiction to come. For the film, Wells adapted his own history of the future, *The Shape of Things to Come* (1933), and was involved throughout the production. He hoped that *Things to Come* would illustrate the "social and political forces and possibilities" presented not only in his novel but also in his analysis of socioeconomics, *The Work, Wealth, and Happiness of Mankind* (1931; see Wells 1935, 9). Though one is fiction and the other is not, both books involve meticulous extrapolation and complex critical analysis, and they are almost indistinguishable in style. *The Shape of Things to Come* is presented as a college history textbook from the year 2106, its pages dreamed into the present day and transcribed by a visionary diplomat to the United Nations, Dr. Philip Raven. The novel and its film adaptation reflect anxieties surrounding the rise of fascism in Europe, and both begin by anticipating the Blitz and the destruction of London. The major historical eras of the film roughly correspond to those outlined in the novel, such as "The Modern State Militant: 1978–2059" and "The Modern State in

Control of Life: 2059 to New Year's Day 2106," the titles hitching the project's concern with the modern to a deeper investment in authoritarian ascendency as neither militancy nor state control of life are regarded as fascist dispositions. Surpassing the book's emphasis on terrestrial utopia achieved through benevolent dictatorship, the film aims humanity's destiny toward the stars, adding a space gun mission to the moon after the last gasp of reactionary Luddite protest on Earth.

There are several other significant differences. Though both the novel and the film begin in familiar historical territory, the script replaces London with the generic Everytown. And in contrast to the novel's academic scholarship, which distances the presentation of global events from the daily lives of real people, the film documents a series of architectural set pieces in the allegorical city, joined together by newsreel styled montages that segue between the major epochs, often jumping entire decades at a time. The major narrative moments depict Everytown's destruction during the air raids of World War II; the social devolution of humanity into tribes occupying the city's ruins; the arrival of a group of reconstructionists based out of Basra, Iraq, who call themselves Wings Over the World; and the construction of a shining new underground city, at which point something that had felt like prewar London turns into a now-global utopia, a true Everytown in more than just name. Central to the history of the future, Everytown acts as the primary novum of the film. It embodies Wells's argument for the manufacture of a modern utopia through a benevolent authoritarianism. Surveying Earth from their mighty airships, Wings Over the World conquer disease and, with the help of their peace gas, finally reverse the condition of barbarous tribalism to which humanity had devolved after the forty-year war that began with the aerial bombing of Everytown on Christmas Eve 1940. Wings Over the World redirects the dictatorial fantasy of world domination into that of a benevolent global technocracy built on what one character calls "a common order and a common knowledge." While the film only implies it with images of angelic togas and airy translucent furnishings, Wells's interest in the "common" has nothing to do with the communal or the proletariat. His book makes clear that the eventual utopia has everything to do with a forced upward mobility that essentially engineers a culture of middle class intelligentsia. The allegorical elements of the film keep all of this rather vague, whereas Wells's novel describes in great detail this stage of centralizing education, establishing English as the lingua franca of the new world order, and finally eradicating all world religions in the name of science. Given the conditions in Europe when Wells wrote his book, and with England on the brink of being drawn into the war, it may be surprising that he would propose a system of authoritarian rule. For Wells, it appeared sufficient to counter nationalism with a cooperative globalism that eventually transcends the limits of world state, and there is no irony in his utopia of genius supermen, achieved after centuries of vanquishing outmoded forms of the sociopolitical organization of human culture.

The novel's academic feel is preserved in the film's frequently didactic tone, which accounts for its most consistent sonic feature. There are few natural exchanges of dialogue. Instead, characters give speeches; they instruct and teach, rant and rally. The ponderous orations of Raymond Massey's two characters provide the film's dominant voice: first as John Cabal, a businessman turned fighter pilot turned spokesman for Wings Over the World, and then his grandson, Oswald, head of Earth's governing council in 2036. Massey would later note that Wells's deliberate formalization of the dialogue made *Things to Come* "fantastically difficult to act. . . . Emotion had no place in Wells' new world" (in Frayling 1995, 22). The grand scope and global scale of events that concerned Wells left the emotive and psychological characterization of individuals largely ignored. However, the musical score by popular composer Arthur Bliss was meant to compensate for this, according to Wells, and as film sound scholar Gregg Redner argues in his extended analysis, the music "clearly added the dimension of human-ness" otherwise absent from the film, particularly so from its dialogue (2011, 142). Though Bliss would not agree, Wells conceived of the recitative insertion of human speech part of the musical vocabulary of its operatic architecture. The film would shift from extended oratories, largely devoid of musical accompaniment, to atmospheric set pieces, the tone and pace of which would be carefully established by an arialike orchestral score (Frayling 1995, 36). The author's film treatment reveals an elaborate personal vision, which includes specific directions regarding the sonic shape and rhythm of the narrative:

THE ORIGINS OF SONIC SCIENCE FICTION • 75

The spirit of the opening is busy and fretful and into it creeps a deepening menace. Then come the crashes and confusions of modern war. The second part is the distressful melody and grim silences of the pestilence period. In the third, military music and patriotic tunes are invaded by the throbbing return of the air men. The throbbing passes into the mechanical crescendo of the period of reconstruction. This becomes more swiftly harmonious and softer and softer as greater efficiency abolishes that clatter of strenuous imperfection which was so distinctive of the earlier mechanical civilization of the nineteenth century. The music of the new world is gay and spacious. Against this plays the motif of the reactionary revolt; ending in the stormy victory of the new ideas as the Space Gun fires and the moon cylinder starts on its momentous journey. The music ends with anticipations of a human triumph in the heroic finale amidst the stars. (in Manvell and Huntley 1957, 50)

With the musical score intended to play such a huge part in the overall conceptual scheme of *Things to Come,* the film's producer, Alexander Korda, did well to get a respected symphonic composer on board for his first movie score. Bliss's motivation was decidedly commercial, but despite his sense that a cinematic score was not quite serious music, he must have been pleased when a singular "*Things to Come* Suite" managed to satisfy critics on the grounds that it could be "understood as 'pure music,' unattached to the cinema" (Redner 2011, 141). First published in 1936 and still performed to this day, the condensed suite acted as an early legitimizer of film music as a sophisticated art form in its own right, even while skirting around the contaminating influence of commercial entertainment. A three-record set of the entire score, performed by the London Symphony Orchestra conducted by Bliss himself for the Decca label in 1936, was one of the first British film scores released independent of its film.

Ultimately, however, the popularity of Bliss's music is far less important than his role in the creative development of the film. Bliss met with the production crew—a rarity in the filmmaking practices of his day, and an anomaly, given the crew's previous experiences of films being driven by the producer, director, and maybe the writer. "In this as in so many respects," Wells wrote, "this film, so far at least as its intention goes, is boldly experimental. Sound sequences and picture sequences are closely interwoven. The Bliss music is not intended to be tacked on; it is part of the design" (Manvell and Huntley 1957, 49–50). Unfortunately, despite Wells's recollection of bold experimentation, the music is strikingly down to earth, quite practical in style and function, and often derivative of familiar passages from the works of Edward Elgar, Richard Wagner, Richard Strauss, and Igor Stravinsky. When depicting scenes of world war and its aftermath, for instance, or as it punctuates the motivational speech "arias" delivered by John Cabal on behalf of Wings Over the World, the music turns martial in the brash mode of British symphonic fanfare. Occasionally dissonant and faster-paced tempos associated with images of global disaster and gradual recovery suggest modernist sensibilities, but in truth, the score can hardly be considered experimental, even for the mid-1930s. Wells's statement to the contrary more likely reflects the underlying conservatism of his own musical tastes. For his part, Bliss was at best ambivalent about modernism, which eventually led to his absorption into and ascendency through the ranks of Great Britain's musical establishment. A popular composer and conductor for years to come, he was appointed as director of music at the BBC from 1942 to 1944, was knighted in 1950, and was named Master of Queen's Music in 1953. As they related to his work on *Things to Come,* the conservative nature of Bliss's sensibilities informed his worrying over the distinctions between two types of machine music called for in Wells's treatment of the rebuilding of Everytown from postwar disaster zone to underground utopia. One was an overly representative music, a sound effect really, to capture the noisy extraction of the Earth's resources, and the other an abstract, absolute music capable of conveying the sublimity of future industry with an impression of effervescent, almost invisible beauty.

It will turn out that the most modern aspect of the sonic experience of *Things to Come* has little to do with Bliss's score and everything to do with the new techniques of mechanical synchronization of sound and vision. Musicologist Matthew Riley rightly notes that if it is a foray into modernism, *Things to Come* is more vital because of Wells's vision of new forms of cinematic spectacle made possible by the synthesis of sound and vision. Riley situates *Things to Come* in the context of early modernist efforts to revitalize aesthetic experience by counteracting the institutional compartmentalization of art and culture through a "total work of art," something like the Wagnerian Gesamtkunstwerk for the cinema, or what Wells splices together as "spectacle–music–drama" (2010, 249). Wells sought to confront the dominant tendencies of commercial cinema by making a film with a far more serious purpose, one more educational than entertaining. By combining elements of prophetic warning with testaments to the power of modern science to build a better world, Wells sought to convey his hope for the future, his trust in science and technology, and his belief that humanity shaped its own destiny. Wells's desire to avoid commercial motivations were matched by his resistance of dramatic tendencies as well, which he thought would tug his film in the direction of the stage. Treating cinema as "spectacle," on the other hand, would result in a new synthesis of the arts, "deploying all possibilities of the media of sound and moving image for the sake of a deeply serious purpose: the communication of his political message. This new art form would be both high-minded and popular ('broad-brow')" (252). Discussing the film in *The King Who Was a King* (1929), Wells described what he called "the art form of the future" (1). Here he often strikes a militant, if not altogether fascist, pitch: "The Spectacle will march to music, sink to silence or rise to thunder as its effects require" (12). Keep this silence in mind. But first, the thunder.

In a montage sequence running longer than five minutes, the rebuilding of Everytown begins with the "mechanical crescendo" that Wells desired in his treatment. Hardly a single diegetic sound accompanies images of giant machines excavating the hills, and the noises that are there play very low in the mix. The music, on the other hand, approaches diegesis by pairing low, pounding timpani with a higher-pitched percussive sound, like a metallic pickax on stone. The orchestra, not sound effects, represents the explosions of Earth, and in several precise instances, rolling drums and blasts of brass horns are perfectly synchronized with the footage of bursting hillsides. After this sonic apogee of what Wells's treatment labels "the earlier mechanical civilization"— with its historical "clatter" of percussion and trumpeting crescendos— the sound of *Things to Come* begins to change, becoming "harmonious and softer and softer." The mighty propulsive explosions of percussion and brass rapidly shift into fluttering winds and rushing strings, all suggestive of a gradual refinement from tectonic noise to the gentle music of industrial manufacturing. The music itself is more sonically efficient as it undergoes a conceptual noise reduction, veering from whimsical airiness to a looping phrase of rising and falling strings—anticipating nothing so much as the Muzaklike blandness of industry training and promotional films soon produced by corporations like AT&T, General Electric, and General Motors—before being propelled along by one of Bliss's beloved marches.

At one point in the production, the montage was to have included some special visual effects created by experimental filmmaker Laszlo Moholy-Nagy using his kinetic sculpture, the Licht-Raum Modulator. Without a doubt, shots of his metal sculptures emphasizing the raw play of light and shadow and various lens tricks would have taken the film into the abstract territories of Bliss's musical impressionism. But Wells didn't like them, and all but a few seconds were cut. The sounds alone would provide the images their weight—or rather their absence of weight, as the montage mounts toward the clean white walls, simple architectural lines, and the clear plastic furnishings of the new Everytown. For Bliss, the sequence had to convey a grand advancement beyond base human survival to the heights of cultural evolution through technology, the ethereal music of industry reinforcing the film's argument for a calming technocratic order that sonically resolves the martial rhythms and horns associated with times of conflict, strife, and suffering. From the propulsive explosions of its birth in percussive noise to the glorious winds and strings of its ascent, and despite the fact that Everytown is in fact subterranean, everything from the translucent furniture to the pantless tunics and capes of its inhabitants suggests a technoutopic heaven.

Bliss's progressive sonic refinery, his achievement of an impression of ultimate lightness and transparency of force, may well offer an outright critique of the harsh and noisy machinery evoked in Huppertz's *Metropolis* score. Wells was certainly vocal in his distaste for *Metropolis*. He thought it dreadful. In an early memo to Korda's production crew, he dismisses Lang's film as "balderdash" and instructs, "As a general rule you may take it that whatever Lange [*sic*] did in *Metropolis* is the exact contrary of what we want done here" (in Frayling 1995, 48). The writer particularly took issue with Lang's thematic emphasis on the machine:

> "Common people" generally in the past were infinitely more uniform and "mechanical" than any people in the future will be. Machinery has superseded the subjugation and "mechanization" of human beings. *Please keep that in mind.* The workers to be shown are individualized workers doing responsible co-operative teamwork. And *work will be unobtrusive* in the coming civilization. (in Frayling 1995, 48)

Though Wells had most likely never heard the Huppertz score, his comments in fact highlight a key contrast between the sonic dimensions of the two films. The atonal sounds and accelerated rhythms of *Metropolis* signified the machinic depredation of the human, generally denoting a pace and scale of technical forces that eclipse the capacities of human perception. Modernist rejection of harmony and melody underscores the narrative contest between the human and machinic sounds. The former is coded as musical event and the latter as sound effect, even if only the sublimated, nondiegetic musical noise that stands in for another kind of diegetic noise. At its most expressionistic, the music of *Metropolis* did not externalize interior human states of consciousness; rather, they evoked new artificial states of being engineered through the machine's complete penetration of the human psyche, first through new modes of mechanical labor and then through the sounds of popular music, which brought the alienation of the human labor force into the spectacular extravagances of the upper class. The impressionist elements of the *Things to Come* score offer something quite different—indeed, the "exact contrary" that Wells desired. Bliss creates an ambience of larger-than-human forces and energies, in this case the power of progress itself channeled toward the technocratic reordering of the whole world, directing social evolution, conquering nature, and reauthoring history. As an impressionist ambient device, sound detaches from specific human characters and the range of their emotions to become a measure of historical progression that plays toward the human ideal and a sonic ascension into the beyond—but rather than spiritual, even this beyond is a domain for human history, conquest, scientific discovery, and destiny. A contrast of spectacular visual elements in *Metropolis* and *Things to*

Come—in fact, two distinct approaches to cinematic montage—makes the corresponding shift from machinic expressionism to industrial impressionism more vivid. In *Metropolis* a kaleidoscopic mixture of abstracted machine parts, fragmented bodies, and excised human organs (eyes, mouths), creates spectacular densities that exceed the narrative to express the grotesque reassemblage of new machine-bodies, almost already cyborgs. In *Things to Come,* the montage works along a historical time line to denote narrative compression and an excision of humans almost entirely. The impressionistic aspects of Bliss's industry theme not only create a specific atmosphere but also imply the presence of unseen forces, the pace and rhythm of progress that subsumes the human within the virtual posthumanity of history beyond Earth.

With construction complete, the new underground city of Everytown is introduced with a short drum roll and trumpet fanfare, then silence. We hear very little music again until the conclusion of Cabal's last speech. Images of the gleaming white Everytown, with its artificial light sources, underground towers, and suspended walkways, are accompanied only by the murmur of the crowds and other faint diegetic sounds. Contrary to all of the talk of the Luddite, rabble-rousing sculptor, Theotocopulos (Cedric Hardwicke), who declaims that "talk, talk, radio is everywhere, this modern world is full of voices," Everytown 2036 is shockingly quiet, devoid in fact of any sound other than the human voice, and even this is rendered as a bubbling murmur. It as if along with their refinement of furniture and devices to translucent plastic, the designers of Everytown have also silenced the crude materiality of the old mechanical world. Only the space gun will emit any noise before the end of the film, first with a faint electric hum that underscores the smooth glide of pistons as the so-called space bullet is loaded into place. After the leader of Everytown, Oswald Cabal, warns the mob to beware the space gun's concussion, Bliss's score returns with a fury, blustery and dense with drums that override the anger of the crowd as we approach the impending moment of propulsion. The music becomes quiet as the space gun is cocked back. A lever is pulled on a control panel, accompanied by an expulsion of air and then the thunderous blast of the space gun itself, the volume slowly fading as the screen fills with smoke. It's noisy, sure, but a necessary last, crude burst of mechanical noise before silence.

Then, as the smoke clears to reveal the starry sky above, the orchestral score returns with its final solemn and majestic theme underscoring a last, overwrought Cabalism: "All the universe or nothing! Which shall it be?" As Cabal repeats himself twice more, a rising chorus of voices echo against the stark and starry sky, "Which shall it be? Which shall it be?" In the end it seems that only the human voice in chorus can convey what Wells called "that exultant shout of human resolution" as well as "the marching song of a new world of conquest among the atoms and stars" (in Frayling 1995, 39). Ascending to the cosmos at last, Bliss's score resolves with a secular, choral apotheosis of unforeseeable human potential rendered as cold speculation and faith in science.

"I want to end," Wells concludes in his treatment, "on a complete sensuous and emotional synthesis" (in Frayling 1995, 40). He believed this was something that could only happen when the musical elements were treated from the outset as part of the film's overall design. The strident tones meant to signify human destiny at the end of the film—to convey Wells's "heroic finale" without a hero, in fact, but rather another human-eclipsing ideal, "triumph"—sit rather harshly against the flat images of a painted star field. The scene is a somewhat shrill reminder that Wells was unable to guide to its completion the unifying synthesis of *Things to Come* as he had hoped. As Bliss recalls, "The financial necessity of having to appeal to a vast audience meant a concession here and a concession there, a watering down in one place, a deletion in another, so that, instead of having the impact of a vital parable, it became just an exciting entertainment" (1970, 105–6). The writer's investment in political proselytizing through artistic spectacle hinged on the technical refinement of the "effective practical synchronizing of sound with film," which he was certain would lead to the conjoined art forms being conceived of and composed together (1929, 12)—at least in theory. In practice, Wells exerted the same "philosophy of planning and central control" that invested his utopian vision with its liberal as well as authoritarian principles, at times calling on the latter in service to the former (Riley 2010, 256–57). But as far as filmmaking went, Riley notes that Wells "lacked precisely the quality the film celebrated—expert technical knowledge" (257). He really had no idea of what was involved to realize his wishes for perfect synthesis in service of the new spectacle. Take, for instance, the newly developed audiovisual synchronization transforming cinema. The synchronization of image and sound was in fact a remarkable feat that required a tremendous precision of human mastery over time. In his autobiography, *As I Remember,* Bliss recalls watching the film's music director, young Scottish conductor Muir Mathieson, leading the London Symphony Orchestra through their performance of his music. "It is a fatiguing and anxious job fitting music to a film," he writes, "and I used greatly to admire Muir at work, baton in one hand, stop watch in the other, one eye on the film and the other on his players" (1970, 106). But perhaps this careful mechanization went contrary to Wells's ideals of a grander synthesis, itself an impressionistic, abstract, and absolute critique of the mechanical.

The distinction that Wells would repeatedly make in correspondence and interviews between intent and result points to his ultimate dissatisfaction with the final product. Wells's original plan was that Bliss would compose and record the score prior to shooting, so that the crew would use the music as a guide to the development of the scenes in production as well as postproduction; typically the musical elements were composed and applied to the film at the last stage of editing (Bar-Sagi 2013). In a letter to Bliss, Wells vigorously defends his belief that the musical score should guide the production of the film rather than come after the final editing cuts have been made. In this respect, Wells is ironically akin to Lang, who had Huppertz play his music on a piano during the shooting of *Metropolis* to help set the mood and tempo of the scenes. For Wells, however, the musical sensibility behind *Things to Come* was less an emblem of mood and tempo than of structure and order. Arguing that "film is a composition" and therefore requires the sensibilities of a "musical composer," Wells faults Korda, the film's producer, for not having "much of an ear but I want the audience at the end not to know what it sees from what it hears" (in Frayling 1995, 40). This is in fact a quite uncinematic idea, one working completely against sound's ability to magnetize sonic events to the image to such an extent that what we hear—the entire "auditory field"—seems to be the "function of what appears on the screen" (Chion 2009, 249). Wells would silence sound's emergent power.

Wells's design of *Things to Come* would celebrate the purposefulness of synchronization over the actual sounds themselves. As often as not, Wells demands extended sequences without any underscore at all. This silence was in fact something new to cinematic experience. The silence of synchronized film demonstrated a dramatic weight that was quite different from the constant musical accompaniment heard during so-called silent films, or the noise of the audience, or the whir of the projector. Wells takes a unique approach to sound design at its outset, arguing for an absolute minimalism that in fact offers us a naive prediction of the approaches to SF sound design that several auteur filmmakers would revisit in the 1960s. Using not music but silence to emphasize the futuristic atmosphere anticipates these filmmakers' interest in manufacturing environments as a way to convey the otherness of future, alien, and outer spaces. Considered independently of the Bliss score, then, *Things to Come* suggests ways in which sound editing can contribute as much as musical composition to the construction of the sonic novum. Sound editing negotiates divisions between dialogue, voice-over, diegetic atmosphere, and nondiegetic accompaniment in often stark ways, in sequence and without much overlap. In *Things to Come,* Bliss's themes don't bubble along constantly. Rather, the music is interspersed among scenes with dialogue and monologue, diegetic sound and noises ranging from the bombing of the original Everytown to the nearly silent mall-like interiors of its later incarnation. The sound editing reinforces the logic of the film's structure as future documentary, the gaps in the underscore making it feel as if we move from actual historical event to a newsreel montage before suddenly and selectively emphasizing the prophetic demagoguery that comprises Wells's vision with its militant, modern, and ultimately anthemic tones.

Abstraction and absolutism work together in Wells's theory of the cinematic spectacle, but as artistic practice, they canceled each other out. Wells thought that the ideal resolution of "the distinction between art and science" would make *Things to Come* an exemplary form of "new sound drama upon the screen," one that would "ultimately supersede opera and theatre" (in Riley 2010, 268). However, modeling a new symbiotic relationship between art and technology after an absolute music, which would bring about the total aestheticization of science through cinematic spectacle, merely amplified the most troubling aspects of

Wells's "liberal fascism" (see Coupland 2000, 541–58). The audiovisual montage that depicts the rebuilding of the modern Everytown glosses over an extended section of Wells's novel: the era of the Wings Over the World's putatively benevolent dictatorship. "Instead of engaging with the knotty problem of political means and ends that is raised at this point," Riley provocatively concludes, "the sequence invites the viewer's assent for the new world order through mystification, images of colossal power, and a dazzling play of music, light and motion" (2010, 268). The few remaining sequences that feature the kinetic art of Moholy-Nagy's Licht-Raum Modulator device, paired with the gentlest elements of Bliss's score, depict the industry of the future as "an abstract pattern of pleasing forms rather than a purposeful process of production," Riley asserts, until the scene seems on the verge of resolving into images and sounds of "purposeless beauty" (265). As absolute music corresponds with the spectacular flow of industry, rendered together as nothing other than the playful flow of forms, Bliss's score is certainly most vivid when its impressions correspond to extramusical elements of an equally abstracted nature. Interestingly enough, the rebuilding of Everytown is thought to be the only scene in which film edits were absolutely matched to the music (Bliss 1970, 105). Yet when the composer debuted this sequence of the score for Wells, the writer responded, "I am sure that all that is very fine music, but I'm afraid you have missed the whole point. You see, the machines of the future will be *noiseless*" (105)!

1927–50 | THE THEREMIN

Not quiet noiseless, in fact. We have one last entry in this prehistory of sonic science fiction proper to consider: a brief study of the electric instrumental sound that would define the genre in 1950. Coming into its own as an innovative sonic novum in several films before exhausting itself as the genre's most characteristic audible cliché, the theremin brings with it significant conflicts between established musical sensibilities and alternative aesthetics probing the place of new sound technologies. I mean "place" quite literally. Where do new sounds and the technologies that make them belong? Is it in properly orchestral contexts, as part of avant-gardist practices, or, particularly after World War II, within a mass media shaped by its insatiable hunger for novelty and disposable entertainment? As it glides through all of these categories, the theremin exemplifies the bond between electronic instrumentalities, changing aesthetics, and new listening sensibilities that will transform popular culture throughout the history of the SF film.

In search of new listening experiences, John Cage heard the theremin as emblematic of a broader cultural clash between those who embrace original sonic possibilities and those who would censor emerging auditory sensibilities by clinging to past idioms. However, most of what Cage heard played on the theremin fulfilled neither his desires nor speculations regarding the future of music and sound. Rather, in concert and exposition halls around the world, the theremin had been shoehorned into traditional classical settings that could accommodate its wandering tones only with great difficulty. While mastering the theremin's quirky interface indicated a new class of virtuosity for some players, Cage was frustrated by the conceptual and performative constraints that the theremin's most prominent advocates placed on the instrument:

> When Theremin provided an instrument with genuinely new possibilities, Thereministes did their utmost to make the instrument sound like some old instrument, giving it a sickeningly sweet vibrato, and performing upon it, with difficulty, masterpieces from the past. Although the instrument is capable of a wide variety of sound qualities, obtained by the mere turning of a dial, Thereministes act as censors, giving the public those sounds they think the public will like. We are shielded from new sound experiences. ([1937] 2004, 26)

As Cage laments, the earliest theremin recitals typically consisted of a familiar fare of so-called masterpieces, and slower ones at that, like Schubert's "Ave Maria," Saint-Saën's "The Swan," and Rachmaninoff's "Vocalise." Despite early advocates like Leopold Stokowski—the first conductor to incorporate electronic instruments and amplification during his tenure with the Philadelphia Orchestra—most musicians, composers, critics, and audiences of early twentieth-century orchestras remained unconvinced that the theremin or other electronics had a place in the concert hall.

Léon Theremin, who referred to himself as a technician rather than a musician, thought that his invention pointed to a future of sound beyond the classical and romantic repertoire. Yet partly as a result of his own training as a cellist, and partly as a result of his desire to market the instrument to home parlor musicians as well as orchestras, he stuck to a repertoire of recognizable melodies with which he might prove the instrument's value as such. However, the quirkiness of the theremin's sound and the stylized manner of its playing technique would ultimately guarantee that it could never become more than a fad. The serious Thereministes, as Cage called them, thus found themselves having to combat the trivialization of the instrument even when it was finally on the cusp of the popularity that Theremin had hoped for, contributing to countless radio plays and then film soundtracks. These biases stuck. When Robert Moog interviewed thereminist Clara Rockmore in 1977, he asked her to summarize her decades-old approach to virtuosity. Her response: "I am interested in making beautiful music rather than sound effects. That is the core of my approach to the Theremin" (Rockmore 2002). Similarly, Lucie Bigelow Rosen expressed "the earnest desire of those who are working with this instrument that it shall cease to be a novelty" (in Holmes 2002, 57).

Despite being an early advocate of the theremin's capacity for less conventional sounds, Cage is not known to have used the instrument beyond a version that Robert Moog modified for *Variations V,* Cage's 1965 collaboration with Merce Cunningham's dance company. Moog's modifications consisted of a set of long antennae, mounted on the floor. The proximity of dancers during the performance triggered raw and barely controlled squeals of electric sound. However, back in 1937, the theremin was central to Cage's thoughts about electrified sound and music. The instrument promised both to break from the musical past and to usher in an era of new possibilities for composition and performance. Cage wasn't the only adventurous composer interested in the emancipatory capacities of the theremin. French composer Edgard Varèse and Percy Grainger, an Australian, also heard within the gliding tones of the electronic instrument the possibilities of a new "free music," as Grainger called it. Varèse and Grainger would embrace glissando and "non-harmonics," characteristics of sounds in nature combined with the newly expressive capacities of machine music (in Kahn 1999, 90). Yet as avant-garde approaches to electronic sound would elude, confound, and upset the ears of popular audiences even more than the sounds of electrified instruments in the orchestra, the edgiest composers of free music found an altogether different kind of shortcoming in the theremin. It too closely imitated sounds of the familiar world. As Kahn explains, composers pushing the limits of Western art music sought to "expand its resources in the changing auditive environments" of the twentieth century (1999, 102). This typically involved expanding the definition of composed sound to include noise while maintaining the integrity of music as an art form that could carry significant meaning. One category of sound resisted their efforts to bring all that was otherwise extramusical within the purview of musical premise: worldly sounds. As will also be the case in the context of musique concrète, any form of recognizable and imitative sound was treated with suspicion, including reproduction through phonographic recording and program music's instrumental mimicry of familiar noises. Sounds made by strange contraptions and objects such as spoons, balloons, or the edge of crystal wine glasses were, according to Kahn, "banished to the circus, variety theater, novelty music, vaudeville, theatrical sound effects, and folk traditions, and even quotation from musics outside one's own tradition could be an exercise in extramusicality" (102–3). This would seal the fate of the theremin, which for years was more often than not exhibited as an oddity in expositions, technical demonstrations, and novelty shows.

Even as a handful of classically trained virtuosos on the one hand and avant-gardists on the other attempted to integrate the theremin's first electric waveform generator into the context of significant musical performances, the instrument appeared destined to be paraded about as "a freak," in the words of Theremin biographer Albert Glinksy, its trembling howl and screeching relegated to "scenes of mystery, terror, or the macabre" (2005, 253). So it went in several early films, beginning with the Russian movies *Odna* (Alone, 1931) and *Komsomol—The Patron of Electrification* (1934); horror films like *King Kong* (1933) and *The Bride of Frankenstein* (1935); the surreal musical *Lady in the Dark* (1944); and thrillers *Spellbound* (1945), *The Spiral Staircase* (1946), and *The Red House* (1947). In the radio adventure *The Green Hornet* (1936–50), the theremin added the signature hornet buzz to the theme of Nikolai

Rimsky-Korsakov's "Flight of the Bumblebee." It was not until its use in science fiction radio plays and films in the 1950s—when distant planets and alien beings, strange devices, futuristic crafts, and robots demanded electric sounds all their own—that the theremin finally announced to the imagination of a substantial public that in fact the future of sound had arrived. It may be that audiences of American SF films in the 1950s were predisposed to accept the new kind of sound experiences described by Cage, caught up as they were in the Cold War rush toward outer space and possessing a general sense of technological promise, even purpose (see Taylor 2001, 72–95). This new generation of listeners was likely unaware of the earlier phases of the theremin's history. However, hearing the theremin as part of a science fiction film actually retrieved cosmic themes that many critical ears had heard upon its debut in Russia and then on through tours of Germany, France, England, and the United States, when the sobriquets of ether music, music of the future, music out of space and of the spheres, first greeted it.

Even though the New York Thereministes found something distasteful about an emphasis on technical novelty for its own sake—particularly the noisy, experimental, and atmospheric explorations of electronic sound in general—it was clearly the cinematic turn of the theremin that gave them the most precise vocabulary for their reproach of its use in Hollywood recording studios. While Rockmore (2002) had long denounced the popularization of the Theremin as a novelty on the vaudevillian stage, the cinema became the primary target of her ire:

From the beginning of electronic instruments, the interest of composers, instrument builders, and performers, is that of a search for eerie, new or strange sound effects. . . . With an electronic instrument the way you present it is the way people think of it. Ninety-nine percent of people think of electronic instruments as something for new, eerie, strange, ugly, strident sounds. Now, that is completely the opposite of my approach. I am a violinist and a musician. I wanted to see if it were possible to use the Theremin to make real music.

These divisions between "real music" and "sound effects" surface repeatedly throughout the history of SF cinema, prompted in part by the ability of electronic tone generation both to mimic familiar sounds and to create new ones, and to play the weird space in between. It was precisely a search for exotic sounds that blasted the trajectory of the West Coast theremin players past the shields of the Thereministe censors that Cage described. The most important of these pop thereminists was Samuel J. Hoffman, a former New York bandleader who performed under the name of Hal Hope. Hoffman retired from the club scene to Los Angeles to start a career as a foot doctor, but he ended up playing the theremin on close to thirty major Hollywood scores. Hoffman also worked with pop composers, recording several space-age bachelor pad albums with Les Baxter and Harry Revel. Space-age pop repackaged the techniques of terrestrial exotica, right down to the album covers with their propensity toward glamorous model shots. Where on an exotica lounge album some unique indigenous instrument might appear for a short solo or add flavor to a traditional combo setting, the theremin represented the exotic and unusual on the albums *Music Out of the Moon* (1947), *Perfume Set to Music* (1948), and *Music for Peace of Mind* (1950). These were the first recordings to associate the theremin with what would become its signature themes—outer space, atmospheric ambience, and states of consciousness—although few would be as romantically inclined as these.

As a pop musician, Hoffman treated the theremin as neither part of the classical establishment nor the avant-garde, and he fit his sound easily into small jazz combos and pop orchestras. Whereas Rockmore and Rosen approached the theremin from an art patronage model, and the avant-garde briefly treated it as the future of liberated music, Hoffman and the composers that he worked with were untroubled by the ongoing novelty of the theremin. They were instead interested in its capacity to function both musically and as a startling sound effect. However, even those quick to embrace the theremin because of its uniquely untamed tonal characteristics had difficulty explaining the appeal of raw electronic sound in affirmative ways. When prodded to explain what the theremin sounded like, Hoffman succinctly replied, "It's controlled static" (in Glinsky 2005, 279). Hoffman typically settled for humorous responses that played on, rather than combated, the instrument's growing reputation as a novelty device. In 1938, when still a practicing doctor in New York moonlighting as a pop bandleader, Hoffman offered "how to play the Theremin" lessons as part of performances with the Hal

Hope Orchestra, broadcast live on CBS radio. "Technically speaking," Hoffman explained in a particularly illuminating lesson, "you hypnotize it by waving the hands in front it, and out comes the music" (199). The unsteady, wavering hand was exaggerated during the theremin lessons that Hoffman conducted on radio and TV variety shows to humorous effect.

In contrast, Rockmore's conservative repertoire was crafted to emphasize the fact that she didn't merely wave her hands around. Rather, she was a steady player who could overcome what were frequently described as the theremin's two major detriments: the vibrato that riddled individual notes and the portamento glide between precise pitches. This led critics to wonder why one should bother with the device at all if the primary challenge was to overcome, rather than exploit, its unique tonal properties. Deciding that the time of the theremin had not yet arrived, many early reviewers would forestall their final verdict, like Ernest Newman, who concluded his 1927 London *Sunday Times* account of Theremin's Albert Hall demonstration this way: "The Theremin invention may have results fifty years hence, of which we can at present form no conception. . . . The pity of it, for us of today, is that we shall not enter into the Promised Land" (in Glinsky 2005, 69). It would in fact be less than fifty years by almost half, and the Promised Land was Mars.

• CHAPTER 2 •

Ambient Novum, Alien Novum (1950–59)

The year 1950 was such an auspicious one for the science fiction film, the beginning of its golden age, that it also marked the end of a cinematic space race. Kurt Neumann's underdog B movie, *Rocketship X-M*, beat George Pal's big-budget production, *Destination Moon*, to the screen by a month. The competition had been so fierce that once Pal got wind of another moon movie, he threatened to sue Lippert Pictures for stealing his story. In reality, few similarities can be found between the films other than the lunar destination and a scene in each film in which a comical engineer pulls out a harmonica and is shushed by his more serious counterparts. All the same, Neumann revised his script at the last minute, adding in a meteor storm that knocks the rocket off its original trajectory to the moon and sends it to Mars instead. With a meager $94,000 budget, *Rocketship X-M* was shot in eighteen days and then rushed to theaters to capitalize on the buzz surrounding Pal's film. The producers at Lippert made sure audiences took note of this. The film's trailer proudly proclaimed that this is "the Screen's *FIRST* Story . . . of Man's *FIRST* Conquest of Space!"

Both films are interesting sonically. They feature scores from high-profile composers, somewhat surprisingly so in the case of *Rocketship X-M*, which boasts a theme sketched out by Ferde Grofé, famous for his popular *Grand Canyon Suite* (1931), though the work was ultimately

• 91

completed, orchestrated, and conducted by Lippert's music director, Albert Glasser. *Destination Moon* features a mildly adventurous, occasionally elegant score by frequent George Pal collaborator Leith Stevens. Being the first sonic ventures into the new era of science fiction cinema, both works established trends that would continue to define the SF film, for good and ill, for the next fifteen years. Even though familiar instrumental sounds presented within familiar cinematic contexts dominate these films, each also introduces distinctive new sounds and sonic sensibilities that have been shaped by the introduction of electronic tonalities. One sequence of the score to *Destination Moon*, accompanying an extended visual survey of the lunar landscape, is processed through an effects device known as the Sonovox, which lends a warbling, phasing effect to the strings and woodwinds. For *Rocketship X-M*, Glasser adds Samuel Hoffman to the studio orchestra and brings the theremin to the SF cinema—*"FIRST"*—even though by 1950 the instrument had played a substantial role in radio, motion picture scores, novelty acts, and pop albums for some years. But the theremin does something new in *Rocketship X-M*. Over the course of a lengthy, sepia-colored sequence showing the *X-M* crew trekking across the surface of Mars, Hoffman's theremin glides between the orchestral elements. Its wavering electronic tones are vaguely musical, but they also hint at something that is not music but almost a diegetic noise. Much like the reddish tint added to the film, the electronic timbre of the theremin conveys the alien planetary atmospherics of Mars.

During the otherworldly sequences of *Destination Moon* and *Rocketship X-M*, musical accompaniment is called on to provide something other than music per se: ambience. *Destination Moon* makes the case that we never hear another world on its own terms and without the technological prosthesis that gives us sensory access to that world. *Rocketship X-M* portrays a ghostly sonic psychogeography radiated by the ravages of unwieldy atomic technologies. Both films use electronic timbre in particular as a way to establish the "out of this world" otherness of alien landscapes. This chapter maps out the origins of the ambient novum in *Destination Moon* and *Rocketship X-M*. Ambient sound in the earliest SF films tends to come from the musical score, where the science fictional circumstances and alien environments are conveyed through electronic timbres: mild sound processing of orchestral voices in the *Destination Moon* score and the contributions of the theremin in *Rocketship X-M*. In both cases, sounds hover between the musical and noisy ends of the sonic psytech spectrum, but their electronic timbres have different consequences. The Sonovox processing gives a technical sheen to the listening experience, providing an auditory point of view during the extended pan of the lunar surface. It helps us imagine how an astronaut might perceive things and feel in such a situation. The theremin that we hear as the crew members of the *X-M* explore Mars sustains something more complex. It is not simply a concrete effect to suggest that this is what Mars sounds like; rather, the soundscape contributes a troubling psychogeographical depth to the most disturbing dimensions of the film's narrative by way of its ambiguous position between music and noise.

Like the ambient novum, the alien novum emerges as electric sounds glide across familiar ontological boundaries of cinematic diegesis. Its history also begins with the theremin. In a singular sonic invasion, the instrument tears through the familiar 20th Century Fox fanfare introducing Robert Wise's *The Day the Earth Stood Still* (1951). The graceful matte paintings of cosmic nebulae backing the opening credits only slightly temper the impact of the single piercing, descending, and sirenlike tone—the "warning and an ultimatum" that the original lobby poster promised would come "from out of space." Aggressive and startlingly loud, the out-there sound of the theremin immediately puts the audience on high alert. Years before its use in the SF films of the early 1950s, the theremin contributed to several film scores in ways that associated its electric voice with psychological distress and aberration. Here, the theremin declares a new theme peculiar to the science fiction film, but which will also draw on these prior associations: alien visitation. *The Day the Earth Stood Still* begins when a flying saucer lands on the White House lawn, its occupants the alien ambassador of an interplanetary federation, Klaatu (Michael Rennie), and his robot companion, Gort. Klaatu has come to administer a galactic litmus test now that humanity possesses advanced atomic technologies. That a frightened soldier quickly shoots Klaatu doesn't bode well for Earth's admission into the cosmic community. It turns out that Klaatu is indistinguishable from an earthling in appearance. He is not human, however, in the way he sounds. "For the cinematic spectator," writes Rebecca Leydon, "the only consistent evidence of his alien origins is the halo of otherworldly sounds with which the musical score envelops him" (2004b, 30–31). Though the alien can blend into the human population, observing and acting without raising suspicions, for the auditor, Klaatu emits the fundamental difference of vibratory extraterrestriality. Of course, we are hardly to believe that Klaatu actually emanates theremin-like sounds, or that "the sound of Klaatu" is heard by other characters within the film's diegetic sound world, with the possible exception of Gort. Gort also emits an audible aura, courtesy of a lower-pitched theremin, which in a couple of key scenes even performs a duet with Klaatu's theremin. Here, the theremins convey the peculiarities of alien consciousness, which become quite complex not only as they extend the extraterrestrial aura of the otherwise humanoid Klaatu into domains of telepathic ability, they also provide an audible basis for the unusual affective relationships between the alien being and the advanced technologies of his robot and spaceship.

The theremin would become the most recognizable sound of science fiction throughout the 1950s, even as the film genre took an abrupt U-turn from the off-world adventures of *Destination Moon* and *Rocketship X-M* to concentrate on tales of alien visitors and invaders from outer space—and there were plenty of them. The roster of new arrivals includes: *The Man from Planet X* (1951), *The Thing from Another World* (1951), *Invaders from Mars* (1953), *Phantom from Space* (1953), *It Came from Outer Space* (1953), and *It! The Terror from Beyond Space* (1958). The preponderance of alien visitation stories is partly a consequence of studio economics. It was far more cost-effective to bring aliens to familiar Earth locales than to incur the expense of set design and special effects required by off-world settings, never mind the science and logistics of the space travel involved. Even more significantly, a thematic shift occurred as American film studios dominate the genre. The SF film became a way to capitalize on Cold War anxieties, even though the specter of nuclear war found in *Rocketship X-M* quickly took a paranoid turn. As Keith Booker describes, the "invisible alien in our midst" motif more often than not validates the McCarthy-fueled hysteria of identifying enemies hidden among us (2006, 35–39). Whether exploiting xenophobic fear in *The Thing from Another World* and *The War of the Worlds* (1953) or endorsing some degree of tolerance toward difference thanks to the cosmic guilt trips of *The Day the Earth Stood Still* and *It Came from Outer Space*, these films consistently use a compelling sonic novum that expresses "by its sonority alone . . . an alien or monstrous presence" (Wierzbicki 2002, 131). Wierzbicki suggests that the theremin presents filmgoers with "the actual voice of the extraterrestrial Other" (130), though alien visitation or invasion films only occasionally give the extraterrestrial its own language in the way that *The Day the Earth Stood Still* includes Klaatu's imperative, "Gort! Klaatu barada nikto!" Fewer films of the period incorporate new, unusual, or electronic sounds as a way of representing the alien voice, and none do so as compellingly or as literally as Edgar G. Ulmer's *The Man from Planet X*. The alien speaks using a raw, modulated electronic sound of unknown source before an astronomer, Professor Eliot (Raymond Bond), and his assistant, Dr. Mears (William Schallert), come to realize that a better communication will be achieved through the universal language of science and mathematic formulas.

Most films of the era, however, present us with a surrogate rather than literal, diegetic voice of the alien, and more often than not, this approximate, nondiegetic voice is provided by the theremin or instruments such as the electric violin, played in a gliding, theremin-like manner. The theremin exemplifies what I call a tonal rather than a thematic or melodic motif, setting up a dynamic by which acousmatic sonic novum represent the unseen and incomprehensible powers of extraordinary alien minds and the advanced technologies of extraterrestrial civilizations. A new sonic atmosphere comes with the alien in the manner of the "halo of otherworldly sounds" that Leydon also calls an "aural aura" (2004b, 31), and which I call the vibe. Incorporated in countless scores, and invariably performed by Samuel J. Hoffman, the theremin's alien vibe plays out as part of the nondiegetic composition as composers exploit its atmospheric qualities. However, as it drifts from planetary ambience to the alien character itself, the theremin's timbral motif prompts a deeper engagement with sound's role in first the psychological and then psychotechnological dimensions of SF films. The theremin is at its most brutal in Christian Nyby's *The Thing from Another World*. The raw, screeching noise of the theremin evokes an inhuman thingness that comes from some place well beyond even the structured families or organized noise languages of futurism and musique concrète. In this way, the theremin affectively sonifies issues of identity, estrangement, alienation, technological vitalism, the alternative states and abilities of extraterrestrial consciousness, and posthumanity typically explored in alien visitation and invasion narratives. This chapter tracks the sonic emergence of the alien novum in the form of the theremin heard in two early alien films—*The Day the Earth Stood Still* and *The Thing from Another World*—with a slight aside on Jack Arnold's *It Came from Outer Space*. This third film continues to associate the theremin with the unseen alien in our midst, but it also implicates the developing sonics of the alien novum within the expedient demands of a film studio system exerting its own monstrous influence over the auditory experience.

The theremin or things pretending to be theremins are not the only agents of the alien novum. This chapter also establishes the role of tape mixing techniques in the development of new sonorous objects. Direct manipulation of sound on a recorded medium—changing its speed, which also changes its pitch; reversing its directionality; cutting off the attacks and decays of sounds—render unrecognizable sounds gathered from the real, concrete world. For SF film sound designers and composers working in the space between musical score and diegetic sound, their tape compositions significantly alter or avoid altogether any resemblance to their earthly origins in order to attain instead the worldliness of the alien. How this otherworldliness sets a sound effect apart from a musical noise concerned composers like Bernard Herrmann, whose tape mix accompanying the "day the earth stood still" sequence ranks as a neglected masterpiece of tape music, as does Akira Ifukube's score for Ishirō Honda's *Gojira* (1956). The use of tape composition and sound design in both *The Day the Earth Stood Still* and *Gojira* proves the creation of the alien novum to be a conceptual and theoretical art form in its own right, one not completely accounted for by musical instrumentality. This is due to newly emergent electronic technologies other than devices like the theremin as well as to the embrace of various musical primitivisms, as heard in Ifukube's use of processed acoustic and recorded sound library material in the *Gojira* score, and in the electronic tonalities created for

Fred Wilcox's *Forbidden Planet* (1956) by Louis and Bebe Barrons, with their cybernetic circuit-bending audio patches and magnetic tape–based manipulations.

Alien sounds blur diegetic distinctions as well as suggest new layers of diegesis, such as the subdiegetic domains of psychotechnologial space and the self-reflexive technodiegetic domain in which new forms of alien consciousness take shape as technological processes. Whittington argues that the theremin's blurring of "the line between music and sound effect" sketches the boundaries of an even deeper anxiety within the sonic palette of 1950s science fiction films (2007, 100). The sonic collision of music and electricity—expressed both as a generated force and through the sound-sculpting dimensions accessed through magnetic tape recording and manipulation—triggered feelings of "uncertainty, skepticism, and fear" due to their sonic instabilities alone (100). SF filmmakers put this tonal instability to use in ways that resonate with golden age SF as normative values and human ideals are invariably destabilized when put in contact with alien forms. Timbral distinctions between harmonic tones and noise repeatedly underscore the basic differences between human and the technological Other in the science fiction film. This dynamic plays out in the wake of the theremin as composers sought different types of tonalities and sonic cues not only to express the alien and monstrous aspects of science fiction but also, through the electric sound of the theremin and its cousins—the various electric violins, guitars, and other simple electronics—to indicate that these are explicitly technological enemies. *Gojira* presents a pair of characteristic sonic effects—the creature's thunderous steps and roaring screech—which anticipate the monster and the devastation it will wreak. The production of these sonic objects is still performed in the context of a composed orchestral setting, as we find Ifukube's notes regarding the effects included in his handwritten score. The diegetic looseness of these sounds do not so much attach to the image of Gojira but rather his presence off-screen. In fact, the footsteps and screech presciently anticipate the creature's impending visual arrival. The scale of noise here is largely responsible for the creature's transhistorical presence. Like the hybridity inherent to his name (literally, "gorilla-whale"), and his amphibian nature, Gojira also straddles the primitive eras of deep prehistory and the immediate future of the atomic era. Ifukube's score plays specifically within this tonal space, combining primitivism with a postwar polyphony of musical styles and sensibilities, including an understanding of the expressiveness of sonic restraint, minimalism, and silence. That the noise of Gojira is product of both simultaneous musical performance and diegetic function reinforces the nature of the ancient alien as an uncanny mixture, possessing no clear identity of its own, and to some extent ultimately undone by the specificity of naming.

I find that *Gojira* presents a compelling way to begin reconsidering the debates about music and noise that shook up the avant-garde after World War II, particularly in regards to the identity of the recorded sound object, including concerns about its validity, its authenticity, and its nature as simulacrum. These become even more pronounced in the case of *Forbidden Planet,* where cybernetic circuit design creates sonic artificial life-forms as part of a larger, autopoietic, sonic psytech ecology. Directly inspired by the work of Norbert Weiner, composers Louis and Bebe Barron built their own sound-generating circuit patches, which they conceived as living organisms for them to torture and burn out in order to speed up the process of creating interesting sounds. This process eerily mimics both the narrative and the major themes of the film, which is concerned with technology's ability to transmit and expose otherwise suppressed psychic content. In this respect, the electronic tonalities of the score (MGM refused to credit what the Barrons had done as music) tread across diegetic boundaries, sonically activating corresponding boundary crossings between mind and matter, illusion and reality, desire and fact, and alien and human. Beyond the disagreements between the schools of musique concrète and electronic music that this film resolves, it also points quite problematically to an emerging cybernetic biomedia, which I explore through an array of unconventional theoretical lenses—Felix Guattari's work on second-order cybernetics and Dr. John Lilly's discussions of noise, cybernetics, and cross-species communication—that I believe shed new light on what Louis Barron achieved when working from Norbert Weiner's *Cybernetics, Or Control and Communication in the Animal and the Machine* (1948). I also briefly consider Deleuze's work on the "virtual image," which I understand to be the sonorous object itself, in order to reflect on the rather despairing cosmos philosophy of *Forbidden Planet*'s oversaturated syntheses.

This chapter's tour through the golden age of science fiction concludes with a left field turn from SF film proper to consider the collaborations of experimental filmmaker Jordan Belson and electronic music producer and disc jockey Henry Jacobs. The pair produced a number of pioneering audiovisual performances for the Morrison Planetarium in San Francisco in the latter part of the decade. They described their Vortex Concerts as a theater of the future that immersed the audience in an abstract cinema of pure light, visual effects, and film loops combined with a mix of unusual sounds from the avant-garde, traditional music gathered from around the world, and isolated audio effects that swirled about the planetarium by means of an early form of surround sound reproduction. These concerts were at once a prototype of the psychedelic happenings of the 1960s, the Laserium planetarium shows of the 1970s, and the rave scene's chill-out rooms of the 1980s. As a form of science fiction, the live audiovisual cinema of the Vortex Concerts anticipates the transformation of the living human through technical interfaces and integration with the complex cybernetic systems of space exploration. As the planetarium becomes a literal ambient novum, providing a cultural buffer for the impact of technological change on the human bodies and minds of its virtual astronauts, it also provides a ritualistic and synesthetic vehicle for the manifestation and mobilization of an alien cosmic consciousness.

1950 | *DESTINATION MOON, ROCKETSHIP X-M*

Destination Moon and *Rocketship X-M* gave audiences their first inkling of how the SF genre could tap into the contemporary spirit of scientific discovery and technical competition underwriting the burgeoning space age even as it reflected the mounting anxieties of the atomic Cold War. However, these are quite different films that neatly recast for the big screen tensions that had already divided written science fiction into two camps: serious science fiction—whether hard SF, based on the natural sciences and engineering, or soft SF, informed by social sciences such as anthropology and psychology—versus pulp "sci-fi," a disparaging term applied to tales of adventure and melodrama. *Destination Moon* emphasizes hard science, but nothing so complex that a short Woody Woodpecker cartoon on the basic logistics of rocket science couldn't handle it. Throughout the film, technical accuracy and convincing detail are much more important than human characterization and dramatic narrative, beyond a few moments of light comic relief and incredulity voiced by the radio engineer, Joe Sweeney (comedic actor Dick Wesson). Played mostly for simple-minded yucks, Sweeney allows the other crew members plenty of opportunities to declaim on important space travel topics like weightlessness in the vacuum of space. There is little bandwidth for emotional needs and psychological well-being. Distress brings on the occasional emotional overload, as when Sweeney angrily rattles off the ways he would rather have killed himself back in Yonkers than be stranded on the moon with an egg-headed rocket scientist, an industry pioneer, and a general. And when he pulls out his harmonica for a little down-home music, Sweeney is quickly silenced. By contrast, the other members of the crew exhibit nothing but the calmest demeanor even as they consider who should be left on the moon when they discover that, given their current payload, they lack enough fuel for the trip home. Science and technology render the human players as parts of the machine, though a little ingenuity and know-how save the day for all. While this lack of character development isn't necessarily a flaw in the film, it does seem that *Destination Moon* fails to develop thematically when its scenarios are in fact ripe for critical engagement.

On the other hand, *Rocketship X-M* is a cautionary tale about the dangers of atomic weaponry that sits somewhere between soft SF and pulp romance. Its story of mishaps and peril, of human passion and tragedy, offsets the few moments of scientific declamations with a potent undercurrent of sociopolitical critique. The makers of *Rocketship X-M* care little for persuasive technical detail, much less educating the audience with the kind of expository space facts that the characters in *Destination Moon* tend to drop at every turn. Instead of a popular cartoon character acting as advocate and industry spokesperson, the leader of the *X-M* crew gets a chalkboard. And where in *Destination Moon* human ingenuity overcomes all obstacles—including Cold War paranoia (industry in league with the military is the big winner) and ethics (the film's atomic rocket science relies on Nazi Germany's V-2 rocket program)—the *X-M*'s mission is plagued by technical malfunction, miscalculation, and an unexpected meteor storm. A series of mistakes and bad luck attends the mission—and (major spoiler alert) everyone dies. The cascading failures that make *Rocketship X-M* such a dramatic narrative constitute a sharp critique of scientific endeavor. Faced with the realization that a once-advanced Martian civilization had blasted itself back to its own stone age, the outlook is grim for a civilization armed with atom bombs. Both the filmmakers and their surrogate characters in *Destination Moon* dismiss the dangers of radiation as so much communist propaganda. *Rocketship X-M* is far more humanist in its overt criticism of atomic power. It is in fact the first instance of a pacifist science fiction cinema, one that would soon include *The Day the Earth Stood Still, The Man from Planet X,* and *It Came from Outer Space,* each of which puts our own planet's nascent atomic age up against a kind of cosmic litmus test (Erickson 2011, 27). In contrast to those countless expository moments of rocket and space science encountered in *Destination Moon, Rocketship X-M* includes several speeches about the dangers of nuclear war. Moreover, the characters, even if stereotypical, express a broader swath of humanity as well as a more diverse range of emotions, often voicing concern and care for each other. Even on the *X-M*, however, the limit of camaraderie appears to be the harmonica, as the gentle flight engineer from Texas, Bill Corrigan (played by popular character actor Noah Beery Jr.), is silenced once he overcomes the weightless conditions to wrestle the instrument to his lips and blow a couple of notes. In terms of its narrative arc, *Rocketship X-M* plummets toward an apocalyptic outburst of passion during the final embrace of the two remaining crew members—the pilot, Colonel Floyd Graham (Lloyd Bridges), and the ship's chemist, Dr. Lisa Van Horn (Osa Massen)—as the rocket plunges to destruction over Nova Scotia.

No wonder that a *Rocketship X-M 2* never got off the ground, despite the fact that when the earthbound project lead, Professor Ralph Fleming (Morris Ankrum), discovers that the mission is a total loss, he announces without hesitation, "Tomorrow we start construction of *RXM-2.*" But his words ring hollow in contrast to the dour faces of the other men in the room, the descending tones of the score, and the stark closing titles, "the end," another sharp contrast to the overall optimism of *Destination Moon,* its own closing titles proclaiming that "this is The End of the Beginning." What could follow the error and devastation of this tragic and ultimately condemning portrait of human ambition and frailty, encapsulated by the Wagnerian immolation of a doomed lovers' embrace? All of this makes for a narrative intensity that *Destination Moon* never attains, while *Rocketship X-M's* astounding box office return of almost $500,000 in its first year proved, for better or worse, that science fiction cinema's popular success would have little to do with scientific accuracy (Erickson 2011, 28).

Sounds of new technologies in George Pal's *Destination Moon* are part of its overall extrapolative agenda, meant to convince the audience not only of the film's plausibility as a narrative but also, more grandly, the plausibility of spaceflight and lunar exploration in reality. Seeking to accurately document emerging space technologies, Pal assembled a dream team of consultants while writing the script, including German rocket scientist Herman Oberth, science fiction writer Robert Heinlein, and visual artist Chesley Bonestell, known as the father of modern space art, whose paintings were influencing NASA's design sensibilities. With an educational and workmanlike feel, the movie comes across as a paean to private industry, speculative capital, technological optimism, and finally corporate imperialism. The numerous sounds of space rocketry and related equipment reinforce the realistic nature of the film, and one of the most original and convincing sonic details is the feeding of the astronauts' voices through radio devices embedded in their space helmets. A telecommunicated edge filters and modulates the dialogue exchanged between astronauts during space walks or excursions on the moon.

Science fiction filmmakers may struggle more than those working in other genres "to create credibility," according to Vivian Sobchack in her groundbreaking study of the America SF film (1987, 216). Sobchack attributes a general turn to sound effect design in SF films to the filmmakers' "innate desire for authenticity," especially when tasked with "documenting the incredible" (216). Indeed, with greater demands for technical veracity than emotional complexity, the sonic experience of hard SF comes from "a soundtrack built primarily from elements within the image, and not imposed on it from without" (216). These are the sounds of rocketry and related gear in *Destination Moon* and *Rocketship X-M,* but SF films would soon be filled with the sounds of more fantastical flying saucers, laser pistols, robots, and aliens, which present new challenges and opportunities for creative sound design and sonic world building. Attention to the audible elements of each important diegetic detail lends tangibility to the story, and it supports the filmgoer's extrapolative investment in events even as it elevates our sense of wonder. Sound design does this in ways that the musical score does not. Sobchack offers a summary dismissal of the music heard in the SF films of the 1950s and '60s, which typically fail to keep pace with the "narrative and thematic preoccupations with the 'future,' with innovation, with 'otherness'" (207). By this account, sound effects compensate for inadequacies of the musical score, even to the point of taking on dramatic and emotive properties that the music lacks. More importantly, however, technical sonic details provide what Chion calls synchresis, the glue that keeps audio and visual experiences synchronized into apparent simultaneity. Sound projects value onto the image by appearing to come from within it. By crafting "an immediate and necessary relationship between something one sees and something one hears," Chion argues, synchresis points to the powerful ability of sound to provide images with material substance and weight (1994, 216). Synchresis becomes especially important in the case of the extrapolative elements of SF films, where Hayward notes that sound must prop up and infuse the speculative narrative through "musical—or other sonic—signifiers that could evoke the various futuristic, scientistic and/or alien themes" (2004b, 7). *Destination Moon* may contain only one experiment with synchresis, but this singular moment typifies the efforts of early SF filmmakers to supersede the otherwise familiarizing dimensions of musical scores and so participate in the film's investment in technical innovation and scientific adventure through sonic novum.

The most mysterious and awe-filled moment in *Destination Moon* is the camera's pan of the lunar surface, rendered in a gorgeous matte painting by Bonestell. The scene runs for more than a minute. Composer Leith Stevens's recording of the orchestra has been processed through a Sonovox effects device and rerecorded, bringing to the midrange woodwinds and strings a warbled phasing quality, as if the magnetic tape wasn't quite playing at a consistent speed. The distortion here is mild but nonetheless manages to signify the otherworldly wonder of the scene through this technological sonic gloss. Though several sequences were in fact recorded through the processing device, this is the only one that retains evidence of Stevens's experiments during postproduction (David Schecter, personal correspondence, August 7, 2013). Here is how this unusual unit works. The device consists of a pair of small speakers and a vocalist. The vocalist holds the speakers against the sides of the throat and then modulates the sound playing through them by changing the shape of the mouth. The sounds emitting from the mouth are then amplified and recorded. A precursor to the talk-box, which runs amplified sound into the mouth through a hollow plastic tube, the Sonovox was a short-lived novelty device usually featured in live settings for maximum visual as well as sonic impact. As professorial bandleader Kay Kyser explains in his introduction to the device in the 1940 comedy *You'll Find Out,* "The Sonovox unit gives diction to the tones of the instruments as they play. Harry forms the words," and here Kyser points to one of his band members, "but the instruments sing them!" (MisterScott99 2007).

I find it fascinating that a cyborg of sorts performs here at the beginning of the history of sonic science fiction, joining the human mouth to electric sound reproduction technologies. The Sonovox filters amplified sound sources directly through the phonemically differentiated arrangements of musculature, bone, teeth, and skin. In the case of *Destination Moon,* despite its unique use of the human mouth as a way to modulate a sound source, the Sonovox does not lend an intelligible voice to the moonscape. Rather, it provides an alien edge that atmospherically alters the listening experience as we view the panorama. An inversion of mouth and ear takes place, as well as a kind of remediation. Filtering sound through a human–technological hybrid creates precisely what Chion claims sound film typically lacks: the "*symbolic mediator of our hearing* embodied in the cinematic apparatus" (2009, 293). While film provides a fixed visual point of view, sound can come at us from any and all directions. This can make it more difficult to determine the point from which sounds emerge, particularly in the case of broadly atmospheric and environmental diegetic sounds, as well as in the case of nondiegetic music, which has no point of origin in the film world at all. *Destination Moon* goes out of its way, as it were, to provide a point of audition during the survey of the moonscape. But other than giving the scene a slightly uncanny edge, what is the point of the Sonovox? Wouldn't the nowhere-place of the musical score alone be enough to convey the emotions of wonder and awe intended to accompany the scene? Not really, for in keeping with the film's emphasis on hard science and technology, we have to witness the moonscape as a site/sight that can only be experienced and appreciated technically.

Just as the microphone and speaker units of space helmets remediate human communication within the new technological environments of space travel and off-planet exploration, the Sonovox in turn functions as that "symbolic loudspeaker," which represents "the mic as a mediating third party" and so transforms affect into mediation (Chion 2009, 293). As a biotechnical cyborg novum, the Sonovox entangles embodied perception, emotional experience, and inhabitation of the moon by filtering what is surely meant to be a moment of wonder, discovery, and mystery through the interface of a technical surrogate that calls attention to itself as mediator. We can't hear the moon, but we can hear the filters and modulating gloss that stands between it and us. The Sonovox filters human awareness of the new lunar reality in ways that exceed our unaided sensory capacities, but ultimately the technical effect conveys less what it feels like to be on the moon than what it is to be technological. This is a hard SF conquest of human experience. By filtering and modulating nondiegetic affective cues through an audio effects processor in order to convey alien space, the Sonovox sequence is not so much about cosmic difference per se as it is about our perception of difference through mediating technical forms. That is, even as the Sonovox gives voice to an experience of awe and wonder, it confirms technology's total permeation of our place in the cosmos.

• • •

In retrospect, *Rocketship X-M* may be most memorable simply because it's the first American science fiction film; or perhaps because it features the amiable Lloyd Bridges in an early lead role; or maybe even because at least part of the script was written by Dalton Trumbo, blacklisted at the time and not given a credit. Back in 1950, contemporary critical reception in the likes of *Variety*, the *Hollywood Reporter*, and the Los Angeles *Daily News* tended to dismiss the film but singled out its "eerie" musical score. For *Downbeat* movie critic Charles Emge, "*Rocketship X-M* wouldn't intrigue even comic book readers" if not for the music written by the unpretentious but popular "light music" composer, Ferde Grofé (in Tibbetts 2010, 197). To secure a composer of Grofé's reputation for a measly $1,250 was one of Lippert Production's biggest coups during their frantic race to beat George Pal's space picture to the screen. To be fair, Grofé was likely both a bit desperate and more than a bit reluctant to get back into Hollywood film scoring even though his music for the documentary, *Minstrel Man,* had been nominated for an Academy Award ten years earlier. But his first major score after a dry spell of seven long years, for Robert Siodmak's noir thriller *Time Out of Mind* (1947), ended up being rejected by the film's producers. Grofé expressed his unhappiness with a scoring process that typically rendered the composer's music more or less inaudible in the final mix, "dipped under," as he called it, the more pronounced dialogue and sound effects, or chopped up into the briefest of cues and stingers (in Tibbetts 2010, 201). All the same, Grofé's apparent need for some income led him to score two last films in 1950: *Rocketship X-M* and another Lippert Pictures production, *The Return of Jesse James.*

For the most part, the *Rocketship X-M* score reveals less affinity for Hollywood music conventions than the influence of modernist composers, an out-of-the-ordinary idiom for this composer of light symphonic music. In a study of the score, John Tibbetts compares Grofé's use of "unusual instrumental textures and ambiguous tonalities for the weightless, free-floating scenes in space and the crashing discords of the liftoff and crash sequences" to Edgard Varèse's construction of "soundscapes" (2010, 204). The theremin and other electric noisemakers, as well as various electroacoustic effects, all played a significant role in Varèse's work. However, the modernist inflection of the music heard in *Rocketship X-M*—particularly its electronic instrumentation—is most likely due to the contributions, if not interventions, of Albert Glasser. A veteran of low-budget B-movie scores since 1944's *Monster Maker* and credited as music director on both of Lippert's films featuring Grofé's scores,

Glasser was the person responsible for including the theremin as well as an early polyphonic synthesizer, the Hammond Novachord, in the soundtrack recording sessions (Larson 2012, 208–9). Glasser proved a fitting intermediary between Grofé's work and the realities of Hollywood sound production. The choice of the two "nontraditional 'effects' instruments" are particularly appropriate as a way to convey the spacey and otherworldly atmospheres of the film, but it also provided a timbre that would stand out, given the limits on frequency range and volume of the film's final mix (Tibbetts 2010, 199). The technical detail would likely have eluded Grofé, an industry outsider, even as it addressed his fears about the impact of the limits of film sound reproduction on his work.

I think that Grofé would have been amenable to Glasser's incorporation of the Novachord. He had performed on one as part of the New World Ensemble, a futuristic group comprising four Novachord players and one Hammond organist that Grofé led through daily concerts at the Ford Exposition during the 1939 New York World's Fair (Brend 2012, 15). The first all-electronic instrument to incorporate subtractive synthesis—a process by which the tone of an oscillating waveform is attenuated by filtering out parts of its frequency—the Novachord featured multiple oscillators, inaudible low-frequency oscillators that added vibrato to the audible sounds, voltage-controlled amplifiers, band-pass resonance filters, and sophisticated envelope controls that determined how a tone played out over time, controlling its attack, decay, sustain, and release. The Novachord mimicked strings, voices, pianos, organs, and vibraphones; it could also create new sounds with more unusual timbres. The frequent adjustments that had to be made to the array of industrial Bakelite controls lined up above the full-length keyboard made the Novachord notoriously difficult for pianists and organists trained to play in traditional ways. While these design features ultimately contributed to the Novachord's falling out of favor with film music composers, arrangers, and performers, the characteristic timbre of the instrument made it a good fit for the strange and otherworldly qualities required of the SF film.

In *Rocketship X-M,* the Novachord provides the subtlest sounds in a film score that several times demonstrates the overly synchronized effect known as Mickey Mousing. The countdown to launch sequence, for instance, features rumbling bass strings and horns on top of which a higher metronomic piano key marks out the passage of time. A steady click grows gradually faster, the string section rising and falling in pitch behind it. As the time of launch looms closer, the strings and brass become louder and ever more frantic. A bit of theremin is brought into the mix here, warbling and swooping upward, rising in pitch as the ascending strings begin to shimmer with the addition of the Novachord to accompany the rocket launch itself. As used here, the strangeness of the Novachord comes from the fact that it is hardly a sound on its own but rather blends with the other instrumental voices to the point of near inaudibility. Its sonic textures work rather like an echo effect around the strings and horns to create an ambience that grows more pronounced as the rocket breaks free of Earth's gravity and attains orbit. According to Brend's history of pop culture and electronic music, the sounds of the Novachord are "all characteristically indistinct in outline" (2012, 15). Adjectives such as "indistinct," "blurred," and "misty" typically describe the vague, atmospheric properties of the Novachord, and oddly enough these properties become even more pronounced the closer the instrument gets to taking on the prominent role of a solo or lead instrument. This imprecision of sound is precisely what Glasser takes advantage of during his sonic depiction of outer space, when a sequence of shimmering, suspended harmonics accompanies the rocket's escape from Earth's gravity.

Leith Stevens achieves a similar effect for similar purposes during scenes of weightlessness in *Destination Moon,* but he does so without the use of electronic instruments. The new sounds of weightlessness are important for our understanding of both of these film scores given their emphasis on ambience and musical atmosphere. In a section of his score titled "Out in Space," Stevens creates his own "unreal effects with strange orchestral color," achieved by a number of impressive modern techniques (Rosar 2006, 400). The weightlessness of space is conveyed through a suspension of musical time, a feeling created as the prominent violins loop through a series of harmonic fourths (ostinato, polytonality), performed with the trembling effect produced by the rapid reiteration of notes (tremolo). The woodwinds as well as a harp, celesta, and glockenspiel all perform the same rising and falling tones with a great deal of glissando. The trembling suspension of the strings along with the gliding of the other instruments suggest an impressionistic "tone painting," its ethereal sounds meant to "correspond with the scintillating appearance of the stars" as well as "evoke the mystery of outer space, the empty void through which the rocketship is traveling" (404). Appearing to stall the progression of musical time through polytonal harmonics and gliding notes, Stevens's orchestration brings to the otherwise visually flat paintings of outer space a grandeur and even spaciousness that they would not possess otherwise. In his study of Stevens's compositions for *Destination Moon* and another popular George Pal film, *The War of the Worlds* (1953), film music scholar William Rosar describes this moment this way: "The music imparts not just mood qualities but *spatial* qualities to the visuals, specifically a sense of *depth*, such that there would be no feeling of the vastness of outer space without the music in this scene. . . . With his music Stevens was thus not duplicating what is on the screen but was instead enhancing or adding qualities not present at all" (2006, 404–5). Rosar, who conducts research in physiognomic perception and body image disorders as well as film music, makes a compelling argument relevant to our prior consideration of added value. During my earlier discussion of *Metropolis,* I argued that a gap of poetic distance, which Chion locates between the pit and the screen of silent cinema, is relocated rather than resolved in the era of sound synchronization. For sound to become an added value to image, it first must be distinct from it. Rosar situates what I consider to be a corresponding gap between our perceptual experience of and emotional response to film sound. The role of music in film is not associative and interpretive, according to Rosar's work on physiognomy, but rather is part of the expressive nature of the work. As far as the perceptions of the auditor goes, music in film behaves in an inherent way, as part of a film's "gesture, intonation, and mood" (1994, 154). Whether the music makes the leap to trigger a corresponding emotional response in its audience is actually less relevant than identifying its expressive properties in dynamic and experiential terms. Writing about the ways in which composers describe their work of adding depth to a film, as well as conscious of the way that film music often works on us whether we are even aware of it, much less whether we want it to or not, Rosar concludes, "We are probably aware of the mood of a piece of music before we can identify or specify which musical features characterize the mood, rather than first noticing certain musical features and then somehow inferring expression from them. With film music, we may not even be conscious of the presence of music, let alone whether dramatic qualities are referable to it or the film as a whole" (1994, 161–62). Musical themes that provide spatial qualities and ambient depth take advantage of this ambiguity, this eluding of conscious awareness and dramatic presence, as if these sounds are not only indistinct but indifferent. Tonally, the fuzzy not quite referentiality of the Novachord as well as Stevens's trembling, gliding, polytonal music are "characteristically indistinct in outline," to repeat Brend's phrase, "as if the sound blurs into silence at the edges" (2012, 15). As they push toward the borders of sonic perception, or as they play in the space between otherwise distinct tones, these sounds of weightless outer space extend beyond the affective, sonic physiognomy that typically situates film music within an explicitly human frame of reference. They make clear perception difficult; in addition, the odd foregrounding of blurred and indistinct sounds sets both them and us adrift toward the depths of cosmic indifference.

The theremin in the *Rocketship X-M* score points this indifference toward particularly malevolent ends. After its brief incorporation into the launch sequence, the theremin is not heard again until an unexpected meteor storm knocks the rocket from its lunar trajectory and sends it to Mars. There is something to both the subtlety and tentativeness of Glasser's introduction of the theremin, especially so when compared to the way that Bernard Herrmann and Dimitri Tiomkin will feature the instrument so prominently in their main title themes to *The Day the Earth Stood Still* and *The Thing from Another World,* both released the following year. Where these two films capitalize on the theremin's immediate connotations of extraterrestrial mystery and menace, the significance of the theremin in *Rocketship X-M* depends on a gradual accumulation of its associations with Mars. Once the *X-M* is in space and knocked off course, the theremin is only audible when Mars is visible outside one of the ship's portholes. As Mars looms larger, the theremin becomes more prominent in the mix. Its dissonant, warbling tones cut like a sonic beacon of doom through the orchestral backdrop that we hear during shots of the ship's interior. After the rocket lands on Mars and the crew members begin their trek across its surface, the theremin is heard continuously.

While the theremin contributes a compellingly eerie tone color in the context of nondiegetic accompaniment, its movement toward the diegetic fascinates me the most here. Just as seeing Mars requires a shift to sepia tints—a perceptual shift indicating that this is what Mars looks like, in comparison to the black-and-white of Earth—the theremin signals a corresponding perceptual shift in hearing. This is what Mars sounds like. The theremin's quavering sonic tint filters both the familiar orchestral fare of prancing strings and melodramatic minor keys as well as diegetic atmospheric sound effects, such as the torrential Martian thunderstorm that prompts mission leader Dr. Eckstrom (John Emory) to declare, "Mars extending us a welcome!" But the real welcoming package comes in the form of deadly radiation, which would have sealed the fate of the landing crew even if an attack by angry Martians tossing boulders and stone axes at them, their own mistakes, and simple bad luck had not. The theremin acts as a sonic barometer of escalating horror as the crew realizes that not only had there been life on Mars, its once advanced civilization had destroyed itself with atomic weaponry. This realization prompts the most devastating dialogue in the film, also courtesy of Dr. Eckstrom: "This is definitely blast effect coupled with intense heat. Ironic, isn't it, the highest attainment of intellect, always diverted to self-destruction? What a lesson for our world. One blast, and an entire civilization is wiped out. I should hate to think that any survived." They have, of course, but the remains of this once advanced civilization have devolved into mutant tribes that attack the astronauts with mindless savagery. The full orchestra punctuates this moment of Eckstrom's pathos with a violent eruption of discordant notes before the music drops back in intensity and the theremin returns. Now noisier than ever, with too many spectra in the air, the theremin's singular but wildly unsteady voice multiplies through another Glasser innovation: a delay-generating effect device, the Echoplex, which uses magnetic tape to record and then repeat incoming electric signals with varying amounts of delay. Amplified and replicated, the theremin does not simply color the planet's otherwise familiar physical landscape of desert canyons and barren hills, which look for all the world just like Zabriskie Point in Death Valley National Park. It saturates and irradiates it. Gliding around bits of dialogue such as, "The radioactivity is at the danger level," the theremin sonifies contamination by radioactive fallout.

Most often too faintly audible in the film to build suspense directly and so contribute to narrative momentum, the theremin works along the fuzzy edges of diegetic ambience. It never fulfills the nondiegetic function of traditional cues, and so eludes provision of affective or emotional resonance, even in the scene depicting the mutated Martians, whose attack on the Earth crew is accompanied by low strings, rumbling brass, and loud drums that convey a brute, primitive menace. The theremin hovers around these overtly dramatic phrasings, offsetting the low tonalities with its briefly wailing outbursts. The theremin suggests a kind of summoning here, calling up a ghost of Martian civilization that is more haunting than the crude mutants, its attack both more subtle and devastating. An evocative aspect of the theremin's instrumentality, the use of cryptic gestures rather than physical touch, has suggested the act of summoning or conjuring sound to many scholars of the early SF film. Leydon directly associates the instrument's "'action-at-a-distance' method of sound production" with its cinematic role as a "sonic marker for 'unseen forces'" (2004b, 31). Hayward considers the theremin "a *virtual* instrument" because it extracts tones out of thin air, draws sound out and calls it forth, actions that make the device a perfect sonic fit for the tales of mesmerism and the supernatural with which it was associated before its use in SF films (1997, 31). Schmidt emphasizes the theremin's earliest associations with the idea of ether, that medium without substance through which electromagnetic waves were thought to travel, and which blurred a variety of early twentieth-century notions about science, electromagnetism, invisible influences, the otherworldly, and the supernatural (2010, 29). However, in *Rocketship X-M,* the theremin does more than represent the ethereal weirdness or ghostly vibe of the devastated alien planet. The instrument's invisible and radiating "ether waves" represent the dangers of technology more specifically while retaining its associations with the otherworldly.

This "action-at-a-distance" prompts a reconsideration of the theremin's ghostly presence during the launch sequence. If it is consistently associated with Mars, had the planet already exerted its influence on the mission to the moon, pulling the rocket away from its destination to lead the crew of five to their demise? Indeed, the theremin is a siren in at least two senses of the word, both summoning and warning. The instrument's association with sirens and alarms is quite literal, as the instrument was initially a by-product of Theremin's research into proximity burglar alarms. With its unique tonal qualities and style of playing, however, the theremin also exploits the siren effect of modernist glissando. Though a premodernist means for extending tonality on traditional orchestral instruments, glissando was nonetheless novel enough at the turn of the twentieth century that Schoenberg could claim in 1903 to have invented the trombone glissando for his difficult symphonic tone poem, *Pelleas und Melisande* (Albright 2004, 7). Yet something more fascinating happens when the glissando technique comes to be associated with mechanical and electrical technologies by which a rotary action can induce sonic glides along the scale of audible frequencies. These modern glissando-generating sources had included Russolo's *intonarumori* as well as the variable-speed phonograph record and film reels favored by Cage. There was "none more glissando" than the siren, and few more compelling than the theremin. It was the theremin that proved most capable of leaving the familiar sounds of nature behind to gain new worlds altogether.

By the time of *Rocketship X-M,* the theremin sonically actualizes another important element of Schoenberg's work, which Ross calls the "Martian breeze" evoked in the Second Quartet of 1908. For the last two movements, Schoenberg had set to music two poems by the symbolist writer Stefan George. A soprano soloist sings about "the wind of another planet" (2007, 55). The lyrics of the final movement evoke "a state of profound estrangement," Ross writes, "with the alienation of the individual turning universal." This estrangement is then "mimicked," Ross continues,

> in soft, sinister streams of notes, recalling the episode in [Schoenberg's] *Salome* when Herod hallucinates a chilly wind. Special effects on the strings (mutes, harmonics, bowing at the bridge) heighten the sense of otherness, as singing tones become whispers and high cries. . . .

> The strings dwell on sustained chords, most of which can be named according to the old harmonic system, although they have been torn from the organic connection of tonality and move like a procession of ghosts. (2007, 55)

Ross's language here captures the postimpressionistic qualities of Schoenberg's composition, which sits somewhere between abstract tone poem and sonic nature painting of the most alien landscape. It pushes everything further and further, toward cosmic alienation. Sustained and wavering notes, working at the edges of harmonic systems, continue to evoke an alien world in *Rocketship X-M*. The sympathies between avant-garde modernist experiment and later SF film scoring is a telling example of the way in which, as Brend (2012) and Schmidt (2010) claim, SF films have smuggled avant-garde sensibilities and experiments into popular culture. These atonal ghosts, hovering like hallucinated wind on the uncanny threshold between the supernatural and psychological disturbance, return with the radiated breeze of the theremin that blows through the score of *Rocketship X-M*. The Grofé and Glasser material tugs the ghost of modernism, with its use of "unusual instrumental textures and ambiguous tonalities," toward the more literally alienated states of science fiction (Tibbetts 2010, 204). Here, the theremin appears as part of a compositional imperative not only to associate the soundscapes of science fiction with the most alienated, modern psychotechnological instrumentalities but also to make them culturally ubiquitous.

• • •

In the context of the SF film, the theremin takes up the modernist challenge to referential sounds and representational music by exploring the otherworldliness of noise. Well into the twentieth century, composers approached glissando as a means of moving beyond the limitations of musical pitch in order to exploit the expressive possibilities of the alien spaces between notes. Varèse attributed his own evolving approach to glissandi to the discovery of "beautiful parabolas and hyperbolas of sound"—in his word, "music"—in the industrial environmental noise of foghorns and whistles from New York's river traffic (in Kahn 1999, 86).

His interest in the siren as an instrument was sparked while reading the work of German physicist and philosopher Hermann von Helmholtz, who was developing his own sirens as part of clinical investigations into acoustics and physiology. New York regularly presented Varèse with a symphony of sirens, impossible to ignore. Kahn explains, "Sirens cried out in public in an already abstracted sound, scanning the auditive range in order not to leave anyone out and, in the process, created a unique push–pull signature yelling *come here* or *stay away* that people failed to take notice at their own peril" (1999, 84). The push–pull panic of the siren was too prevalent a feature of modern urban experience for the composer to ignore, suggesting "the perfect modernist anthem" of dread, alienation, and dangerous, dehumanizing technologies (84). Varèse sought something a bit different, however, which may have been what led him away from actual sirens to the sirenlike but ultimately more complex oscillators of the theremin.

Reference to modern urban noise sources for specific representational purposes would have led Varèse to use glissandi as part of a program music in imitation of the outside world of rivers and cities. On the contrary, the composer believed that sirens, whistles, and eventually the theremin possessed inherent properties of world making that went well beyond representation and referentiality. Divorced from traditional instruments, the glissando devices created a nonreferential music that could be drawn directly into the abstract sound worlds of the modern composer. Varèse used both the siren and the theremin to create what he called a "spatial music," and due to their revolt against fixed points of pitch, these glissandi generators could project a world "outside the narrow limits imposed by keyboard instruments" (in Kahn 1999, 86). The unstable and widely resonant sound waves activated by stroke of the hand around a theremin's antenna releases the "auditive world unto itself" that dwells in glissando and reveals itself through the theremin's electric glide (83). As Kahn goes on to explain, glissando was one of several ways in which "extramusical material" was drawn into compositional practices of the twentieth-century avant-garde. Glissando took one beyond the known range of fixed pitches with "a gestural sweep stringing together the more disparate and wayward elements of a composition. Noise was an atomistic element that signaled an abundance apart from itself, whereas the glissando contained infinity itself while attracting elements in its vicinity. Noise invoked the world, whereas the world dwelt within the glissando" (84). Extramusicality appears to also signify the otherworldly. Even as "the sounds of the world" came to be heard as organizable materials by all sorts of twentieth-century composers, composers like Russolo and Cage, as discussed earlier, divided them into categories in ways that the word "sound" typically signified something that retained its referential capacity, while the word "noise" pointed to something that was areferential. Most of the avant-garde composers sought to exploit areferential noise in lieu of the referential evocation of noise that program music had accomplished by using traditional acoustic instruments played in imitative ways. Music described as imitative was a shadowy duplicate, a false version of the modernist impulse toward noise, which overstated its likeness to reality. The apparent mimetic connectedness to the world provided in program music was in fact artificially extramusical, though the suspicion of the imitative and referential plagued modernist composers who sought to distance themselves from programmatic sensibilities. This deeply affected Varèse, Kahn writes, as the composer had to "maintain his criticism of imitation in the music of others since joining his glissandi too tightly with specific sounds in the world would have removed them from their mapping of the infinite gradation of nature" (87).

The spaces opened up by glissandi define noise according to its placeness relative to a world, even though this world might be of a new and previously unknown nature. In *New Musical Resources* (1919), American composer Henry Cowell argued for including glissandi and sliding pitches in the composer's tool kit for just these reasons, exploiting its vastly expansive capacities to discover new worlds. A compositional art of "sliding pitches" could match nature's function without copying its products, Cowell speculated ([1919] 1996, 20). While drawing on the principle of natural sounds, "such as the wind playing through trees or grasses, or whistling in the chimney, or the sound of the sea, or thunder," Cowell thought that glissandi could be abstracted and so avoid too strong a mimetic element. Musical scales, because "based on steady pitches hardly to be found in nature," are in fact unnatural. By contrast, a composer interested in "abstract music" could draw on gliding sounds that were categorically, rather than mimetically, like the sounds of nature—that is, free of fixed pitched and part of "a new tonal foundation" (20). Such emancipatory rhetoric is encountered again and again in the practice as well as the theory of early twentieth-century composers, and glissando persistently is heard as the singular means of liberating music from what Theremin himself called the "despotism of the twelvenote tempered piano scale" (in Glinsky 2005, 56). The theremin would prove the most important of the "new instruments of the future" that Italian composer Ferruccio Busoni called for in his manifesto of 1893, "Insufficiency of the Means for Musical Expression" (in Kahn 1999, 85). Busoni argued for the development of new devices that would expand the breadth of orchestral sounds and techniques while transcending the limitations of the pitch-segmented keyboard, which he later labeled an "impure medium" in 1911's *Sketch of a New Esthetic of Music* (in Kahn 1999, 85). Again, nature provides a categorical measure as Busoni implores, "Yet Nature created an *infinite gradation—infinite!*" (in Kahn 1999, 85). The theremin opens up a space of infinite gradation for the composer, performer, and listener alike, the push–pull of atmospherics an invisible touch at a distance, a compensation for the device's handsfree gestural interface by means of alien, oscillating waves. The theremin plays this out with the areferential gesture of an ontological blurring, acousmatically here and there, its eerie sonic affectedness achieved through glissando and tremolo, each a movement between tonal spaces rather than the accurate positioning of a tone within a singular space.

The theremin's electrically tainted alien atmospheres, like those of the weightless Novachord, the harmonically suspended tone poems of stellar vistas, and the Sonovox's technical filtering of the lunar landscape, offer sonic ambiences unique to the SF film. They demand a new kind of listening experience by smudging the contours of more familiar orchestral sounds. This sonic blurring confuses and deflects the locative processing supplied by the ear, especially pertinent to cinematic experience. Chion describes some of the places in which we are accustomed to locating sound relative to film:

> Some are embraced as synchronous and onscreen, others wander at the surface and on the edges as offscreen. And still others position

themselves clearly outside the diegesis, in an imaginary orchestra pit (non-diegetic music), or on a sort of balcony, the place of voiceovers. In short, we classify sounds in relation to what we see in the image, and this classification is constantly subject to revision, depending on changes in what we see. Thus we can define most cinema as "a place of images, plus sounds," with sound being "that which seeks its place." (1994, 68)

Always restless and in search of "its place," and with its diegetic location invariably "subject to revision," cinematic sound is underwritten by a deep ontological instability. Sound is an added value, not inherent, and this fundamental detachment from images means that sound can move almost anywhere else at once within the untethered space of the acousmatic screen of cinema. The syncretic value of sound becomes more expressive as it seeks new roles beyond giving a particular image materiality or weight but also all sorts of "sensory, informative, semantic, narrative, structural or expressive" values (Chion 2009, 212). The theremin, Novachord, modernist atonality, and Sonovox exploit this instability in ways that lead to an expansion and diversification of the acousmatic ecology of the SF film. Even as their new sounds speculatively stabilize the unusual places depicted on the screen, making them both present and presentable, they deepen the alien ontology of the alternative world, pull it away from us, and make it into a world apart. The ambient novum can thus be said to reinforce our ability to imagine another world, but only as it separates us from that world.

We found that in *Destination Moon,* a technological filter mediates this gulf between worlds. In ways typical of the hard SF of the golden age, the consequences of the mediating prosthetic of technological innovation for the human psyche are left unexplored. In contrast, *Rocketship X-M* draws out the significance of that profound alienation and universal estrangement that Schoenberg had first associated with a cosmic wind. In several sequences, the theremin registers not only the planet's unusual physical landscape, contaminated by radioactive fallout, but also the emotive and psychological undercurrents of the film, which likewise become contaminated by the doom that befell Martian civilization. It certainly seems to be the case here, as Sobchack suggests, that the most emotive sound in SF cinema "derives from the objectively posited and photographed narrative world of the film" (1987, 216). For Sobchack, the sounds of machinery and technology are science fiction's equivalent of the emotive surf or wind of more earthbound genres. The barrier between alien landscape and human consciousness provided by the Sonovox in *Destination Moon* ultimately makes the astronauts' experiences more convincing, if less passionate, as technological interfaces dampen and filter human response. *Rocketship X-M* blends the weird extraterrestrial nature of Mars with the emotional and psychological registers of its explorers through a singularly characteristic new sound, the technologically irradiated wind of the theremin. Where *Destination Moon* depicts technological adventures largely bereft of any psychological concern for the space explorer, *Rocketship X-M* is about the alien edge between the two.

I want to conclude with some thoughts on "psychogeography," particularly as the term suggests some unexpected resonance between *Rocketship X-M* and the roughly contemporary theory of the French artists and cultural subversives known originally as Lettrists and then as situationists. The term originated in the Lettrist international journal, *Potlach*, in a 1953 essay by Ivan Chtcheglov called "Formulary for a New Urbanism," though the idea had informed the art, theory, and urban practices of the Lettrists early on. In "Introduction to a Critique of Urban Geography" (1955), Guy Debord defines "the study of the precise laws and specific effects of the geographical environment, consciously organized or not, on the emotions and behavior of individuals" ([1955] 2006, 8). Where Debord weaves together history, sociology, Marxist critical theory, and game theory, Chtcheglov's work draws explicitly on the language of science fantasy and futurism. "The latest technological developments," Chtcheglov argued, "would make possible the individual's unbroken contact with cosmic reality while eliminating its disagreeable aspects" ([1953] 2006, 3). The speculative and cosmic turn of Chtcheglov's theory underscores its anticipation of an emerging "unitary urbanism," a revolutionary take on architecture and urban design that centered on "the synthesis of art and technology" (Sadler 1998, 15). Encapsulating formulas for "modulating reality" as well as "engendering dreams," psychogeography positioned technology's synthesis with art as a means of creating new urban ambiances and what Debord called "distinct psychic atmospheres" ([1955] 2006, 10). Urban space is occupied not only by literal police forces but also by controlling geometries that both dictate human action and code emotions within shared living spaces. To resist this spatial programming, Lettrist and situationist psychogeographers favored the *dérive*, or drift, as a "technique of rapid passage through varied ambiances" (Debord [1958] 2006, 62). The glide works here as a navigational method, a strategy for cutting across prescribed points of power in order to reveal new spaces within the familiar city and so uncover what Chtcheglov called "the Other Country" ([1953] 2006, 1). The various emphases on ambience, drifts, psychogeography, synthesis of art and technology, and the manufacture of new worlds found in these Lettrists and situationist works illustrate the sympathetic capacities that the sonic novum will possess in the history of the SF film, particularly in terms of the genre's ability to provide both spaces of technocultural accommodation and methods for navigating rapidly changing cultures and encounters with difference. It would take several years before SF cinema would draw the most pronounced concern of the situationists, the city or urban geography, into the equation and suggest something like Chtcheglov's "symbolic urbanism," though with a markedly dystopic turn ([1953] 2006, 2); later chapters will discuss several of these films, including Godard's *Alphaville* (1965), Kubrick's *A Clockwork Orange* (1971), John Coney's *Space Is the Place* (1974), Scott's *Blade Runner* (1982), and Maeck's *Decoder* (1984).

Without pushing this connection much closer than a speculative provocation, I do want to emphasize the ways in which SF cinema's use of electronic technologies to create new kinds of soundscapes connects with the experimental urban futurism of situationist attempts to spark what Chtcheglov calls the "consciousness of the cosmic" ([1953] 2006, 6). Both converge around psychogeographical experience, but the SF film develops sonic novums that capitalize on the areferential aspects of electronic film sound as it seeks its place within blurred acousmatic ecologies, exploiting the powerful capacity for music and expressive noise to trigger drifts and glides into the unknown. As the theremin of *Rocketship X-M* merges headspace with landscape during the extended sequence on the surface of Mars, we encounter something similar to the sonic landscapes of horror films, where ambience functions within horror's psychogeographical tool kit, particularly in the case of haunted spaces or locations of psychic residue, pain, and lingering malevolence. Certainly the sonic psychogeography of Mars becomes more and more agitated as it rids itself of the unwanted guests to whom it had earlier given a welcome, in Eckstrom's words, with a thunderstorm. Anticipating the deep bond between unnatural sounds and planetary intelligence later explored by Russian composer Edward Artemiev in his score to Andrei Tarkovsky's *Solaris* (1972), the theremin exploits new ambient music compositional strategies that take a psychogeographical approach to sounds that reside somewhere between nature and psyche, between diegetic noise and nondiegetic motif. By replacing the instantly recognizable melodies of the classic leitmotif with a technical tonality, the signature electric sound of the theremin monitors the mood of the Martian planetary consciousness that has been fundamentally altered by technological disaster and now pulses around the landing crew before eventually coming back to haunt them.

The theremin triggers a whole cascade of fears around the dangers of nuclear disaster by turning our attention back to the difficulties facing an atomic-age Earth. This is, after all, SF cinema's first cautionary tale (Erickson 2011, 27). The conclusion of *Rocketship X-M* brings everything together with startling consequences. The ghostly anti–life force that pulsed in the atmosphere around the landing crew eventually comes back to haunt them, for it proves a tenacious sonic presence. The theremin drops out of the soundtrack as three surviving astronauts, one mortally wounded, regain the temporary black-and-white, orchestral haven of the *X-M.* The weepy violins of Glasser's "Homeward Bound" sequence take over, just before the score swells into the disastrous gloom of the fatal finale, "None Came Back," once the film's original title that doubtlessly gave a bit too much away. During this closing musical movement, the theremin makes its last, though most pronounced, melodic statement. It renders a sorrowful theme that closely follows the plucked strings just before the full orchestra begins a series of plummeting phrases as the rocket crashes to Earth. Here, as the ambient noise of Mars falls into music, its descent would seem to get close to Cage's desire "to elevate the sound effect to the level of musical instruments" (in Kostelanetz 2003, 164). But there is no elevation here, only falling. What is it that prompts Glasser to push the theremin into this explicitly composed turn, and such a maudlin one at that?

While the sudden, startlingly musical expressiveness of the theremin seems to retreat from the otherwise innovative approach to ambient soundscape design in the earlier parts of the film, it now registers the final malevolent influence of Mars. The radiation has contaminated the score. The distinct noise of Mars has become a recognizable motif, and the tone has no respect for place. As stated earlier, it is a tonal rather than musical motif—that is, a motif that is not established by a particular melodic sequence of notes but rather a recognizable type of sound, a tone color that can invade other melodies or tint harmonies with its strange, electric harmonics. As an instrumental voice announcing the persistence of the memory of the devastated Martian civilization, the theremin continues to blur diegetic and nondiegetic functions with a final gesture of its uncertain placeness. This doesn't merely exploit the acousmatic, black box hardware design of the instrument, it turns it into the dominant aesthetic of the device, the hidden core of an areferential black hole, which dissociates gesture from sound event in the same way that timbral character has become dissociated from musical sequence. Wierzbicki attributes the theremin's "tantalizing ambiguity," which is the essence of its appeal to SF filmmakers, to its existing neither subjectively nor objectively in relation to a precise and visible source (2002, 130). Demers likewise emphasizes the invisibility of its sound creation that makes the theremin performance "inherently mysterious to watch, because there was no vibrating resonator and no visible site of sound production" (2010, 40). Technoacousmatic screening sets sound adrift, makes it pliable and uncanny, forever seeking but never quite finding its place. The invisible, destabilizing acousmatics of the alien sound is thus one way of explaining why a correspondence finally develops between new sound-generating technologies (particularly those that obfuscate their means of production), the articulation of atonal sonic vocabularies, and the need to evoke the psychogeographical ambience of unknown alien worlds in science fiction cinema. The timbral motifs of the theremin will quickly suggest a distinctively alien vibe, not just alien ambience, establishing that indexical convention of the SF film described by Leydon (2004b). What begins as a confusion of sound spaces in 1950, triggered by sounds that won't stay in their place and so end up confusing diegetic and nondiegetic events, becomes an increasingly sophisticated trope in later SF films.

1951 | *THE DAY THE EARTH STOOD STILL,*
THE THING FROM ANOTHER WORLD

By the 1950s, the theremin had already been used in films for several years to evoke the dramatic states of consciousness brought on by hypnosis, mesmerism, and dreams as well as psychotic fugues, pathological impulses, fixations, and alcoholism (see Wierzbicki 2002, 128–29). Its use in the horror film draws the theremin toward abhorrent experiences and points the way to the expressionist soundscapes of the more troubling psychogeographies of the unconscious. The theremin can be heard in the scores for Max Steiner's *King Kong* (1933) and Franz Waxman's *Bride of Frankenstein* (1935). In both cases, however, the effects are subtle, either by the intention of the composer or by virtue of the low-fidelity recordings. The theremin made its most significant film debut in one of the bizarre dream sequences in Robert E. Dolan's psychoanalytic musical, *Lady in the Dark* (1944). But it is in the following year that the theremin really comes into its own as an instrument that can sonify the unseen mind, as we hear in two film scores by Hungarian-born composer Miklós Rózsa. The first accompanies Alfred Hitchcock's psychological mystery, *Spellbound* (1945), and the second Billy Wilder's dramatic account of an alcoholic writer, *The Lost Weekend* (1945).

When charged by Hitchcock to come up with a new sound that would convey *Spellbound*'s paranoid atmospheres, Rózsa immediately suggested the theremin. In a test sequence composed for the approval of Hitchcock and producer David Selznick, the theremin underscores a tense scene in which the amnesiac, John Ballantyne (Gregory Peck), stands armed with a straight razor in the bedroom of his psychiatrist, Dr. Constance Petersen (Ingrid Bergman). The director and producer were both enthusiastic about Rózsa's demonstration of the theremin's capacity for underscoring the unspoken psychological drama in the scene, and they asked Rózsa to incorporate the instrument throughout. For much of the resulting score, Rózsa's parts for the theremin double the melodic lines written for the violin section. This required a professional thereminist who could not only read sheet music but also could meet the demands of precision playing with a well-tuned ear and steady hands. Such crucial qualifications led Rózsa to call on the most famous thereminist of the day, Clara Rockmore, but she refused to participate in the Hollywood film score as a point of "principle" (in Glinsky 2005, 254). She attributed her subsequent rejection of the use of the theremin as a movie "sound effect" to her "life-long" desire to treat the device instead as "a musical instrument, as a musical possibility, a new voice on which to . . . interpret serious music, not frighten people" (254). The part would go to the only sheet-reading theremin player listed in the L.A. musicians' union, Samuel Hoffman, who made his film soundtrack debut when picked by Rózsa to perform in lieu of Rockmore. For her part, Rockmore eventually revised her assessment of Rózsa's score, concluding that the music for "*Spellbound* happened to be a very charming melody. I wouldn't hesitate to play it today" (253). Even though in retrospect the melodic properties of Rózsa's score won her over, at the time Rockmore's bias against the use of the theremin in film and radio dramas caused her to overlook the fact that the instrument can not only play musical themes but also at the same time convey unusual, psychological states of terror far more complex than what she calls "this *woo*, voodoo thing" (253). Contrary to Rockmore's fears, Rózsa's score provides genuinely melodic content for the theremin, exploring its expressive range as an instrument with motifs that echo the other instrumental voices as well as engage them in harmonic interplay. At the same time, Rózsa's use of theremin even more remarkably exceeds what Rockmore called the "musical possibility" of the device in order to establish its significance as "a new voice" (254). In fact, Rózsa's principal achievement with the *Spellbound* score was his realization that unusual instrumentation can trigger psychological entanglement through a combination of musical expression and timbral forms characteristic of something neither nondiegetic nor diegetic: the shadowy middle ground of the psychotechnological that I refer to as the subdiegetic.

Few films used the theremin "to plumb the shadowy recesses of one man's inner terror," as Rózsa describes it in his autobiography (1983, 129), in more harrowing ways than *The Lost Weekend*. The composer recalls that the film was nearly shelved after screening for a test audience featured "a disastrously inappropriate temporary score" (129). A bit of Gershwinlike classical jazz accompanied an early scene of the writer Don Bimam (Ray Milland) fishing in his whiskey bottle, prompting bouts of uproarious laughter from the audience. The hilarity quickly evaporated when it became clear that this was to be a stark account of alcoholic desperation, and many left disappointed and startled by what seemed an abrupt change in the film's tone. After conferring with the director, Rózsa composed a score in which the theremin would provide what he would call "the official 'voice' of dipsomania," something that conveyed "the utter despair of this man, his craving for alcohol," and which "is only told to you by the sound of music" (in Glinsky 2005, 255). As one of the new generation of serious Hollywood composers, Rózsa realized that associating particular characters with specific timbral motifs make the audience susceptible to minute variations in the score. Subtle changes in dissonance or consonance, sonic tension and resolution, keep us in touch with the fluctuating psychological states of characters.

Rózsa's innovation is emblematic of the profound changes to Hollywood film scoring practices that occurred near the end of World War II, particularly a growing distaste for the Wagnerian leitmotif and its one-dimensional sonic characterization. Already by the end of the 1930s, in fact, populist American composer Aaron Copland had claimed that the significance of the film score was related directly to its capacity for "underlining the psychological states of characters"(Frith 1996, 115), and so he turned from late romantic style leitmotif and character-based themes to instead match musical themes to the pace of action, both exterior and interior. Sociomusicologist Simon Frith (1996) notes that as the new composers explored more complex relationships between music and the minds of characters on the screen, they opened their scores to noise, atonality, and electronic timbres. Bernard Herrmann noted in 1945 that the film score should "seek out and intensify the inner thoughts of the characters" (in Smith 1991, 122). In his scores, atmospheres of terror, mystery, grandeur, and misery extend interior characterization into a much wider, "enveloping" psychological space shared by characters and audience alike (122). Previously, Hollywood's orchestral sensibilities had been firmly rooted in nineteenth-century models of "leitmotif technique, uninterrupted scoring, dense orchestral textures, and associative use of key-centers," while the string section typically provided a "normative, unmarked sonic term in film music practice" (Leydon 2010b, 40). Film composers of the 1940s started to experiment with new tonalities and technologies and thereby participated in the avant-garde's challenges to classical and romantic norms while pushing the film score beyond some vaguely defined quality of character toward specific psychological states, thus establishing the basic principles of a sonic psychotechnology.

Münsterberg's *The Photoplay* ([1916] 2002b) mapped out the ways that cinematic mechanisms could express cognitive drama through an exaggerated and effects-driven exteriorization of the mind into the film's visible world. These same effects, he argued, would trigger an affective transfer that seizes the audience member "by the strange emotion" (108). Herrmann would agree, describing music as "the communicating link between the screen and the audience" (in Smith 1991, 122). Herrmann and others among the new generation of film composers propel Münsterberg's theoretical expressionism into sonic domains, as a "truly musical interpretation" of the narrative becomes part of "the total world of the film," just as Münsterberg had anticipated in 1916 (2002b, 203). But what Münsterberg had not anticipated was the extent to which composed sound would express, exteriorize, and trigger specifically psychotechnological relationships. In 1945, Rózsa's scores for *Spellbound* and *The Lost Weekend* offered the most intriguing exploitation of a sonic psychotechnological relay yet. Unstable electronic timbres not only portray the mental distress of the characters on screen but also provoke the discomfort, unease, and anxiety of audience members. With a variable timbral motif that works according to intensities rather than melodies, the sound of the theremin is not so much audible throughout a score as a continual and general musical voice but is rather used in very specific contexts for timbral effects and their corresponding affective triggers.

While Rózsa's scores are the first to realize the theremin's capacity to serve as a psychotechnological apparatus, others would soon follow suit. In the wake of *Spellbound*, enough psychological thrillers featured the theremin in their score for the instrument to gain a reputation as "the official instrument of psychosis" (Sotiropoulos 2010). Roy Webb's score to Robert Siodmak's *The Spiral Staircase* (1946), for instance, uses the theremin to signal the murderous impulse of the film's serial killer, Professor Warren (George Brent), while Rózsa turned to the instrument once more to create the haunting space of psychological torture in Delmer Daves's *The Red House* (1947). Visually, psychological thrillers draw from the traditions of both expressionism and surrealism, as in the Dalí-designed dream sequences and hallucinatory fugues for *Spellbound*, the house of shadows and its vertigo-inducing stairway in *The Spiral Staircase*, and the delirious visions of *The Lost Weekend*. But perhaps the most unique power of the sonic apparatus—the theremin, in these cases—is its capacity to charge scenes with strange and startling psychological tensions against minimal, stark or even absent, visual cues. Pointing to the precision that associates the theremin with discrete events rather than a sonic element that plays throughout an entire film's score, Wierzbicki attributes the "highly discriminate usage" of the theremin to its becoming such a potent barometer of abnormal psychological conditions (2002, 130). The theremin sonifies the subconscious drama, invisible and inaudible to most characters on the screen, while at the same time prompting a psychosomatic or psychotomimetic grafting of "physical or psychological entities" (130) to the listening bodies of the audience. Because these subconscious sonic entities are "unsettling by the very nature of their pitches and rhythms" (130), and work us over by a kind of touch from a distance, they replace the mimetic or representative figures of the Wagnerian leitmotif, which associates sound with characters on the screen to create sympathies or antagonisms, and work on the listener directly as affective agents. The science fiction film will take very specific advantage of this agential sonic entity.

As the theremin drifts from the psychological thriller to the SF film, it takes these affective subconscious entities with it. The lineage is acknowledged outright in a promotional trailer for *The Day the Earth Stood Still*, which proclaims, "They came 250 million miles *out of space* . . . to hold the world *Spellbound* with New and Startling Powers from Another Planet!" The allusion to the Hitchcock film is certainly unintentional, for the only possible cinematic connection would be the prominence of the theremin in both film scores. At the same time, the language of the trailer captures precisely the theremin's transfer of its psychotechnological resonance to the SF film for a new effect: the actualization of otherwise invisible, startling alien powers. The film suggests that these powers are both mental and technological. In fact, the theremin plays out the unseen connection between the two. In *The Day the Earth Stood Still* specifically, music actualizes the alien psychotechnological interface that links Klaatu to his technology. Inside his flying saucer, Klaatu executes control over the ship's controls both by verbal commands issued in his native language and by waving his hands at doors and over blinking instrument panels. Most of the consoles we see in the spaceship interior are operated through gestural controls, and Klaatu at times suggests nothing less than a first-rate thereminist as the instrument is featured prominently during such scenes. But the theremin is as contextual as it is suggestive; it sonifies the mysterious, alien technologies and incomprehensible power sources without ever quite becoming a diegetic element. Rather, even while the theremin hints at the pulse and hum of an advanced technology, it stays removed and distanced from the terrestrial setting of the film. In other words, the theremin never sounds like it comes from around here but always from an extraterrestrial out there.

• • •

We get our first look at Klaatu's alien environment as he retreats into his spaceship to trigger the titular "day the Earth stood still." Here we get our first listen to this environment as well. The theremin featured in this sequence becomes far more melodic than at any prior point in the film. With Klaatu back in his saucer, which we might think of as a little piece of his home planet here on Earth, the theremin seems to settle back into its "natural environment" and breaks out into a brief celebratory homecoming song (Leydon 2004b, 36). This is certainly an uncanny sound event that combines the invisible timbral motif-driven vibe that marks Klaatu as alien with the diegetic and ambient noises generated by his advanced technologies, including the robot Gort. The association of the theremin with images of alien technologies becomes particularly poignant whenever Gort speaks or acts. Though humanoid in shape, Gort is smooth, metallic, and faceless, a kind of knight in shining armor whose thin visor opens to reveal a single pulsing glow or to emit an incinerating ray. Like Klaatu, Gort is marked by a sonic aura, but its vibe is distinct, playing at a lower pitch and with more extreme glides from one pitch to another than Klaatu's theremin. Again, it is probably far-fetched to presume that characters in the film, particularly merely human ones, hear the sounds of Gort as actual diegetic events. Perhaps this is exactly what Gort and the otherworldly technology sound like, but audible only to alien ears—ears that the audience occupy by proxy. The melodic turn of the theremin when Klaatu boards his saucer, however, suggests that something else is going on, a psychotechnological exchange that is further advanced in other sequences.

The expressive musical and affective qualities of alien psychotechnological interfaces become most pronounced whenever Klaatu and Gort communicate. The timbral motif's turn toward the melodic occurs as Klaatu establishes an invisible telepathic correspondence with Gort. While Klaatu remotely programs the robot with a set of staccato flashlight commands, a pair of theremins cycle through a sequence of interlocking half steps. The more highly pitched theremin associated with Klaatu is performed with full-throttle vibrato, and the second theremin, Gort's lower-pitched instrument, plays as steady and calm a note as a theremin can muster, though still with notable warbles and trembles. This pairing of distinct electronic frequencies emphasizes the instrument's instability at both ends of its range while amplifying the fringes of pitch at either end of the spectrum (Leydon 2004b, 35). This lends a kind of weepy, whimpering quality to the exchange between Klaatu and Gort, with the robot at times sounding almost like a big, moaning dog. Along with its basic two-note melody, the rhythmic call-and-response interaction of the theremins suggests to Leydon "the secret channels of communication between Gort and Klaatu" (39). Whether audible as such to Klaatu or Gort, or a kind of telepathic duet, alien and robot do indeed sing to each other in a way that manifests the emanating transmission of sonic psychotechnologies. Mapping the psychotechnological dimension of the sonic novum here back to its source, Harry Bates's "Farewell to the Master" (1940), highlights the ways in which a cinematic form not only differs conceptually and narratively from its textual counterpart but actualizes its affective agency through new sonic materials. After a pair of alien visitors lands their spaceship on the lawn of the U.S. Capitol, "Farewell to the Master" recounts the experiences of Cliff Sutherland, a freelance journalist of the future who hopes to get the shot that will land on "the front page of every paper in the Solar System" (Bates 1940, 60). The aliens are remarkable. One is an eight-foot-tall green metal robot, "the powerful god of the machine of some undreamt-of scientific civilization," named Gnut (59). The other, Klaatu, is strikingly "godlike in appearance and human in form," with a face that radiates "kindness, wisdom, the purest nobility" (62). Upon the aliens' arrival and despite the "graciousness and dignity" that made it clear to the thousands gathered that their guests came in peace, a deranged gunman shoots Klaatu with a laser pistol. The alien is soon buried in a marble mausoleum, while the spaceship and the motionless and silent robot, Gnut, become the central exhibits of a newly constructed interplanetary wing of the Smithsonian. These details are presented as backstory, conveyed during Sutherland's first visit to the museum as he pauses to watch an audiovisual documentary playing at the entrance to the new hall. The extended transcript of the recording's content isn't just for purposes of exposition, however, as the narrative will eventually turn on this seemingly inconsequential detail.

Eager to keep this sensational story alive with a picture of Gnut that would cast the statuesque robot in a "weird and menacing" light (59), Sutherland sneaks into the museum one night, only to discover that Gnut is active. Detected but ignored by the robot, Sutherland hides in the shadows as the robot enters the spaceship on unknown business. It is here that we encounter one of the most extraordinary sequences in the story:

> There was a faint whir of wings, soon followed by the piercing, sweet voice of a bird. A mockingbird. Somewhere in the gloom above his head. Clear and full-throated were its notes; a dozen little songs it sang, one after the other without pause between—short insistent calls, twirrings, coaxings, cooings—the spring love song of perhaps the finest singer in the world. Then, as suddenly as it began, the voice was silent. (68)

At first Sutherland is taken aback by the anomaly of hearing a mockingbird sing in December. The mystery only deepens as Gnut emerges once more from the spaceship. A soft thud on the museum floor announces the demise of the mockingbird. The robot retrieves the fallen bird that "had lost its song forever" and returns to the spaceship (68). With the dark interior thwarting his efforts to snap an award-winning photograph, Sutherland is at a loss when another "peculiar series of muffled noises reached his ears. . . . Animal noises—first scrapings and pantings, punctuated by several sharp clicks, then deep, rough snarls, interrupted by more scrapings and pantings, as if a struggle of some kind were going on" (68–69). Suddenly, an enraged gorilla emerges from within the spaceship, battles Gnut, and wrecks the museum before falling to the floor and dying—dead not from its scuffle but as the result of some mysterious weakness that overtakes it.

This pair of dramatic incidents, both strongly encoded by expressive sounds, sets the stage for the revelation of this SF text's primary novum: Gnut is using the museum's audiovisual recordings in an effort to re-create the murdered Klaatu. The robot's experiments are fatally flawed, however. During his second night of investigation, Sutherland encounters a doomed reconstruction of a man named Stillwell—the very man, it turns out, whose voice was heard on the documentary recording welcoming visitors to the Smithsonian's otherworldly exhibit. Sutherland watches as Gnut makes a pile of failed experiments: the mockingbird, the gorilla, and, to his horror, not just one but two dead Stillwells. Fleeing in a panic, Sutherland is apprehended by the police. The reporter's testimony leads to the containment of Gnut in a cage of futuristic plastic, surrounded by armed guards and military-grade weaponry. But Gnut escapes his containment unscathed and, grabbing Sutherland on the way out, heads off into the night to the mausoleum, where the remains of the "unspoken visitor from the great Unknown" are interred in a plastic coffin (83). Rather than the body, however, Gnut is interested in a small box at the foot of this coffin that contains records of his arrival, including a roll of "sight-and-sound film" (83). Gnut grabs the box of recordings and returns, Sutherland still in tow, to the spaceship, where the robot sets to work on several apparatuses arranged near another coffinlike box.

Sutherland is in for another shock when Klaatu's physical form appears in the box and begins speaking in an alien tongue to Gnut, who replies at length in the same unknown language. Klaatu also speaks with

Sutherland, clarifying that not only is he not the same Klaatu as the one encased in the tomb, but that this duplicate form is in fact dying. Confronted by Sutherland's incomprehension, Klaatu explains:

> Although unlike us, Gnut has great powers. When the wing was built and the lectures began, there came to him a striking inspiration. Acting on it at once, in the night, he assembled this apparatus . . . and now he has made me again, from my voice, as recorded by your people. As you must know, a given body makes a characteristic sound. He constructed an apparatus which reversed the recording process, and from the given sound made the characteristic body. (85)

When Klaatu informs him that his reconstructed body is doomed to failure because of "imperfections" (85) in the recording media, Sutherland realizes that the animal forms he encountered earlier had been re-created from a collection of filmstrips "recording the speech of various world fauna" (85), just as the Stillwells were extracted from his voiceover on the exhibit documentary. Sutherland suggests to Klaatu a strategy that might compensate for the flawed recordings. By tracing the imperfections in the audio back to the recording apparatus itself, he hypothesizes, Klaatu might then figure out a means of cleaning up the recording, canceling out the flaws, and at last creating a viable life-form. Sutherland quickly gathers the recording apparatus that Gnut needs for this inspired feat of backward engineering, which the robot plans to conduct back at its home planet. Before leaving, Sutherland offers Gnut, on behalf of Earth, an apology to be delivered to the successfully reconstructed Klaatu, Gnut's "master yet to come" (87). Gnut then speaks for the first and only time in the story, delivering the surprise ending, "You misunderstand, *I* am the master" (87).

This rather too clever remastering of our misperceptions of the robot's true identity underscores the issues of sound and fidelity in this classic golden age story by *Astounding Science Fiction*'s founding editor; the story of course also happens to be the basis of one of the most iconic films in SF history, *The Day the Earth Stood Still*. Variations between the short story and the film range from the mildly superficial (a loincloth-clad humanoid Gnut with metal for muscles becomes the metal-encased Gort) to the substantive. The film takes place in a contemporary setting rather than the futuristic Earth of the short story. There is no Sutherland character in the film, the protagonist of which is Klaatu. At his arrival, Klaatu is shot by a soldier, not a rogue assassin, but is merely wounded, recuperates quickly, has a widowed love interest and befriends her son, is shot again, this time fatally, and then is more successfully, though not explicitly sonically, resurrected by Gort. The surprise ending is cut out; the humanoid Klaatu is clearly the master of the robot.

Sound plays a different role altogether in the film, though both the short story and film are concerned with the nature of recorded sound and what can be done with it. Beyond the use of the theremin in the score, *The Day the Earth Stood Still* is one of the first SF movies to explore the expressive capacity of electronic tonalities generated through the manipulation of magnetic tape recordings. The sounds are situated nondiegetically, as an integral part of the music scored, conducted, and realized technically by Herrmann. Only occasionally do strange sounds emit from the alien visitors within the diegetic world of the film, like Gort's eyebeam, but these aren't drawn from the short story, with its own cache of possible amazing sounds. Rather, the film sublimates those aspects of the fiction into its score. Now, though, I want to consider the text of "Farewell to the Master" in just a little more depth, as Gnut's sonic regeneration device provides an example of the fictive novum that pushes to the limits of Suvin's original formulation. In fact, it necessitates an expanded concept of the novum that is not only receptive to the romanticism of pulp science fiction—perhaps at its most hackneyed—but which is nonetheless expressive of sophisticated post-human psychotechnologies.

In "Farewell to the Master," the sonic regeneration apparatus cognitively oscillates with the recording media technologies of the reader's familiar world, evoked throughout the story through numerous references to journalistic multimedia: photographs, filmstrips, newspapers, sound recordings, and, slightly ahead of its time, television. The story is set during a time of media saturation if not yet convergence, but the most interesting twist comes with Bates's extrapolating the possibility of using such media—and sound media in particular—to reconstruct physical duplicates of living things. The text draws a correspondence among sound, body, and some kind of ethereal life essence. In the two passages from "Farewell to the Master" quoted at length above, a figurative sonic novum provides the opportunity to reflect on the relationship between sound and variously animal, human, and alien identities. While the narrative deals with the practicalities of high-fidelity sound recording, the sonic novum triggers its own thematically charged analogies of other kinds of fidelity: that which should ideally dictate the fair terms of relationship between greater and lesser beings, for instance. Ideas about mercy, the maturity of the human species, and cosmic responsibility; the capacity for advanced technologies to act as agents of destruction or connection; notions of war or peace—these also circulate through the text. Such themes can be found in both the short story and its cinematic adaptation, but they work out in significantly different ways.

In its literary form, the sonic novum situates speculations concerning the intersection of sound technologies and the alien psyche or soul, though we can't really call it that. Bates (1940) offers us this instead: "As you must know, a given body makes a characteristic sound" (85). With the original body of Klaatu still encased in plastic, the sonic regeneration device doesn't resurrect but rather reconstructs a body from its recorded duplicate. The accuracy of this reconstruction is verified not by the recognition of some mysterious psychic essence but rather by its "characteristic sound," something that in the parlance of the pulp fiction sounds kind of scientific rather than spiritualistic, suggesting an invisible radiating by-product of the tangible body, a waveform rather than a soul. Even a robot could be said to possess a characteristic sound; even the particular mockingbird, we are told, doesn't so much lose its life but rather its song, the thing that made it unique not as an individual but as a species, and that could be, and was, lost forever. Gnut's initial experiments with the sonic regeneration device fail, but the inexplicable shortcomings of futuristic sound engineering are at last countered by good old human ingenuity as the journalist comes up with the solution to Gnut's problems: the robot must remaster the source tapes. The surprise ending is supposed to shock us into recognition that this "god of the machine" (59) is in fact superior to the "benign god" (62), which we are told three times Klaatu resembles. The penultimate gesture toward Sutherland's technical resourcefulness, well intentioned though it may be, vaguely undercuts the presentation of Gnut as a benevolent caretaker—remember, Sutherland had wanted to cast the robot in a "weird and menacing" light (59)—and so recuperates into a comfortable familiarity any potential the story may have had to challenge the presumption that the human form of life would be superior to all others.

Admittedly, the sonic regeneration device is a relatively weak example of Suvin's novum. With its existence apparently known only to Sutherland, it hardly reflects a major historical transformation. Gnut better exemplifies the traditional novum, though even the impact of the robot's appearance on humanity is at last hardly earth-shattering. The sonic regeneration device is, however, a powerful example of what I have called the new novum, for where the traditional novum triggers an estranged reconsideration of the present course of history, the new novum provides a space to reflect on technical instrumentalities and new modes of being in a highly technological world. In contrast to the film that it inspired, Bates's 1940 short story submerges its cosmic ethics beneath an assumption that science can duplicate the function of faith, resurrecting the godlike dead. Dropping out direct references to the sonic regeneration device, eliminating Sutherland, and shifting Klaatu into the role of the novum turns the film into a tale of a wounded cosmic savior, a techno-Christ (Klaatu even takes on the name, "Mr. Carpenter") who declares us not quite ready for galactic brotherhood. The figurative sonic novum of "Farewell to the Master," which links Gnut to Klaatu through sonic characteristics, is ported into cinematic form in *The Day the Earth Stood Still*, with the pair of theremins recalling the relationship between sound and higher beings, alien technologies, and the nature of both human and alien consciousness. Though absent from the film's narrative, the sonic regeneration device is recast through Herrmann's score, which effectively distributes the sonic elements of the original short story along nondiegetic registers. By no longer treating the sound object as an analogous device, the film increases the disorienting cosmic dimensions of the ethereal substance, the characteristic vibe that surrounds the alien. Here we experience the sonic novum's ability to modify its own mechanism by remediating from text to film, shifting from an imaginary device within a narrative world to an actual sonic object that occupies the peripheries of the cinematic narrative in the form of music.

Here, the sonic novum is encoded within a nondiegetic space that ultimately gestures toward a more removed subdiegetic space, the cinematic space of invisible psychotechnological imbrication.

Reconsidering the duet of Klaatu and Gort's respectively characteristic sounds, the doubled theremins allow Herrmann to establish alien communication in a fairly direct way by suggesting extraterrestrial psi powers such as telepathy and telekinesis—powers functionally invisible but fundamental to many SF narratives of the period, especially those about alien invasion. These sounds occupy a subdiegetic zone of the film, where sounds are not so much offscreen and extracinematic but rather emit from the deep subconscious interiors of characters on the screen while also working affectively on the bodies of the listening audience. The theremin had already technologized the subconscious in the thriller, where it conveyed the particular disturbing psychotechnological subroutines of suppressed memories and alcoholism. Herrmann's score for *The Day the Earth Stood Still* exploits these aspects of the instrument pioneered by Rózsa. Like Rózsa, Herrmann thought that "film music must supply what actors cannot say. . . . It must really convey what the word cannot do" (in Fiegel 2003, 25). Here, the theremin goes from one kind of voice to another, from Rózsa's "official" voices of alcoholism and psychosis to the extraterrestrial nonvoice of psychic vibration and telepathic exchange, sonifying the "New and Startling Powers from Another Planet" that the film's trailer promised. Herrmann's score turns subconscious diegetic sounds into a cosmic force. The film's narrative builds toward this singular event.

On the day the Earth stands still, Klaatu's psychotechnological reach extends well beyond the walls of his flying saucer and into the cosmos of which he is an ambassador. The sonic novum extends into new territories, as well. Klaatu deactivates all human machines and technologies during a sequence referred to in Herrmann's composition as "The Magnetic Pull." Klaatu's ability to manipulate time, space, and the very physics of electromagnetic attraction leads to a grand scene of cinematic stasis, achieved throughout a sequence of stock footage street scenes depicting cities all around Earth, where everything—washing machines, dairy equipment, printing presses, factories, vehicles of all kinds—has stopped working. The film's director and Herrmann alike knew that the score had to provide a sense of the invisible, alien forces at work at the film's dramatic crux. Rather than overcompensate for the stillness of the sequence with a frantic score, Herrmann creates a minute of frozen music using what he recalled as having been "the most experimental, avant-garde techniques" of any film that he had scored (1971, 36). The composer oddly asserts, "At that time, we he had no electronic sound, but the score had many electronic features which haven't become antiquated at all: electric violin, electric bass, two high and low electric theremins, four pianos, four harps and a very strange section of about 30-odd brass" (36–37). In retrospect, Herrmann's subtle distinction between "electronic sound" and "electronic features" must be his way of indicating that in 1951 they had lacked the analog synthesizers that would become widely available by the mid-1960s. While the scope and unusual combination of instrumentation alone places Herrmann in the company of avant-garde composers like Varèse, Herrmann's tape composition—the first of its kind in a Hollywood film—predates all but Schaeffer's works of musique concrète in terms of developing tape manipulation and mixing practices as artistic activities in their own right. As an early example of sound design in the SF film, Herrmann's work demonstrates a keen ear for effective sequences of film music accompaniment with very specific thematic resonances and consequences.

The final mono soundtrack of *The Day the Earth Stood Still* possesses a sonic clarity that Herrmann achieved due to his use of multiple tracks during the recording and mixing processes. More than a matter of sound reproduction, this involved some of Herrmann's most compelling design techniques. One of his signature practices involved the isolation of the sounds of acoustic instruments. Distinct instrumental voices would normally resonate with each other, creating a rich field of harmonic overtones that sound like they occupy the same physical, natural space. "Acoustical instruments interact with everything around them in nature," Stephen Husarik writes in his treatment of the film, "even other instruments. They 'hear' each other, adjust to each other, and tune up" (2010, 172). At the time, film music was typically recorded in a unified studio setting, which contributed to the natural instrumental interaction that Husarik describes, rather than the product of overdubbing and mixing. This same music was fated for delivery over a mono channel in the movie theater, along with all the other sounds in the movie, adding to an even denser blend of voices and sounds. Herrmann effectively cancels this interplay, limiting the range and ability for instruments to communicate with each other during recording. By alienating each instrument from the others, Herrmann thwarts the natural resonance of interinstrumental communication, first isolating distinct acoustic sound events in the recording studio and then capturing them on separate channels of magnetic tape. Instead of mutual strands of instrumental voices "listening to each other" as they tune up in the play of acoustic space, Herrmann negates "acoustical color" by denying "the interaction between overtones" (Husarik 2010, 173). This provides further opportunity to recompose a kind of musical communication in an artificial and alien sound space—one of a predominantly electronic timbre—and within which the wide and unstable bandwidth of the theremin in particular stands out. Herrmann's treatment of other instruments is even more compelling. He often cuts off the actual attack of an instrumental sound on tape, emphasizing what Husarik calls "the residual ambience of each note" and making that ambience its own compositional element (172). Through processes of "harmonic nullification, rhythmic confusion and acoustical cancellation" (168), Herrmann further removes the original timbral properties of sounds from their source material. As he reverses, filters, and remixes his recordings of different instruments, both acoustic and electric, the magnetic tape recordings come to operate in the manner of electronically generated sounds.

These practices play out the film's thematic exploration of humans and aliens. The numerous "human" instruments heard throughout *The Day the Earth Stood Still* tend to emphasize an emotional subcurrent but also erupt into moments of brute, grossly hands-on performance, a particularly vivid counterpoint to the hands-free and ethereal theremin. Human beings lack the refined sonic aura that sets the alien sound apart. Especially harsh due to Herrmann's sound isolation techniques, the violent and ugly banging on pianos, drums, and gongs that provided the source content for "The Magnetic Pull" sequence portrays humans as "musical primitives" (Husarik 2010, 171). This aggression isn't removed once these sounds are captured by the magnetic pull of the tape recording, but rather electrified and made susceptible to alien manipulation.

Husarik describes this as an invisible refinement of sound made possible by electricity, which metaphorically resonates with the film's dramatic climax and its depiction of "the influence of alien electronic technology over Earthly mechanical power" (172). As the Earth succumbs to Klaatu's alien command, the score can only be heard in terms of its alien electronic sensibilities. Husarik concludes, "Even though there are acoustical instruments playing, they have been absorbed into the electronic world through multiple recording techniques and tape manipulations. Nothing purely acoustical is allowed to thrive in the electronically controlled environment" (173). Manipulated by the same sonic psytech that links the alien directly to the vast cosmic reserve of power over time and space, earthly sound collapses into the black hole of an auditory alienation; an affective distinction between music and electronic timbre as such then emerges to reveal the materiality and thingness of subdiegetic, psychotechnological sound. Alien sonic psytech confronts music's evolutionary potential like a resonating shadow from the future now cast back onto the crude, crumbling foundation of terrestrial sound palettes. By contrast, the theremin, with its sublimated and voiceless vibe of the alien, is aligned with the beauty and grandeur of outer space itself, electrically at home with "the celestial harmony of the movement of the planets which Earth's factionalism and arms race threatened, and which had prompted Klaatu to be dispatched as an ambassador to Earth, to invite us to change our ways" (Hayward 1997, 38). Hayward's (1997) analysis of *The Day the Earth Stood Still* plugs the cosmological evocation of the theremin directly into the sociopolitical thread of the film's narrative. The theremin performs a note of cosmic nostalgia, then, calling out Earth's alienation from a galactic civilization that is enlightened and inclusive, proactive rather than reactionary, and empathetic to the expressivity of the unknown.

• • •

The use of theremin as sonic aura in *The Day the Earth Stood Still* is not that different from the sonic taint that radiates around the weird creatures in Jack Arnold's *It Came from Outer Space*. These aliens take possession of human bodies and would walk about undetected if not for their inability to properly mimic the affective behaviors of their hosts—they also tend to take off all their host body's clothing. But the audience can pick out the victims of alien possession well before the other human characters in the film, thanks to the theremin's sonic disclosure of each otherwise hidden alien. Though ultimately benevolent, the alien minds hidden inside human bodies are exposed because they evoke the wrong feeling. With its distinctive electronic tones offering a technological solution to a problem of narrative production, the theremin's job in such instances is to identify the otherwise familiar-looking alien in our midst and to open up a new domain of sonic diegesis that maps out the extraordinary powers of alien beings. It did this in *The Day the Earth Stood Still* as well, and in both that film and *It Came from Outer Space,* the end result seems to be a simultaneous empathy and alienation of the human from the visitors from outer space.

We have no opportunity to feel empathy for the Thing from another world in Christian Nyby's film of that title. In this film, a sentient, vegetable-like life-form that seeds itself through nourishment of human or animal blood—what one character calls "some form of super carrot"—takes on a lumbering humanoid form courtesy of James Arness. Regardless of its body, the Thing's presence is always given away by a set of stingers provided by some of the theremin's most aggressive and clamorous shrieking ever recorded for film. More than the fact that the monster is mostly a shadowy and offscreen menace, the main barrier to any affective connection to the alien come from the unsettling tonalities of the theremin, performed yet again by Samuel Hoffman in a score by Dimitri Tiomkin. We can either barely hear the theremin except as something lurking in the final mix, or it blares out and attacks us outright. Hoffman offers up his most hard-core work yet for *The Thing from Another World,* his contributions heard even more clearly on the original soundtrack album's tracks, such as the high-pitched vibrato barrage that concludes the "Melting Sequence," and the outrageous, sustained screech that hovers above the thundering orchestra of "The Thing at the Door." In its loudest sequences, the theremin acts like an electronic space invader of the acoustic orchestra. Brash, wild, and uncompromising in its extreme oscillations, the timbral motif heard here is as far as one could get from the single vibrating waveform that conveys the genteel melodicism of Klaatu's theremin halo vibe. On the other side of an existential, perhaps even ontological, divide, the Thing is not a being as such. The Thing cannot be sonically represented, and just as it is most frightening when not quite visible but obscured by shadows, and despite all the aggression of the theremin stings, the Thing is actually most terrifying when not quite heard as such. This is where the sound of a simple Geiger counter comes into play. Hinting at a Thing and yet not the thing itself, the Geiger counter sonifies that which cannot sonify itself.

The American scientists and Air Force crew who discovered The Thing near their arctic outpost have known from the beginning that the creature is slightly radioactive. This is how they discovered its frozen bulk in a block of ice after accidently blowing up its buried flying saucer. Once the revived Thing has begun to roam the outpost, the Geiger counter alone announces the proximity of the otherwise invisible and lumbering horror. It is a great, practical plot detail, and in its few usages such a successful sound design decision that it threatens to render Tiomkin's score beside the point. The accelerating ticking possesses far more potential peril than the theremin outbursts, which simply come upon us, shocking us rather than building suspense. Sobchack suggests that, far more than the composed score, the Geiger counter delivers "a recurrent and sinister aural motif"—what I would label a concrete motif—of clicks and ticks that provide a more intense emotional bridge to the human characters in crisis than musical cues (1987, 216). When we measure the Thing as diegetic Other—its radiating, dangerous vibe registering on our sensitive technical device as a steadily accelerating tick—the Geiger counter in fact captures a nonpresence, a radiating vibe around another thing, a thing that is the absence of music, that cannot be heard on its own terms, and that is sonically invisible. This isn't the same thing as silent. Rather, the sonically invisible exploits the acousmatic properties of both the black box, hands-free technology of the theremin and the conditions of theatrical presentation in the cinema. Even as the theremin's suggestive, invisible vibe is eclipsed by the compelling Geiger counter sound effect in *The Thing*, it was also heading toward another kind of invisibility in golden age scores—one symptomatic of a more familiar kind of monstrosity, the Hollywood music industry.

By 1953, the theremin was quickly becoming functionally invisible even as the talents of SF film composers were increasingly taken for granted. In the patchwork score for *It Came from Outer Space*—composed by Herman Stein, Henry Mancini, and Irving Gertz, none credited on the screen—the familiar Hoffman theremin continues to identify otherwise invisible aliens among us through short sonic cues and timbral motifs. As it reinforces an increasingly familiar genre boundary, however, the theremin seems more obligatory than necessary, exploratory, or alienating. Rather than a carefully crafted element of a score designed to be integral to the whole experience of the film, the soundtrack plays more like incidental music. In fact, bits of the music created for *It Came from Outer Space* become part of Universal Studio's sound library and are used well into the 1960s. Even in its viral afterlife, this score goes on to ensure the theremin's erasure through its overfamiliarity as a generic sonic gesture. The theremin can hardly be heard at all against the sounds of a more compelling electric string quartet in the soundtrack of *Project Moonbase* (1953). The theremin sound, as it were, lingers briefly in the atmospheres of SF films, longer than the actual instrument itself, as its timbral motif becomes not only functionally automatic but a kind of style that other instruments capable of producing a thereminesque sound could mimic. Working in the SF genre came to mean that composers would treat acoustic, electric, and human voices in ways that suggest or imitate the theremin's signature warble and glissando to evoke ethereal and cosmic sounds. The solo electric violin was particularly popular and can be heard in the scores to the films *Kronos* (1957), *It! The Terror from Beyond Space, Missile to the Moon* (1958), and *The Cosmic Man* (1959), where the electric strings both evoke the glissando of the theremin and serve up shimmering atmospheric effects. The Novachord is heard in several films and even more often on TV's early SF shows, including the themes to *The Twilight Zone* (1959–64) and *The Outer Limits* (1963–65), along with the Ondes Martenot, a highly expressive keyboard invented in 1928 that was also capable of portamento glides and unusual electronic textures. The most intriguing thereminesque moment of the golden age is heard in William Cameron Menzies's *Invaders from Mars* (1953). Raoul Kraushaar's score builds toward an extended cosmic movement featuring an unaccompanied choir, their voices sustaining a rhythmic, almost atonal flutter and glide that dramatically expands the scope of instrumental voice to reflect the frightening plurality of would-be conquerors indicated in the film's title. Near the end of the 1950s, trombonist Paul Tanner developed the Electro-Theremin, which replicated the timbre of the original theremin while bringing its pitch and volume under more formal and precise control through sliders, switches, and knobs. The Electro-Theremin is heard on the theme to the TV show *My Favorite Martian* (1963–66), where it also provided the sound effect for the rising and falling antennae of the Martian, Uncle Martin (Ray Walston), and perhaps most famously in The Beach Boys' "Good Vibrations" (1966).

Even in the best case, however, the thereminesque function becomes a familiarizing sonic force rather than an alienating one. Its ubiquitous timbral motif reinforces genre identification and, ultimately, stereotypes. Particularly in American SF films, fewer composers sought legitimately new and weird sounds. One of Samuel Hoffman's last film scores reunited the aging doctor with composer and bandleader Les Baxter, who had conducted the recording sessions for the early space-age lounge album, *Music Out of the Moon* (1947). The film was Roger Corman's *X: The Man with the X-ray Eyes* (1963), in which Dr. James Xavier (Ray Milland) uses experimental eye drops to extend the power of his vision and ends up, as you can guess, with X-ray vision. The theremin gives voice to Dr. Xavier's vision, representing the mutation of the X-ray gaze and giving us a way to see the world through his eyes, as it were. This synesthetic loop effectively closes the psychotechnological circuit by which the electronic instrument had once generated compelling sonic novums. Caught up in its own gaze, the theremin sounds exhausted, overheated, and trapped in the black hole that replaces each X-ray eye. "All one has left is a resonance chamber well on the way to forming a black hole," Deleuze and Guattari write of the overheated sonic refrain. "A material that is too rich remains too *territorialized*: on noise sources, on the nature of the objects" (1987, 344). Turned into a schizophonic vision of the gap between a sonorous object and its source in the contemporary soundscape, with a black hole at its center, even the chance of a synesthetic exchange shuts down, and the theremin loses its voice. The now characteristic, rather than new, sound of the theremin is emptied of meaning and becomes devoid of value as all the potential sonic territories of the new, once powered by their own areferentiality, collapse into a singular sonic tonality that can no longer be made into a motif beyond its own self-referential echo. With the end of its psychotechnological relevance in range, any remaining bit of the theremin's capacity to contribute meaningfully to the sonic novum will be limited almost entirely to irony and self-referential kitsch, as in Howard Shore's use of the instrument in Tim Burton's *Mars Attacks!* (1996). Here, as it retroactively evokes the sounds of the golden age, the theremin is eclipsed by the film's more significant sonic novum: the Martian head-exploding power of Slim Whitman's "Indian Love Call." As Hayward observes, Whitman's yodel is at once more "aberrant" and, with its "melodic leaps and oddness," its devastating glides far more alien and otherworldly than the theremin could be at this point of its decline (2004a, 179, 186n7). At once iconic and ironic, the theremin is now science fiction's quintessential sonic motif, a stock cliché of the Other sound, and its normalizing tonalities can only reinforce our expectations of the conventions of 1950s science fiction films.

The codes for hearing the theremin in such specific ways developed over time. Its precinematic history as an innovative technological form of musical instrument had garnered its first associations with the music of the spheres. The theremin prompted aesthetic distinctions between the sonic avant-garde and classical traditions even as emerging popular forms of music recast such distinctions through its association with science fiction on film and television. But with satire and kitsch, the theremin hits a limit, in part because overuse and appropriation wear it out. Its gradual acculturation and depletion as a sonic novum is a by-product of the historicity of science fiction and the time line of innovation that the very newness of the sonic novum seems to necessitate. Without a doubt, the experience of a sonic novum depends on previous episodes of listening and prior associations and expectations, while the repetition of a once unusual sound over time—and in multiple, reiterative contexts of a similar nature—has a familiarizing effect. It turns a type of sound once considered highly unusual into a way to normalize, define, and understand a genre. The old "new sound" thus becomes conventional.

But time is only one way to measure the newness and difference of science fiction, sonic or otherwise. As Zepke (2012) notes, the genre requires not simply a "new" new, but something that is "untimely." The term comes from Nietzsche and represents for Zepke a way to think of science fiction beyond the mechanism of cognitive estrangement and its underlying investment in a critical investigation of the present and its historical limits. Rather than "a reflection of current modes of being," the untimely designates "an alternative future, a future undetermined by the present" (2012). Untimeliness triggers a radical eruption of becoming so different from present conditions that drawing the estranged imagination back to reality, through a utopian vision of possibility and hope in the present, cannot critically reduce it and make it known otherwise. Here Zepke pits a dystopian science fiction against the utopian versions of Suvin, Jameson, and others who, given their desire to prove that SF is a relevant genre capable of critiquing the present through defamiliarization, end up rendering the actual future with a "shock of otherness" that, to reiterate the words of Jameson, does nothing more than "dramatize our incapacity to imagine the future" (2005, 288–89). The plight of the theremin, its turn first from specific instrumentalities to a quality of thereminesque tone that other instruments could evoke, and then to the dead end of the cliché, has gone through precisely the crisis that Jameson describes. By his account, science fiction becomes "a contemplation of our own absolute limits" (289) as well as "a meditation on the impossible, on the unrealizable in its own right" (232). In contrast to this utopian impasse, Zepke (2012) proposes a theory of more radical dystopias that "confront the present with the unhistorical and ontological force of becoming itself, and so open the present onto its immanent outside, onto what there is in it that escapes it." By reconsidering human values altogether and embracing Otherness, Zepke argues, a radical dystopian science fiction shifts analysis from Jameson's epistemological pessimism toward a form of Nietzschean "ontological optimism," which overcomes the seeming necessity of the human scale of history, ceases to mirror present conditions, and renders something altogether different. Cue up the great, thunderous footsteps of an unseen force, a piercing shriek, and wait for it; oh no, it's . . .

1954 | *GOJIRA*

The SF film has provided a site for composers and producers in search of the unusual, the different, and the untimely sound. Where the sounds of the new become increasingly associated with emerging technologies, the sounds of radical alterity and the untimely can come from many unusual methods and means of production, including the use of so-called primitive or exotic instruments and styles, handmade devices, prepared and otherwise modified versions of traditional instruments, and postproduction manipulation of recorded sounds. All of these are encountered in Akira Ifukube's score to *Gojira* (1954). I am interested in how these technical approaches shift SF cinema's sonic sensibilities from a futurist perspective to those of the untimely Other.

Gojira begins with a pair of distinctive sonorous objects: thunderous footsteps and piercing shrieks. With only the Toho studio logo on the screen, there are three stomping thuds. After a short beat, a single screech accompanies the appearance of the film title, the monster's own name. These repeat. We hear three more footsteps and then three more of the torturous screeches before the repetitive string motif of the music proper begins. Even this will continue to include the percussive footsteps and monstrous screams. It is one of the most ominous and harrowing main title themes of any work of science fiction, but particularly so in the 1950s. The various apocryphal accounts of the source of sounds and their assemblage is itself fascinating, indicating just how much sonorous objects resist clear identification of their origins. The cries of the creature are usually attributed to the rubbing of the loosened strings of a double bass with a coarse, resin-coated glove. But Shuhei Hosokawa's study of the *Gojira* score explains that the production of the unusual sounds was much more involved. Ifukube not only transformed the contrabass into "an imaginative and creative sound maker," but the composer and his crew also used magnetic tape manipulation to further distort what Honda's sound engineer, Ichiro Minawa, already deemed "very ugly" sounds (in Hosokawa 2004, 48). Echo was added and the tape sped up in order to shift the pitch of the bass string higher so that it would be distinct against the lower frequencies that dominated Ifukube's "Main Theme," and which were intended to impart both heaviness and solemnity to the giant monster's presence (54). The source of Gojira's other signature sound, its heavy stomp, is a bit more difficult to attribute. A variety of ideas have been suggested, with the most common being that Ifukube and his crew banged on kettledrums with a knotted rope (Matthews 2007, 96). Hosokawa (2004), on the other hand, recounts a story of Ifukube stumbling over a wooden box in the studio, perhaps an early amplifier cabinet. Liking the sound, Ifukube then recorded onto tape while banging on the box with his fist to produce the echoing whomp (Kobayashi 1998, 89). Tim Martin (2014) incorrectly attributes the sound of the footsteps to the manipulation of the double bass. Other Japanese texts report that the sound was made by taking a recording of an explosion found in the Toho Studio's sound library, cutting off the attack of the sound so that only the decay of the sound was audible, and then feeding that taped sound into a reverb box to give it additional weight and presence (Ryfle 1998, 32). Hosokawa repeats this account as well, but adds that rather than a single explosion, the foot stomp was mixed from the sound of Japanese fighter jets, firearms, bomb blasts, and other sound sources transferred from Toho's collection of wartime optical soundtracks. Understanding *Gojira* as a key critical film about Japan's fate during World War II, Hosokawa suggests that this last detail represents the film's "material debt to the War . . . since the Toho sound archive results from the company's close connection with the military during wartime" (2004, 49).

With these last accounts of appropriated field recordings corroborated in multiple sources, *Gojira* appears to be one of the first Japanese films to feature tape manipulations for its unusual sounds, situating Ifukube and his sound engineers, like Herrmann, among the vanguard of tape experimentation and composition in the 1950s (Hosokawa 2004, 49–50). However, there are still some fascinating discrepancies about exactly when and how the sounds of Gojira were added to the "Main Title" theme, and whether we should regard them as diegetic, nondiegetic, or something in between. If Hosokawa's account is the most accurate, Gojira's foot stomps and screeches were added in postproduction editing. The original soundtrack recording suggests that this is correct, as it offers an isolated track of the "Main Title: Footsteps & Cries," noted as "M2," while the initial track, "Main Title," is noted as

M2+M1. Both versions are included in the *50th Anniversary Godzilla Soundtrack Perfect Collection* box set with running times of 2:11 (Toho Music Corporation, 2014). But another fiftieth anniversary edition of the soundtrack separates the two differently, starting with a track titled, "Godzilla Approaches (sound effects)," with a running time of 0:49, followed by "Godzilla Main Theme," running 1:31 (La-La Land Records, 2004). This begs the question as to why, in his handwritten score, Ifukube includes notation for the two sound effects: a semibreve for each stomp, labeled "Magic Box," and a descending squiggly line noted as the "Song of Gozila." (An image of the score is available in Rathford 2014.) The score suggests that when Ifukube's ensemble performed the "Main Title," the more traditional musical elements coincided with the performance of the noisier effects. This would be similar to the theremin's coexistence with orchestras during the recording sessions of the scores to *Rocketship X-M, The Day the Earth Stood Still*, and *The Thing*, even though its role in the film glides across diegetic boundaries. On the other hand, just as Herrmann's graphic score outlined the time-suspending assemblage of backward tapes and edits altering sonic timbre and dynamics in the tape composition, "The Magnetic Pull," the score for Ifukube's "Main Titles" may indicate a conceptual unification. Acknowledging that "composition" meant more than the arrangement of precisely musical elements, the coordinated timing of concrete effects is now an essential part of the film's sound design.

The acousmatic screening of sounds during the opening titles of *Gojira* makes them attributable to neither nondiegetic nor diegetic sources. In fact, the only thing these sounds are indisputably associated with is the name "Gojira." More than its Americanization, Godzilla, Gojira is a telling and significant portmanteau of the Japanese words *gorira* (gorilla) and *kujira* (whale). The neologism of the "gorilla-whale" emphasizes the suspended differences, if not quite oppositions, of its parts, while the incompatible, elemental mixtures render a sonic and semantic identity of any kind almost always problematic. I contend that a similar incompatibility of elemental parts shapes Ifukube's score, particularly as it intersects with the film's thematic presentation of the ancient creature awoken by atomic blasts. Here, atomic testing plays a role similar to that of atomic power in *The Day the Earth Stood Still,* announcing a new stage of planetary evolution that forces a check on human morality and puts us in our place relative to larger cosmic scales. Stylistically, "Main Titles" points backward and forward just as the film does historically. The piece points back to the kind of manufactured primitivism of the Russian composers, particularly Igor Stravinsky, whom Ifukube championed to the extent that he wrote the title of his score to *Gojira* in Russian. Stravinsky's reliance on atonal sound clusters and fantasies of tribal rhythm in *The Rite of Spring* were particular influences on the "Main Titles." Ifukube also participated in the emergence of a future music made with electronic recordings and magnetic tape. His approach in this regard differed from Bernard Herrmann's, who modified his own isolated recordings of acoustic and electronic musical instruments; Ifukube, in contrast, used prepared instruments, abused effects units as instruments, and sampled from the Toho sound effect library. The combination of these within the singular "Main Titles" prompts Hosokawa to describe Ifukube's score as a form of "high-tech Primitivism" (2004, 47). He also characterizes the composer as self-consciously monstrous to the extent that Ifukube stylistically merges European modernism and Japanese aesthetics at the expense of postwar, nationalistic sensibilities (52). Similarly, Hosokawa retrieves the sonic elements of *Gojira* most linked to primitivism and folklore, which he claims have been largely neglected by critics more concerned with the film's critique of atomic weaponry (44). In part this neglect is due to the relative brevity of the scene, only a minute or so, in which we see the Odoshima islanders dance ritualistically in hopes of calming a supernatural being from the ocean depths—crude, premodern "antics" scoffed at by the film's contemporary Japanese reporters. For Hosokawa, this scene treats Gojira with "awe and reverence," an ancient creature of folklore that turns out to be real and deadly for the out-of-touch-with-its-roots city of Tokyo (53). As we follow the monster's "trajectory from an abyss at the edge of Japanese territory to the metropolis," the narrative of this ancient creature confronted with the high-tech dangers of atomic blasts splices together "archaic past and emergent present, . . . nature and civilization, myth and science, fantasy and reality" (44). The high-tech primitivism of Ifukube's score thus participates in a sensibility of strange mixtures that we experience in the film's narrative, its themes, and of course in the hybrid name of the hybrid creature, Gojira.

Despite the fact that uncanny hybrids proliferate throughout *Gojira*, dominating the film's underlying logic and structure, the creature is unique among SF movie monsters of the 1950s. Unlike the typically nameless "thing," "creature," "it," "them," "X," and so on, Gojira has a name. For Hosokawa, this naming both accounts for the longevity of Gojira as a recurring hero of *kaiju* cinema even as its name morphed into the Anglicized "Godzilla." But naming is also responsible for the monster's downfall, as Hosokawa concludes: "Naming is taming and classifying the unknown in order" (2004, 43). Along with naming, Hosokawa points to "the aural triptych (music, stomping and roaring sounds)" without which the monster would not "have become an outstanding icon in film history" (43). Both the name of Godzilla and its consistent, repetitive timbral motif of paired sound effects would transform the creature from ambivalent protagonist to cinematic hero over the years and into the foreseeable future, with a franchise of more than twenty-five films, remakes, and serials, as well as countless products in every media imaginable. The score's fate and Godzilla's iconic sound logo did not go unchanged over the years. In Toho Studios' 1955 release, Motoyoshi Oda's *Godzilla Raids Again,* the score by Masaru Satoh replaces Ifukube's minimal, three-note motif with a thin gong sound, recordings of which are on occasion stretched out and run backward. While Godzilla's cries remain the same in this first Japanese sequel, the Americanized remake, known as *Gigantis, the Fire Monster* (1959), not only renames Godzilla as Gigantis but also completely modifies the sounds made by the creature. This was perceived as a failed experiment, and never again would the American studios try to pass Godzilla off as another creature altogether. As far as the original Japanese films go, the next four—from *King Kong vs. Godzilla* (1962) to *Invasion of the Astro-Monster* (1965)—reunite director Ishirō Honda and composer Akira Ifukube. Though Honda nudged Godzilla more and more in the direction of a terrestrial culture hero fighting off other monstrous threats, Ifukube's scores would retain the ponderous, minimal triad of notes as well as the characteristic sounds, particularly the scream, emitted by the creature.

Even from the start, Gojira was never quite like the alien invaders and monsters of American SF. Gojira is "an internal alien," and like his classic nemesis, King Kong, is a kind of "noble savage, a compound trope of irrational barbarianism and sublime innocence, violence and vitality, the pristine and the pure, the pagan and the passionate" (Hosokawa 2004, 54). This is a trope that the makers of the American version, *Godzilla: King of the Monsters!* (1956), seem intent on reversing by placing their own familiar alien on the scene, reporter Steve Martin (Raymond Burr), whose commentary positions Godzilla and Japan, for that matter, as external forms of Otherness rather than semantic forms different by nature of the incongruities they internalize. Gojira is unique among the canon of SF film monsters, especially in the original 1954 release, because it is the film's protagonist, emblematizing and embodying the work's politically charged allegorical content. Even Gojira's defeat by the "oxygen destroyer" weapon plays bittersweet, is portrayed as somewhat awful in fact, and is at last undercut by the sentiment that another creature would rise, though even the consequences of this are regarded with some uncertainty. This ambiguity gets at the essence of the film's lasting sublimity, mostly conveyed through Ifukube's requiem-like theme as the monster is destroyed. The solemnity of the score holds together and suspends, rather than resolves, the conflicting aspects of Gojira's destruction, both that which he wreaks, which is after all a kind of ecological vengeance, and his own demise, which is more tragic than just (Hosokawa 2004, 56–57). That there is no real certainty that the monster has even been defeated in a way that would prevent his return or the appearance of another like him—no final vanquishing of evil, for who could be certain that Gojira was in fact evil?—makes the film highly uncharacteristic of the numerous SF/monster movie hybrids of the 1950s. It simply works on an altogether different scale.

That Gojira always appears first as an approaching sound object is testimony to the mind-boggling grandeur of the creature's existence compared to that of the human. The sonorous object is a way of measuring the creature in time as well as space. Other than the heaviest of Gojira's sonic signature, his footsteps, Ifukube evokes a cosmic scale of heaviness in several places of his score with rolling timpani, aggressive piano stabs at atonal clusters of keys, low, slow, and menacing horns, and the pitches of wind instruments that always rise or fall in a little whirling scale of whole notes, as if sent adrift in the aftershock of the heavier sounds. With few exceptions, and with hardly any variation once Gojira actually appears in the film, there's not a lot of nondiegetic sonic real estate left for other music. Human music, by contrast, plays a strictly diegetic role in the film, first during the brief ritual on Odoshima, the other in Tokyo. One of Honda's few lighter turns in the original film occurs as we hear a brass fanfare accompanying some exciting action shots of Japanese navy boats getting into position for battle. However, the whole sequence turns out to be showing on TV, and the brave and patriotic music is meant to hide the fact that the troops are scared to death. A little bit of nondiegetic trickery plays out on the evening news and is quickly undercut through a reporter's voiceover. Other than that, when human characters speak in *Gojira,* the underscore is minimal or, most often, not there at all. These silences make their own essential contributions to the atmosphere of the film, putting us in a space of constantly waiting with dread anticipation for that next great footstep to drop, listening for the moment at which Gojira will once more shatter the silence. This effect is considerably diminished in the Americanized version, where the reporter, Martin, narrates in voice-over during all of the otherwise silent gaps. This loud and busy Americanization misses the point of Ifukube's score and sound design sensibility, which favors the ways in which minimal rhythms and repetitive tonal sequences work on "the auditory sense," which is, the composer claims in his own *Introduction to Music* (1951), "the most primitive among the senses serving the arts" (in Hosokawa 2004, 44). More basic sounds tap into "the primordial, the intuitive and the instinctive" (44) quite differently from complex orchestral harmonies and melodies, much less nonstop blathering exposition. Gojira calls the listener back to a time before the scientific rationalism of the modern televisual age, a time when hearing rather than seeing cued the primitive human to environmental dangers. The ear is the only order of sensory mechanism by which silence can be filled with such dread, the unseen possessed of an ancient hope, both senses spliced together in equal, uncanny measure by neither the thing not yet present nor the body not yet affected. This means that we should always hear Gojira long before we see him, and we should grow used to silence as a place at once full of fear, reverence, and anticipation of the thing to come.

1956 | *FORBIDDEN PLANET*

By the middle of the 1950s, SF cinema's need for entire libraries of new sounds expanded as rapidly as the genre itself. Composers continued to mine glissando, vibrato, and the shimmering tonalities of electric instrumentation to develop the atmospheric music of science fiction, while other sound makers were called on to represent not only new worlds but also alien beings, monsters, robots; spacecraft, transporter devices, and laser guns and other futuristic weapons; and the wonders of lost civilizations, interstellar vistas, and cosmic disasters. As composer-technicians and sound designers tapped into new audio technologies, unusual sound-making practices, and new electronic tonalities, their work would destabilize differences between music and noise even more aggressively than the theremin had before, consequently leveraging sound into the thematic heart of SF's ontological and phenomenological tropes. None did so more radically than Louis and Bebe Barron's score for Fred M. Wilcox's *Forbidden Planet.*

Generally regarded as one of the greatest science fiction films of the 1950s due to its brilliant colors, widescreen presentation, sophisticated visual effects and animations, alien sets, as well as its dramatic narrative and themes, *Forbidden Planet* was also the first SF film to feature a completely electronic score. MGM Studios was more than a little reluctant to call it music, so they settled on the term "electronic tonalities." Pragmatically speaking, this let the studio dodge the fact that Louis and Bebe Barron worked out of their home studio in Greenwich Village and weren't members of the local L.A. musicians union. The wording itself is vaguely sci-fi and futuristic, and doubtless some new kind of terminology was necessary to convey the unconventional degree to which odd electronic sounds permeate our experience of the film. Though still occasionally misattributed to the theremin, the sounds are in fact the products of the pioneering circuit-bending synthesis and magnetic tape manipulations of the Barrons. There are plenty of siren decrescendos and accelerations, but these are raw, short, and gritty compared to the smooth, swooping lines of the theremin. It is still surprising that MGM Studios would go for such an unconventional score, created by a quirky pair of outsider artists. But popular culture was primed for an invasion of out of this world sounds, due both to prior exposure to new sounds through SF films and to a growing expectation that the SF film needed ever newer sounds of a futuristic sort, sounds that most SF films were no longer providing, especially where the music was concerned. *Forbidden Planet* delivered something that proved the genre could still be adventurous, raw, and deeply unsettling (as did Don Siegel's *Invasion of the Body Snatchers,* released the same year), and not even the Barrons could believe that their sounds would be used so extensively in the film. They had initially been asked to provide electronic sounds for about twenty minutes of the total film, and assumed, as did most of the producers at MGM, that their work would supplement a more conventional orchestral score (Wierzbicki 2005, 9). But the project's executive producer, Dore Schary, proved to be a fan of the Barrons' unusual style of audio production, and it was ultimately due to his advocacy that the Barrons' work was used throughout the film (10).

The strange, overdriven sounds created by the Barrons are ultimately inescapable. They are heard everywhere, in at least some portion of every scene, variously screeching, thunderous, bubbling and humming, and they do everything that sound or music can do in a film, constantly confusing diegetic distinctions. The electronic tonalities do the things that music does, providing leitmotifs around the film's main characters. They act as conventional sound effects, helping to animate spacecraft, a robot, and several alien devices and places, such as the long abandoned facilities discovered on the planet of Altair IV. They provide the alien music of the ancient Krell, initially intended to be the product of the unusual musical instruments built by American composer, Harry Partch (Wierzbicki 2005, 159n70). They sonify an invisible psychic monstrosity, the creature from the Id of the mad Dr. Morbius, as well as the Krell Mind Booster, the alien psytech that gives its wearer the power of mind over matter. Either because the Krell equipment was old and breaking down or because this is what happens when human minds try to use alien technologies, *Forbidden Planet* presents us with a tale of planetary disaster and individual pathology. The plot echoes Shakespeare's

The Tempest, pushing the psychosexual undercurrents in the direction of alien sonic psytech and thereby expanding SF cinema into invisible domains and inhibited areas of consciousness. Given these narrative and thematic concerns with the interpenetration of the minds of Earthlings and the technologies of aliens, sound provides a subdiegetic layer to the film. Drawing on golden age science fiction's fascination with mind over matter, psionics, mad science, and the consequences of scientists playing God, these themes play out not only because of the dangers of humans using ancient alien technologies but also through the more distant history of doom that befell the ancient alien civilization of the Krell. As in *The Day the Earth Stood Still*, the narrative of *Forbidden Planet* plays along a psychotechnological substrate. Where *The Day the Earth Stood Still* posited psychotechnology as a form of refined alien achievement, in this later film, in which the unseen and menacing Id monster roams for much of the film as nothing other than invisible electronic sound, there is something deeply and altogether unsettling about psytech entanglement.

Insofar as they constitute a musical score, the ultimately inhuman electronic tonalities of *Forbidden Planet* contrast sharply against the conservative nature of the majority of SF film scores. The humanist sonic sensibilities of Universal's *This Island Earth* (1955) provide a particularly high-profile case in point. Although *This Island Earth* set the bar for big-budget science fiction films at the peak of the golden age, the score comes across like an afterthought. It is attributed to Joseph Gershenson, but what we hear is in fact a mishmash of studio properties. It includes short compositions by Henry Mancini, Herman Stein, and Hans J. Salter, all uncredited on screen, and all destined to have their scores join the Universal Studio sound libraries for recycling in numerous Universal B movies. Some of *This Island Earth*'s soundtrack includes Mancini and Stein recordings originally used in *It Came from Outer Space*. While there isn't a theremin in earshot, the music acquires some spacey pathos thanks to the Novachord, though even this electric keyboard contributes in ensembles of instruments providing conventional emotional triggers and familiarizing affective cues that underscore dramatic events. Beyond the Novachord, there is nothing to associate the film's musical experience with the futuristic, alien, or technological sounds that the narrative evokes. That novel electronic sounds were confined to the diegetic realm was quickly becoming the norm in SF film sound; here they provide the noise of alien technologies, particularly the "interocitor," a mysterious, advanced technology that combines telecommunications, autopilot, surveillance, and a weapon of directed energy beams. Listening to *This Island Earth*, it is clear that every sound has its place along the diegetic strata, and futuristic electronic sound design happens strictly in support of the film's world building, while musical cues support nondiegetic emotional engagement through the use of instrumental voices that in no way differ from what we might hear in any kind of popular film. This belief in music as familiar emotional trigger, in fact, turns out to be a uniquely human virtue and the key to survival on this island Earth, which is in the end saved by the power of music: after the alien Exeter (Jeff Morrow) learns to appreciate Mozart, he foils plans for an invasion of Earth.

Against the typical film studio scoring practices, and literally at the expense of a more conventional theme by composer David Rose (Wierzbicki 2005, 159n69), the Barrons' work for *Forbidden Planet* eclipses such humanist sensibilities and terrestrial values with the raw voice of electric circuits. It does so specifically as a means to explore theories and methods introduced in mathematician Norbert Weiner's *Cybernetics, or Control and Communication in the Animal and the Machine*. Louis, a self-taught electrical engineer, sketched circuit diagrams based on Weiner's designs, which he and Bebe would then assemble in their kitchen studio. Patched onto wooden boards, Louis's components incorporated the same vacuum tube oscillators as the theremin, but the resulting sounds differed significantly thanks to elaborate feedback paths. The circuits were frequently overdriven to produce more dynamic, aggressive, and less predictable sounds, and their patches inevitably burned out quickly and dramatically. The recorded tapes of the sound circuit sessions were further processed as the Barrons changed the speed, reversed tapes, looped tapes, sliced tape to envelop the attack and decays of sounds, and created manual effects like echo and delay. Though these techniques would become part of the sound-sculpting capacities of modular synthesis and effects units, there were no controls on the circuits themselves. The Barrons' sensibilities and methods ran counter to emerging trends in electronic instrument design. Greater emphasis was being placed on precision of pitch achieved through ribbon controllers and keyboards and range of sound-altering controls, as on Raymond Scott's keyboard theremin, the Clavivox (1952–56), Paul Tanner's Electro-Theremin (1958), and the Siemens Studio for Electronic Music (1959). These design innovations would eventually converge on the work of Robert Moog, whose first modular synthesizer was produced in 1964, along with a growing assortment of analog filter-based subtractive synthesizers, rhythmic sequencers to trigger notes and other controller events, and increasingly complex ways to process electronic sound in real time. I will come back to consider how the Barrons' cybernetics rejected too much human control over the behavior of the circuits, favoring instead the generative nature of the work as a form of artificial life programming. First, however, I want to establish the space that the Barrons occupied between abstract electronic music and concrete tape music, as these will largely determine the range of their contributions to the film by blurring its diegetic borders.

The Barrons worked in both a conceptual and practical space between the two major branches of their contemporaries. The composers of *elektronische Musik* built on the traditions of atonal music, twelve-tone serialism, and absolute music, valuing works that were not representative, referential, or programmatic in nature, and thereby marked by abstraction in ways that they believed concrete sound and noise could not be. By contrast, Schaeffer's work arguably made listening to sounds more important than their composition. Beyond any questions of representation or referentiality, musique concrète confounds the categories of making music and the concentrated, deliberate hearing that he labeled "pure listening" (2017, 66). In the acousmatic conditions prescribed by Schaeffer, how sounds are heard, through what kind of mechanism, and beyond what sort of screen, overrides questions of source identification and the methods of sound generation that largely shaped the practices of the composers of *elektronische Musik*. The sonorous object, in this situation, becomes an agent in its own right. Distinctions between created music and found music contrast states of subjectivity and objectivity, but also signification and agency, human or otherwise. In fact, the authenticity of a particular sound typically revolves around the signification of its own agency, which Schaeffer to some degree grants to the sonorous object.

The agency of the sonorous object becomes even more urgent in the case of the electronic tonalities encountered in *Forbidden Planet,* which were initially composed not through a written score but rather by the manufacture of sound-generating circuit boards, the behaviors of which were wildly unpredictable. Such unpredictability will concern us throughout this analysis as the film transports these significant debates from the musical avant-garde to the domains of popular culture, where it finds meaningful, if short-lived, purchase. Bringing with it auditory points of view that are new not only to cinematic experience but also to technoculture, *Forbidden Planet* fosters the new sonic ecologies of the technoacousmatic imaginary. Sobchack's taxonomy of the sonic novum in SF cinema is useful here. She identifies the sounds of technology that seem to have "created their own music for the genre" and which consist of the "various beepings, tappings, tickings, hummings, and thrummings, songs sung by rocketship gauges, levers, and engines, by cyclotrons and atomic reactors, by computer consoles" (1987, 222). Immediately, Sobchack's catalog of noises recasts debates in modern music practice and theory, specifically those around sonic authenticity and representation, in ways relevant to the science fiction film and its need for both technologically futuristic and alien sounds. Typically, authenticity implies some prior familiarity, as we must be familiar with a sound before we can judge whether or not it is actually the sound that we think it is and thereby determine whether that sound is authentic to the listening experience. This usually means being able to identify the source that produces a particular sound. Knowing where a sound comes from requires further differentiation between what Sobchack calls either objective or subjective sounds, the former being recognizable sound "things" or effects, the other more typically musical in nature. In terms of their identification and referentiality, objective sounds are in a sense discovered rather than made. They express an aesthetic value only through a monstrous reconceptualization of what music means in the first place. Whereas noises are "found" and "externally based (and therefore objective)," music is typically "created" and "emotionally derived," according to Sobchack, "and therefore subjective" (216). The case is not as clear as this dualism suggests, of course, as Sobchack's own descriptive language blurs this distinction from the start. She ultimately concludes that what makes SF sounds unique is their confusion of precisely such binary oppositions. While Sobchack's evoking of long-standing antagonisms between forms of objective, found music and subjective, created music may give us a way to understand the boundary blurring sounds of *Forbidden Planet*, it still does not adequately capture the specific tensions that the film exploits between the sonorous object orientation of musique concrète and the abstract electronic compositions of the students of European serialism. Combining a unique, generative method for electronic sound making with tape mixing techniques, the unfamiliar thingness of the sonorous objects encountered in the *Forbidden Planet* score destabilizes the presumed value of distinguishing between electronic music and musique concrète along with other differentiations between subject and object, the abstract and concrete, and human or object-oriented agencies.

Schaeffer's concept of the sonorous object of musique concrète describes a sound that is never reducible to the particular media that produces and reproduces it; this sonorous object exists somewhere between the recording media and listening subject, with the sound object proper manifesting between the medium of sound reproduction and the ear, the one separated from the other by an acousmatic screen. Detractors of musique concrète like French composer Pierre Boulez attributed the form's failure to the inability of the sound material to escape its representational value and so function as something other than a familiar noise, namely as music. For Boulez, the recognizable, material source signification of found sounds constantly undermines the composer's efforts to exert control over every element of the musical work, including all physical parameters and properties of sound. Musique concrète struck Boulez as regressive, a new kind of "program music," with either an explicit narrative or obvious theme derived from its material source content. This in turn established the limit of the sound's representational capacity. However, the Barrons and MGM producer Schary discovered during a test screening of *Forbidden Planet* the exceptional ease with which the radiophonic techniques of tape music worked well in the new context of science fiction. For their test audience, a rough cut of the film, not yet overdubbed, was screened with the Barrons' music, played on a tape deck only "more or less synchronized with the film projector" as a "technician fairly improvised the manipulation of volume levels and equalization" (Wierzbicki 2005, 10). The response was so enthusiastic that MGM opted to release the film without any other editing, the electronic sound running over the occasionally sloppy blending from one scene to another and accommodating for the "rather draggy pacing" (in Wierzbicki 2005, 10). Precision of sound proved less important than a general atmosphere. This effectively flips Boulez's program music into a remediating mirror as the representational capacity of sound is loosened and reversed. Rather than pointing back to the noise source at its origin, the new sound is unmoored and then vaguely mapped onto narrative objects, events, and spaces, which in turn become the virtual sources of sounds in the technoacousmatic imaginary. These electronic tones also prove instrumental in the opening up of new spaces beyond traditional diegesis.

More than a reconciling of programmatic and absolute aesthetics is at stake here. The synthesist composers of electronic music like Eimert and Stockhausen believed that they had fulfilled the aesthetic goal of the "absolute music" of their teachers, the serialist composers, by having found a music that represented nothing but itself (Taylor 2001, 54). This allowed them to short-circuit a historical conundrum. The first wave of electronic musicians, particularly Eimert and Stockhausen, at once extended and exhausted the possibilities of what had been, before and during the war, the major new music of the day: the serial music of Arnold Schoenberg, Anton Webern, and Alban Berg. In 1923, Schoenberg proposed a "method of composing with twelve tones which are related only with one another" (in Ross 2007, 212). Avoiding the traditional tone structures of the major and minor scales, the twelve-tone approach involved arranging the complete chromatic scale (on a piano, a full octave including all the black keys) into a series or row; typically, only when each of the notes in a row had been played could the composer reuse a note to start a new serial row. Though often atonal in effect, twelve-tone composition was in fact a reaction against freely atonal forms, providing the structural premise of an original row and its various inversions (the row flipped upside down), retrogrades (the row reversed), and retrograde inversions (reserved and upside down). Whereas the original twelve-tone technique applied only to pitch, serialism extended such control to the duration of notes, sound dynamics, and so on.

Villainized by the Nazis, the abstractions of twelve-tone music and serial composition could come back after the war both as a "truer" history of serious Western art music and as a historical and technological advancement that continued to reject the antimodern romanticism favored by the leaders of the Third Reich (Taylor 2001, 47). The music made from oscillating circuits might escape the historical baggage that still linked serialism, even though in opposition, to the war, worn-out traditions, history, and horror. Electric sound offered a clean slate. Empty of programmatic signification and therefore outside of one kind of history, electronic music could both reclaim one and newly claim another. Certainly serialist techniques made sense given the emerging electronic technologies of the day. Composers faced with the increasingly complex nature of sound-making opportunities in the radio laboratories in which they worked—the modular nature of which was always open to the insertion of new components—turned to systematic composition in order to exercise control over every aspect of electrically synthesized sound (duration, attack, dynamics, and timbre). In the assessment of composers like Boulez, electronic music was thus viewed as the logical and most rigorous outcome of the serialist project (Taylor 2001, 50). Serialism provided the inspiration to shape the flow of oscillating current by extending the idea of twelve-tone composition to other sonic parameters, including a sound's duration, attack, decay, and other dynamics, all capable of manipulation through the physical resources of the radio-engineering booth with its oscillating signal generators, filters, ring modulators, rotary speakers, echo and reverb chambers, multichannel mixers, and tape machines (Holmes 2016, 67–68), More complex sounds could be achieved through additive compositional processes that subsumed electronic synthetic timbre into serialized design. The electronic synthesis of sound, then recording and further manipulation through tape mixing, all became part of the composer's tool kit. Each stage of the process included something that a composer could take into consideration when using the precise programming of sonic events that serialism made possible. Taylor understands this chiefly as an issue of "human agency in the face of technology," with the creators of *elektronische Musik* maintaining "control over the work by devising the most complicated and abstract modes of formal organization ever. In the realm of purely electronic composition, they advocated synthesizing sounds so that listeners could not bring previous associations to them" (Taylor 2001, 53–54). Without adequate control, the composition was, according to Boulez, "consigned to nonbeing" (in Taylor 2001, 51). The failure to control all facets of a musical composition negated the creative act and rendered an object with neither abstract presence nor aesthetic significance. "Composers advocating 'determinacy' thus viewed the relative looseness of *musique concrète* as highly problematic," Taylor concludes, "with the composer as much a discoverer as creator and, in Boulez's eyes, not a creator at all" (51). A concern for human agency underwrites Boulez's approval of electronic music. Moreover, the formally organized, abstract modality of electronic music, like serialism before it, avoided the limits of prior romantic and program music as well as the perceived shortcomings of the contemporary musique concrète. While the synthesis of sound extends the composer's control over all sonic parameters it also prohibits listeners from recognizing the sound and bringing with them previous associations and subjective interpretations about what the sound represents. In fact, makers of musique concrète also sought to liberate the sonorous object from the listener's associations with sound sources and so prohibit the a priori representational capacity of sound.

The ability to recognize a sound—and thereby attribute to it not only a source but also a significant meaning—was problematic to composers of *elektronische Musik* and musique concrète alike. For Schaeffer, the emergence of the sonorous object depended on his making recorded sounds unrecognizable and thereby both extract and "abstract the musical values they were potentially containing" (Taylor 2001, 45). The challenge presented to the composer of musique concrète comes from what Taylor calls "residual signification" (46). Taylor explains, "Recognizable sounds might evoke residual meanings that listeners might associate with the sounds' origins, which would mean that the composer is neither creating, nor in total control of, a self-contained aesthetic object" (46). Schaeffer sought to alienate the recorded object from its source, peeling the sonic event away from what he labeled "dramatic or musical context" (47), in order to derive the new aesthetic form of the sonorous object through feats of sound engineering. He intended to circumvent the listener's recognition of sounds. "If I succeeded," he concluded, "there would be a *musique concrete*. If not there would be only trickery and procedures of radio production" (46). Schaeffer differentiates two basic types of sound sources: "noises, which always tell you something—a door cracking, a dog barking, the thunder, the storm; and then you have instruments," which tell you "la-la-la" (in Taylor 2001, 46). For Schaeffer, the key innovation of musique concrète consisted of avoiding notation and compositional planning. This was not a musician's art per se, but rather that of the radio engineer experimenting in the studio with new techniques for listening that involved modification of the sound signal (Schaeffer 2017, 66). The manipulation of the recorded medium itself—changing speed (which also changed the pitch), reversing directionality, looping sounds, cutting off the attacks and decays of sounds, and so on—all became ways to render sound unrecognizable. Sonically estranged through these processes applied to the recorded signal, the listener's tendency to hear the residues of signification is circumvented in ways that "reexert control over the 'quality' of the sound itself" (Taylor 2001, 47). Schaeffer openly struggled toward a music free of preconceived associations, emphasizing the creation of isolated sound objects that a listener could explore in a moment of "reduced listening" while attempting to conceptually separate timbral qualities as such from the identification of sound sources. When there wasn't simply some kind of flaw in the manufacture of a musique concrète, it was the residual worldliness of the sound that most often rendered it as something other than composed music. The electronic music composers also thought the residual worldliness of a recorded sound object a failure to adequately abstract sound and thereby aestheticize it in the ways that would turn it into music rather than noise. As much as any of his detractors, Schaeffer clearly hoped to avoid creating sounds that might be regarded merely as a kind of sound effect rather than music as such. And though he thought it more promising than the new serialism, even he was ultimately as

164 • AMBIENT NOVUM, ALIEN NOVUM

dismissive of his outcomes: "Some of us were working at constructing robots, others at dissecting corpses. Living music was elsewhere, and only revealed itself to those who knew how to escape from these simplistic models" (in Taylor 2001, 54–55).

• • •

The "elsewhere" to the impasse of the technoacousmatic imagination described by Pierre Schaeffer, as well as the robots and the corpses, has a surprisingly precise location: Louis and Bebe Barron's kitchen studio. Here, the couple worked without the official military-grade technologies of their institutionalized counterparts in state-sanctioned radio stations and university labs. The gear in the Barrons' home was mostly a homemade affair. Their prize possession was a first-generation Ampex 2000 tape recorder, a gift to the couple on the occasion of their marriage on December 7, 1947. And while their studio tended to take over most of their Greenwich Village apartment, it was in the kitchen that "living music" was being cooked up, patched together, dissected, and reassembled through methods that radically reconciled the aims and methods of electronic and concrete music. In contrast to the precision required of the electronic serialists, the Barrons were decidedly noninterventionist. They preferred to patch together circuits and tubes, turn on their tape recorder, throw the switch, and then sit back and listen to the results until the patch burned itself out. If they grew impatient, they might overdrive the signal to get quicker, more extreme results.

Considering the *Forbidden Planet* recordings as a cinematic object recasts some of our earlier concerns with signification of sound in both electronic music and musique concrète, here reconciled within a singular practice that takes advantage of the autopoietic properties of overdriven circuit feedbacks as a manner of chance operations before rendering a final product through tape manipulation and mixing. In the cinematic context, sounds with reduced residual signification prove especially ripe for creative appropriation and resignification relative to the cinematic event to which they add value, as the Barrons and their producer Schary discovered to some astonishment during the screening of the film's rough cut. Lacking residual associations, new electronic sounds prove especially apt at attaching to the unusual images and events of the SF film, even those of an invisible psychic or psytech nature. Schary—who apparently "got a big kick out of those two kids," the Barrons, and found himself "captivated by the sounds and fascinated by their account of how those sounds were produced"—thought that their "electronic tonalities" (his words) would be a particularly good fit not just for MGM's first science fiction feature, but one with "a different slant and a different villain—not a creature or a humanoid with an odd look but rather a psychological villain, the beastly id of a rational man that ultimately destroys him" (in Wierzbicki 2005, 8). Working first from a rough cut of the film sent to them in late December 1955, then a longer cut in color, the Barrons created circuit patches with the film in mind, occasionally creating their own versions of the "weird, very primitive sound effects" included on sections of the workprint (Bebe Barron in Wierzbicki 2005, 8). Bebe Barron recalled, "We set down a list of characters and approached it like a director would, directing the actors. We would build a circuit for each character" (in Brend 2012, 63). The Barrons considered their patches to be circuit doubles for the film's main characters, including Robby the robot, the Id monster, and Morbius, while other circuits and collections of taped sessions were organized around distinctive objects or settings, such as the recording of ancient Krell music or the Krell power station.

The greatest difficulties the Barrons faced came on the heels of MGM's rejection of the leitmotifs that they had created for the sole female character in the film, Altaira. Though the Barrons typically erased sounds that too closely recalled the timbres of actual instruments, they did come across some passages that suggested the deep strings of a viola, overdubbed these more or less at random onto the tapes of their "love music," and created the romantic sounds—that is, the harmonic relationships of "pure, stable pitches"—that they associated with the film's love interest (Leydon 2004a, 74). While a few sections of the soundtrack possess some semblance of normalized Hollywood film scoring conventions, there is none of what we might call humanist music in the film, and the overall tone of the film is different because of it. Leydon argues that the closing musical sequence for *Forbidden Planet* is particularly uncharacteristic of 1950s science fiction. We lack the sort of "soaring strings and tonal grounding," that would otherwise resolve "the Krell's legacy of dystopic cyborgism" with a triumphant expression of humanist tonalities (75). More than a gesture against narrative closure, the soundtrack presents a radical view of psychotechnology and the hidden life of cybernetic circuits that avoids the expectation for "sonic resolution" (75) and presents us instead with the catastrophically open-ended demise of a subdiegetic electroacoustic ecology.

The Barrons' own reflections on their work are fascinating documents of human encounter with alien life. At times, Louis or Bebe will refer to the "characteristic activity pattern as well as a 'voice'" of a particular circuit (in Taylor 2001, 94). This is the most conventional of the terms and metaphors with which the Barrons document their encounter with the idiosyncratic behaviors and overdriven life cycles of their circuit patches. The Barrons attribute their interest in the behavioral aspects of electric circuitry to the cybernetic theories of Norbert Wiener, not only *Cybernetics* (1948), as I noted earlier, but also *The Human Use of Human Beings* (1954) as well as Clark Hull's *Essentials of Behavior* (1951). The Barrons considered their circuits to be a basic kind of life-form, noting similarities between electronic and psychological functionality. This might be a stretch from Wiener's association of "the physical functioning of the living individual and the operation of some of the newer communication machines," which he felt were "precisely parallel in their analogous attempts to control entropy through feedback" ([1954] 1988, 26–27). This stage of Wiener's work emphasizes the physiological function of the living system as sensory receptors provide a "special apparatus for collecting information from the outer world" that then makes this information available to the operation of the creature or machine through a complex feedback system interacting with a "central regulatory apparatus" (27). What makes the Barrons' work such a compelling, although eventually horrific, extension of the circuit designs that Louis copied from Wiener's *Cybernetics* (1948) was their substitution of death wish for life cycle. "We would do the craziest things," Bebe describes. "Those circuits were really alive: they would shriek and coo and have little life spans of their own. It was just amazing. They would start out and reach a kind of climax and then they would die and you could never resurrect them" (in Leydon 2004a, 70). Louis likewise biomorphizes their circuit patches: "We design and construct electronic circuits which function electronically in a manner remarkably similar to the way that lower life-forms function psychologically. . . . Most remarkable is that the sounds which emanate from these electronic nervous systems seem to convey strong emotional meaning to listeners" (in Taylor 2001, 94). This evocation of affective emanations and psychology supplants Wiener's physiological emphasis in ways that resonate with the film's excised material about Freudian psychoanalysis and what Bebe Barron called "all the psychological stuff about dreams" (in Wierzbicki 2005, 9). The Barrons' practice retains a certain degree of Freudian subtext even as it develops a psytech design scheme of some complexity, pointing beyond the usefulness of psychoanalysis, and culminates with a form of interspecies communication. I have found the work of Félix Guattari, particularly where his ethicoaesthetic paradigm meets with the onto-genetic machinism of second-order cybernetics, valuable in this context along with the unorthodox, extraterrestrial cybernetics of John Lilly.

The schizoanalytic mechanisms outlined in philosopher and psy-chotherapist Félix Guattari's *Chaosmosis* (1992) prove especially sug-gestive for an exploration of the subdiegetic territories of *Forbidden Planet*. Guattari establishes his concern with the "phylogenetic evo-lution of machinism" by framing two overlapping and mutually con-tingent forms, the mechanosphere and biosphere, both of which are in fact autopoietic "living machines" capable of generating, maintaining, and expanding their own internal organization and external boundary limits (1992, 40). Guattari prods Francisco Varela's thoughts about the biological constraints of autopoietic organization to get at something more inclusive of nonorganic systems and the idea of machinic het-erogeneity. This broader category of autopoietic production and dif-ferentiation suggests some of the ways by which machinic "autonomy accommodates diverse mediums of alterity" through various, contingent processes of ontogenesis, the production of being through social systems and technical machines (40). The Barrons' practical contributions to this speculative cybernetics are largely overlooked, and here I am interested in their production of the *Forbidden Planet* score less as an endeavor in music making, however unconventional, than as an experiment in sonic cybernetics that stages an actual alien encounter. In this respect, the Barrons operate along the same fringes of sonic psytech praxis that

Dr. John C. Lilly would later occupy. The protocols documented in Lilly's 1968 psytech handbook, *Programming and Metaprogramming the Human Biocomputer*, yielded significant interspecies contact with dolphins. Both projects followed from Lilly's contributions to a panel about Communication with Extraterrestrial Intelligence that took place at the 1965 IEEE Military Electronics conference. In this paper, Lilly first outlined the steps to achieve what he calls "interlock," the synchronization of two biocomputers, which Lilly refers to as a "dyad," coexisting within a shared communication network (1968, 91). Lilly proposes a "participant theorist" approach that would establish "interlock with a non-human computer by whatever modes are possible. . . . Corrections are introduced in context almost automatically by reward-punishment interactions in response to errors on each side of the dyad" (96). Lilly repeatedly emphasizes the responsibility of participant theorists, who must act with an "open-ended, non-species-specific" contingency in mind, and always with "mutual respect, voluntary dedication," to the alien biocomputer (99).

With implications for the ethicoaesthetic dimensions of biomedia research, these aspects of interspecies communication—articulated in Lilly's plea for future work that would develop "a theory of the communicator, human type, faced with a nonhuman communicator with a brain and presumed mind of high quality" (99)—were ignored by the Barrons, whose encounter with the alien life-form manifested through their circuit patches was polluted by the unchecked nature of their experimental process. Bebe's description of the monster circuit, for instance, outlines a clinical psytech depth analysis of the patch, using tape manipulation as a means of uncovering otherwise hidden sonic depths, behaviors, and psytech subroutines:

> This was an amazing circuit: the sounds which came out were tinkly and bubbly—very high-pitched with lots of complex activity. I was sure that, if we slowed them down, lots of activity we weren't able to hear would come to the foreground. So we slowed it down fifty or sixty times, which was a very laborious process because the only thing we could do at that time was to record it at 15 ips and then play it back at 7. Of course you build up staggering amounts of tape noise. It was

just amazing what came out of it. A whole rhythm emerged, because obviously when you slow down reverberation enough times, you get rhythm—that was the only way we had to get rhythm. (in Leydon 2004a, 70)

Variable tape speed manipulation uncovers the latent patterns of "echo rhythms" and other artifacts of the recording process (72). In the case of the monster, these echoes and unconscious microglissandi come to function as a leitmotif that repeats periodically throughout the film. This slowing down of the recorded object constitutes a form of depth analysis searching for buried material "held in dynamic storage," a sonic antithesis "entirely strange to one's conscious self" (Lilly 1968, 67). Listening to the recordings of burnt-out circuit patches, plumbing them for characteristic signs of a distinct voice and unique life-form that is already deceased, never to be resurrected, ended up exposing what Lilly calls "the potentially lethal aspects of certain unconscious, protohuman, survival programs" (1968, 67). Lilly's thoughts about consciousness hinge on the storage capacity of the deepest levels of consciousness, protohuman survival programs, most of which run not silently but with a muffled roar of noise among the lower layers and corners of the unconscious. Unconscious survival programs tend to be "wordless" and reside in the "emotion–feeling–motivational storage parts of the computer" (68). Slowed down and with the pitch shifted, the rhythmic pulse of such intense protohuman survival programs must be unearthed carefully as a result of their potentially destructive power over the self-metaprogram. Because of the obstinacy of alien psytech survival programs, the sound recordings of the Barrons tended to be "poor representations in the *modeling*, clear thinking and verbal portions" of consciousness, instead allowing certain agencies of the human biocomputer to trigger the "breakdown of the barriers between the emotional-wordless systems, and the wordfilled modeling systems by means of channeled uninhibited feeling and channeled uninhibited action" (68).

Throughout Lilly's documentation of his experiments with LSD-25, sensory deprivation, and floatation tanks, one consistent thread is the presence of noise. Noise is a generative force as well as a substance ripe for metaprogramming: "With a bit of proper programming under the right conditions, with the right dose, at the right time, one can program almost anything into the noise within one's cognitive limits; the limits are only one's own conceptual limits, including limits set by one's repressed, inhibited, and forbidden areas of thought" (77). Noise stores added value in surplus, and in many ways gets the most interesting—that is, it reveals the furthest limits of the repressed, the inhibited, and the forbidden—on the verge of circuit overload. While Lilly valued noise as a site for meaningful generative potential, what makes the Barrons' discoveries so simultaneously innovative and harrowing is their exploration of what amounts to a kind of "black noise," a sonorous object-oriented event that takes place among the "muffled objects hovering at the fringes of our attention" (Bogost 2012, 33). For game designer and philosopher Ian Bogost, black noise frames our experience of alien objects and phenomena. Bogost's formulation usefully pulls back the concept of alien phenomenology from an experience of the alien as other person, as an alienist or existentialist philosopher might have it, or even another creature, as Lilly would have it, but rather concludes, "The true alien recedes interminably even as it surrounds us completely. It is not hidden in the darkness of the outer cosmos or in the deep-sea shelf but in plain sight, everywhere, in everything" (Bogost 2012, 34). Faced with this world in which the alien is everywhere, Bogost contends that the materialist philosopher's job "is to amplify the black noise of objects to make the resonant frequencies of the stuffs inside them hum in credibly satisfying ways" (34). Even if it didn't echo the Barrons' practice as much as it does, there is something vaguely menacing in Bogost's amplification of alien feedback circuits to make them sing. For the Barrons, recognizing the motific expressivity of overdriven circuits had everything to do with metaprogramming the affective leitmotif at the expense of alien life.

To consider the Barrons' circuits capable of life, consciousness, and the agonies of death necessitates some form of the vitalistic machinism of Guattari, which he also brought to his collaborations with the philosopher Gilles Deleuze: "Not every organism has a brain, and not all life is organic, but everywhere there are forces that constitute microbrains, or an inorganic life of things. . . . But, in the final analysis, the same ultimate elements and the same withdrawn force constitute a single plane of composition bearing all the varieties of the universe" (1994, 213). The cosmic "varieties" that Deleuze and Guattari evoke reside in the background radiation of black noise, suffusing many different "organisms" (both biological and machinic) with those aspects of sensation—"the vibrations of the stimulant on a nervous surface or in a cerebral volume" (211)—that might constitute a life force. So why not the life of a circuit patch actor, dying invisibly but very audibly offscreen? Deleuze and Guattari's descriptions of "sensation" parallel the interests of Stockhausen and Eimert in the purity of electronic sound, which is known by "the contracted vibration that has become quality, variety" (211). The electric conduction of a psychotechnological aesthetic force reveals the contemplative nature of matter that operates "on a plane that is different from mechanisms, dynamisms, and finalities: it is on a plane of composition where sensation is formed by contracting that which composes it, and by composing itself with other sensations that contract it in turn" (212). This compositional process, by which the Barrons' circuit-based leitmotifs would be drawn into signification through the images that they compose, finally destroys life by means of a catastrophic inflation of added value.

Questions remain concerning the role of torture, abuse, and autopsy in the alien encounter and what this has to do with the elimination of residual significance in the sonorous object. The Barrons didn't simply work as close to the point of burnout as possible; they plunged full on into the spawning and exploitation of short-lived life-forms, hastening their cybernetic offspring to a violent demise. Tape decks captured the throes of cybernetic overload and fried circuitry. The death glitch gives the listener a glimpse of sonic intelligence, a kind of intention to express what was hidden deep in the psytech program. Black noise triggers an otherwise invisible structural disintegration of sound caught too fast in the grip of cybernetic materials. The circuitry of the Barrons echoes the Krell's music technology, which is heard in the film as a recorded artifact discovered by Morbius. The ancient music, made half a million years before the time of the narrative, is the only diegetic music—in fact the only music labeled as such—heard in the entire film. This alien music is subtle, droning, and hardly there at all, the product of long delay loops, suggesting to Leydon a metaphor of the Barrons' own lost sound technology and their "obsolete music-making skills" (2004a, 62–63). But I think that there are more than metaphorical synchronies at work, not only between the music of the Krell and the Barrons' quirky and quickly outdated equipment but also between the Krell Mind Booster and the sonic life-forms generated by the Barrons' circuits. There is one significant difference, however, that must be immediately acknowledged. Whereas the ancient Krell technology led to the creation of matter from thought, the Barrons' circuits created consciousness from matter and electricity. The very plurality of the circuit entities, which the Barrons brought forth and encountered, is a telling reversal of the doom of the Krell. The Mind Booster. At least when interfaced with the mind of Dr. Morbius, the device results in an overwhelming singularity, one mind to rule them all, and one mind to ruin them. The Krell mind-expanding technology seems to have led to what Leydon calls "a world without instrumentalities" (65), but the world is revealed to be nothing more than the instrumentality of consciousness. Morbius's fate is driven by the mechanical drives of his own unconscious and the monstrous by-product of a repressed and subconscious will. Morbius's overprotection of his daughter, Altaira, borders on the incestuous. Further, he wants to keep the discovery of the Krell civilization and technologies to himself. In both cases, his distrust of the alien earthmen who have come to his planet leads to murder. Whether Morbius has "gone Krell" or not, we can only guess, as Captain Adams (Leslie Nielsen) does for us, that the entire Krell civilization had been destroyed by its own monsters from the Id, in which case the planetary cataclysm that concludes the film would be the end of a long line of disasters at once cosmic and psychological.

To go with the flow of the film, we either have to make constant microdifferentiations among sonic events or we have to let everything blur into a sonic singularity. This conceptual blur that renders everything overly connected comes easily in *Forbidden Planet,* as individual sounds sync up to images or events in imprecise ways, and as sounds in general tend to glide across visual cuts and so further challenge our ability to situate them consistently. Leydon hears the film soundtrack as a network that interconnects sonic elements in competition with each other: "'irrational' affective music representing *Eros* and *Thanatos,*" while another "broad category of leitmotifs," suggests the presence of "rational technology" (2004a, 71). This differs significantly from what we heard in the case of Klaatu and Gort, where the collective subdiegetic plane extrudes affect as a kind of telepathic psytech communication. In this case, though, the subdiegetic connection is between a human mind, that of Dr. Morbius, and the machinery of his already alien psyche. Leydon again looks toward metaphorical connections when she concludes, "This permeability of the diegetic/nondiegetic sound boundary acts as a kind of metaphor for the monster/Morbius situation, where the boundary between mind and matter is similarly porous" (71). But the reality-generating properties of the psytech link between Morbius and the monster from his own mind are more than metaphor; in fact, they trigger an even greater overcoding of sonic eventfulness that takes the whole movie with it into the black hole of black noise. The direct link of Morbius and the invisible monster is sonically revealed when the sound of the "monster circuit . . . ceases at the very moment that Morbius wakes up in his study, that is, with Morbius's 'return to consciousness'" (71). Even moments of silence are thus caught up in the continuum of a collapsing sonic psytech. Silence adds value by prompting our attention to the otherwise unseen connection between the linguist and the deadly manifestation of his own unconscious mind. This breaking of the web of sonic connectivity snaps the movie in two, and from here on out, everything moves toward death and destruction. Even from the day of the film's fateful test screening, the score turns out to have been a very apt premonition of this overconnectedness, which relies on the vagueness of sound synchronization, and this complete burnout of the capacity for either abstract or concrete sounds to signify differently. "While individual circuits could be used to represent characters, the story also suggested a web of interactions among the leitmotifs," Leydon concludes, "the ancient Krell and their technology are reactivated by Morbius; Morbius *is* the monster; the monster is conjured up by Altaira's emerging desire for Adams. None of these connections is made explicit in the narrative until near the end of the film, but hints and clues are worked into the soundtrack throughout" (71). Leydon works out a schema of sonic permeability by which implicit and invisible connections are made, through which silence too becomes the added value of the invisible, and by which the entirety of the forbidden planet Altair is ultimately indistinguishable from the entirety of Morbius's Krell-broken mind.

The cinematic principle of sound's added value is so out of control in *Forbidden Planet* that it in fact reverses the usual situation so that the image becomes that which adds value to the sonic event. That is, rather than sound reinforcing and situating the image, the image here must help us make convoluted distinctions between diegetic musical cues and leitmotifs, nondiegetic sounds, sounds of the invisible subdiegetic drama, and alien music heard as a diegetic artifact. This radical over-coding and reversal of cinematic values suggests the "virtual image" that Deleuze differentiates in his writings on cinema and Henri Bergson, and leads me to conclude that the virtual image is in fact sound:

> Ever vaster circuits will be able to develop, corresponding to deeper and deeper layers of reality and higher and higher levels of memory or thought. But it is this most restricted circuit of the actual image and *its* virtual image which carries everything, and serves as internal limit. We have seen how, on the broader trajectories, perception and recollection, the real and the imaginary, the physical and the mental, or rather their images, continually followed each other, running behind each other and referring back to each other around a point of indiscernibility. But this point of indiscernibility is precisely constituted by the smallest circle, that is, the coalescence of the actual image and the virtual image, the image with two sides, actual and virtual at the same time. (1989, 68–69)

This strikes me as a bit too tidy for *Forbidden Planet,* given the horrific nature of the Morbius disaster, although it does suggest some of the boundaries that collapse as Morbius's Krell-boosted mind begins invisibly to unravel the fabric of the local universe. Consider the death of the Morbius circuit. The electronic circuitry that represents the invisible Id monster—sounds that are perhaps diegetically emitted by the monster and audible to the characters—gets into a vicious and deadly feedback loop as it mixes with the Morbius circuit. The Morbius circuit burns out. Morbius's death scene is scored with the sounds of "the actual dying of that circuit," Bebe recalls; "you can hear it going through agonies of death and winding down. It was really sad, very pathetic. We could never get that circuit to do anything afterwards" (in Leydon 2004a, 71). Along the subdiegetic realm of the film's Id, living circuitry burns out in sync with the pretend death of on-screen characters. Dr. Morbius bears the brunt of this judgmental cautionary tale. He dies in the grip of mind-blowingly complex alien psytech, having accessed forbidden zones of biocomputer programming. A twofold death thus plays out in parallel, both in the speculative imagination as we observe the character in a dramatic narrative but also, perhaps more tragically, in the demise of the one-of-a-kind Morbius circuit off screen. The two deaths converge in subdiegetic space. Another meditation by Deleuze gets to the point of such dire cinematic consequences:

> Between the two sides of the absolute, between the two deaths—death from the inside or past, death from the outside or future—the internal sheets of memory and the external layers of reality will be mixed up, extended, short-circuited and will form a moving life, which is at once that of the cosmos and of the brain, which sends out flashes from one pole to the other. . . . But between the two, what flashes of lightning there will have been; these were life itself. From one pole to the other a creation will be constructed, which is true creation only because it will be carried out between the two deaths, the apparent and the real, all the more intense because it illuminates this interstice. (1989, 209)

As with Deleuze and Bergson, the Barrons have realized the conditions by which the virtual image that is sound has everything to do with death and the disastrous doubling that is the remembering of the dead, including the long-dead alien Krell.

Sometimes I doubt just how far to read into this language that the Barrons were so fond of when describing their cybernetic circuit bending. They do, however, undeniably and very usefully push past simple anthropomorphism to comprehend instead a form of biomedia and work from the presumption that their circuits were living beings. But their recollections often turn morbid. Louis and Bebe Barron agree that "'you have to be free to abuse the circuit.' Fortunately, 'Tubes are forgiving'" (in Leydon 2004a, 68). Louis goes on to reflect, "We can torture these circuits without a guilty conscience—whereas if we did it musically we might have to torture a musician . . . we look on these circuits as generally suffering, but we don't feel compassion" (in Brend 2012, 54). In the most extreme case, the Barrons describe their work in terms of a calculated cruelty: "The thing would just be tortured to death. You could really hear it." The sounds of a tortured homemade circuit suggested "the last paroxysms of a living creature" (in Leydon 2004a, 68). The abdication of conscience and compassion in the face of alien suffering, abuse, and torture underpin another side of humanist music that is, at last, deeply suspicious of new technologies and potentially dehumanizing cybernetics. In such cases, the turn of language suggests that perhaps we should follow Lilly's lead and sketch out the bioethics of alien encounter at any scale of contact across difference, even when dealing with temporary sound objects.

The SF film soundtrack provides a space in which the sonorous object is capable of an authentically alien expression. The monstrous Dr. Morbius and the Id monster, much like the Thing, the creature, the monster from space, or Gojira from the ocean deeps, have sonic equivalents, each achieved through the manufacture of new ways of making sound in excess of conventional instrumentation and technique. In a key passage, Sobchack speculates on "the possibilities of using music *as* an alien language, one indecipherable in its particular meanings yet emotionally communicative" (1987, 208). Without quite proposing the use of music in order to render alien emotional experiences beyond normative human terms, Sobchack is on the verge of concluding that the sound effect has generally taken over the emotive expressivity of music in the SF film; she ultimately envisions "altering the shape and instrumentation of music so as to create a disorienting and dissonant physical and emotional response in the viewer" (208). This is not only disorienting but also tragic in the case of *Forbidden Planet*. We can hear the dead, or at least we can hear their technological proxies perform again in a recording, just like those of the ancient Krell, even as we can uncover the mysteries of dying circuit consciousnesses in bits of tape-recorded black noise and rhythmic bursts of decelerated static. The Barrons' sonic entities are different, even among aliens; they come not from afar but from somewhere close at hand, out of the interstices of nowhere at the edges of phenomena, and they die horrible deaths at the hands of their human parents.

The conceptual space of the sonic novum facilitates a fatal interlock of the cosmological imagination and the sonorous object with disastrous consequences that unravel the narrative, particularly as a tale of parenting. Who is to say with absolute certainty that Morbius's daughter Altaira is not a product of the Krell Mind Booster, the offspring of a lone human survivor and the planet Altair's insanity-inducing technology? Certainly the final annihilation of not just Altair IV but the entire Altair system suggests that two events—Morbius's death and cosmic destruction—are the result of a catastrophic psytech meltdown. Chion notes that "music in sound films is generally discontinuous; music cues are dispersed throughout, and they are interwoven with other sound elements. These factors allow music to play a more significant structural role and to create 'zones' of segments with music and segments without" (2009, 407). Not so in *Forbidden Planet*, where every zone is a forbidden one. Everything is too connected and oversaturated; there are no distinct timbral zones and few pauses between the sounds brought to shots of spaceship interiors or the Krell power station or a rampaging invisible monstrosity or space blasters or Altaira's theme or recordings of ancient Krell music—and so on. All the sounds clearly derive from the same kind of technological source, even though we may not know exactly what that source is. It's the overwhelming continuity of everything that we hear that glues this world together and tears it apart in an obsessively self-reflective holocaust of a film. All of this runs as rampant as Cook's (Earl Holliman) bottles of booze, which come mass-produced out of Robby as the robot demonstrates its rather unlikely imitation of the Mind Booster's power, making primitive earthly wishes come true. Everything is overcoded, overdriven, and finally overwhelmed. The all-encompassing psytech failure is cosmic. What if this is all a dream of the Krell, the fulfillment of their forbidden death wish? After all, the humans are the dangerous alien visitors here, the aberrant Others who arrive in a flying saucer bringing death in its wake.

1957–59 | THE VORTEX CONCERTS

Over a three-year span, San Francisco's pioneers of planetarium arts, disc jockey Henry Jacobs and experimental filmmaker Jordan Belson, produced almost forty Vortex Concerts at the California Academy of Science's Morrison Planetarium in San Francisco. The concerts combined music drawn from Jacobs's tape collection of musique concrète, experimental electronic music, and various forms of music from around the world, with a performance of projected patterns, images, and film clips. The program notes for Vortex 4 described "a pure theater appealing directly to the senses," an abstract audiovisual cosmos composed of lights, optical effects, electronic sound, and multichannel audio reproduction utilizing thirty-eight speakers distributed around the perimeter of the planetarium's sixty-five-foot dome (Golden 1995). Jacobs and Belson worked with special interface technologies developed for them by Morrison Planetarium staff and a lead engineer from a Stanford think tank (MacDonald 1998, 72–73). With a rotary controller that enabled him to direct sources to specific speakers, Jacobs could make sounds constellate across discrete regions within the space or even put the whole sound mass into a circular motion, the favored effect that gave the concerts their name. Belson used keyboards, faders, and remote controls for the lights and up to thirty projection devices, including kaleidoscopes, strobes, prisms, diffraction slides, interference patterns, and the star field projector in the middle of the planetarium. As they transformed equipment intended for popular space science entertainment into new performance interfaces, both artists felt as though the dome itself had become "an exquisite instrument," as Belson recalled (in Youngblood 1970, 388). A language of instrumentality—of keyboards, consoles, joysticks, and potentiometers—underscores the direct appeal of the Vortex Concerts to the senses through a kind of swirling, high-definition, surround sound form of phenomenal science fiction. Belson would go on to recreate the live visual instrumentality at home in his own cosmic cinema, using a handmade optical bench that Gene Youngblood describes as "a plywood frame around an old X-ray stand with rotating tables, variable speed motors, and variable intensity lights," which allowed the filmmaker to create and capture slit-scan interference effects, kaleidoscopic mandalas, and more (1970, 158).

Considering the lack of media documentation, what an actual Vortex experience might have been like comes to us, if not in the retrospective interviews of Gene Youngblood and Scott MacDonald, then in the form of the frequently hyperbolic language of Belson and Jacob's contemporaries. These include the exhilarated San Francisco art critic

Alfred Frankenstein, who describes the way in which one of Belson's visual works had "the extraordinary effect of lifting the spectator right off his seat to traverse that sky-space in a wonderfully disembodied way" (in Keefer 2008, 4). Harriet Polt and Roger Sandall offer a more sober assessment in the spring 1961 issue of *Film Quarterly*: "The combination of space, light, color, and sound creates an enveloping audio-visual experience in a completely controlled environment, in which the audience, once admitted, is not allowed to leave until the performance is over" (36). And an unnamed correspondent for *Time* magazine provided readers this account in February 1959 under the title "Music: The Sick Machine":

> B-z-z-up. Whoo. Whoo. Twitter. Z-o-o-om. ma-a-a-chine! The sounds whooped and wallowed in the semidarkness, seemed to race one another, swooped head on into ear-splitting collisions. Under the domed ceiling, lights wriggled and flickered, reeled and burst in dazzling, flaky showers. A voice came booming in: matchwood splits into matches!

The significance of the passage of the Vortex Concerts into textual descriptors is not to be overlooked. It is part of the Vortex Concerts' becoming what I will describe as an unconscious heritage resonant with concurrent developments in theoretical space sciences and astronautics, and anticipating aspects of consciousness studies, psychedelic research, and poststructuralist philosophy. I contend that the Vortex Concerts contribute to our understanding of performative, audiovisual media but also humanity's relationship to outer space through technology, the body, imagination, and a form of psychotechnological spiritual practice that I dub "cyborg ritual." It is this overlap of various sciences, technologies, and philosophies with an emergent form of live, speculative media that warrants consideration of the concerts within the context of the ambient and alien novums of a sonic science fiction.

As the planetarium becomes an instrument for visual music, it situates its occupants (performers, technicians, and audience alike) within an affectively driven cybernetic system. As Frankenstein suggests, this becomes an uplifting, cosmic ritual for attendees. The emerging psytechnician exploits the parallel function of spiritual and technical counterparts not so much as a means of artistic communication but rather as a tool for personal exploration and insight. Much like the yogic practices that would increasingly inform Belson's films, the poses of cyborg ritual entrain "our autonomic systems to live in harmony with our old heritage, as well as with our new exploration of outer, and perforce, inner, space," in the words of Manfred Clynes, a space science researcher and musician whose work plays a particularly important role in my treatment of the Vortex Concerts as kind of science fiction for spiritual cyborgs ([1970] 1995, 42). Clynes's 1970 essay "Cyborg II" evaluates the role of the astronaut's emotions, autonomic affective postures, and the activities of the unconscious mind in ways that had been neglected by other researchers publishing in the space sciences. The essay is a sequel to 1960's "Cyborgs and Space," by Clynes with Nathan S. Kline, which was first published in *Astronautics,* the leading journal in the field. Clynes and Kline consider the astronaut a form of cybernetic organism, and they coin the simple portmanteau neologism, "cyborg," in the process. Because it was more logical than trying to reconstruct earthly environments for astronauts in outer space, "bodily functions" would be made to accommodate "the requirements of extraterrestrial environments," an approach deemed "more logical than providing an earthly environment . . . in space" ([1960] 1995, 29). The design of "artifact–organism systems" builds the astronaut right into the spaceship (29), as various regimes of mechanical, pharmaceutical, and environmental programming support the "self-regulating man–machine systems" during space travel (30). Clynes and Kline considered the mind of the astronaut a human–machine hybrid of "symbiotically combined" parts, which would be prepared for the mental rigors of space travel through "pharmacological and hypnotic approaches" to brain programming (31). This was actually a pretty standard approach in early astronautics. Robert W. Driscoll's report on NASA's Biotechnology and Human Research, "Engineering Man for Space: The Cyborg Study," concentrates on the use of "artificial organs, hypothermia and/or drugs in adapting man to a space environment" ([1963] 1995, 76). Particular attention is paid to sensory deprivation, both as psychological crisis and strategy for coping with the duration of flight. The consensus at the time presents the mind of the astronaut as something to lull, depress, hypnotize, and put to sleep.

The mind would be regulated, called to attention when needed, and put down for long periods of time of otherwise tedious wakefulness. This was the environment in which Clynes's own "Cyborg II" took shape and reacted. His appeal to emotional well-being and affect-based programming stands out as a singular consideration for not only the astronaut's mind but also for mood and mental health. "Cyborg II" was ultimately too far out there. *Astronautics* rejected the article.

The insistent concern for the emotional and imaginative life of the space traveler makes Clynes's research unique among his contemporaries. Other researchers introduced biomechanical and pharmaceutical methods to manage the astronaut's body. Where Clynes worked from the mind and body outward toward machine systems, bionics computing tended to work toward the mind from the opposite side of cyborg research. It is nonetheless closely related in its similar regard for mind–machine hybridization. In "How Do We Get There?" (1960), Major Jack E. Steele of the United States Air Force approaches the emerging field of bionics as an interdisciplinary partnership of biology, mathematics and engineering with the common goal of building a living computer system. Steele describes the bionic heritage of "vital" computing and the design of "devices and systems which to the naïve observer might well appear to be alive" ([1960] 1995, 55). These advances in vital, complex cybernetics are then used to model the human brain. In contrast, Clynes sequences the development of the computer brain according to specific stages of the human brain's life span, noting milestones in psychological development:

> The virtual body images associated with each emotion have an unconscious origin. They are not wilfully created by each individual— they represent his heritage. So do essentic forms. This unconscious heritage travels with us into space. But we have seen that the autonomic and the unconscious meet. Through understanding our unconscious heritage consciously, we may be able to teach our autonomic systems to live in harmony with our old heritage, as well as with our new exploration of outer, and perforce, inner, space. ([1970] 1995, 40)

Despite numerous methods for controlling brain function, little consideration was given to what might be going on in the mind of the astronauts, and less still the emotions. In order to exercise the emotional range of the astronautic cyborg, Clynes comes up with the idea of "sentic cycles." These are based on the relationship between bodily expressive patterns and certain states of mood. Clynes calls these body-emotion memories "essentic forms" ([1970] 1995, 38), which are constituted by the emotion recorded in autonomic arrangements, such as the set of facial muscles that constitutes a smile. This is the unconscious heritage that Clynes describes. The heritage of earthly memory residing within the physical form of the astronaut predisposes the body toward specific postures, gestures, and motions. Clynes held that affect could be stimulated and regulated by certain postures, repetitive motions, and autonomic reactions. He suggests that these emotive states might be orchestrated into routines that would be classified initially according to physical, and then later tonal centers (38–39). Clynes programs "a sequence of 30 to 40 expressive actions of a particular emotion" that covers "the entire spectrum of emotions," including "no emotion, anger, hate, grief, love, sex, joy, reverence" (38). The technology is subtle, a sequence of poses of forefinger and thumb that relate to specific emotional states, or what he calls E-actions. Through subtle adjustments of pressure and angle, the finger and thumb could be made to exercise its emotional counterpart on demand. Arguably, localized gestures would compensate for the hampered affective range of the confined body of the astronaut. Clynes describes an optimal state of "psychologic homeostasis" (36) through which the mind programs its own emotional content, generating affective embodiments by rewiring the physical heritage connected with the astronaut's emotional life. E-actions compensate for the deprivation and routine of astronautic experience—perhaps an ironic compensation given the systematic programming of the E-action routines themselves.

Ultimately, Clynes suggests a kind of cyborg programmer/composer type, and we should consider E-actions as a kind of mood music. Certainly music epitomizes for Clynes the sentic "communication of emotions in the present moment" ([1970] 1995, 37). It has the same ability as E-actions to shape specific forms of essentic recall. As "a generalized mode" of real-time emotional expression, music doesn't depend on the "specific situation or individuals" (38). More important, music is a form of touch. Its generalized emotional communications are "capable of generating and discharging emotional states through its vibratory touch forms, which we call sound" (38). Sound waves physically touch us, something that Clynes sought to exploit as a means of programming new sentic behaviors for the astronaut. Clynes's stress on the emotional body of the astronaut is met, therapeutically, by this idea of sound's vibratory touch, which is capable of triggering the discharge of emotion. Clynes's emphasis on the vibratory makes emotion a matter of sensation and thereby something that can be manipulated, synthesized, and controlled.

When I suggest that the Vortex Concerts supply precisely the kind of unconscious heritage described in Clynes ([1970] 1995), I point to the simultaneously physical and mindful postures that predispose us—bodily as much as imaginatively—within the planetarium toward a certain kind of cyborg spirituality. We encounter a kind of deep muscle memory, an autonomic pose, in the supine form of the reclining stargazer. There comes with this pose the deep memory of Clynes's essentic forms, which impress mood and affect onto the body, and which manifest here as nostalgic longing for the pure night sky, undiminished by light pollution and unblocked by construction. The Vortex Concerts facilitate the embodied experience of the cosmic listener, determining the poses that accompany a deeply self-reflective process for the individual while also programming an emerging mode of social gathering or "happening," an improvisational collective embodiment that uses multimedia to purposefully evoke or trigger unusual states of group consciousness. In the era of a nascent psychedelic culture, the artist's role began to shift, becoming both programmer of group interactions and situations and a self-conscious explorer of the psyche. In conversation with Youngblood, Belson proposes that the artist must function as a scientist of inner cosmic experience, and he references his past use of substances like peyote and LSD, subsequent work with meditation and other body technologies like yoga and breath work, and filmmaking and contributions to the Vortex Concerts:

> The new art and other forms of expression reveal the influence of mind-expansion. And finally we reach the point where there virtually is no separation between science, observation, and philosophy. The

new artist works essentially in the same way as the scientist. In many cases it's identical with scientific exploration. But at other times the artist is able to focus more in the area of consciousness and subjective phenomena, but with the same kind of scientific zeal, the same objectivity, as scientists. Cosmic consciousness is not limited to scientists. In fact scientists are sometimes the last to know. They can look through their telescopes and see it out there, but still be very limited individuals. (in Youngblood 1970, 174)

The Vortex Concerts retrieve stargazing from science by pushing beyond the planetarium's function as a virtual, imaginary duplicate of the space observatory. Jacobs and Belson take space back from the hands of astronomers, as it were, and give the night sky back to the artist, the myth maker, and the philosopher while collapsing distinctions between outer space and inner space, macrocosm and microcosm, cosmos and psyche. While the collapse of such binaries would in some ways underscore the enterprise of space exploration as a whole (as I will discuss later in reference to Al Reinert's 1989 film, *For All Mankind*), its significance was largely ignored within the context of military, industrial, and scientific initiatives to get off-world and land on the moon. These collapses would play out, however, as a popular cosmological agenda within the Vortex Concerts, which most palpably capture these dissolving binaries through the synesthesia of the audiovisual performance, making them far more significant as a reflection on space, philosophy, and the arts than as a legendary and now irreproducible notch on the time line of obsolete media ancestry. To conclude that the Vortex Concerts can never happen again, as Cindy Keefer (2008) of the Center for Visual Music is wont to do, is to go against the futurist impulse of the project, summed up by Belson's own assessment that "its pure, nonobjective use of light, color, and sound make Vortex the most advanced form of theater yet developed," and in fact, "a prefiguration of the theater of the future" that reveals film itself to be "simply a transitional form between conventional theater and whatever theater will be in the future" (Polt and Sandall 1961, 36–37). To the contrary, Keefer concludes that when Belson refers to the Vortex Concerts as "a sacred memory," he means that they are "not possible or desirable to be re-created" (2008, 4). However, the sacred memory that Belson evokes in fact resonates with the unconscious heritage that Clynes describes as a necessary tool for ritualistic cyborg navigation of the emerging future. The primary concrete media of the Vortex Concerts—a pure theater of lighting and optical effects combined with new and unusual sounds dispersed throughout the immersive, highly dynamic sonic space of the domed theater—celebrate audiovisual materiality as a necessary mode of cybernetic cosmic consciousness that retrieves the past and points to the future.

Jacobs and Belson's synesthetic programming through immersion, sensory manipulation, and noise recall our earlier discussion of Lilly's cybernetic practice. Lilly constructs complex media ecologies of biomechanical interfaces and psychoactive agents in order to transmute outer space to inner space through the systematic deprivation and redirection of what he called the "circuitry in one's computer usually occupied by perception of external reality" (1968, 33). Lilly situates the brain within a larger unit, the human biocomputer, which extends the domain of exactly what could be systematized in cybernetic regimens—the entire body—as a means to profoundly alter consciousness. Lilly assembles a network of mind-altering substances, isolation tanks, sensory deprivation methods, dream/sleep research, and esoteric and Eastern spiritual practices, which he combines in the form of scripts and programs for psychological development and transspecies communication. Lilly describes the autoamputation of the cyborg in terms of radical adjustments of the human sense ratio. Throw one sense out of whack, and at least one other sense will overcompensate for that imbalance in a flood of alien phenomena. Lilly brings this process under the control of measurable experimentation in the laboratory, and he presents his findings in terms of the transformation of the human into a programmable biocomputer that relies on a complex system of embedded psychotechnological subroutines that are at once physical, sensory, cognitive, and emotional. I am condensing this greatly here, but what I want to apply to our consideration of the Vortex Concerts is the shift that Lilly makes from the outer space of the senses to the inner space of the cybernaut's mind without disregarding the body's holistic investment in emotive and imaginative functionality. When deprived of its traditional formats of sensory input and their complex aggregates of experience, the human body and mind undergo a compensatory rush of false impressions. Their corresponding affects fill the void of the senses in an autonomic effort to regain equilibrium.

The human biocomputer, when engaged in this process of affective realignment, produces the "self," an entity capable of becoming lucid in such moments and then engaging as a coparticipant (re)engineer/ programmer of the human biocomputer in which the self is embedded (Lilly 1968, 92). Borrowing language from cybernetics and computer sciences, Lilly raises the prospects for a new space-age set of philosophical and spiritual or religious practices—a kind of mind-focused programming he called metaprogramming—as the cybernaut participates first in the cognitive transformation of identity and then the interlock of transspecies communication. These high levels of sentic identity and communication follow from the subtraction of sensory input. Deprivation of sense input incurs the compensatory processes of the inner-sense organs and ghost limbs that function in our dreams and other hypnogogic states of consciousness. Lilly describes this process in terms of random bursts of noise: "The increase in *white noise* energy allows quick and random access to memory and lowers the threshold to unconscious memories (*expansion of consciousness*)." Lilly continues, "In such noise one can project almost anything at almost any cognitive level. . . . The major operative principle seems to be that *the human computer operates in such a way as to make signals out of noise and thus to create information out of random energies where there was no signal*" (1968, 76–78). Lilly's sentic space travel is likely far beyond what Clynes had in mind, but it is space travel through a sonic cosmos nonetheless in which the cybernaut's own body and consciousness project imaginary alien novums to fill the void of sensory deprivation. Clynes reduces the self to little more than pure emotional postures that can be managed by a set of responsive behaviors. Lilly, on the other hand, allows for a much wider range of possible cognitive behaviors and activities in which the cybernaut can engage, including the exploration of new extraterrestrial spaces and contact with alien life. Accessing the new and alien domains opened up through synesthetically altered affect, Lilly's individual experiments suggest a speculation on the collective role of consciousness and bodies in the Vortex

Concerts, which provide a ritualistic tool for the cybernetic reprogramming of the inner space traveler.

As the planetarium becomes a visual music instrument, a kind of cybernetic emotive system takes shape that nudges the planetarium's usual representative, mimetic, and educational functions toward a simultaneously abstract expressiveness achieved through concrete experiment with equipment in the new emotive, aesthetic, imaginary, and speculative registers of a cyborg ritual. The primary media of the Vortex Concerts—the futurist theater of "electronics, optics, and architecture" (Belson in Polt and Sandall 1961, 35)—the venue of the Morrison Planetarium itself becomes the instrument and vehicle handled by Jacobs and Belson, situating the Vortex Concerts within a larger field of artworks devoted to a "total environmental experience," which Youngblood calls "intermedia works." Intermedia represent a blend of audiovisual technology, conceived through the arts rather than science and engineering, and "grounded in the fields of psychology, information theory, and communication engineering" (1970, 348). As interest in multichannel audio and video technologies combined with developments in early networked community and real-time telecommunication, intermedia art was from the beginning deeply influenced by the research and theory of behavioral scientists looking at the systematic ways in which humans engage their spaces, as well as interact with others within those spaces, in order to understand the regulation and control of those spaces and the people within them. Intermedia, in other words, is art's most immersive and expansive branch of cybernetics.

Youngblood predicts intermedia's move toward "that point at which all the phenomena of life on earth will constitute the artist's palette" (1970, 348), accurately anticipating new media trends in data mining, visualization, sonification, and real-time data processing. Intermedia also looks forward to a general cultural shift among public art institutions that fulfill an outreach and educational goal through entertainment, something that we see in institutionalized venues of intermedia such as IMAX theaters, digital domes and planetariums, and interactive museum displays. Even as it institutes interdisciplinary relationships, however, intermedia is also about a mutually informed, highly speculative, synesthetic movement toward "inner and outer space, the microcosm and the macrocosm," Youngblood writes. "On the one hand, intermedia environments turn the participant inward . . . , providing a matrix for psychic exploration, perceptual, sensorial, and intellectual awareness; on the other hand technology has advanced to the point at which the whole earth itself becomes the 'content' of aesthetic activity" (348). Youngblood attributes an intuitive sensibility to the newly emerged global citizens of the 1960s who realize that "life could be a process of non-ordinary realities" propped up by the intermedia network, and in which the inner processes of the mind no longer have to be merely dreamed but can be lived in embodied space (348). He concludes,

> In this forthcoming global activity of continual myth-generation, dramatic-fiction cinema will find a new and vital role to play. Although obsolete in one respect it will become enriched in another. While videotape cartridges and cable television will bring conventional cinema into the home on an individual level, society will seek its communal mythic experiences in elaborate intermedia environments found today only at world expositions where the average citizen is able to experience, for a limited time, the wealth and inventiveness that is kept from him in everyday existence. (352)

This cybernetic intermedia is realized within the embodied sentic space of the Vortex Concerts, where the spiritual cyborg self, already embedded in complex systems and engaged in self-aware metaprogramming tasks, launches toward new forms of community and coalition that extend across species to include alien consciousnesses. Lilly's (1968) sentic cyborgization hooks the human biocomputer into existing fields and media of communication typically blocked by the primary senses and the habitually aggregated worlds that have built up around those senses. A sentic rechanneling of unconscious heritage into already inhabited, preexisting systems (such as dolphin or extraterrestrial biocomputers) may be more in line with the community model put forward in practice by Jacobs and Belson. While Clynes does suggest a parallel of outer and inner space explorations sympathetic to this discussion, he never allows for the philosophical and the dreaming mind. This is ironic, for meditative inquiry, insight, and rejuvenation, as well as hypnagogic reverie and lucid dreaming, are precisely the unique states of consciousness known to be most enhanced by the mind-altering technologies incorporated into bionic space design and cybernetically engineered vehicles for extraterrestrial travel, exploration, and habitation. Lilly provides an alternative route into inner space, but the Vortex Concerts appeal to both. The Vortex Concerts anticipate these trajectories by not only opening up channels of sentic reaction and deep human response to the night sky and cosmic spaces both beyond and within, but also by treating this cybernetic process as a community event. When applied to cultural bodies, sentic forms manifest through ritual postures and actions. Cosmic philosophy is embodied thought, shared among participants in a controlled environment that prohibits premature evacuation, triggered by the lurch and spin of the Vortex machine. This Vortex marks our sentic heritage, a shadow cast from the theater of the future onto an audience of imaginary space-age cybernauts. There, the bodies ready for liftoff—each interfaced through the technological nervous system of the planetarium, the ambient novum of the future theater—extend senses programmed by new synesthetic intensities to form a global self poised for encounter with the expanded planetary consciousness embedded within the alien intermedia environment.

• CHAPTER 3 •

Cosmos Philosophy and Thought Synthesizers (1959–68)

As the decade of the 1950s came to a close, electronic sound was a well-established convention for outer space and psychic space in the science fiction film. SF cinema exploits this sonic trope in rather literal ways, making the otherwise "intangible spaces, both cosmic and psychological," the stuff of its narratives, imagery, and atmospheres through the indexical presence of electronic sound (Leydon 2004a, 64). The previous chapter established the ways in which electronic sounds functioned atmospherically to create the new spaces, or ambient novum, of the SF film. As science fiction narratives shifted toward tales of alien visitation and invasion, new electronic sounds traveled with the alien in the form of sonic halos, timbral motifs, or vibes that identified the visitor or monster as different. These alien novums developed a complex form of sonic psytech that opened up new domains of cinematic subdiegetics along which psychological and technological events played out. While the primitive and minimal sound designs of *Gojira* avoided the electronic instrumentation of its North American counterparts, creating an audible footprint that suggested a clash of ancient and impending atomic realities, *Forbidden Planet*'s extreme electronic tonalities turned from traditional instrumental interfaces to instead develop a prototypical form of circuit-bending, cybernetic programming, and the artificial life of biomedia. Finally, Belson and Jacob's Vortex Concerts revealed

• 191

a new sonic cosmos—or psonicosmos—of psychotechnological inter-media; maintained by the synesthetically programmed sonic psytech of the collective audience, a new scale of cinematic apparatus provided both an immersive dive into deep consciousness and a launch into a mythic cosmos. The Vortex Concerts pushed science fiction not only in the direction of intermedia art but also toward a burgeoning psychedelic subculture. Interviewed by Scott MacDonald, Belson recalls the rapid-ity with which an audience developed for the Vortex Concerts: "People were ripe for it apparently. This was just on the brink of the era of the light shows and the happenings. The audience was a real cross section of the population. In fact, some of the people were a probably a little too colorful for the planetarium's staff" (1998, 73)! This proved problematic for Morrison Planetarium's first director, George Bunton, who was dis-turbed by "the composition of this audience, roughly one-half of whom he described as 'Bohemian,' or belonging to the beat generation and widely regarded as 'denying themselves nothing in the way of worldly pleasures and sensations'" (Marché 2005, 142). By the end of the 1950s, electronic instrumentalities and new sonic experiences created an inter-face between the mind and an emerging technocosmos that would push further toward the expanded consciousness of psychedelic experience over the next ten years. Of course, science fiction films paved the way for it.

This chapter is concerned with the trajectory of the SF film over the course of the 1960s. Several significant transformations take place. The genre becomes noticeably more international, for one. Whereas in the 1950s, over three-quarters of science fiction films were the exclusive product of American studios, in the 1960s the majority of films were either from other countries or were joint studio productions. Among the seventy or so films marketed as U.S. productions, several were in fact overdubbed and edited versions of international films, with the product of the Soviet bloc being a particular target during producer Roger Corman's tenure at American International Pictures (AIP). The science fiction films of the Soviet Union, East Germany, Poland, and Czechoslovakia warrant consideration on their merits, as they consis-tently demonstrate quite sophisticated sonic novums that incorporate alien sonic artifacts into their plots. However, as these films are worked over in the studios of AIP or Crown International Pictures, their distribution for American markets demonstrates what Goodman calls "audio virology," which I discuss as a form of appropriation caught up in the throes of the Cold War through which the films undergo the "engineering, incubation, transmission, contagion, and mutation of sonic culture" (2010, 129). Subsequently, the sonic novum both amplifies the genre's capacity to promote a form of cosmic music and locates an ideological contest. The SF films of the Eastern bloc countries pose questions about how Soviet filmmakers heard American SF films, but conversely, they demonstrate how codes as well as modes of listening to the SF film became institutionalized for American audiences. This chapter thus suggests some of the ways in which SF films not only become a place of sonic defamiliarization but also familiarize the role and range of accepted unfamiliar sounds. My earlier discussion of the theremin and its trajectory from multifaceted sonic novum to the major cliché of SF indicates the depletion of the relevance of a certain type of sound. Corman's versions of the Soviet SF films for AIP turn this sonic depletion into the weaponized "*modulation* of preemptive capital" (Goodman 2010, 155).

Faced with this viral institutionalization of the sonic experience, the SF filmmakers of the French new wave and later Stanley Kubrick would react against electronic tonalities altogether to forge new relationships between sound and science fiction. Electronic sounds become suspect musical devices, not only due to their familiarity in SF films but also due to their saturation in pop music and rock. Further, as moments of novelty shift from musical composition toward sound editing, and a film's soundtrack becomes more a part of the postproduction assemblage of the film, the creation of the sonic novum is often achieved through a final, comprehensive edit and mixdown of all audiovisual material into a single cinematic experience, often executed by the film's director. This change begins with two French films from the early '60s, *La Jetée* and *Alphaville*. The directors, Chris Marker and Jean-Luc Godard respectively, conduct radical experiments in sound editing that yields an experience at once fragmented, disjointed, multilayered, and often disconnected from the visual content, yet they beg multiple layers of viewer cognition and engagement. They also explore the capacity of cinema to transform time and consciousness through a common dedication to the assemblage of vast but ultimately broken sonic novums that completely permeate the cinematic experience.

Science fiction at this juncture is in fact a tale of not just one but two new waves. The French new wave films exhibit an element of structural experimentation within the genre that is comparable to the UK literary new wave. As science fiction hit the '60s and left behind its golden age, the genre became both a serious vehicle for mature content and a site of formal experiments. Science fiction came crashing down to earth and a range of ambiguous and often contradictory philosophical themes, speculations around sociological issues, particularly drugs, sexuality, and youth culture, and experimental approaches to narrative style and language converged on the page early in the decade, fueled in part by J. G. Ballard's 1962 guest editorial in *New Worlds* magazine. Ballard sought to redirect science fiction toward more immediate and psychological concerns, asking, "Which way to inner space?" Novelist Michael Moorcock resoundingly replied, "This way," as he took over editorial responsibilities for the magazine in 1964. With Moorcock at the helm, *New Worlds* responded to Ballard's manifesto with a contemporary science fiction that completely abandoned "straightforward tales of interstellar adventure" in favor of "more oblique excursions into shadowy realms of the psyche" (Latham 2011, 128). The content and themes of SF were quickly transformed by writers interested in the experimental techniques of avant-garde writers like William S. Burroughs, particularly his use of the cut-up and other unconventional techniques, and Thomas Pynchon, with his densities of language and references to pop culture.

Unless ironically played, the masculinist rocket men, the distressed women, and the disinterested scientists were gone. *New Worlds* was suddenly replete with stories that fulfilled Ballard's original shopping list for contemporary SF writing: "More psycho-literary ideas, more meta-biological and meta-chemical concepts, private time-systems, synthetic psychologies and space-times, more of the somber half-worlds one glimpses in the paintings of schizophrenics, all in all a complete speculative poetry and fantasy of science" (in Latham 2011, 129). The scientific rationality and technical accuracy at the heart of serious SF was thought "boringly square," and writers and publishers of such stories were deemed "complicit agents of a faceless, amoral technocracy" (129).

A largely transatlantic divide between U.S. and U.K. audiences appeared as American SF editor Donald A. Wollheim accused Moorcock of launching a crude "crusade" of "shock words and shock scenes, hallucinatory fantasies, and sex" (in Latham 2011, 129). The British new wave also triggered a generational split in the field. New wave writers tended to be younger and hip, embedded in the psychedelic scenes at the UFO Club and the rowdy Ladbrook Grove, where they could be sonically jettisoned into the cosmos by space rock bands like Pink Floyd and Hawkwind. With extended jams both atmospheric and hard rocking, and accompanied by hallucinatory light shows, these bands took the listener through space-themed material that bore science fictional titles like "Astronomy Domine," "Interstellar Overdrive," "Set the Controls for the Heart of the Sun," "Silver Machine," "Master of the Universe," and "Time We Left This World Today." *New Worlds'* promotion of formal experimentation and the cultural ethicoaesthetics of the London underground found their archetype in Brian Aldiss's "Acid Head Wars" stories, a Joycean romp through a psychedelic bioweapons war serialized in *New Worlds* and collected as *Barefoot in the Head* (1969), as well as Moorcock's own Jerry Cornelius novels, with their fever blend of speed, psychedelics, sexual taboo, and acid rock.

Aldiss's book is one of those rare works of science fiction that gives the entire novel over to neologistic play and formal experimentation. I discuss it here along with a very brief foray into the experimental linguistic SF of Anthony Burgess's *A Clockwork Orange* (1962), not only to suggest that the sonic novum can exist in text as well as film or audio recordings but more importantly to point to the sympathies among forms and media that reveal larger technocultural imprints on the genre as a whole. The written SF of the British new wave shares something of the French new wave's interests in science fiction as a means of disorientation, experiment with form, irony and self-reflexive criticism, and the subconscious undercurrents of pop culture, both its suppression of and overt appeal to sexuality. I am interested in how these commonalities tug the SF film toward a collision with psychedelic culture in the latter half of the decade, where the cosmologies of outer and inner space become increasingly technologized and entangled, and the sonic novum is used to actualize a form of cosmic philosophy. Here, I continue

196 • COSMOS PHILOSOPHY AND THOUGHT SYNTHESIZERS

to conceptually modulate Deleuze and Guattari's work on the refrain, thinking through the highly self-reflexive mobility of the "thought synthesizer," which both "makes audible the sound process itself" and makes "thought travel . . . in the same way as one makes sound travel" (1987, 343). *Barefoot in the Head* begins in this accelerated zone of sonic travel, where our nineteen-year-old hero, Colin Charteris, hops out of his Banshee for a brief stretch though his mind still moves at "fantastic speeds suddenly swallowed by car and human frame with that sneering sloth of the super-quick, where anything too fast for retina-register could spend forever spreading through the labyrinths of consciousness" (1969, 14).

Aldiss's book depicts the aftermath of the "Acid Head Wars," when hallucinogenic drugs were used as weapons and turned Europe into "a randomised freak-out" (Aldiss, n.d.). The writing in *Barefoot in the Head* slips in and out of various literary modes: Joycean streams of consciousness full of puns and spliced-together words; acrostic poems, anagrams and palindromes, concrete poetry, and other word games; pages of shattered text thrown roughly back together; cubist-inspired experiments with multiple perspectives; and something akin to the surreal rock lyrics of Bob Dylan, the Beatles, and Syd Barrett. Contextualized by such a barrage, even the moments of straightforward clarity take on an additional charge of affectation and illusion:

> Turning her tormented head, she saw the ocean weakly flail the macadam margins of shore bearing in change, long, resounding, raw—and knew again as some tiresome visiting professor of microscopic sanity made clear to her that hear again repetitively iron mankind zinc was on the slide between two elements. . . . Such sounds seemed sexplicable, nexplicable, inexplicable, plicable, lickable, ickable, able, sickable. She was able to differentiate the roar into eight different noises, all flittering towards her under the cover of each other. (Aldiss 1969, 176–77)

The most intriguing sonic novum in the book comes from Aldiss's development of literary technique from his research into the phenomenon of auditory stabilization. Aldiss cites the influence of Dr. Christopher Evans of the National Physical Laboratory and his study of the

Warren-Gregory effect, which described the effect of listening to words played repeatedly on an endless tape loop. In Evans's account, one of two things occurred: fragmentation (the loss of part of a word) or distortion (a new word appears to insert itself into the tape loop). Aldiss composed large sections of poetry and prose through this auditory technique (Sneyd 2010). The neologistic composition of *Barefoot in the Head* thus borrows directly from sonically triggered cognitive processes and puts them toward neosonic speculation in the material form of language. Aldiss's use of auditory stabilization makes the case for an alternative to Suvin's a priori form of novum, creating a new novum that feeds back into itself and, open to the cognitive noise that this feedback introduces, works that noise into the mix rather than filtering it out. In contrast to the totalizing novum of analogy and parable that Suvin postulates, this new sonic novum is highly contingent on immediate material context and play, and in this way it more closely resembles moments of actual historical change—the impact of hallucinogens on consciousness as well as culture—rather than their representation. Such moments, Csicsery-Ronay explains, aren't always products of organization and intention but rather may well be viewed as "undecideable events, capable of progressive, regressive, and even lateral or chaotic consequences, depending on their contexts of interpretation and their pragmatic issues" (2008, 54). The SF text, in this case, is the alien artifact.

Music historian and critic Ted Gioia notes that there is an entire branch of "linguistic science fiction," which combines inquiries into language's relationship to society with formal experimentation and self-reflexivity (Gioia 2012). Gioia is mostly thinking of works in which linguistics and semiotics become part of the fiction's speculation, such as Samuel R. Delany's *Babel-17* (1966), in which the weaponized language of the title transforms the learner's perceptions and thoughts; this is one of the first SF novels to include a poet and linguist as its protagonist. Stanislaw Lem's *His Master's Voice* (1968) tells of extraterrestrial messages and the rival team of linguists and scientists vying to translate them. But for all their extrapolations about language, these books mostly play out and read in familiar ways. It is uncommon to find written science fiction so devoted to neologisms that a new language thoroughly permeates the work, but notable exceptions like *Barefoot in the Head* and

A Clockwork Orange confront readers with both their unfamiliar scenarios and new forms of writing. Burgess's novel features the fictional Nadsat slang, a polyglot blend of English, Russian, and other elements drawn from sources ranging from the King James Bible and schoolyard puns to pop lyrics and advertising jingles. Presented through the first-person narrative point of view of fifteen-year-old Alex, the unusual language here both establishes character and creates the ambience of the fictional future through an intensive mesh of neologistic play:

> The Korova Milkbar was a milk-plus mesto, and you may, O my brothers, have forgotten what these mestos were like, things changing so skorry these days and everybody very quick to forget, newspapers not being read much neither. Well, what they sold there was milk plus something else. They had no license for selling liquor, but there was no law yet against prodding some of the new veshches which they used to put into the old moloko, so you could peet it with vellocet or synthemesc or drencrom or one or two other veshches which would give you a nice quiet horrorshow fifteen minutes admiring Bog And All His Holy Angels And Saints in your left shoe with lights bursting all over your mozg. (Burgess 2012, 7)

This excerpt is certainly still readable, and the neologisms either decipherable (e.g., *synthemesc*, "synthetic mescaline"), translatable (*veshches*, alluding to Russian *věšč*, "things"), or mostly understandable in context (prodding = producing). While pointing to its own evolution, or possibly devolution, the language is immediately striking as an artifact of the future even though this future is actually set in the past of Alex's reminiscence. It is further notable that, as text, "text" itself seems an outdated form for a generation that no longer reads, and we are to treat what we read in *A Clockwork Orange* as an oral, rather than written, testimony.

The drug-addled minds of Colin and Alex set the stage for consideration of a psychedelic sonic novum in cinema that, by and large, is more figuratively related to a broad transformation of consciousness in 1960s technoculture than to any literal, documented impact of hallucinogens on SF films. The most overtly psychedelic (barely science fictional) film is the "fifteen minutes into the future" hippie exploitation flick, *Wild in the Streets* (1968). Here, the fate of the United States is changed after a charismatic rock singer, Max Frost, rallies youth across the country and manages to get the legal voting age changed to fourteen. Frost is subsequently elected president, immediately retiring over-thirty oldsters to prison camps where they are prescribed mandatory daily LSD ingestion. Frost even enforces a dose on his mother (Shelley Winters), who freaks out and is left clawing at a chain-link fence. The film speculates partially on the revolutionary force of electric acid rock, and the 13th Power's major theme song, "Shape of Things to Come," echoes science fiction's past. Most of the soundtrack was not in fact composed by young garage rockers but rather by space-age bachelor pad veteran Les Baxter, and was performed by a variety of L.A. session musicians. The music is not at all futuristic but rather sounds exactly like the songs you would expect to hear from any number of West Coast garage bands in 1966–68. But the lyrics tell a different story, one about a "new sun rising up angry in the sky," "new dreams crowding out old realities," and a "revolution sweeping in like a fresh new breeze." Max Frost and The Troopers sing of an inevitable tomorrow that belongs only to youth.

Among the exemplary instances of the sonic novum that conclude this chapter, few ask us to listen more attentively and youthfully than the prerecorded musical selections that Kubrick used in *2001: A Space Odyssey*. Consider, for instance, the extended, slow-paced space station docking sequence. Kubrick chose Johann Strauss's "The Blue Danube," he explains, because it "gets about as far away as you can get from the cliché of space music" (Agel 1970, 88). While this specific recording ran the risk of being too familiar to some of the film's audience members, the director was confident that it would be heard differently not only in the context of the SF film but particularly among the young audience to whom the film would likely appeal: "Most people under 35 can think of it in an objective way, as a beautiful composition. It's hard to find anything much better than 'The Blue Danube' for depicting grace and beauty in turning" (88). The beauty of "The Blue Danube," its sonification of astronautic mechanics, typifies a kind of shutting up, which is not quite a shutting down, of the sonic tropes of the SF film as the director upsets and retools expectations for the science fiction film. This achieves a particular resonance within a film that repeatedly downplays or undercuts the spoken word, whether through the frequently extended scenes of silence or the gradual shutting down of the HAL 9000's voice synthesis function. Instead of adhering to the rules of cinematic semantics, in which sound enunciates things like emotional resonance, temporal flow, or expository meaning, Kubrick's audio works in a manner described by literary theorist Richard Doyle as a rhetorical adjunct for the turned-on ear. Discussion of multiple psychedelic evolutionary accessories pervades Doyle's *Darwin's Pharmacy* (2011), but here I want to emphasize his reading of the LSD experience in terms of voice, silence, and "an entire cosmos of sound" (114). For Doyle, the voice serves as the principal attractor for human evolutionary selection. Eloquence is a "rhetorical amplification" meant to attract the listener, and Doyle suggests that the psychedelic is an eloquence adjunct that silences the ego and allows for transhuman receptions, "a hailing by and hospitality toward an entity that is anything but human" (115). Citing psychologist Stanley Krippner's compilation of the many varied effects of psychedelic substances on linguistic functionality, Doyle suggests that language's inability to articulate the psychedelic experience must be met by a conceptual shift from speaking to listening. Listening—and particularly the ability to listen to sounds never heard before—is more important than the abilities of the human orator to speak in moments of transhuman exchange. "Listening, of course, is anything but passive," Doyle writes. "But nor is it a doing of the usual sort, and often involves the blockage of the self rather than its cultivation, a shutting up that is not a shutting down" (111). An adjunct to transhuman rhetoric, the eloquent psychedelic amplifies the ear, blocking the self, in order to facilitate the polyphonic subjectivities and temporal multiplicities that are the goal of poststructuralist psychotherapies and shamanism alike.

The sparse and almost inconsequential human dialogue of most of *2001*—the extended silences, the sounds of breathing, the HAL 9000 unit's artificial voice, the various vocal sounds of the hominids, and the final unintelligible whispering of aliens—conspire to silence the human ego in ways consistent with Doyle's analysis of the expanded ear:

> By dialing down the ego toward a vanishing point, human subjectivity is pulled inside out and the transhuman other broadcasts on that track usually labeled "interior" but whose very experience is itself contingent

on an opening to a state in which inside and outside dissolve: the ego, that static aspect of the self that knows what is possible and impossible, must lose its sound track, which dwindles to nothing but the "chattering monkey." (2011, 111)

The evolutionary potential that confronts the "chattering monkeys" at the beginning of *2001*, and resolves with a chorus of chattering aliens near the film's conclusion, is in fact heard in all three of the major SF films of 1968: Kubrick's *2001*, Roger Vadim's *Barbarella*, and Franklin Schaffner's *Planet of the Apes*. This sonic potential has everything to do with the shutting up of the conventions of electronic music as such and the concomitant turning on of new sonic novum as sites of engagement with the cosmos, the socius, and the affected body, each traversed by powerful transhuman forces. This chapter concludes with a consideration of the sonic novum involved in these three films relative to the technocultural forms that they upset. A dynamic expansion of sonic psychotechnologies, capitalist virologies, and alien hypersensitivities runs throughout this chapter's survey of the psonicosmos.

1959–63 | THE SOVIET GOLDEN AGE

Though Eastern bloc studios never produced films at the volume or rate of the Americans, their films did achieve a unique sophistication of visual effect and sonic ingenuity. The first was the work of the special effects cameraman Pavel Klushantsev, *Doroga k Zvekdam* (*The Way to the Stars*, 1957). With its voice-over narration, occasionally strident and jaunty, but ultimately inconsequential, orchestration, and some shimmering electronic cues during spacewalk scenes, the film plays like a Soviet counterpart to the George Pal productions *Destination Moon* (1950) and *Conquest of Space* (1955), as well as the "Man in Space" and "Tomorrow the Moon" episodes of *Disneyland* (1955). *Doroga k Zvekdam* went into production at the Leningrad Film Studios for Popular-Scientific Films in 1956, and it presents a stark ideological contrast to the corporate orientation that invests the pseudo-documentary realism of these American films with the spirit of industrial capital. But even underwriting its realism and scientific verisimilitude with Soviet nationalism did not completely protect *Doroga k Zvezdam* from a skeptical state film administration. Studio management and state authorities in Moscow advised the film's director to drop the project because "it had nothing to do with the 'everyday working people' and instead to make a popular-scientific film about increasing the crop yields of beets" (Kaminskij 2013, 275). Klushantsev persisted and would become the hero to SF filmmakers for years to come. As the film soared into theaters on the tail of the *Sputnik* launch in 1957, it resonated with Cold War reality in a way that *Destination Moon, Conquest of Space,* and the Disney films simply had not. Less science fiction than speculative documentary, *Doroga k Zvezdam* was the only Soviet space-related film to gain international distribution without Americanization. Though triggering anxiety among its American audiences about their country's inability to beat the Russians to space, and coinciding with a glut of predominantly lower-quality American SF/horror hybrids, *Doroga k Zvezdam* would inspire Stanley Kubrick, George Lucas, and Robert Skotak, the multiple Academy Award–winning special visual effects supervisor of *Aliens* (1986), *Terminator 2: Judgment Day* (1991), and *Titanic* (1997), among others (275). For its admirers, the film's convincing technological details, coupled with the recent exciting turn in space exploration heralded by Sputnik, overshadowed the incompatibility of its ideological factors with the foundational Cold War narratives, which cast a paranoid pall over America's SF films and their tendency to code the alien as a force of subtle infiltration or outright invasion.

As the '50s headed into the '60s, some of the most sonically adventurous science fiction films of the period include the Soviet films *Nebo Zovyot* (1959), *Planeta Bur* (1962), and *Mechte Navstrechu* (1963); the East German–Polish coproduction *Der Schweigende Stern* (1960); and the Czech film *Ikarie XB 1* (1963). In their original form, the last two rank among the most intriguing and sophisticated works of any SF cinema produced in the 1960s, and they make significant contributions to our growing catalog of compelling science fictional sonorous objects, primarily due to the role of sound and sonic artifacts within the films' narrative worlds. These films tend to be slow and thoughtful, and though there are elements of hard SF that recall Pal's *Conquest of Space* or Klushantsev's *Doroga k Zvezdam,* they are frequently underscored by a romantic tenderness that manifests in shots of natural beauty and song. Dialogue attains an occasional lyrical bent both poetic and philosophical. Generally, issues of history, society, and Cold War dynamics play out as realistic reference points in these films, rather than as the allegorical displacement that we experience in most American science fiction. The Soviet bloc films argue for the superior project of a socialist future, and they would consistently remind their audiences that only the Americans had been foolish enough to use atomic weapons of war. A broadly international sensibility of collaboration also characterizes the films, in which the Americans are not so much played as outright villains but rather as greedy capitalists with only their own financial investment and gain at stake, and whose shortsightedness is a source of bemused pity. But all of this is lost in translation, and not one of these films would be improved by its Americanization.

Once in the hands of their American distributors, the Eastern bloc films were edited down, overdubbed, repackaged, renamed, and "ideologically re-adjusted" (Kaminskij 2013, 280), losing much of their important sonic qualities in the process. To the utter detriment of their narrative contribution and thematic complexity, sound and musical content would be swapped out with little regard to a film's original score, while efforts to match the movement of lips to new English dialogue often resulted in a surreal disconnection from events and emotions. New musical cues, sound effects, and atmospheric elements pulled from library collections would frequently be recycled among the films of a particular producer. When Roger Corman bought *Nebo Zovyot,* for instance, he dropped the project in the lap of a young assistant by the name of Francis Ford Coppola, who, under the pseudonym Thomas Colchart, made his directorial debut with the film, now renamed *Battle Beyond the Sun* (1962). The Coppola film had little to do with the original. Corman was mostly interested in the quality of the visual sets, matte paintings, and special effects. Rather than having dialogue translated, Coppola's lip-synched script eliminated the framing narrative as well as the Cold War aspects of the original. America and Russia were replaced by generic states that had split the world into northern and southern hemispheres after a nuclear war. The characters were given Anglicized names. The cosmonaut helmet insignia was changed from CCCP to IIST (International

Institute of Space Technology). Many dialogue-laden scenes were cut entirely, and new interiors were shot with new American actors, whose parts were also often dubbed with new voices. The consequences for the film's original impact were dire. One somber and poignantly emotional scene takes place on an asteroid after the Soviets have made a well-intentioned but disastrous effort to save a stranded American. Coppola recalls the producer telling him to "jazz it up for American audiences," which he did by adding a pair of battling moon monsters that resembled male and female genitalia (Kaminskij 2013, 280).

The original version of Valery Fokin's *Nebo Zovyot* (*The Sky Is Calling* or *The Heavens Beckon*, 1959) blends documentary-inflected speculation around impending space travel with a more adventurous narrative; the story is framed as the dream of a young writer visiting a space research laboratory. Lectured by a professor and inspired by the model rockets and cosmic paintings of the professor's assistant, the reporter's reveries are launched into space with a crescendo of strings. The bulk of *Nebo Zovyot* is about a Soviet science mission to Mars that goes awry as a result of their overly zealous American space program counterparts. While both missions to Mars are scheduled to launch from a Soviet space station in orbit around Earth (the film is ideologically bolstered by Nikita Khrushchev's foreign policy of peaceful coexistence and fair competition), the Americans hope to beat the Russians to Mars. They ignore warnings of a meteorite storm and launch before they are fully prepared. The American rocket goes off course and heads toward the sun, and the Russians must turn their science expedition into a rescue mission, only to end up with both nations' crews stranded on the asteroid Icarus. After a failed attempt to use an unmanned rocket to deliver fuel to Icarus, a second Russian cargo rocket, supplied with fuel but also not intended for human occupancy, is piloted by a brave cosmonaut who arrives successfully, though at the cost of his own life.

In several scenes, *Nebo Zovyot* sonically pits Soviet science and altruism against American corporate capitalism. As the Americans rush to launch their rocket, wind instruments give the scene an almost comedic lightness before rising strings, bursts from the brass horns, and rolling timpani suggest the heaviness of the Americans' dangerous course of action. The score then takes a brief somber turn as the cosmonauts discover that their comrade has been injured on the launch pad during the rash takeoff; it is the very same man who will give his life to come to everyone's aid in the final rescue. Shattering this sad fade is a particularly cacophonous scene set in New York's Times Square as brash swing music and the braying voice of a TV announcer shares the news of the "sensation in space": America's rocket *Typhoon* is on its way to Mars even as the "stars are winking at our guys" and "The Big Bear constellation is waving with its paw!" Brilliant neon advertises the Mars Syndicate, which is selling off shares of land on Mars at ten dollars an acre, "so, so cheap," but sure to turn today's poor into tomorrow's millionaires. While an animated billboard shows a bubbly drink pouring from the tip of a rocket into a glass of sparkling bubbles, another announcer exhorts her audience to drink a new space cocktail, guaranteed after the second glass to deliver "the condition of total weightlessness" and render its imbibers capable of producing "only one sound: Drink. Drink. Drink." Finally, audiences are exhorted to tune in every thirty minutes for live transmissions from space, which are in turn interspersed with advertisements for the *Cosmos Typhoon* being read by one of the American crewmen. His commentary consists of comparing the sun to a "red-headed girl, smiling and welcoming our victory in space." Both scenes have their musical counterparts, first as the Russian mission launches and then during its aftermath, as news of the launch is reported to the Russian people. In the first case, rather than the prancing flutes and reckless thunder of brass and drums that accompany the Americans' frantic launch, the Russian sequence features an evenly paced anthem as the two cosmonauts pass a long line of their comrades in solemn procession. The music peaks in a moment of late romantic, Wagnerian passion.

Nebo Zovyot features the U.S.S.R. State Orchestra performing appropriately stately music, created by the Stalin Prize–winning composer of Kremlin-approved operas, Iulii Meitus. As Kaminskij explains, Meitus's score reinforces the film's plot with the "dramaturgical expertise" of socialist realist music; it is not only familiarizing but also functions in an "ideologically-tested" fashion (2013, 278). However, orchestral themes are not the only music heard in *Nebo Zovyot*. Once the cosmonauts are on board their rocket and have checked their instruments, we experience in real time almost the full minute of their countdown, scenes cutting between the rocket's cockpit and mission control, and during which we hear nothing but the metronomic click of the countdown clock. After the rocket blasts off, the musical score consists of an electric organ, its notes trembling with vibrato through a brief melodic sequence. All of these sonic events are fairly in keeping with scoring traditions and recall nothing so much as Glasser's work on *Rocketship X-M*. The most extraordinary thing happens as the scene shifts to a brief shot of Earth from space. All is silent for several seconds; then a simple little electronic tune begins to play, a calm call to attention, and we see a couple of images of the Kremlin. In contrast to the garish lights of Times Square, it is dusk in Russia, and statues and state buildings are seen in silhouette against the evening sky, reflected in water. Against images of the sunset over the sea, a spokesman from Moscow calmly addresses the rocket crew, "The Soviet people congratulate you on the space ship *Motherland*." Rather than the noise and bluster of the Americans' announcing their own rocket launch to an invisible radio and TV audience, the Soviets quietly thank their cosmonauts.

Where the U.S.S.R. State Orchestra provides the more traditional sequences of film accompaniment in *Nebo Zovyot*, Vyacheslav Mescherin and his Orchestra of Electro-Musical Instruments supplies music for the other scenes. Mescherin's career as an electronic musician began while he worked for state radio during the day and played with his colleagues late at night. First they attached amplifier pickups and microphones to balalaikas, accordions, guitars, pianos, and violins, and then they added theremins, electric organs, the thereminvox (Theremin's electronic harmonium, which brought more precise control to the original design), a vibraphone, and Andrei Volodin's complex, duophonic synthesizer, the Ekvodin, invented in the late 1930s but not commercially available until the middle of the 1950s (Maynes 2003). The Ekvodin was quite advanced for either decade. The pair of velocity-sensitive keyboards provided for precise and expressive playing, while other features included a touch-sensitive ribbon for glissando, a built-in reverb effect, and both automatic and player-controlled vibrato (Volodin 1997; see Smirnov 2013, 95–96). It is likely the Ekvodin that we hear during the most cosmic sequences of *Nebo Zovyot*, while in an earlier Soviet rocket launch sequence, brief shots of the space station feature music by Mescherin's orchestra. Rather than diegetically representative, these highly atmospheric passages are metaphorically suggestive of both the cosmos and the sophisticated, electrically powered technology required to get there in much the same way that electronic textures contributed to the earlier American films. Vaguely recalling the scene from *Rocketship X-M* in which a view of Mars was accompanied by the wavering tones of the theremin, when we first catch sight of Mars through the main portal of the Soviet ship, we hear a vibrato-laden chorus of human voices and then what sounds like a tenor voice, which brings a tone of mystery to the scene. Later, when Mars looms above the silhouetted forms of the cosmonauts stranded on Icarus, a trembling thereminvox or Ekvodin is played to maximum thereminesque effect along with a shimmering vibraphone, adding both cosmic atmospherics and a sense of technological mediation to the scene much as the Echoplex-filtered accompaniment does for the lunar vistas of *Destination Moon*. While the function of electronic sound works in similar ways in the American and Russian films, the significance of a Soviet electronics lies elsewhere.

Mescherin had apparently fantasized about a new Soviet sound since the mid-1950s, and his group had been around for only a couple of years before they were asked to contribute to *Nebo Zovyot*. Though initially derided and parodied, the ensemble was at the start of what would become a lengthy and popular career. Shortly after *Nebo Zovyot* premiered, Mescherin's orchestra would begin to create what reporter and radio producer Charles Maynes (2004) called the "quirky sentimental soundtrack to daily life in the Soviet Union" as Mescherin's space-age sound was played on the radio and could be heard in countless TV cartoons and films. Like Muzak years later, it was piped into factories, convention halls, and grocery stores. Mescherin's ensemble would even play live for Soviet troops in occupied Afghanistan, on nuclear submarines, and at Soviet outposts in the arctic (Maynes 2003). But well before the ubiquitous presence that Mescherin's group would achieve in all homely corners of Soviet life, his electronic sounds were explicitly born of the space age. In 1959, Mescherin was taken to KGB headquarters and commissioned to record an electronic version of "The Internationale" that would be "broadcast into the cosmos" as the recognition signal of the *Sputnik 3* satellite. This wasn't the first futuristic take on

"The Internationale"; the modern Russian composer Dmitri Shostakovich had arranged a version for theremin in 1935 for a patriotic film about the civil war (Kaminskij 2013, 279, cf. 20). But by the late '50s, the timing was right for a cosmic, electronic, and ultimately Soviet sound. When Mescherin met Yuri Gagarin in the 1960s, the cosmonaut apparently told the bandleader that he had heard "celestial music while orbiting the earth" and that it sounded "similar to those of electronic musical instruments." Likewise, Aleksei Leonov, the first cosmonaut to make a space walk in 1965, claimed that "the music made by the electro-musical instruments corresponded closely to his state of mind in outer space" (Kaminskij 2013, 279). A Soviet television documentary made upon Leonov's return included footage of the rocket crew and the space walk accompanied by Mescherin's orchestra. "The perception of Soviet television viewers," Kaminskij concludes, "along with that of the cosmonauts, was that the sound of the electro-musical instruments had virtually become the sound of the cosmos" (279). This is a state-sponsored psonicosmos, a turn of that quintessential, otherwise intangible index of outer space and psychic space into the approved ideology of the Soviet space program. The electronic sonic novum could be familiarized as the signature of the new even as it was underwritten by socialist realism and drawn into the state apparatus, where it would support not only the future of Russia but belief in a Russian future.

• • •

The ideological turn would not completely dispel the mystery of alien sounds and their capacity to draw the mind and the cosmos together through new psychotechnologies. Russian and other Soviet bloc movie production houses would feature sonic artifacts as part of their narrative devices, in part recalling the radio engineer Los of *Aelita,* and to realize these strange new sounds, they would draw upon the Soviet counterparts of Western Europe's and the United States' experimental radio studios and electronic music labs. Polish composer Andrzej Markowski, a contemporary of Krzysztof Penderecki, created the sounds of the alien sonic artifacts for Kurt Maetzig's *Der Schweigende Stern (The Silent Star,* 1960). Markowski and Penderecki worked in the Polish Radio

Experimental Studio, founded just a few years earlier, utilizing new electronic and magnetic tape editing technologies to discover what Barry (2011) calls "a new universe of sounds." Given the biographical portrait of Markowski in Andrzej Wajda's *Dyrygent* (*The Conductor,* 1980), the opportunity to create far-out sonic novum for science fiction films was likely a welcome escape for composers working "under the constraints of a nationalized culture industry" (Kaminskij 2013, 281, cf. 30). At the time of his work on *Der Schweigende Stern,* Markowski was seated as art director and principal conductor of the Kraców Philharmonic Orchestra. He had also founded a chamber orchestra for performances of new music, championing the work of challenging composers, both fellow Poles like Penderecki, and others from around the world. Markowski composed his own material for more traditional orchestral settings as well as for film, including several electronic pieces for experimental films. Finally, he is recognized as the first Polish composer to create concrete music for use in the theater (Oron 2012). His contributions to *Der Schweigende Stern* combine elements of all of these areas of his practice, ranging with great sophistication from stirring themes written in a late romantic style, patriotic music, and various electronic sound effects designed for use as diegetic elements.

A joint effort of East German and Polish studios, presented in German, and based on Polish science fiction writer Stanislaw Lem's *The Astronauts* (1951), *Der Schweigende Stern* presents a dramatic contrast to the Cold War–infused paranoia of the American science fiction of the 1950s, replacing the alien allegories of those films with a general basis in actual history. At the same time, like *Rocketship X-M* or *The Day the Earth Stood Still, Der Schweigende Stern* ultimately offers a cautionary tale against atomic weapons. Presenting a moment of international unity in the face of the first evidence of alien life in our own solar system, the story follows a team of scientists and academics drawn from all parts of the globe: a Chinese biologist and linguist, an Indian mathematician, a Russian cosmonaut and professor, and an American nuclear scientist. Logistic support for the mission is rounded out with a Polish engineer, an African TV technician and communications expert, a Japanese physician, and our heroic lead, Raimund Brinkman (Günther Simon), an East German rocket jockey and ace cosmonaut. The interracial crew of the rocket *Kosmokrator* represents an Earth united not by military force but through the cooperative spirit of scientific investigation and collective enterprise. A similar theme would be articulated in American SF with Gene Roddenberry's TV show, *Star Trek* (1966–69), which debuted six years later, although *Star Trek* doesn't play its own nationalistic legacies quite so literally. *Star Trek* also doesn't carry with it the historical weight that *Der Schweigende Stern* captures, set as it is in 1970 but with the American bombing of Hiroshima and Nagasaki still fresh in everyone's minds.

With its elements of alien linguistics and extraterrestrial recording media, *The Silent Star* proves to be anything but silent. Human communication in the film is regularly mediated by futuristic technologies: spaceship consoles, computers, and the communication devices that allow the *Kosmokrator* to communicate with moon station Luna 3 over an insistent underscore of Morse code and Klaxon calls. Sound in fact plays a remarkable role throughout the film. Narrative events are triggered when engineers seeking to irrigate the Gobi Desert discover a "cosmic document"—a magnetically recorded "spool" of otherworldly origin—that had arrived on Earth aboard a wrecked flying saucer that turns out to have been the real cause of the Tunguska meteor impact of 1908. A team of prominent linguists utilize the "world's largest computer" and eventually commandeer a space mission otherwise meant for Mars to decode the message and uncover its origins in a Venusian sound library. Some of the most intriguing sounds in the film are the reversed, modified, and electronically filtered voices that make up the content of this alien spool, which we hear as both the linguist–biologist and the mathematician run a language-analysis program on the *Kosmokrator*'s onboard supercomputer, the Marax.

Once at their destination, the increasing hostility of the Venusian environment is matched by the wavering audibility of the dramatic orchestration and its replacement by more unusual sounds and effects. Weird electronic elements proliferate through the soundscape and seem a product of the planet's atmosphere and the abandoned but still operative technologies of the native Venusians. As a large landing party arrives on Venus, a clicking Geiger counter pulses beneath a sustained, hovering electronic tone that evokes the theremin with its slightly melodic, solitary wandering line. Near the end of the film, louder and more dissonant orchestral music with occasional ascending bursts of electronic tonalities are cut with violent blasts of ambient wind. The combination of steamy bursts and howling wind, unsettling electronic tones, anxiously beeping equipment, and electronically modulated communications chatter anticipates the sonic tensions of Ridley Scott's *Alien* (1979). The crew finds evidence of planet-scale catastrophe on Venus. Elongated but humanoid shadows burned onto walls of buildings point to nuclear devastation. The investigators determine this to have been caused by a radiation weapon, now aimed at Earth, and which a clumsy move on the part of a crewman inadvertently triggers. An electronic interface screen in the control room—"a Venusian nerve center"—for the atomic ray weapon emits electronic sounds and manipulated voices, which take on a singsong quality that, when almost synchronized with the orchestral score, suggests an alien ghost chorus.

Der Schweigende Stern's narrative of "an alien civilization that overreached and destroyed itself" recalls *Forbidden Planet* (Erickson 2011, 162), particularly through its sonic association of variously chattering and bubbling electronic tonalities with alien artifacts and extraterrestrial atmospheres. As in the case of *Forbidden Planet,* it is frequently difficult to tell to which images the electronic sounds should be anchored, particularly the scene in which the pilot, Brinkman, encounters a nest of little chittering biomechanical creatures, alien spiders apparently made of circuits and wires. One of these emits two clear electronic tones as Brinkman catches it, and again later as he hands the captured creature to the linguist. Upon dissection, the little creature turns out not to be "a form of life" but rather a microcrystal. The device is fed into the Marax. Visualized on oscilloscope, a short sequence of bubbling and skittering electronic music and what sounds like backward, sped-up voices play over the ship's speakers. Recalling the sounds heard on the original alien spool, these are deduced to be the voices of the Venusians. The "strange metallic insects had a way of storing sound in their crystalline nuclea," the team linguist concludes; the Venusians use them "to record both speech and sound." These creatures are a historical record. As in the discovery of the spool and the living sound library, linguistic discernibility drives the narrative, frequently whenever ideas about hearing and comprehension, noise and language, butt up against alien technologies. As the Polish engineer Saltyk (Ignacy Machowski) speculates about a large, golf ball–like structure encountered on the surreal Venusian surface—"Is it life or a machine?"—the American professor Hawling (Oldrich Lukes) responds, "Can't say. No idea. Everything is so strange here. It's as if we tried to read a book in a foreign language. It'll take days. Maybe then we'll understand."

The Americanized version of *Der Schweigende Stern* seems particularly designed to thwart understanding across linguistic or cultural boundaries. Shorn of close to twenty minutes of footage, the Crown International production led by Hugo Grimaldi, *First Spaceship on Venus* (1962), comes across as nothing so much as an amalgamation that clumsily riffs off of previous American films. There is not only *Forbidden Planet* with its huge alien structures, still actively capable of devastation, outliving a doomed civilization, but a neighboring planet destroyed in an atomic war (*Rocketship X-M*), the space mission threatened by meteor storm (also *Rocketship X-M*), a dangerous spacewalk for inflight repairs (*Destination Moon*), as well as elements from *Conquest of Space* and 1954's robot film *Gog* (see Erickson 2000). "Perhaps," as Erickson (2000) writes, "this Eastern-Bloc space opera consciously intended to restate and transcend all the American space movies they had seen." More likely, these elements come across as more blatant borrowings due to the botched editing and overdubbing, which strips them of context, isolates them dramatically, and tosses out almost all of the character-building backstory and intrigues that had made this a compellingly human drama. The originality of Markowksi's score and sound designs are also lost. The electronic tones that, once on Venus, had provided a dense tapestry of new diegetic-blending sounds, in the remake mix abruptly with stock orchestral cues and themes accompanying fragmented scenes or bridging significantly recut footage. Much of the original score was removed and replaced by uncredited and unlicensed cues from previous science fiction films, including Leith Stevens's score to *Destination Moon,* Herman Stein's *This Island Earth,* and even pieces from Stein's cues and stingers composed for *The Wolf Man* (1941), as identified by Kaminskij (2013, 282). In his review, Erickson (2000) describes the new accompaniment as "an obnoxious needle-drop collection of stock cues that chimes in with a goofy comical tune for the robot and predictable 'oriental' music for the introduction of Sumiko." The more nuanced themes about song and sound that play such an important role in their original form are also targets of Grimaldi's "major film surgery" (Erickson 2000). In place of musings on the nature of language, which in Maetzig's film provide a unifying cultural force, the American variation emphasizes technical and meaningless space jargon and narrative exposition, much of it pilfered from older science fiction films as well (Erickson 2000; also see 2011, 160–63).

Unlike its American reworking, the original story is serious to the point of being somber and played that way, without a hint of the camp that led one early reviewer to quip in the pages of *Variety* that Venus was "no place to spend a summer vacation" (in Erickson 2000). With an astounding number of academics on the roster—the *Kosmokrator* boasts four professors among its crew—key characters are given emotional depth to go along with their complex intellectual sensibilities. The sexual tension between Brinkman and the Japanese medical officer Sumiko (Yoko Tani), the sole woman among the crew, is downplayed until finally laden with trauma—the death of Sumiko's husband on the moon, and her own sterility, induced by atomic radiation in Hiroshima. The involvement of the American nuclear physicist, Hawling, comes against the objections and interference less of the world party designing the space mission than it does of Yankee investors and businessmen, one of whom Hawling lambasts, "My dream is the stars, not your old dream, which was Hiroshima." The only thing close to comic relief in this mysterious and often grim film is the duping of Hawling by Saltyk, whose robot Omega continually thumps the competitive Hawling in chess. The real joke on this dumber-than-a-robot, overachieving American comes when Saltyk, at Sumiko's urging, reprograms Omega to lose at chess and so bolster the disconsolate crew member's morale. Finally, comradely behavior extends across the technical divide. Brinkman, the first of the crew to explore the surface of Venus, and Omega talk to each other during their survey. Omega's responses to questions and commands are little more than electronic chirps and trills, but these anticipate R2-D2's language, as the machine's intelligibility is established through little pitched sequences conveyed within emotively appropriate contexts, such as a descending set of notes to denote sadness or fear. Without a doubt, a Soviet suspicion of American interests and activities brings a very different ideological perspective to *Der Schweigende Stern*. Even when contrasted against the industry-fueled capitalism, hawkish attitudes, and paranoia of the American films, however, it is difficult to regard the film as "100% Soviet propaganda" just because of its frequent juxtapositions of "the futility of American aggression with the harmony of brother nations working in a common cause" (Erickson 2011, 161). America is continually berated, and the use of atomic weapons is repeatedly presented as proof of U.S. barbarity, though this can just as easily be seen as the source of *Rocketship X-M*'s pacifist protest. At any rate, the not-so-silent stars of *Der Schweigende Stern* are clearly language and sound themselves. In both of its versions, the film crystalizes issues regarding the transmission of meaning and noise across nationalist borders as the film in its original form exploits science fiction's capacity to uphold ideological perspectives while, in its Americanized response, translation, revision, vocal dubbing, and substitution of original musical cues and effects with generic counterparts become key components of a sonic weaponization of the remix.

• • •

Pavel Klushantsev's second feature science film for the Popular-Scientific Films division of the Leningrad Film Studios, *Planeta Bur* (*Planet of Storms*, 1962), involves another Soviet trip to Venus in which the Russian crew must once again help stranded American astronauts. Based on a novella of the same title by Russian SF author Aleksandr Kazantsev, the film realizes "a literary model much indebted to sound experiments" (Kaminskij 2013, 282). These experiments play a significant role as the astronauts of both nations face man-eating plants that sing, fight dinosaurs and dragons that can only be defeated by ultrasonic weaponry, and most significantly detect the mysterious voice of the planet itself over the microphones attached to their helmets. Sound also led to the film's condemnation and the end of Klushantsev's career. For the ideological error of having female cosmonaut Masha "cry in the cosmos and . . . lose her self-control in her hour of hardship," the U.S.S.R. minister of culture, Ekaterina Furtseva, made sure that Klushantsev would never make another feature film (Kaminskij 2013, 285–86, cf. 40). Kaminskij notes that while Klushantsev "de-ideologized the plot as much as he could" (283), downplaying the spirit of American–Russian cooperation in a way that neither *Nebo Zovyot* nor *Der Schweigende Stern* had managed, some of the most fascinating sonic aspects of the film consist of its smuggling in of ideologically suspect elements of American musical culture.

The film's score was the work of Leningrad composer Aleksander Chernov, while its sound design was largely the product of Mescherin's Electro-Musical Instruments ensemble. An educator as well as a composer, Chernov helped popularize jazz idioms in the Soviet Union, and in *Planeta Bur* is given an opportunity to write a little bit of swing music that plays from a loudspeaker mounted on the American's robot, John. Chernov also composed the film's title song, a pop number performed by actor and singer Vladimir Troshin, which became a hit in the Soviet Union. However, the voice of the planet is most striking. With Klushantsev hoping to create astounding sounds that would nonetheless be recognized as emanating from "the sphere of the feminine-magical and the exotic" (Kaminskij 2013, 283), the film also features the voice of popular Peruvian American singer Yma Sumac (known as the Queen of Mambo and a Hollywood icon). Sumac's famous four-octave vocal range was the centerpiece of Les Baxter's exotica production, *Voice of the Xtabay* (1950), though some of the most impressive moments of the album's vocals were later revealed to be the result of postproduction work by Baxter and his engineers. When Baxter found a short phrase that he liked but wanted to end the sequence on a high note that the singer would not be able to jump to on her own from the previous phrase she was singing, he made it happen by cutting and splicing the tapes (283–84, cf. 36). Leydon (1999) hears Baxter's work on *Voice of the Xtabay* as comparable to his earlier, prototypical space-age album, *Music Out of the Moon* (1947), claiming that the later LP "exploits Sumac's status as a kind of human theremin" (66). For *Planeta Bur*, Mescherin and his Electro-Musical Ensemble likewise took advantage of Sumac's vocal range combined with less than conventional editing. Rather than working with the singer directly, Mescherin manipulated recordings of

Sumac, editing and mixing her already "idiosyncratic vocal modulations" until they became the tones of the Venusian soundscape (Kaminskij 2013, 284). Mescherin then composed a melodic sequence for other instruments based on his tape mix of the Sumac recordings. His planetary music featured a theremin performance by Russian virtuoso Konstantin Kovalskij, an original member of Mescherin's ensemble whose part on *Planeta Bur* mimicked the taped arrangement of Sumac's voice, largely replacing the human vocal part with electronic overtones. Processed in both instances by magnetic tape editing that allowed the composer to achieve unnatural effects, Sumac's voice and the theremin ultimately reverse their relationship, going from Baxter's use of the exoticized folk instrument of the human voice as a kind of living theremin to Mescherin and Kovalskij's use of the theremin as Sumac's voice of the exotic Venus.

After contributing to the script of *Nebo Zovyot,* Mikhail Karzhukov went on to cowrite and direct with Otar Koberidze the SF film *Mechte Navstrechu* (*Toward Meeting a Dream,* 1963). Produced by Odessa Film Studio, the project enjoyed a bigger budget than previous Soviet SF thanks to the celebratory atmosphere that followed Yuri Gagarin's successful spaceflight. Like *Nebo Zovyot* and *Planeta Bur,* this film is also about a Soviet rescue mission, though instead of a rash American crew, the subjects of the rescue are alien visitors from the planet Centurion, who have crashed two spaceships, one on Mars and the other on Phobos, one of Mars's moons. Also recalling *Nebo Zovyot,* the rescue rocket piloted by the cosmonaut Tanya Krilova (Larisa Cordeichik) is damaged by a surge of solar radiation and lands on Mars, where it lacks fuel for the return voyage to Earth. This necessitates a second rescue mission, this time with Krilova's lover, Andrei Sayenko (Boris Borisenko), on board. Sayenko sacrifices his life while his comrade Ivan (Otar Koberidze) saves a Centurion female, Etinaya (T. Pochepa), from near death, then makes it to Mars, rescues Krilova, and returns to Earth. Though requiring a dear sacrifice, the success of Soviet cosmonautics translates into an uplifting and heroic tale.

Sonically, *Mechte Navstrechu* is most significant because it features for the first time contributions from the Russian composer Eduard

Artemiev, performing on the ANS synthesizer, a device invented by Yevgeny Murzin in the late 1950s that allowed the composer to draw his scores and create sounds with images and light. Inspired by the theosophical mysticism of Russian composer Alexander Nikolayevich Scriabin (the device takes its name from his initials), Murzin's technology allows for visually generated musical composition; the composer draws sine waves and other shapes onto glass plates, which are then read by a light-sensitive trigger. Artemiev would later work with director Andrei Tarkovsky on several films, using the ANS synthesizer to much more profound and provocative effect, especially in the 1972 film, *Solaris*. I will reserve my most substantial discussion of the ANS synthesizer for that film, which I treat in the next chapter. For *Mechte Navstrechu*, the ANS device is used to design the sound of a radio signal from another world. Just as the theremin had provided both a mobile, atmospheric halo around Klaatu and Gort in *The Day the Earth Stood Still*, and filled the alien home of Klaatu's spaceship, shots of the intriguing Centurion interiors, with dramatically lit spheres and various, mysterious technologies, are distinctly accompanied by Artemiev's atmospheric ANS score. While the aliens are mysterious, they are ultimately friendly; nonetheless, the Soviet-dominated Earth becomes a beacon of light, with gloriously scaled architecture seen in sunny exterior shots compared to the gloomy interiors of the Centurion spaces. Many of the structures on Earth are mythic in scale, dwarfing their human crowds with soaring statues, such as the lithe female form holding either a sun with rays or, more likely, a *Sputnik*-style satellite in one hand while the other lifts heavenward. Gigantic view screens allow for public address and a global broadcast of the triumphant rescue of the Centurion female. Sound drives the film's plot and characterizations. *Mechte Navstrechu* begins with an engineer receiving a mysterious signal from space, which is processed by a team of scientists. At the same time, daydreaming cosmonaut Sayenko shows off his iPod nano–sized Crystalphone to his lover Krilova, playing her a musical celebration of spaceflight. This remarkable Crystalphone attracts the attention of the alien Centurions. The Centurions are always silent as they slowly amble through the electronically bubbling and swooshing sounds of their mysterious interiors (homes seems too

218 • COSMOS PHILOSOPHY AND THOUGHT SYNTHESIZERS

generous a word). Summed up by Sayenko's ballad to the stars, earthly identity is essentially sonic and draws the alien to it through its hopeful and charming tonalities.

• • •

Possibly the greatest SF film of the Soviet studios is Jindrich Polák's *Ikarie XB 1* (1963), an adaptation of Lem's 1955 *The Magellanic Cloud.* Unfortunately circulated for years in its AIP variation, *Voyage to the End of the Universe,* this original film is in fact a prescient instance of the maturing of the genre that would culminate near the end of the decade with Kubrick's *2001: A Space Odyssey. Ikarie XB 1* is frequently, apocryphally considered an influence on Kubrick, which is certainly plausible considering the similar visual feel and pace. Particularly unfortunate given the nonsensical turns of the AIP version, *Ikarie XB 1* is intended to be sophisticated fare for adult viewers, a serious platform for a complex and critical set of intertwined stories about the various crew members aboard *Ikarie XB 1.*

With *Ikarie XB 1,* Czechoslovakia's Barrandov Studios showed that the kind of lavish expenditure that American studios only occasionally devoted to SF films could result not only in stunning visual design but also stories with complex character development, psychological depth, and a narrative sophistication that went far beyond the pulp orientation of most American golden age films. The deconstructed time line of the film starts out with the dark star radiation–crazed Michael (Otto Lackovic) running amok on the ship, threatening the mission, and observed calmly by other crew members through remote cameras. The ship's captain (Zdenek Stepánek) recollects the launch from Earth, and we have seventy-five minutes of flashback until we return to Michael and his space madness. Numerous subplots, including the romancing of the already married Bridget (Irena Kacírková) and a pregnancy would take the film from space to soap opera in less able directorial hands, but here these narrative threads contribute to a film that explores the everyday nature of existence in space, which will also include extended sequences in the gym, dining facilities, and a dance club. AIP dropped all of these plotlines while also eliminating what few anti-Americanisms were present. The ones that were there were significant and serious, as the film also takes place in the shadows of American use of atomic weaponry, though without the heavy-handed dialogic processing of *Nebo Zovyot* and *Der Schweigende Stern*. On their voyage to Alpha Centauri, the *Ikarie's* crew comes across a derelict vessel from Earth. Once on board, the investigators discover the American crew of the *Tornado*, a military craft from 1987, long dead, attired in decadent bourgeois evening clothes. An apparently armed quarrel over cards and gambling had deadly results for all. To the investigators' further shock, they find that the *Tornado* has a payload of nuclear devices and chemical weapons bearing names like "Tigger Fun." An accident by the *Ikarie* away team causes the derelict craft to self-destruct.

Ikarie XB 1 is compelling sonically. As Robert Barry (2013) notes, composer Zdeněk Liška's score turns SF-scoring conventions on their head in the opening title sequence, mixing orchestral and electronic tones until they are almost indistinguishable. Throughout the film, the composer uses acoustic instrumentation in diegetic space, almost as a sound effect, "while the electronics carry the tune." In its reach for realism and plausibility, *Ikarie XB 1* is also about evolving musical sensibilities. Music is thoroughly integrated into the life of the *Ikarie's* crew. Four months into the voyage, the crew's morale is low, and few go to the gym anymore. As music begins to play over the ship's loudspeakers, the crew leaders host a dance with dinner jackets and formal dresses. Some crew members drink and sniff a vapor drug that contains scents and memories of Earth ("November?" "Earth!"); others dance to musical styles that are at once hip and routine, slightly sexy while also cultured, "a sort of dissonant future mambo" that works within the overall eclecticism of the score's mixture of impressionist passages with "tense late romanticism," droning strings and electronics, and "furious machine rhythms" (2013). The dance music is familiar yet different, slightly off beat, evoking through its difference a kind of nostalgic gap that a more straightforward incorporation of familiar music and dance steps would not have achieved. Likewise, when one crew member on board the American *Tornado* discovers a grand piano with a vaguely futuristic design of a pair of wings for its lid, he picks out a few chords of Arthur Honegger's strikingly modern composition, "Le roi David." Rendered as such a brief fragment, the tune is at once challengingly eclectic and lyrically beautiful; it comes across not as modern but as part of distant antiquity.

There is a good deal of silence, or at least of open, reverberating space, in *Ikarie XB 1*. This is a space in which nostalgia breathes, or is breathed in, though life aboard the *Ikarie* has become something of a general condition without many specific links back to Earth history other than a few references to war crimes, Hiroshima among them. Beyond a sniff of Earth scent, a snippet of Honegger, or the derelict American craft, there is little in the film to remind us of Earth in any substantial way. No mention of governments or religion or other institution provides a backstory for this twenty-second-century voyage to Alpha Centauri. Without such reference points, the film takes on a mythical aspect as it depicts the spaceship's voyage to a White Planet in orbit around that star, its path through the dangerous domains of a radiating Dark Star, with all the madness and death it would bring upon the crew, and the saving graces of the White Planet's benevolent alien race, which shields the crew at last and greets their arrival just as a baby is born aboard the *Ikarie XB 1*. Erickson points out the uncanny foreshadowing "of *2001*'s staring Star Child" and of the pitched emotion of awestruck faces and rapturous score that concludes Steven Spielberg's *Close Encounters of the Third Kind* (Erickson 2011, 202). These new beginnings are both dulled and upended by the American version, *Voyage to the End of the Universe* (1964), which shortens the closing musical theme and cuts most of the shots of the wonderstruck faces. The spacecraft is recast as an alien vessel of unknown origin, searching for the Green Planet. The encounter with the derelict *Tornado* is also revised, no longer depicting an American spaceship but something that can be vaguely dismissed as the primitive craft of an ancient militant civilization. The ending becomes a real shocker as well, with the spacecraft arriving at the Green Planet, which of course turns out to be the Earth, as confirmed by a grainy shot of the Statue of Liberty on one of their ship's monitors. All roads lead to America, which ambiguously recasts the crew of the *Ikarie* into alien invaders, a device that AIP would recycle in their update of the Italian film, Mario Bava's *Terrore Nello Spazio* (*Planet of the*

Vampires, 1965). Without either the silence of space or the grandeur of Liška's closing themes, the dread and hope of mythic human spacefarers, the film is overwhelmed by an awful and nonsensical revision. That this new version is credited to the direction of "Jack Pollack," and then copied by a 1965 Robert Lippert production, *Spaceflight IC-1*, shows just how deaf the Western world was becoming to Soviet innovations in the field. With its weak mutiny plotline, a disturbing subplot in which the ship's captain attempts to make a pregnant passenger abort her baby for vaguely defined medical reasons, and a completely inconsequential hack of a score, we have truly arrived at the dead end of the universe.

In his analysis of this largely overlooked era of Soviet SF films, Kaminskij points out that while these films "developed promising and innovative approaches toward creating an acoustic identity of the genre" (2013, 287), their subsequent Americanization instead reinforces an unfortunate realization first noted by Sobchack (1987). With rare exceptions, American SF appears to be "disinclined toward experimental electronic music" (Kaminskij 2013, 287). Its filmmakers tend to treat music as a familiarizing force, while sound effects prove the exception and allow for a defamiliarization that is, nonetheless, at the same time and for all practical purposes aestheticized and anesthetized by being magnetized strictly to the diegetic world. Interestingly enough, the Cormanization model of recycled footage and familiar sounds does not change this basic dynamic of American SF as we head through the 1960s. On the other hand, the reliance on overdubbed and other piecemeal content, rarely presented in a unified way with the original narrative, has surprising consequences that involve the innovation of new audiovisual production practices: namely, the emergence of postproduction editing that relied on new sound and film editing technologies allowing for the rapid repurposing of existing content and other elements to be reused in new productions. Soundtrack and visual content are split, with the latter occasionally "requiring" revision, such as the elimination of CCCP logos from space helmets or the replacement of a female lead because the original actress looked "too Russian" for American viewers, as Kaminskij describes it. Moreover, newly recorded voice-over and dubbed dialogue erased and replaced unwanted ideological content.

What is perhaps most perplexing in the case of these revisions is that even "the 'non-ideological' electronic music of the socialist films was interfered with significantly . . . [and] replaced by a mere compilation of existing soundtracks consisting of classical Hollywood orchestrations" (Kaminskij 2013, 288). This erasure was not typically followed by the addition of American ideologies beyond that of erasure itself and the pragmatic repurposing of cheaply appropriated content for financial gain. This results in what Kaminskij calls "a type of cinematic fast-food" (288). This "exploitative integration" (285) of Soviet bloc films—which are relatively more sophisticated and sensitive than their American counterparts, especially so given the requirement of ideological compliance and the threat of censorship—forces them into the lowest bracket of SF film production in the United States.

Planeta Bur would suffer greatly from its Cormanization at American International Pictures. It was first cut into Curtis Harrington's (as John Sebastian) *Voyage to the Prehistoric Planet* (1965), with new sequences shot for the remake along with new music culled from Ronald Stein's score to the low-budget 1960 film *Dinosaurus*. Other snippets from *Planeta Bur*—and some of the same ones, for that matter—would join outer space and rocket sequences from *Nebo Zovyot* and yet another Soviet film, *Mechte Navstrechu*, to become Harrington's 1966 film, variously titled *Queen of Blood*, *Planet of Blood*, *Planet of Vampires*, and *The Green Woman*. Initially a story of peaceful alien contact, *Mechte Navstrechu* begins when alien eavesdroppers overhear an Earth woman singing to her lover. In his remake, Harrington cuts the opening premise and makes a vicious alien vampire film. *Voyage to the Prehistoric Planet* was later recut into the *Voyage to the Planet of Prehistoric Women* (1968) by Corman's protégé, Peter Bogdanovich (credited as Derek Thomas), who also combined space footage from *Nebo Zovyot* and *Mechte Navstrechu*, and added several sequences featuring young women from Carillo Beach, dressed as mermaids, including Miss Palm Springs 1948 and former Universal Pictures sex symbol Mamie Van Doren. By the end of the 1968 film, Van Doren's voice is added to the Sumac–theremin hybrid in a scene that exemplifies the most "dubious practices" of overdubbing and resynchronization but also, Kaminskij rightly notes, of cultural relations and business ethics (287). With *Queen of Blood* and *Voyage to the Planet of Prehistoric Women,* we witness the decline of American SF cinema that would make Kubrick's *2001: A Space Odyssey* such an unexpected shock in 1968, premiering just four months after *Voyage to the Planet of Prehistoric Women,* which would also be the last of the Corman films built mainly from Russian footage, though by no means the last of his exploitative cinema.

As they lay claim to Soviet SF films, Roger Corman's variously named production companies, along with AIP and Crown International, foster what Goodman calls "predatory brand environments" (2010, 131). This space is not rendered audible through an open conflict of cognitive estrangements meant to reinforce incompatible nationalistic vectors but rather by the total fracturing of "ideas, beliefs, and values" (131). The shattering and pilfering of Soviet films negates the translation of their cinematic language and other sonic innovations by means of a capitalist predation that can no longer even be labeled ideological. To ruin a great, or even just a decent, film demands both an engineered sonic infection that negates the sonic texture of the original film while also adding further decontextualized sound cues that result in the complete disruption of the inherent, designed "rhythms, frequencies, and intensities" that sound otherwise provided the initial cut of the film (132). The point here is not that music and sound simply mean more in the original Soviet films—with or without their initial ideological premises, promise, and shortcomings—for certainly "their intensity" was already "transduced by regimes of signification" (132). As they become Americanized, however, these films lose the flexibility of a complex sonic glide across the realms of cinematic perception, affect, and being, and which they had previously engaged and enjoyed in much the way of their American golden age counterparts. This restriction of sound manifests at least partly as an inability to glide across the visible edits of the film, a function that sound typically performs as a way to generate continuity across scenes. Perhaps the greatest consequence of the radically cut up and reassembled nature of the Americanized Soviet SF films is that their scores and sounds become as inconsequential as the material they join, which effectively fixes each sonic moment in time as nothing more than a functional bit of sound that has little, if anything, to do with the bits of sound before or after it. This strategy of conceptual and material isolation, the nailing down of each thing in its place, is fundamental to the American colonization of audio space.

At the same time, we witness in the Cormanization process an early form of studio composition, dub, and remix culture that is hard to completely villainize because it emphasizes the useful elasticity of the relationship between audio and visual content, and it valorizes the act of postproduction as a highly creative space in its own right. Musician and producer Brian Eno would point to parallel developments in popular music production during the mid-'60s as the technical edge of studio practice increasingly shaped the aesthetic and compositional sensibilities of musicians. In his reflections on "Ambient Music" (2004a), Eno writes of this initial era in which "psychedelia expanded not only minds but recording technologies as well. But there was still an assumption that playing with sound itself was a 'merely' technical job—something engineers and producers did—as opposed to the serious creative work of writing songs and playing instruments" (95). For the "recording composer," a new class of producer who is at once sound editor, designer, and engineer, the studio itself becomes a kind of musical instrument or, in Eno's case, a tool with which to realize "the distinguishing characteristics of new music" made possible by recording technologies that explored "the development of the texture of sound itself as a focus for compositional attention, and the ability to create with electronics virtual acoustic spaces (acoustic spaces that don't exist in nature)" (95). Recording detaches sound from its source and space, removing the recorded sound from its original ambience and location and thereby making it available anywhere. Magnetic tape takes this in a more specific direction, making the recorded object distinctively more malleable than, say, a vinyl disc recording. The emphasis on both sound texture and virtual acoustic ambience has a common effect "that takes music out of the time dimension and puts it in the space dimension" (Eno 2004b, 127). This effect transforms composition completely. Recording takes the essentially improvisational elements of a live studio performance and lends them a sense of compositional significance, purpose, spatiality, and continuity that they may not have had originally, as Eno heard in Teo

Macero's productions of the electric Miles Davis records. Rather than simply postproduction editing or mastering, the work of Macero and later Eno himself constitutes a form of "in-studio composition," where the use of studio equipment for sound editing, effects processing, mixing, and overdubbing all get tied up in there own improvisational assemblage of material: "You can begin to think in terms of putting something on, putting something else on, trying this on top of it, and so on, then taking some of the original things off, or taking a mixture of things off, and seeing what you are left with—actually constructing a piece in the studio" (129). Problematic as they are for their crass exploitation of appropriated materials, the Corman and other distribution groups nonetheless were also participating in this newfound compositional space in which the edit became a creative gesture in its own right. We encounter a similar practice of composing films and film sound through studio assemblage, though with significantly more sophisticated and challenging results, in the pair of SF films of the French new wave to which we now turn.

1962–65 | *LA JETÉE, ALPHAVILLE*

Two of the most adventurous SF films of the 1960s are products of the French New Wave, Chris Marker's *La Jetée* (1962) and Jean Luc-Godard's *Alphaville* (1965). Experimental in form and subject matter, these auteur productions were made outside of the hierarchical economies of the French film studio system and managed to dodge the wary eyes of French state censors, who had aggressively cracked down on anything that might contribute to the social and political tumult of the era. Both Marker and Godard had films banned during the peak of state censorhip around the colonial wars in Algeria. In 1953, Marker's short film collaboration with Alain Resnais had disparaged French colonial exploitation of African cultures, while his sympathetic portrayal of the Cuban revolution in the 1961 documentary, *Cuba, Si!*, was deemed "ideological propaganda" and "a menace to public order" by the film board, which feared that the work might incite similar upheaval in the French Carribean; their letter, signed by the Minister of Information, accused Marker of treason (in Hilliker 2000, 4). Godard's 1960 film, *Le*

Petit soldat (*The Little Soldier*), was banned for references to torture in the Algerian conflict. In his astute analysis of the two SF films, largely neglected in scholarship on the New Wave, film historian Lee Hilliker suggests that Marker and Godard turned to science fiction for similar reasons and as a direct consequence of their run-ins with the national film review board. Both films constitute deeply personal sensibilities through original narratives that "speculate on the shape of a future French society" (2), in which manipulation by technocratic order plays out in imaginatively oblique ways. The first takes place after a nuclear war has ravaged Paris, and a cabal of scientists goes to any ends necessary to save their class at the expense of their less fortunate, imprisoned test-subjects; the other takes place in a sterile, automated future in which civilization is programmed and managed by a vast computer and its various machine and human agents. Both films also demonstrate a degree of formal experimentation not seen before, and rarely since, in science fiction cinema. Surprisingly, Hilliken talks only obliquely about the sound designs of either film. In fact, their creative sound design, especially the unusual placement and sequencing of sounds, contribute substantially to the distinctive assemblage and overall effect of these films.

Though different in overall tone, narrative, theme, and speculation, both *La Jetée* and *Alphaville* feature a sonic experience that is fragmented and disjointed, arranged according to a predominately sequential and diachronically singular sensibility rather than multilayered, sonically synchronized and made cohesive either by being shared among or clearly distributed across diegetic boundaries. Sound is disconnected from the visual content in ways that multiply rather than diminish the dimensions of our audiovisual engagement with the films. I would argue that the films anticipate Eno's insight into compositional mixing in the recording studio, which I discussed earlier, and run parallel to William Burroughs's extensions of the cut-up text to image, film, and sound editing. Both films establish the capacity of the SF film to manipulate the flow of time, radically spatialize perception, and alter consciousness by exploiting the instrumentality of studio composition.

In Marker's *La Jetée,* the manipulation of time and the altering of consciousness pose dilemmas for its unnamed protagonist (Davos Hanich), prisoner of a group of scientists seeking to recover from the nuclear devastation of the Third World War. Forced to conduct time-travel experiments, the prisoner is selected because of his powerful, even obsessive memory of a woman (Hélène Chatelain) whom he had once noticed on the jetty of Orly Airport just before seeing an unknown man die there. The scientists believe that the strength of their prisoner's memory might protect him as they try to send him into both the past and the future in search of resources and assistance. Once the prisoner travels into the past, he meets the woman of his memory and they have a brief relationship that is disrupted by the scientists sending him into the future. After successfully attaining a future power source that will help rebuild his civilization, the prisoner realizes that the scientists plan to kill him. The prisoner rejects further assistance from the people of the future and returns to the prewar past instead, in search of the woman at the jetty. Tracked by an assassin sent by the scientists, however, he realizes too late that the death he had seen as a child was in fact his own murder.

In this short film about the psychotechnology of memory, Marker goes to unusual lengths to explore the capacity of the cinematic apparatus to affect memory and our perception of time. By creating a fragmented form of still images, Marker deconstructs the usual flow of film and disrupts our sense of cinematic time in ways that reflect the unusual experiences of the prisoner, whose time-travel experiments cut back and forth throughout episodes in his life, from childhood to death, all linked together not by clear causality but in repetitions, dislodgings, and staggering returns. The sound is mostly disjointed as well, consisting of a disembodied voice-over narration, extended silences, a record album (choral music), library music (orchestral cues), and isolated heartbeats, whispering voices, and birdsong. The film begins with a few seconds of black screen accompanied by jet engine noises, followed by the first still image of Orly's observation deck. Because Marker zooms out rather quickly, the opening shot appears conventional and the sound natural. But when the image freezes, we realize it is a still photograph. As the first titles appear, and the jet engine sounds morph into a solemn, requiemlike piece performed by the Russian Orthodox Cathedral Choir of Paris, it feels more like something has just ended than begun. Throughout this title sequence, slight fluctuations and occasional drops in volume reveal the recorded object as an artifact, and an aged one at that, before the phonographic sounds and still photograph of the airport fade out together. Conducted by Piotr V. Spassky, this particular recording of "Tropaire En L'Honneur De La Sainte Croix" (from *Musique Liturgique Russe,* 1957) will return, several minutes into the film, when we see images of a devastated Paris; in reality depicting the damage caused during World War II, here the historical images are used to illustrate the devastation of the nuclear war that occasions the film's imaginary future. The repetition of such recognizable artifacts, like this recording of the Russian choir, is essential to the film's logic of return.

Back to the initial shot at Orly, an introductory voice-over sets up the narrative, reading the text that covers the screen against a stark black and silent background, and we then return to still images of the airport and again hear sounds that seem natural in this context—in this case, the isolated voice of a woman making an announcement over the airport's public address system. But after the narrator begins to speak over these announcements, then becomes the sole source of sound, the film holds onto the image of a young woman's face for more than twenty seconds, one hand held at her lips, her hair blown by the wind. The long shot of this image serves to lodge it into memory even though we do not yet understand its significance. What is of particular sonic importance in these first several minutes is the relationship that Marker establishes between his unconventional use of still images and isolated sound events. Rarely do we hear sounds layered on top of each other, with the exception of the voice-over that occasionally speaks over another sound. For the most part, sounds are as singular as a photographic still: a heartbeat, a whisper, the narrator's voice, and the musical cues consisting of the selection of Russian liturgical music or the stock compositions of BBC composer Trevor Duncan heard during the park and museum scenes ("The Girl (Prologue)" and "The Girl (Theme)," both from the Boosey & Hawkes sound library, early 1950s) as well as the time travel sequence near the end of the film ("Vastness of Space," from The New Concert Orchestra's *The Challenge of Space,* 1954). Romney (2007) points out that Duncan's library music—"Eerie, romantic, and obsessive in its repetitions"—always seems to be heard from afar, from a distant point in space as well as from the past. These sound objects stand out less as sonic events and more as constructed artifacts, frozen in their isolation and artificial enhancement: the heartbeat could only be heard over a stethoscope, the whispers by the unusual proximity of lips to a microphone, and the album on a record player. As the film progresses, sounds become increasingly unmoored from specific relationships to the still images. While by its nature sound flows in ways that the images do not, the audible events and music do not ground the movement of vision, failing to provide transitions between images or smooth over visual cuts. The sounds of *La Jetée* also do not help the audience navigate between diegetic and nondiegetic experience as everything collapses into the distance of recorded artifacts and memories. Alteration to the speed of transition from one still image to the next in fact does more than sound to determine *La Jetée*'s pace—a function usually given over to the musical score—as in the scene near the end of the film when the protagonist rushes toward the realization of his own death (and his having witnessed his death as a child), as well as in a scene showing the woman's eyes opening so quickly that the flickering illusion of traditional motion film is almost achieved.

The unconventional assemblage of *La Jetée* resonates with Marker's previous experience making short documentary and travel films. Certainly *La Jetée*'s reliance on still footage and voice-over bring with them a documentary-like atmosphere, while the narrative suggests the particular skills of the documentary filmmaker, embodied in both the protagonist's ability to obsessively focus on an image and the film's exploration of the image as site of trauma and concealer of otherwise hidden sociopolitical process (in this case, the imprisonment and assassination of the prisoner by an agent of the scientific cabal). Considering *La Jetée* a particular variation of Marker's autobiographical travel films of the 1950s, Hilliker argues that the film reverses the time of the image, which in the travel film usually comes after the journey; the documentation of a place and time resigns both geography and event to the past and holds them in safekeeping, as artifacts, for a future in which that space and time may be destined to disappear. In *La Jetée,* however, the image not only permits travel to past and future alike but also can be said to originate the voyage in the case of the lingering photographic shot of the woman on the jetty near the start of the film. As both documentary agent and its subject, "the bearer of the image," the prisoner, becomes the "voyager . . . in this documentary on the future," even while he is "subject to manipulation by elements beyond his control, and his ability to fixate on an image from the past makes him a pawn in the struggle for the control of history" (Hilliker 2000, 6). The images of the woman's face and the death of the man become triggers for travel into a past that is just as active and mysterious as the future. The structural disconnections between image and sound facilitate and reenact these slippages and reversals of time. Given his emphasis on the ways that Marker destabilizes the formal integrity of experience in the event of time travel, it is particularly surprising that Hilliker doesn't address the function of sound in the film.

Marker's use of sound recordings, the artificial and isolated nature of which emphasize their presence as isolated sonorous objects, hardly provides the kind of continuity and familiarity of traditional film music and sound. Whittington (2007) is correct to point to the important role that sound plays given the fragmentation of the image, though crediting the sound track with the narrative structure and "formal unity of the images" (62) suggests a more conventional function than the experience of *La Jetée* warrants. Contrary to Whittington's claim that *La Jetée*'s sounds "unify and comment on the imagery" (2007, 63), sound in fact takes place in another world and time altogether and so obeys the disjointed sensibility of the still imagery and the narrative. The narrator's commentary and other sonic events in *La Jetée* create a gap between image and sound, and this gap is the space in and through which the time traveler loses his moorings in the present and shifts into the past that is also a future, and vice versa. While the powerful images stored in memory function as a psychotechnological anchor to the prisoner's past, sounds are vehicles for distance, a launch pad into the future, and agencies of travel that cause slippages through time. Sound adds value to the images here not by fixing them in space but by loosening them, so that even the potentially diegetic sounds (of the airport, the heartbeat, the whispering voices) come to us far removed from the sources that made them, which we hear as if across vast gulfs of time, in memories yet to come. Hilliker makes the rather astounding but convincing argument that given the degree to which Marker's own images, films, and documentary work had become "subject to control by state powers beyond his influence,"

La Jetée provides the artist a space of expression that is "part metaphorical autobiography, part traumatic sociohistorical allegory" (12). Marker has developed, by combining the semantic codes of science fiction, documentary, and travel films, "a process that effectively renders the film unrecognizable as a threat" even as it facilitates "a subtextual space" in which artist and audience can meet in mutual understanding beyond the threat of the censor (12). Given the dire consequences of events for the film's protagonist, and the film's narrative and structural resolution of a paradox through a kind of doubled death that is at once a coming together and an erasure, we are left with questions about the prisoners of the technocrats, those who can still "imagine or dream another time," as the narrator characterizes them. Against the pessimism of the film's narrative and its narration, the fragmented sonorous objects provide the subdiegetic space in which a message is transmitted, even if a broken one, that eludes censorship with the stealth of an antinovum, a contest of historical allegory that has voided its own history, but which actualizes our apperception of the new in the now.

• • •

Jean Luc-Godard's *Alphaville: A Strange Adventure of Lemmy Caution* (1965) also expands the expressive capacities of science fiction cinema through a powerfully fragmented form of audiovisual poetics. As in Marker's film, the gaps created in moments of disconnection between audio and visual content resist the totalitarian omnipresence of the technocratic system, and in this film about the barely escapable automatization of language and human behavior, the fragmented sound design becomes a primary force of elusion through its unpredictability. This strategy is fragile, however. Where fragmentation in *La Jetée* ultimately allows formation of a subdiegetic zone that slips below the technocratic censure of temporal immobility, the ubiquity of the Alpha 60 computer that controls Alphaville is combined with an inability to see and hear it completely, which turns fragmentation into a tautological force of control within what is not so much a totalitarian but, if you will, a "fragmentarian" state.

Examining the potential dangers of computerization and cybernetic control, *Alphaville* combines elements of film noir and science fiction within a "future is now" urban environment. The film avoids the traditional tropes of the popular science fiction of its day—there are no rocket ships, flying saucers, aliens, or robots—and lands somewhere in a world of pulp, comics, and serials that the SF genre had mostly left behind in 1950. The hard-boiled detective lead, Lemmy Caution (Eddie Constantine), is especially out of place, driving from the Outlands to Alphaville in his interstellar cruiser, a Ford Galaxy. *Alphaville* can be viewed as a critique of an already dehumanized present, represented by the cold modern architecture of Paris, the gloomy industrial districts, and computer rooms and recording booths, while Caution's gear—his Galaxy (actually a newer-model Ford Mustang), pistol (a M1911 Colt Commander), cigarette lighter, and Instamatic camera—suggest that the hero hasn't so much traveled from the 1960s into the future but from the 1940s into the mod '60s. *Alphaville* drops this bare-fisted, tough-talking pulp detective into a scenario that recalls nothing so much as Franz Kafka's stripped-down worlds with their mysterious bureaucracies and George Orwell's omnipresent, totalitarian state in *Nineteen Eighty-Four* (1949), but played like a decidedly parodic, occasionally slapstick comic strip of a film.

Alphaville's narrative revolves around Caution's undercover mission as secret agent 003, disguised as a journalist, Ivan Johnson, working for *Figaro-Pravda*. Caution hopes to track down another agent from the Outlands, Henry Dickson (Akim Tamiroff), who has gone missing in a seedy hotel on the outskirts of Alphaville. Caution is also gunning for Professor von Braun (Howard Vernon), the creator of the generally unseen, but frequently heard, Alpha 60 computer. Alpha 60 has outlawed love as well as freedom of thought and expression, and it has banished poetry, music, and the arts. Showing signs of emotion is punishable by public execution, with criminals shot, then dropped into a swimming pool where synchronized swimmers finish them off. Other groups of undesirables are executed en masse at movie theaters, while the riffraff are allowed to waste away in poverty, strung out on drugs and alcohol, and goaded to kill themselves in the cheap hotels along the perimeter of the city. Organized with the impeccable logic of the machine, Alphaville is divided according to social classes with their own internal hierarchies, such as various levels of the Seductresses, each tattooed with a different number, and features carefully regulated zones of artificial night or day and fixed temperatures. The harsh voice of the Alpha 60 computer can be heard anywhere at any time, while neon signs flash mathematical formulas like "$E = mc^2$" and traffic signals constantly appear in an overbearing fashion, typically taking over the entire screen while accompanied by a blasting fragment of the musical score or harsh, isolated noises. Following Dickson's lead to Professor von Braun, Caution navigates this strange new world and eventually meets the professor's daughter, Natasha (Anna Karina), who he gradually deprograms as he engages Alpha 60 in verbal contests, kills the professor, and eventually destroys Alpha 60. Caution and Natasha leave the inhabitants of Alphaville in a collective daze as the city comes to a standstill.

Godard's genre-mashing film relies heavily on the mystique of Lemmy Caution, already a well-established character that had been portrayed by Eddie Constantine to popular acclaim in France since 1953. Originally an American FBI agent, then later a private detective, Lemmy Caution was created by British writer Peter Cheyney in 1936. The character's popularity was solidified through numerous media outlets—books, radio, and film—around the world: ten Lemmy Caution novels were published in the U.K. between 1936 and 1945; his radio series ran in Australia and New Zealand throughout the 1940s; and seven European films were made before Godard deconstructed the character (and actor Eddie Constantine) in *Alphaville*. According to Constantine, Godard purposefully projected Caution into "a future world with which he was unable to cope" in order to "kill off" the character. "And we succeeded too well," Constantine concludes; "I never worked again in French films" (Darke 2005, 22). This is not entirely true, as Constantine would reprise his role in a made for TV movie in the late 1980s and appeared in what would be his last turn as Lemmy Caution in another Godard film, *Germany Year 90 Nine Zero* (1991), where Caution disconsolately wanders around a recently reunified Berlin. Without a doubt, as *Alphaville*'s "strange adventure" subtitle claims, the film was a major departure for Lemmy Caution. Before Godard got hold of him, Caution had been strong and upbeat, an against-all-odds kind of pulp character who never shied away from a brawl and always got the girl, or two, or

234 • COSMOS PHILOSOPHY AND THOUGHT SYNTHESIZERS

three. While he did these things as well in *Alphaville*, he comes across like a parody of the trench-coated Bogart, dumpy, depressed, worn out and spaced out. Constantine had starred in a more traditional Lemmy Caution film only two years earlier—the French–Italian film *Your Turn, Darling*—but he seemed to have aged at least ten years by the time *Alphaville* was in production. Godard turned Caution into a monochromatic comic strip character, namechecking a lineage that included Dick Tracy and Guy Leclair (the French name for Flash Gordon), both of whom we find out had disappeared during their own earlier missions into Alphaville.

The transformation of Lemmy Caution is accomplished in part by Godard's transporting the detective into different genre settings that present him not only as a cartoon spoof of earlier incarnations of the character but also a vehicle for sophisticated reflections on cybernetic technocracy and an update of the myths of both Orpheus (see Darke 2005, 19, 94–96) and Prometheus (Silverman and Farocki 1998, 60). In the form of poetry and cigarette lighter, Caution bears the ancient gifts of music and fire. Godard's treatment of the pulp detective is at once a purification and a reduction to essence, Darke suggests in his discussion of the film, noting that Godard often referred to Constantine "as being like a 'block,'" and all the extraneous pediments that attached to Lemmy Caution—the whiskey, dolly-birds, and punch-ups—are either stripped away or thoroughly remodeled by the director" (2000, 20). Constantine was perplexed by Godard's approach, which often treated his character as more of a prop than protagonist. "He was shooting, but without a story," Constantine recalls. "So, for three days, I was walking the streets of Paris alone in my hat and raincoat and he was doing panoramic shots of the ultra-modern buildings of La Défense" (in Darke 2005, 20). Where Constantine described the "Lemmy Caution formula" as "five punch-ups and three girls," Godard had Caution shrug off a trio of Seductresses and, like Orpheus, single-mindedly pursue his sole love interest in a chaste and poetic relationship. The requisite fight sequences are also reduced to almost nothing, with one rough up in an elevator simply showing Caution knocked about by invisible blows, and a brawl in a hotel bathroom is shown reflected in a mirror. The popular actor's existing French audience was also alienated by the experimental cinematic contexts of *Alphaville*. Godard reflected in 1965, "I really can't see how my films could work [with the public]. I've the impression of doing exactly the opposite of what people want" (in Darke 2005, 22). Though there are still fisticuffs, and though Lemmy still gets the girl, he does so thanks to poetry and being in touch with the sensitive core of his own flawed humanity. Upon rescuing his Eurydice, Natasha, from the hell of Alphaville, it is Caution who tells her not to look back at the city of the dead as they head out on what he calls their "night drive across intersidereal space" and to home (Darke 2005, 94). While flipping the Orpheus/Eurydice relationship on its head, maintaining the dynamics of the tough-guy and dame relationship is less important than Caution's teaching Natasha the meanings of "conscience," "tenderness," and "love," while his assassination of her father, the villainous computer programmer von Braun is similarly less consequential than the verbal gymnastics that short-circuit the Alpha 60 computer, proving at last that poetry beats logic and death.

Like Marker in *La Jetée,* Godard "transposes his social critique to an allusive, traumatized futuristic version of contemporary Paris while avoiding direct representation of contemporary political material" (Hilliker 2000, 12). In this film, mythological subtext and "a volatile genre mix" of science fiction and film noir, with its high contrast black and white shots, mostly captured in the city at night, evoke the film's polarized extremes of not only good and evil, even life and death, but also of the human and machine, poetry and computer logic, and sound and silence. Sound in *Alphaville* works on several layers, and whether diegetic noises and voices or nondiegetic score, sonic events frequently disrupt and alter the film's narrative flow. When taken on its own terms, the film's score by popular French composer Paul Misraki fulfills the tropes of the noir source material with music that is on occasion romantic (both Misraki's "Thème d'amour" and "Valse triste" ride on achingly beautiful strings) and at others dramatic (such as the repetitive horns and drums that begin "La ville inhumaine," heard first during the film's opening titles). Even though Misraki's music was composed for *Alphaville,* the titles of specific pieces suggest the most traditional of library cues, but in either case, Godard mixes the music in a completely unconventional manner, cutting against the image in unsettling ways and often starting and stopping the cues in what seems to be a completely arbitrary manner. Musical cues are often used in Godard's work with such brevity at any given time that they fail "to bring purely musical codes into play," and even when played at length, "the music is too separate from the action to allow conventional cinematic musical codes" to function as we expect (Cormack 2006, 27). While the nondiegetic music heard in *Alphaville* may lack the "added indeterminate meaning" that recordings of classical composers and free jazz musicians brought to Godard's later "fractured thriller-comedy," *Détective* (1985), they resist both emotional and cognitive determination in ways that are consistent with Godard's aesthetic of sonic disruption and fragmentation.

The noises heard throughout *Alphaville* behave according to a similar aesthetic. Abrasive electronic beeps, like Morse code, blurt out throughout the movie, often interrupting dialogue. These sounds have no apparent, visible source, but like the various flashing neon formulas and signs, they may be construed as auditory evidence of the ubiquitous presence of Alpha 60. Just as startling is the sudden dropping out of sound altogether, which happens so abruptly that it seems as if something has gone wrong with the film itself. Such moments strike me as the most self-reflexive in the entire film. Not only do they foreground the activity of watching a film but they also foster an atmosphere of instability and worry, both mirroring the unexpected demise of the unassimilated audience of foreigners who are electrocuted while visiting a movie theater in Alphaville and anticipating the breakdown of the machine that will conclude *Alphaville*. All of these sound practices go against the grain of standard cinematic editing practice, which typically "consists essentially in the art of smoothing rough edges by degrees of intensity" (Chion 1994, 42). Godard was already challenging this dominant sensibility in the early 1960s, and his style of sound editing can be construed as a "demystification based on discontinuity," cutting sound and images in ways that reveal their existence as discrete units, which the practices of fades, cross-fades, dissolves, and other mixing strategies typically hid. "Godard unmasks conventional sound editing," Chion concludes, "all the more in the way he avoids the usual practice of mixing many tracks at once such that our attention is not grabbed by breaks and cuts in the sonic flow" (42–43). Instead, isolated sounds, often foregrounded through sudden jumps or drops in volume, emphasize the unnaturalness of their relationship to the cinematic image; rather than fostering the "appearance of continuity and transparency," they disrupt the temporal flow as well as the space of cinematic experience (42). Where sound in cinema would provide a sustained flow as well as a rhythm to the visual experience, Godard's sounds obey the same logic of cuts, ruptures, and sudden jumps that are more common to cinema's sequencing of the moving image.

Godard's rejection of sound editing conventions suggests the development of a language of sonic fragments—what Chion calls a sound shot—that resist not only each other but also the images to which they would usually become attached. There is little spatial magnetization of sound to image in *Alphaville*, in part because the sounds work so much in their own space, but also because sonic events within this space cannot be attributed to specific sources, causes, locations, or triggers. In this context, Darke's analysis of Godard's visual architecture is useful. The "strangely elastic sense of space" that Godard achieves through partial shots and reflections, such as we find in Lemmy's hotel room, creates a sense of "off-screen space that is pregnant with possibilities" (2005, 62). Cinematic "dislocation" (Michelson 1971) and disorienting visual perspectives (Roussel 1989) "combine to suggest another, potentially infinite, off-screen space" (62). I am surprised that Darke does not discuss sound here, as it contributes significantly to the development of the potentiality and possibility of this space beyond the screen. This is where Lemmy's noir-inflected voice-over comes from but where Lemmy never is, so to speak. It is also the nonlocation of the Alpha 60's voice, which is also simultaneously nowhere and everywhere. Both voices are typically presented against moments of stark "silence, as Godard empties the soundtrack of dialogue, music and ambient sound" (Chion 1994, 48) in order to set up the sound shots. I am interested in how the sound shot functions as a nonplace.

Working from the ethnographer Marc Augé's concept, Darke suggests that all of Alphaville has become a "non-place," the "transitional space such as one finds in airports, service stations, supermarkets and hotels. These are spaces devoid of ancestral features, historical associations and private meanings—all the things that combine to give 'space' a sense of 'place.' Non-place is full of signs, instructions, advertising and images. Non-place serenades the stroller with piped mood music" (33). While the architecture of cinematic spaces arguably resists the voiding of context that affects actual nonplaces, because of their necessary function within narrative dynamics, the labyrinthine "patchwork of transitional zones—corridors, staircases, offices, hotel rooms—liberally interspersed with their characteristic signage" that we encounter in Alphaville warps the city beyond the space of the screen and into the unseen domain of sound, which tends to come to us with all the apparent lack of purposeful connection as the contents of the "jukebox that sits incongruously in the corner dispensing soporific mood music" (34) during Caution's bathroom brawl, likewise incongruously set in the mirror.

The creation of the space of isolated visual and sonic fragments coincides with the emptying out of that space, turning the domain of lived human experience into a dimension that really exists nowhere at all. Chion seems reluctant to conclude that Godard successfully achieves a sound shot, a specific unit of sonorous object that resists the temporality that tends to dominate our perception of sound. "What strikes the listener instead is the dynamics of the break between the two fragments," Chion writes. "The explanation of this mystery is that when we talk about a [visual] shot we are lumping together the shot's space and its duration, its spatial surface and its temporal dimension. While for sound pieces the temporal dimension seems to predominate, and the spatial dimension not to exist at all" (1994, 44). Chion confronts what I perceive to be an essential paradox in Godard's approach to sound editing in *Alphaville*, which simultaneously creates a specific, disconnected space for sound, and yet a space that is also a kind of nowhere, like the Outlands from which Lemmy Caution appears from across intersidereal space and to which he returns, leaving Alphaville behind him.

The nature of the sound shot is not only commensurate with that of the sonorous object, which according to Schaeffer is equivalent neither to the means of its production, the method of its transmission, nor the apparatus of its hearing, but also the science fictional novum. As Jameson explains, the novum embodies the utterly new characterized by an "absolute and intrinsic unpredictability" (1972, 126). But to the extent that its newness is so unpredictable, the novum is also immaterial.

Materialization or actualization into lived history short circuits the novum's potential. Even as it embodies utopic energies, the novum thus figures the limit and failure of utopia. O'Donnell (2007), writing about Jameson, emphasizes that the failure of the utopic novum is "necessary for the form itself, and it is this failure that points to the limits of representation and the empty place of the not-yet. The utopian text is therefore a simultaneous revealing and concealing of contradictions." This describes the condition of the sound shot in Godard's *Alphaville*, where the sonorous object does not magnetically ground the image so much as it reveals the limits of sound's representative capacities. Alphaville, the imaginary city, is a utopia, which strictly defined means "nowhere" or "no place" rather than "good place" (Darke 2005, 23). *Alphaville* the film is the utopic deconstruction of the imaginary city, reveling in the various irreconcilable contradictions and oppositions that underwrite as well as undermine it. The chief characteristic of the utopic text is that it is "a failed amalgam" of incompatible elements (O'Donnell 2007), what Anthony Burgess suggested would better be called "a cacotopia—on the lines of cacophony. . . . It sounds worse than dystopia" (in Darke 2005, 24). If we recall that the essence of the novum lies in its relationship to liberatory, utopic possibility, then the novum, like the utopian, is "a mode of thinking structured by various oppositions," which has implications for understanding the role of textual as well as sonic, or cacophonous, forms:

> The overt purpose of the utopian text, to imagine difference, really conceals its true function, which is to delimit the present. The value of the utopian for Jameson is that it enables us, against the text's own overt intentions, to gauge these limits, thereby opening up the possibility of an awareness of that which can be neither thought, nor imagined, except as an empty possibility, namely the novum. (O'Donnell 2007)

Form, according to O'Donnell, opposes content in the utopian text, contradicting that which is represented by playing in the space of formal possibility. But as Zepke (2012) points out, there are limits to the usefulness of Jameson's approach to the utopic novum, represented by his claim that rather than keeping the future alive, SF's "deepest vocation is over and over again to demonstrate and dramatize our incapacity to imagine the future" (Jameson 2005, 288–89). This fundamentally pessimistic way of knowing the world is the quintessential element of utopian fiction, which can at best only "succeed by failure" in revelation of our "our own absolute limits" (289). As I have noted, Zepke's analysis refutes this position, arguing that SF requires—and in fact makes possible—not only a new but an inhuman future, without which we are condemned, as Nietzsche writes in *The Genealogy of Morals,* to a "present lived at the expense of the future" (2006, 7–8). How the cacophonic enables the realization of the sonic novum beyond even the nonplace of utopia is our immediate concern.

Reconsideration of the familiar human values that SF tends to uphold—particularly its valorization of scientific and technological forms of knowing the world coupled with a utopian rendering of the impossible future as a critique of the present—allows for a shift away from the epistemological pessimism that underwrites Jameson's critical project. In contrast, Zepke (2012) moves SF toward an "ontological optimism . . . far beyond humanity's epistemological frame or the formal analysis of science fiction." Here Zepke shifts SF criticism away from its investment in cognitive estrangement and toward theories of affect and posthuman becoming, which will reconfigure the genre's ability to engage "the appearance and political efficacy of the future." Zepke points to the love scene in *Alphaville,* featuring Caution and Natasha, in which Godard's "narrative formulaically rehearses the classic dystopian scenario pitting human emotion against the coldly rational machine, [while] the film's aesthetic construction works against these critical allegiances." The scene is a strange one. In voice-over, Natasha recites bits of poetry derived from Paul Éluard's *Capital of Pain,* Misraki's love theme playing quietly underneath it. In a series of extreme close-ups, Natasha and Lemmy stand alone and stare straight into the camera, lit from behind or against a blank gray, nondiegetic backdrop, or almost stiffly embracing, with frequent fades to a completely black screen. We already know that Natasha barely understands the vocabulary of love, much less the emotion, and Godard is hardly concerned with action at all. Rather, this is the emotional/emotionless equivalent of the fighting action sequences, in which actors freeze in a dramatic pose, caught in a series of snapshots, rather than engage in fisticuffs. Zepke claims that this scene presents "not an *alienation* of the image but rather its *abstraction*. It does not carry with it a meaning that could resolve the dystopian opposition of man and machine, of logic and love; instead, it uses this opposition to construct a strange and beautiful sequence without cognitive or emotional coherency; not the representation of the new but its actual emergence." The love scene works in neither the realm of diegetic representation nor the space of the formal device, according to Zepke, opening instead "onto the outside of the rational logic of *Alphaville* (as dystopian society and as diegetic film) but which has nevertheless been produced by it. The abstraction leading to a new future is in this sense a method rather than a program or a formal device. We do not know what the future is because the future is precisely that part of the now that has no being, but only rather a becoming." The simultaneous emptiness and excessiveness of the scene situates it both beyond the narrative and the form of the rest of the film, becoming an abstract moment of poetry functioning as an equivalent to the nowhere space of the sound shot. The nonplace of Natasha's voice-over facilitates this movement beyond the cinematic space here as in other voice-over sequences in *Alphaville*, which insert gaps into the narrative and form that use emptiness as a way to signal their strange relationship to sonic bodies that are ultimately incongruent to the film.

The computer blips and beeps that are frequently interjected over bits of dialogue suggest this strangely nonlocative sound and the difficulties that it poses for hermeneutic approaches to *Alphaville*. Do these sounds simply point to Alpha 60's ubiquitous monitoring of human activity throughout Alphaville, as Whittington argues (2007, 65)? If so, why do the characters never react or respond to these interruptions and the surveillance that they represent? These sounds might not be specific signs of surveillance (their randomness belies their diegetic purposefulness) but merely indicate the omnipresence of Alpha 60, something so everywhere that it might as well be nowhere. If these sounds are nondiegetic events that are inaudible to characters in the film, then we have to consider the ways in which they interfere with the audience's perception of the action and reception of the dialogue, functioning as a kind of cacophonous control mechanism that orders reality through the nonsensical by means of a rational program of unexpected disruption. Or do

242 • COSMOS PHILOSOPHY AND THOUGHT SYNTHESIZERS

they implicate a degree of control so far beyond the human that it only seems irrational as a result of our limited points of view and audition? Perhaps this random cacophony is an act of directorial resistance against the forces of control embodied by the Alpha 60 and therefore part of the potentially liberatory elements of the film that are in turn embodied by Lemmy Caution. Such questions cannot be resolved, in large part because there is neither space nor place for their resolution.

Few sonorous objects expand beyond the categories of diegesis and nondiegesis as completely as the voice of Alpha 60. The computer speaks in a series of amplified gasps, gurgles, belches, and croaks, which are in fact produced by an uncredited man whose larynx had been destroyed in the war and so speaks from his diaphragm (Silverman and Farocki 1998, 60–61). These are not the sounds of "a man with a mechanical voice box replacing his cancer-damaged larynx," as erroneously claimed in Darke's study of the film (2005, 39)—not, in other words, the product of a cyborg voice—but rather the production of a human body that stretches our conception of what we mean by the artificial voice in the first place. In a comparison of technocratic sonic utopias, David Metzer (2003) pits the "dead voice" of Alpha 60, which "had become almost inhuman," against the "world of pure electronic sound" (153–54) underscored and resolved by the steady, amplified, and technologically manipulated breathing of Karlheinz Stockhausen as a conclusion to his union of electronic music and musique concrète, *Hymnen* (1966–67). Metzer highlights the disruptive eventfulness of the breathing that produces the words of Alpha 60, provocations never resolved beyond their function as sonic irritation, and the steady, wordless breathing of Stockhausen, which ultimately resolves the various electronically produced sounds, both synthetically generated and magnetically taped and edited, of his sonic utopia, Hymnunion. Despite the timbral differences in these instances of artificially accentuated breath, there are marked similarities in the sonorous objects. Chion's description of the voice of Alpha 60 as "closely miked, cavernous, and out-of-space (i.e., impossible to locate spatially)" can just as readily apply to the closing breaths of Stockhausen (2009, 332). Technologically enhanced in the mixing process, Stockhausen's breathing exceeds the pattern, rhythm, and length of most normal human breathing, even in meditative states, particularly with the unnaturally combined inhalations without intermittent exhalations (Metzer 2003, 153). But herein lies their difference from the gulping voice of Alpha 60. Where the breath of Stockhausen draws the listener into the sonorous body, the guttural sounds of Alpha 60 expulse from the body, at once turning the breath into an artificially regulated apparatus even while attaching it to a damaged body. Something similar is achieved in the sound space between apparatus and body in Marker's *La Jetée*, in which the sound of the heartbeat links the present time of the scientists with the prisoner's past and future. Only across great temporal distances, however, can we associate the sound of the heartbeat and the body that contains it with the images of the mind, dissociated and out of time. Within this nonplace gap we experience not a critique but an avoidance of censure.

As is the case in Marker's *La Jetée*, sound synchronization and the unity of sound and cinematic image are no longer desirable in Godard's film. The expulsion of magnetic connection between sound and image allows the filmmaker to create suggestive audiovisual events that, through their disconnection, allow for the possible interaction of cacophonous elements. The forces of potential becoming, of the emergence of possibility, exceed being. For Marker, the methodology of the potential of the nonplace has to do with his explorations of memory, which collapses in a gap between sound and image to become a hidden zone of becoming beyond censure. Marker's emphasis on the sonorous artifact, like the visual artifact of the photographic still, in a work that slips provocatively critical messages past the disapproving eye of the state's film review board, proves fixity to be an illusion of the object in time. Godard is less concerned with time than with issues of control in space. *Alphaville* both expresses and resists rational order while putting the mind and body in touch with irrational processes and intuitive emotions. This is the straight line that moves in a circle, and the nonplace essence or meaning of Caution's riddle. Both Marker and Godard are concerned with the relationship of the body to the spoken word. Both destabilize that relationship. Whereas Marker and his unnamed narrator are at war with the controlling capacity of technocratic command, whispered in secret murmurs, Godard's Lemmy Caution valorizes the word's poetic properties not because of what it means but because of its interpretive ambiguity and potential. Throughout the film, Lemmy Caution's narration, a staple of film noir, competes with the voice-overs of Alpha 60, and there are conflicts between the poetry recited by Natasha and Alpha 60's aphoristic speech (much of it appropriated from the work of Jorge Luis Borges). *Alphaville* is ultimately a contest of voices, and Lemmy Caution slowly breaks down Alpha 60 by answering its questions as an aesthete:

> ALPHA 60: Do you know what illuminates the night?
> CAUTION: Poetry.
> ALPHA 60: What is your religion?
> CAUTION: I believe in the inspirations of conscience.

A simple question asked by Caution during this exchange, a question in response to a question, becomes another riddle that sticks with Alpha 60 throughout the remainder of the film: "I admit I might have reasons to lie, but how can you differentiate between lies and truth?" Though Godard quickly opted not to stick with his first title, *Tarzan versus IBM,* we shall remember this poetic tough guy, whose direct confrontation of Alpha 60 is nothing like astronaut Dave Bowman's tender dismantling of the HAL 9000 that we will soon encounter in Kubrick's *2001: A Space Odyssey.* Erickson (2002) points to the reappearance of this trope of the tough guy verbally outwitting a supercomputer through philosophical trickery and sociopolitical conundrums in episodes of *Star Trek* and the existentialist spy thriller *The Prisoner* (1967–68). But something else is going on here. Rather than trying to prove his own philosophical or sociopolitical perspective, much less answer his own question, Caution at last poses a living riddle—something like, "Do you accept our proposal?"—before riding off with Natasha, his "pretty sphinx," a phrase repeated multiple times in the film, but not in order to prove his human superiority but by making the machine aware of its own misfortune as Caution's imperfect equal. Some things are best left unspoken, some riddles unsolved.

1966 | *FANTASTIC VOYAGE*

The Disney-ride aesthetic of the 1966 Cold War SF thriller *Fantastic Voyage* was probably not what science fiction writer J. G. Ballard meant when he asked which way to inner space in his editorial for *New Worlds* magazine, the flagship publication of the British new wave. The film's early psychedelic vibe comes from the Academy Award–winning lava lamp–alicious set design, the mod scuba wear, and the occasionally unhinged twelve-tone score by popular composer Leonard Rosenman. As SF cinema goes, *Fantastic Voyage* not only feels like a Disney production, but it also shares director Richard Fleischer with Disney's classic Jules Verne adaptation, *20,000 Leagues Under the Sea* (1954). But with Raquel Welch in her skintight explorer's suit and groped by seaweed, *Fantastic Voyage* feels like a sexed-up variation of the undersea adventure played out inside the human body. Equipped with a miniaturized submarine, the *Proteus*, and laser operating tools, a crew of five is injected into the bloodstream of their comatose patient, Dr. Jan Benes (Jean Del Val), a Soviet defector with information that will help the Americans get ahead in the inner space race by allowing their miniaturization technology to work for indefinite periods of time. After a failed assassination leaves Dr. Benes with a blood clot in his brain, the rescue crew and ship are shrunk with the current technology, which limits miniaturization to a single hour. Against a doomsday clock, the rescuers must navigate the weird and frequently hostile terrain of inner space on their way to the brain where they must perform their sensitive operation.

Fantastic Voyage begins with a short sequence of weird electronic tonalities during the opening credits. These tones establish that the cinematic experience is science fictional, perhaps thought to be necessary in a film that initially plays its narrative of Cold War espionage and intrigue so close to the reality of its contemporary audience. The next forty minutes of the film are largely devoid of science fictional elements, visually and sonically; sounds are stark and diegetic, and it is absolutely silent where we might expect musical accompaniment and cues. This was Rosenman's plan: silence until the miniaturized submarine is injected into the comatose body of the defecting scientist, when the transformation of visual scale is matched by a tonal shift into dissonant twelve-tone composition. Given the technical sheen and hyperrealism of the opening sequences of the film, that there should be music inside the body at all is the real surprise. But that the music should be so musical is just as surprising. More than an atmospheric transformation, the

246 • COSMOS PHILOSOPHY AND THOUGHT SYNTHESIZERS

score emphasizes a structural change of tone that gets at the heart of sound's physiological intrusion. Compared to the other kinds of Western music, twelve-tone composition possesses a startling sonic precision; this precision of movement from note to note is even more unfamiliar in the science fiction film, which by 1966 still tended to feature the kind of gliding lines and unsteady sustains of the theremin, or the blurry, shimmering notes of something like the Novachord or electric organ. Rosenman's score evokes instead mathematics and computation through a spectral miniaturization of tonality to match the narrative's processes of microcosmic perception and action. Along with a change of scale to match the change of the crews' bodies, the musical composition also reorganizes the psychological atmosphere of the crew through its various phases of physiologically triggered wonder, horror, fear, and awe. This is emblematic of psychogeographical discovery in SF cinema, which ambient music amplifies as a way to create psychological analogs for the genre's unusual worlds.

Science fiction film music negotiates the relationship between the psychological states of characters and audience during their encounters with new and unknown landscapes and their inhabitants. In *Fantastic Voyage,* the body becomes a hostile alien domain, something that the music achieves through its atonal chromatics. *Fantastic Voyage* wasn't Rosenman's first foray into atonality. He composed his first twelve-tone score for *The Cobweb* in 1955, the same year he scored more traditional themes for *Rebel without a Cause* and *East of Eden.* But for Vincente Minnelli's *The Cobweb,* the edgy and unfamiliar sounds of twelve-tone music took the place that the theremin had occupied in the psychological thrillers of the previous decade, bringing a remarkably disturbing edge to the otherwise innocuous new window drapery that triggers so much interpersonal dysfunction when installed in a psychiatric asylum. We hear a similar approach to dissonance and unusual mental states in Jerry Goldsmith's score to John Huston's *Freud* (1962), which links atonal sequences to the destabilized psyche revealed through surreal dreams and hypnotic fantasies. To Goldsmith's chagrin, Ridley Scott would later substitute bits of the *Freud* soundtrack in lieu of new material that Goldsmith had written for *Alien* (1979), the consequences of which are discussed in the next chapter.

As it shifted from psychological thrillers to science fiction—again, much as the theremin had before it—twelve-tone music brought the charge of the unfamiliar to a particularly earthbound science fiction of the mutants among us. We hear one characteristically atonal tag in a 1963 episode of *Outer Limits*, "The Man with the Power." The episode has more than a coincidental sonic link to *Fantastic Voyage*, dealing as it does with experimental brain surgery and featuring the actor Donald Pleasence, whose characters are more than they seem on the surface. In "The Man with the Power," Pleasence plays a mild-mannered and harried professor who discovers that he can focus Earth's electromagnetic field into beams. Fueled by conflict with his overbearing wife, disastrous consequences come when his suppressed anger manifests as psychic attack. Before each outburst, an unsettling bit of dissonant music played on string and brass instruments presages the frightening psionic damage. Twelve-tone composition is a fitting choice for invisible psionic/sonic attack, evidenced by physics as much as culturally reinforced ways of listening. In Ross's (2007) discussion of twelve-tone innovator Arnold Schoenberg, the writer attributes the occasionally apocryphal accounts of riot and scandal of concerts by Schoenberg and his students Alban Berg and Anton Webern to "the physics of sound" itself (60). Atonality emphasizes the harmonic intervals that composers had believed to attack the ears physiologically since at least the 1863 publication of Hermann von Helmholtz's *On the Sensations of Tone as a Physiological Basis for the Theory of Music.* Helmholtz attributed harmonic variations to the interactions of multiple sound waves at varying intervals, creating pulsating "beats" that either please or perturb the ear with "a sensation of 'roughness'" (in Ross 2007, 61). The rapid beats produced by semitones were thought to be particularly distressing, which Helmholtz likened to strobing light or a scrape on the skin (in Ross 2007, 60). Semitonal assaults proliferated through the work of twelve-tone composers and are potentially the cause of infamous revolts in Europe's most hallowed concert halls. While hardly the psychedelic exploration of psychic interiority that Ballard and others in the new wave envisioned, Rosenman's score for *Fantastic Voyage* anticipates the extent to which SF filmmakers would generally reject new electronic sounds, and even sound altogether, in their creation of sonic novum. As we head toward the end of the 1960s, the silence of outer space becomes especially stark against the precision of twelve-tone compositions and the skin crawling smear of atonal overtones, all of which we will experience in Kubrick's *2001: A Space Odyssey*. As far as *Fantastic Voyage* goes, the film's most sonically compelling narrative sequence is in fact utterly silent, as members of the medical team and other personnel must remain absolutely quiet as the *Proteus* and its crew pass by Dr. Benes's eardrum.

1968 | *BARBARELLA, 2001: A SPACE ODYSSEY,* *PLANET OF THE APES*

Our representative science fiction films of 1968 expand the genre in very different and ultimately incompatible ways by means of a conceptual psychedelia. The turn from "-delic" to "-delia" indicates a shift from psychedelic substances proper to the appearance or suggestion of the psychedelic through image or sonic equivalents and proxies. Each film stimulates a separate component of what Guattari (2011) calls the "machinic unconscious," activating three distinct but related "hypersensitivies" that are very much in tune with the kind of psychotechnological operations unleashed through the perceptual and cognitive adjuncts of the psychedelic agent:

> The unconscious works inside individuals in their manner of perceiving the world and living their body, territory, and sex. . . . In other words, not simply an unconscious of the specialists of the unconscious, not simply an unconsciousness crystallized in the past, congealed in an institutionalized discourse, but, on the contrary, an unconscious turned towards the future whose screen would be nothing other than the possible itself, the possible as hypersensitive to language, but also the possible hypersensitive to touch, hypersensitive to the socius, hypersensitive to the cosmos. (2011, 10)

Guattari's four hypersensitivities resonate within new psytech forms poised in the cosmos of the sonic novum, suspended between past and future, individual and technoculture, bodily affect and psychic effects. I will treat these hypersensitive stages of the machinic unconscious in terms of psytech operations defined by the distinct subroutines at work in these three films, each attuned to the formation of the following forms of sonic novum: the socius in Vadim's *Barbarella*; the cosmos in Kubrick's *2001: A Space Odyssey*; and touch, which I treat as a general equivalent to affect, in Schaffner's *Planet of the Apes*. These three hypersensitivities correspond to largely unconscious mechanisms by which listening subjects perceive and inhabit the world around them in terms of their sex, bodies, and territories. The correspondences that I describe here may be only the most obvious arrangement of the triads. Other forms and equations are possible, so that touch and the cosmos, for instance, may correspond more than the socius to sex throughout *Barbarella*. The flexibility of these arrangements reveals that their contingency revolves around the initial hypersensitivity that Guattari identifies: that of language, which under the influence of psychedelics must undergo a significant retooling, as ethnobotanist researcher Terence McKenna explains: "Once we set ourselves the task of describing the psychedelic experience, it will become more accessible, because if we each gave our best metaphor and then all used those metaphors to produce a better metaphor, we eventually would retool our language so that we would be able to handle these modalities" (1992, 77). Rather than propose a class of psychedelic science fiction film per se, the expansion and retooling of language here suggests the ways in which the SF film might function as a rhetorical adjunct in the manner of a psychedelic. These three films emphasize, encourage, or struggle with new modes of listening through the expansion and amplification of the ear, as it were, over and against new modes of enunciation and expression. It is in their capacity as virtual psychedelic that these films reverse human subjectivity, dissolve the ego and its "sound track" (Doyle 2011, 111), and open the ear to alien chatter along transhuman channels.

Roger Vadim's *Barbarella* is an orgy of seemingly incompatible sonic styles: space-age bachelor pad music full of hip Herb Alpert–style horns and Nelson Riddle string sections; weird blips and beeps and outbursts of dissonance directly drawn from SF cinema's past as well as the more spaced out fringes of psychedelic noise being explored by Pink Floyd, Hawkwind, and the Grateful Dead; and the raw fuzz guitar, Farfisa organ, and tambourine of Swinging London's freakbeat groups, mod rock, and L.A.'s underground and garage nugget bands. As campy science fiction that brings together the worlds of French comics and Italian cinema, *Barbarella* has very specific predecessors in the freaky kitschedelic exotica of Antonio Marghereti's *Gamma One* quadrilogy, all four films produced by MGM in 1965 and released in English as *Wild, Wild Planet, War of the Planets, War between the Planets*, and *Snow Devils*, along with the rather improbably titled ... *4* ... *3* ... *2* ... *1* ... *Morte* (*Mission Stardust*, 1967), the sole SF film from Primo Zeglio, a stalwart director of spaghetti westerns. In the Gamma One series, Angelo Francesco Lavagnino's scores intersperse exotic orchestral cues with edgy and unsettling electronics, occasionally adding the twanging guitar familiar to Italian westerns. Getting into a James Bond vibe, Zeglio's film loosely adapts a space action novel, full of spy thrills and sexy intrigue, featuring the popular German character, Perry Rhodan. Like many of the songs heard during opening Bond credits, composer Anton Garcia Abril's main theme, "Seli," achieved crossover success as a single for radio broadcast. This mostly wordless song was a collaboration of some major Italian talent, written by the prolific Marcello Giombini and sung, with occasional thereminesque glide, by the popular soprano Edda Dell'Orso. Throughout Zeglio's film, electronic interludes unexpectedly burst into groovy psychedelic pop, and where *Barbarella*'s music may sound a bit tamer than the Italian film scores, the role of the electronic underscore is much the same. Power-line drones, echo-laden and processed voices, and all kinds of weird burbling and bleeping noises coalesce within an altogether futuristic, ambient soundscape. Taken as a set, these films convey a kind of international mod culture built from the sonic fragments of the past decade or so: the space-age instrumental lounge music of the 1950s; more contemporary vocal pop songs that nonetheless feel dated and slightly disingenuous; fuzzed-out freakbeat pastiches composed by writers of the previous generation (rather than songs by actual, current bands, as we find in the Yardbirds' barnstorming appearance in Michelangelo Antonioni's *Blow Up*, from 1966); and lastly electronic experimentation that works squarely in the tradition of the SF film. Electronic sounds often function independently, even inconsequentially, of whatever else is happening in the musical score, and they sit easily between diegetic and nondiegetic spaces. This independence turned inconsequence will become a particularly telling feature of *Barbarella's* hypersexual sonic dynamics.

The instrumental interludes, pop songs, and weird electronics heard throughout *Barbarella* are mostly the work of the American hit record producer and songwriter Bob Crewe along with popular TV and film composer Charles Fox. The material was performed by a studio ensemble calling itself the Bob Crewe Generation Orchestra, as well as by a minor psych pop group, The Glitterhouse. With their horns, flutes, guitars and, most importantly, drums, the instrumental themes bring the space-age lounge music of 1950s staples, Les Baxter and Harry Revel, into the psychedelic era, while the songs with vocals—the title track, with its refrain of "Barbarella, psychedella," and "An Angel Is Love," sung by Bob Crewe, along with Crewe's songs, "Love, Love, Love Drags Me Down" and "I Love All the Love in You," performed by the Glitterhouse—land the film score clearly in psych pop territory. *Barbarella's* synthesis of the sounds of the space-age bachelor pad with the psychedelic pop of the '60s nightclub suggests a form of armchair psychedelia, offering virtual travel into the original underground rave scene but with an untimely lounge in the back of the room, where stoned patrons mix it up with martinis served straight. Though the key to its kitschedelic sensuality, *Barbarella* was hardly alone in its particular blending of what would otherwise be two antagonistic music cultures, and very distinct generations: the hi-fi lounge scene of the 1950s and the acid-inflected sensibilities of the 1960s. Similar blends are heard in the Burt Bacharach music composed for the campy James Bond film, *Casino Royale* (1967). And several LP recordings of the era—among them Dan Sebesky's *Distant Galaxy* (1968), the 101 Strings Orchestra's *Astro-Sounds from Beyond the Year 2000* (1968), Enoch Light's *Spaced Out* (1969), and Dick Hyman's *The Age of Electronicus* (1969) and *MOOG: The Eclectic Electrics of Dick Hyman* (1969)—combine early modular synthesizers, fuzz guitars, rumbling percussion, strings and sitars as they run through a line-up of proto-electronic covers of popular hit songs amid a handful of original tunes bearing overtly science fictional or spacy titles. When the arrival of the Moog synth in 1964 put unusually robust electronic tones under the control of a piano-style keyboard, quirky electronic covers of pop music and movie themes were suddenly ubiquitous (check out The Moog Machine's *Switched-On Rock* (1969), for example, or Hugo Montenegro's *Moog Power*, also from 1969, with its rendition of the title song from *Hair* and the popular "Aquarius"). This formula of tonally quirky but ultimately familiar Moog mood music would stay this way well into the 1970s, even though some albums took a more edgy, experimental approach. Sebesky's *Distant Galaxy* is particularly interesting in the context of *Barbarella*, as abstract electronic interludes like "Martian Storm" or "Spiral Nebulae" segue between unsettling renditions of Simon and Garfunkel's "Sounds of Silence" or Dylan's "Mr. Tambourine Man." Crewe and Fox's work demonstrates a comparable blend of popular song styles rendered psychedelic by the introduction of odd, electronic noises that disrupt more often than sustain the melodic sensibilities of the music proper.

The Moog-showcasing and other early electronic pop records of the 1960s don't merely update the space-age bachelor pad albums of the 1950s, they suggest an unceasing line of sonic experimentation along a continuum in which new electronic tonalities are associated with both outer space and the female form. A collection of all original material, Harry Revel's *Music from Out of Space* (1955) offers a fairly conventional blend of orchestra and chorus to deliver songs with cosmic titles like "Vibrations from Venus" or "Cosmic Capers," while other works feature proto-electronic music covering jazz and pop standards, like Paul Tanner's *Music for Heavenly Bodies* (1959), which showcases his ribbon-controlled electrotheremin in more familiar song settings like "Over the Rainbow," and Frank Comstock's *Music from Outer Space* (1962), which sets jazz and pop classics with obvious cosmic allusions in their titles like "Stella by Starlight" and "When You Wish Upon a Star" against the electronic exotica of the theremin, electric violin, and Novachord. As much as the musical content, the packaging of these albums points to the psychedelic electronic space pop of the 1960s, *Barbarella* in particular. Like lounge exotica before it, with its pictures of frequently bare shouldered women from Hawaii, Tahiti, India, the Andes, and elsewhere, space-age bachelor pad album covers typically feature images of women suspended or stretched across cosmic backgrounds, visualizing the suggestive, off-color puns of song titles like "Uranus Unmasked," from Revel's *Music from Out of Space,* or the album title of Tanner's *Music for Heavenly Bodies.* In case a prospective bachelor might miss the point of the front cover's image of a fully nude woman, stretched out above a galactic vista, the liner notes of this last album make the connection obvious: "*Heavenly Bodies,* whether it be the type that whirl about us in space, or those that have the glitter of Monroe, Mansfield or Bardot, have always had a magnetic attraction for man. The cosmos, infinite galaxies, lunar bodies suspended in space, glittering stars light years away from the Earth . . . all of these are both stimulating and staggering to the imagination" (in Taylor 2001, 89). Where front covers explicitly link the naked female to the otherness of outer space, the back covers of space-age bachelor LPs associate the male with the technologies that put women in their place and bring space itself under control, ultimately colonizing it through technological superiority (87–88). These back covers were not only filled with cheeky puns but also very technical details about the album's production and instructions for the proper settings for reproduction over the home stereo. The combination of "babes in space," masculine posturing, and technical know-how is no subtle subtext but rather a realization of the capacity of the hi-fi stereo itself. As Taylor explains, the complex technical operations of the home stereo sound system allowed a man "to reclaim some domestic space and authority in the home" after a hard day at work, drowning out the noise of the wife and kids with the volume and stereophonic presence of hi-fidelity sound (2001, 79–80). The stereo could also play into the bachelor's mechanisms of seduction by cuing up a choice cut of mood music by the likes of Les Baxter or Harry Revel.

The female Other constructed by the stereo hi-fi systems of men, whether husband or bachelor, had been part of an effort to colonize and conquer Otherness through the "consumption of new technological forms" (Bartkowiak 2010, 137). Rather than simply claiming that a man's place is technological, while a woman's is not, what we rather experience is a technoculture that places gender along a spectrum of devices. While the stereo hi-fi, with its multicomponent, modular design, is identified as the properly sophisticated domain of men in leisure, in their dens or pads, the push-button functionality of devices in the kitchen and washroom is presented as easing the workload of the woman in her home. This works out sonically as the opposite of the masculine stereo is the absence of the stereo but rather a very different type of stereo system made specifically for women. Lacking the equalizers, balance potentiometers, and proper stereo placement of the hi-fi, these devices for women, Taylor tells us, featured a simplified, push-button functionality in attractive packaging, a sonic equivalent to a new dishwasher (2001, 81), though this was soon replaced altogether by the transistor radio, which took even the selection of material away from the listening woman. In this way, "*complex* technology was defined as the proper domain of the man" (81), and simple, easy to use technology was the proper domain of the woman.

Barbarella makes such technocultural distinctions ambiguous when the film reverses Marshall McLuhan's idea that we are the sex organs of technology as he writes in a section of *Understanding Media* called "The Gadget Lover": "Physiologically, man in the normal use of technology (or his variously extended body) is perpetually modified by it and in turn finds ever new ways of modifying his technology. Man becomes, as it were, the sex organs of the machine world, as the bee of the plant world, enabling it to fecundate and to evolve ever-new forms. The machine world reciprocates man's love by expediting his wishes and desires, namely, in providing him with wealth" ([1964] 1994, 46). In contrast to McLuhan's phallic extensions, *Barbarella* proves that the machine world has essentially whored itself out to the woman, who pimps the machinic unconscious in the name of what would otherwise be a technocultural evolution—after which "the role of humans would be seen as little more than that of industrious insects pollinating an independent species of machine-flowers that simply did not possess its own reproductive organs" (De Landa 1991, 3)—if it were not for the fact that sex in *Barbarella* is a specifically nonreproductive deterritorialization and retooling that reclaims both sex and technology as a woman's place. Standard Earth practice, we are told twice in the film, involves the use of "exaltation transference pills" and nothing but palm-to-palm contact is required once a couple's "psychocardiograms" show compatibility. This practice is repeatedly shown to be dissatisfying, but this does not mean that Barbarella is left to have sex the old fashioned way. *Barbarella* rejects the evolutionary thrust of technocultural procreation by

COSMOS PHILOSOPHY AND THOUGHT SYNTHESIZERS • 255

means of adjuncts that take the place of any originary organ, advocating sexual encounter as a recreational end in and of itself. Even the names of two of the men that Barbarella encounters—Hand (Ugo Tognazzi) and Dildano (David Hemmings)—suggest substitutes for traditional intercourse.

Barbarella decenters social programming for bodies and displaces the feminine by means of technological proxies. Both as an icon of space age pop and its psychedelic Other, *Barbarella* overloads complex sonic technologies through ultimately purposeless activities that are devoted solely to sensation. In the turned-on psychedelic terrain of its cosmic social body, *Barbarella* traces out constellations of sonic influence among the "flows of commodities, flows of expression, flows of embodiment, and flows of affect" (Shaviro 2003, 193–94) that likewise traverse the machinic unconscious. Shaviro's outline of flows suggests that we should consider the psychedelic properties of erotic psytech as a momentary modulation of affect. He writes, "Postmodern social space is traversed by financial, informational, and biological flows; the flows of affect modulate and shadow these other flows, repeating them in the mode of felt experience. And this is precisely the function of psychedelia. . . . *Sentio*, rather than *cogito*, is the psychedelic first principle of postmodern consciousness" (194). Sexy space-age psych pop provides a cognitive adjunct to the machinic unconscious in the form of a backdrop of indifferent, generic, vaguely dispensable music that is completely oblivious to the action on screen. It seems so inconsequential that listening would become a harrowing experience, an overzealous record of emotional neglect, if it were not for the sonic desynchronization that lends the activities of transspecies sex, otherworldly sex education, and sexual torture the atmosphere of a slapstick comedy. While the space age lounge music heard in the score could be seen as a familiarizing counter-irritant to the dissonance of the film's electronic noises, a source of relief, "the sounds of the lounge and the sounds of the psychedelic combine into a polysemic and polysonic orchestration that delivers mixed messages at best. Are we seeing and hearing an empowered sexual being or are we seeing and hearing the continued exoticization of other places and the primitive sexual mores that must exist in such places" (Bartkowiack 2010a, 145)? Bartkowiack is correct to suggest that given all of its ambiguous historical contingencies, "*Barbarella* occupies numerous ideological potentialities" (146), and none of them are satisfactorily resolved as the overly affected individual sonic body saturates the social body in this film, overloading its technologically coded territories.

The opening title sequence of *Barbarella* plays almost like a space-age bachelor pad album cover come to life as Barbarella (Jane Fonda) strip-teases her way out of her aluminum space suit to the sounds of the Bob Crewe Generation Orchestra. As Bartkowiak characterizes it, two forms of hipster culture collide here in a single "concentrated and consumed mode of escape that could be used as recreation. . . . Both could also be considered challenges to dominant social and cultural life, though both re-emphasize the systems they attempt to escape through the consumptive habits built around them" (2010a, 138–39). Herein lies both the unique problem and potential for *Barbarella*'s audience. When originally released, *Barbarella* generated split opinions, especially among women reviewing the film, which grasped this paradoxical suspension between problem and potential. Some downplayed Fonda's acting skills, "stretched to the breaking point along with her clothes," concluding that her character "was a representation of the timeless consumption of women as a sort of cultural capital" (Bartkowiak 2010a, 141). Others saw in Fonda a radicalized and liberated woman who "capitalized on free love and sexual pleasure as shocking and therefore resistant" (141). This provocative, liberated, and healthy Barbarella struck Pauline Kael, writing about the film in the *New Yorker*, as "playfully and deliciously aware of the naughtiness of what she is doing" (in Bartkowiak 2010a, 141). The resolution of these multiple, conflicting approaches are beyond the scope of the current analysis, and perhaps beyond the resolute. We are left instead to examine what role the music and sound of *Barbarella* plays given this dynamic uncertainty, particularly by amplifying it simultaneous independence and insignificance.

Throughout the film, the songs of the Bob Crewe Generation act as a beacon that both calls out for and forestalls physical action. For Bartkowiak, *Barbarella* reveals itself in the now familiar form of the paired indices of the sonic novum as the late bachelor pad style of Crewe's albums is "jettisoned not only into an interstellar journey, but also into the inner journey of the psychedelic experience. The unknown corners of the galaxy and of the inner mind provided . . . a sense of dissonance and playful potential" (2010, 135). I am interested in how this sonic novum both defines and breaks the outer/inner limits and boundaries of the film, though I want to avoid Bartkowiak's reinstatement of the masculine gaze, which he does with his references to Crewe's previous orchestral mod releases, *Music to Watch Girls By* (1967) and *Music to Watch Birds By* (1967). Rather, the space-age "bird" songs of Barbarella deterritorialize the gaze by the force of an obfuscating cosmic body sound, which comes from what Deleuze and Guattari call—though in the context of an altogether other birdsong—"the territorial assemblage of a bird species [that] opens onto interassemblages of courtship and gregariousness, moving in the direction of the partner or 'socius.' But the machine may also open the territorial assemblage to interspecific assemblages, as in the case of birds that adopt alien songs" (1987, 333). The passage from terrestrial birdsong, through the psychedelicized domains of the machinic unconscious, to the alien song concerns us now.

In the 1950s, exotic lounge music suggested that "the strange and the unknown could be conquered through the consumption of new technological forms," whether the hi-fi at home or the rocket in space; both are coded as masculine domains within the lounge and bachelor pad (Bartkowiak 2010a, 137). Psychedelic culture, on the other had, was invested in mind-altering music and drugs for male and female users alike, consumed in the shared social spaces of the discotheque, the go-go club, and the happening. Even as problematic social and sexual codes persisted in these spaces, the profound destabilization of psychedelics experienced through music and electronic sounds, along with provocative light shows, exaggerated the expansion of affect, letting loose sonic adjuncts for bodies getting it on through an equivalent use and consumption of the Other. In this respect, *Barbarella's* sonic cues do not simply update the sexual sensibility of 1950s lounge exotica, with its codes for masculine technical superiority, they make a frequently exploitative appropriation of the body of the Other available to feminine perspectives that are coded, in very complicated and at last unresolved ways, according to new forms of heterosexual, homosexual, and transsexual encounters, the last including unexpectedly casual experiences with alien species and machines. Discussing sound, music, birdsong and territory in *A Thousand Plateaus* (1987), Deleuze and Guattari theorize that "sexuality may appear as a territorialized function, but it can just as easily draw a line of deterritorialization that describes another assemblage" (325). In *Barbarella,* this transition from territorialized sexuality to different assemblages typically begins with the traditional role of the damsel in distress, with sex offered in reward for rescue or other favor, but it ends with Barbarella freewheeling her way through a large number of sexual partnerships without lasting consequences. Where the globe-trotting record collection of the space-age bachelor argues that female partners are fundamentally interchangeable, *Barbarella* reverses this by making its female lead a collector of partners, several of them remarkably alien. She is not better than her male counterparts but rather simply different.

McKenna (1992) has tracked the longevity of the idea of sex between human and nonhuman beings at important evolutionary pivots, and while Doyle (2011) suggests a more specific sexual relationship between humans and plant beings, psychoactive plants in particular, we can understand the human to provide a symbiotic reproductive capacity to specific machine assemblages as well. Borrowing from McKenna's account, we may conclude that *Barbarella* describes both the synthetic and vaguely erotic turn of the sadomasochism that many alien abduction narratives bring to ufology. McKenna attributes the simultaneous eroticism and terror of the alien probe to the desire for a rapturous relationship to the Other given highly complex technocultural entanglements that manifest at crucial stages of evolution. This is something that the human species has traditionally associated with plant guides, though McKenna updates this to include synthetic psychotechnologies that epitomize the space age. Shifting the production of chemical guides from the jungle to the lab brings on a general crisis within the extended social body of technoculture: "It's as though by passing into the psychedelic phase—the space-faring phase—the entire species were passing into adolescence and becoming aware of the possibility of something like a sexual completion with an Other, with an intelligent, nonhuman species. . . . One dimension of the culture crisis is a collective erotic drive for a connection with the Other" (McKenna 1992, 73). Propelled by the simultaneous fear of, and hope for, the "apocalyptic transformation" of its human subjects, the machinic assemblages of technoculture amplify the affective encounter with the Other—now formulated along erotic lines—and culminates in a dyadic fusion and transspecies connection through new and exotic technologies (76). "To date," McKenna concludes, "the cultural engineers have not stressed enough that the erotic element be included in the design of the human future" (76).

Something of this dyadic fusion between the human and Other resolves over the course of *Barbarella,* with the film's heroine cast alongside the alien angelic lover, Pygar (John Phillip Law) or against the demonic Great Tyrant (Anita Pallenberg), but most importantly inside of the simultaneous orgasm/death-inducing Excessive Machine, the literal sex organ of the villainous Dr. Durand Durand (Milo O'Shea). The device encloses its female victims within a sexually stimulating device that is controlled by an odd kind of keyboard. While showing an unusual bit of sheet music featuring the modernist visual score for a piece entitled "Sonata for Executioner, and Various Young Women," the scene is set up with a soft riff on Bach's "Toccata and Fugue in D minor." Durand Durand tenderly places his gloved fingers on the backlit plastic controls, which results in a quick outburst of rhythmic percussion and electronic tones, and as the camera pans up the surface of the Excessive Machine to Barbarella's face, a very brief segment of psych pop plays on distorted electric guitar and bass. The rapid cuts from one type of sound to another is quite typical of the film, though of particular interest here because they have nothing to do with the sound of the Excessive Machine itself, and the scene will continue to exhibit a barely cohesive mixture of orchestral horns and woodwinds, electronics, psych pop horns, electric guitar, and increasingly frantic drums. These sounds are, in their own way, utterly excessive cues that create a kind of irrelevant milieu just when we expect to hear an emphasis on diegetic music and noise as the Excessive Organ plays on Barbarella's body. Barbarella obviously enjoys it, which she expresses with a couple of quick gasps and surprised outbursts, but her pleasure is not the goal of the villain. At first Barbarella cries out in wide-eyed wonder before Durand Durand informs her, "When we reach the crescendo, you will die . . . of pleasure." As the camera pans back to show the entire Excessive Machine, little in the musical accompaniment matches the frantic movement of Durand

260 • COSMOS PHILOSOPHY AND THOUGHT SYNTHESIZERS

Durand's hands across the organ's controls. The rhythm speeds up, dominated by the drums and becomes more intense even as Barbarella's facial expressions calm, her eyes closed, mouth agape, but making very little sound before one last cry, almost drowned out by the drums. The musical score now takes a different turn after a cacophonous clash of drums and instruments, gradually slowing down as processed male voices, low in the mix, slowly moan as the music takes its last turn as an atonal freak-out. The Excessive Machine overloads as Barbarella's orgasm does not drown out the organ—she is now completely silent as events internalize—but breaks it altogether. "You've undone it! You've undone me!" Durand Durand cries. "The energy cables are shrinking. You've turned them into faggots. You, you've burned out the Excessive Machine!" Whether vocal or silent, Barbarella's orgasms—the only synchronized audiovisual element of the sequence—are an auditory supplement for a physical response to postevolutionary technocultural assemblage. They manifest her capacity to entertain what Guattari calls "the polyphony of modes of subjectivation" through a silent adjunct to the "multiplicity of ways of 'keeping time'" (2011, 15) that the noisy mixture of incompatible sounds would otherwise revel in as a mode of torture if it were not so dependent on meter and tempo rather than rhythmic variety.

The ironically overwhelming sonic presence of Barbarella's silence, which is not that of her death but her life, causes the Excessive Machine to lose that which had defined it: its strict adherence to meter and time signature, which can be accelerated but not varied and which is undone by its gradual breakdown into free rhythmic play and atonality. In their discussion of "milieu components" and "territory"—the former dealing in "a quality and a property," the latter in "a matter of expression"—Deleuze and Guattari describe the emergence of territory when "milieu components cease to be directional, becoming dimensional instead, when they cease to be functional to become expressive" (1987, 315). Barbarella's orgasmic overwhelmings (the plurality is awkward but necessary) of the assemblage of score and organ known as the Excessive Machine "makes aggressiveness the basis of the territory, . . . which has dangerous political overtones" (315–16) that ultimately prompt Durand Durand to announce that he must resort to the lash. By contrast,

Barbarella's bodily organs "presuppose a territory-producing expressiveness. In this sense, the territory, and the functions performed within it, are products of territorialization. Territorialization is an act of rhythm that has become expressive, or of milieu components that have become qualitative" (315). Where Durand Durand sought to change Barbarella's tune, turning the cries of orgasmic pleasure into a death moan, through a rapidly increasing tempo, a quantitative change, Barbarella does just the opposite, turning her orgasmic pleasure into the death of the machine by moving according to her own, qualitatively expressive rhythms. Territorial functions are in fact the product of the "becoming-expressive of rhythm or melody" (316). Where meter is a matter of strict dogma, "rhythm is critical" (313), and the expressive capacities of the latter—which Deleuze and Guattari also call "the refrain"—propel bodies beyond territories and territorial functions, such as "sexuality, aggressiveness, flight" (315). Sexual embodiment for Barbarella is a movement from evolutionary territorial form to deterritorialized forces, a shutting down of "the tonal system" that takes us "from assembled refrains (territorial, popular, romantic, etc.) to the great cosmic machined refrain" (350) of the rhythmic, orgasmic noise that breaks the Excessive Machine in an excessive deterritorialization of Barbarella Psychedella. We should hear her as an embodied cosmic thought synthesizer. The deterritorializing power of sound, according to Deleuze and Guattari, comes neither from its signifying and communicative values nor its physical properties, but rather it works along "a machinic phylum that operates in sound and makes it a cutting edge of deterritorialization. But this does not happen without great ambiguity: sound invades us, impels us, drags us, transpierces us. It takes leave of the earth, as much in order to drop us into a black hole as to open us up to a cosmos" (348). If it weren't for the winged Pygar informing Barbarella, upon rescuing her and the villainess Great Tyrant from the destruction of their city, "that an angel has no memory," we might be tempted to conclude that Barbarella at last resides somewhere between the "memory of an angel, or rather the becoming of a cosmos. . . . Produce a deterritorialized refrain as the final end of music, release it in the Cosmos—that is more important than building a new system. Opening the assemblage onto a cosmic force" (350). With a woman under each arm, Pygar ascends into the heavens on the flute-driven winds of Bob Crewe's most overtly Bacharachian refrain, a snappy, if ultimately inconsequential, little number, "An Angel is Love," a soundtrack for trysts to come.

As psychedelic science fiction goes, *Barbarella* and *2001* offer significantly different trips: the first sexy and recreational, the second metaphysical and spiritual, but both clearly about turning on the sonic novum to psychedelic hypersensitivities. Whereas *Barbarella* sonifies the hypersensitive body, *2001* sonifies an encounter with new cosmic territories at the intersection of outer and inner space. Acknowledging their substantial differences, however, it is worth noting that the sensations of psychedelic hypersexuality that culminate with the burning out of the Excessive Machine in *Barbarella* have much the same function as planetary alignment will in *2001*, where the musical accompaniment lacks most of the traditional cues for empathetic response even as it overwhelms the listening body through affective intensities and pure sensations that aren't typical of cinematic experience. During the three moments of cosmic alignment in *2001*, each accompanied by Strauss's "Also sprach Zarathustra," Redner suggests that "the separate elements have returned as something new, something that retains the elements of its 'original matter' but now returns not as a copy, but as a new manifestation of the same separate affective sensation. They have in their recurrence 'become' an assemblage of perceptive and affective sensation" (2011, 185). The sonic novum in *Barbarella* works similarly by turning affective sensual alignment into the postevolutionary sex drive of an autoerotic musical language that plays in blind disregard for visual and narrative counterparts. This is evidence of what Deleuze and Guattari call the "catalytic function" of the refrain "not only to increase the speed of the exchanges and reactions in that which surrounds it, but also to assure indirect interactions between elements devoid of so-called natural affinity" (1987, 348). The modes of psychedelic transcendence here depend on a break from inherent affinities or significations, including those that govern the familiarity of sonic conventions in the science fiction film. It is time to depart from the kitschedelic embrace of transcendence as a mode of sexual escapism to reach the cerebral and spiritual modes of awareness triggered by cosmic events in *2001*.

COSMOS PHILOSOPHY AND THOUGHT SYNTHESIZERS • 263

• • •

Stanley Kubrick's *2001: A Space Odyssey* is easily the science fiction film with the most pronounced psychedelic reputation, deserved or not—mostly not. Kubrick dismissed drugs, and LSD in particular, in a 1968 interview with *Playboy* magazine. Not only had he never taken acid, but Kubrick announced that he thought drugs were worthless: "The pervasive aura of peace and contentment is not the ideal state for an artist. . . . The artist's transcendence must be within his own work; he should not impose any artificial barriers between himself and the mainspring of his subconscious" (Agel 1970, 346). It turns out that *2001*'s association with psychedelic culture has more to do with its reception, popular and critical. But even this reception seems exaggerated. Very few of the film's contemporary reviews and reactions collected in Agel's comprehensive *The Making of Kubrick's "2001"* (1970) recount actual psychedelic drug experiences during screenings of the film, with the wry exception of some comments published in the "subterranean newspaper," *Rat*: "*2001* is the head flick of all time. Note the faintly resinous spoor of the audience, the people fighting at intermission to get those 50-cent chocolate bars, the spaced-out few who contemplate the curtain for long minutes after the movie ends" (247). Nonetheless, a psychedelic reputation persisted as reviews, advertisements, and press releases took a sharp turn from the film's original line of publicity—the first movie posters proclaimed "an epic drama of adventure and exploration" and "highlighted technology and science in both words and visuals," as Chion (2001, 35) explains—to exploit instead pop references to psychedelic culture. *Time* magazine labeled it a "psychedelic experience," while one commentator, quoted in *Variety*, said the movie was "for groovin', not understandin'" (Agel 1970, 241). Most famously, the *Christian Science Monitor* called *2001* "the ultimate trip" (in Chion 2001, 35), which became the tagline for a new set of psychedelic posters that accompanied a 70mm release of the film in 1970. But even as some viewers and reviewers coded the film in psychedelic terms, just as many, if not more, adopted a language of personal and spiritual transformation devoid of the tropes and substances of psychedelic culture. Kramer's critical work on the film retrieves its mainstream success and popularity, citing numerous letters to Kubrick and MGM testifying to deeply affective and philosophical experiences. While *2001* resonated with a countercultural desire to hasten spiritual evolution through psychedelic drugs, in Kramer's interpretation, the film was in fact part of a pervasive "dream of true human transformation" in America at this time (2010, 77). In *The Sixties Spiritual Awakening*, religious scholar Robert S. Ellwood goes so far as to call the film a "Sixties parable" of these far-reaching concerns and hopes (in Kramer 2010, 89).

Media reception clearly shaped *2001*'s identity as a film of psychedelic or transformative experience. So did the various technical formats in which the film was presented. The writer of the aforementioned *Variety* review claims the film's psychedelic effect actually depended on whether one saw it in 70mm Cinerama or 35mm format, with the former emphasizing the film's "mind-bending complexity" in contrast to the smaller format's "fable-like simplicity," which was "not the psychedelic 'trip' so promoted by many, but a tight, closely-knit, rigorously-structured narrative that basically takes the form of an anecdote" (Agel 1970, 241). In this case, while audience testimonies and critical reviews, along with statements by the director, cowriter, and crew, may merely hint at an underlying psychedelic potentiality lurking within SF cinema, the various cultural and critical receptions must have less to with its effect than material affordances of the cinematic psychotechnologies involved. Shaviro claims, "Psychedelic drugs and electronic technologies affect the sensorium in strikingly similar ways" (2003, 188). Indeed, Shaviro's extended description of the affinities shared between psychedelic drugs and new electronic technologies reads like a description of *2001*:

> They both disperse and decenter subjectivity. Consciousness is scattered all across space, and yet in a strange way intensified. Concentration is no longer possible, for too many things are happening all at once. Forms are fragmented, and context is erased. Each event seems to stand by itself, throbbing with its own singular halo. Objects turn into hyperreal doubles of themselves: dense clouds of information, pulsing with bright, saturated colors. Yet, despite the isolation and fragmentation, everything seems to be mysteriously connected. You

are in direct communication with the most distant forces of the cosmos. (188)

Kubrick's film functions according to its own psychedelic regimen, silencing the orating ego (as I will discuss, a key decision was to eliminate a voice-over narration penned by cowriter Arthur C. Clarke) and substituting sonic adjuncts that can access the hypersensitives of the machinic unconscious and aim it toward a cosmic deterritorialization. This takes shape in the film as an oft-noted desire on Kubrick's part for *2001* to have some kind of "transformative effect" on the audience, and for the movie experience to resemble contact with the film's evolution-instigating monolith (Kramer 2010, 53–54). Sound plays a particularly important part in this process.

Kubrick's use of prerecorded material throughout *2001* went against Hollywood scoring practice, and his treatment of film composer Alexander North, who had worked previously with the director on *Spartacus* (1960), left something to be desired (Chion 2001, 24). Though there had been signs of trouble as Kubrick stopped communicating with the composer during editing, North did not realize that Kubrick hadn't used any of his original score until he attended the film's premiere. The final state of the film shouldn't have come as a complete surprise to North, however, as Kubrick had frequently expressed his desire to use excerpts of classical and avant-garde recordings in the finished film despite MGM's pairing him with North relatively early in production. Kubrick used audio guides throughout the creative process, and even while writing *2001* with Clarke, it was Carl Orff's *Carmina Burana* that inspired the filmmaker more than the seasoned science fiction author (12). Much of the music that made its way into the film had been picked as early temp tracks that Kubrick used to find a scene's "inner rhythm" and to determine the relationship between various shots (24). North ultimately wrote Kubrick something close to his inspirational sources, and parts of his score come across as pastiches of both the Strausses. Overall, as heard in the recorded performance of North's full score by the British National Philharmonic Orchestra, conducted by Jerry Goldsmith, and released on the Varèse Sarabande label in 1993, the resulting film would have been very different if North's work had replaced Kubrick's temp track. For despite the fact that the film studio and North agreed that a single score would act as a sonic unifier of the otherwise disjointed pieces of the grandly scaled film, Kubrick had rejected North's score precisely in order to challenge traditional cinematic codes, particularly those concerning the role of sound as a provider of narrative momentum and emotional cues.

Kubrick's recorded selections, often isolated from other sonic elements, do both more and less than provide an existential continuity across shots and edits. Sound editing typically hides the many divisions, both little and great, that really define film (Chion 2001, 66). Kubrick brings the disruptive and dissociative properties of film to the fore, creating what Chion calls "a cinema of discontinuum" (70). All of Kubrick's pieces of music seem to be oblivious to each other: stylistically, historically, instrumentally, and tonally (97). This is precisely what North's score would have abolished "through its symphonic unity," which would have tied everything together into a tidy, consistent package. Chion concludes, "The samples of borrowed music both tear the film apart, isolating its different parts from one another, and create its unity through their very incommensurability" (97). This very different unifying capacity of incommensurable sound pieces is key to understanding Kubrick's sonic cosmos, in which incompatible scales of experience never synthesize into new wholes but rather align themselves in arrangements, juxtapositions, and patterns. Kubrick's use of "some of the most dissimilar musical pieces imaginable" accentuates not only their sonic discontinuity, then, but also significant gaps in human culture and history (96).

Kubrick's use of album cuts was also part of his attempt to move the film away from what he confessed to Clarke was the threat of "silly simplicity" and facilitate instead a mind-expanding experience (in Kramer 2010, 50). This led Kubrick to radically transform the sonic expressivity of the film, which North's score would not have achieved on its own. North's theme titles, like "Space Station Docking" or "Trip to the Moon" give a clear sense of where North's cues would have been used, and his music often apes Kubrick's temp tracks to a degree clearly uncomfortable for the composer and also occasionally the listener, particularly his "Main Title" theme, with its mimic of the low opening tones and rising horns from Richard Strauss's "Also sprach Zarathustra," then replacement of the timpani hits with a flourish of strings followed by more melodic phrasings. Critical reception is divided over how this score would have changed *2001*. Gene D. Phillips concluded that it would be "difficult to see how North's music would have been an improvement on the background music that Kubrick finally chose for the film" (2016, 464). In contrast, in the liner notes for the Goldsmith recording, Kevin Mulhall asserts that "there is no doubt" that *2001* would have been bettered by North's score. "Even if one likes some of the choices Kubrick made for certain individual scenes," Mulhall (1993) concludes, "the eclectic group of classical composers" that Kubrick favored "resulted in a disturbing melange of sounds and styles overall." Both responses miss the point.

In the first case, Kubrick's selections can hardly be situated in the background, as they are typically placed front and center, with little to no diegetic sounds competing for attention. Kubrick's sound editing rarely stacks different sounds vertically; rather, sounds tend to move horizontally, with distinct breaks between the sequences of nondiegetic prerecorded selections, dialogue and minimal diegetic sounds, amplified and thereby foregrounded diegetic sounds (such as Bowman's breathing), and silence. The second perspective, articulated by Mulhall (1993), privileges the unifying role of the film score. Agreeing with Kubrick's rejection of North's score is not just a matter of preferring the quality of the prerecorded selections to North's pastiches or even his more original material, however. Something more significant is at work in Kubrick's survey of twentieth-century composition practices, which covers compositional styles ranging from romanticism and early modernism to the contemporary avant-garde and early electronic music. This has to do with the various disconnections and alignments of differentiated sonic materials that turn the music into "an alien language to translate and experience," as Whittington asserts (2007, 40). It is less important that the music itself is new—as in newly composed for the film, but also as in the various tropes of "new music" that have concerned us so far in this book—as it is that the film demands a new kind of listening.

Before this "rhetorical amplification" can take place, as we have learned from Doyle, we must have the "shutting up that is not a shutting down" (2011, 111). Kubrick struggled with early versions of the film conceived with Clarke, which cast *2001* as a documentary or educational science film. The film would establish its conceptual credibility through ponderous voice-overs and interviews with practicing scientists, while a more straightforward narrative would be delivered through spoken exposition. The most complex, enigmatic points of narrative were to have been guided along by lines like, "Now he was master of the world," which Clarke penned to accompany the arrival of the Star Child, a character of essentially ambiguous identity in the film but clearly identified in Clarke's writing as the transformed astronaut, Bowman (Kramer 2010, 47). Kubrick silenced all of these voice-overs, interviews, and expository moments as he pared the film experience down to something approaching a "purely visual experience" built on the foundation of extended musical and sonic sequences (52). Instead of Clarke's documentary, *2001* attains a kind of hyperreal sheen during long moments of nondiegetic silence, sustained recordings, and amplified, isolated bits of sound design that emphasize the sonic details of the futuristic, diegetic landscape.

Kubrick's investment in new sound experiences was intertwined with an equivalent fascination with new visual experiences, something that would shift the scale of his film toward the expanded cinema experiments of Jordan Belson and the Whitney brothers. Clarke's original draft called not for a monolith but a huge cube that would show little educational movies on its surface. Kubrick was then faced with the challenge of showing what was playing on the cube. He decided to avoid the issue altogether and planned to focus on the hypnotized faces of those staring at the cube, depicting their mental transformation by expression (Kramer 2010, 48). Kubrick kept the cosmic cube idea but morphed its shape into the thin black rectangular monolith, which would eventually become a gateway into completely abstract visual cinema. Once he had this idea, he wrote Clarke, he began finding ways to make his film an encounter equivalent to contact with the cosmic object, one that would imbue the same kind of ambiguity and mystery. Kubrick was obviously aware of the intermedia culture emerging in art galleries, festivals, global expositions, and concert venues, and he saw potential in the large-scale formats of expanded cinema for creating the immersive experiences fit for a new form of serious science fiction film. The three keys to transforming the cinematic SF experience toward this end were: first, his erasure of the documentary and narrative elements; second, his use of the immersive scale of Cinerama projection; and third, the film's

COSMOS PHILOSOPHY AND THOUGHT SYNTHESIZERS • 269

sonic character. Music became crucial to Kubrick's plan, and he finally announced that he "intended the film to be an intensely subjective experience that reaches the viewer at an inner level of consciousness, just as music does" (in Whittington 2007, 120). Kubrick thus took a scientifically and technically plausible extrapolation regarding the conditions for extraterrestrial encounter and cosmic destiny, which would validate extrapolation by adopting the reasonable form of an educational science film, and turned it into an art film. Many of Kubrick's decisions were made only a few weeks before release date and without Clarke's knowledge, much less approval (51). In the SF community, Kubrick's treatment of Clarke's original vision was discussed as typical of a wider generational divide in the field, and it reinvigorated debates about new wave science fiction within the SF community (Latham 2011, 133). As is evident in the editorials of time-honored SF magazines and a new generation of fan publications, well-established, older writers tended to disparage the film for precisely the reasons that the writers of the British new wave, their American counterparts, and younger readers praised the film: "The mystical subordination of rationality and merits of synthetic self-transformation" appealed to a younger audience that "embraced the film, not despite but *because* of its enigmatic, oracular qualities" (128, 131).

Kubrick crafted an affect-oriented cinematic hypnotism (Kramer 2010, 49–51) over the course of several edits and cuts, with Clarke in tepid agreement with the drastic changes to their initial concept. Despite Kubrick's insistence otherwise, the film seemed destined to be perceived as not only deeply artistic, if not mystifying, but also as emblematic of psychedelic culture. The film meshed perfectly with the psychedelic visual arts culture of the so-called acid cinematiques that Stafford and Golightly survey in their early analysis, *LSD: The Problem-Solving Psychedelic* (1967). The writers track the dissemination of the powerful hallucinogen from the laboratory and professional therapeutic use throughout popular culture. Citing *Life*'s cover story of September 9, 1966, about psychedelic light shows, Stafford and Golightly conclude:

> The youth of the country is responding enthusiastically to this "total assault on the senses." Attempts to produce a "drugless trip" often consist of "acid-rock" music played at monumental volume,

270 • COSMOS PHILOSOPHY AND THOUGHT SYNTHESIZERS

> accompanied by the incessant play of strobe lights, kleig lights, rapidly flickering images in swirling colors, projections from an "infinity machine" and other artificial sensory effects. (252–53)

Not only did *2001* provide a movie theater equivalent to the light show, it was also part of a widespread change among film scoring practices, which played out along the same generational divide that the new wave science fiction writers detected, as more and more directors treated the film's musical accompaniment as a compilation of audio selections. To this extent, the sonic experience of *2001* is not that formally different from *Easy Rider* (1969), though the latter reinforced the timeliness of the new music of its younger generation of moviegoers, where the former played off of the fact that its selections of classical and avant-garde music would likely be unfamiliar to youth audiences. Chion explains that both the sudden dominance of popular music in films and the absorption of avant-garde and experimental sensibilities into mainstream cinema brings to an end "the noble pretense" that film music would "absorb and embrace all musical styles within a single mode" (2009, 104). That a younger audience could hear this as evidence of a new kind of sound, but also as an agreeable format for film sound to begin with, again links the sonic experience of *2001* to that of other films of the time, including *Barbarella,* which also held together, but barely, an almost incompatible array of musical fragments. At any rate, this desire for a totalizing musical unity is precisely what MGM hoped North's score would do, though it is rather telling that he never took a crack at the various Ligeti works that Kubrick used throughout his temp track. Some sounds just lie beyond the scope and scale of absorption and embrace. The idea that a single musical mode could somehow represent all musical modes ran directly against Kubrick's desire for the unsettling discrepancies and, ultimately, silences, arranged across the film's extended soundscape.

While the vast majority of science fiction films typically avoided this degree of formal experiment with visual music, psychedelic spectacle, and sonic novum throughout the 1960s, we have encountered something of this in the works of experimental SF cinema discussed earlier in this chapter. In Marker's *La Jetée,* the rhythmic interplay of almost entirely still images and sparse sound design provides a formal corollary to a narrative of disjointed time travel as well as the potentially disastrous collapse of the spaces of inner personal and outer collective memories. The play of light, reflection, color, gases, and textures in Jordon Belson's cosmic films strongly suggest their own cinematic language and a concrete symbology. Sounds turn into signs of "celestial mechanics" at work in the "deep structure" of not only Belson's films but also *2001*, where the subdiegetic domain of a cosmic unconscious is formed by the "spectacle of alignment [that] emerges as a leitmotif throughout the film" (Whittington 2007, 39, 47). For Whittington, solar alignment with the monolith suggests a specific meaning and value—in his account, "the notion of order out of chaos and celestial progression" (48)—against which the entire history of humanity is just an elided blip between bone as weapon and spaceship. This is a classic example of the overcoded values that are added sonically and that work on Whittington's ears as an expansive agency. In another instance, music is overloaded as an emotional associative. Whittington's subjective sonic experience is altered by an expectation for emotional corollaries, and so he hears Aram Khachaturian's "Gayane Ballet Suite (Adagio)" as diegetic music that plays (over loudspeakers, I suppose) during an astronaut's workout and so provides the audience with a "desolate and soothing . . . portrait of the character" (51). But these examples could strike us in completely different ways in both of these scenes, where they may in fact suggest nothing so much as Chion's "anempathetic music"—"music whose ostensible indifference to the situation on screen, implacably continuing no matter what, creates an expressive contrast" (2009, 94)—but written on a grand scale of cosmic indifference. Whether or not we imagine that the "Adagio" is blasting from the spaceship's interior speakers or simply plays for nondiegetic effect has everything to do with how much think that Dave Bowman (Keir Dullea) is consciously participating in the creation of this nostalgic and tender mood. In either case, as a form of running music, the piece comes across as profoundly indifferent to what the character is doing on screen.

Anempathetic to the narrative events, Kubrick's recorded musical selections here and elsewhere illustrate a profound, extraterrestrial form of "schizophonia," R. Murray Schafer's (1977) term for the splitting of sounds from their sources. Recorded media brought acousmatic rupture to the modern and postmodern soundscape, making every sound indifferent and detached and poised for realignment. In *2001*, Kubrick represents the twentieth century as an alignment of radically variant sonic forms. It is really the only sense of the twentieth century that the movie gives us as it elides everything between the evolutionary transition of the hominids from prehistory to the cusp of a celestial posthumanity. Rather than foster narrative continuity or the uniformity of added sonic values that would absorb and unify everything that went between these unfixed, transitional emergences, Kubrick exploits the recorded artifact's capacity to serve as an adjunct to absolute visual experience and so spatially align, rather than merge, differences. Sound reminds us of ourselves through its capacity to act as an agent of multiple returns and becomings, syntheses and refrains. The musical recordings used in *2001* operate transparently as rhetorical adjuncts and points of cosmic juxtaposition of the anempathetic and the "intensely subjective experience" that Kubrick described. They overcharge sound's capacity to add value by revealing the contingent and constructed nature of sound in cinema, playing with sound's inability not to enter into significant relationship with images, to which it adheres even if not precisely synchronized. Music excessively overcodes any given sound–image relationship as a site of potential meaning; that is, the potential to be meaningful overrides any actual meaning conveyed, which is what I believe Kubrick meant by a film that works like music; "to 'explain' a Beethoven symphony would be to emasculate it by erecting an artificial barrier between conception and appreciation. You're free to speculate as you wish about the philosophical and allegorical meaning of the film" (in Whittington 2007, 120). Rather than present the results of a speculation in the way that Clarke's initial, future documentary would have done, Kubrick offers the film up as the grounds for speculation. Accordingly, sounds are presented in terms of their effects rather than meanings (Chion 2001, 92). Kubrick's musical selections not only reverse the sensibilities of the typical science fiction film soundtrack, it also voids them, empties them out, silences them completely, especially in those sequences in which we are most accustomed to hearing musical cues. As Chion writes, "most of the action passages such as space walks and murders go without; the music seems to be reserved for contemplative sequences" (90). It is also

COSMOS PHILOSOPHY AND THOUGHT SYNTHESIZERS • 273

unusual to encounter a science fiction film given over entirely to such new kinds of images and visual effects that they become a form of "visual music," so much so that the entire film begins to feel like an artifact of the future, when even the material medium of the cinematic content has changed, or an object from the alien world that it depicts. Like the film's hominids and astronauts, rather than looking at a cube showing educational movies, we are confronted by a mysterious rectangular monolith that we must see and hear in an equivalent moment of hypnotic encounter while undergoing some form of inner transformation.

• • •

Released shortly before *2001*, Franklin Schaffner's *Planet of the Apes* (1968) enjoyed redoubled interest after the success of Kubrick's film. For the next several years, *Planet of the Apes* morphed into one of the first full-scale science fiction franchises, spawning multiple generations of sequels, remakes and reboots, TV shows, action figures, lunch boxes, cartoons, comic books, Halloween costumes, and LPs. Its contorted time-travel narrative provides a minor shock to the system with a story full of action, passion, and declamations courtesy of American astronaut George Taylor (Charlton Heston)—participant in the first interspecies kiss, even if only with a costumed proxy (Kim Hunter) and completely platonic in effect. Compared to the major commitments, temporal, cognitive, and aesthetic, that Kubrick's film asks of its audience, with a slow, methodical, puzzling, and variously astoundingly silent or unsettlingly atonal soundtrack, *Planet of the Apes* hardly seems psychedelic in any usual sense of the term. It does, however, resonate with those aspects of the psychedelic experience concerned with the hypersensitivities of touch as its primate, if not quite primitive, bodies get caught up in the tug of a devolutionary return and future mutation.

With its gritty, earthy sets and wild array of primitive analog sounds courtesy of the composer Jerry Goldsmith, *Planet of the Apes* is the shrooms to *2001*'s acid. Although it does so through a pop vernacular that brings crashing down to earth *2001*'s cosmic pairing of hominids and astronauts at key points of technocultural evolution, the original *Planet of the Apes* brings to the psychedelic era of SF cinema something like McKenna's "archaic revival," its astronauts and apes triggering the retrieval of "what we knew in the beginning: the archaic union with nature that was seamless, unmediated by language, unmediated by notions of self and other, of life and death, of civilization and nature. These are all dualisms that are temporary and provisional within the labyrinth of history" (1992, 18). These dualisms are eradicated linguistically and physically, according to McKenna, by psychedelic adjuncts introduced to embodied consciousnesses thrust out of time (18). In this film, humans have lost language, a key to its psychedelic shutting up of the ego, while the apes have evolved their own multifaceted technoculture. Of course, *Planet of the Apes* hardly offers as idyllic a resolution as McKenna's account, playing out this moment of suspended dualisms as high anxiety and ending in despair with its reversals of our sense of time and the dawning (or dusking?) conceptualization that this *Planet of the Apes* is not another world but our own, devastated by nuclear war.

The film bridges two generations of science fiction, with a script by *The Twilight Zone*'s Rod Serling that harkens back to the Cold War themes of the 1950s even as it casts more contemporary concerns with racial and animal rights through its speculative lens. The Earth of 3978 leads both elsewhere and backward as time unravels and historical cause and effect twists and knots back into "nothing other than the possible itself," as Guattari describes the workings of the machinic unconscious, "these *abstract machines* [that] traverse various levels of reality and establish and demolish stratifications" (2011, 10–11). Guattari's work here implicates the machinic unconscious within the "material and/or semiotic" (11) deterritorializations of sound in its archaic revival. Rather than simply retrieving primitive psychotechnological states through a retro-futuristic approach to technoculture, Guattari's schizoanalysis bypasses "causalist or finalist extrapolation" and, in the name of apprehending "relations and systemic balances" in bodies, minds, families, society and history, asks us instead to "think time against the grain, to imagine that what came 'after' can modify what was 'before' or that changing the past at the root can transform a current state of affairs: what madness! A return to magical thought! It is pure science fiction, and yet . . . " (10–11). In *Planet of the Apes,* the most narratively inflected of sonic components approaches this process of going against the grain in the most basic way, with humans mute while all other primates can speak. Why the apes speak English, much less why the various primates—chimpanzees, orangutans, and gorillas—speak the same language, is not explained. It ultimately may be beside the point given a film that matches the schizoanalyst's trajectory of escape from language—"Its 'structure' results from the petrification of a sort of grab-all through which the elements come from borrowings, amalgamations, agglutinations, misunderstandings" (Guattari 2011, 27)—to the postlinguistic "time of the refrains" (108). More succinctly in *The Machinic Unconscious* than he and Deleuze would later develop the term, here Guattari defines the "refrain" as the "simplification of the basic rhythms of temporalization" (108), and insofar as Guattari's refrain traces the contours of the machinic unconscious, it can be heard to revel in the "mute dance of intensities that is simultaneously played out on the social body and the individuated body" (32). Against the grain of time, the "future-primitive" (Miller 2010, 212) sound of *Planet of the Apes* "contributes to an evolution in the opposite direction" (Guattari 2011, 108–9). Guattari's discussion culminates with the conclusion that it is within "the domain of animal ethology that we shall have to base the existence of a problematics of innovation, creativity, and even freedom concerning the components of the refrain" (114). This involves two fascinating outcomes: a relative assemblage of, first, hierarchies of "instinctive components" (here, sounds that trigger affective, bodily responses) and of "nervous centers" (the physical receptors and aggregators of those triggers); and second, refrains that move among "stratified systems" (in my reading of the film, the instruments in performance together) and "diagrammatic processes" (Goldsmith's written scores and notes on his unusual instruments and methods of playing), which in combination lead to "mutations in the order of spatio-temporal coordinates, social coordinates" and so on (115). But this linguistic reprogramming—ultimately bypassed in the film by the astronaut Taylor's speech, which tends toward conservatively humanist testimony, diatribes, and curses—is only a small part of the film's compelling sonic novum.

To really get at the complex ways in which time cannot be thought, but must be heard, against the grain, the sonic primitivism of the film's score bypasses language altogether, and in this way it melds McKenna's

276 • COSMOS PHILOSOPHY AND THOUGHT SYNTHESIZERS

revival of the archaic with Doyle's psychedelic blockage of the ego and subsequent tuning into alien frequencies. Several themes from Goldsmith's score confront the listener with a primitive and distorted rite of martial sounds performed on culturally imported, modified, and otherwise unusual instrumentation. This was Goldsmith's first science fiction score, but he immediately recognized that *Planet of the Apes* would necessitate a different approach: "The obvious way would be to use electronic and all sorts of synthetic means of reproducing the music, and I feel, without trying to sound pretentious, that the resources of the orchestra had just barely begun to be tapped" (in Larson 1985, 245). The future-primitive setting and narrative of *Planet of the Apes* provided just such an opportunity to tap into the unexplored capacities of orchestral sound, avoiding already well-established SF tropes and introducing something at once very old and new, though new here in the sense of the estranged. Pitting music against noisy effects, Goldsmith describes the score using terms that have become familiar to us over the course of this study. "I felt it was an exercise for myself to see what I could do to make some strange sounds," the composer recalls, "and yet try to make them musically rather than effect wise" (245). Though not always obvious based on sound alone, the instruments used in Goldsmith's score are outlined in his notes to the score. These include: a ram's horn for battle calls; the vibraslap (a manufactured version of the jawbone with a wooden ball connected to a resonator box, which creates a rapid fluttering); the Brazilian cuica (a friction drum with a bamboo stick penetrating an animal hide skin used to produce squeaky tones that suggest the cries and hoots of apes); bass slide whistles (the gliding rise and fall of their notes also suggesting ape vocalizations); and stainless steel mixing bowls (tuned to create percussive sounds). Goldsmith also repurposed conventional instruments through unusual playing techniques: French horn players reversed the mouthpieces on their instrument; string players used the wood of the bow on their strings; and clarinetists audibly clicked the keys of their instruments. The only electronic effect used in the score's performance was the Echoplex processor, which provides a reverberating quality to plucked strings or percussion, as if pushing them into a cave where the notes mixed together with an almost overwhelming complexity of overtones. Making such unconventional demands on his performers—both changing the type of instruments they played as well as how they played familiar instruments—reshaped the sonic experience of the SF film from the ground up. The result is often a frantic, dense and distanced atonal rumble pierced by raw blasts from the ram's horn and thundering decrescendos pounded out on piano.

For all of its borrowings from other sound cultures, Goldsmith's exploratory incorporation of primitive acoustic instrumentation and methods does not play out at all like the "exotic" voices of instruments heard in the lounge music discussed earlier, in which absorption of unusual sounds within otherwise familiar settings created a formal homogeneity that could accommodate, and anesthetize, any sense of cultural variance. "Western music has claimed to become a universal model, occasionally absorbent and with some 'folklorish' condescension," Guattari (2011) writes. "Particular styles of music were no longer related to territories, unless via the mode of exotic seduction" (109–10). Though reflecting here on the musical codes of the Baroque era, Guattari's comments could not evoke any better the phenomena of lounge exotica but also the formalized appropriations of ethnic instruments in the work of Pierre Boulez and Karlheinz Stockhausen. Where the exotic stood for an interchangeable Other in lounge music that produced a universal sameness through a combination of common popular music codes, technical production values, and album packaging aesthetics (Taylor 2001, 92), Stockhausen's recordings of ethnological instruments collected at the Musée de L'homme in Paris in 1952 disregarded the traditions and methods of playing those music to turn them into raw sound materials; that is, Stockhausen's recordings of the instruments of Indonesia, Japan, China, and elsewhere became nothing more than a matter of understanding their "frequencies . . . and the dynamic level of the partials of the spectra, in order to know what the sound is made of, what the sound is, as a matter of fact; what is the difference between a lithophone sound or, let's say, a Thai gong sound of a certain pitch. And very slowly I discovered the nature of sounds. The idea to analyze sounds gave me the idea to synthesize sounds" (Stockhausen 1995, 33–34). Here, all sounds are brought under the universal regime of frequencies, which in turn points to the further totality of electronic frequency synthesis. Built from the sounds of the African mbira, Boulez's 1952 composition,

"Étude sur un son," was described some years later by Vladimir Ussachevsky as a "'tour de force' of planned transmutation of a single sound of an African drum into an austere linear landscape delineated by a sort of unsmiling musical logic" (in Taylor 2001, 57).

In contrast to these totalizing absorptions of ethnic instruments into a universal sound, Goldsmith's *Planet of the Apes* score builds on the dissonant and percussive sensibilities of modern composers like Bela Bartók and Igor Stravinsky, most prominently noted in music historian Jon Burlingame's Goldsmith retrospective and obituary (in Miller 2010, 212; see also Burlingame 2004a). I find even more compelling relationships between Goldsmith's score and the primitive dimensions of Pierre Schaeffer's work. Particularly in regards to musical "primitivism, and conceptions of otherness more generally" (Taylor 2001, 55), Schaeffer again becomes the conceptual and practical pivot for divisions between the French makers of musique concrète and the mostly Austro-German *elektronische Musik* composers. Early in his practice, Schaeffer had incorporated the sounds of non-Western instrumentation and voice into his work. His first piece of musique concrète, from 1948, included a number of thin-metal instruments such as the African xylophone, mbira, bells, and toy whirligigs. None of these instruments or Schaeffer's work with them yielded sounds that hid or distorted their sources. In this way, Schaeffer's approach to African instrumentation differs significantly from the use of the mbira by Boulez. Having founded Ocora, a record label for traditional African music and worked with technicians in African radio in 1954, Schaeffer was invested in preserving what he heard to be "vulnerable musical cultures—lacking notation, recording, cataloging" (57) while at the same time learning from and drawing on African techniques such as bricolage, which he then updated for the modern recording studio. Boulez had lobbed the term "bricoleur" at Schaeffer as an insult, somewhat akin to the disparaging use of "technician" over "composer" (for his part, Schaeffer would call Boulez "a pretentious boy, a kind of musical Stalinist" in a 1987 interview with Tim Hodgkinson for *RēR Quarterly*). Schaeffer, however, accepted Boulez's snide remark "not as an insult but as something very interesting," and he found in the practice of patching things together what he thought was responsible for the origins of music itself (in Taylor 2001, 57). Bricolage retained humanity within music with "a process that is shaped by the human, the human ear, and not the machine, the mathematical system" (57–58).

What disturbed the ears of the postwar school of electronic musicians was the fact that Schaeffer's "experimental music" presented the ear with such an untidy conglomerate of source materials (Taylor 2001, 56–57). Schaeffer's process was considered flawed because his work took shape at the mixing desk rather than as the result of a prior compositional form. Essentially revisiting longstanding tensions between the theories of Schoenberg (the rationalist of logical historical progression in the field of composition) and those of Stravinsky (the primitivist), electronic musicians after serialism sought rigorous control and organization over all sounds. As Taylor not only teases out tensions between the work of Schaeffer and Boulez but also within the work of the French anthropologist Claude Lévi-Strauss, he highlights the latter's differentiations between the primitive bricoleur and the modern scientist: "The bricoleur begins with materials at hand and makes a structure out of them. The scientist, on the other hand, begins with an overall structure, a concept" (2001, 58). For Lévi-Strauss, science is like composition. It is primarily a conceptual, hypothetical, and theoretical process that renders conceptual events concrete, whereas bricolage, like musique concrète, recycles and repurposes the concrete. Summing up the process of bricolage, Lévi-Strauss writes that "earlier ends . . . are called upon to play the part of means: the signified changes into the signifying and vice versa," while the scientist works with concepts, "hypotheses and theories," creating "its means and results in the form of events" rather than the other way around (in Taylor 2001, 58). As an example of primitive, "Mythical thought," bricolage works with vitally charged, concrete objects, or "signs" (58). Significantly influenced by the anthropologist's work, Schaeffer's formulation of artistic practice is itself a bricolaged hybrid made out of the otherwise oppositional perspectives encountered in Lévi-Strauss. In much later reflections, Schaeffer developed two contrasting versions of music: "musique habituelle," an ordinary music in which composition precedes realization, and "musique nouvelle," a new music in which realization works backwards, thinking time, as Guattari suggests, "against the grain," so that what comes after does in fact modify what was before (10).

Goldsmith's practice—composition no longer sounds like the most compelling term—embodies the bricoleur's concrete science, working with whatever materials might be at hand to create an unusual sound, but with a gritty, primitive materiality that avoided the abstract aspect of electronic music and effects as much as possible. Goldsmith's penchant for unusual sounds is summed up in a running gag attributed to a longtime collaborator, Arthur Morton, who was fond of saying that anytime he heard a strange noise outside the scoring stage, he would call out, "Find out who that guy is and bring him in here. We can use that in Jerry's next picture" (in Burlingame 2004b). But do cinematic scores so readily normalize the avant-garde in this respect, and resolve its deepest disputes through a combination of expediency and creative problem solving? Goldsmith once described twelve-tone music as "not avant-garde anymore; it's sort of old hat, but for film it is still sort of new" (in McGinney 2013, 221). This being "sort of new" is what *Planet of the Apes* is all about. "As with modern art," McGinney writes, "most mainstream audiences found such music puzzling and unsettling because of its unfamiliar, dissonant sounds and its cerebral aesthetic. However, they could accept sounds like those of twelve-tone music more easily when they were included as part of a movie score, especially for a horror or science fiction film" (2013, 222). Goldsmith's work in this respect expands the sonic territories that Bernard Herrmann and Akira Ifukube had introduced into earlier SF films but toward different ends. As much as it echoes the violent banging about on pianos and drums in the score to *The Day the Earth Stood Still*, which you may recall suggested that humans were musically primitive in contrast to the ethereal electronics of the theremin, the percussive primitivism of *Planet of the Apes* is all encompassing, lacking any instrumental counterbalances other than taut moments of silence, which are fraught with peril and propel the frequently disturbing impact of an aggressive sonic touch—an ape-like vocalization or blast of the ram's horn—so sudden and extreme that it seems as if the humans in the film hear it, and attempt to run and hide as a result. In this respect, Goldsmith's work also recalls Ifukube's original combination of unsettling silences and off-screen diegetic noises, blending aspects of modern primitivism and atonality with an affecting use of minimalism and silence. Throughout *Planet of the Apes*, we are made to wait anxiously before we hear both subtle sonic cues, such as the wing like fluttering of the vibraslap, which suggests avian life agitated by an invisible predatory presence, and more violent events, like the blasts of the ram's horn and rattling percussion that announce the arrival of the gorilla soldiers.

The sonic archaic revival here involves a reverse engineering of instrumental modes, which implicates the search for the sonic novum in a return to the uncanny capacities of the acousmatic sonorous object. Cynthia Miller (2010) describes the physical, affective properties of Goldsmith's *Planet of the Apes* score in ways that recall my earlier discussion of twelve-tone music in Rosenman's score to *Fantastic Voyage*. In spite of any skepticism the composer may have had about twelve-tone's originality, Goldsmith's music achieves a similar kind of audible roughing up of the listening body. Not only the assorted percussive sounds, but all of the instrumental voices in Goldsmith's thoroughly deterritorialized orchestra, are "both rhythmic and decidedly arrhythmic," the unusual nature of which engages "the futuristic imagination" of the science fiction film while also provoking "the body's sympathetic tone and most basic, primitive responses—apprehension, panic, flight, anger—as well" (Miller 2010, 214). The emphasis on primitive modes of hearing, where the entire body is poised in a state of relative shock, not only replays tensions fostered throughout the history of SF cinema as well as debated within the postwar sonic avant-garde, it highlights the ways in which these tensions and debates more broadly define the boundaries of a technocultural body in moments of historical crisis, whether this be the threat of nuclear devastation or catastrophic racial conflict.

Though the ultimate consequence of such a crisis, and its trigger, is not even fully known at the very end of *Planet of the Apes*—where evidence of the old Earth's destruction is matched only by the ultimate anempathetic sounds of the surf—this narrative culmination, the end, turns out to have been the cause. Everything in the film leading up to this moment has been retreating from it, rife with bodily peril, all causes at last turned out to be effects: enslavement, punishment, torture, crucifixion, lobotomization, and vivisection among them. The film's exploration of animal and race rights target white bodies almost exclusively, as the only African-American among the astronauts, Dodge (Jeff

Burton), is shot and killed by a band of marauding gorilla soldiers early in the film. Goodman shares a fascinating account of sound and dread, of white bodies and guerrilla warriors in the late eighteenth century, as the tribal nation of the Maroons managed several surprising victories over English colonialists in Jamaica. "The abeng, a fashioned cow horn, had two uses," Goodman writes; "by slave holders to call the slaves to the cane fields and a 'traditional form of communication among the communities, warning them and sending messages across difficult terrain.' The Maroons used the abeng in tandem with their other special techniques—drum communication, the ambush, and camouflage—in order to outwit the British" (2010, 65). The primitive elements of the film's score exacerbate its racial codes through the kind of sonic warfare that, Goodman notes, relies on "the sonic activation of the affective sensorium [that] produces an autonomic response" (70), not only through its arrhythmia but also by means of tonal intensities in which distortion is both tactile and tactical. Goodman speaks specifically to the affect-oriented psychotechnological mechanisms of film sound design:

> In the cinematic experience, the frisson that acute fear produces—the sensation of chills, waves of shivers up and down the spine, goose bumps and hairs standing on end (piloerection)—is actively pursued. The interplay of fear and threat is evoked by narrative tactics of tension such as suspense, a gradual buildup through delaying the arrival of the event whose occurrence resolves the tension, and surprise, working on the effect of the unexpected, the unforeseen, a shock. Film sound modulates affect by tapping into and rewiring the line of attack, the line of flight, and the line of fright. (73)

The sonic novum instigates the archaic revival but also mobilizes an ambiguous critique of the future by means of an acoustic terrorism that revels in the very concreteness of sonic experience, the effect that precedes its own cognition. For Boulez and other detractors, this time reversal had doomed musique concrète to be a kind of "music of primitives, or, perhaps worse from their perspective, civilized people who had 'gone native.' It was in the position of oral music rather than written; bricolage, not science, premodernity, not modernity" (Taylor 2001, 60). The archaic revival shifts the questions of the primitive from the modern to the postmodern, and doing so conducts a McLuhanesque retrieval of the primitive and preliterate, of a space-age orality, which privileges "acoustic space" and affect over the "visual, linear, rationalized, and homogeneous" aspects of the serialized "culture of industrial modernity" (Shaviro 2003, 189–91). *Planet of the Apes* reconstructs this archaic drift by means of a war between the senses, which sound ultimately dominates because of its capacity to trigger precognitive affective states, to touch its listeners, in a concrete way that visual cinema typically does not. Affect, Goodman informs us, is neither "supplement" nor "replacement" to cultures of representation; rather, affect "inserts itself ontologically prior" to representation, "thereby examining the very conditions of possibility for a sonic materialism and the ethico-aesthetic paradigm it would entail" (2010, 10). Goldsmith understood this explicitly, concluding that film scores must do more than complement narrative action: "I try for emotional penetration" (in Miller 2010, 213). At this point, penetrating sound still reinforces the colonial territories of white bodies, and even though it seems clear that Taylor's final words condemn the human "maniacs" who destroyed their own world, not the apes who inherited it, that he gets the last word, delivers it against the relatively silent backdrop of the natural world, conserves the film's affective sonic potential for some future time. As Goodman advises, "While sonic mood modulation becomes another dimension of the ambiences of control, it would be foolish to ignore the complex affects of the ecology of fear for the sake of a too hasty politics of silence" (2010, 73). The touch of time against the grain, skin rubbed the wrong way, will be the end of an abstraction, and the beginning of things.

• CHAPTER 4 •

Sonic Alienation and Psytech at War (1971–77)

It is surprising how quickly science fiction turned from the grandeur and mystery of *2001*, or even the campy romp of *Barbarella*, to such a dark, cynical form of cultural critique. By 1971, three films—George Lucas's *THX-1138*, Stanley Kubrick's *A Clockwork Orange*, and Robert Wise's *The Andromeda Strain*—resolutely shut down the expansive psytech mobilized three years earlier to plunge into the most aberrant political, physical, and psychic domains of the human condition. I am of course concerned with the sonic dimensions of this turn, specifically as it involves a malfunction, if not the eradication, of the earlier hypersensitivies of the machinic unconscious. *THX-1138* restricts all three with a narrative that limits the socius forbidding sex and touch, and contracts outer space into the cold, white interior of the cell—a constriction acoustically matched by sound designer Walter Murch's dense headphone mix. Kubrick's *A Clockwork Orange* offers a complete refutation of the sonic experience of his own earlier film, *2001*. Kubrick's new film concerns the abuse and anarchic destruction of the hypersensitive by nullifying the body (through drugs and ultraviolence), territory (home invasion), and sex (rape). Finally, *The Andromeda Strain* brings the macrocosmos crashing back into the body with its alien viral invasion of the microcosm even as any potential of intergalactic transcendence and cosmic metaphysics are blunted by intrigues of the body politic. While

• 285

science fiction could still play to a young audience, it was growing up, forced to confront a world with serious earthly problems even as its previous fascinations with outer space were quickly becoming reality.

Science fiction cinema in the 1970s also experienced a brief return to electronic music and unconventional sound design before George Lucas's *Star Wars* and Steven Spielberg's *Close Encounters of the Third Kind* significantly changed the sonic novum in 1977 through a very clearly delineated differentiation between realms of diegetic noise and those of nondiegetic scores of a classically orchestral flavor. Prior to 1977, however, electronic tonalities returned to SF films, which reintegrated electronic and synthetic sounds into the music as well as the world of science fiction cinema. Once again, new sonic devices synthesize and electronically process sounds in ways that implicate the unseen presence of extraterrestrial entities or forces, which has profound consequences for humans and extraterrestrials alike. Alien psychogeography is the explicit theme of Andrei Tarkovsky's *Solaris* (1972), in which both the score and ambient sound design at once delimit and open up new dimensions of the psychotechnological properties of cinema. The unusually synthesized sounds of the ANS synthesizer, programmed and performed by Eduard Artemiev, are responsible for constructing not simply an auditory point of view but an alien one. To this extent, the film explores alien psychotechnological entanglement in ways that go well beyond the prior linguistic and musical encounters of earlier Soviet SF, although *Solaris* also probes issues of incompatible languages.

The 1974 Sun Ra film *Space Is the Place* is also about language, which plays a mythic role in this strange gospel of the Arkestra's enterprise due to its amalgamation of culture, sound, and music. *Space Is the Place* recasts the sound of the alien in terms of racial conflict, both within African American culture and with white culture. Sun Ra's sonic myth science not only provides an escape route from these culture wars but also figures a return to the alien novum as a place of resistance and exodus. Armed with sonic psytech (Sun Ra's electronic keyboard, which he uses to navigate his interstellar Arkestra), Sun Ra transforms the consciousness of inner-city black youth, turning them on through cosmic vibrations, and leading them back to their extraterrestrial origins. As he promises a return to the otherworldly origin planet, Saturn, Sun Ra reclaims the diasporic tribe by recuperating the slave narrative. In both *Solaris* and *Space Is the Place*, what makes a sound authentically alien has more to do with the ways in which new technologies and methods for making, processing, and reproducing sound bring with them innovative ideas about what kinds of sounds are possible rather than predetermining what sounds are desirable or even what those sounds might signify and mean for the human audience of the science fiction film. The "human" also becomes a contested category split along both planetary and racial lines. Historically, the SF film has incubated the technologies needed for making new cosmic sounds, a narrative that Sun Ra's Arkestra takes up literally, as an engine of interstellar travel and the key to the liberation of black people, where the ANS synthesizer, like the planet Solaris, facilitates cosmic drama as technological analogy, spiritual allegory, and psychotherapy. In these very different films, the genre seeds development and application of new artifacts, instruments, and sound-making practices, which both works also investigate in terms of their liberatory capacities. New science fictional spaces of accommodation take shape as much on a distant planet of the imagination as in the inner city in these two peculiar takes on the alien visitation narrative.

Strange new sounds become part of the speculative processes of SF, but as they play an important role in narrative as well as in developing the psychotechnological entanglements that film enacts, they open themselves up to significant cultural anxieties around the encounter with genuine agents of alterity rather than sonic simulacra. Over the course of the 1970s, the enclosure of sonic experience in the service of immersive spectacle increasingly polices our ability to avoid distinctions between music and noise, often mobilizing entire regimes by which sound is coded as musical or not and is determined as permissible or otherwise. In the scores by John Williams heard in the twin blockbusters of 1977—*Star Wars* and *Close Encounters of the Third Kind*—music has much the same effect even though the former features the composer in his most highly romantic Wagnerian mode, while the score to *Close Encounters* ranks among his most atonal work. In either case, sound largely demonstrates the same sensibilities and values even while the films absorb the otherwise incompatible sonic novums of past SF cinema. The most conservative nondiegetics of classic big budget films like *This Island Earth,* as well as the pulp serials and swashbuckling adventure genres, return in the case of *Star Wars,* while the dynamic musical range of *2001* is brought at last under a unifying total score in the case of *Close Encounters of the Third Kind.* Further, these films play out the differences between music and noise to support a nostalgic agenda, but they also develop a new kind of sonic novum, one that takes advantage of the design of sound on multitrack editing stations and made for playback over new high-resolution and multichannel theater sound systems. An aesthetic of sonic immersion emerges that favors cognitive saturation over estrangement. Not only does this leave the filmgoer little leverage for critical engagement, it also tends to support patriarchal mythic forms hitched to the nostalgic longing for films of old, products of putatively simpler worlds, whether that of the light comic strip style of the early serials or Disney features. The content of this mythos is culturally conservative rather than progressive even though it is technically innovative. These, then, are sonic novums in conflict.

A sharper contrast could hardly be made between our exemplary SF films of 1971 and 1977, despite the fact that two of them come from the same director, George Lucas. Rather than antagonistic, the later films are merely the fulfillment of the end of the utopian imagination that the earlier had put into motion. *Star Wars* recasts the metaphysical hypersensitivities of the psonicosmos by establishing and policing rigid territorial distinctions between worldly noise, even otherworldly noise, and mythic music. *Close Encounters of the Third Kind* recasts the primitive hypersensitivities of sonic affect and embodiment in terms of childhood fears ranging from monsters under the bed to abduction, even as these lie alongside adult fantasies of returning to idealized childhood freedoms and mythic irresponsibility. As Williams restores "the mythic qualities lost in most film music" (Lerner 2004, 98) while effectively quoting Lucas's favored serialized westerns and proto–space operas, the composer's use of distinct leitmotifs for each character in *Star Wars* eschews psychological depth, development, and connection to instead emphasize each character's alignment with mythic and predestined Forces. In *Close Encounters,* the sonic urtext comes with the climactic quotation of "When You Wish Upon a Star" from Disney's *Pinocchio* (1940). While *Star Wars* and *Close Encounters* derive their musical master narratives from popular culture, they also adhere to strict divisions between domains of musical expressivity and technical sound effects.

With *Star Wars* and *Close Encounters*, SF cinema can no longer present anything substantially new or different except for the crisis of the new. Given the propensity of Lucas especially but Spielberg as well to edit, revise, and suppress certain aspects of their archive, the endlessly "remastered" copies of copies not only negate the historical authenticity of the archive but also constitute a form of empire that glorifies nothing so much as the recursive cultism that Walter Benjamin first labeled an "aestheticized politics," which replaces critical awareness with a mystifying cult of power ([1936] 1968, 217–18). Zepke (2012) describes the collapse of the utopian imagination in science fiction films that "either cynically exploit wish-fulfillment fantasies masquerading as political narratives . . . or return us to essentialist human values through the reduced narrative of escape. In both cases these utopian fantasies are symptomatic expressions of our political powerlessness and of our inability to imagine a future of anything else." Overcharged by new levels of volume, mixed with greater resolution and a wider range of frequencies, and multidimensional in theatrical reproduction, sound becomes spectacle, an immersive perversion of the sonic "space of accommodation" of new technological conditions that Bukatman (1997, 8) argues the SF film provides. Bukatman emphasizes SF's provision of a formal as well as cognitive space that facilitates actual and figural technocultural transformation. What I wish to establish here is how the trauma of the machinic consciousness, brought on as the psychedelic space age of SF cinema comes to an end, plays out sonically over the course of the 1970s to culminate with the blockbusters of 1977 and their obsessive, hyper-regulation of noise. "Noise," Goodman explains, constitutes "the outside of a regime of coded sound, continuously perturbs music, threatening its regulation of sonic flow" (2010, 51). Beginning with John Williams's aesthetic mission to control the total sonic experience of *Star Wars* and *Close Encounters*, along with technical innovations in surround sound mixing, high-resolution audio reproduction, and noise reduction technologies, the regulation of noise in psychotechnological apparatuses is increasingly managed within the movie theater rather than in the imaginary spaces of a science fiction film's narrative. As all sounds become elements within the spectacular ecology of the SF film experience, the outsider and alien value of the noisy Other is eliminated. This reverses a previously necessary development by which noise "not only plays a crucial role in the creation-destruction cycles of musical evolution, setting in motion the mutation of sonic culture, but also . . . anticipates broader social crises and transformation" (52). By policing the sonic novum, SF's blockbuster films recast the tensions between music and noise that have concerned us throughout this book in terms of emergent technologies of audio fidelity. By distributing sounds around the acoustically immersive but also highly active and mobile spaces of surround theatrical reproduction, the sonic domain itself comes to act as a kind of motif, a motif of a spatial rather than timbral nature. This posttonal motif of sound as immersive control structure shapes and directs hearing. It also ideally models the listening subject, sustaining a structuralist myth of the singular self who must now be centered within the vastly expanded headspace of the theater. But before we can get to this exterior that poses as an interiority, we must first get inside of some uncomfortable soundscapes.

1971 | *THX-1138, THE ANDROMEDA STRAIN, A CLOCKWORK ORANGE*

George Lucas's first film, *THX-1138* presents the utter annihilation of the three hypersensitivities of the machinic conscious. The cosmic domains of *2001* are instantly negated within the stark, anesthetically white walls of the living quarters/prison cells of *THX-1138*. The equally expansive interiorities accessed through the monolith's star gate, along with the simultaneous exhilaration and terror of the psychedelic trip, are also canceled out by *THX-1138's* mind- and mood-regulating regimen of pharmaceuticals, surveillance, and ubiquitous media communications, frequently delivered in the tight quarters of headphonic space that completes the total limitation of movement that this film explores. The sterile autoeroticism and sexual dysfunction of *THX-1138* replace the frequent couplings, whether evidence of a sexual liberation or exploitation, witnessed over the course of *Barbarella,* and which challenged our notions of social space and its technocultural coding through sexualized bodies. The archaic revival and evolutionary reversals of *Planet of the Apes* are confronted by the stark temporal dead end of *THX-1138*, not only with its "future was now" sensibility but also its distillation of physical touch, which always worked on the affected skins of primates, into an interiorized simulacrum of essence. *THX-1138* is an allegorical distillation of its contemporary world, as Alexandra DuPont (2004) concludes in her review, in which one of the most prophetic aspects of the film is its anticipation of cable television's segregation of viewing markets into "sex," "violence," "comedy," and "smart" channels, all of which are equally vapid imitations of a substantial outside reality in the same way that mood-regulating pills imitate psychological substance or individualized interiorities.

Lucas cowrote the film with Walter Murch, who also designed the film's unique sonic experience. For both, it was less important that *THX-1138* extrapolate forward in time as it was for the finished film to feel like an artifact from the future, a product of a future that was, but never is, now. Lucas will revisit this extrapolative historical sensibility in *Star Wars*, where the film hermetically seals its subject matter from the real world through the nonplace of fantasy, myth, and fairy tale. Regarding *THX-1138*, Murch elaborated that he and Lucas wanted to make "a film *from* the future rather than *about* the future. We're looking at a film from a foreign country, whose custom and habits and cinematic language we're really not familiar with. . . . This did make for a little confusion in the audience that did see it—but that was, to a certain extent, part of our intent" (DuPont 2004). I can think of few SF filmmakers or sound designers who describe their project in such a way; the novum here is not new but rather already old, well fixed in its ways and casting a long shadow back onto a rather dismal present from an even more dystopic future. The film's sound design was key to this process, providing Murch a language of broadcast or transmission. As Murch notes, "The concept was to find the future through the sound design and bring it back, without alteration or explanation" (in Whittington 2007, 81). Of course, Murch's conceptual and practical approaches must be juggled around here as the sounds that we hear in *THX-1138* are indeed altered and manipulated in order to sound like documents from the future. Murch approached voices, for instance, in this way: "We had one Nagra tape recorder with the clean voices on it. We ham-radioed them into the universe, received them back again as if they were coming from another country, fiddling with the tuning so that we could get that wonderful 'sideband' quality to the voices. Then we rerecorded them on another Nagra and cut them into the final sound track" (in Whittington 2007, 74). Murch called this worldizing, and the sound world that he created assaults the listener with an endless stream of voices, radio broadcasts with fragments of Muzak, commercials, official warnings, regulatory reminders, and broadband surveillance chatter.

Murch's notion of the film as foreign country plays out in his sound design and edits, with the soundscape one of few elements in the film that brings texture and grit to the smooth white walls, the occasionally indistinguishable human bodies, and the reflective chrome faces of the likewise indistinguishable members of the police force. Murch's concept of sound design as broadcast makes every diegetic sound seem as though it were emitting from over a loudspeaker somewhere in the world of *THX-1138* or, even more likely, played over headphones directly into the minds of each isolated, but thoroughly synchronized, member of its populace, each steeped in an individually directed soundscape that shares the same collective message through an endless broadband saturation. Sound locks each mind into a place at once common and isolated. As the sound of an outside space, its ambience, invades the interior domains of the mind, the headphone mix keeps the sonic action close to the auditor and more susceptible to its ambient rhythm. Chion (2009) notices that "the mixture of different sound *tempi*" in the film gives it "a markedly polyrhythmic character" for a monophonic recording, as "collisions of different speed can occur constantly within a single scene or as an effect of crosscutting that opposes contradictory rhythms" (121). Instead of providing breaks in the sonic flow, however, the various collisions, crosscuts, oppositional sounds, and contradictory rhythms make the overall sonic character of the experience that much more comprehensive—that is, more invasive, more imprisoning, and completely inescapable. Lalo Schifrin's somber, religious choruses and musical atmospheres in *THX-1138* are no exception, and though technically nondiegetic, they work completely within the totalized soundscape of the film. Heard in the context of the radio chatter, advertisements, instructions, prescriptions, computerized beeps and industrial noise, they become part of the future artifact as well. There is no place of escape or relief, a point emphasized in Murch's original mono mix of *THX-1138*, which plays best over headphones. Not even stereo separation provides a space in which the mind can move and dodge the sonic mass. With headphones on, listening in isolation, we become the ideal auditor, inhabiting the film's telecommunicated sound world and subject to its broadcast programming and ubiquitous, manufactured consciousness.

Along with directors like Lucas and Francis Ford Coppola, Murch was an instrumental part of "the postproduction revolution" as filmmakers approached the editing of the film as "a site of vigorous experimentation" (Whittington 2007, 72). Postproduction no longer referred to work done with the oversight of the studio, often by producers only involved during the last stages of a project, but rather it became an essential part of the director's vision and practice. In the case of *THX-1138*, Lucas edited the film footage for almost half a year while Murch worked on the sound design. Editing their work simultaneously and then collaborating on the final mix promised that the sound and visuals would best influence each other (72). For his own part, Murch's contributions involved a staggering complexity, with "approximately twenty different layers of sound effects, dialogue, and music" involved in the sound mix of *THX-1138* (73). Just as it drew these various layers of sonic event together, Murch's "sound montage" work—a kind of musique concrète for film that produces the singular sonorous object comprising the entirety of what we hear over the course of a film's runtime—followed from the "convergence of recording, editing, and re-recording duties" and involved "conscious experiments in each of the traditional areas of sound production, blurring their distinctions" (73). Murch's sonic innovations combined the new technological resources of Hollywood sound craft, the spirit of freewheeling collaboration from the California film schools that nurtured the postproduction revolution, and the experimental approaches of the French New Wave. "From the fragments of the past and the influences of the present," Whittington concludes, "the sounds of the future were now audible" (74).

It is a testimony to Murch's abilities that many of the pioneering film projects in which he was involved are about sound and listening.

After *THX-1138*, he provided the mix of pop hits, doo-wop, and radio personality chatter than made up the radiophonic collective consciousness of Lucas's *American Graffiti* (1976). He also did sound for two films by Francis Ford Coppola, *The Conversation* (1974) and *Apocalypse Now* (1979). The films with Coppola effectively launched the field of sound design in name and not only practice—Murch was the first to receive on-screen credit for such in the opening titles of *Apocalypse Now*—and elevated film sound from a craft to a form of sonic artistry. For all four of these films, Murch contributes a sonic dimension that encourages "cinematic play, self-reflexivity, and shifts in subjectivity" (Whittington 2007, 21), and which I consider an intertwined form of subdiegetic consciousness and technodiegetic space. In *American Graffiti*, for example, with Wolfman Jack as guide, pop radio creates the teenaged collective unconscious through the combined technologies of the automobile and broadcast, with pop hits represented less as a homogenous backdrop and more as a wide range of musical moods for make-out sessions and hot rod competitions. Sound is never merely atmospheric in *American Graffiti*, and in fact, it does something quite similar to sound in *THX-1138*, taking the various, independent experiences of those in their separate, automotive headspaces and uniting them according to a ubiquitous soundscape that constantly leaks beyond diegetic space with the presence of something more like a musical than a traditional drama. The placement of musical cues within the diegetic world over time suggests that the characters are in fact creating their own soundtrack, even though they have to go through the proxy of Wolfman Jack to do so; music is their affect generator and a tool for the management of consciousness and mood alike. Both of the Coppola films reflect on the relationship of sound to specific states of consciousness; they are also about sonic psytech and rely on the mixing of new diegetic spaces that sonify both the mind and technologies. Throughout *The Conversation*, the obsessive and paranoid listening to surveillance tapes reveals "the unstable, subjective, and constructed nature of recorded sound" (20), while for *Apocalypse Now*, Murch designs an entire technoacoustic ecology of psychological warfare. Tape recordings and loudspeakers conduct a war of words during lulls in combat, channeling obscene taunts, rock music, and Wagner, while recitations of Eliot become acts of terror as well as routes of temporary escape, a sonic hallucinogenic gateway out of hell. Before these films, almost as their collective prototype, *THX-1138* involved a radical fragmentation and reassemblage of sound sources that postproduction technologies mediated, filtered, processed, and combined into new compositional and aesthetic forms. This not only actualized the film's themes, it made them something that we must inhabit.

• • •

Released twenty years after his film *The Day the Earth Stood Still*, director Robert Wise's *The Andromeda Strain* is a largely pessimistic science thriller about a microscopic alien organism that arrives on Earth aboard a crashed satellite probe. Devastating the population of a small Arizona town, the virus becomes the subject of investigation by a group of scientists over the course of which human ingenuity and technological invention frequently pose more dangers than the virus itself. With elements of government conspiracy and cover-up—the underground base in which the core science group attempts to decode the Andromeda strain turns out to be a facility for biological weapons research—human frailty, intuition, luck, and circumstance prove more salient to the survival of the species than our technologies.

Gil Mellé's score to *The Andromeda Strain* is an anomaly in an era of filmmakers doing everything they could to get away from the biggest sonic cliché of the SF film: weird electronic shit. Mellé's music for *The Andromeda Strain* was the weirdest science fiction score since *Forbidden Planet* even though built from a broader range of source materials (McEneany 2010). Mellé built his own electronic instruments, and he also had a fondness for musique concrète, manipulating recorded buzz saws, trains, and bowling alleys for the film's accompaniment. Mellé described the resulting music as a "sheet of sound" selected and arranged according to more personally defined sonorous principles rather than on "Western scales, or major and minor, or the normal things that people get involved with" (in Larson 2012, 435). The resulting sounds jump among heartbeat rhythms and pulsing noises, analog computer beeps and blips, and more aggressive jackhammers and percussive outbursts. Rarely do we hear familiar instrumental tones, and even when

296 • SONIC ALIENATION AND PSYTECH AT WAR

timbral elements recall piano, electric organ, drums, or horns, the little fragments of sound do not bring to the score any kind of recognizable melody, thematic motif, or consistent rhythm. It is even difficult to call Mellé's work "atonal," taking such a complete departure from not only traditional film music but also the twelve-tone composition of *Fantastic Voyage* or the primitive dissonance of *Planet of the Apes*. Mellé's noisy soundscapes are far more industrial and abstract, with few contemporary parallels other than the film and television soundtracks made in the BBC Radiophonic Workshop for *Doctor Who* (1963–89) and other projects, where even non-SF programming like quiz shows and commercials frequently featured all-electronic scores comprised of electronic tones, ambient atmospheres, and mutant melodies made without any apparent basis in known instrumentation.

As a recording jazz artist since the age of nineteen, Mellé knew instruments, playing saxophone in variously sized ensembles for Blue Note and Prestige throughout the 1950s. His ensembles were almost always unconventional, bringing together unusual timbre combinations, such as the low-register balance of his own baritone sax with trombone, bass, and guitar heard on *Patterns in Jazz* (1956) and the tuba and French horn included on his *Gil's Guests* sessions (1956). Mellé's songs and transcriptions often feature unusual rhythms and time signatures, while overall, the material emphasizes tone clusters and patterns of sounds—what he referred to as "Bartók's architectonic thinking" (in Steinberg 2002)—rather than the traditional melodies or even modal techniques of jazz. With their spacious, open harmonic groupings of detached notes, somewhat in the manner of cool jazz, Mellé's 1950s recordings have been loosely identified as "Third Stream" music. Composer and musician Gunther Schuller (1986) coined the term in the 1950s to describe the hybrid of jazz and classical forms pioneered by Duke Ellington and George Gershwin, and which remained relevant as modern jazz artists probed what Schuller referred to as "the future of form in jazz" (18). Schuller insisted that there was no "Third Stream Jazz" (120) and sought to delineate the characteristics of an entirely new genre, "a *fusion* of these two forces" that detractors considered a "hybrid intruder" (114). Perhaps meaning to conjure up similar musical fusions, Mellé called what he was doing "primitive modern," a sound exemplified on the 1956 album of that name but also heard on the 1957 follow-up, *Quadrama*. Mellé's liner notes to *Primitive Modern* describe "a wedding of the classics with the more modern developments native to jazz," as well as "the perfect admixture of classical techniques with jazz emotions and beat" (in Harrison et al. 2000, 628). While his recordings never quite warrant the occasional appellation of Third Stream, differing significantly from the work of Schuller and most other practitioners due largely to the use of "dissonant counterpoint and bitonality" (629), it does exhibit a fascination with form and sonic "superstructure" (Schuller 1986, 19). Mellé's band work often pushes against the limits of jazz hybridization into unknown territories with unusual touches like vocalist Monica Dell's low, spacey moan on one of Mellé's first recording, "Four Moons" (1952), or the strange sounds and structure of "Iron Works," from the *Primitive Modern* album. On this composition, drummer Ed Thigpen used pieces of metal pipe in his kit, lending the recording its industrial "machine-shop sound," while an "unexpected break in the tune" occurs in which every player suddenly drops out and guitarist Joe Cinderella "emits a beam of abstract sound—a totally static moment and an early echo of Mellé's future in electronic music" (Steinberg 2002).

Even by the mid-1950s, Mellé was "looking toward a musical future that never occurred" (Yanow, n.d.). He moved to Los Angeles in the 1960s to start writing music for film and television. His bold approach to acoustic jazz worked well within the context of crime dramas, and Mellé composed themes and incidental music for the Sidney Poitier film *The Organization* (1971) and such shows as *Ironside* (1967–75), *Columbo* (1968–78), and *The Six Million Dollar Man* (1973–78). American film studios continued to favor predominantly orchestral or pop musical sensibilities, with a music director, composer, and ensemble all involved. Mellé was at home in this market, expanding the role of the composer in popular television shows, which presented a microsonic environment that demanded quick bursts of iconic sound, eventually sound logos, typically placed at either end of a commercial break. Mellé's ability to compose in short but dynamic, tonally adventurous phrases was a good fit for TV. This sort of synthetic music making that Mellé practiced also facilitated the consolidation of soundtrack creation to a single producer responsible for composing, performing, and postproduction mixing.

Others working in similar ways in SF cinema would include Wendy Carlos, John Carpenter with most of his own films, Howard Shore's work on David Cronenberg films, Vangelis, Larry Fast's Synergy, Brian Eno, Tangerine Dream, Clint Mansell, and Hans Zimmer. For Mellé, the attraction of the independent synthesist on the part of film studios was purely financial: "It's a way to eliminate the orchestra and do a score very cheaply, because the synthesizers are used to simulate and duplicate the instruments that we've all had in the orchestra for years. There's nothing *different* about it" (Larson 2004). Mellé reminds us more than once that he came before "all this." His point is that any reasonable understanding of what electronic music is, with all its familiar names like Moog and Arp and "all those things," must cast its shadow back onto film history, when "one had to build one's own equipment." It would seem that one must also make a value assessment that privileges the kind of scoring practices involved in making the "electronic music" of *The Andromeda Strain* stand out against the noise of electronic tonalities heard in *Forbidden Planet*. Subsequently, we must cast our ears back from what he characterizes as an era of ubiquitous, cheap mass production of the synthesizer to a time when handmade equipment meant one must be a technician as well as a composer in order to create unique music that no one had ever heard before.

This was not an unusual trajectory for jazz composers and musicians, particularly, it seems, the predominantly white male artists of the Third Stream, who produced more commercially conventional works that drifted into a watered down experiment with form opposed to, or at least out of touch with, their African American contemporaries creating the aggressive, bluesy edge of hard bop and the outer limits of free jazz alike (Toop 1995, 191). In *Ocean of Sound,* David Toop suggests that the combination of "commercial acumen" with elements of modal "colouration, impressionism, counterpoint and self-conscious rhythmic experimentation," made them fitting for the ambient as well as expedient necessities of TV and film scoring (192). While most of Mellé's popular scores for media demonstrate this fusion of the commercial and experimental, at least some of his compositions continued to demonstrate a kind of sympathy to the space jazz of Sun Ra and later experimenters, like Eric Dolphy, whose *Out to Lunch* (1964), Toop suggests, offers an enduring blend of eclectic sensibilities "integrated into music which sounds at once utterly familiar yet from another dimension"(191). Closer to the end of the 1960s, Mellé's music would leave the "familiar" further and further behind.

Mellé had been making his own synthesizers as early as 1959, back in New York when recording for Blue Note and then Prestige, but once he moved to L.A., he began incorporating them into his practice. His group, the Jazz Electronauts, performed at the Monterey Pop Festival in 1967 and released their only LP, *Tome VI*, in 1968. Mellé's liner notes herald "the first album of electronic jazz," promising something significantly different than amplified guitars or electric organs, "instruments that synthesize or modify" existing sound sources but ultimately don't "produce sounds strongly indigent to themselves" and subsequently "expand the tone and dynamic spectrum of what would ordinarily be a standard jazz quartet instrumentation." Rather than a precursor to what would become known as jazz fusion, which involves a blend of jazz and electric rock, Mellé introduces five new instruments, each designed and built by himself, that are "much akin to those used in electronic classical music," a hybrid suggesting what the jazz critic Leonard Feather apparently dubbed "Fourth Stream" music, which Mellé's notes explain means "a melding of three vital musical forces to produce a fourth." Synthesizing aspects of modal and free jazz with very abstract electronic tones that suggest nothing so much as the *Forbidden Planet* score (check out the extended spaced-out sequence in the middle of "Blue Quasar," the album's opening track). If anybody, the Electronauts most readily recall Sun Ra and His Arkestra, but the smaller size of Mellé's ensemble allows for an openness in the performance that brings the various electronic elements to the foreground of the mix. *Tome VI*'s back jacket introduces each of Mellé's instruments, many of which he would also use in the production of his score for *The Andromeda Strain*: "The Electar," a "theoretical" approximation of stringed instruments with no strings, but which lets the player control pitch, decay, and volume; "the Envelope," an effects module used to "mutate" bass and cello lines in order to create rhythmic pulses; "Tome VI," a transistor circuit providing oscillator, modulation, and envelope processing built into a "tubular perforated extension grafted" to Mellé's own soprano saxophone; "Effects

Generator," a console that generated arpeggiated passages and complex polyrhythms; and the "Doomsday Machine," a "low register electronic 'cymbal'" capable of producing a "most ominous and sinister quality that at times can sound like total decimation." Mellé never recorded again with the Electronauts, but his scores for *The Andromeda Strain* and Rod Serling's *Night Gallery* (1969–73) would feature all of this primitive futurist gear and more, including a new 8-voice analog percussion synthesizer that he made, the Percussotron III, one of the earliest drum machines in electronic music history (Steinberg 2002).

Mellé is quick to proclaim several firsts: the first white bandleader signed to Blue Note records; the first electronic jazz band; the first electronic drum machine; the first all-electronic score for a motion picture (*The Andromeda Strain*) and television (*Night Gallery*). At least one of these, the film score, is not entirely accurate, though Mellé's ([1983] 2004) qualifications for coming to such a bold conclusion are significant, and he is quick to anticipate the obvious objection to come in an interview with Randall Larson conducted in 1983:

> I'm very familiar with *Forbidden Planet*. *Forbidden Planet* was not a *score*. *Forbidden Planet* was described, on the picture, as electronic sounds ["tonalities"], and the sounds were generated by ordinary test equipment that you would find in any television repair station. Ordinary test sign-wave generators and that's *not* electronic music. There's another important thing: *Andromeda Strain* also incorporated elements of *musique concrète* [natural sounds used musically], quite extensively the main title included recorded sounds of bowling balls hitting pins, sounds from lumber mills, and so on. I spent two days with Robert Wise at the Jet Propulsion Lab taping all sorts of *musique concrète* sounds that would be incorporated in the score. That was another first. I don't know of anyone else who's used *musique concrète*, even yet. Of course, it's dangerous ground you're getting into sound effects, so you have to handle it very delicately.

Though my earlier consideration of *Forbidden Planet* treated a similar pairing of electronic tone generation and tape-mixing composition, Mellé's problems with the film revolve around two distinctions: instrumentality and performance. The earlier liner notes to *Tome VI* emphasize both and effectively outline the strategy and practice relevant to Mellé's work on *The Andromeda Strain*. Each one of Mellé's inventions produces its own "strongly indigent" voice—"the effects generator . . . is as unique as a trombone"—which can and must be performed in real time just like any other instrument in the quartet. Mellé dismisses the tape music of the electroacoustic tradition—"picture yourself applauding a tape recorder"—and insists "no tape or overdubbing techniques are used" on *Tome VI*. More important to Mellé, "Musical intuition is as essential to a jazz musician as to the electronic composer in such exploratory musical ventures. Improvisation is the common denominator." Not only does *Tome VI* represent the first electronic jazz album, then, it is a culmination of the birth of "live electronic jazz," and the "eloquence of electronically generated tones" was validated for the bandleader by the favorable reception of this new music at the Monterey Jazz Festival. Synthesizing practices of electronic music and musique concrète—which we must now identify as a Fifth Stream!—revolves around the use of "music" in both terms, something that Mellé finds missing in the Barrons' productions, and it encapsulates notions of instrumental voice and performance, which for Mellé are more vital than the idea of composition, or writing music, per se.

The Andromeda Strain presented particular, significant challenges for Mellé, who was instructed by Robert Wise to deliver a score "with no themes, no recognizable sounds. . . . No harmonies! In short, what he wanted was a kind of a non-score." Mellé recorded material for over ten weeks, building up a "stockpile of ideas" in the form of tape recordings, which he then mixed together in a real-time performance with a twenty-four-track console. The expansion of the mixing desk made it possible to play back and combine tapes in a kind of improvisation, something prohibited by the single-track editing stations used by the Barrons and Bernard Herrmann, for that matter. In Mellé's hands, musique concrète became a performance art in its own right. He continued to struggle with the fear that not only might audiences mistake his music for sound effects, but the director might take his score for music: "How to keep my music, which was a kind of a non-music, separate from the sound effects in the picture was not easy. How do you know which is which?" The film score would seem to suggest what now must be our Sixth Stream, something so synthetic that it goes well beyond music and effect, a kind of music that is also a kind of nonmusic, at which point cues evoke not so much the invisible but the microscopic. This is nothing less than the nonspace of the Andromeda strain and its motif, a "kind of chirping, bassy rhythm" that we hear when the alien spore might be nearby. Again, Mellé recalls another first:

> It's interesting you mention that, because that was actually a forerunner of the ostinato that was used in *Jaws*. The idea was to communicate to the audience that the virus was in the vicinity and posing great danger, but one you can't see. We want to make the audience aware, and the way to do that was of course to use an ostinato that they would recognize immediately. It was literally a repetitive sound, it was not a musical sound in any sense, far less musical than what John Williams used in *Jaws*, but *Jaws* had the same principal: you've got a fish in the water and it's dangerous and you want the audience to know it but you don't want to show it. It was the same thing. (Larson 2004)

Appropriately in the case of the postbop jazz musician, a raw new form of motif—a rhythm motif—emerges that is essentially devoid of the timbral qualities that had distinguished earlier SF motifs from melodic counterparts. The rhythm motif possesses a superstructural architecture, something like the distinct formation of the hexagonal Andromeda cells.

The unusual nature of Mellé's music at first seems particularly bizarre, given the not-so-out-there setting of *The Andromeda Strain*. Much of the film takes place in labs and other sterile and highly controlled environments. The tense opening title is hardly a main theme in any sense of the word. With its skittering rhythms approaching static velocities and sudden dropouts, I find it one of the most unsettling bits of music put to film, much less during opening titles. Other than the titles, Mellé's music is typically heard only in important technical action scenes, and little of it is heard at any length—we are faced with an economy of microbursts of sound—making it particularly shocking when they are. There is much more music to be heard on the vinyl LP released in 1971, infamous for the hexagonal cut of the packaging and the vinyl record itself. Threatening the ruin of needles, as announced in a bold red warning label included in the album package, this artifact in fact adds a further dimension to our consideration of the film's theme of intuition and human error against highly technical constraints and of alien virology, here taking the form of a sonorous object from the future. Heard on the album as sustained flows rather than micromovements, Mellé's work feels even more ahead of its time. The last half of the track "Hex" includes an extended sequence of ambient space music not too far removed from the work of Tangerine Dream and other Berlin School musicians. Mellé's electronautic future jazz appears in the plucked bass lines of "Andromeda," from which the virus's rhythm motif was extracted. The closing track, "Strobe Crystal Green," anticipates Intelligent Dance Music or ambient techno with Mellé's rapid drum machine, programmed sequences, jackhammer samples, and feedback-drenched synth lines. The LP package is a weirdly alien artifact as well. Pressed to vinyl in the shape of the Andromeda virus and released in a reflective silver six-panel gatefold jacket that opens like an iris shutter, the LP suggests a strange new strain of mutant jazz that didn't come from around here. The distortion of sounds and album material alike speaks to contamination by an alien source that has transformed the sonorous object into a sonic anomaly, an antiobject that, like the nonscore itself, could not be played without the risk of systemic damage across the full range of hypersensitivities but that of language most of all.

As part of an improvisational performance, Mellé's new instrumentalities and live musique concrète initiates a rhetorical amplification that shuts down and redirects our earlier queries into the primitive and cultural appropriation. Deleuze and Guattari differentiate between a deterritorialization, which the old kind of musique concrète had triggered and what must be heard as a reterritorialization in Mellé's work, which "must not be confused with a return to a primitive or older territoriality: it necessarily implies a set of artifices by which one element, itself deterritorialized, serves as a new territoriality for another, which has lost its territoriality as well" (1987, 174). Mellé's practice of proliferating streams, each synthesis moving sound matter further and further away from the territories of singular and separate sound forms, never ends as the rhythm of reterritorialization can only accelerate with ever greater density. Older categories fall away, while something new lurks within something old, as the pianist John Lewis explained to Gunther Schuller:

"It isn't so much what we see (or hear) in the music of each idiom; it is more what we do *not* see in the one that already exists in the other" (1986, 116–17). The SF film has forever been the zone of a similar, inevitable cross-fertilization of forms, but in Mellé's score for *The Andromeda Strain*, it appears to have a reached a certain threshold, an ultimate distance, that reveals its status as "anti-pedigree and anti-establishment," as well as "the ultimate anti-label music" (120), even doing so at what Goodman calls the "intersection of sonic culture with the virological pragmatism" (2010, 131–32) of studio capital. Schaeffer argues that "the sound object is not a state of mind" (2017, 67), and though it strikes me as ultimately improbable that our encounters with the sound object could avoid subjectivity to the degree that Schaeffer proposes, the degree of objectivity that he describes makes of sound a profoundly alien object, unmodified "either with the variations in individual listening or the incessant fluctuations of our attention and our sensibility" (68). The sonorous object is its own thing. At the same time, Schaeffer's sonorous object must be partly constructed out of what each listener brings to the encounter at the moment of contact. It may well turn out that the opposition between mind and external reality that Schaeffer describes is responsible for our experiencing a sound as new and the mechanism by which the sonic novum cognitively estranges us and manufactures new psychotechnologies. "Concrete machines," Guattari writes, "relaying resonances of black holes carried by semiotic components cannot be classified or labeled according to general categories. They are organized only within the framework of particular arrangements specific to each type of assemblage which themselves escape any taxonomic systematization" (2011, 105–6). Remember, Robert Wise asked Mellé for something never asked, at least in his estimation, of "any composer in the history of the world": "music that had no themes, no chords, no harmonic structure, and with totally new sonorities" (Larson 2004). Mellé's score not only shows that signification is inseparable from the materiality of sound, it argues for the essentially alien nature of both. What may be the most remarkable thing about Mellé's nonscore with its nonmusic is that it draws attention to the alien sonic superstructures of an invisible microcosm without standing in for them. It is almost as if it wasn't there at all.

SONIC ALIENATION AND PSYTECH AT WAR • 305

• • •

A Clockwork Orange absorbs Stanley Kubrick's previous film, *2001: A Space Odyssey,* so completely within its distorted reflection of the future-as-the-present that in the record bins of the Chelsea Drug Store—the very one where Jagger went to get your prescription filled in the 1969 Rolling Stones song, "You Can't Always Get What You Want"—you just might find not one but two different copies of the *2001* soundtrack. As Alex (Malcolm McDowell) strolls the aisles of the local "disc-bootick," the sequence is full of recognizable, many now iconic, LP cameos: Tim Buckley's *Lorca* (1970), Neil Young's *After the Gold Rush* (1970), the Beatles' *Magical Mystery Tour* (1967), Stray's first self-titled album (1970), Pink Floyd's *Atom Heart Mother* (1970), and of course the different albums related to *2001,* one MGM's official soundtrack release (1968), and the other a Polydor compilation, *Theme Music for the Film "2001: A Space Odyssey" and Other Great Movie Themes* (1970). As Alex chats up a couple of young "devotchkas," Sonietta (Gillian Hills) looks at Mungo Jerry's 1970 hit, "In the Summertime," while Marty (Barbara Scott) namechecks Goggly Gogol, Johnny Zhivago, and Heaven Seventeen. The names of two of these imaginary bands are displayed on the record shop's colorful Top Ten list, nine years before the Sheffield synth-pop band took the name Heaven 17 for themselves; at least two other bands—Johnny Zhivago and The Humpers—got their names from the film, as if the movie might seal their future success or at least their notoriety.

Timelines collapse as we take the pulse of future pop music charts in the midst of actual product. Judging by their late-mod clothing and hipster hairstyles, Alex, Marty, and Sonietta would not look out of place in Chelsea in the early 1970s, while the record boutique's vaguely futuristic décor was fully in the moment and of its time as the '60s collapsed into the '70s. More importantly than the scene's confusing time signatures (to which I will return), this is one of few instances in which Kubrick incorporates imaginary music in a manner akin to Burgess's novel. Even the names of Marty's bands are sourced from the book, with the exception of Johnny Zhivago, which replaces the more sedate

Luke Sterne. For the most part, however, Kubrick ignores not only a few imaginary composers that play a more significant role in the novel but, most importantly, the "invisible realities" that the imaginary music represents (Rabinowitz 2003, 109). Early in the novel, Alex describes a moment of sonic ecstasy (there are several in both the book and the film), as he recalls listening in rapture to Geoffrey Plautus's one-movement violin concerto: "a bird of like rarest spun heavenmetal, or like silvery wine flowing in a spaceship, gravity all nonsense now, came the violin solo above all the other strings" (Burgess 2012, 39). The reader is driven to appreciate the eloquence of Alex's poetic turns in such moments, and if any element in the narrative moderates our loathing and gives us a tinge of despair at Alex's eventual cognitive reprogramming and loss of free will, then it is the glimmer of the higher self evident in such passages. As there is no such concerto, nor its American composer Geoffrey Plautus, nor the violinist Odysseus Choerilos—nor several composers, pieces, and ensembles associated with imaginary "classical" works, for that matter—Rabinowitz (2003) probes the function of imaginary music in *A Clockwork Orange*. He tracks this music in three ways: its use in world building, as a corollary to neologism; its role in emotional modulation, moderating our antipathy to Alex toward ambivalence; and its contribution to Burgess's aesthetic argument.

In the novel, imaginary music functions in a way indistinguishable from Burgess's invented language, Nadsat, estranging the reader with an equivalent of the young person's slang, and in this case, shocking us with the notion that any of the youth in this violent new world would listen primarily to classical rather than pop music. Whether the works of Plautus and another fictional composer, Friedrich Gitterfenster, are contemporary or very old, perhaps from some alternate romantic era, their presence suggests that the novel's infection of the timeline runs both ways, removing the reader from "any historical milieu" (Rabinowitz 2003, 110). Brief references to imaginary ensembles like the Claudius Birdman String Quartet or even the pop blues of Ike Yard's "Honey Nose" remove the novel from "any historically specifiable musical environment" (110) other than the very, very old but enduring works of Beethoven and a handful of other composers long since dead. In the case of Burgess's novel, the incorporation of actual contemporary recordings and artists risked dating the extrapolation in the same way that utilizing actual slang from the Teddy Boy culture that partly inspired Burgess's work would have; rather, a new polyglot language, often of unknown or only partially known elements, had to be crafted, accompanied by an unfamiliar list of new music, composers, and musicians. Kubrick's interest in history will turn out somewhat differently and will explain why an actual record shop can be full of new and recent releases that sit alongside a Top Ten list of imaginary bands or bands yet to come.

This does not yet justify Alex's sonic reverie of Plautus's "heaven-metal" music, and Rabinowitz attributes a more significant rhetorical function than imaginary world building. Imaginary music—such as the phrases from the fictional *Das Bettzeug* of the fictional composer Gitterfenster that triggers Alex's fight and falling out with his droog Dim (Warren Clarke)—catalyzes action, whether it be causal sex (rarely), violent brawls (frequently), or violent sex and rape (most frequently). It does so in both the book and the film, though again with significantly different consequences. Rabinowitz argues that Burgess's novel is "very profoundly a book about music," and more specifically, "an exploration of certain violent undercurrents in the German musical tradition, an exploration tied to certain philosophical claims about the act of listening" (114). Moreover, Burgess's novel not only probes the relationship between violent atrocities and the Austro-German symphonic tradition (118) but also in contemporary British youth culture and the violent conflicts among gangs of aging dandy Teddy Boys as well as an emerging generation of stylish Mods and leather-clad Rockers (114). While not quite creating empathy, the description of imaginary music does in fact "moderate our antipathy to Alex's violence and thus helps support the fundamental ambiguity on which the novel's complex moral effects depend" (111). Through his narration of the novel, Alex provides a point of audition through which we hear and aesthetically judge different forms of music. Rabinowitz makes useful distinctions between the technical attributes of music: its existence as "a concrete entity" (those characteristics of sound like rhythm and timbre that can be expressed through written notation and, I would add, through recording), and its "attributive" aspects, "the application of shared, culturally determined interpretive conventions that assign meanings to the actual sounds" (115).

308 • SONIC ALIENATION AND PSYTECH AT WAR

Between these two poles, the concrete sound and the cultural codes that regulate sound, is "listening" itself, "an active interpretive process" that involves both the technical and attributive levels but actualizes them as music in a culminating synthetic act (116). *A Clockwork Orange* focuses on two different attributive screens used by Alex. Singling out German classical music, one screen develops along a "cultural-historical" axis that "encourages us to listen to music in terms of musical history, national borders, and a series of charged hierarchies, including the distinction between popular and classical music" (119). The other takes shape along a spectrum of "competing ethical screens" (119), which runs the gamut from, on one end, music as a goad to actual violence, as well as self-critical replays and fantasies of violent actions in Alex's imagination, to another end, which Rabinowitz identifies as an "alternative way of listening that redeems music as a cultural practice, and Alex's spiritual journey" (120). There is of course a lot of conceptual diagramming going on here that does not stick with Kubrick's film. Even though it is built from the same basic components, the film ignores this spectrum and maps out instead a "far different historical-cultural attributive screen" (122) with a surprisingly one-dimensional consequence.

Kubrick erodes the precision of the classical canon that Burgess worked with both literally and imaginatively. Again and again, his musical selections cut against the scenes with which they are paired—a pompous bit of Elgar heard in a prison corridor or state hospital, a sprightly "Singin' in the Rain" for rape and assault—but not in a random, inconsiderate way, nor even to create a sense of what Rabinowitz calls "emotional counterpoint" (121), where music would play like a joke that "neutralizes" or "serves to soften the violence" through satire and irony (125). Rather than reveal the "trace of something dark and dangerous lurking within Beethoven" (126), the glorious nature of the Ninth Symphony that plays against Alex's fantasies of sex and violence reveals an ironic distance within the very core of Alex's character, one which has largely replaced complexity of character altogether (125). Gengaro (2013) suggests an altogether different reading of these scenes, arguing that music is of far greater importance in the film than in Burgess's novel, where it serves "a largely symbolic function," while in Kubrick's film "the music is transformed into a structural element, an aesthetic standard, or an emotional hook. It ceases to be simply a symbol. Instead, music is a visceral connection to the actions on-screen, the cuts in the film, and the experiences of the main character" (108). Rather than grant a critical function to the imaginary music and composers of Burgess's novel, Gengaro considers them an ineffectual symbol that misses out on the effectiveness of Kubrick's music selection, picked precisely because it is "enjoyable and familiar, packed with its own cultural meanings" (108). This disregards the many layers of cultural attribution, however, particularly in a film that associates Alex's love for classical music as part of his perversity, as one movie poster makes explicit when it describes the film as "the adventures of a young man whose principal interests are rape, ultra-violence, and Beethoven" (in Gengaro 2013, 108). Given the exclusivity of Alex's tastes, music becomes either a symbol of his free will or "his only redeeming characteristic" (109). He is repeatedly depicted as a musical outsider, a snob who dismisses Marty and Sonietta's music as "fuzzy warbles" and "teeny pop veshches" (Burgess 2012, 48), an aesthete among plebeians like his parents, his fellow Droogs, the "devotchkas," and Dr. Brodsky, who admits that the only thing he knows about music is that it heightens emotions (128). All the same, I think we must be wary of overselling music as a mechanism that "allows the viewer to forge a connection to Alex, even subconsciously" (Gengaro 2013, 109), especially to the extent that it might become an empathetic forge rather than an anempathetic forgery.

The philosophical and aesthetic arguments that Burgess develops through his use of imaginary music, Rabinowitz suggests, are altogether missing in Kubrick's film, which at the least distorts if not reverses Burgess's approach. For as Kubrick cuts out references to Plautus, Gitterfenster, and the rest, he also eliminates the impact not only of Burgess's imaginary music but of the imaginary. Kubrick consistently associates Alex's inner-thoughts with masturbatory mind-movies that are as violent as anything else in the film, depicting the total colonization of Alex's consciousness by an ultraviolence against which classical music can hardly be heard as an ironic, much less a modulated antipathetic counterpoint. Kubrick acknowledged that his use of music stylized the violence in order to substitute for Burgess's writing style (Rabinowitz 2003, 125). In her close treatment of the film's music, Gengaro elucidates this point, calling the music a stylized buffer for the violence that specifically fulfills the function of the fictional Nadsat language, which according to Burgess, was "a Russified version of English . . . meant to muffle the raw response we expect from pornography" (in Gengaro 2013, 129). For Rabinowitz, on the other hand, Kubrick misses the point of Burgess's novel as a philosophical inquiry into music and its connections to violence. Rather, the film draws on "prepackaged associations with music to manipulate the viewer's relation to the violence" (2003, 126) and so completely "reverses the argument of the book, for it uncritically participates in precisely that cultural phenenomon" (126). If true, this would be quite a dramatic contrast to Kubrick's use of music in the earlier *2001*, which relied on the lack of associative attributes and cultural-historical contexts among the young viewers it assumed would be its audience.

Kubrick's inclusion of the Moog-driven work of electronic composer Wendy (at the time, Walter) Carlos involves the development of "alternative, medium-specific mechanisms" (Rabinowitz 2003, 112) that would make up for the loss of Burgess's imaginary composers and flights of fantastical prose as Alex described their music. Rabinowitz concludes that Kubrick muddles the attributive screening process, remapping the novel's various canonical distinctions between national modes of classical music as well as between classical and pop, the change of medium from novel to film subsumes music within the technical attribute (125). This eliminates the various coding practices derived from culture, skipping over the domain of listening proper, the synthesis of human-driven, active interpretation that takes place in between the technical substance of the music and its various cultural codes. In the novel, this is epitomized by the imaginary music, which we only experience as synthetic interpretation. But in the film, this is the very role of Carlos's equally synthetic renditions. Returning now to the distinctions formulated by Schaeffer, I would suggest that where "pure listening" and "listening to effects" equate to Rabinowitz's technical attributes of the material sound object, and "variations in listening" to the cultural construction of subjectivity, what we experience in Kubrick's *A Clockwork Orange* is the subsuming of the imaginary point of audition by synthetic "variations in the signal," in which a previously conceptual and affective synthesis literally becomes the space of technical process.

In the novel's last chapter, cut from the American edition and ignored by Kubrick if he knew it was there at all, Alex learns to appreciate music that is "very quiet and like yearny" (Burgess 1995, 199). Without this particular way out of the book, Kubrick comes to different conclusions about music as a means of cultural programming and control. The problem for Rabinowitz lies in the fact that "the emotional counterpoint between sound and image, the stylization that moderates the impact of the violence" (126) relies excessively on cultural codes: Beethoven's Ninth Symphony is an iconic work of great art, while Rossini's "William Tell Overture" is a Hollywood cliché for sped-up action sequences, probably more familiar to many of Kubrick's viewers as the theme to *The Lone Ranger* (1949–57) than a piece of opera. This familiarity not only forbids critical interrogation of musical codes, it turns them into fully technical elements of the work (125). Gabbard and Sharma hear in the film an inscription of "the aesthetic ideals of Romanticism and Modernism," which rejects the standard cinematic scoring conventions of music that is functionally invisible or inaudible and most effective when hardly there at all (2003, 93). This suggests that the film essentially continues the project of *2001*. But as it shuts down the hypersensitivities involved in a cosmic deterritorialization of SF space music tropes and cultural assumptions and expectations, *A Clockwork Orange* suggests that music is rather a primary mechanism for cultural control precisely because of its secondary nature to the image and due to its programming of things through the background of things.

This subtlety is both pervasive and perverse. Senior director of the IEEE History Center, Michael Geselowitz (2016), points out that *A Clockwork Orange* is the first film to feature Dolby sound. Dolby A, created for noise reduction in professional recording studios, boosted high frequencies before recording in order that they would mask the high-end hissing typical of signals recorded on magnetic tape. "When recorded music is loud," he explains, "the hissing is not as noticeable, but when the music is soft or there is silence, most of what is heard is the hissing. If the recording level is adjusted so that the music is always recorded loud, then it could be turned down later, and the noise volume would also be turned down." Struggling only a bit with the fact that *A Clockwork Orange* is not only a deeply troubling film but was also rated

X when released, Geselowitz explains that rather than high profile revolutions of sound technology, most innovations happen "while our backs are turned." One such instance of the "innumerable small changes" that shape the history of sound technology then is not only the introduction of Dolby A in recording studios but also its home consumer counterpart, Dolby B, which prompted the "emergence of the cassette as a high fidelity medium." Wendy Carlos was an early adopter of Dolby A, which allowed her and producer Rachel Elkind to better manage the dramatic drops between the loud and quiet sections of her material as well as accommodate the range of electronic timbre with which she worked. It was Carlos, Elkind, and Dolby Laboratories' Ioan Allen who convinced Kubrick that *A Clockwork Orange* should be the test case for using Dolby noise-reduction in cinema. Geselowitz attributes the film music's impact, even if only as a sonic supplement to the visuals, to the successful use of noise reduction and the way in which it boosted the overall "auditory experience" without audiences even knowing why. Who did notice this new "technological infrastructure" was the film industry, and Dolby technology would soon become standard. It remains for us to determine why such a traumatizing film was the agent for this move toward high fidelity in cinematic sound reproduction.

As Alex undergoes his reprogramming through the Ludovico treatment, he protests the use of the second movement's "Turkish March" from Beethoven's Ninth Symphony against scenes of marching Nazis, Luftwaffe bombings, and images of warfare and destruction. His cry that "It's a sin!" is met not with disdain but puzzlement as the doctors attending him calmly dismiss it as a "background score" (in Gabbard and Sharma, 102). Whether it is more upsetting because of its association with Nazism, because it has been rendered as background music, or because what we hear in this sequence is Carlos's synthesized version, gets squarely at the tensions that the film exacerbates around the issues of synthetic listening. As Gabbard and Sharma conclude, "Kubrick would dignify the struggles of Alex by invoking this tradition of the Beethoven myth" (103), creating a character ultimately deprived of free will after repeatedly using his love of Beethoven to indicate that he is the only one in the film's world who still possesses "a finely developed aesthetic sense" (102). I am convinced then that the use of Beethoven's Ninth to accompany scenes of Nazi rallies and warfare would not bother Alex in the least. Rather, an issue of sonic fidelity and presence is at stake.

Not only is Alex a music snob, he is also a hi-fi snob. When he picks up Marty and Sonietta from the record shop, he promises them an "all proper" sonic experience that will blow away their own "pitiful portable picnic players." Likewise in the film, thanks to the use of Dolby A noise reduction, the music of *A Clockwork Orange* possesses a startling range, reproducing the Deutsche Grammophone recordings of Beethoven and Rossini in full hi-fidelity. Compared to the massive presence of the sounds of orchestral and choral performance, what we hear during Alex's final breakdown in the Ludovico treatment is a short fragment of Carlos's Moog brass and winds, which provides a stripped-down and even cartoonish accompaniment to the footage of marching Nazis. Arguably, the Dolby A system that Carlos and Elkind had recommended worked against them here, revealing the relatively simple, narrow-bandwidth purity of the synthesizer against the more complex overtones and broader presence of the previous orchestral music. The comedic effect is exacerbated by the introduction of the vocoder-like voice, along with images of the Barmaley Fountain, a statue of six schoolchildren dancing in a ring before the ruins of Stalingrad, and Alex is at last reduced to incoherent screams. Gengaro argues that the Moog music ultimately suggests "an ungodly transformation" and "mechanical 'contamination'" (139). Though Gengaro admits that this conclusion seems out of step with both the popularity of Carlos's *Switched-On Bach* and Alex's seeming enjoyment of Carlos's music at the record shop, I would suggest that the context of the record shop contaminates Beethoven, heard in its synthesized pop variation, rendering the composer as ubiquitous and plastic as would the use of the opening notes of the Fifth Symphony as a doorbell chime or a bust of the composer as a desperate weapon. Alex's own use of Beethoven, otherwise rendered so devoid of aura, as fuel for ultraviolence is an attempt to bring some grandeur back to the music, even if only the depraved and rotted "glories" of Nazism and deadly fascist hooliganism.

The terms of psytech warfare in the film's narrative are thus largely defined by whether or not Alex struggles against the anempathetic nature of the music around him, whether music is a meaningful call to action and feeling or rather an empty, interchangeable commodity of what Kubrick (1972) calls the culture of "the new psychedelic fascism—the eye-popping, multimedia, quadrasonic, drug-oriented conditioning of human beings by other beings." Gengaro concludes that the Moog music offers a sign of the future, "a time in which the cutting edge of technology is used to play music," suggesting a sonic novum of the mechanical future, but to me this feels incompatible with its function as "a part of setting the scene as costumes and furniture" (140). Rather than a sign of a future yet to come, now heard in retrospect, Kubrick's "future" is never more than "a quaint retro-future vision" (141) of the timeless "horrorshow" of reality. In respect to this draining of reality, the role of music is not the only way in which *A Clockwork Orange* shuts down the sonic novum of *2001*. Kubrick's earlier film is structured around distinct vocal epochs: the hominid voice, the human voice, the synthesized machine voice, the avant-garde voices of Ligeti's choirs, and bare human breath. Where the intelligible human voice is almost completely absent in *2001*, *A Clockwork Orange* not only features a first-person narrator that prattles on in Nadsat, but is full of loud human vocalizations. Its characters, particularly Alex, sing, shout, yell, moan, cry, and otherwise make plenty of noise. *A Clockwork Orange* seems frenetically, overwhelmingly, and almost distractingly loud when compared to *2001*. The use of diegetic song is also important. Alex delivers a gleeful rendition of "Singin' in the Rain" during an act of home invasion, rape, and murder; this same song renders the chief irony near the end of the film, when Mr. Alexander (whose wife had been murdered by Alex) unknowingly lets a "cured" Alex back into his house. Mr. Alexander's posttraumatic collapse is triggered by Alex's exaggerated, insanely chanted version of "Singin' in the Rain" while taking a bath, even as the soundtrack to Mr. Alexander's revenge comes from the Ninth Symphony. Kubrick packs the song with multiple layers of irony so dense they began to cancel each other out, which he describes initially as "comical sadism" and then later as "magic coincidence" (in Walker 1971, 229, 296). The Ninth Symphony is the harshest sonic pharmakon, part of Alex's cure as well as his illness. Was his loving use of the Ninth as a personal soundtrack to violence merely a copy of true Nazi horrors, a watered-down pop form of genocide? Or is it the only redeeming glimpse of free will, of the eloquent and poetic independence of the ear in a time of synthetic, musical homogeneity? Disturbing visuals and Carlos's synthesized variant of the fourth movement of the Ninth make Alex sick, unable to disassociate the two in the collapse of the imagination and the rise of the purely technical, to the point that he is driven to an unsuccessful suicide attempt. The Ninth Symphony thus becomes a psytech battleground. By the end of the film, we cannot be sure which of Alex's mental states we witness when he responds at last without affect to the music that had once elevated or emptied his existence and concludes, "I was cured all right."

1972 | *SOLARIS*

Revisiting the Cold War dynamic between American and Soviet SF films, Andrei Tarkovsky's *Solaris* was originally billed in the West as Russia's response to *2001*, and without a doubt, the film has long been commercially, and occasionally critically, contextualized in contrast to Kubrick's film. The first use of this phrase apparently came from a review of the film in the U.K.'s *Spectator* magazine, from which it was picked up and added to U.K. movie posters. Italian and Spanish posters followed suit. Despite Tarkovsky's outspoken dismissal of *2001, Solaris* is even treated as more of a cousin than an antagonist, as Phillip Lopate (2011) suggests: "Both set up their narratives in a leisurely, languid manner, spending considerable time tracking around the space sets; both employ a widescreen mise-en-scène approach that draws on superior art direction; and both generate an air of mystery that invites countless explanations." A similar argument could be made for the musical sensibilities, with the Bach prelude heard throughout *Solaris* reminiscent of Kubrick's use of traditional classical selections, while the more outré elements of Artemiev's score recall the cosmic atmospheres of Ligeti's atonal compositions. However, this comparison threatens to gloss over the significant differences of these two films and their sonic vocabularies. Kubrick's initial impulse was to move as far away as possible from what he heard as the clichés of space music and the electronic scores of SF cinema, which led him to construct his own soundtrack from existing recordings that ranged from classical waltzes to atonal choruses. The relative variety among Kubrick's musical selections is the only thing that testifies to a human history over the course of his great elision from hominids to starfarers. For Kubrick, the recorded object offers some measure, limited though it is to Western traditions within a hundred-year span, of human tonal diversity, and in its way it reveals the capacity for music to become new again. In fact, the ability for music to become new again, through a kind of Nietzschean eternal return, appeals more to Kubrick than either hackneyed ideas about a future music or the recorded object's role in the collective memory and archive. As it becomes new and different, music makes as much a case as the monolith for the cosmic transformation of humanity across both generational and extraterrestrial gulfs. The sound of Tarkovsky's film will differ completely, avoiding the variety of human music and the scope of cosmic phenomena, as it plunges into a singular account of extraterrestrial contact and alien psychotechnology.

Based on Stanislaw Lem's novel of the same title, Tarkovsky's film tracks the encounter of space psychologist Kris Kelvin (Donatas Banionis) with the planet Solaris. Kelvin is sent to Solaris to check up on the mental health of the crew of a space station orbiting the distant planet. Though scientists have been investigating the oceanic planet for decades, their research has made little progress, some scientists have disappeared, and one returned investigator, the space pilot Henri Berton (Vladislav Dvorzhetsky) has reported disturbing encounters that point to either madness or unusual properties of the planet itself that warrant further study. Upon his arrival, Kelvin finds Solaris Station, built to hold eighty researchers, dilapidated, and its crew members are in bad shape. One scientist has killed himself, and the two remaining are on the verge of total mental collapse. Kelvin's own situation soon deteriorates as he begins to encounter his wife, Khari (Natalya Bondarchuk), who had killed herself several years before his current mission. Kelvin learns from the station's cyberneticist, Dr. Snaut (Jüri Järvet), and astrobiologist, Dr. Sartorius (Anatoli Solonitsyn), that all members of the crew have encountered "visitors" like his wife, and they suspect that these are in fact products of the planet's activities in response to the scientists' presence.

The film develops the increasing psychogeographical entanglement of Kelvin and Solaris as the planet re-creates his wife again and again. In the first instance, Kelvin kills Khari by shoving her into a space capsule and ejecting the craft, burning himself in the process. This launches a repetitive cycle of Khari's returns and failed suicides. Sartorius theorizes that the bodies of the "visitors" are composed of "neutrino systems," and there appears to be something about this unusual corporeal makeup that allows Khari's body to return and to heal itself, once after tearing through a metal cabin door and another time almost immediately after she drinks liquid oxygen. Although initially tethered to Kelvin's physical proximity, Khari gains autonomy both physically and cognitively over the course of the film, resulting in one of its most troubling mysteries: given this independence, why does Khari persistently attempt to end her own life, and fail? The neutrino manifestations appear to be less re-creations of Khari in her own right and more versions of Khari lodged in the subconscious of the psychologist, a deep memory or projection distorted by Kelvin's longing for his dead wife and feelings of guilt for their failed marriage. Suicide trauma plays out repeatedly as Kelvin's encounter with Solaris turns into the psychodrama of a lone man working through his loss, grief, and depression. While the re-created Khari is locked into the vicious death-wish cycle, Kelvin's psyche also manifests additional, distinctly Freudian content. Khari's final appearance, for instance, follows on the heels of Kelvin's dream of his mother as a young woman worried about his mental state. Upon waking, Kelvin finds a note from Khari requesting that Snaut and Sartorius kill her. Further, bombarding Solaris with Kelvin's brain waves ends visitations from the neutrino constructs, but it also begins to imprint the planet with islands derived from Kelvin's memories, facilitating at last a dreamy reunion on the surface of Solaris with a neutrino version of the aged father he had thought left behind forever on Earth.

One of Lem's major problems with Tarkovsky's adaptation of his film was the addition of scenes on Earth; in the novel, everything takes place around and on Solaris itself. Lem was also displeased with the displacement of science fictional themes in favor of more humanistic and psychological concerns, turning the work into a weirdly existentialist morality tale. For Lem, a "sphere of cognitive and epistemological considerations" was central to the book (Beres 1987), which took the form of a new field of scientific study and research, Solaristics, much of which concerned the nature of the Visitors, a phenomenal form of alien life that may manifest through contact between the planet and human minds. Lem argued that Tarkovsky rid the film of Solaristics and turned the fate of the scientists embroiled in study of the planet into nothing more than an "existential anecdote" about human life on Earth rather than a "grand question" concerning our place in the cosmos. By focusing on the mental and emotional impact on Kelvin triggered by the reappearance of his dead wife—what should remain "a strange and incomprehensible appearance," Lem writes—Tarkovsky substitutes a narrative of human conscience for a depiction of and inquiry into human encounter with the impenetrable, "the Unreachable, the Thing-in-Itself, the Other Side" (in Beres̀ 1987).

Considering the narrative without sound, as story and image, Lem's criticism of the film has some merit. The addition of opening scenes set on Earth, and its return, if only by proxy, by the end of the film as an island appears on the planet Solaris with Kelvin's home and aging father, emphasizes the human ability to impose its existence on the otherwise ambiguous mystery of the alien Solaris. Things are still weird—rain falls inside the house rather than outside—but this anecdotal and biblical testament, as the father receives his prodigal son with open arms, overwrites the original Solaristic potential with what Lem dismisses as "just some emotional sauce into which Tarkovsky has submerged his heroes" (in Lopate 2011). For the director's part, the sequences and images of Earth were added to provide "an equivalent of something beautiful in the viewer's mind. A subject of one's longing," Tarkovsky (1972) announces. "So that after he plunges into the mysterious fantastic atmosphere of Solaris, when he suddenly glimpses Earth he again feels normal, at home. So that he begins to feel longing for this ordinariness. In other words, he feels the beneficial influence of nostalgia." It is unclear whether the effects on this "he" that Tarkovsky mentions refers to the viewer or Kelvin, and perhaps the difference is inconsequential, given Kelvin's overwriting of the cinematic apparatus with the imprint of his psyche. Tarkovsky is explicit about the goal of this revision to Lem's narrative, retrieving what he calls "the deeper meaning" of science fiction, which isn't science fictional at all, it turns out, but rather a tale of moral dilemma. "This is a novel not only about the clash between human reason and the Unknown," Tarkovsky (1971) argues, "but also about moral conflicts set in motion by new scientific discoveries. It's about new morality arising as a result of those painful experiences we call 'the price of progress.'" The language of progress here, the human journey of discoveries and consequences, situates *Solaris* within the traditional territory of the historical novum.

Given how frequently critical responses to Tarkovsky's *Solaris* conclude that the ocean planet is a sentient entity, it certainly seems that one key element that the film eliminates is the role of ontological ambiguity, the overwhelming mystery that surrounds the nature of Solaris, which at last prevents us from being able to articulate exactly what Solaris is. The "relatively blank center" (Freedman 2000, 110) of Lem's novel, Solaris raises the possibility that there is a kind of life completely different from what humans know, a life of the thing rather than the being, which is measured not by scientific knowing but unresolvable inquiry. By joining together the processes of science with those of religion and philosophy, Solaristics suspends the ability of its observers to contact the alien planet, the "Thing-in-Itself," and so determine whether Solaris acts with intention or automatically. This ambiguity leads Csicsery-Ronay to designate Solaris "a pure novum," a limit case of the single novum, which "has no significant qualities other than its newness and difference" (2008, 68). Solaristics will never resolve whether the Visitors are products of "anomalous, possibly inexplicable natural causes" or "anomalous, possibly inexplicable behavior of mind" (67). This doubly anomalous novum confronts us with a pure difference that cannot be drawn back into human history; it represents no new roads but rather "a void into which all human hypotheses fall," Csicsery-Ronay concludes. "It separates the history of human meanings, ideologies, projects, and successful experiments with existence, from the blank novum that signifies only that these things do not apply" (68). Tarkovsky's additions of the earthly home as a frame for the film draw the limit case of the pure novum of difference back into the stream of human history, or perhaps worse, of spiritual idealism, myth, and nostalgia.

The ontological blank of the anomalous novum complicates Tarkovsky's intent as we turn our attention to the auditory experience of *Solaris* and seek to characterize the nature of the sonic novum produced through Artemiev's work with the ANS synthesizer. Sound in *Solaris* repeatedly takes the visually familiar and renders it sonically different in ways that are consistent with the blanking out of the novum as a site of pure difference. This is a challenge given a film in which Tarkovsky's familiar visual sets and sequences suggest that the present is already estranged (Lopate 2011). Few scenes do this more so than the nearly five-minute sequence in which the rocket pilot Berton, back from Solaris with his own unusual and traumatic memories, drives around an unnamed city. The segment plays thirty minutes into the film, featuring what turns out to be a minor character who has just had a verbal argument with Kelvin, and ultimately goes nowhere. Recalling Godard's use of modern Parisian architecture and cars in *Alphaville*, where Lemmy Caution drives his Ford Galaxie from the Outlands to the planet of Alphaville on the highway of "intersidereal space," the scene features the superhighways of Akasaka district, Tokyo. Where the Caution driving segments are played as wry, comic-strip spoofs, Berton's driving sequence is defamiliarizing in every way. Visually, the scene switches between color and black-and-white for no obvious reason, while sonically, the sequence is compelling for the gradual transformation of highway noise into the strange wash of ANS sounds that will come to signify Solaris and its disorienting point of audition (Barry 2011). Berton's driving through tunnels even recalls Dave Bowman's journey through the infinite in *2001*, and in both films we note a similar switching from point of view shots to close-ups of the men's faces, surrounded by flashing lights and accompanied by atonal scores (Underman, n.d.). Artemiev's biographer, Tatiana Yegorova, suggests that the goal of this "long and static episode is the alleviation of the abrupt transition from audiovisual images of habitual earthly existence to unreal images of the Cosmos," though this neglects the fact that another five minutes transpires back at the dacha of Kelvin's parents, where Kelvin burns most of his belongings before voyaging to Solaris (1997, 231). Certainly, in both *Solaris* and *2001*, extended scenes in the psonicosmos are among the most defamiliarizing in their respective films, and the journeys that they undertake shift from a futuristic novum to one of pure alterity.

All cinematic sound exists beyond an acousmatic screen and is initially unmoored from the image. As it attaches to the image, giving depth, materiality, consistency, and a whole range of other values to what we see, sound is never fully in its place, much less in the space of the screen where we often situate it. The ambience of science fiction films frequently benefit from this fundamental placelessness of cinematic sound, which amplifies the otherworldliness of the genre into profound ontological crises. Electronic sound imbricates the effect of a psychological alienation and affective estrangement within auditory points of view (or points of audition) that withdraw from us, preventing our ability to recognize and know them other than as experiences of the deep alterity of neosonic physiognomies. Few SF films explore this with the sophistication and self-reflection of *Solaris*. The nature of alien psychogeography and the efforts of humans to understand their relationship to that space is the explicit narrative concern of the film; it also completely imbues the film's sonic novum.

Composer Eduard Artemiev's synthesized score for *Solaris* provides one of the keenest encounters with the complex intensities of alien space, which either exhibits a new form of planetary consciousness or its simulacrum, and establishes the ways in which contact with alien space modifies the human psyche. The music heard during the film's main titles—a solemn rendition of Bach's Choral Prelude in F-minor for organ, "Ich ruf zu Dir, Herr Jesus Christ," which is the only traditional form of music heard throughout the soundtrack—gives us little indication of the kind of sonic experience we will have as the film progresses. Some musical themes are extracted from the Bach prelude, suggesting at times a leitmotif of the planet Earth and other times of specific characters, but most of the score combines subtle sounds derived from orchestral instruments as well as recordings of natural phenomena, along with more extreme, abstract washes of electronic noise and sound processing effects. With the exception of the Bach prelude, these elements do not provide thematic motifs through recognizable, recurring melodic lines but, just as the theremin had in *Rocketship X-M,* develop tonal motifs—Artemiev (1993) calls them "leit-timbres"—that reinforce the alien dimensions of ambient world building in the film. As synthetically generated and processed sounds tonally color the experience of *Solaris* as a visual, narrative, and philosophical object, they also expose the alien nature of the cinematic apparatus itself. Sound renders the film's psychotechnological reflection of unconsciousness likewise alien to normative human experience and the conscious mind.

322 • SONIC ALIENATION AND PSYTECH AT WAR

Sonically, *Solaris* measures the entanglement of the human mind with alien space in terms of complex polyphonic multiplicities that combine elements of classical music, atonal dissonance, synthesized electronic sound, ambient noise, and profound silence. The initial performance of Bach's prelude, played on a solitary organ during the opening titles, is the only instance in the film in which we hear the piece in its unadulterated form. As the prelude repeats, or attempts to repeat, three more times over the course of the film, it acts like an obsessive and singular prayer of despair, resembling nothing so much as the film's other obsessive repetition: the visitations from Khari that recur throughout the narrative. The choice of this particular prelude seems full of personal meaning never explicated, already reverberating in the echoing interiors of Kelvin's mind and imbricated with guilt, agony, isolation, anger, despair, and perhaps hope. The fragmented and processed variations of the theme provide a kind of leitmotif of Kelvin's depression—heavy, oppressive, and beautiful—in which love and loss are enmeshed to such a degree that when asked by one of the manifestations of Khari, "Did you ever think of me?" Kelvin replies, "Only when I was sad." The Bach prelude suggests at times a motif of Earth, at other times Khari's theme, particularly in those moments when Artemiev modifies the prelude into a polyphonic cantus firmus (a preexisting melodic line from which harmonic counterpoints derive). However, the most compelling use of Bach's music is evident when mixed with abstract synthesizer sequences. Here the melodic leitmotif and the tonal motif collide. The synthesizer blurs the Bach piece around the edges, causing it to recede into cosmic cinematic depths, and as the tone colors both come to the fore and fuzz out around the edges of perception, the prelude no longer represents either Earth or Khari as such, but rather acts as the sonic equivalent to the neutrino duplications.

A neutrino construct of Khari is not Khari but rather a projection of Kelvin's memory of her. This version of Khari is never totally accurate in its reconstruction because, filtered through Solaris, the neutrinos mix Kelvin's various emotional distortions into an illusion overloaded with psychic impressions and twisted into a signifier with little relation to reality as such, even as it reveals buried, unconscious correlatives. Likewise, Solaris ultimately reduces the Bach prelude through a process of fractal reconstruction, overwriting each of the iterations with its own noisy mixture. Solaris does not so much pick up on a note and extend it through a long decay process, as an echo would, but builds up an electronic maelstrom around it, amplifying sound as it absorbs it, until the prelude no longer has an identity of its own but becomes another form altogether through the infinite (de)gradations of feedback. By the film's end, when choral voices and other instruments are added to the organ, the prelude comes across as one final effort to bolster human grief, to resist the alien replication, absorption, and dissipation that Solaris causes through its oceanic synthesis.

The unusual electronic sounds turn once-familiar music into a concrete, sonorous object voiding itself of prior associations and values as its self-sustaining feedback loops create a disintegrating vestige of the tonal state rather than music as such. The emphasis on unique tonal spaces was clearly part of Tarkovsky's design. In interviews, Artemiev often reflects on what he learned about Tarkovsky's changing attitudes toward music and sound in cinema over the course of their working together on *Solaris*. Ahead of a larger industry-wide turn toward sound design proper in the latter half of the 1970s, Tarkovsky described an interest in sound painting, a term that foregrounded the spatial aspects of musical composition over the temporal. "He said more than once: 'I do not need music as such, what I need are the states and conditions'" Artemiev (2006) recalls. "Not the music in its traditional understanding, but something closer to natural sounds." Tarkovsky considered it the job of the composer to build the film's sound world, acting not as "an author of music, but the organizer of audio space in the film" (Artemiev 1988). As far as his compositions for *Solaris* are concerned, sound painting resonates in remarkable ways with the workings of Artemiev's ANS synthesizer, which allowed the composer to draw his scores and create sounds with images and light.

Celebrating the unified art of sound and light that Scriabin professed, the ANS allowed the composition of music according to the color spectrum as its inventor Murzin incorporated Scriabin's synesthetic theory of composition into the synthesizer's design. The ANS utilized the photo-optic recording techniques of cinematography, which captured on film the visible image of a sound wave for its later reproduction.

It also allowed for the synthesizing of sound from hand-drawn sound waves. Rather than film, however, the ANS included five rotating glass discs, each with tiny optic phonograms representing pure tones drawn on them. When read by a beam of light projected through the discs and onto a photovoltaic tone generator, phonogram tracks drawn near the center of the disc created low-frequency tones, while those nearer to the outside edge produced higher frequencies. The combination of five discs, each with 144 optic phonograms, allowed the ANS to generate 720 distinct tones. The composer programmed tones by drawing on a large coding area of the ANS interface, a glass plate covered with a non-drying mastic, along which a vertical axis designated the pitch of a tone and the horizontal axis its duration. This mastic-covered glass plate was referred to as the "score" of the ANS. With a handle at the front of the synthesizer allowing the composer-performer to regulate the tempo, the coding field moved past a narrow aperture of light that passed through the images scraped onto the mastic. The exposed portions of the images allowed the modulated light of the phonograms, acting now as frequency modulators, to trigger up to twenty photocells attached to amplifiers and band-pass filters. While the composer could draw traditional sets of tones, far more complex polyphonic sounds could be created that exploited sweeping glissando, microtonal and other unusual scales, and dense explosions of white noise made with a single vertical scratch triggering all 720 pitches at once. Because the resinous material of the mastic did not harden, the design of the image could be modified quickly, allowing for both precision of control and a wide range of resulting sonic spectra (Kreichi 1997).

As Artemiev points out, the ANS synthesizer's polyphonic capacity far exceeded the commercial synths of the early 1970s, such as the popular monophonic Moog modular. Further, the ANS eliminated the gap between composition and music with an instrument that "gave the composer an unlimited palette of sound and freed them from the restrictions of instrumentation and musicians" (Crab, n.d.). Artemiev fondly recalls a transformation of creative role from composer to sound painter, which was just what Tarkovsky wanted. "A composer, working on the score of the synthesizer, is like a painter," Artemiev (2004) notes. "He paints, retouches, erases and deposits code pictures, immediately carrying out an auditory control of the result." By fostering the development of new and unusual sounds, the ANS also proved a perfect match given the director's desire for Artemiev to paint "audio space" rather than compose music as such. Etching the score in mastic presented the composer with a graphic space that rendered the "composition wholly in its dynamics and spectral structure" (Artemiev 2004). The ANS design is thus conceptually and philosophically a kind of Solarian instrument, providing a sonic analog of the alien planet's capture of a psychic image, rendering it visible to human consciousness, and then processing it to release the synesthetic form of the neutrino object.

The spatial orientation of the Solaris instrumentation pits two forms of psychotechnology against one another, which it then refracts into abstract absolutes through the twinning processes of infinitely gradable reflection. One is the reflection of a mirror, which takes a human form; the other is a reverberating ambient ocean, which is the alien form. Tarkovsky's film repeatedly emphasizes the connection between the human and the mirror, with several areas of Solaris Station featuring mirrors and other reflective surfaces. Of course, this can be a practical challenge for a camera crew—one mirror-laden room designed by the film's art director, Russian painter Mikhail Romadin, hid Tarkovsky's cameraman, Vadim Yusov, inside a mirrored dome—but innovative technical solutions reveal still deeper psychotechnological spaces and operations. The part of Solaris that projects into the human psyche, capturing content there and then projecting it back into a reflective space, works precisely like this mirrored sphere with the cinematic apparatus hidden within it. Kittler argues that by its nature, "cinema is a psychological experiment under conditions of everyday reality that uncovers unconscious processes of the central nervous system" (1999, 161). *Solaris* depicts the collision of the unconscious processes of not one but two nervous systems, one human, the other alien, capturing a pair of "involuntary and technological mechanisms at the same time" (162). The film also doubles the doubling of cinematic projection as it reflects the involuntary and self-reflective nature of Kelvin's psychic entanglement with Solaris.

In this respect, *Solaris* can be considered an interplanetary form of doppelgänger cinema, which according to Kittler magnifies "the unconscious in mobile mirrors; they double doubling itself" (155). Kittler has in mind here early film illusions like those seen in Heinz Ewers's *Student of Prague* (1913), which would allow actors to confront their own images on the screen (153–55). This cinematic doubling of the double has everything to do with an "anti-psychology" in which "the imaginary, once the dream produced by and coming out of the caverns of the soul," is revealed to be "a simple optical trick" (168). In some ways, the Solaris instrumentality of a camera hidden by a mirror in a room of mirrors turns the optical trick into a manufactured cavern of the soul. With so many mirrors and so few cameras, a reverberation of the image takes over the space completely, each reflection an echo of another. With the integrity of the double of a double subsequently inferior to its source, the room is made noisier through this visual feedback of duplication and overdubbing. Given the film's new sonic ecology of tone colors and sound painting, here the image functions like sound, amplifying the correspondence between two psychotechnologies. Kittler asserts, "Phonography and feature film correspond to one another as do the real and the imaginary" (119), but where phonograph recordings provide an uninterrupted transcription of auditory events, cinematographic processes from the start involve editing, cuts, and sequencings of essentially still images in order to "reproduce the continuities and regularities of motion," but which are really "phantasms of our deluded eyes" (119). Of course, a similar kind of sound editing becomes possible with the advent of magnetic tape recording, processing, and manipulation, which is where correspondence becomes convergence of media. Likewise, Artemiev's ANS scores remediate a graphic compositional sign that infuses the real with sound, which has actual consequences for our understanding of the film. Is the planet Solaris a thing rather than a being because it processes visual psychic material as if it were sonic? Solaris substitutes the workings of the visual imaginary with those of the sonic real. It does not so much visually mirror but rather sonically dubs psychological content by reducing the fidelity of the source material in order to perform a rudimentary kind of enunciation, if not communication, using alien psychic detritus as the basis of its semantics. This instrumentality points to the thingness of the psychic apparatus lodged within the human nervous system and replicated by Solaris.

Solaris dubs an auditory-oriented psychoanalytic treatment onto the cinematic apparatus and realigns unconscious psychic functionality with alien ontology. Otto Rank's 1914 discussion of *The Student of Prague* is a pioneering but flawed application of psychoanalysis to film that nonetheless remains quite useful to our understanding of how *Solaris* works. Rank compares cinematography to dream work, proposing that if the processes and techniques of psychoanalysis involve "uncovering deeply buried and significant psychic material, on occasion proceeding from the manifest surface evidence," then this approach is agreeable to the treatment of film content (in Kittler 1999, 142). Kittler has some significant reservations about Rank's approach, arguing that this "filmic uncovering, the return from the cinema to the soul, from manifest source or celluloid skin to unconscious latency, from a technological to a psychic apparatus, only replaces images with words" (142). As far as *Solaris* overtly involves psychoanalytic process, Kittler's skepticism is corroborated by the film's tendencies toward wordiness—philosophical debate, monologue, diatribe, soliloquy—presented against a stark backdrop devoid of diegetic and nondiegetic sounds.

Doubled by Artemiev's experiments with spatial sound design, Tarkovsky pushed *Solaris* in the direction of the auditory real by application of sound paintings. He eliminated cinematic "imitation" to favor instead psychotechnological equivalencies between filmic technique and the unconscious acts of the psyche that most powerfully articulate along the sonic strata of the subdiegetic, that special offscreen region in which sound can construct states of extracinematic consciousness in alien space. Kittler argues that cinema, which presented for "the first time in the global history of art, a medium [that] instantiates the neurological flow of data," is less about imitation and copying the real than its reflection, doubling, and dubbing; whereas "the arts have processed the orders of the symbolic or the orders of things, film presents its spectators with their own processes of perception . . . with a precision that is otherwise accessible only to experiment and thus neither to consciousness nor to language" (1999, 161). The provisional, partial nature of this dubbing sensibility contributes to the value added by sounds in *Solaris,* with Tarkovsky substituting the synthetic noise at the center of the film for the blankness noted by Freedman (2000, 110). This is an alien psychogeography in which the psyche does not associate with being as such but with the Otherness of the thing. It cannot be engaged directly, on its own terms, but only through feedback loops and dubs, resulting, Freedman concludes, in "the construction of the fundamentally other ocean that, like the unconscious for Lacan, can be known only obliquely and through its effects" (110). This oblique effect pushes us right back into the sonic domains of the film and its equivalencies in the ANS synthesizer, the instrument that transforms image into neosonic spaces. The filmed image acquires resonance from sound only when the sounds of the visible world are removed, according to Tarkovsky, or when "extraneous sounds that don't exist literally" are added to the image (1989, 158). Sound must be constrained and constructed, an addition that brings something to the film that is otherwise alien to it, and thereby expresses what Tarkovsky calls "an essential element" of the Other rather than merely an "appendage to the visual image" (158–59). Changing the added sound should thus result in a qualitative difference in what we see.

In his notes on *Solaris,* Artemiev describes the sounds of the planet as one of five types of sound that he needed to create for the film, including: ambient landscapes; sound perceptions and points of audition of characters in the film; variations on the Bach theme; and memories of Earth. Despite these clearly delineated categories, however, sounds are rarely what they seem, and they are hardly ever as distinct as these would suggest. Some of the most meaningful sounds are simply products of diegetic events. What sounds like leaves rustling in the wind are in fact strips of paper hung near an air vent on Solaris station in a blatantly self-aware and nostalgic attempt on the part of a crew member to trigger memories of Earth. The artifice of sound in this instance is revealed specifically as Tarkovsky zooms in on the sonic focal point. This emphasis on such diegetically constructed sound is fundamental to the director's meditations on the role of sound in cinema. Tarkovsky stresses that sound's relation to the cinematic image is never natural or naturalistic; if it were, we would simply hear a cacophony. "In itself," Tarkovsky concludes, "accurately recorded sound adds nothing to the image system of cinema, for it still has no aesthetic content" (1989, 162). Naturalistic sounds, then, have no expression of their own but are rather part of an alien sonic ecology of sounds adding their value to cinematic images under fully artificial circumstances. How the constructed sound can at once become the essence of the image and yet be completely alien to it is at the heart of the mystery of *Solaris*. The scientist on Solaris Station who has sonically reconstructed his own nature sound by adding cutout paper strips to air vents does so in order to activate a memory of earthly wind, even though this memory only emphasizes just how far away Earth and its trees and breezes are from those orbiting Solaris. But there are more extreme instances of adding "extraneous sounds" or using sounds that have been "distorted so that they no longer correspond with the image" (162). One of the most disturbing comes after Khari has killed herself by drinking liquid oxygen. As Kelvin holds her frozen body, we hear a sound of cracking glass. In his brief analysis of this scene, Chion explains that, though completely unnatural, these do not strike us as "'wrong' or inappropriate sounds" (1994, 39). Instead, the sonic body in which breaking glass sounds like shards of ice "render both the creature's fragility and artificiality, and a sense of the precariousness of bodies" (39). For Chion, this scene exemplifies the "true *free counterpart*" (39) that exists between image and sound and ensures each one's otherness from the other. This set of sounds could be operating in an overtly symbolic function, nondiegetically suggesting precarious bodies, but it also conveys this iteration of Khari's artificially constructed nature because it fails to mimic the kind of sounds that a human body would make in such a condition. The "fragility" that Chion describes could also be psychological metaphor, analogically representative of the distressed character and her traumatic, flawed humanness. The scene also seems indicative of an alien being coming to terms with its own discoveries that it is not human, not really Khari, but something else entirely, something that is in its essence an artifice, a kind of camera behind a mirror. It could be that breaking glass is what a body made out of neutrinos sounds like after it drinks liquid oxygen; that is, the sounds of the shattering glass are in fact the diegetic sounds made by the spasms of the Khari construct and in this way purely the stuff of science fiction. In fact, this entire polyphony of interpretative options, each generated through the audiovisual counterpoint of image and audio dub, upsets rhetorical presumptions in order to generate difference.

Artemiev's work continues to push deeper into this territory of Chion's "true *free counterpart*" with continual drifts away from one-to-one sound–image relationships and into complex, dense washes of ambient sounds without clear sources or identities of their own. Rather than pointing to something specific or having a meaning attached to them, they really signify nothing other than the listening presence of Solaris. That is, these sounds represent hearing rather than enunciating. Most of what we hear over the course of *Solaris* are sounds mixed with and filtered through another sound, typically the thick, broad-spectrum atonalities generated by the ANS synthesizer. The most overt instance of this comes from the traffic noises that feed back on themselves as they mix with the ANS washes during the Breton driving sequence. Solaris has no sound of its own but is rather constituted by the absorption of the psychic sounds of the visitors from Earth, which it then reflects back to them. The sounds of Solaris, Artemiev notes, are "composed of the sounds of terrestrial life as if processed by the Ocean. . . . The characters of the film hear (or are trying to hear) sounds either similar to terrestrial ones, or sounds which are kind of little cells or islands remaining from the Earth which they manage to identify out of the mass of strange and yet incomprehensible noises" (in Barry 2011). In this respect, all sounds heard over the course of *Solaris* come to us indirectly, already entangled and awash in the ocean of Solaris, defamiliarized by its reverberation and rendered into an unnatural and alien ambience.

$$\bullet \quad \bullet \quad \bullet$$

In *Solaris*, unfamiliar sounds impose difference on perception as they are presented not as alien atmospherics in their own right but rather as an altogether alien substitution of human perception, and thereby consciousness. I have occasionally presented the idea of an auditory point of view, or point of audition, that in the early film *Destination Moon* is provided by the Sonovox processing of the otherwise familiar sounds of the orchestral accompaniment of an extended pan of the lunar surface. In that instance, the Sonovox filters human perception through a technological apparatus, thereby sonically permeating the scene with a sonic analog of the technical interface that allows the observation of the moon in the first place. In *Rocketship X-M*, Martian psychogeography comes from an atmosphere that tints and taints human perception, with the wavering and gliding sounds of the theremin acting as the ambient, radioactive tone color of the alien wind that ends up affecting the melodic score as well. The psychogeographical sounds of Solaris mirror these processes rather succinctly. But instead of an intermediary device between observer/auditor and object, and rather than an exterior atmosphere picked up by human ears, the sounds of Solaris are perceived from the inside of the alien out, where they manifest through an alienated inner ear. That is, what we hear when we hear the sounds of Solaris are in fact the sounds of Solaris hearing.

In his essay on sound in Soviet science fiction films, composer and writer Robert Barry (2011) considers this moment of "experiencing the Earth through the eyes—or rather ears—of the Solaris ocean itself." This offers a prime example of Russian formalist Viktor Shklovsky's theory of "'*otstranenie*'—the experience of one's own everyday lifeworld as observed by an alien being." Introduced in Shklovsky's 1917 essay, "Art as Technique," this idea of the extreme estrangement or defamiliarization of point of view emphasizes the processes by which common objects, which are "taken for granted, hence automatically perceived," can be estranged and made new through enhanced perception (Margolin 2005, 815). Shklovsky proposes this theory as a form of resistance to automatization and formulaic function in narrative. Poetic language, which according to Shklovsky is fundamentally estranging, is "created to remove the automatism of perception; the author's purpose is to create the vision which results from that deautomatized perception" ([1917] 1998, 16). Given the mundane, run-down elements of the Solaris Station interiors, with their homely touches such as vases of flowers, a butterfly collection, wooden furniture, candles, and quilted bed covers, Artemiev's score is, Barry (2011) notes, "one of the sole sources of the sense of the alien and exotic in the film." While perhaps more evident in some scenes than others—during Khari's violent resurrection and the weightless episode in the Solaris Station library—this estrangement saturates the film with its shifts between color and black-and-white, obsessively extended shots (such as the slow pan across the library's painting, Pieter Bruegel the Elder's *The Hunters in the Snow*), and extreme close-ups (most significantly for our purposes, the zoom up to Kelvin's ear near the end of the film). All of these techniques resonate with the estranging formalist techniques that Shklovsky theorized, for defamiliarization involves slowing down and increasing the difficulty of the reading process and its corresponding comprehension while also self-reflectively turning the reader's awareness to the procedures, or artistic devices, that cause the estranging effect (Margolin 2005, 815). Language, according to this approach, must impede understanding.

As defamiliarizing agents, new sounds materialize the formalist, thing-oriented theory of Shklovsky ([1917] 1998), who argues that art's purpose is to transmit the sense of a thing as it is sensed, not as it is recognized, and much less as it is understood. Estrangement comes about by amplifying and exaggerating the difficulty of perception as an artistic aim in and of itself, which is prolonged by formal techniques that emphasize perception while interfering with recognition and understanding. Shklovsky considers recognition an automatic task, while perception is raw and capable of estranging the habitual and automatic associations accrued through familiarizing repetition and stored in memory, and he claims that "art is a way of experiencing the making of a thing," which involves the formal interference with "automatized" responses (16). This might shed light on the narrative of *Solaris*, which plays out this perceptual process as psychological drama. The neutrino visitors projected by the planet Solaris repeatedly fight against automatic psychic recognition by the Solaris Station crew. The repetition of Khari's manifestations does not reinforce Kelvin's recognition of her but rather amplifies her difference, straining against the habitual rut of disconnection that had undermined their marriage. I am intrigued here by the capacity for sound not only to engage this formal element but also to estrange the audience's own experience of the making of the thing that is *Solaris* the film, so that our own habitual recognition of the cinematic apparatus is likewise defamiliarized.

Again, Tarkovsky's reflections on the film are telling, particularly in terms of the role of electronic sound. "Instrumental music is artistically so autonomous that it is far harder to dissolve into the film to the point where it becomes an organic part of it," he writes; "its use will always involve some manner of compromise, because it is always illustrative. Furthermore, electronic music has exactly that capacity for being absorbed into the sound. It can be hidden behind other noises and remain indistinct; like the voice of nature, of vague intimations" (1989, 163). Electronic sound hides within other sounds, just as the camera hides within a mirrored sphere in a room of mirrors. But what is the point of a hidden sound? The answer, I find, has to do with this comparison that Tarkovsky makes between electronic sounds and "the voice of nature." Recall that early advocates of the theremin, or of glissando more generally, sought to discover a sound that could act formally, like natural sounds, through a sympathetic means of generation, rather than by imitating or representing existing natural sounds through unnatural means. The synergies here with Shklovsky's ([1917] 1998) theory—which values the making of a new thing over the representation of a thing we already know, which cannot resist our knowing it, even while we perceive it, unless it becomes estranged—prompt us to reconsider once more Artemiev's compositions. Sounds in *Solaris* constantly border on the inaudible and recede from our ability to hear them, much less know what they might represent. In a revealing interview included on the Criterion edition of *Solaris,* Artemiev discusses his estranging of the sounds created by an orchestra, which he treated as "one giant synthesizer" of such subtlety that it was almost inaudible (Barry 2011). "It occurred to me," the composer recalls, "that we could introduce orchestral sounds, voices, tapping on the strings light as the rustle of grass, very subtle. [Tarkovsky] liked this idea very much. And that's how we slowly created a special musical language. The surrounding world, with the help of the orchestra—the clusters of soft sounds emerge, almost inaudible, sometimes overlapping. The viewer may not even notice them" (Artemiev 1972). Artemiev and Tarkovsky would use a similar technique a few years later in *The Mirror* (1975), where once again the emphasis is on blended sounds of such subtlety that they are hardly sounds at all. Tarkovsky describes "an earthly echo" composed of rustling, sighing, and breathing: "The notes had to convey the fact that reality is conditional, and at the same time accurately to reproduce precise states of mind" (1989, 162). This approach presented a particular challenge for Artemiev, as Tarkovsky was suspicious of electronic music. "The moment we hear what it is," Tarkovsky concludes, "and realize that it's being constructed, electronic music dies. . . . Electronic music must be purged of its 'chemical' origins, so that as we listen we may catch in

334 • SONIC ALIENATION AND PSYTECH AT WAR

it the primary notes of the world" (162). Worldliness returns as an essential value when searching for a sound that is stubbornly unfamiliar in its thingness, possessing more of the nature of sound, and the sound of nature, than something imitating or representing a natural sound.

We might understand the close-up of Kelvin's ear as a closing meditation on hearing Solaris, and *Solaris*—that is, something finally closed off from us. Tarkovsky certainly impedes cinematic language through the formal stylization of the camera work; the slow pace of the film, the extended sequences and close-ups, as well as the variously colored film stock estrange and defamiliarize the narrative cinematic experience. Hearing, however, proves an even more compelling impediment. Artemiev's music and noise at once call attention to themselves and withdraw from us in order to confound the processes of comprehension by reflecting the unseen artifice of Solaris that resides within reflection and thrives on reverberating sound. It hides in order to implicate the inherently alien nature of hearing. What we experience is a shift from comprehension of meaning to alien sensation, from thinking to estranged affects, which fulfills Shklovsky's ideas about formal techniques of defamiliarization: "The purpose of art is to impart sensation of things as they are perceived and not as they are known. The technique of art is to make objects 'unfamiliar,' to make forms difficult to increase the difficulty and length of perception because the process of perception is an aesthetic end in itself and must be prolonged" ([1917] 1998, 16). As much as the psychoanalytic projections of Kelvin, replicated and dubbed by Solaris into psychotechnological ambience, permeate our experience of *Solaris*, the entirety of what we see and hear is in fact a product of alien perception, which presents itself back to us not as an epistemological knowing but as the raw difference of ontological presence, a tone color, a thing within the mirror. This is the only explanation for the sonic transformation heard during Berton's driving sequence, or even the subtle electronic duplications of nature sounds during the initial Earth sequences. In one of his most outrageous comments, Tarkovsky states that his original intention was to have set all of *Solaris* in a shabby Soviet bloc apartment on Earth (1999, 130). It seems at times, however, that the opposite is achieved, and that all of the film takes place on *Solaris*, or at least comes to us through the reconstructed points of view and audition that are *Solaris*. For in those initial scenes that putatively take place on the actual Earth—whether at the dacha of Kelvin's parents or on the highways of the unnamed city—the alien Solaris still resides like a camera hidden inside of a mirrored sphere, giving itself away only through its inexplicable reflections of a visual field treated, through a synesthetic convergence, as sound. Tarkovsky writes:

> Music can be used to produce a necessary distortion of the visual material in the audience's perception, to make it heavier or lighter, more transparent, subtler, or, on the contrary, coarser. . . . By using music, it is possible for the director to prompt the emotions of the audience in a particular direction, by widening the range of their perception of the visual object. The meaning of the object is not changed, but the object itself takes on a new colouring. The audience sees it (or at least, is given the opportunity of seeing it) as part of a new entity, to which the music is integral. Perception is deepened. (1989, 158)

Tarkovsky captures here the estranging properties of sound, particularly when tone color or Artemiev's leit-timbre transforms not the meaning of an object but rather our primary perception of the thing. Tarkovsky's consideration of emotional prompts, I suggest, are related to his desire for Artemiev to create states rather than themes, as these can be complex, subtle, and ultimately alienating rather than familiarizing. In terms of this sonic state orientation, then, Solaris resides in the image and behind other sounds. Only periodically does it reveal its presence as an alien thing through minute repetitions and amplifications of a particular modulating effect, not really a sound at all, that overwhelms both the visual and sonic fields, all the while resisting our efforts to hear anything, especially in a hermeneutic manner engaged with themes and meanings, beyond the repetition of effect. The point at which the sounds of *Solaris* exceed the image and its double is nothing less than the final stage of the conflict that sound painting on the ANS synthesizer resolves between symbolic orders and the order of things.

1974 | *SPACE IS THE PLACE*

John Coney's Sun Ra film, *Space Is the Place,* locates the sonic novum of the Afronautical enterprise on the fringes of pop culture. This was nothing new in Sun Ra films, given the hard bop score to the sociological

336 • SONIC ALIENATION AND PSYTECH AT WAR

documentary, *Cry of Jazz* (1958), the free jazz of an abstract cosmos in *Magic Sun* (1966), and the foregrounded electronics of *Spaceways* (1968). Coney's work is the most narratively structured of the Sun Ra films. Sun Ra visits Earth in his Arkestra spaceship, traveling in time between Chicago in 1943 and Oakland in 1972. Geographical and historical milestones in Sun Ra's own career, the dates denote shifts in musical style and culture; but more importantly, they paint Sun Ra and his archrival, the Overseer (Ray Johnson), as archetypes engaged in mythic struggle for the souls of African Americans on either end of the civil rights movement. While recasting the sonic novum in terms of racial conflict, *Space Is the Place* is more concerned with race-based conflict within African American culture. As far as Sun Ra's battle with the Overseer goes, they mirror and flip each other's iconography repeatedly. Sun Ra, not the Overseer, is associated with eyes; the Arkestra spaceship is a huge pair of eyes, and the eye of Horus adorns Sun Ra (Lock 1999, 68–69). The Overseer, by contrast, controls sound, corrupting the radio network, programming popular announcer Jimmy Fey (Christopher Brooks) against Sun Ra and thereby compromising the one channel by which Sun Ra had hoped to reach the African American community.

Sonic control mechanisms extend to the U.S. government as well, with this villainous entity using constant surveillance and violence against its own citizens. Mass media and news coverage both function as part of the surveillance mechanisms of the U.S. government and the Overseer. Sun Ra tries to break into these channels, and many of his songs function rather as jingles and public service announcements, particularly the "Outer Spaceways Incorporated" segment. The FBI engages in sonic warfare when at one point they capture Sun Ra and torture him by playing "Dixie" repeatedly. They resort to cruder methods at a local community concert, where they try to assassinate Sun Ra at his Minimoog. But armed with sonic psytech of his own—the electronic keyboard used to navigate his interstellar Arkestra—Sun Ra aims to transform the consciousness of inner-city youth, turning them on through cosmic vibrations in order to remind them of, and return them to, their extraterrestrial origins. Sun Ra reclaims the diasporic tribe by recuperating the slave narrative, promising to chain up the reluctant and skeptical and remove them to the origin planet, Saturn, by force. Of course, he isn't really forced to take such desperate measures, as the vibrations of his music are enough to tune the listener to Saturnal frequencies. By the end, the mission cannot be considered a success. Sun Ra is at last able to save only his closest disciples, even the remaining "black part" of Jimmy Fey, but he is unable to redeem Earth as he had hoped. In this respect, Sun Ra is much like Klaatu, who leaves Earth with his mission unaccomplished. Almost like Klaatu, Sun Ra at one point announces that he is a representative ambassador of the Intergalactic Council of Outer Space. Unlike Klaatu's departure, however, Sun Ra's Arkestra exodus is followed by Earth's explosion, though we are left to conclude that this was Earth's doing and not a consequence of Sun Ra's actions. Sun Ra's music is more spaceship than weapon, and his sonic myth science provides an escape route from the culture wars; it does so by returning to the alien nature of the sonic novum as a site of resistance through difference. Rather than situating the novum ahead of us in time, Sun Ra's black myth science puts it out of time altogether. This recodes the film's ending, and though it appears to end with the ending of Earth, we have already been told that it is "after the end of the world," as June Tyson sings. We begin outside of historical time and ordinary space to inhabit the realm of Astro Black Mythology.

Space Is the Place presents us with the futurist sublimation of alienation, reimagining the African diaspora as cosmic and mythic/legendary extraterrestrials. Issues of "separation, escape and otherness" are revisited through SF tropes (Zuberi 2004, 78). In this respect, the film not only seems an appropriate juncture in Sun Ra's evolving musical career but it also reflects his more recent tenure as a teacher of a course called "Black Man in the Cosmos" at UC–Berkeley, where there was interest in both the local and national contexts of black nationalism. It was in fact Bobby Seale and the Black Panther Party who had invited Sun Ra to Oakland, where much of the film was shot in 1971, though Sun Ra's mythmaking and mysticism ultimately proved out of sync with the gritty necessities of African American life in Southern California. Although *Space Is the Place* is praised in circumspect language at best, this merely confirms how out-there and otherly it is. The chaotic mix of humor, prophecy, genre mixing (SF, musical, blaxploitation, documentary), and lack of clear plot amount to the cinematic equivalent of Sun Ra himself, standing before the kids of the Oakland Youth Development Program. They deride him and his mishmash of clothes, doubting whether he is authentic. Sun Ra throws back at them a challenge to their very desire to fit into authentic society, and ultimately suggests that none of them are real: "I'm not real. I'm just like you. You don't exist in this society. If you did, your people wouldn't be seeking equal rights. You're not real. If you were, you'd have some status among the nations of the world" (in Zuberi 2004, 88).

The film is not only a chaotic mix of cinematic styles but of musical forms, including free jazz, space-age exotica, psychedelic soul, and electronic music. Not only was Sun Ra one of the first jazz musicians to incorporate electric keyboards such as the Hammond and Farfisa organs, particularly in a prefusion context, he also test-drove some of the first Moog, Minimoog, and Crumar synths (Zuberi 2004, 82, 81). Using these electronic technologies provided the science to Sun Ra's myth, as the sonic novum developed along "the technology–magic continuum" (Eshun 1998, 160). Part of its revolutionary potential in the context of Afrofuturism, sound, and electric sound in particular, turns this continuum into a "discontinuum" through the alternating electric current that "transmits across gaps and intervals, and not by lineage or inheritance. Traditional culture works hard to polarize this discontinuum. Music willfully collapses it, flagrantly confusing machines with mysticism, systematizing this critical delirium into information mysteries" (161). This discontinuum effect manifests whenever we try to patch together the narrative that seems to thread through *Space Is the Place*, and Zuberi embraces this idea of the productive paradox of the discontinuum when he calls the film an example of "imperfect cinema" (2004, 89). Its so-called flaws in fact provide a means of resistance against imposed cultural norms.

Sun Ra's myth–science discontinuum also destabilizes differences between music and noise, score and special effect, in a way that proves consistent with other examples of the sonic novum. Throughout *Space Is the Place,* Sun Ra's electronic sounds do act as special effects, drawing on the history of SF sound's "familiar scary semiotics of alien presence and space" (Zuberi 2004, 85). Zuberi finds this paradoxical, but it is really another way in which Sun Ra's discontinuum runs throughout the film and throws off cultural codes. For Zuberi, electronic sound effects are no more scary than the horn blowing, screeching, and honking of free jazz, or the use of African, Indian, Islamic, and Eastern sounds, tunings, and instrumentation in new jazz music. What Zuberi calls a yearning element within free jazz had already manifested as a science fictional novum in albums like Ornette Coleman's *Change of the Century* (1959) and *The Shape of Jazz to Come* (1959), Eric Dolphy's *Out There* (1960) and *Outward Bound* (1960), and John and Alice Coltrane's *Cosmic Music* (1968). These records explicitly associate the gliding freedom of tonality that electronics also made possible with synthesis of new tones; liberation from traditional tempos and pitch comes to be associated with the openness of outer space, and technological experimentation with freedom. The "far-out" sounds in jazz involve the use of "volume, texture, grain, tone color, and other sonic variables to create variation and interest, demanding of the listener a focus and appreciation of sound for its own sake" (83). As horn players like Coleman, Dolphy, Coltrane, and Pharaoh Saunders would explore, "attention to aural texture meant stretching the sonic possibilities of existing instruments, producing dissonance and atonality" (83) as part of the larger, liberating escape evoked by titles like Coltrane's "Transition" and "Ascension"—both works so out there at the time of their recording in 1965 that they wouldn't show up on records for years to come. But along the myth–science discontinuum in search of space and alterity, Sun Ra does not readily affiliate with the free jazz scene, which he thought of as alienating instead of alien. Free jazz musicians, Sun Ra concludes, "don't know how to connect with the people. They play music, they are very good at that, but what they are doing has nothing to do with the people. They have no sense of humor. . . . There's humor in all my music. It always has rhythm. No matter how far out it may be, you can always dance to it" (in Szwed 1998, 236). Free jazz hits the terrestrial limits of the sublime, then, while the frequency of Sun Ra's myth–science discontinuum draws the cosmic as well as the comic into a common oscillation. SF sounds and imagery are part of the fundamental accessibility of the Arkestra project, "an optimistic philosophy of universal enlightenment" (Langguth 2010, 160). "It's more than avant-garde," Sun Ra concludes, "because the 'avant-garde' refers to, I suppose, advanced earth music. But this is not earth music" (in Corbett 1994, 7).

What makes a sound authentically alien has more to do with the ways in which new technologies and methods for making, processing, and reproducing sound bring with them innovative ideas about what kinds of sounds are possible rather than what sounds are desirable, or even what those sounds might signify and mean for the humanoid audience of science fiction films. But the human also becomes a contested category split during racially coded episodes of listening. For the Afronaut, the possible sound is more relevant than issues of authentic sounds, and to escape the human continuum, Sun Ra's vibrations function more in terms of the mediality, rather than the technicality, of the SF film, which temporarily isolates the ontological presence of the Other within the special video and sound effects, and emphasizes "moments and intensities more than narrative" (Zuberi 2004, 91). For SF critics like Brooks Landon and Scott Bukatman, SF cinema has always been about itself as a form, with its special effects intensifying reflexive zones of the cinematic apparatus, thereby necessitating a critical turn away from narrative and toward film production as a science fictional mode in its own right (Landon 2002, 40). This is certainly Bukatman's motivation for exploring the special visual effect in two works, and animation in a third, as agents of a technological sublime, something that Zuberi picks up on in the context of Afrofuturist works, where "both the attraction of powerful technology and our fears about it are articulated within the excess of phantasmagorical spectacle" (Zuberi 2004, 92). Most valuably, Zuberi extends the approach to the visual effect found in Landon and Bukatman to consider "music's function as a special effect" in *Space Is the Place*—as "*the* special effect," in fact, "that can transport black people into a higher state of consciousness and being" (2004, 92). While Zuberi perhaps overemphasizes the significance of vocal declamations, poems, lyrics, and refrains in Sun Ra's material, privileging bodily forms of expression, he also suggests that the use of electronic sound in space jazz precipitates a turn toward the material mediality of the technical. Sun Ra exploits the capacity of electronic sound to manufacture the "bodily and mental sensation of musical textures" (92), which is another kind of play on the myth–science discontinuum between affects and effects. This is strikingly modernist, in Zuberi's assessment, which describes the sonic novum accordingly, with its "shock of the new and its non-representational materiality as mediated noise" (93). Sun Ra's cosmic tones for mind and vibrations for the body set the human in motion. The dance floor that Sun Ra evokes points to his role as predecessor to George Clinton's Parliament and Funkadelic, though Sun Ra should also be situated within a larger space music scene that, since the middle of the 1960s, has explored the intersection of science fictional themes, imagery, and sounds with various forms of pop and rock music. Over the course of the 1960s, electronic technologies for "amplification, distortion, and feedback" provided many new means to create "distorted tones and chords" (Zuberi 2004, 83). Subsequently, the "line between noise/sound effects and music in rock, jazz, and other popular music styles becomes blurred," Zuberi concludes, as "popular music 'catches up' with Science Fiction noise only in the 1960s, as electronic instruments and the increasingly elaborate manipulations of the studio console commonly permeate the production and sound of music" (83–84). Much of these intersections came with the introduction of new instruments like the Mellotron and other keyboards, modular synthesizers, step sequencers, and effects pedals, which allowed the performer real-time control over many of the processes that had once taken laborious studio postproduction work. With the transformation of the recording studio into an instrument in its own right, postproduction work also changed rapidly and repeatedly thanks to a steady stream of new gear. Artists and groups like Pink Floyd, Jimi Hendrix, the Moody Blues, King Crimson, Brian Eno, and Tangerine Dream "were creating visionary science fictional environments and narratives with sound alone, stimulating a boom in innovations in mixing-, microphone-, and playback-technologies" (Csicsery-Ronay 2010). With rock fueled by the alterations to subjective space, time, affect, and signification that psychedelics introduced, new vocabularies for sounds were created. Further, sonic experimentation for its own sake was valued as a basic part of this vocabulary, and the immersive, spatial design of sound became as important as melodies or song structures. Sensation took the place of sense, and music and noise were perceived as a means for structuring experience and transforming consciousness (Waksman 1999, 291).

The synthesizer was already associated with the kind of cosmic culture war that could only be summed up, as Pinch and Trocco (2002) note in their history of the Moog synthesizer, as a "moment of sixties freakout" (305). They refer to a scene in Nicholas Roeg's *Performance* (1970), in which Mick Jagger appears as a rock star named Turner. As Turner improvises on a modular synth, Pinch and Trocco describe, Jagger's character becomes "the mad captain at the controls of spaceship Moog" (305). The Moog, as diegetic sound effect, is at once score and prop, a piece of "psychedelic paraphernalia" (305) that represents a change in the mind of the protagonist. In this way, the Moog "was not just another musical instrument; it was part of the sixties apparatus for transgression, transcendence, and transformation" (305). Sun Ra certainly extends these associations into the 1970s, plugging cosmic tones into a technocultural socius through a kind of anticombat combat that cuts in multiple directions at once: his fondness for big band formats points him back to the '40s swing era and nightclubs, while his interest in 1970s-era youth centers situates him in the domains of contemporary jazz and psychedelic soul. Sun Ra's fondness for Disney tunes, his appropriation of biblical style, his references to Saturn and Egypt, on the other hand, continually put him well within the discontinuum of cultural bricolage and deconstructed subgenres (Zuberi 2004, 91).

Whereas SF in the Afrofuturist approach might at times appear complicit with "the scientist industrial technological, culture-sociopsycho babble of a single civilizational paradigm," buying into the worst "colonizing, imperial mission of science fiction," Sun Ra undercuts this complicity through the ambiguities of the myth–science discontinuum (Zuberi 2004, 79). For Sun Ra, there is a problem with science fiction itself, especially alien narratives, which relates to the idea that his electronic noise music should be heard according to ears tuned to the discontinuum: "I don't see any reason why space is horrible. I believe, rather, that people who make these movies show a sort of portrait of the Earth. Moreover, in these movies you often see people from space who are doing something worthwhile, are conquered by Earthlings" (in Szwed 1998, 131). Sun Ra felt a certain validation of his cosmic optimism when he saw *Star Wars*, which he thought to be "very accurate" (in Szwed 1998, 348) and his fondness for both *Star Wars* and *Close Encounters of the Third Kind* underscored his dissatisfaction with the final product of *Space Is the Place*, which he thought was never as beautiful as it should have been, whereas Lucas and Spielberg's films embodied SF's potential to convey "an emancipatory countermyth opposed to the ugliness and banality of the 'real'" (Langguth 2010, 157). Langguth encourages us to hear Sun Ra's endorsement of these non-Afrofuturist films as completely sincere, his humor rarely treading into irony or the disingenuous, but rather possessing the best qualities of the new in science fiction: "visual beauty, sense of wonder, and optimism" (157). By Szwed's account, however, Sun Ra was certain that bits of his ideas were used in both *Star Wars* and *Close Encounters of the Third Kind*—the Force in *Star Wars*, the little synthesized song used to communicate with the aliens in *Close Encounters*—and was suspicious about the fact that *Space Is the Place* had disappeared after only a couple of screenings in San Francisco and New York (1998, 332–33). While this allegedly cosmic plagiarism may demonstrate nothing so much as Sun Ra's "powerfully prescient ability to employ myth as media" (Stanley 2014, 57), it also hints at the appropriative sonic branding that ends up defining the science fiction blockbuster.

1977 | *STAR WARS, CLOSE ENCOUNTERS OF THE THIRD KIND*

The big SF films of 1977 provide an even starker contrast to the psychedelic hypersensitivities of the late 1960s than the films of the early part of the decade. While the sonic novum had become liberated from institutionalized modes of discourse and cinematic functionality in the 1960s, films like *THX-1138* and *A Clockwork Orange* effectively challenged liberatory modes in a flash of critical relevance and artistry. For Guattari, the late 1960s had witnessed a retrieval of the original unconscious of Freud, its "seething richness and disquieting atheism," and we have considered how this plays out for SF cinema, particularly in the pivotal year of 1968. But in the wreckage left after the desolate and dystopian films of 1971, SF cinema in 1977 would largely reinstate the form of structuralist unconscious described by Guattari, predicated "on the analysis of the self, its adaptation to society, and its conformity with a signifying order" (1992, 10). Two of the biggest films of the decade—*Star Wars* and *Close Encounters of the Third Kind*—both defined blockbuster cinematic sensibilities for years to come, including a return to original orchestral scores that took full advantage of innovations in noise reduction and high-resolution recording and reproduction of sound. These are admittedly compelling artifacts that capture the turning of the utopian imagination, which seems to flip over to the dystopian forever despite its apparent celebration of joyous spectacle and nostalgic renewal.

The film known simply as *Star Wars* in 1977 was the beginning of John Williams's dominance of the sonic imaginary, initiating a return to cinema's sonorous past not only in the form of retro sci-fi pulp but also golden age comics with the first *Superman* movie (1978), weird adventure tales with *Raiders of the Lost Ark* (1981), and eventually sentimental coming-of-age stories with the Disneyesque *E.T. the Extraterrestrial* (1982). As we will find, Williams's score to *Close Encounters* is the only sonic anomaly in the bunch, but even it is really about the absorption of past SF film styles, in this case the more uncomfortable atonalities and dissonances of *2001*, which are ultimately absolved by a Disney hook. *Star Wars* in particular precipitated a widespread transformation of science fiction film scores and was responsible for the copycat bluster of Glen Larson and Stu Phillips's *Battlestar Galactica* (1978), Luigi Cozzi's *Starcrash* (1978), Goldsmith's score for *Star Trek: The Motion Picture* (1979), John Barry's *The Black Hole* (1979), the Roger Corman production *Battle Beyond the Stars* (1980), Stanley Donen's *Saturn 3* (1980), and a Toho Studio film, Koji Hashimoto's *Sayonara Jupiter* (1984). The main sonic tropes of the aspiring blockbuster included a highly charged combination of Wagnerian leitmotifs and Straussian tone poems that could dip into dissonant menace but mostly rode on a bed of humanist romanticism and martial time signatures, all performed by large philharmonic orchestras and rarely featuring electronic instruments or markedly synthetic sound.

John Williams's orchestral scores reinforce the directorial desires of George Lucas and Steven Spielberg to return to a golden age of cinema's past. The nostalgic impulse behind these film scores casts us back to the earlier cinematic sensibilities of the matinee serial, especially the romantic ornamentalisms of Erich Wolfgang Korngold's compositions for the swashbuckler adventures of Errol Flynn. Contemporary critical reaction to the *Star Wars* soundtrack often shot past cinematic predecessors to point out where Williams quoted Richard Strauss or Gustav Holst, particularly "Mars, the Bringer of War," from *The Planets*, certainly the most obvious reference point for the cosmic symphonic poems that Williams turned out. Favorable critical reactions to *Star Wars* play up the Wagnerian aspects of the score, with some even arguing that Williams's use of leitmotif restored "the mythic qualities lost in most film music" (Lerner 2004, 98). In any case, Williams's return to romantic orchestration, which precluded the openly futuristic sounds of science fiction, particularly the electronic score, was most often celebrated without reservation or qualification. Neosonics were reserved for the work of the sound design crew and their invention of special sound effects.

Even as sound effects help make SF believable, they have often compensated for the lack of musical novums and so surpass their role as familiarizing agents that both build the science fictional world and contribute to the affective undercurrents of the film. Sound effects present the listener with "the 'music' of machinery," Sobchack claims, and the care in arrangement of sound effects constitutes a form of found sound art or musique concrète (1987, 216). These concrete sounds possess more affective resonance for the science fiction film than any music could, she argues, and they constitute the SF filmmaker's unconscious replacement of "emotionally derived" dramatic music (216). Comments by sound designer Ben Burtt generally validate this idea. "Sound in fantasy," Burtt explains, "can function somewhat like music. You can decide what emotional reaction you want to create" (in Whittington 2007, 107). He goes on to describe the pitches associated with the two major light sabers heard in *Star Wars*: "Darth Vader's laser sword is pitched in a minor key, whereas Obi-Wan Kenobi's is more of a C major chord. When they get together, they don't really harmonize very well" (109). Burtt conceived of sound effects that would affectively engage the iconographic objects, spaceships, and locations, while also adding new layers of meaning to the movie's themes and the underlying archetypes that shape the narrative (107). Specific sounds such as Darth Vader's breathing apparatus or a run of tweets and whistles from R2-D2 "build motifs, accentuate themes, and punctuate dramatic passages" in ways that parallel the function of Williams's musical score. This is how sound effects go beyond merely diegetic function to engage thematic and emotional dynamics.

The more figurative use of noise as a kind of music differs only slightly from the distinctly pitched light sabers to include more subjective ideas about what noises might signify. Again for *Star Wars*, these include variations in the sounds associated with warring spacecraft: "Everybody in the Empire had shrieking, howling, ghostlike, frightening sounds," Burtt recalls, while "the rebel forces had more junky-sounding planes and spaceships" (108). Sound effects become voices in the case of Chewbacca and R2-D2, revealing Burtt's attentiveness to pure vocal affect as an alternative form of the emotive expressiveness of composed music. Through the careful organization of sound effects that "shaped, humanized, and anthropomorphized" R2-D2, filmgoers could easily tell when the droid was worried, afraid, compassionate, distressed, or being rude (108). There is also a programmatic quality to these sound effects, which function like cinematic music by prompting us how and when to respond to the narrative emotionally. In the case of Chewbacca and R2-D2, the sound effect design has the kind of familiarizing and humanizing capacity usually attributed to musical cues.

In Burtt's hands, sound effects also take on the nature of musical motifs, or perhaps a *motif concrete,* like that first anticipated by the work of the Barrons. Burtt describes sounds as characters in the films: "Specific sounds became like animated characters, alive with their own personalities, stories, applications, and function" (in Whittington 2007, 25). However, characters in *Star Wars* come together at a nexus of not only repeated sound effect signifiers but also by means of mythic, melodic leitmotifs, creating doubly striking indicators of a sonic presence often heard just before or as characters take to the screen. After the capture of the rebel ship with Princess Leia on board, Darth Vader's first appearance in the film is "marked by an aggressive and highly dissonant musical stinger that assaults the tonal universe much as weapons fire assaults the soundtrack" (Buhler 2000, 40). Just as his black armored suit and cape stand out against the white armor of the Stormtroopers, the "dissonant musical gesture sets Vader apart from the rest of the Imperial troops precisely because the music suddenly comes forward and takes note of him" (40). While Darth Vader never gets his own theme in the first *Star Wars* film, he does so in the next two films, where his "musical character congeals in the ponderous leitmotif of the Imperial March" (40),

Williams's most strikingly literal riff on Holst's "Mars" composition. This arrangement makes possible "thematic conflict within the score, but even more important, creates the potential for a dialectical engagement within the leitmotif between semiotic and mythical uses of the device" (41). Character development and conflict thus play out along the psychospiritual channels that are the essence of Lucas's mythic narrative and Williams's score.

One reason that Williams's themes may exclude electronic tones, which so dominate the diegetic world of the film, is that openly technological-sounding tones in *Star Wars* are reserved for obviously technological sources on the screen. The zing of an X-wing fighter panning across the stereo field, the zap of a blaster, or the hum of a light saber exists in a sound world of its own. Unusual sounds do not intermingle with the orchestral score in any musical or composed capacity. Rather, such distinctions and sonic interactions become the matter of multitrack sound separation and three-dimensional spatial management. This exacerbates a certain tension in the soundtrack that reinforces the film's divisions between reality and spirituality, technology and myth. Such distinctions of type are not only important to the management of the sonorous *Star Wars* experience but also uphold underlying psychotechnological principles of the film:

> From the camera tilt that initiates the action in each of the films, sound effects are associated with images of technology, radical human interventions in the material world, whereas, after its initial moment of synchronization, music dissolves its bond to the image, allowing it to point to what extends beyond the material reality of cultural mediation, namely the Force. Indeed, the filmic representation of the Force depends crucially on music, which is why it is appropriate to speak of a conflict, perhaps even a dialectic between music and effects on the soundtrack. Sound design is more than a simple question of taste in these films; it is the very means by which the mythical world is constituted as agonistic. (Buhler 2000, 41)

Sound effects (or noises) equate to technology and material reality, while music equates to the Force. Right from the start, when triumphant, horn-blaring music accompanies a simple scroll of yellow text

348 • SONIC ALIENATION AND PSYTECH AT WAR

disappearing into a field of stars, *Star Wars* evokes the gung-ho aesthetic of the Saturday matinee, but presented on a much larger scale, at greater volume, and with new depths of sonic resolution and clarity. Williams skips over the moments of atonal subtlety and gradual build-up of the cosmic orchestra of Kubrick's use of Strauss's "Also sprach Zarathustra" in *2001*, though Williams does go for a similar sense of mystical grandeur conveyed by strings, horns, and starships as the opening text crawl fades and the first shot begins. For the most part, though, Lucas's spaceships rarely move at the slow speed of a Pan-Am shuttle in *2001*. Rather, they dart here and there with their own buzzing roars dopplering about the stereo field. Behind all this frenetic activity, the film demands sharply defined, hyperdistinct instrumental sounds. For this, a handful of leitmotifs were needed that could identify key characters even when they were in the cockpit of a speeding star fighter, and big themes were required that could represent larger, and much starker—well, forces. These included motifs that are broadly representative of the Rebel Alliance, the Empire, and both the good and dark sides of the Force.

More important than the motifs of individual characters in *Star Wars* are the grander musical themes that attach the moral, political, and spiritual resonances of the narrative to a mythic substrate. As individual character motifs interact with these larger thematic figures, we hear a shifting landscape of erosions of commitment, of growing alliances, and ultimately of spiritual journey. Williams's Force motif, which early in the film functions as a free-floating signifier devoid of any clear referent, in retrospect is heard as a way of foreshadowing Luke's destiny to discover the Force. He is sonically marked before we even know him or what part he will play. Buhler's (2000) analysis of the "Binary Suns" cue in the first *Star Wars* film is a particularly keen treatment of "the language-like character of music" and its "self-consciously mythic" function in the film's soundtrack (42):

> When Luke steps outside with the two suns hanging in the sky as background, a full statement of the Force theme accompanies him despite the fact that at this point in the film nothing about the Force has been revealed. The 'primal baptism' that will link signifier and signified does not occur until Ben explains the Force to Luke

later in the film. Moments like this one when the music seems not entirely bound up with its semiotic function are what gives this music its mythical character. The music seems to intuit connections that are beyond immediate rational comprehension. (44)

Leitmotifs, orchestral climaxes, and false finales recur throughout *Star Wars* with "a kind of summarizing power. The mythic quality of the music lies in the perception of a semiosis in flux" (44). That is, the Force must register as nothing other than the failed link between signifier and signified and so become an excess of psychospiritual activity that manifests through the musical expression of extraordinary sources at work within the filmic universe. Just as the theremin became music to communicate the emotive plight of the alien, Klaatu, musical cues in *Star Wars* are "fundamental to the representation of the Force" (44). However, when music merely serves the screened content as another kind of sound effect—typically one of the invisible, such as the otherwise hidden channels of Klaatu's psionic powers or the Force of Obi-Wan Kenobi, for instance—at these points myth itself strives to become an object, an immaterial double, or the material mediation of a convincing speculation of mental and/or cosmic abilities.

As a space opera, *Star Wars* presents a passage through mythic and archetypal systems, which we'll get a better sense of by exploring on-screen characters and their sonic doubles. Where we heard the theremin as the voice of the alien no matter what it happened to be playing—that is, what I have called a timbral motif—leitmotifs in *Star Wars* require something more consistently recognizable as a specific musical expression, a theme. But themes in *Star Wars* are also highly modular. A given motific theme is typically short enough that it can interact with the motifs of other characters or within larger thematic elements of the score without losing its own unique qualities. These themes are also emotionally modular. When played at a different pitch or tempo, the motif can provide an ongoing psychological barometer of a given character. Unmasked and dying, Darth Vader's once ominous theme plays slowly and sadly just as we discover more nuances to his character, prompting sympathetic responses as he undergoes redemption, and just before his characteristic theme is absorbed into the larger musical motif that has signified the Force throughout the film. Of course, Luke also comes into ownership of this Force theme. As Luke comes of age over the course of the first *Star Wars* film (a plotline that the rest of the trilogy merely serves to test and reinforce rather than challenge and develop in any significant manner), the leitmotif does change in some ways, particularly as it mingles with elements of the main theme, perhaps as a way of reminding us of Luke's singular connection to this drawn-out narrative universe. Luke's theme also frequently mingles with the Force theme, suggesting his privileged connection to the mythic layer of the film and its spiritual concerns.

• • •

Though *Star Wars* may be the most obvious SF film of its time to demand an Adorno-styled critique of potentially fascistic sensibilities (see Franklin 2017, 26–30), *Close Encounters* yielded more of this tenor of criticism from contemporary critics. Many pointed to manipulative techniques on Spielberg's part as the director—techniques deeply underscored by Williams's compositions—and found in the film's ideology an authoritarian desire for order that went hand in hand with the privileging of "irrational dogma over scientific reason" (Lerner 2004, 102). Due to its blend of nostalgia, boyhood myths, and spectacle, Tony Williams even labeled the film "a Disneyland version of *Triumph of the Will*" in the 1983 issue of *Wide Angle* (quoted in Lerner 2004, 102). Lerner argues that Williams's use of strong and obvious musical cues "participates in the film's authoritarian rhetoric; it leaves little ambiguity as to how the film demands that it be read" (104). Williams's score develops as a "carefully crafted verbal argument" that moves from an "abstract, melody-less atonal language . . . towards a music of clear, even famous melody. Formlessness yields to form; the threatening yields to the familiar as Penderecki yields to Disney" (105). In *Close Encounters,* dissonant and unfamiliar sounds are associated with the threat of the alien in the well-established ways that they have throughout the history of SF cinema, drawing on the uncomfortable associations between atonality and negative mental and emotional states. In contrast to the role of similarly uncomfortable sounds in *2001,* where Ligeti's music upset our expectations that dissonance equates to something evil on its own terms, Williams resolves the fearful connotations of alien sounds (just as Spielberg does visually as well as narratively) by gradually replacing modernist atonal music with older romantic and operatic sensibilities. In this way, the film score switches out "tonality for atonality just as it substitutes a non-descript heavenly existence for middle-American materialist banality" (102). Williams does not avoid these associations in his score to *Close Encounters*, where "a certain kind of musical modernism . . . encodes that which is meant to be perceived as 'alien'. . . . *Close Encounters* addresses some of the traditional questions of the [science fiction] genre—questions of moral and metaphysical speculation, of cultural identity and one's position in the cosmos (or, at least, the suburbs) while projecting and personifying collective anxieties onto the easy target of an alien" (102). Williams draws on some of the most characteristic techniques of high musical modernism, including aleatoric sections and shimmering tone clusters, emulating the approaches of Ligeti and Krzysztof Penderecki, whose *Threnody for the Victims of Hiroshima* (1960) was used in Spielberg's temp track of *Close Encounters* during the scene of Barry's abduction from his mother's house. Williams sets these modernist tones against other forms of orchestral themes that exhibit the same kind of harmonic, tonal, and romantic sensibilities of his work on *Star Wars*. The culmination of this replacement of uncomfortable, alien atonality by familiar musical themes comes as Williams renders for orchestra clearly recognizable elements of *Pinocchio*'s "When You Wish Upon a Star," quoting this theme nondiegetically in the final scenes of all versions of the film (the original theatrical version in 1977, the 1980 Special Edition, and the 1998 Collector's Edition).

The Disney song is of such importance to *Close Encounters* that it is shocking that it only survives, diegetically, on a music box heard briefly in 1980's Special Edition of the film. In his original script, Spielberg called for the original version from the *Pinocchio* soundtrack to be sourced as Roy Neary (Richard Dreyfus) entered the alien mother ship, and in his novelization, Spielberg writes that as Roy ascends into the alien craft, he "was thinking and hearing a song in his head" and then includes some lyrics from "When You Wish Upon a Star" (in Lerner 2004, 104). This is an important detail for Lerner, who notes that the soundtrack is "intended to be heard within Roy's head," indicating the degree to which the experiences and mind-set of this character models "the intended subjective positioning of the audience," as we are meant to identify with Roy (2004, 104). But Roy not only abdicates his responsibilities as both a husband and father, he also immerses himself in a return beyond childhood to an ultimate infantilization in the womblike interior of the mother ship. In almost direct opposition to what happens to Bowman in *2001*, Roy's return to the star womb signals a nostalgic retreat to the childlike simplicity encoded by Disney films and their dreamy musical scores. As a contest of musical forms, Lerner concludes, the "anti-melodic modernist tone cluster music resonates strongly as the appropriate music to accompany the abduction of a child, the disruption of the familial bonds, for it sets itself in opposition to melodic, tonal music (the music associated with the Disney model of family)" (106). Even as Williams's score becomes beautifully melodic in ways that re-cast the extraterrestrials as not only benevolent but also "familiar and familial" at once, Williams also resolves his score, and thereby the film as a whole, by incorporating Hollywood's traditional signifiers of "epic religiosity and grandeur: harps and textless female choirs" (106). This is a problematic move for Sobchack, for whom *Close Encounters* epitomizes the ways in which special visual effects in SF films have come to represent transcendent states. The film, she concludes:

> initiates a new iconography of beatific human wonder, editorially linking affect to effect. Heads tilted, eyes gazing upward with childish openness and unfearful expectancy—this is the human face of transcendence whose emotion is enacted by what it sees. . . . This alien carousel of a spaceship is not built on principles of economy and rationality, but as a material apotheosis of good feeling, and its presence euphorically fulfills and objectively resolves Roy Neary's intense and incompatible desire both to regain his lost patriarchal power and become a born-again child. Following *Close Encounters,* this narrative and thematic signification of special effect as special affect becomes a major formulation of the genre's mainstream. (1987, 284)

Sobchack's careful breakdown of the visual dynamics in the closing scenes are important to our current understanding of how music also works as spectacle in this film, with its affinities for a kind of "'free-floating and impersonal' (Jameson) affect" that becomes "thematically connected to intense and transcendent states of feeling" (1987, 284). Similar awestruck moments play out in *Star Trek: The Motion Picture, E.T. the Extraterrestrial, The Black Hole, Starcrash, Battle Beyond the Stars, Saturn 3*, and countless others. Accompanied by grand orchestral swells, extended special visual effect sequences become the hallmark of mainstream SF, a genre that has left behind all those "signs of a rational and objective science and technology to representations of a joyous, and 'sublime,' intensity—thematically linking postmodern culture's new 'detached,' 'free-floating,' and 'liberated' sense of emotional transcendence with the transcendental and loving alien" (287–88). In *Close Encounters*, however, the sonic spectacle takes its path through the diegetic world of the film in a narrative that, sonically at least, peaks during the electronic music jam between the terrestrial ground crew and the alien craft before its final anticlimactic ascension into Williams's romanticized orchestral score. To get from this extraterrestrial synth encounter to Williams's apotheosis, we must first determine the significance of five simple notes.

The distinct compositional domains that Williams faced when working with Lucas didn't apply as much to his work with Spielberg. He had already written the two-note minimalist motif for the impending shark attacks in Spielberg's *Jaws* (1975), so five notes for *Close Encounters* should have been a breeze. Spielberg's instructions asserted key differences divorcing diegetic electronic tonalities from music proper: "It shouldn't even be a melody," Williams recalled in a 1998 interview. "It should be more like somebody pushes a doorbell. Like Avon calling—you know. 'Ding Dong.' It's not a melody. It's not even a phrase. It's just musical intervals. With no rhythm assigned to them or anything. Just five notes." These musical sounds were like a TV jingle, a station ID, something not all that different from the constant backdrop of strategically aired commercials and cartoons playing on Roy's family's TV. Such sound cues continually point back to childhood, and this interstellar hello had to be simple enough to play on a kid's rainbow-colored glockenspiel. The story of the creation of these five notes variously attributes John Williams going through hundreds of permutations before coming up with the final combination of notes. Though Williams's hoped to compose a seven- or eight-note motif, Spielberg was insistent on five tones that could be chanted by mass crowds, played on a child's instrument, whistled, and finally synthesized. These five notes are hardly a motif and the sequence of tones barely a communication. It is bereft of all content and meaning, but not of Williams's politics of sonic control and tonal cleansing. The five tones seem to express, as SF films had before, that mathematics are the language of the cosmos, and that music is mathematical, something that the simple chime of five pure tones could get across more than a complex score might, much less a score that might attempt to play back the aliens their own sound, which is apparently dissonant, a little frightening, mysterious, and skin crawling. These simple five tones, one set chosen out of hundreds of options, are a crystal-clear, readily repeatable, easily transmittable, imminently assimilable, and total rejection of atonality. They become the crucial weapon in Williams's war on noise, though only after one last excursion from the lofty domains of the score to the earthly electronics of the diegetic realm.

Played back to the alien mother ship near the end of the film, the five notes of the cosmic doorbell chime announce that we are home and ready for company thanks to the incorporation of an ARP 2500 modular synth, played by Phil Dodds, a technician and later vice president of engineering at ARP Instruments. As in earlier science fiction cinema, electronic tones are directly associated here with the alien voice, a raw communicative gesture lobbed across the void of incomprehension. Deleon (2010, 18) distinguishes the familiarizing musical elements, even played as electronic or synthesized tones, that in this sequence unmask tensions between the organic orchestra and technical synthesizer, as well as between the composer-musician and the technician-engineer. These differences reserve the domain of music proper for the nondiegetic layer of the film, while musical sonic events that emerge from within the diegetic world of the narrative must be retrieved as something that isn't music per se but rather a technological event. In the case of the ARP 2500, the sense that technological music is somehow alien music, and so not quite really music at all, is reinforced here by the look of the synthesizer, which despite its keyboard controller is introduced as a module of an intergalactic communications switchboard rather than a musical instrument. Performed as part of a highly mediated event and spectacle, the musical jam session that results from the five tones is ultimately caught up in an accelerating, out-of-control feedback loop that blows out the terrestrial unit. This proven insufficiency and inadequacy of our technologies to keep up with the alien music, however, is overcome by the five tones' final absorption into the film's closing themes.

The concept of the technologically advanced and enlightened civilization folds back around to the glorified childhood of the alien visitors. Williams asserts a sonic control mechanism that pits nondiegetic and diegetic sounds against each other, then absorbs the diegetic cues within his unifying nondiegetic score. This is the case with the five-tone theme that serves human and extraterrestrial communication as well as "When You Wish Upon A Star." In the latter case, Spielberg had almost trumped Williams's score with a sappy signature tune from his own Disneyfied childhood. When Williams quotes "When You Wish Upon a Star" in order to accompany Roy's final abrogation of husbandry, fathering, and employment to ride off with the star children, the orchestral strings—which ascend ever heavenward through a kind of sustained variation of the everlasting upward glide of the Shepard tone—accompanied by harp, normalize Roy's ascension into a sonic sensibility predicated on the rejection of dissonance, electronic tones, and the resources of mediated memory. This may or may not be part of the cosmic existential crisis that Roy experiences, but it certainly seems to be the case for the sonic imaginations of Spielberg and Williams. Given the equation of normalcy with orchestral instrumentation and the familiarizing function of recurring melodic motifs and modular thematic movements that can be shuffled around in on-going arrangements without losing their sense of belonging to a unified, tonal whole, Matthias Konzett (2010, 101) suggests that the turn toward a singular orchestral sound maintains the illusion of the unified subject and protects the image of subjectivity against fragmentation. This unified subject is always at threat in alien-oriented SF, where soundtracks tend to reject the familiarizing function of sound and take us into far more discomforting atonal ranges. However, in the sonic domains of the cinemas of the late 1970s, even more was at stake for film audiences, where the unification of the listening subject was endangered by the wildly distributed and often hyperactive dimensionality of the multichannel surround sound mix. For Whittington, the immersive qualities of the multichannel mix are at the heart of *Close Encounters*'s nostalgic infantilization: "The surround channels carry the sounds of the alien crafts jetting by, the reverberate radio chatter from the government controllers, and the mutual tones of communication and music. The scene places characters and audiences alike into a visual and sonic playpen of fantasy and science fiction" (2007, 122). This sonic playpen becomes more menacing, however, when Whittington characterizes it—seemingly unwittingly—as an all-encompassing trap, with surround sound providing a sonic equivalent of the hyperreal spectacle of simulation that turns movie theaters into "a total sonic environment, which masks the real environment of the theater space to create a sonic space with no entry and no exit" (122). This totalizing space, the proxy of simulacra that replaces all other spaces, aspires to the status of immersive amusement park ride.

Just as SF films provide a popular conduit for avant-garde practices in new music and sound making, Bukatman (1997) describes a process by which the visual sensibilities of film's early avant-garde persist through changing cinematic tendencies. The narrative modes that have come to dominate cinema—stabilizing spatial codes in ways that subordinate our physical presence within the theater to the fictional spaces and times of the screen—are in fact relatively recent developments in the lineage of audiovisual entertainments. Here Bukatman updates Tom Gunning's (1986) idea of an exhibitionistic cinema, which points back to the early films of Méliès and the Lumière brothers as well as pre-cinematic forms of visual spectacle such as panoramas and magic lantern shows. These early forms of spectacle were presented to an audience as something to look at almost for their own sake, as spectacle, and for the audience's immediate reaction. However, since the domination of narrative modes, the act of presentation becomes secondary to the events depicted on the screen, which are regarded as the "*represented* experiences of the spectator's onscreen surrogate," while affective response and psychological impact largely become vicarious in nature (Bukatman 1997, 13). However, the presentation of the spectacular attraction for its own sake does not simply "disappear with the dominance of narrative, but rather goes underground, both into certain avant-garde practices and as a component of narrative films" (13–14). Gunning (1986) discusses the musical, which puts the brakes on narrative for its song-and-dance numbers, while Bukatman makes a convincing case that in science fiction films, the "spectatorial excess" of the special visual effect likewise halts the narrative impulse during extended moments of revelry in the film's own visual design and technological achievement. Rather than alienating the spectator, such moments actually "*re*-integrate the spatiality of the spectacle with the 'actual' spatiality of the theater to create a phenomenologically significant experience" (1997, 14). The simultaneous distancing of the embodied viewer from the space of the screen and reembodiment of cinematic phenomenology is the neovisual splicing together that has its equivalent in the fictive neologism, with its alienating linguistic newness that at the same time becomes a means for orienting the reader toward the fictional world.

The exceptional nature of the special visual effect accommodates a new mode of subjectivity for the filmgoer relative to a virtual cinematic space made possible by the kind of advanced technologies that the narrative is about in the first place. One of the problems with the electronic and digital technologies of spectacular culture and the information age is that their operations tend to be invisible and inconceivable. The reason that the special effect spectacle and the information age go so well together, particularly where both are concerned with "state-of-the-art" innovations, is that the former presents the latter in "detailed, phenomenologically convincing forms," and in this way "the ontological anxieties of the present are endowed with a concreteness and literalness of form" (Bukatman 1997, 14). The special visual effects of *TRON* (1982) and James Cameron's *Terminator 2* (1991), Bukatman argues, "construct new objects and spaces that visualize abstract cultural concerns and permit a provisional reembodying of the human subject in relation to those concerns" (14). Whittington arrives at similar conclusions and regards the role of sound effect design as a distinctive way in which SF films accommodate new technologies, emerging instrumentalities, and audiences. New means and methods of cinematic sound reproduction tend to make their public debut tethered to the SF film, Whittington explains, so that "sound technology, like special effects technology, has been hard-wired to the science fiction genre. In part, it is a tenet of the genre not only to be about technology but also to *be* its embodiment" (2007, 115). In this cinematic landscape, the conceptual–technical hybrid of SF's sonic novum presents a simultaneous "transgression of existing norms and an attentiveness to its own manufacture" (115). Schmidt also emphasizes SF's sonic engagement with the self-reflexive mode of the spectacle, but her analysis goes beyond sound effect design to consider electronic sound more generally. "The use of a machine to generate electronic sounds is even further appropriate to the genre if we consider the longstanding tradition of spectacle within sci-fi film," Schmidt writes. "Alongside any 'inherent' eeriness they might convey, electronic sounds have a quality of aural spectacle, a sound that is recognized and therefore potentially celebrated as human invention" (2010, 36).

The complex and paradoxical function of newness in science fiction both disorients and orients us during our encounter with its imaginal objects whether in the media of written text, film, digital movie, or recorded sound. The tenor of this critical turn to effect design as a site of technological boundary pushing and reflexivity is common to SF theory whether linguistic, cinematic, or sonic. We could probably very broadly describe an effects novum that operates across all science fiction media—as neologistic word making in literary SF, as special visual effects or neovisuals (including set design, costuming and makeup, model building and matte painting, and CGI), and as sonic effects or neosonics (including sound design and the musical score or cues created by unusual means and processes). In each instance, this broadly defined effects novum would link SF's imaginary worlds to the domains of technical experimentation and creative practice, and it does so through the synthetic and synthesizing properties of language, image, and sound. This realization is particularly important for the critically engaged participant in science fictional modes—whether reader, viewer, or listener—who may want to understand how SF is ported from one medial base to another as well as how he or she may remediate strategies for integration or resistance.

As neosonic phenomenon, the Dolby Surround mixes of *Star Wars* and *Close Encounters* first channeled the various sonic powers across a shared acoustic ecology that made resistance quite difficult. As Williams discovered working with Lucas and Spielberg, the policing of audition within this domain involved "not merely a repressive set of exclusions or limits, but a generative distribution of sensations that identify, channel, and amplify sonic power. What is distributed are those elementary pulses or throbs of experience constitutive of an aesthetic ontology that revolves around vibrational force and the prehension of affective tonality" (Goodman 2010, 189). After the use of Dolby A noise reduction in *A Clockwork Orange*, *Star Wars* and *Close Encounters* both helped secure industry standardization around Dolby Stereo encoding, and thereby guaranteed a certain kind of marketed listening subjectivity, while this format agreement "functioned to commodify science fiction films and provide audio content" in increasingly standardized ways (Whittington 2007, 118). SF hesitates between Dolby's provision of what is presented (though not necessarily heard) as a more "realistic" sound and its tendency to self-reflexively turn on the technologies of its own production, critically subverting the codes of technological adoption in order "to expose their constructed nature" (119). John Williams reveals the spectacular nature of what Goodman calls the "sound signature," the movie theme as a form of "virosonic branding," hook, or jingle (2010, 190). For Goodman, the sound signatures of virosonic branding have everything to do with our experience of time in the domains of "predatory capital." When striking preemptively, in the form of a none-too-subtle, and in fact spectacular sound event that Goodman calls *déjà entendu*, the movie theme as jingle or earworm points us toward future acts of consumption, "mobilizing audio viruses to hook consumers in advance for products that may not yet exist" (189–90). Dolby promotional materials stressed the realism of sounds using their system, and their sonic agenda was roughly the same as not only the SF film aesthetic of Lucas and Spielberg but also their ambitions as builders of commercial empires and licensed franchises.

The *Star Wars* films, particularly the last two of the original trilogy, and *Close Encounters* most fully exploit the new intensities of sound that Dolby systems made available. *Close Encounters* is notable for its long dramatic moments achieved through the expansive near silence of several scenes just before we detect the slow buildup of the mother ship's arrival, or the darting flybys of smaller scouts. These are strategic moves, not randomly added values, and they are not left up to synchronicity.

With every sound in its place, even the five-tone sequence provides a way to regulate noise, to quell the potentially uncomfortable barrage of atonal alien sounds, to train the alien to speak our language of the spectacularly minimal mathematics of surround capital. By institutionalizing rigid distinctions between diegetic noise and nondiegetic music, and managing worlds from the inside out, sound, in other words, can no longer provide a contested field for polyphonic selves but rather becomes the regulatory device of a total point of audition, a kind of pansonicon, as it were. The management of the immersive speaker space—the third kind of sound, if you will, that follows from our prior contact with stereo's seconding of available audio channels—also brings to its absolute end the illusion that there is or ever was a single soundtrack as such. And with the end of this illusion, a new life awaits you.

• CHAPTER 5 •

Sonorous Object-Oriented Ontologies (1979–89)

The SF/horror hybrids of the late 1970s and early 1980s rejected the cleanly delineated sonic novums of the big blockbusters of 1977 while still taking advantage of their expanded spatiality. Exploring the dark side to the serial heroism of *Star Wars* and the countless space operas that trailed in its wake, Ridley Scott's *Alien* (1979) and *John Carpenter's The Thing* (1982) were retro in another way, tapping directly into golden age sensibilities of 1950s SF to mine the unsettling paranoias of alien invasion. The alien noise things of this retro–golden age SF can burst out of any sound, at any second. Mobilized by the demands of the horror film for tones that trigger primal fears and yet meet our demand for neosonic risk and reward, these sound worlds sink into the subconscious domains of fractured, paranoid minds and terrorized bodies while exploring surround sound reproduction as a psychotechnological adjunct for fear of the unknown and unexpected. As they embody the SF/horror film's need for unusual sonic identities, these films often broach the borders of tactile sound and body horror.

Both *Alien* and *The Thing* revisit sensibilities first heard in *The Thing from Another World* and *Gojira,* particularly the ways in which the entire sound field works on us across diegetic domains. The multichannel platforms that both films use compound this effect, leaving us uncertain where sounds might emerge in the space around us, as well as whether

• 361

they will signify an event in the realms of the diegetic, nondiegetic, or both. As with *Gojira*, sounds of the alien are integrated into the musical score through the use of unusual instrumentation and sound editing, particularly in Jerry Goldsmith's score for *Alien*. Here, the alienating auditory primitivism extends beyond the composition of a score to include the poststereophonic design of theatrical surround sound systems. Quiet spaces potentially hide a sound that can either emerge from an increasingly unsettling acoustic background of dripping water, rattling equipment, and beeping monitors, or it can morph out of the backdrop of the musical accompaniment. Layers of technological sounds associated with human efforts at communication, often in states of disrepair or malfunction, also become particularly compelling parts of the sound design, taking us back to the hypermediated technical interfaces of *Destination Moon, 2001,* and *THX-1138*. Placement of the alien sound in expanded psychogeographical soundscapes becomes a startling new means for staging the auditor's encounter with the dangerous unknown. I conclude my analysis of these two films by proposing the existence of sonic xenomorphs. These monstrous sounds are notable for the ways in which they reveal themselves over the course of a continually morphing, sonic becoming, rather than as beings as such. Such alien sonic novums amplify to the breaking point and beyond cultural anxieties around the technologized sonic experience—including sirens and Klaxons, telecommunication signals, and, most egregiously, signal glitches. Blurring categorical distinctions between music and noise as a result of the emotional resonance that noises accrue in the context of SF/horror, diegesis becomes highly unstable, gravitating between almost arbitrary aesthetic differentiations of the expressive capacity of composed music and plausible sound effects. This aims sonorous ontological instabilities toward the interior, unknowable gulfs of abject alien technicities.

While the most sonically audacious science fiction films of the 1970s blocked the three hypersensitivities of the machinic unconscious, the ambient elements of *Alien, John Carpenter's The Thing, TRON, Blade Runner, Decoder,* and *For All Mankind* shift alien sonic geographies toward digital, cybernetic, and hypermediated spaces, and it is through this shift that they sonify the machinic unconscious. Ridley Scott's *Blade Runner* (1982) and West German director Muscha's *Decoder*

(1984) eliminate the blockages of touch (affect), sex, and the cosmos, while Steven Lisberger's *TRON* (1982) and Al Reinert's pseudodocumentary of the Apollo space program *For All Mankind* (1989) maintain them. New hypersensitivies altogether take shape in *TRON* and *Blade Runner*, among the first films to update ambient SF sounds for the digital era, blending and blurring diegetic sounds and nondiegetic scores in ways that access cybernetic and synthetic spaces. Both the musical scores and sound designs for *TRON* and *Blade Runner* participate equally in each film's distinct examination of organic and artificial space, to opposing ends. While the sonic construction of *TRON* ultimately conserves key binary differences between the human and the digital duplicate, with consequences for our capacity to understand virtual worlds and artificial intelligence, *Blade Runner* blurs the distinctions between such binaries—the organic and synthetic, music and noise, the nondiegetic and the diegetic, the virtual and the real—in order to probe the construction of synthetic consciousness and the manufactured cybernetic world. *TRON* and *Blade Runner* approach cybernetic entities from opposite poles: one introducing the human into the cybernetic domain, the other introducing the cybernetic element into the human domain. Sonically, the composers for these films—Wendy Carlos and Vangelis, respectively—approached their themes in similar ways: by exploring the sonic space between acoustic orchestral voices and digitally synthesized sound. Something crucial to these narratives' explorations of the relationship between human and replicated identity thus plays out sonically. I am particularly interested in how these synthesized sounds contribute to the cyberspatial world building of the films, especially to understand how that world building facilitates the manufacture of replicated human consciousness.

A dystopian film from the West German postpunk underground, *Decoder* is also concerned with the ambient sonic programming of human consciousness and will. In this film, music blurs the contours of histories and memories, an ambiguity rendered as technocultural strategy by William S. Burroughs's dream guidance in a couple of scenes of *Decoder*, in which the techniques of musique concrète are espoused as an audiovisual weapon within the media-saturated culture of surveillance and control. In *For All Mankind*, on the other hand, the practice of musique concrète pushes toward transcendent states of consciousness, those existing outside of the control mechanisms of news broadcast and manifesting as outside of history altogether. The zeroing out of preconceptions that Burroughs advises, opening up our experience of history to ambiguity and thus renewed possibility, is how the unexpected connections facilitated by cut-ups, remixes, Tarot decks, and dreams are turned into actions. This ambiguity at the heart of action, rather than the purpose behind it, is the antiessence of these hybridizing techniques, that which makes them viable as a way of resisting control and rewriting history. An ambiguity of affect appears to be a precondition for the effectiveness of the cut-up and other noise rituals. *Decoder* is thus about the manufacture of consciousness and the inherent struggle between the real and the replicated. Here, ambient space becomes socially contested through an exploitation of sonic cultural warfare, with order maintained through Muzak while rebellion takes the form of hard-core industrial music. *For All Mankind* explores the relationship between ambient music and the manufacture of collective memory, through which moments of transcendental epiphany overwhelm the record of technological achievement. Where sound in *Decoder* contributes to a culture war by altering the minds of listeners, changing behaviors, and instigating riot, sound also transforms our ability to evaluate lived experience and inhabit screened space in more subtle ways. *For All Mankind* thus suggests that sound, by adding and altering the values through which we make that evaluation and so access the acousmatic, largely determines our sense not only of what is real but what is. Mediation, in this sense, is not only a matter of process, of mediating, but also of differentiating—of not simply becoming, but of becoming Other. Along these lines, Kember and Zylinska negotiate a key conflict between Bergson's accounting for "difference as immanent differentiation from within that drives the production of 'forms ever new'" and Derrida's argument, in their words, for "difference as a (quasi)transcendental place of absolute alterity that cannot be subsumed by the conceptual categories at our disposal" (2012, 27). Describing media as a vital process, Kember and Zylinska inadvertently provide a new definition of a kind of "mediating novum": "the *lifeness* of media—that is, the possibility of the emergence of forms always new, or its potentiality to generate unprecedented connections and unexpected events" (xvii). Through its reconceptualization of diegetic music and nondiegetic ambience as a mechanism for posthistorical transcendence, Reinert's documentary fabricates a collective cultural memory of space exploration.

Novums measured by the situations in which we encounter SF film during the 1980s can no longer apprehend difference per se but rather operate along a spectrum of variously positive or negative effects. This is a rather traditional function of the novum, which, according to Suvin, satisfies its subjects through "critical analysis or utopian longing" (in Csicsery-Ronay 2008, 55). However, as we have seen repeatedly, the immersive sounds of SF open up the novum to an engagement with a much wider variety of states of consciousness than Suvin allows. Suvin's situationally determinate and functionally limited novum reduces the experience of "optimal SF" to those that deliver the "tacit paradigm of parabolic, critical freedom" (52). All other SFs are filled with ineffectual novums that he deems "pessimal," "banal," "incoherent," "dogmatic," "invalidated," and "inauthentic" (52–53). For Suvin, the best kind of SF is characterized by a singular effect on the reader's consciousness, a cognitive estrangement that yields, through the shock of the new, a specific kind of gain that can best be "judged by how much new insight into imaginative but coherent and this-worldly, that is *historical,* relationships it affords" (1979, 81). The soundscapes of SF/horror in *Alien* and *The Thing* charge up and amplify the shock factor by conceptualizing the novum as a point of potential and unexpected eruption of dangerous sonic entities. The other films considered in this chapter are also concerned with the nature of sound as a space of being, an ontology attached to very specific forms of sonorous object. Becoming so object-specific in their orientation, the films explored in this chapter in fact open up the novum to more varied cognitive states in addition to not only the critical mode favored by Suvin but also the nostalgic modes first articulated in *Star Wars* and *Close Encounters. Blade Runner* revisits film noir with its retro-cyberpunk Los Angeles and detective narrative trappings. *For All Mankind* is among the first handful of films to revisit the moon landings. *Decoder* looks back to a West Germany before the commercialization by corporate America. *TRON* tries so hard to be of the moment and on the cusp of the digitalization of popular culture—programmer chic, video arcades, an emerging graphic design aesthetic, narratively inconsequential, compressed '80s rock courtesy of Journey—that it ages itself with every passing second. While *The Thing* is the only remake of the lot, Carpenter approaches his project by specifically embracing the trappings of golden age science fiction, but through the liquid lens of body horror, updating the Cold War atmosphere of enclosure, isolation, and paranoia in ways that suggest both an AIDS-era narrative and a breakdown of masculine stereotypes. Also destabilizing gender codes in SF films, *Alien* turns the nationalisms of golden age SF in on themselves, its horrors that of the alien within us, the deadly by-product of shadowy military–industrial–corporate interests.

The repeated convergence of sonic becoming and the cosmological imagining that this book has located at the site of science fiction cinema indicates an ongoing need for critical inquiry into the genre as a means of understanding three things: the dynamics of technoculture by means of an aesthetic investigation of the conceptual and physical spaces shared among new sonorous objects and their listeners; the function of sonic spaces as adjuncts to consciousness that alter the operations of psychotechnologies; and the negotiation and management of difference within these spaces. Sound becomes ever more crucial to our engagement with the media of contemporary technoculture as it develops what Dyson (2009) claims are "notions of immersion and embodiment," which are ubiquitous in contemporary cinema and instrumental in the development of new media, and which are in fact founded on "a conceptual model and a set of technologies," first delivered and then naturalized by "reproduced and transmitted sound (that is, audio)" (3). One of the most tenuous developments of new cinematic formats and other new media lies in their approach to "aural territories, including not just the frontiers opened by audio technology but the close associations sound has with embodiment (via synesthesia), with the sublime (via music), and with alterity (via metaphysics)," Dyson concludes. Reterritorializing "aurality's mythos, sound is simultaneously neglected and appropriated by the complicated rhetorics of immersion and embodiment that have inaugurated new media discourse and have announced new media as 'new'" (6). Our encounters with SF films yield such substantially variable cognitive effects and affective states that we have begun to categorically distinguish films according to their specific effects on consciousness (Powell 2007, 4–5). As Powell argues, mainstream and conventional cinema are notable for their ability to integrate the more radical effects of an experimental and expanded cinema on their audiences, a corollary to its capacity to smuggle in the otherwise outré sounds of the avant-garde, primitivism, atonality, electronic music, and so on. "Altered states are at once idiosyncratic and subject to changing fashions like the film technologies used to present them," Powell concludes (13). That the sounds of a film could be designed in order to trigger specific effects on the minds and bodies of its auditor-viewers is the most interesting consequence of this conclusion. As both object and functioning ecology in this respect—and this chapter is largely devoted to unfolding the relationship between these two—the sonic novum is both "an imagining system" (Harper 2010, 114) and a place to think. The real appeal of the technoacousmatic setting is the way that technology emerges as a sign of new ways of being in the world while spatially accommodating the new listening subject it demands, a subject balanced on what Harper calls "the tightrope between new and familiar musical languages" (115). Listening to new sounds necessitates the training and habituation of the ear to hear the world around it in certain ways, but it also always demands their overturning, upsetting, violation, remaking, transforming, and renewal.

1979–82 | *ALIEN, JOHN CARPENTER'S THE THING*

Significant examples of SF/horror hybrids and the "body horror" subgenre, Ridley Scott's *Alien* and *John Carpenter's The Thing* present tales of alien encounter that push toward cinematic extremes of graphic bodily transformation, parasitism, and unnatural destruction. With the first film set on a deep space vessel, the second in an Arctic research station, the narratives concern a chance encounter with alien artifacts that trigger the awakening of a deadly life-form. As the titular Alien and Thing morph their ways through the bodies of the majority of each film's characters, the films become rather dire accounts of human isolation, paranoia, distrust, and conspiracy. Both films combine fear-inducing musical cues, hyperrealistic sound designs, and innovative multichannel

368 • SONOROUS OBJECT-ORIENTED ONTOLOGIES

presentation and surround sound reproduction to locate the body of the listener within the hypersensitive domains of SF/horror and the unknown. Not only can the alien sound emerge from within any sound source, it can also manifest from singular speaker locations in the movie theater. Immersive and yet fragmented, these unsettling sounds overload the point-of-audition of the listening subject with dread and thereby monstrously extend the unsettled vibratory field of the ear across the entire body. Here, among confused "layers of coding and construction," the relationship between sounds and their alien sources is "overdetermined and embedded by the production process and structures that support it" (Whittington 2007, 148). I am concerned here with the multilayer space of the sonic novum and its mutation of listening bodies through cinematic experience. Recalling my earlier consideration of Dolby A noise reduction, which worked its way from the background of sound reproduction processes into theaters through the disturbing resolution of *A Clockwork Orange,* I continue to explore why the reconfigured listening subjects of Dolby Surround systems have such an affinity for places of sonorous body horror.

Incongruously, the sonic grit of *Alien* is actually attributable to the clarity provided by Dolby noise reduction, which, Chion explains, "lends tangible reality to a future where the equipment is not always in the best of shape" (2009, 127). Carefully crafting and reproducing the sounds of diegetic equipment, always in a state of disrepair, as well as crew member's telecommunications, transmitted in distressing and less than ideal circumstances, brings to *Alien* an element that Lucas had called for in *Star Wars*: the feeling of inhabiting a used future. Jerry Goldsmith had pioneered this exploration of used-future aesthetics in his score for *Planet of the Apes,* and once in sync with Ridley Scott's demands for a nonromantic score, he would bring not only this sensibility to bear on the *Alien* project but also his cache of future-primitive instruments (here, the conch shell, didgeridoo, and the wooden and brass horn known as a serpent) and the unusual techniques that he had developed more than ten years earlier for *Planet of the Apes.* By the end of the 1970s, the seasoned composer had become reluctant to work beyond the tropes of what SF film music had become in the wake of Williams's *Star Wars* themes: big, bombastic, often militant, and fully orchestrated romanticism. Goldsmith's original title cues for *Alien* are almost as sweepingly romantic as the main theme he composed for *Star Trek: The Motion Picture* that same year. Scott never liked the Goldsmith score, rejecting entirely the initial theme that would have accompanied not only the main titles but also the opening shots of the sleeping spaceship, *Nostromo*. Though it featured a more melancholy turn than the new *Star Trek* theme, the unused title sequence for *Alien* has an inappropriately uplifting and overall majestic feel, with moments of bombast and percussive crescendos clearly inappropriate for what was essentially a horror film in outer space. Scott had something else in mind entirely, and he asked Goldsmith to rescore this scene in its entirety in order to give the film a less romantic and more suspenseful tone from the start. Having just heard Tomita's electronic rendition of Holst's *The Planets*, Scott had originally wanted the Japanese synthesist to score *Alien* (Scott 1979, 15). Perhaps when settling for Goldsmith, Scott had hopes for something like the hybrid of dramatic orchestration with the deep Moog-filter inflections and tense ARP 2600–driven sequences that Goldsmith composed for Michael Anderson's *Logan's Run* (1976). Ultimately, though, it is difficult to imagine *Alien* bearing much of a musical footprint at all, and in any case, nothing of Goldsmith's score is heard in the film as he had composed and sequenced it to the original cues. In the end, much of what Goldsmith wrote went unused.

It was not just the thematic music that Scott found lacking. The director also disliked Goldsmith's atonal segments (see Brigden 2017), which often come across as too tightly synchronized to visual events and so make the film's action cartoonish and over the top, even manipulative. One example is the scene in which Science Officer Ash (Ian Holm) is revealed to be an android sent to protect the alien at the crew's expense. While Ash begins to malfunction and attempts to suffocate Ripley (Sigourney Weaver), a close sync of nondiegetic stinger music with the action on the screen threatened to overcode the shocking scene like the schlockiest of horror flicks. Scott, his film editor Terry Rawlings, and music editor Robert Hathaway simply cut the musical score for this scene, while throughout the project they chopped up and resequenced the score, rendering Goldsmith's music a strangely fragmented, vaguely ambient, highly unstable, and altogether menacing sound experience.

370 • SONOROUS OBJECT-ORIENTED ONTOLOGIES

This would give the production crew more flexibility in terms of which elements of Goldsmith's music they would keep, if any. In several places, the editors stuck with the temporary track that Scott had used to guide him through the initial editing pass. This included pieces of Goldsmith's earlier score for John Huston's *Freud* (1962) and selections from Howard Hanson's Symphony No. 2 "*Romantic,*" which is heard during the final battle between Ripley and the Alien, as well as during the closing credits. Much of what we hear of the new Goldsmith cues were recued by Scott and his sound designers, displacing stingers, if not eliminating them altogether, in ways that produced more tension because there was no guaranteed placement of a pending sonic event. Almost every sense of intention, location, direction, or synchronization of the sounds was removed, making the potential for sonic encounter highly uncertain and unpredictable.

Now an integral part of the aesthetic design of the entire editing process, this new "aesthetic of imprecision" (Chion 2009, 126) governs the diegetic sound space of *Alien* as well. Sounds in the film are frequently both "bad" (126) and "dirty" (127), Chion notes, referring to the muted engine sounds of the *Nostromo* and the weird, distorted hootings and cavernous spaces of wide-open Echoplex effects heard in Goldsmith's revised main title theme: "Right from the opening credits . . . we hear dull, pale, lifeless, and life-sapping sounds throughout the film, but this dullness, rather than being the consequence of 'maxed-out' audio technology, is in fact intentionally *created* by technology" (127). Throughout the film, human voices are also dirty, scuffed up, mumbled and hacked out as the actors draw attention to the "wheezing, breathing, puffing, and panting between words," even while words themselves are always in danger of being drowned out by some cacophony of ship noises: steamy expulsions, dripping water, the pulse and roar of distant and unseen machines, sirens, computer sounds, telecommunication interference, or alien attack itself (128). The numerous audio and video communications among *Nostromo* crew members are likewise noisy, full of static and atmospheric interference, doomed by technical malfunction, which generates much of the film's anxiety.

As it became apparent that sounds in *Alien* would be fragmented, displaced without visible or apparent sources in diegetic or nondiegetic space, and distorted through additional postproduction desynchronization, Goldsmith likewise took apart the orchestra and added minimal and unusual sound sources that let him treat musical instruments like sound effects. The unsettling nature of the film's psychotechnological terror comes from this virtually sourceless approach to music, which renders timbre unstable and ultimately without clear origins. We wait for subtle cues and musical movement that will suggest the unseen presence and forewarn us of invisible menace (Whittington 2007, 155). At points so subtle that some might not hear it at all, the heartbeat sound that precedes the attacks of the alien, for instance, functions as a concrete motif, though it is the opposite of the Geiger counter in the original version of *The Thing*. Where the Geiger counter constituted a diegetic aura for a creature so alien that it had no sound of its own—its silent gap of antibeing triggering dread and escalating anxiety among the human characters and audience alike as all listen and wait for the alien to close in on them—it is never exactly clear from what auditory point of view we perceive the heartbeat. Whittington implies that the sound's musical role is a way of getting close to the mind of the alien itself, suggesting that as the xenomorph gets "in tune with the body rhythms of its prey," it uses the human heartbeat as "a targeting mechanism" (2007, 159). Emerging uncontrollably from the human interior, this sound of bodily function imbues the film's exterior spaces with an affective dread somehow filtered through the alien's perspective. These sounds borrow heavily from the sensibilities of the horror film score, of course, where filmmakers have developed musical conventions to convey the disjunctions of narrative, the fracturing of character, the unexpected non sequiturs of scenic atmospheres that keep filmgoers poised in anticipation and fear, and spectacles of excessive violence and horror (132). But this process turns particularly malignant in *Alien*, in which "sound effects take on elevated status" as music becomes an atmospheric sound effect, tangling together to become a singular "organism of sound" (143). We never know from what space this neosonic xenomorph will emerge, and so we become hyperaware of the sonic field while at the same time guarded to the point of paranoia.

As music and sound effects alike tend toward dissonance, discordant and primitive instrumentation, as well as minimalist cues—like the heartbeat in *Alien* and, as we will find, the throbbing synthesizer lines of Carpenter's *The Thing*—these hypersensitivities of the body that trigger disorders of affect and set most filmgoers on edge become characteristic of the sonic novum of SF/horror hybrids. Goodman calls this "uneasy listening": "Affective tonality can be felt as mood, ambience, or atmosphere. As film sound designers know only too well, certain frequencies can produce an affective tonality of fear in which the body is left poised in anticipation, expectant of incoming events: every pore listens for the future. Just think of the *uneasy listening* of atonal or discordant sound, or the sense of dread induced by low-frequency drones" (2010, 189). Dolby reaffirms the presence of precisely the kind of sounds and noises (ambient background hums and wind, for instance) that had largely been dropped from the soundtracks of early cinema in order to make dialogue, musical cues, and other important sound events audible within the limited frequency range of mono- and stereo-equipped cinemas. It is not only a matter of tonality, however, but also of sonic placement. One of Murch's innovative contributions to sound design was the use of polyrhythm and polytonality to suspend multiple sounds in a shared space and so fill the sonic novum with "multiple centers of attention" (Chion 2009, 123). Before Dolby Surround made this ubiquitous, Murch's practice had already created "a profound shift" in cinematic listening by "dispensing with the idea of a single rhythmic center to a film" (123). Dolby Stereo mixing takes advantage of this proliferation of polyrhythmic events and decenters the film, allowing multiple types and intensities of simultaneous sounds to inhabit the same cinematic space. Dolby potentially "grants more importance to *sound effects* as elements of setting, punctuation, and expression," Chion suggests (124), and the technology indeed seems especially fit for the demands of SF/horror hybrids, which thrive on the expressive and affective dimensions of concrete sound.

In the case of *Alien,* Dolby multichannel sound design allows for startlingly rapid transformations of diegetic space. This prompts Whittington to conclude that "the sound design is an organism that is much like the Alien in the film—part human, part machine—mutable, metaphoric, and very elusive" (2007, 147). The expanded spatial sound design contributes to this elusiveness while at the same time fosters a concrete realism. Exploring the constructed nature of real sounds—which in cinema are typically artificial, produced, processed, metaphorical, and representative rather than real as such—Whittington's argument builds on Amy Lawrence's *Echo and Narcissus* (1991). As Lawrence writes, "The myth of 'objective' sound reproduction ('mechanical neutrality') disguises the ideology of the apparatus, including (a) the ideology into which the apparatus is inserted, and (b) that which it promotes and organizes itself around" (in Whittington 2007, 148). Rather than abandon realism, science fiction requires the manufacture of realistic codes as a way to promote the audience's investment in the fantastic, futuristic, and alien. In this way, SF relies on what Lawrence calls the "camouflage [of] its materiality behind a myth of realism" (148). The codes for "realism" are created, then "passed along from production to production," reinforcing themselves over time in ways that formulate cinematic methods as well as audience expectations (149). The composite nature of the soundtrack "hides much of the material work of the mode of production" as sounds morph among specific cuts, fades, and effects in ways that make their isolation for analysis difficult to achieve (149). This is partly why Whittington frequently turns to visual, particularly spectacular, modalities to explain what is happening sonically and hence invisibly. He inherits this particular rhetorical move from Alan Williams's "Is Sound Recording Like a Language?" (1980). Here, Williams offers a semantic approach to audiovisual content, which exists at a remove from "the full, material context of everyday vision or hearing" even while it offers "the signs of such a physical situation" (in Whittington 2007, 150). This activates the perceptual foreground of sound while removing us from deeper contact with sonic materials withdrawn inside the background of the audiovisual experience, for "in sound recording, as in image recording," William writes, "the apparatus performs a significant perceptual work for us—isolating, intensifying, and analyzing sonic and visual material" (in Whittington 2007, 149). Where Williams emphasizes the recording process, Whittington correctly considers that the "crucial post-production processes of sound mixing and editing" do not merely participate in but ultimately determine "the true nature of any sound construction" in the cinema (150). Of particular relevance when listening to *Alien* and *John Carpenter's The Thing*, the manufacture and manipulation of sound objects intensifies their isolation into small, moveable fragments that are more connected to the way sound works in everyday perceptual contexts than imaginary ones. Instead of borrowing from semantics, which treats sound as language and primarily about the making of meaning from the visual, which treats sound as a form of spectacle, or from ideology, which treats sound as part of an unreal camouflaging of material apparatuses, we need a way to think about sound as simultaneously real, mechanical, and alien.

Lawrence and Williams reveal that all listening is somehow horrific, a deeply alienated activity in its own right, as we are challenged by "the hidden structures and influences" lurking behind cinematic sounds (148). For Whittington, it is a matter of revealing "production ideology (recording practices, processes, and the history of reading codes) as well as the influence of genre codes, considerations, and expectations" (148). Williams emphasizes the construction of "a specific point of view" that is "mediated by the recording apparatus and the technical choices that the recordist [sic] makes" (in Whittington 2007, 150). These technical decisions determine and, at least as applied in the final film narrative, delimit "sound perspective and spatial cues" (150). Whittington's analysis usefully goes beyond recording to consider the manufacture of sound during editing and mixing, "which are highly manipulative processes by which sound is further isolated, intensified, and analyzed" (150). Against a manufactured "realism," Whittington argues for the expressionistic development of an "audio-biomechanics" that melds together "sound, body, and machine" (150) and provides a sonic corollary to the movie's narrative, images, and themes. After his careful analysis of sound effects, ambiences, music, and voice, Whittington concludes that *Alien*'s fusing of SF/horror conventions transforms "even the most 'realistic' sound effects . . . into organisms of the fantastic, which stalked and eluded audiences in the corridors of the narrative diegesis" (164). But as he deflates the argument by simply pairing up a pleasurable "dark lyricism" of horror with the SF film and its "concerns about technology" (165), Whittington is faced with the conclusion that "seemingly 'realistic' sound effects . . . transform into expressionistic constructions" (147). In fact, just as diegetic realism trumps nondiegetic aesthetic cues in *Alien,* this at last seems antithetical to the reality of sonorous objects, their alignment with actual and original technologies—that is, their origin in technicity.

As an agent of simultaneous cognitive estrangement and hypersensitive affective engagement, the sonic xenomorph directs us toward "the thing" that resides "beyond the instrumental dimension of technology," as Sarah Kember and Joanna Zylinska describe the originary technicity of media (2012, 14). In possession of their own vital processes beyond mere use, technologies mediate human being, emergence, essence, and becoming. They also reserve something for themselves. The interpenetration of biological and technological vitality goes beyond instrumentality and user-based perspectives. Screened by the "technological set up for the world," with our being and our ability to change determined by it, mediation as life process is profoundly alien to begin with, involving nonhumanist agencies, influences and forces beyond human control (14, 9). The thingness of the sonic novum partly reveals itself in the form of the numerous new things that mediate the music and noise of science fiction—that is, instruments, circuit components, tools, material hardware, and loudspeaker configurations—and so entangle the histories of the sonic xenomorphs of SF/horror with that of music technology design and development. In the early days of the home VHS market, *John Carpenter's The Thing* prompted its audience for a sonic upgrade to achieve new dimensions of cosmic horror. *The Thing* was not only one of the first videotapes with stereo sound, it was the first to announce on its packaging that it featured something called a "matrixed surround track." This was a word to those savvy home sound technicians who had figured out how to mode their VHS tape decks so that they would decode the matrixed surround track on Dolby Stereo films and thereby play back their tapes in multichannel sound on homemade rigs. Video hacker lore collected at IMDb.com considered the sonically active, directional sound design of *The Thing* to be one of the best tests of the home matrixed surround system. It appears that the spread of immersive multichannel sound technology necessitated a neosonic terror, something edgy and unexpected, explosively loud enough from any potential direction, to put its audience in its place.

With their pre-CGI effects, *Alien* and *The Thing* occupy a transitional cusp between analog metamorphosis and digital modulation. As xenomorphs, they take the appearance of the former while actuating the latter. Shaviro (2010) has mapped out the postcinematic landscape in which modulation supersedes metamorphosis: the latter is "expansive and open-ended, while modulation is schematic and implosive" (14). Properly and distinctively digital in procedure, "modulation requires an underlying fixity, in the form of a carrier wave or signal that is made to undergo a series of controlled and coded variations" (14). A concurrent transition from the industrial modes of disciplinary regimes and rhythms to control society ensures the flexibility of forms in the moment. "Metamorphosis gives us the sense that anything can happen, because form is indefinitely malleable," Shaviro concludes, whereas modulations

> imply that no matter what happens, it can always be contained in advance within a predetermined set of possibilities. Everything is drawn into the same fatality, the same narrowing funnel, the same black hole. There is no proliferation of meanings, but rather a capture of all meanings. Every event is translated into the same binary code, and placed within the same algorithmic grid of variations, the same phase space. (13–14)

A well-established component of the cosmic thought synthesizer, modulation is an Other form of metamorphosis, or xenomorphic: "The only fixed requirement is precisely to maintain an underlying *flexibility*: an ability to take on any shape as needed, a capacity to adapt quickly and smoothly to the demands of any form, or any procedure, whatsoever" (15). This is precisely what both the Alien in Scott's film and the Thing in Carpenter's do; it is how they become. It is also telling of the films' sonic novums. The entire soundscape of these films becomes what Shaviro calls "a relational space," a vast sonorous hyperobject that continually "varies from moment to moment, along with the forces that generate and invest it" (17). Alien modulation works against "the constraints of locality" (23). Alien sounds thus flourish through nonlocality, and in both *Alien* and *The Thing*, the sonic xenomorph dislocates time and scale, without apparent origin or source, and without a particularly evident goal in mind beyond unanticipated attack.

SF/horror depends on the tension between the alien sonorous object in acousmatic presentation, along with the relational attachments of sound to cinematic visuals, in order to create the unique auditory point of view that is the sonic novum, opening up a space for cognitive play and speculation as well as unleashing a force of threatening and dangerous alien contact. The methods and processes of listening are every bit as important to our experience of new cinematic sounds as the properties of the alien sonorous object on its own terms. Chion describes the cinematic experience in terms of an "audiovisual contract" (1994, 126) that governs sound's modulation of our perception of visual movement, speed, time, and space, as well as our empathetic attachments. Chion defines three modes of listening—the casual, the semantic, and the reduced—that involve varying degrees of passive and active perception. While we might assume that listening with "conscious and active perception" is most important to the student of film sound, Chion argues that there is a larger "field of audition that is given or even imposed on the ear; this aural field is much less limited or confined, its contours uncertain and changing" (33). The visual experience of cinema is "contained by the screen" (33) and works within the limits that fix our field of vision; the screen gives us things to see, but we can also always choose to close our eyes or look away. Sound works beyond this limit; it imposes itself on our ears from all directions and with a physical force of volume and frequency that the image lacks. It is hard to selectively hear or tune things out. "There is always something about sound that overwhelms and surprises us no matter what . . . and thus sound interferes with our perception, affects it," Chion concludes. "Surely, our conscious perception can valiantly work at submitting everything to its control, but, in the present cultural state of things, sound more than image has the ability to saturate and short-circuit our perception" (33).

In John Carpenter's films, minimalist, droning synthesizers—something between a humming power line and a human heartbeat—are the basis of terror that burns out perception with the primal techno-diegetic capacity of the electronic signal. Carpenter reduces music to a raw electric undercurrent, as if the only thing his version of *The Thing* really retains from its 1951 source is the electric carrot zapper that blows out the original invader. Carpenter had already gotten into such minimal musical performance because of its ability to evoke "the fundamental psychology of primal sound" (Donnelly 2010, 165). An ambient accompaniment to unseen malignant natures in his 1980 film, *The Fog,* "the eponymous fog of the film is sounded by synthesizers, forming as much a *sonic* as a visual threat. These atmospheric affordances stem from the properties of sound itself—invisible, enveloping, and potentially disturbing" (165)—which are particularly dynamic in the kind of immersive, multichannel environments that fog the minds of the listening subjects of Carpenter's films. The ambient ecologies of the SF/horror film are full of such primal triggers. Desolate arctic winds, undercut by the synthetic drone in *The Thing*, as well as the out-of-place water sounds in the depths of a spaceship or the "alien wind," created by Goldsmith's conch shell sourced through the Echoplex, in Scott's film, emphasize the terrestrial roots of xenomorphic alien "foreboding and dread" (Whittington 2007, 139). In *The Thing*, the wind initially conveys the isolated location, but it eventually becomes a sign of psychogeographical duress in the arctic research station. "Once again," Whittington concludes, "sonic expressionism establishes layered meaning, an external and internal landscape of fear and dread" (138). Ambient sounds like wind and water not only sonically demarcate diegetic spaces and locations but also "traverse the psychological and intellectual terrain" of the film (139). The SF/horror film makes us hyperaware of the need to listen when surrounded by and being attuned to the presence of sounds so quiet that only a techgnosis of the ear—that is, a knowledge that is exclusive to technological means—could make them available to us. Whittington explains that new surround sound technologies have "reconfigured the cinematic experience" by showcasing multichannel systems, reveling in moments of sonic excess when it was still an emerging technology (2007, 116). The reality of surround sound system technology necessitated an aesthetic form that would simultaneously turn listening into a spectacle, something calling attention to itself as a new way of listening, but something that would also disappear into a more realistic imaginary world. In this way, ambient music comes to the foreground, "constituting a *primary* effect rather than mere incidental background," and so inverts our sense of auditory point of view (Donnelly 2010, 165).

Charging the atmosphere with its synthetic presence and insistent, heartbeat pulse, this music acts as the unseen but ever-present, metamorphic Thing that rides on the hi-fidelity, multichannel carrier wave of the Dolby system, which here provides what Shaviro calls the "underlying fixity" (14) of modulation. The range of postcinematic affect that Shaviro (after Brian Massumi's 2002 *Parables for the Virtual*) outlines are preeminently sonic—that is, they are "primary, non-conscious, asubjective or presubjective, asignifying, unqualified and intensive" (3)—and they work on us, in the way that sound does, with "affective flows that the subject is opened to, and thereby constituted through" (5). As it relates to the sonic xenomorph, I believe that this affective construction of subjectivity accounts for the occurrence of signature electronic heartbeat motifs in both films, "the essence of the synthesizer, its primal electronic tone, throb, or pulse" (Donnelly 2010, 164). This electronic heartbeat is the basis of the terrorizing affect of sonic psychotechnology in SF/horror, and in both *The Thing* and *Alien*, it constitutes an alien point-of-audition through the biotechnologies of the xenomorph.

What literature exists on the sound of these two films is nothing if not consistent in its emphasis on these signature concrete motifs. Writing about *The Thing*, Billson (1997) takes note of the "tonic heartbeat" (24), while Conolly (2013) describes the "heartbeat motif" (60). This "darkly insistent pulsation . . . never quickens, suggesting an alien presence from the outset that is alive, calculating and prepared to take as long as it takes. The music often lapses into a fixed landscape of fundamental tones, frequently centering on a monotone that can be felt as much as heard" (60). In his study of *Alien*, Luckhurst (2014) describes the use of the heartbeat to "slice through aesthetics and hot-wire the nervous system itself" (41). Suggesting that the heartbeat motif is a modulator of the audience's physical response, Frome (2010) tracks the acceleration and then fall of the heart rate during the chest-bursting scene, in which synchronization between sound and screen is less important than between sound and the embodied viewer, subjected here to a kind of "emotional contagion" (162). More obliquely, Chion's discussion of the "continuum of bodily physicality and . . . the technological setting" of *Alien* also has to do with the heart, though less its consistent beat than its sudden bursting apart in moments of what he calls the "spray effect" (2009, 128). Similarly, Whittington sets the sound of the heartbeat against that of the scream, which collide in the most effectively devastating fashion as Captain Dallas (Tom Skerritt) makes his way through the *Nostromo*'s ventilation shafts, hoping to seal off the Alien's escape routes. As other members of the crew watch his progress on a computer monitor, the heartbeat syncs up with a little blip on the screen.

When Dallas suddenly meets the creature, we hear its piercing scream blast through the ship's communication system. More than any other sequence in the film, the introduction of these technological mediators suggest that the heartbeat is at once the Alien's "targeting mechanism" and the effect of the crew's sonar tracking device used to search the *Nostromo* (2003, 159).

In each instance, we experience the synthetic biotechnology of the xenomorphic sound object. I will draw briefly here on Timothy Morton's (2013) work on hyperobjects. This is immediately useful as a way to pursue unusual sound entities, partly because Morton's work is premised on a critique of the visual orientation of Western art, philosophy, and media studies that ends up articulating the emergence of hyperobjects, which shift to the sonic and tactile, the affective, and the material or thingness of the world. Morton introduces five terms to sketch out a taxonomical topography of the hyperobject: viscosity, nonlocality, temporal undulation, phasing, and interobjectivity. Sonorous hyperobjects are at once deeply and expansively alien to a human scale, presenting radically different modes of being, and perhaps also of knowing the world. Viscosity speaks to the stickiness of the sonorous hyperobject, which surrounds us (and in fact leads to new loudspeaker configurations in theater and home to better do so) and engulfs us, but it does so while attached to narratives about disassembled, fragmented, and discontinuous beings. Viscous sound exploits the complementarity of uncanny sounds, which sit clearly neither here nor there, forming an invisible, quantum connectivity between them over the course of a film. As sounds begin to point to each other within a kind of alien goo of residual signification, everything points to everything else, but only to signify the potential that any one of them could suddenly reveal a quantum link to an elsewhere that might burst out in the form of renewed alien malevolence.

In his discussion of Carpenter's use of synthesizer in *The Fog* (1980), Donnelly rather awkwardly backs into a posthumanist argument, suggesting that Carpenter's synthesizer score reveals "a high degree of technological determinism" (160). Identifying a human-centered orthodoxy, or "hyper-humanism," Donnelly notes that it is "difficult to see processes that evacuate human activity as having much validity. It is not terribly fashionable to point to the foundations in human physiology of music"

(160). He then goes on to map the "primary sounds" of pumping blood, breathing, "the high pitched whine of our nervous system," and even tinnitus. As far as human perception goes, the sonorous hyperobject can never be perceived as more than the traces of a thing, not the thing itself. Undulating through time, "hyperobjects are time-stretched to such a vast extent that they become almost impossible to hold in mind" (Morton 2013, 58). In most instances, the nonlocal nature of the sonorous hyperobject ensures that when we perceive the trace of it, we are in fact listening into the past, like hearing stars. The undulation works with and against the phasing effect, another process of nonreferentiality by which sonorous hyperobjects end up removed from anything other than the concrete self-reference of "the thing." As sonorous hyperobjects phase in and out of human narrative space-time, "gaps and ruptures" signal particular tension and promise, "the invisible presence of the hyperobject itself" (76). That this sonorous hyperobject sticks to us owes much to its capacity for nonlocal interobjectivity. In hyperobjective space, sonic objects attuned to human scale become the subject of interobjective influence, such as the mixing, processing, and re-presentation of sound events. These are not hyperobjects. Rather, we come to detect hyperobjects in part through their interactions with and mediations of other immediately evident entities and human scaled events. All are fascinating aspects of the alien sonic novum, particularly in the two retro SF/horror films that concern us here. The withdrawn and incomplete pieces of a massively distributed sonorous hyperobject verify the reality of the sound objects that it invades, modifies, and morphs, even as it threatens to ruin them completely. Listening struggles to become a precognitive activity, but the general affect of the encounter is measured by the collapse of worlds and being, of self into thing: "The proximity of an alien presence that is also our innermost essence," Morton at last ascertains, "is very much its structure of feeling" (139).

The story behind the musical score to Carpenter's remake of the 1950s classic extends some of these questions of body invasion and mutation, of relational spaces and the modulation of sonic xenomorphs, into the economies of the Hollywood studios. Carpenter had had several hits with virtually independent films, *Halloween* (1978) and *Escape from New York* (1981). His remake of the golden-age classic, *The Thing*, was

382 • SONOROUS OBJECT-ORIENTED ONTOLOGIES

his first big-budget entry. The studio would also provide for a composer. Jerry Goldsmith's name was mentioned, but Carpenter got his choice with famous Italian composer Ennio Morricone. Early in the process, Morricone wrote a score based on the script rather than a cut of the film. Carpenter recalls getting twenty minutes of recorded music from Morricone for him to use wherever he wanted, and a main theme. "I told him that he was using too many notes for the title track and that he should simplify it," Carpenter explains. "He did simplify it, and the title track that you hear is his" (in Boulenger 2003, 144). Morricone's score never had the particular vibe that Carpenter was looking for, however, which was the John Carpenter vibe: low, thudding bass; minimalist and repetitive phrasing; primitive electric hums and a raw synthetic edge. Carpenter's frequent collaborator, Alan Howarth, recalls the director playing Morricone the *Escape from New York* soundtrack that he and Carpenter had made, hoping it would get Morricone to understand what the director wanted. "It didn't hit the core moment of John Carpenter," Howarth explains of Morricone's score, "until he had him imitate John Carpenter" (in Stockford 2011). Accordingly, Morricone ditched the orchestra and created the synthesizer-based variant score. "That's when Morricone came up with this very memorable theme with that electronic pulse," Howarth continues. "It's almost like Morricone doing John Carpenter."

Even this would not fully satisfy Carpenter, and several scenes feature work that he and Howarth rushed off to produce. "Since we needed something, I secretly ran off and recorded in a couple of days a few pieces to use," Carpenter recalls. "My pieces were very simple electronic pieces—it was almost tones. It was not really music at all but just background sounds, something today you might even consider as sound effects. I used these pieces as unifying moments because structurally we had to redo *The Thing* at one point in the centre. I put them in there to glue together the film, but in no way was I trying to compete with Ennio's score. The score is his" (in Boulenger 2001, 144). As the synthesizer renders melodic themes less vital than sound effects and minimalist textures, Carpenter's work, Donnelly concludes, "emanates from the basics of acoustics, furnishing a *primal* sonic character to the film. This process is far closer to sound design than it is to traditional music" (164), a perspective validated by Carpenter's claims about the music of *The Thing* being more like sound effects. But while Carpenter's insistent attribution regarding Morricone's role as composer seems clear enough, it appears that the old distinctions we have so far considered between musical composer and sound effect technician are coming back as a defensive mechanism, a way of saving face given that one of cinema's most respected composers, and indeed one of Carpenter's heroes, was not up for the minimalist synth noise of a sonorous object that Carpenter wanted for his film. Looking at the documentation of the soundtrack suggests something different as well. The official "Original Motion Picture Soundtrack" recording is a long out-of-print album that credits "Music Composed and Conducted by Ennio Morricone." However, several tracks are attributed to John Carpenter and Alan Howarth, including the main title. The frequency with which the names of Alan Howarth and Larry Hopkins are appended to Morricone tracks suggest postproduction additions and modifications to Morricone's material. The contemporary, in-print release of *The Thing* soundtrack includes Alan Howarth's digital re-creation of the Morricone score. "The orchestral cues I've done with Larry Hopkins [use] Digital Orchestra Tools to recreate them," Howarth says of a recent disc, "and in some ways the performances are better in our version than they were in the original. It's like an upgrade" (ScoreKeeper 2011). The convoluted, entangled, morphing history of Morricone's score and various recordings thus plays out a xenomorphic possession by the Carpenter upgrade, until it becomes a music that isn't even music, but also something that is not even quite a sound effect but rather merely a kind of sound thing.

1982 | *BLADE RUNNER, TRON*

The unusual ambiences of science fiction films often blur sounds by gliding across those diegetic borders that typically allow listeners to differentiate between types of sounds and so determine where sounds reside relative to the images on the screen. As far back as *Destination Moon* and *Rocketship X-M,* this has taken on an ontological dimension, as electronic timbres foreground the significantly different forms of the technological found in each film, with the former making a case for the extrapolative plausibility of world building and the latter revealing the

384 • SONOROUS OBJECT-ORIENTED ONTOLOGIES

unintended consequences of scientific discovery and the ethicoaesthetics of becoming Martian by the proxy of deadly radiation. Where electronic filtering of sound in *Destination Moon* triggers a subtle embedding of human perspective through the technical interface, *Rocketship X-M* aligns the electronic timbre with a contaminating alien difference. In *Solaris*, synthesized sound does a bit of both, representing the speculative psychogeographical nature of an alien planet that is also a lifeform while reflecting and reinforcing the psychotechnological elements of the cinematic apparatus and so human apprehension of difference. The qualitative struggle with new and synthetic sounds, and especially the treatment of electronic sounds as equivalents to worldly sounds that are also set apart from that world—in other words, to reveal without revealing their conditional and constructed nature, and thereby link them up to the "precise states of mind, the sounds of a person's interior world" (Tarkovsky 1989, 162)—is essential to our experience and understanding of Ridley Scott's *Blade Runner*. As it had before in *Solaris*, a tension informs our experience of *Blade Runner* as cinematic, narrative, and sonorous object, particularly in terms of the film's erosion of distinctions between organic and synthetic, natural and artificial, sounds, and the consequence of such an erosion for consciousness.

Based on Philip K. Dick's novel *Do Androids Dream of Electric Sheep?* (1968), *Blade Runner* is a noir-influenced cyberpunk thriller set in 2019 Los Angeles. The environment is at once devastated and yet filled with activity, and many humans have moved to colonies off world, though much of the labor force there consists of artificial humanoids known as replicants. After a deadly mutiny on an off-world colony, several replicants escape to Earth in order to confront their designer, Dr. Eldon Tyrell (Joe Terkel), of the Tyrell Corporation, about the limits of replicant existence. They are hardwired with a fixed life span of four years. These synthetic humans are illegal on Earth, where they are "retired" by so-called blade runners. The narrative revolves around a former blade runner, Rick Deckard (Harrison Ford), who is forced back onto the job to hunt down the dangerous replicants. Early in his investigation, Deckard visits the Tyrell Corporation, where he meets Rachel (Sean Young), Tyrell's personal assistant. Deckard has been tasked with testing one of the latest generations of replicants, the Nexus-6 models, with a device called the Voight-Kampff analyzer, an employee-vetting tool that measures emotional responses and affective changes to triggering questions, and which traditionally distinguishes between human and replicant. With the Nexus-6 models reportedly capable of feeling emotions and possessing implanted false memories, Tyrell insists that Deckard run the test on a human to yield a negative response before testing one of the new replicants. He offers Rachel as the test subject. Only after asking over a hundred questions does Deckard realize that not only is Rachel a replicant, but also, possessing memories based on Tyrell's own niece, she doesn't know she is a replicant. This event sets off a philosophical chain of reactions around the distinctions between the human and replicant that intensifies as a sexual and romantic relationship develops between Deckard and Rachel. As the blade runner hunts down the rogue replicants, several clues lead us to wonder whether Deckard himself could be a replicant.

Blade Runner's exploration of the new states of virtual existence being vividly contextualized by emerging digital technologies prompts a confrontation of the boundaries between natural and synthetic sounds, and between interior and exterior worlds. Diegetic and nondiegetic sounds in the film continually drift in and out of each other and so create a singular, mostly undifferentiated ambience that recalls the gliding sounds investigated earlier while also employing a new kind of sonic gauziness achieved through the use of digital reverberation effects. New synthetic sounds reflect from either end of the diegetic spectrum toward a middle ground in which tones and noises of a common digital timbre serve as both subjective registers of affect, which may in fact be artificial, and objective measures of the unusual futuristic spaces, events, characters, and other objects encountered in the film. As several, if not the majority, of characters may in some sense be objects, the purposeful confusion of the type and function of sound plays out sympathetically with a narrative about the blurred distinctions between living human beings and synthetic replicants. This core confusion also reinforces the film's main philosophical themes, which problematize the nature of consciousness, memory, emotion, knowing, and being.

The music heard in *Blade Runner*, most of it composed and performed by Greek musician Vangelis, presents an indistinct soundscape, often as grimy as it is celestial, which blends a wide palette of sonic sensibilities that includes romanticism, electronic drones, blues, film noir soundtracks, space music, Asian and Middle Eastern music, and ambient styles. These frequently combine in what I call a "downturned" fashion, with sustained portamento notes that drop in pitch from higher to lower notes as the volume also fades out, giving the film its overall tone of heartbreak and melancholy. This downward drifting mood is sustained by Vangelis's use of reverb and echo across the entire soundtrack as well as through the hazy amalgamation of instrumental voices from his preferred analog synthesizer, the polyphonic Yamaha CS-80, and electric Fender Rhodes piano. The "aftertouch" feature of the Yamaha CS-80 keyboard gives the performer control over the inflection and modulation of every note by changing the pressure applied to a given key. This not only makes the playing more expressive than other synthesizers of the time but also allows for compelling timbral instabilities and subtleties that open up new tonal spaces around and between those of more traditional instrumental voices. This real-time expressivity was essential to Vangelis's work and extended to his processing of instruments and recorded sounds through devices such as the digital reverb effect unit, the Lexicon 224; the expansive sound-processing components of the digital FM synthesizer, the Yamaha GS-1; and the digital sampler, the E-mu Emulator keyboard. Not only was there a synthetic combination among different sources of musical timbre, then, Vangelis's practice approached instrumental and effect processing devices as equivalent resources for improvisational performance.

Unable or unwilling to write or read music, Vangelis composed his score to multitrack tape while watching parts of the movie on a video screen set up in his studio, which played short cuts on VHS tapes delivered from Scott's studio on a daily basis. A similar live-to-tape approach was used when Vangelis brought in guest performers, including the English Chamber Choir, vocalists Mary Hopkin and Demis Roussos, and saxophonist Dick Morrissey, all of whom would improvise around and often replace altogether synthesizer lines sketched out by Vangelis and demonstrated on tape or live in the studio. Instinctive and spontaneous, Vangelis let his music unfold in reaction to the visual textures of scenes rather than originate from his understanding of or ideas about the script. He later recalled, "What interested me the most for this film was the atmosphere and the general feeling, rather than the distinct themes. The visual atmosphere of the film is unique and it is that I tried to enhance as much as I could" ("Vangelis Scoring Blade Runner," n.d.). In this respect, Vangelis's music is highly situational, providing varying contexts for characterization rather than the sonic representation of simple, repeatable qualities of character per se. Individual cues are less expressive than ambience and overall atmosphere, as cues are never repeated so consistently that they turn into full-on leitmotifs.

There is a slight looseness—a lack of fixedness, if you will—between vision and sound in *Blade Runner* that also results from Vangelis's particular scoring process as he proves adept at responding to and capturing the general movement within a scene. Consider, for instance, the shifting discordant elements that cut in and out of the sultry saxophone of the film's noir-inflected love theme, mixed with the sounds of thunder and rain, and Vangelis's electric piano, when Rachel goes to Deckard's apartment. Full of conflicted emotions, forced affections, and Deckard's unwanted sexual advances, the scene problematizes the issues of aggression and rape of a nonhuman replicant by having Deckard program Rachel, instructing her to "Say kiss me" and "I want you." As Rachel finally complies, if not fully consents, the scene resolves sonically with another of Vangelis's long glides of descending bass tones that takes us into an exterior shot of the city. Short electronic bleeps and blips often accompany shots of buildings, vehicles, and other technological devices along with longer drones, for instance, matching the floating quality of the sustained synthesizer pads with that of the police car, the Spinner, as it hovers and flies between skyscrapers. Vangelis uses subtle shifts in intensity of these sounds during transitional moments, with adjustments to the volume and to the amount of reverb moving us from exterior to interior spaces, or even among different densities of space along a crowded street or inside a building. The gauzy blur around sounds and between them lends both a murky quality to the mix as well as a kind of underlying restlessness as sounds wander within active, reverberating space. While taking advantage of several new digital instruments and devices, as well as working with the latest noise-reduction devices for mixing in multitrack settings, Vangelis also performed his final mulitrack mixes

388 • SONOROUS OBJECT-ORIENTED ONTOLOGIES

in real time, applying reverb from the Lexicon 224 to the master tapes as he combined sounds and mixed them down. As with his original sessions, this mixdown phase was performed to footage on VHS tapes, which had now been edited and sequenced in close to final form. Vangelis did not have access to the kind of digital mixing board automation or, more importantly, time-code synchronization that would become ubiquitous by the end of the 1980s, and so the strategy of long falling notes, drones, and reverberating washes blurred from one scene to the next. The use of sonic gauze in the final mix and the related management of vision–sound synchronization prove significant to our experiences of ambient space and our subsequent understanding of virtuality in *Blade Runner.*

• • •

I want to establish the significance of Vangelis and Scott's approach by means of a remarkable contrast to another high-profile science fiction film of 1982, Steven Lisberger's Disney film, *TRON.* Both films are sonic anomalies in the wake of the immensely popular orchestral scores that Williams composed for *Star Wars* and *The Empire Strikes Back* (1980), as well as for Spielberg's *Close Encounters of the Third Kind* (1977), and which quickly became the dominant form of SF film music. Moreover, the overall sound management of SF films had shifted with the release of these three movies, as growing crews of sound designers, engineers, editors, and managers typically preferred clearly separated sounds. This clarity is the case both in respect to the tonal distribution of sounds in a well-equalized final mix and in regard to sounds reproduced and presented across the multichannel speaker systems cropping up in movie theaters. Even more to the point, the separation of sounds relevant to their diegetic status would reposition the electric and synthesized sounds that had typified the genre by the middle of the 1970s but had also solidified the science fiction film's ability to interject avant-garde sensibilities regarding timbre, sonic representation, noise, and electronic sound into popular media forms. After *Star Wars,* however, electronic tonalities and new synthetic sounds were typically situated within the imaginary world of the film, while the musical cues tended to recuperate the timbres of orchestral romanticism, now associated with broadly melodramatic themes and presented with the Wagnerian grandiosity of scale designated by the term "space opera." Given that both *Blade Runner* and *TRON* reject these operatic tropes while continuing to explore the new spaces of hi-fidelity, theatrical sound reproduction, I now want to explore further the intersection of emerging digital sound technologies and the ambient novum, particularly as these have consequences for postnatural, cybernetic psychogeographies.

Like *Blade Runner*, *TRON* also features a score by a notable synthesist and composer who both scores and performs much of the music, and who is responsible for producing the final soundtrack mix. Wendy Carlos was chosen for *TRON* on the basis of her reputation for modular synthesizer versions of classical music as first heard on her popular album, *Switched-On Bach* (1968) and its sequels, as well as the album, *Walter Carlos' A Clockwork Orange* (1972), which presented in full the music she and Rachel Elkind recorded for Kubrick's film. For the project's sound management, Disney hired Michael Fremer, a comedic disc jockey with a degree in industrial labor relations, and who had worked with *TRON*'s director, Steven Lisberger, on an Olympic-themed animation project, *Animalympics,* for Warner Bros. in 1980. Fremer immediately envisioned a score in which orchestral music would signify the real world while electronic music would represent the computer world. A fan of Carlos's work, Fremer proposed that she would produce the synthesizer music for *TRON*'s computer interiors. Eager to compose for orchestra, Carlos countered with the suggestion that she should write the orchestral music with her synthesizer elements in mind, advising "a combination of symphony orchestra and synthesizer for the computer world, and just a string orchestra for the real world" (Moog 1982, 54). Fremer agreed, though this not only broke down his original binary equation in which the orchestral equated to the real world and the synthetic to cyberspace, but also led to complications in the production that would demand his skills in labor relations.

At stake now for Carlos was the creation of a seamless score, which would feature "a blending throughout of electronic and acoustic colors, with no harsh, artificial separation of timbres" (Moog 1982, 54). The combination of the distinct tonal "colors," with synthetic sounds adding to rather than clashing against the strings, and eventually several choral parts, struck the composer as "a natural, *simpatico* idea that exactly complemented the way the film combined live action and video graphics" (54). Carlos's synthesizers would thus provide the sonic equivalent to the unique animation techniques by which *TRON* maintains if not necessarily rigid, then certainly precise, distinctions between the ontological spaces that its characters inhabit. There is no mistaking a human programmer—or User—in the real world for a digital program in the virtual world, even though the latter person is physically modeled after the former in the imaginary domains of cyberspace. Rather than animations, the software programs running within the mainframe computer are anthropomorphized duplicates of their real-world programmers, outfitted in costumes designed by French comic book artist Moebius (Jean Giraud), and given abbreviated names vaguely indicative of their computer world function. For instance, game developer Kevin Flynn (Jeff Bridges) is Clu (Codified Likeness Utility), while Flynn's former partner and programmer, Alan Bradley (Bruce Boxleitner), is Tron (initially Lisberger's abbreviation of "Electronic Man," but later equated to the "Trace On" function). The same actors portray both the programmers and their programmed counterparts, but they are filmed using a difficult and expensive technique of backlit animation for the computer world sequences. The actors perform on a completely black set, filmed in black-and-white, for this footage, which is then reproduced in a large, high-contrast film format developed by Kodak. Animations are added to multiple layers of sheet film on top of this live footage using rotoscopic processes that trace graphics over and around the filmed footage. This process is done by hand. Even though *TRON* was often heralded as pioneering because of its incorporation of computer animation, less than 20 percent of it is actually digitally animated. The editing and assemblage of the film ended up being more labor intensive than traditional cel animation, and the costly backlit process of animation was never used again in a feature film. Further, the final cut revealed flaws in the backlit technique in the form of flickers and glowing outlines around characters and other components on the screen. Lisberger initially incorporated these flaws into the release by adding sonic zingers to suggest that these are in fact technical glitches in the computer world, but he would later remove them for the restored Blu-ray edition. At any rate, the point here is that the difficulties of fitting analog and digital worlds together posed significant problems throughout the making of the film. Similar difficulties challenged its sonic world building.

Just as the film replicates characters across worlds while visually distinguishing between the real world and the imaginary world of the digital computer in the form of added, animated layers, so does a corresponding approach link and differentiate the two sound worlds. Remarkably different from both Artemiev's electronic sounds, which subtly hide behind or within barely audible natural and acoustic noises, as well as Vangelis's blurry, improvised impressions, the synthesized radiance of Carlos's score calls attention to itself as a compatible addition to and electronic outfitting of the orchestral instrumentation. But whether in the real world or the computer world, human expressivity underscores the music we hear. Carlos's synthesizer parts are for the most part played within traditional tonal constraints and timbral contrasts, and there are no programmed sequences, meaning that Carlos plays chords and melodic runs on the keyboard controlling her Moog modular analog synthesizer as well as a Crumar GDS (General Development System), an early digital synthesizer. Each instrumental component is recorded separately and then mixed together to assemble a whole piece. Rather than the "long, sweeping musical lines" she had originally imagined, however, Carlos discovered while viewing a short demo reel that *TRON* would feature a fast-paced style of editing that demanded brief musical cues (Moog 1982, 54). Carlos chopped up her score into sequences of short compositions based on two basic themes. One is a strident martial theme including a quote from Igor Stravinsky's *Rite of Spring* that is used during battle and chase scenes, the other a melodic love theme, which shares its melody and chord changes with the main *TRON* anthem. Carlos generated a database of cues that would be concisely clocked to the visual sequences through the use of digital synchronization interfaces. As Moog (1982) explains, Fremer and Carlos were among the first producers and composers of film music to utilize the digitally time-coded, multitracking technologies and Society of Motion Picture and Television Engineers (SMPTE) master code generators for exact synchronization of music and sound effects with visual content and dialogue. This does not mean that the sounds themselves were in digitized format, for they were still recorded to analog tape. Rather, the innovation was in the use of the digital SMPTE clock, which displayed time down to the second and indicated the specific frames of film or video. The SMPTE interface could also correct any slipping of the sync between the audio and visual sources. Developing a control mechanism in this audiovisual middle ground proved especially important for Carlos.

Similar to Vangelis's work on *Blade Runner,* Carlos composed and edited her cues to the video footage, though using Fremer's equipment to synch precisely to the SMPTE code within a shot where Vangelis preferred a looser combination. So that she could manage all of these short cues, Carlos also wrote a cue locator program on her Hewlett-Packard 9825 computer, which let her enter the times of events within a one- or two-minute visual sequence, then enter the meter and tempo of her musical accompaniments. Her program would then suggest the variations of the tempo required for the music to fit the visual footage. This had some unintended consequences, however. With the exception of a few atonal, atmospheric stretches, many of the cues are almost pushed too hard toward the hypercinematic synchronization effect by which Carlos got "the sound and picture to fit like a hand in a glove. Things fit perfectly in the score," she recalled. "It's just as if the film were shot to the music, not the other way around" (Moog 1982, 55). In a number of sequences, however, Carlos's music is overly synchronized and gains precisely the cartoonish quality that she wanted to avoid, such as in the passage of the Solar Sailer over the treacherous grid known as the Sea of Simulation. Despite his fondness for the score, Fremer later recalled that the digital precision of time-code synchronization seems a bit strange and "almost campy," lending such an exaggerated quality to the animations that they threaten to break the artifice of the sequences altogether (Fremer 2014). At other moments, given the brevity of Carlos's cues and the quickness with which visual and sonic elements cut from one to another, the cues feel even more disconnected from the cinematic events than the song by the rock band Journey, "Only Solutions," which plays over the closing credits in lieu of a Carlos composition—and much to her chagrin. It is a telling moment of diegetic breakdown, as the Journey song had originally played on the jukebox at Flynn's arcade, as the programmer beat his own high score on the game *Space Paranoids*. But abrupt, tagged-on "needle drops," as Carlos (2001) calls them, would end up replacing much of her score and certainly render her various cues as a form of nondiegetic effect in the final mix by Mike Minkler, who tended to jump back and forth from short musical phrases to special sound effect sequences, with a fondness for the latter.

Carlos was particularly upset about Minkler's cutting out her musical accompaniment to a light cycle race, keeping only the synthetic sound of the computer-generated vehicles. Fremer and Frank Serafine, the sound designer on the project, initially recorded these sound effects as Fremer raced his Saab Sonett along Mulholland Drive. Typical of their process, the two made their own field recordings—a pair of microphones in the engine compartment of the Saab, recorded on reel-to-reel (Fremer 2014), or the sound of the twin propellers captured while riding in a Goodyear blimp (Moog 1982, 57)—and then further processed and manipulated them, often using one of the first digital sampling synthesizers, the Fairlight. For Fremer, almost anything could be a sound source. "The inside of my frost-free refrigerator provided the sound for the Solar Sailer," he explained. "We recorded lots of video games, and even got an engineer in here to program those chips for new sounds. We recorded motorcycles, cars, hundreds of different things," and they made countless noises on the Minimoog and Prophet-5 synthesizers. Each of these effects was not only recorded and transferred to the sixteen-track mixer that would produce the final mix for the film but the effects were also cataloged on an Atari 800 computer, which helped them quickly pull up just the right sound at just the right length for rapid deployment in the mixing stage: "Every sound was described by some word like 'bang' or 'whoosh,'" and mapped according to the number of the reel of tape on which it was recorded, its track on the multitrack, the SMPTE time code, and a brief description of the sound" (Moog 1982, 57). Confronted by all these different types of sounds, each one of which required precise synchronization with corresponding images and narrative moments, Fremer came up with a solution every bit as innovative as the computers used to animate the film.

As with Carlos's programming of a sound database management

tool that nonetheless required her to achieve the final stage of precise synchronization, we find here a human–machine hybrid strategy to manage the audiovisual divide for the sound effects and subsequent creation of the film's diegetic world. The most persistent problem with the project, which led to Carlos's greatest displeasure, was the piecemeal delivery of the audio and visual assets, with sound effect producers often working with unfinished backlit footage and thus with no sense of the animated elements to which the sounds would ultimately come to be attached. Meanwhile, scheduling and budgetary constraints led to a complete reversal of Carlos's plans to create her synthesizer work first, then record and overdub the orchestral and choral material. Additional problems with the quality of the recordings and some of the performances also disappointed Carlos, so in addition to adding her "synthesizer colors" to the recordings, she also had to double and replace elements of the orchestral recordings that had either been played poorly, missed, or not correctly recorded (Moog 1982, 56). While Carlos completed her score, Minkler and his crew set about mixing down the special sound effects to the finished film footage, and it was at this point that the imaginary sound of *TRON*'s diegetic space took over the project. Fremer recalls this as a key turning point in the film's production:

> There was no strong musical spokesman on the dubbing stage. It was a blueprint for disaster. Instead of letting the music carry the emotions, they gave priority to the effects and mixed the music down or out. It's too bad. I believe that the film could have been stronger if the soundtrack had used more music and less effects, if the music were allowed to reach out and grab the emotions. (in Moog 1982, 57)

Fremer's assessment of the problems between *TRON*'s sound worlds is typical of the post–*Star Wars* approach, which largely differentiates the domains of the speculative imagination (sound effects) from affect and emotion (music). Disney had hired Fremer to act as sound supervisor, "planning music and sound effects together, since they represent complementary aspects of the soundtrack's impact" (Moog 1982, 53). But Fremer breaks down the distinctly different functions of music and sound effect, the latter having "an impact that is literal, whereas music carries the emotions on a higher plane" (53). Fremer further believes that attention to the score was particularly important for his contemporary audience in the early 1980s, when filmmakers and movie studios still had to contend with a wide variety of cinema facilities. Whereas big dramatic sound effects will lose their impact over smaller speaker systems, enough music gets through to "still communicate emotion. In small theaters," he concludes, "a film will degenerate into a cartoon if it doesn't have a powerful score" (53). Of course, the analogy to cartoon music is particularly poignant in the context of *TRON,* one of the first Disney films to both visually and narratively challenge precisely what it meant to be a cartoon in the digital era.

For Fremer, *TRON*'s music was particularly important, given that so much of the narrative took place in unfamiliar, imaginary environments. "The music," he explains, "has to guide the audience through emotionally alien territory, to cue the viewer to the desired response" (in Moog 1982, 53). In retrospect, Fremer characterizes the *TRON* score in terms of sonic temperatures. The film includes a mild love story of sorts between two computer programs, TRON and Yori (Cindy Morgan), whose real-world counterparts had once been lovers. While the online chemistry between the two is by no means hot—in fact, a scene featuring Yori's seduction of TRON was cut from the final film—the score makes up for it, according to Fremer (2014), because it "packs cinematic musical heat and strong emotion." In an era when home computing had yet to catch on, Fremer understood that most of his audience would never get a film that takes place in the "cold, electronic environment," and so "the last thing we needed for a musical score was the obvious Kraftwerklike electronic chill, especially given the script's suggestion of an electronic flame between TRON and Yori" (2014). In retrospect, the sliced and finely cued but still "grand, sweeping gestures" of Carlos's love theme proved too much for the "cold computer world and the spark-free relationship between the two computer programs," and Fremer concedes that the score is "almost too hot for what ended up on the screen" (2014). Emphasizing the emotionally familiarizing role of the score, Fremer's comments highlight the consequences that separation of types of sounds can have upon the development of the space of the sonic novum.

Of course, the varying familiarity or newness of sounds shapes critical reception of SF films, as well, and it is possible that familiar musical cues and accompaniment are needed to stabilize the film. Deleon claims that music emotionally grounds a viewer otherwise confronted by unfamiliar images and unusual narratives. "If the musical score mimicked the world itself," Deleon asserts, "the viewer would be lost" (2010, 15). The conventional aspects of the musical score "maintain a solid foundation in order to allow readability of the unfamiliar," and arguably not only intelligibility but also affective resonance hinge on the familiarity of musical cues (15). This clearly aligns the function of the score with humanist perspectives and values, as without the affective cues of the musical score, the reader, viewer, or auditor would have no prompts to understand the nuances of character, relationship dynamics, or stages of drama such as moments of peril, tranquility, anger, fear, and anticipation. However, these kinds of sonic cues work with just about any form or genre of movie, and they are responsible for providing essentially normative, although varied, emotive agencies in cinematic sound. Science fiction or fantastic films may have an even more urgent need for a familiar score, Deleon suggests, by "providing the needed comfort for viewer accessibility and the freedom to present worlds that are fantastic in nature" (20). In this interpretation, the musical score does not simply smooth over visual edits—the cuts and jumps and other visual discontinuities that might snap us out of any cinematic illusion. Rather, familiar music becomes the ground floor of the known and the knowable. Keeping us grounded in the humanizing flow of emotional events, psychological drama, character relationships, and other affective dimensions of situational atmospheres makes it possible for us to accept the unfamiliar sights and stories of the SF film. Unfortunately this reading prohibits the formation of the sonic novum in music entirely, prohibiting the listener's encounter with sonorous alterity.

In *TRON*, nondiegetic music expresses familiarizing humanist values, measuring the affective temperature, while the diegetic noises, even though participating in the unusual and alien sensibilities of the film's world, ultimately contribute to the aesthetic of immersion within the computer world by fostering our suspension of disbelief. When the sonic temperature fails to match that of a narrative scene, or when nondiegetic musical cues match the visual events with too close a degree of synchronization, an affective Mickey Mousing occurs. This overly hot point of synchronization violates the binary but complementary oppositions of figurative music and literal noise, and it fails to provide an encounter with difference beyond normative, human space. As *TRON* cuts quickly back and forth between synthetic diegetic noise, nondiegetic orchestral musical cues, and nondiegetic orchestral and synthetic cues, a kind of sonic flicker effect disrupts the film rather than holds it together. In *Blade Runner*, by contrast, the audio mix produced by Graham Hartstone, Scott's primary sound engineer, reinforces rather than resolves Vangelis's compositional sensibilities and so creates an ever more dense, multidiegetic soundscape conceived at once symphonically and organically, figuratively and literally. Reverberation draws diverse sounds together into a common and constant soundscape. That is, reverb causes the pitch and transient frequencies of sounds to converge by blurring otherwise distinct frequency bands around vague tonal centers. With sonorous objects drawn as much from the diegetic world as from Vangelis's score, audibility of sounds thus becomes of primary importance in the mix as *Blade Runner* combines its underlying, frequently subaquatic ambience with the regular and rhythmic appearance of distinct and individual sounds in the sonic foreground.

The final soundtrack mixes produced by Minkler for *TRON* and Hartstone for *Blade Runner* could not be more different in terms of their respective approaches to rhythmic interaction and pattern formation across both simultaneously occurring and sequential diegetic domains. Minkler tends to keep musical cues and sound effects distinctly in the foreground, often presented against stark and silent backdrops, and set apart from one another both temporally and tonally. This allows him to use musical cues and sound effects in much the same way, needle-dropped in and synced up tightly to short bursts of image. The peculiar effect of *TRON* in this respect is that the would-be emotional registers of the music, which tend to act as affective triggers while also regulating the pace of the image, come across as either too cold and distant or too hot and forced. In Hartstone's *Blade Runner* mix, by contrast, Vangelis's replicant orchestra, electronic keyboards, and processed sounds drift into and through the ambient space of the film like a flying Spinner vehicle and in more subtle and shadowy ways than *TRON*'s light cycles, ripping along their vividly constrained grids. Carlos's music is likewise precise and bouncy, its clearly delineated micro-motifs distinctly interspersed among special sound effect sequences and cut sharply against a stark black background of silicon silence. Another crucial contrast against the sonic world building of *TRON*: the spaces of *Blade Runner* are never silent, and the background seems to recede forever.

• • •

The combination of Vangelis's digital score and Hartstone's sound design create dense layers but never overload the perspective of our point of audition or upset our diegetic orientation in ways unsympathetic to the density of the film's visual design and its themes of confused ontological identification, self-awareness, and virtual identity. In his discussion of *Blade Runner,* Chion describes the film's sonic recuperation, in the post–*Star Wars* era, of science fiction's earlier requirement of "an 'other' music, involving a blurring of the line between sound effects and music," as evident in films like *Forbidden Planet* and *Solaris* (Chion 2009, 139). For Chion, "a material analogy between the electronic sound effects and the synthetic music of Vangelis" takes shape both in the film's tonal textures and its interacting rhythms. Rather than *TRON*'s shifting among diegetic noise and nondiegetic music, *Blade Runner* not only perpetually blurs sounds but also establishes "a sort of rhythmic pyramid that extends from big waves of sound in low registers to rapid electronic beepings in the ultrahigh range" (139). This attention to sonic architecture, which mirrors the monolithic Tyrell building, is key to the film's investment in the manufactured and synthetic ambient novum. Lawrence Paull, production designer of *Blade Runner,* describes the film's "additive architecture" (in Sobchack 1987, 263), a term drawn from the realm of audio synthesis that plays out as both visual and sonic fractals. Ever finer and greater orders of magnitude replicate through the noisy haze of the city, an audiovisual equivalent to reverb that blurs everything perceivable at such density as to suggest spaces that trail off forever through infinite gradation.

This fractal retreat renders even the most noticeable sounds in *Blade Runner* through an acousmatic blind, even those situated diegetically. The interiors of the Tyrell building, Deckard's apartment, or J. F.

Sebastian's (William Sanderson) rooms in the Bradbury Building are always filled with notable sounds, but their sources are never apparent. This sensibility confronts us with what Bukatman calls the "limitless complexity of the film" (1997, 58). Bart Mills also describes Scott's approach to the film in terms of its uncountable textural layers, "so that the visual information is imparted in every square inch of screen. Details proliferate" (in Sobchack 1987, 263). Even so, rather than building up a world, these details fall back, retreating holographically in much the same way that Deckard explores a digital photograph through a potentially endless fractal zoom. Rather than indicative of the real world, the fractal operations of the programs that have created this world are highly artificial, themselves products of "massively repeated, simple operations" running within a chaotic system (Bukatman 1997, 58). Sound in *Blade Runner* also proliferates through fractal repetition. This is what all the reverberation brings to (and takes from) the film's sounds, creating echoing replications that trail off into the never completely quiet background or suddenly amplify into the foreground via the additive repetition of a signal turned into a swelling feedback loop. Vangelis's reverberation unit performs in the manner of a "fractal machine," as Guattari (1992, 50) describes, and which, like Deleuze's (1989) time-image, draws cinema into a recursive discursion with profound implications for our understanding of beings, human or otherwise. "The cinema does not just present images, it surrounds them with a world," Deleuze writes before making explicit connections between ambient world building and cybernetic design as cinema "looked for bigger and bigger circuits which would unite an actual image with recollection-images, dream-image and world-images" (68). It is generally my impression that what Deleuze calls the time-image is in fact the sonorous object that crystallizes the image, puts it in its place, and adds value to the otherwise invaluable and empty ghost of the filmed image. Bukatman discusses this proliferation of ambient circuitry in terms of the "fractal environment" that pervades the film, in which visual and sonic urban tableaus draw similar structures across dramatically different scales (1997, 58). We experience, then, a continual ontological echoing of the "functional or signifying role" of discursive sounds activated within dense reverberating ecologies, in which, according to Guattari's idea of the "chaosmos," "the existentialising function of pure intensive repetition is called the refrain function" (1992, 53). The fractal repetition of reverb is an excessive form of the refrain. It is not the repetition of playing something over and over again, but rather a copy of the original technicity of a sound, then a copy of that copy, and so on, an echo that lives in the circuitry of electric and digital audio processing, a transient memory of living sound captured in a reverberating feedback fractal.

One of the more remarkable sonic features of *Blade Runner* is just how musical the diegetic world is in its own right. The snake dancer's music in the strip club, the piano in Deckard's apartment, the torch song, "One More Kiss, Dear," that plays on what sounds like a scratchy 78 record broadcast from who knows where—are all situated diegetically even while remaining profoundly out of place and, perhaps more importantly, out of time in the film's imaginary world, at once futuristic and nostalgic, but ultimately more like neither than both. *Blade Runner* provides an exemplary case of sound's ability in film not to reproduce but render the visible world, and the invisible world as well, which it withdraws from us. Chion suggests that "certain high, jagged electronic motifs that populate the film's sonic landscape do not represent actual sounds heard by the characters so much as they suggest the micro-activity of machines that make up their world" (2009, 244). These are signs of the deeply artificial and synthetic nature of the world of *Blade Runner,* and are evidence of the replicated, programmed, and implanted nature of the film. Part of the synthetic quality of the (replicant?) narrator and point-of-view character, Deckard, is reflected in the synthetic sound world, which triggers a knockoff noir fantasy of the detective film or police procedural while sonically reconstructing the audience's memory of prior cinematic representations of what it means to be noir. When overly coded in the film's original theatrical release by Deckard's voice-over, *Blade Runner* plays out its tropes in a more self-aware, and ironically self-reflective, way than other nostalgic SF films such as *Star Wars,* which points back to westerns, swashbucklers, and 1930s science fiction serials, and *Close Encounters of the Third Kind,* which looks back to Disney family fare of the 1950s. *Blade Runner's* sound world offers a prescriptive media history of film noir scores and soundtracks, with all of its constant rainstorms and lonely saxophones, strip club exotica, and police sirens. Suggesting a programmed amalgamation of a cinematic genre, *Blade Runner* is the representation of a synthetic delusion, a frequent theme of Philip K. Dick's work, particularly its source novel, *Do Androids Dream of Electric Sheep?* This is something explicitly along the lines of the noir implants used by the lead character of the disturbing novel *Noir* (1999), by K. W. Jeter, who would go on to write the only official *Blade Runner* sequels. In *Noir*, Jeter's lead character, a detective named McNihil, has had media-based technology inserted into his eyes, where something like a real-time microcomputer reprocesses actual reality into a black-and-white virtual counterpart that tints and recodes everything along film noir motifs. As in Jeter's novel, the noir-themed elements of *Blade Runner* are arguably a manifestation of Deckard's own implanted memories and synthetic consciousness. The original theatrical version with Deckard's voice-over makes almost too obvious the film's recasting of '40s noir stereotypes, its forced detachment and upbeat cadences approaching a campiness that the film doesn't really warrant, particularly near its conclusion. The most significant problem with the voice-over, however, is the clarity of the audio, which stands too far out and away from the reverberating mix that otherwise mingles all sounds.

What Scott's film gains when he strips out the voice-over and lets us hear the complex ambient sound world is far more compelling as psychogeography, a field of vision and audition permeated by the kind of emotional resonances required of the film noir script as genre and for the goal of affective programming. Diegetic sound cues function as prompts for the artificial consciousness of the blade runner. These sonic reinforcements provide props for the noir fantasy, an aural counterpart to the world that Deckard has been programmed to perceive and believes himself to inhabit, and that intercept and tint the audience's reception of events on the screen and recast them through a synthetic filter of implants, false memories, and virtually cinematic events, so that our experience as filmgoers is also that of a synthetic replication. Chion notes that the soundscape of *Blade Runner* suggests "a kind of loose musical score" based on the "thousand individual and collective rhythms . . . that make up the city" (2009, 244). A manufactured mood becomes exteriorized through the invasive billboards and loudspeakers, traffic sounds, and video monitors, all of which combine within a singular soundscape coded along classic noir lineages. As these diegetic noises also push toward the status of constant, ambient music, they reveal the thoroughly manufactured and synthetic nature of the world of *Blade Runner*. Most rooms in the movie hum and beep with a looping regularity, particularly Deckard's apartment, which "features a constant low-pitched pulsating electronic oscillation and a ghostly sound similar to breathing-in with an asthmatic wheeze," and which "smoothly glissandos up a fifth and then down again over a period of three seconds . . . repeated at approximately four second intervals" (Hannan and Carey 2004, 161). Similar upward and downward sweeping notes are also heard in *Blade Runner*'s diegetic world in the form of police sirens, almost always heard as if from afar and falling still further back into the vast, ambient soundscape with its floating, gritty, and expansive urban texture. Recalling SF cinema's lineage of sirenlike glissandi, with the contradictory attractions and dangers of their otherworldly alienation, Vangelis's processed piano and synthetic sirens, but also his music as such—the gliding saxophone riffs, the distantly heard and outdated torch song, or exoticized Asian and Arabic motifs—mix together to create the nostalgic dimension of a psychocybernetic space that modulates the world of *Blade Runner*.

As sound shifts from functional signifier to ambient effect, it becomes ontological in nature rather than phenomenological. Yet this is not an ontology of fixed truth and essence but rather one of contingent situation and presence; nor is it an epistemological apprehension of "a univocal truth of being through techne" but rather "a plurality of beings as machines" (Guattari 1992, 53). In *Blade Runner*, this has consequences at once empathic and cartographic based on the psychotechnological operations of the ambient sonic novum. Its blurry, synthetic, sonorous psychogeography retrieves a key detail from Dick's novel otherwise missing from the film. This is the mood organ, a device by which human users dial up preprogrammed, synthetic states of consciousness on demand. For Dick, this sonic metaphor of technoconsciousness—a fairly transparent metaphor for psychopharmaceuticals—is the key to the novel's wearing away of distinctions between human and replicant. The mood organ resonates with the sonic experience of the film through Vangelis's synthetic replications of noir mood-enhancing music, as well as his gestures toward romantic motifs and science fictional glissando, which clue us into the preprogrammed nature of the otherwise affectless personality of Deckard, who may himself be a replicant. Vangelis's use of digital simulations—musical replicants and digital models of orchestral instruments—as well as the existence in his score of sounds and drones that seem of a kind with the sound effects and diegetic ambiences replicate the film's blurring of humans and replicants (Hannan and Carey 2004, 160). The authenticity of human experience and consciousness is at stake here.

Questions of the authenticity of sounds do not apply merely to musique concrète and sound effect design. The synthesizer is also suspect. Schmidt provides a critical account of the aftermath of the monophonic Moog and other analog synthesizers on the sonic SF experience. What she calls the "electronic/atonal conventions" of the alien sound first emerged in the 1950s, then were reinforced through the 1960s and 1970s, with some notable exceptions. While *2001* and *Planet of the Apes* rejected electronic music conventions but retained atonality as a measure of the alien, *Star Wars* and *Close Encounters* largely rejected both or found ways, in the latter film, to absorb and resolve them. By the 1980s, SF film soundtracks "morphed into something much less obviously alien" (2010, 34) and begin to oscillate, often in the same film, between large ensemble orchestration and synthesized electronic sounds. It really is not until after *Star Wars* that the authenticity of the synthesizer would come into question, even if still analog in nature (like Vangelis's CS-80). As we hear in Vangelis's score to *Blade Runner,* the sonic uncertainties triggered by synthesized sounds allow the score to participate in the narrative and thematic study of humanoid-looking robots, cyborgs, and other category-blurring entities. In films like *Total Recall* (1990, based on a short story by Dick) and *The Matrix* (1999), entire artificial realities blend the organic and the virtual properties of sound in new and interesting ways. These films assure us that, even when fully digitized, it is the capacity of the electronic sound to hold within it contested and even incompatible meanings that makes it characteristic of the SF genre: "The electronic, even in some innocuous backbeat or ambient pulse, thus accesses both the powers and the horrors of technology, the nostalgia for a more authentic past and the terror of the perfect but soulless copy" (Schmidt 2010, 35). Schmidt associates the electronic sound with the spectacular, that element of cinematic experience that calls attention to itself and celebrates its own manufacture. We should unpack some of the suspicions of this manufactured sonic "thing." Electronic sounds, she concludes,

> can take on a considerable array of different sonorities and moods, yet there is one quality that it can never entirely shake. As a musical instrument, the computer or synthesizer is suspect; while a violin or drum is no less a product of human technology than a synthesizer, electronically-generated music tends to connote a relative lack of authenticity. When it purports to "copy" the sound of an acoustic instrument, the synthesizer is deemed by some to be lacking, even as others would equate this achievement with the heights of technological progress. (36)

Synthesized woodwinds and strings, by this account, are instantly inferior to their acoustic equivalents (and by acoustic, I mean wood, brass, and strings). In this regard, "technological progress" is measured by imitative rather than originary capacities. The reduplicative properties of synthesized sounds are particularly problematic, and precisely what Vangelis's score exploits, as we will find. That a manufactured sound could pass for an actual acoustic sound is a challenge to neurological processes, Schmidt argues, citing Robert Jourdain's popular science book, *Music, the Brain and Ecstasy: How Music Captures Our Imagination* (1997):

> The particular timbre, loudness and pitch of a sound are created by minute changes in the sound; it is these alterations rather than any continuity in sound which our auditory cortex interprets and such changes which are lacking in a synthesized sound (Jourdain 54). Thus, no matter how pleasing it may be to the ear, the electronic may always signify both itself and an anxiety about authenticity, and might have always been pre-destined to be alien. (36)

Its purity has become the very limit of electronic sound and the ultimate determination of its ability to function expressively as nondiegetic musical accompaniment or diegetic sound effect. This does not quite sit well with my experience of *Blade Runner,* in which the less differentiated sounds that define its fractal densities confuse any clean binary that would equate the human to the musical motif and replicant Other to the electronic, analog, or otherwise synthetic sound. The fractal soundscape reveals a programmed and designed world that thoroughly encompasses all of the film's characters and all modes of being and thinking in their world.

Of course, cinematic music is traditionally used as a way to trigger specific emotional reactions and states of mind and mood, as is the case in *TRON*, and for some reviewers of *Blade Runner*, Vangelis's score is considered to be pathetically typical in function and form. Andrew Stiller hears the music as "an unobtrusive background to help set the mood of each individual scene" (1991, 196). Stiller argues that the music is both cliché and purely functional, "there simply to make sure that the audience keeps furiously chewing their popcorn" (198). The music becomes particularly formulaic in two important scenes: the murder of the replicant's inventor, Tyrell, where the score signals a Wagnerian culmination that implies a fated death and sets the course for the rest of movie, and the tragically heroic welling up of music that should cue sympathy at the death of the replicant, Roy Batty (Rutger Hauer), "a thing that would be by no means assured without that musical nudge," Stiller concludes (198). In each case, the point of such programmed background music is "to cue the audience as to how they're supposed to react" (198). Stiller treats the musical score as affectively functional, a programmatic prompt toward emotional responses given scenes that, left on their own, might be ambiguous and polyvalent. But for the most part, Stiller fails in his discussion to consider what role the diegetic music and sounds play in the characters' world, particularly given their psychotechnological enmeshment within that world and with each other. When he does consider the more blurry sounds of *Blade Runner*, Stiller overvalues the emotive significance of particular sound effects. Discussing the breakdown of distinctions between diegetic and nondiegetic sound, Stiller describes the ambient hum in Deckard's apartment. For Stiller, this sound "radiates stability, calm, and self-understanding as it quietly oscillates" (200). However, he doesn't explain why these particular emotional prompts are needed in these scenes, and his adjectives point to a kind of emotional underscore that I have never picked up on in *Blade Runner*, much less in Deckard's apartment scenes. Rather, these strike me as deeply unstable, tense, lonely, doubtful, seething, constrained, and artificial. Synthetic ambient sound becomes an occasionally oppressive presence, but if anything, it tends to come across as indifferent.

Moments of diegetic music—again, the "One More Kiss" segment, the strip club music, Rachel playing the piano in Deckard's apartment, Deckard alone at the piano—also present a peculiar indifference. Diegetic sounds like those of the androids in replicant toymaker J. F. Sebastian's rooms or the atmospheric wheezing of Deckard's apartment, the rain sounds and traffic noise, also take on a role usually reserved for nondiegetic cues. However, these cues from the film's diegetic world likewise reinforce how far outside they are, how much distance there is between Deckard and the world around him. For Chion, these sounds reveal a peculiar lack of normal affect. "This juxtaposition of scene with indifferent music has the effect not only of freezing emotion but rather of intensifying it," Chion concludes. "I call this kind of music anempathetic" (1994, 8). In *Blade Runner*, every single sound is anempathetic, separated from emotion except when emotion has to be programmed as part of the SF film noir script. The indifferent nature of sound objects, the fractal world in which they blur and fade away forever, reveals the scripted, inorganic, ahistorical, replicated, and implanted nature of our experience of them. Stubbornly acousmatic, always withdrawn and withdrawing, sound here does more than add value, which is what the otherwise sourceless sound does when it "interprets the meaning of the image, and makes us see in the world what we would not otherwise see, or would see differently" (34). Instead, sound in *Blade Runner* makes us doubt the authenticity of what we see, or it makes such distinctions between the authentic and synthetic glaringly beside the point. Sound supports the imagination of characters and audience alike with persistent and peripheral sound props that build a world rather than encode it with emotion. The sound objects heard in *Blade Runner* are profoundly indifferent to the events around them and rarely attach to a specific image or visual object on the screen; they rather pervade the film as ambience. Such sounds do not provide the filmgoer with a means of emoting within the imaginary world but instead seem to be there in order to remind us that every detail has been seen to, that this is a complete world and yet also a fraud, right down to the electric stage-set atmosphere and the background hum of a manufactured sonic cosmos.

1984 | *DECODER*

Set amid the real-world sleaze of Hamburg's Reeperbahn district, West German corporate headquarter sprawl, and the industrial wastelands of Berlin, Muscha's obscure science fiction film, *Decoder*, is a tale of sonic terrorism that pits a young industrial noise artist against the corporate fascism of the Muzak music company. The film follows the sound experiments and interventions of an urban noise freak, F.M. (indeed, a human "frequency modulator," played by F. M. Einheit aka Mufti of West Berlin's Einstürzende Neubauten). Fueled by an industrial postpunk form of Burroughsian tape experiments and chaos magic, F.M. learns to resist the synthetic sonic atmospheres of contemporary mass consumption through tape experiments and lifestyle modification. Though it never circulated far from its underground origins, *Decoder* is in fact one of the quintessential cyberpunk films. Directed by punk filmmaker Muscha (Jürgen Muschalek), from Düsseldorf, *Decoder* was mostly producer Klaus Maeck's brainchild; he was the film's producer and primary writer, and he wrote and published the *Decoder Handbuch* (1984) that laid out the resources, theories, and most importantly the strategies at work in the film. A Hamburg journalist and part-time filmmaker, Maeck had covered the early industrial music scene while running the Rip-Off record shop in 1979. Rip-Off quickly folded, but for a while it was the center of Hamburg's punk underground. This scene was the source for Maeck's first Super 8 film, *Amok* (1979). The film had no dialogue, the director recalled, because "the music explained everything; German punk and 'avant-garde' tunes, some English classics and Throbbing Gristle. Elements from *A Clockwork Orange,* punk attitudes and the almighty power of television were the themes" (Maeck 2008, 201). With Rip-Off gone and sick of journalism, Maeck started work on a project about Muzak that would eventually result in *Decoder.* Against the mood-conditioning and mind-controlling sound environments produced by the Muzak corporation, *Decoder* would pit the noise of industrial music and synth

408 • SONOROUS OBJECT-ORIENTED ONTOLOGIES

pop—England's Throbbing Gristle offshoots, Psychic TV and Coil, Soft Cell, The The, Hamburg's Abwärts and Einstürzende Neubauten.

Maeck's research took him to several corporate offices in the major West German cities, and he managed to interview a Muzak company director. It was a strange meeting for Maeck, but it convinced him that Muzak worked. The "provocative questions" he had meant to ask melted away under the influence of the sonic Valium, and over the course of the meeting, he became calmer and talked more gently than his earlier desire for confrontation had warranted (Vague 1985). This is just what the Muzak corporation would expect. Muzak wasn't music; it was "scientifically-engineered sound" that changed consciousness for production and relaxation. The writers of the Muzak corporate handbook would not dare to call it music, though Muzak might bear a certain resemblance and could be said to possess musical properties. But it is definitely not, the handbook qualifies, "music which is meant to entertain. Because music is art. But Muzak is science. So it does not require a conscious listening effort. Yet it has an enormous effect on those who hear it" (in Vague 1985). As Maeck discovered during his interview, Muzak does indeed work like a powerful antianxiety agent, and he conceded that its use in hospitals to calm patients and mitigate worry was a noble one. However, the centralized distribution of Muzak content over telephone cable lines to subscribing customers meant that the Muzak corporation sent the same content to hospitals, the dentist's office, supermarkets, fast food chains, factories, and offices. Its ubiquitous nature—characterized in the company's catchphrase, "Muzak is more than music. It's an environment" (in Vague 1985)—was the aspect of this corporatized sound science that most disturbed Maeck.

A tool for collective social control, Muzak synchronized the human biorhythm as well as conditioned mood, and it extended this affect everywhere through its pervasive presence (West 1989). Muzak at 8 a.m. would calm you down for work; around 11 a.m. it would get more stimulating in preparation for your lunch break; by afternoon, it would calm you down as you completed the second half of your work day; and then it would get a little exciting again in anticipation of your being done for the day. It would send you home with a smile on your face. The mood-regulating sounds would not stop there; they were waiting in your car to greet you, Maeck surmised, pointing to the Muzaklike central programming of FM radio stations that similarly mapped out daily mood cycles for their listeners. Muzak could instigate different types of affective mood responses, not simply provide stress relief or a sense of relaxation; it was also a motivating agent. Whether it was piped into restaurants, department stores, malls, or the grocer's, Muzak made "shopping more pleasant and less hurried" while at the same time it kept the customer happily consuming. "The entire process is known as Muzak Stimulus Progression," the company handbook announces, which "provides an overall feeling of forward movement, can mitigate stress and produce beneficial psychological changes" (in Vague 1985). For Maeck, the franchised burger joints that had invaded West Germany—he had originally intended to name the project, *Burger Kreig* (*Burger War*)—epitomized those episodes of mass capitalism and gross collective consumption that Muzak was meant to sonically gloss for us, creating an ambience of bubbling soda pop contentment (Maeck 2008, 201). At the same time, Muzak dulls the awareness of patrons, making sure that they are unaware of the constant surveillance and manipulation of their lives through medial forces of control.

We first see F.M., working as a clerk at a local burger joint, in a bit of black-and-white surveillance feed under review by an employee of the Muzak corporation, Jäger (Bill Rice), whose perpetually dour expression belies the mood-altering properties of his employer's product. F.M.'s experiments in tape manipulation, audio cut-up, white noise, and low-frequency infrasound are troubling to the corporate heads at Muzak. Tasked with F.M.'s assassination, Jäger will end up in a kind of bizarre love triangle with the noise artist's girlfriend, Christiana (Christiane F.), a model at the peepshow that Jäger frequents to the tune of Soft Cell's "Seedy Films." Things get serious when F.M. notices that there is a direct correlation between the playing of Muzak and the contentment of the customers of H-Burger—a one-letter pun, according to Maeck, on heroin, "horse," and the horsemeat that European burger chains were thought to substitute for beef (Maeck 2008, 202). In one early scene set in the restaurant, we hear Muzak just as we would expect, supplying a faint, barely audible but still omnipresent score to mundane activities. It is a simulacrum of instrumental pop hits, the familiarity of

410 • SONOROUS OBJECT-ORIENTED ONTOLOGIES

which is completely manufactured and yet even more effective because of the way it eludes precise identification. After getting his hands on one of the Muzak cassettes and modifying its content, F.M. conducts his first experiment in noise intervention at H-Burger. At first, while the unaltered Muzak plays over H-Burger's speakers, couples happily eat their burgers, drink their sodas, swallow, and smile at each other in their mutually vacuous enjoyment; visually, these scenes are saturated with a red/pink filter. Things change when F.M.'s own anti-Muzak plays. First, we hear a warping of the tape's original speed before the Muzak turns into an abstract, metallic sheet of distortion; the lighting filter changes to a sickly green and shadows increase until the expressions on the faces turn noticeably sour and ill at ease. Oddly, this transformation appears to be triggered by F.M. plugging his ears, for as soon as he moves his fingers away, the Muzak returns as before, the lighting regains its red/pink glow, and the expressions of contentment return as well. This flexibility between, or at least entanglement of, psychic and social spaces is key to the film. This change of sonic atmosphere is primarily a psychological affect that only F.M. experiences. One of the mysteries of the film is that this decoding and projection of internal affect should manifest outwardly through subliminal sonic psychotechnologies; it is in fact a direct reversal of the lines of influence that Muzak exerts by using external sound sources to control the inner behavior and emotion of their human subjects.

In the first shots of F.M. working in his apartment studio, he wears headphones and manipulates a small frequency-generating device while watching two men with briefcases interact on the street below. We are given no explanation for what is transpiring, but as F.M. continues to watch and generate noise that presumably only he can hear, the film speeds up so that the two men become more and more erratic, walking in circles, leaving and returning, setting down and swapping their cases without any apparent purpose. This is the first indication we have that there is some kind of subliminal connection between sound and human action, and it is the randomness of F.M.'s sound experiments that puts him in Muzak's crosshairs as the company seeks to monopolize the soundtrack to daily experience and so dictate purposeful and profitable behavior. All of *Decoder* takes place in the psychogeographical middle ground that results from media saturation and ambient sonic psytech. The film is startlingly prescient regarding the emergence of contemporary network culture, although Maeck is quick to qualify that the "many 'hints'" that could be taken as "a wise prophecy" are in fact "nothing other than one transcription of the zeitgeist at the time" (Maeck 2008, 205). The most compelling aspect in this respect consists not only of the ubiquitous presence of media but also in the ways in which media interact, not simply literally but conceptually, so that the function of one media (say, environmental Muzak) can be used to modulate our understanding of another media (television screens). Video monitors are in fact everywhere and have become an ambient media. Early on in the film, when we follow Jäger into the video surveillance room at Muzak headquarters (leaving unexplained exactly why a corporation like Muzak should even have some kind of video surveillance room), a bank of monitors shows all manner of disparate content including not only closed-circuit surveillance footage but news footage of street riots and police repression, a shot of England's Princess Diana and Prince Charles in a motorcade, and a scene from Fritz Lang's *Metropolis* (specifically, Freder's dream of Maria's robotic duplicate, dancing lasciviously before a crowd of leering men, their eyes gradually resolving into a swirling, kaleidoscopic montage). While this suggests a kind of attention-deficit mentality that demands stimulation and oversaturation for its own sake, it also suggests the possibility that the viewer might detect unexpected connections and relationships across the set of screens. This is something that Maeck borrows from William Burroughs's theory and practice of the cut-up, which turns on a synchronicity engine that makes unexpected connections among randomly associated sets of material and promotes precognitive awareness.

Burroughs writes frequently about the ability of the manufactured soundtrack, juxtaposed, often sharply, against existing visual spectacle (whether as media, film, or television), or against society, as an urban tactic for disrupting political events, lectures, rallies, and other large gatherings. As the mainstream news media takes up this antimedia footage, it becomes a catalyst for its own change or destruction. This was just the kind of sonic warfare that Burroughs had both fantasized about in *The Ticket That Exploded* (1962) and *The Wild Boys* (1971), and advocated in "The Invisible Generation" (1961), *The Electronic Revolution* (1970), and *The Revised Boy Scout Manual* (1970). In a lecture delivered at the Naropa Institute in 1976, Burroughs (1986) describes the cut-up techniques of Brion Gysin in terms of their revelatory power: "When you cut into the present, the future leaks out." He proceeds to articulate a system of divinatory processes that incorporate multiple media of composition (paper, magnetic tape, film). Ultimately Burroughs proposes a system in which prophecy becomes indistinguishable from memory, the random from the intentional. "How random is random?" he asks of his work with audio tape recorders, which he distinguishes from textual practice by calling it a "cut-in" rather than a cut-up. "We know so much that we do not consciously know that we know, that perhaps the cut-in was not random. The operator on some level knew just where he was cutting in. . . . So cut-ups put you in touch with what you know and do not know that you know." As early as 1961, Burroughs had extended the practice of literary cut-ups to tape recordings and film, proposing that "anyone with a tape recorder controlling the sound track can influence and create events" ([1961] 2004, 336). Burroughs's theory follows from the basic premise that sound cannot help but add value to visual content, which we previously discussed in terms of the cinematic experience but which Burroughs proposes as an experiment with television:

> What we see is determined to a large extent by what we hear. . . . You can vary this proposition by a simple experiment. . . . Turn off the sound track on your television and substitute an arbitrary sound track prerecorded on your tape recorder, . . . street sounds music conversation recordings of other television programs . . . , you will find that the arbitrary sound track seems to be appropriate and is in fact determining your interpretation of the film track on screen people running for a bus in piccadilly with sound track of machine-gun fire looks like 1917 petrograd. . . . You can extend the experiment by using recorded material more or less appropriate to the film track for example take a political speech on television shut off sound track and substitute another speech you have prerecorded . . . hardly tell the difference isn't much. (2004, 335)

Initially the experiments that Burroughs devises are really about personal liberation and autonomy. Sound recording and playback activates "a past time set by precise association," while tape manipulation liberates the mind from "old association locks" (2004, 335). Prior associations lock us into certain modes of behavior and obsession. Anticipating Marshall McLuhan's central thesis in *Understanding Media* (1964), Burroughs claims that "a tape recorder is an externalized section of the human nervous system . . . you can find out more about the nervous system and gain more control over your reactions by using the tape recorder than you could find out sitting twenty years in the lotus posture or wasting your time on the analytic couch" (338). Mixing tapes recorded in the present with tapes from the past projects the "future rising out of old recordings" (338). But experiments in self-discovery quickly turn into experiences of external forces of control, of finding that there are "agencies official and non official" operating "without your awareness and very much to your disadvantage," those who would program you and who would decide for you which of your tapes should play, and when (339). From this point, Burroughs begins to argue for tape experiments of a more confrontational manner.

Burroughs contributes to two short dream sequences in *Decoder*. Both of F.M.'s dreams inspire advances in his tape experiments; they also link his work with electronics to magic, particularly in the first instance, where the beginning of his dream segues from a scene in which Christiana's numerous frogs try to climb up their metallic silver bedsheet while her voice intones the witches' incantation from Shakespeare's *Macbeth*. With the witches' spell still audible, the scene drifts into a green-tinted landfill, where Christiana, covered in her bedsheet, sits among bloated plastic trash bags. As the camera pans back, we see an old man in a trench coat and trilby, walking with a cane along the top of the landfill. Christiana rises to follow him, and Burroughs pauses and turns to her. We hear his voice, spliced in with the sounds of crows cawing, and a sample of one of his own tape cut-ups: "Word Falling, Photo Falling, Break Through in Grey Room. He has gone away to invisible morning, leaving a million recordings of his voice behind." Christiana runs to catch up with Burroughs, and the two recede as they cross the trash-strewn ground toward the pink-lit and otherwise featureless horizon. Near the end of the dream sequence, the image shifts from film stock to an image captured on a TV monitor, the colors now in higher contrast (the sky a more vibrant pink, the land blue), a faint line of video distortion running across the screen. As the camera pans back, we see that we are looking at the image on a TV set. The distortion lines begin to scroll, accompanied by bursts of visible and audible static, and we cut to a close-up of the sleeping F.M., colored deep blue, the static from the TV set still audible, along with the musical score that accompanied the dream with a low synthesizer rumble and a bell-like keyboard sound meandering around in the high end. As F.M. wakes up and wanders across his apartment, lit in the same deep blue and pink color palette of the dream, toward the TV, which shares the same camera shot of F.M.'s apartment, his racks of audio gear, and eventually the TV set itself, the image on the TV screen begins to feedback and falls away into infinite regression. F.M. turns off the TV, and the dream soundtrack stops immediately. He plops down at his mixing desk and plays back one of his own earlier cut-up experiments, which combines bits of Christiana's previous dialogue, looped into strange patterns, with sounds of virtual warfare from a video arcade and manipulated bits of Muzak from the H-Burger.

An extended scene with Christiana and her frogs also sets up the second dream sequence (Maeck explains the significance of frogs in his handbook). It begins with a close-up of plants in the strange apartment garden that she has created, the sounds of the frogs gradually mixed with a steady drum machine beat and a piano trill that sets up the sexiest music sequence in the film, a bit of seductive synth pop by Dave Ball and Genesis P-Orridge called "Sex and the Married Frog" (1985). With a fancy cocktail in hand, Christiana reclines on her bed in a short gown, surrounded by herpetology books open to pages with drawings of frogs. There is also a deck of Tarot cards on the bed, and to one side a recently dealt spread, again suggesting her connection to the occult. Christiana plays tenderly with a frog, letting it crawl to her crotch and across her breast, before gently holding and caressing it near her face, her mouth slightly open in pleasure. This love scene is broken by a thunderstorm and F.M.'s return. F.M. is eager to share his experiments. He begins playing her some of his distorted Muzak, but she wants nothing to do with it and drops despondently to the bed. We cut immediately to

F.M.'s next dream, presented as a video feed rather than film stock, and accompanied by the same music as his previous dream. F.M.'s second dream encounter with Burroughs takes place in a small electronic parts shop, where Burroughs sits busily picking away at a cassette recorder with a screwdriver. With faint lines of video distortion evident throughout the dream, most of the sequence is shot in the near black-and-white of surveillance monitors; when first entering the shop, F.M. is seen on such a monitor, which turns out to be situated in the dark recesses of the shop behind Burroughs's desk. When asked what he wants, F.M. drowsily replies, "Nothing special," which Burroughs repeats a few times as he works. After F.M. absently knocks over a bin of diodes, Burroughs, annoyed, hurries over to impart advice to F.M.: "Look, you got a problem, you start from zero preconceptions. You want 'nothing special.' Here it is." Burroughs hands F.M. the dismantled device. As Burroughs directs F.M. to the door, the lines of video distortion grow noisier before being replaced by a video color bar, which turns out to be on the TV in F.M.'s apartment. F.M. wakes up from the desk where he has been sleeping, turns off the screen, which silences the dream music as well, and enters into a creative frenzy.

Two very interesting things are going on in these dream sequences that inform our understanding of the relationship between sound and image, and sound and sound. First, they reclaim the space of the TV monitor as an ambiguous zone and not simply a space of cultural control. In several parts of the film, Maeck notes, television screens, like fast-food chains and Muzak, appear to be "a symbol of cultural colonization and control" recurring like a motif throughout the film (199). Maeck points to a short scene in which F.M. and Christiana drop off for beers at a small pub. The scene is indeed strange, almost pointless, but charged with an unexplained force of potential signaled by a sudden outburst of pigeons that lift off as F.M. darts toward them just before the couple reaches the pub's door. The sound of the birds' wings splices immediately into an explosion heard in the next sequence as we see a black-and-white war movie playing on a television set mounted on a wall inside of the pub. While the couple stands at the bar and orders their drinks, the camera cuts to the TV screen, showing antiaircraft artillery taking down a plane. Maeck treats this as a sign of American cultural imperialism based on the fact that this is an American war movie, and its sounds of gunfire, airplanes and explosions, intercut with the dialogue of Anglo-American actors, almost drown out the voices of F.M. and the bartender. This is not quite nuanced enough, for while TV screens do participate in new forms of cultural control, they do so more often by means of their ambient presence and not necessarily their specific content.

A scene in a video arcade also suggests that ambient noise trumps coherent interpretive strategies. Certainly, the games that F.M. and his friends play depict an aggressive, militarized America as images of the game graphics are spliced together with images of military operations. When game players adjust a joystick or rotate a knob on their game, an actual missile launches, and a series of massive explosions precede the announcement of the game's "Ende." This is one of the most science fictional sequences in the film, in fact, as it is seems that rather than playing for entertainment, F.M.'s time at the arcade is part of conscripted military duty, a conclusion based partly on a decidedly ambiguous verbal exchange between F.M. and Christiana. After finishing their meal, and with Christiana having the feeling that F.M. will do something that day, she seems to be reluctantly sending him off to war as she holds his shoulders and announces, "You really have to go." He then informs her, "If you do not know exactly who the enemy is, you must be very careful." He wears a military dress uniform and marches to the arcade in the accompaniment of a growing squad of camouflage-outfitted soldiers, while images of other players in the arcade show all of them wearing military attire. The scene could also be treated as part of the cultural colonization that Maeck explores in the film as he points to the imbrication of the military and culture industry. However, the imagery here is once again deeply ambiguous. As F.M. and his friends march in lockstep to the arcade, they are accompanied by an intense piece of industrial music by F. M. Einheit, composed of clattering metallic sheet percussion and marching boots ("Riots," 1985, from the *Decoder* soundtrack). Rather than provide evidence of any actual military service in some dystopic science fiction film, the uniforms could simply be what this group of young men wears to the arcade, as paramilitary dress and iconography were frequently part of the early industrial music scene. The images of warfare shown in the film footage cut into the video game sequences seem oddly antiquated, signs of a time when you knew who the enemy was, compared to the present, in which an unseen war was being waged between the forces of corporate control and a corresponding sonic terrorist resistance.

The second element that the dream sequences reveal is the surreal psychogeography that the characters in fact inhabit throughout the film. Most narrowly, this is a domain cohabited by Christiana and F.M., as the two dream sequences provide extended transitions from one character to the other, linking their consciousnesses by the occulted link of video dreamtime. Indeed, in their first conversation in the film, after a long and awkward silence as the couple eat some unidentifiable meal, Christiana asks F.M. to tell her something that he had dreamed that night. He says he dreamed nothing, and she says that while she did dream, she can't remember what it was; it was more of a feeling about something that he would do that day. Maeck suggests that the relationship between F.M. and Christiana is a key to the manner in which the film repeatedly sets up pairs of thematic oppositions only to let them slide into one another ambiguously rather than become fixed polarities (2008, 199). Maeck neatly unpacks the ways in which F.M. is identified with sound, Christiana with vision (she is a peepshow model, after all, and an object of the male gaze). F.M. is a user of electronic media and technology, which is represented by his apartment room, filled with stacks of equipment and shot in blue and pink, and he manipulates the sound science of Muzak into its noisy antithesis. Christiana, usually shot in green, is a user of magic and associated with the organic, represented by the many plants in her room, and more specifically, her frogs. But these possible polarities become confused, violated, all as a way to cut lines of control otherwise fixed in opposition. In one of the only scenes of intimate conversation between F.M. and Christiana, they are blindfolded and speak to one another on the phone. As the camera pulls back, however, we find that both are in the same room, and the blindfolds are Christiana's rejection of the power of the gaze that she exploits (and which exploits her) in the peepshows. Maeck notes that the telephone conversation, when F.M., unseen, "is in the ear," is the only intimacy that the two can share. "Hearing is feeling," Maeck concludes. "Hearing the pure word, with no images to distract the mind" (Maeck 2008, 205).

418 • SONOROUS OBJECT-ORIENTED ONTOLOGIES

One form of media thus becomes a kind of antidote or countermeasure to abuse in another. As Christiana and F.M.'s interactions become more volatile, the first indication that she may feel sympathy for Jäger comes from the confessional conversation that they share through a glass wall, subverting the intention of the peepshow.

In the battle for ambient sonic psychogeography, Muzak seeks to design and impose while F.M. and his growing cadre of noise terrorists hope to disrupt. *Decoder* plays out the conflict between music and noise in a very ambiguous way. Rather than simply reversing their values and thereby continuing to make sharp contrasts between music (Muzak) and noise (industrial music), *Decoder* reveals how either can be used to manage or disrupt the urban environment. Muzak is, by its producers' own definition, not music but science; the goals of F.M. and others is not to defeat this science that poses as music by retrieving humanist, musical values (which is what Eno hoped to do with his own ambient music project, as I will discuss below in the context of his contributions to Reinert's *For All Mankind*); rather, the goal is to create a kind of anti-Muzak, an opposing form of sound science that produces exactly the reverse effects than that of the Muzak corporation and its subscribers, but by manipulating their own methodologies. If Muzak uses the science of sound as a means of human engineering, developing patented techniques for sound filtering, mixing and sequencing in order to stimulate or soothe as they desire, then the exact opposite could be achieved through reverse engineering. As Lessour (2013) writes, the primary goal of *Decoder* was to reveal "the techniques of manipulation to get at the real information beneath" and "unscramble the codes of manipulation so that they could be re-appropriated to subvert their originators." This is true not simply of F.M.'s subversion of Muzak cassettes but also of his discovery that noise works two ways. In one scene, when a group of disruptive punks (followers of the Black Noise priest, played by Genesis P-Orridge) come into H-Burger, the manager puts on a tape of loud noise to run them out of the café. Maeck notes, "The only valuable political work must use the enemy's techniques" (2008, 201). This goes both ways. After this sequence, however, either having been inspired by or actually recording some of the noise used against them for his own mixes, F.M.'s noise assaults escalate to include attacks by additional noise terrorists beyond H-Burger and into McDonald's and Burger King. F.M. thus turns the sounds of control against themselves and their constituency. This is consistent with the actual sound-making practices of Psychic TV, F. M. Einheit, and Einstürzende Neubauten.

In a 1983 essay by Genesis P-Orridge, "Muzak: A Concept in Human Engineering" (the title comes from Muzak corporation literature), he discusses his collaborations with another member of Psychic TV, noise collagist Monte Cazazza. Cazazza is credited with coining the term "industrial music," which Genesis P-Orridge (1983) declared would be "an anti-muzak that, instead of cushioning thee [*sic*] sounds of a factory environment, made use of those very sounds to create rhythmic patterns and structures that incorporated thee [*sic*] liberating effects of music by unexpected means." In the recordings of Psychic TV and Einstürzende Neubauten, we encounter the diametric opposite of Muzak's engineered intention "to disguise stress, to control and direct human activity to generate maximum productivity and minimum discontent in order to give large corporations and industrial complexes thee [*sic*] highest possible profit with thee least responsibility" (P-Orridge 1983). As Genesis P-Orridge describes the procurement of the Muzak corporation handbook "by nefarious means," in order to better understand and subvert the goals of the sonic enemy, we find the culture war already well under way. These are precisely the approaches of the members of Einstürzende Neubauten, who experimented, Maeck explains, with "the very limits of sound and music." Exploring the percussive potential of scrap metal and grabbing sounds from the urban-industrial landscape—concrete bridges and tunnels, drills, even burning oil—and then utilizing the techniques of musique concrète to alter the recording process itself, the group directly engages, again according to Maeck, "the musical potentialities of electricity and the mixing desk itself" (2008, 207).

The power of the tape cut-ups and noise experiments essentially brings magic ritual to sound engineering, which becomes evident as F.M.'s antics grow wilder and more disturbing while working at his mixing desk. After his second Burroughs dream, F.M. begins to use the movement of his body to manipulate and interfere with his tape recordings. Later, in the most disturbing sequence in the film, he tortures one of Christiana's escaped frogs, recording its screams, and finally squeezes it to death. He ends up going into a spastic frenzy of motion, swinging his arms wildly, spinning around, banging his fists onto his equipment, and at last smearing what appears to be shit onto his face and into his mouth. In this scene, F.M. seems to be engaged in a variation of Aleister Crowley's frog ritual, in which Crowley consecrated a frog as Christ, then sacrificed it on a cross in order to claim the high rank of Magus of the Aeon. The ritual is described, along with a discussion of ethnographer Henry Wassen's work on the role of frogs in native Amazonian mythology, in the *Decoder Handbuch,* the companion piece to the film edited by Maeck and Walter Hartmann (1984, 43–47). In F.M.'s case, the frog rite combines with the "musical alchemy" attributed to Genesis P-Orridge, Psychic TV, and the Temple ov Psychick Youth, also discussed in the *Decoder Handbuch* (34). These magical practices are not presented in the context of adherence to ritual and formula, however; rather, they are part of the general do-it-yourself sensibility of chaos magic, a kind of postmodern practice that encourages the individual to borrow and combine different belief systems (such as various world religions, mythologies, theosophy, Gnosticism) with science fiction, fringe science theories, shamanism, and psychedelics. What F.M. experiences as his tape science moves in the direction of chaos magic has been described by Genesis P-Orridge, who explains that the cut-up is "a contemporary, non-mystical interpretation of Magick. The aim is reclamation of self-determination, conscious and unconscious, of the Individual. The result is to neutralize and challenge the essence of social control" ([1987] 2010, 164). Here P-Orridge recalls the original impetus of Burroughs and Gysin's cut-up experiments, which were geared more toward individual liberation from rational forces, prescribed lines of associative thinking, and internalized control than sociocultural intervention. In a section titled "The Person," P-Orridge writes: "The picture we get [of the person] from Cut-ups is more accurate than any traditional description. What has always been presented as the irrational becomes far more accurate and plausible than the Rational explanation we are endlessly urged and bullied to accept. The psychology of the unconscious explores the background of the so-called rational mind both by disciplined investigation and hysterical dissociation of thought habits" (161). The behavioral cut-up through hysterical dissociation ultimately taps into the "psycho-integrative" properties that P-Orridge attributes to Magick (161). This process resolves polarized oppositions, particularly by means of an alchemical reuniting of masculine and feminine, science and magic, technological and magical practices, which takes place in the psychogeographical dreamtime of the media-saturated environment. There are elements of waking up involved here, but it is more in the manner of lucid dreaming than actual waking life.

The individual engaged in behavioral cut-up, according to P-Orridge, requires "The Room," a special space in which "to grow and develop," and which is both "a physical place" and "a metaphor, too," of the mind ([1987] 2010, 158). The Room functions as a special psychotechnological interface, and in *Decoder*, F.M.'s home recording studio taps into the weird history of recording studios as special kinds of rooms associated with unusual states of consciousness. This is the case in the discoveries that began in the latter half of the 1960s by the Beatles, Brian Wilson, Pink Floyd, and Jimi Hendrix, among countless others, that the recording studio could do more than capture live performances, manufacturing auditory experiences by mixing and manipulating tape recordings, summed up by Eno's pronouncement that psychedelia expanded the capacity of recording technologies as much as the minds of its users. The Jamaican dub producer, Lee "Scratch" Perry, practiced a "MythScience of the mixing desk," a sonic magic used to "sculpt space" by means of the multitrack mixer and various technical effects, reverb, echo, and tape flange (Eshun 1998, 62). While other dub producers used similar tools, Perry's work was especially connected to a form of sound-induced madness, which explored what Eshun describes as "routes through a network of volumes, doorways and tunnels connecting spatial architectures" (1998, 63). Before finally burning down his own studio, Perry himself described the Black Ark facility as a kind of "space craft" and his mixing board a cybernetic interface: "I put my mind into the machine and the machine performs reality" (in Eshun 1998, 62). There are numerous descriptions in Pinch and Trocco (2002) of pioneering engineers, electronic instrument designers, and performers for whom modular synthesizers not only led to a lot of what Robert Moog himself called "weird shit" emanating from basement studios but also electronically expanded minds, and even drove some mad, as these technicians of

422 • SONOROUS OBJECT-ORIENTED ONTOLOGIES

space interfaced with new configurations of electric circuitry and tapped into what Moog termed a "cosmic network" of the "ideas and concepts [that] permeate our universe and our consciousness" (2002, 26, vi).

How does *Decoder* itself participate in—rather than simply depict—this culture war and the role of the cosmic sonic network that permeates all we know and are? For one, we know that Maeck wanted his viewers "to feel the movie!" Inspired by Burroughs's instructions for the use of infrasound in *The Revised Boy Scout Manual* and Throbbing Gristle's use of extremely low frequencies, Maeck entertained the possibility of provoking physical discomfort among his theater audience, especially in the scenes set at the H-Burger (Maeck 2008, 202). This would accomplish something like one of the attacks depicted in the film and would make the theater itself a place of intervention and disruption, rather than a place of entertaining compliance and consumption. This would also be another instance of an anti-Muzak. Muzak achieves its mind-numbing effects precisely because it lacks both high and low frequencies. Accordingly, Maeck attempted to include recordings of "low, low bass frequencies" (202) and infrasonic sound throughout the film's score, but the movie theater loudspeakers were too limited to reproduce them (West 1989). With that said, *Decoder* does begin in a sonically disturbing fashion with a pair of sounds that are particularly unsettling when taken together. Desolate electronic wind noise occupies the high range of audibility, and a sustained low-frequency (though by no means infrasonic) tone rumbles underneath. There are no midrange frequencies at all—already an anti-Muzak occupation of the audible terrain. The film's minimalist assault on the body thus begins immediately, even before the stark blue letters, scaled from the top of the screen to the bottom and spelling out "DECODER," scroll across the black screen from right to left, then appear again, still blue on black, small and faded before zooming forward to sit squarely in the center of the film. It is a cheap visual effect, but the starkness of the words, their minimal primary color against the darkness, anticipates the frequent use of monochrome filters throughout the film, and indeed matches the sudden switch to a scene showing the upper half of Jäger's body, shot from below and at an odd angle, occupying only the right half of the screen, and filtered blue against the same black backdrop. Still the synthetic wind and uncomfortably low drone are heard, for more than a minute now, and as Jäger (the image slowed down somewhat), begins to turn and walk off, the scene fades to a purple tinted parking lot, the sun shining behind buildings low on the horizon, and gradually pans left to reveal a tall, glass-fronted building, which will turn out to be the offices of the Muzak Corporation. As the windy sound becomes a gradually rising jet engine roar, the character walks past a guard into the building. The jet roar is silenced abruptly as the scene cuts to an interior elevator and then a long, nondescript hallway. Running for more than three minutes, the low throb threatens to modulate and distort other sounds, such as that of the electronic drum machine that fades into the mix as the scene opens in Muzak's headquarters. While lending a certain amount of the ominous to the proceedings, we really have no idea who Jäger is, or even that he is entering Muzak headquarters, and so the point of this opening scene is not about what the music adds to the visual experience; rather, it testifies to the ability of music to invisibly alter other sounds—to act as added value not to image but to sound—and hence gets at the elements of infrasound and the subliminal that *Decoder* explores and exploits. Operating at the outer extremities of electric tonality, this is not music but anti-Muzak, something that adds overtones to frequencies where Muzak operates through sonic cancellation. It is subtractive rather than additive.

The subversive properties of sound's additive value return near the end of the film, when F.M. and other noise terrorists trigger riots with their weaponized cassette players. As Burroughs instructs, added sounds never play in a vacuum, or simply against visual footage, but along and within a continuum of sounds. This reaches its pinnacle in the film with its incorporation of footage from actual Berlin riots against a state visit from Ronald Reagan, emphasizing the rioters' use of boom boxes to play gunshot sound effects rather than fire actual guns. Even by the time Burroughs published *The Electronic Revolution* in 1970 (originally printed in West Germany in a dual-language edition), the cassette tape recorder had become a "front line weapon" that could be used "to produce and escalate riots" ([1970] 2001, 20). Demonstrators armed with portable tape recorders could wreak havoc by playing prerecorded noises of riot and violence, instigating further chaos that could in turn be recorded in

424 • SONOROUS OBJECT-ORIENTED ONTOLOGIES

an immediate cut-up of the past and present, where fantasy and reality amplify the noise of one another in an ever-escalating feedback loop. Maeck's intent for his film was always situated somewhere between an instruction manual for a revolution of media and corporate technoculture, and a technospell that would make its images and sounds become reality by sympathetic magic. Perhaps it worked. For Reagan's pending visit to Berlin—the epitome of political spectacle that was merely the surface for a far more pervasive invasion by the American culture industry of fast food, luxury goods, and media—Maeck planned to stage his own sonic intervention, with actors carrying around cassette players. But reality preceded them. Local anarchists and other protestors were already on the scene, playing tapes with recordings of gunshots, explosions, and helicopters. Maeck recalls, "They put tape recorders in windows, and if you're in the street and you hear all these noises and you don't know where it's coming from and you think where is that fucking helicopter? Where is that shooting coming from? People got confused and more and more angry" (Lessour 2013; also see Maeck 2008, 204). Police broke or confiscated two hundred tape recorders, by Maeck's estimation. Such moments readily validate SF writer J. G. Ballard's assertion in his introduction to his novel *Crash*, that "modern science fiction became the first casualty of the changing world it anticipated and helped to create." Now the SF writer finds it "less and less necessary . . . to invent the fictional content of his novel. The fiction is already there. The writer's task is to invent the reality" (1974, 4).

Decoder maintains SF cinema's function as a conduit for a future that is already now. As Burroughs argues, cutting into the flow of an audiocassette tape puts you in touch with what you didn't know that you know; cutting up the past (the recording) lets the future leak out in the form of unexpectedly powerful synchronicities and coincidences. *Decoder* is meant to be a novum that prompts action, both a moment and a means for the further eruption of the new into corporately scripted reality. The film's accompanying manual and cassette release of the music expanded the theoretical underpinnings of the project by facilitating audiovisual cultural resistance. No longer analogic extrapolation, the actual Berlin riots render *Decoder*'s vision a moment of the past before it is even filmed.

1989 | *FOR ALL MANKIND*

First released in 1983 under the title *Apollo,* Al Reinert's poetic treatment of NASA's moon missions suffered through a short life as an underappreciated art film. This original cut consisted of visual footage from the Apollo missions set to the ambient music of Brian Eno, his brother, Roger, and the guitarist Daniel Lanois. The film was otherwise silent. After tepid audience response, Reinert and editor Susan Korda spent the next six years remaking the film, radically resequencing the visual footage and rearranging the soundtrack. They culled content from six million feet of raw film and over eighty hours of archival audio documentation, along with new interviews with the astronauts. The resulting film, with its now relatively steady stream of voice-overs derived from historical exchanges between mission control and the flight crew, as well as Reinert's own postmission interviews with the astronauts, radically recontextualizes the Apollo missions. Two particularly important things happen in this regard. Reinert collapses all six of the Apollo lunar landings into a single mission to the moon. He also tends to sacrifice factual clarity for poetic juxtaposition. Reinert is not concerned with either historical or scientific accuracy. A translunar injection sequence, for instance, is actually a rocket's reentry. Space-walk footage comes from the Gemini missions. At one point, a key shot that Reinert was looking for—a view of Earth from the window of the space capsule—was not available in the archive, so he simply pasted a photograph of Earth to the window of a capsule on display at the Smithsonian Institute and created the shot himself. Even the film's title comes from Reinert's remixing of President Kennedy's 1962 "space effort" address to Rice University. Kennedy proclaims, "We set sail on this new sea because there is new knowledge to be gained and new rights to be won, and they must be won and used *for all people.*" Reinert edits the clip, splicing it with another point in Kennedy's speech. Replacing "people" with "mankind," the phrase anticipates the text on the memorial plaque that the *Apollo 11* crew left on the moon, which announced, "We came in peace for all mankind," as well as with Neil Armstrong's "one giant leap for mankind."

The sonic experience of *For All Mankind* is the source of an occasionally delirious confusion. The voice-overs are often at odds with the

426 • SONOROUS OBJECT-ORIENTED ONTOLOGIES

film footage of specific crew members and mission footage. Rarely do we see on screen the person whose words we hear. A historical acousmatics thus takes shape in which snippets of human speech serve as a kind of *dialogue concrète* to create the film's overall atmosphere. As sound is detached from a specific source of attribution, these memories come across as universal. History becomes a matter of ambience. *For All Mankind* thus loses its moorings in all of the documentation, sacrificing referential accuracy to recreate the Apollo experience as a form of mysticism. Rather than technical or logistic logs, in fact, Reinert's final mix reveals a predilection for the affective flight log, as it were, with the astronauts' descriptions of their personal impressions, moods, emotional reactions, liminal states of consciousness, and minds expanded in the direction of the universal and mystical territories of waking dreams, hypnagogic trances, and episodes of transcendence. Without attribution, even the most intimate and personal of each astronaut's experience becomes a statement of collective knowledge gained "for all mankind."

In his liner notes to the *Apollo: Atmospheres & Soundtracks* album (1983), Eno recalls his own experience of the first televised Apollo moon landing and how it shaped his sonic reimagining for the soundtrack. The television coverage left him less than satisfied, he writes. First, the difference of scale between event and coverage was "quite inadequate to the vastness of space," while a small television screen with its poor range of color made the moon landings look to him like a bad episode of *Star Trek*. Second, and rather more egregiously, "the fear of boring the general public had led the editors and commentators to present the transmissions from space in an up tempo, 'newsy' manner that was unsympathetic: short shots, fast cuts and too many experts obscuring the grandeur and strangeness of the event with a patina of down-to-earth chatter." In Eno's assessment, the film that Reinert pulled together from so much footage would be the "definitive" account of the Apollo missions. Silence the chatty coverage of reporters and slow down the pace, and the mystery of space travel returns. As composition, the project would provide Eno with "an opportunity to explore the feelings of space travel, being weightless, seeing the night-time campfires of Saharan nomads from high above Earth, looking back to a little blue planet drifting alone in space, looking out into the endless darkness beyond, and finally, stepping onto another planet." This wasn't to be "adventure music," Eno concludes. Quite the contrary. "What this film can do is to present a set of moods," he writes, "a unique mixture of feelings that quite possibly no human had ever experienced before, thus expanding the vocabulary of human feeling just as those missions had expanded the boundaries of our universe." This interest in composing moods as ambient atmospheres had guided Eno's work since the mid-1970s, first with his tape loop deconstructions of Pachelbel's Canon, then his collaborations with loop guitarist Robert Fripp, and finally his own ambient series. In his liner notes to an earlier album, *Music for Airports* (1978), Eno defines a sonic ambience "as an atmosphere, or a surrounding influence: a tint." Here, the creation of sonic ambiences follows the impressionistic sensibilities discussed earlier in the context of the fantasy of a moon landing depicted in *Destination Moon*. Maximizing a composition's capacity to act both as atmospheric noise and composed soundscape designed to reflect specific moods, ambient music must also be sonically pliable, working well when played as background but also compelling when listened to in a more focused and intentional context. The four tracks on *Music for Airports* were a representative set of what Eno imagined would become a series of music created for different spaces and contexts. Conceiving ambient music as a site-specific art, a sonic psychogeography of pieces composed "for particular times and situations with a view to building up a small but versatile catalogue of environmental music suited to a wide variety of moods and atmospheres," Eno immediately distinguishes his project from the output of Muzak and other "canned music companies," which regulate environments by "stripping away all sense of doubt and uncertainty (and thus all genuine interest) from the music." His music would retain mystery, uncertainty, and doubt, as well as act in calming and soothing ways, and these would reflect the mind of the listener as well as the space filled by the composition.

Eno places particular significance on the transformation of listening that comes from the introduction of new recording technologies, considering the range of compositional options that recording studios since the latter half of the 1960s make possible. His ideas gravitate around two areas of innovation, as I discussed earlier but will expand on here: "the development of the texture of sound itself as a focus for

428 • SONOROUS OBJECT-ORIENTED ONTOLOGIES

compositional attention, and the ability to create with electronics virtual acoustic spaces (acoustic spaces that don't exist in nature)" (2004a, 95). Immersive effects are particularly important for Eno, who sought to create "music to swim in, to float in, to get lost inside" (95). The mood-conditioning potential of ambient music was a response to changes in listening habits brought on by radio, record players, and cassette tapes: "People were wanting to make quite particular and sophisticated choices about what they played in their homes and workplaces, what kind of sonic mood they surrounded themselves with" (94). This too presented an overt challenge to the Muzak system, which preprogrammed the sounds of social spaces from corporate headquarters and which, by the end of the 1970s, had extended its reach into the increasingly centralized FM radio broadcast. But for all that, Eno discusses his ambient music in terms of mood-space catalogs; his ambient recordings tend toward a gauzy vagueness, and their overall affective charge is distant and anempathetic. Even at its most musical, the nondiegetic ambient music heard in *For All Mankind* lacks the empathetic charge that exudes from scenes in which we hear what the astronauts actually listened to in the space capsule—country and western by Buck Owens and Merle Haggard, tremolo and slide-heavy rock and roll by Santo and Johnny—truck driver music, really. In one scene, the de facto theme to Kubrick's *2001*, Strauss's "Also sprach Zarathustra," plays on a portable cassette tape unit, floating and spinning in the weightless conditions onboard the craft. Armstrong is known to have taken Les Baxter's space-age pop LP *Music Out of the Moon*, featuring Samuel Hoffman on the theremin, with him on *Apollo 11*, along with Dvořák's *New World Symphony*. In one particularly poignant scene in *For All Mankind*, Ken Mattingly, not really a fan of country and western music but rather a self-proclaimed "classical music nut," listens to Berlioz's *Symphonie Fantastique* while orbiting the moon, alone in the command service module, as the other *Apollo 16* crew members explore the lunar surface. Mattingly recalls the experience: "People are always expecting you to say it was lonely, but it wasn't. It was incredibly peaceful, it was *wonderful*. It was just me and the stars and the *Symphonie Fantastique*" (in Reinert 1979, 175). This is the emotionally charged music of *For All Mankind*. It carries the weight of cultural memory and plays out the emotions as an immediate diegetic effect rather than the nondiegetic music that, as Chion describes it, "participates directly in the emotion of the scene, moves in sympathy with it, envelops it, prolongs and amplifies it" (2009, 430). By contrast, in the case of the music of Eno and Lanois, the more their music turns toward the melodic, the more distanced and detached it becomes from human events and character.

For All Mankind includes several such melodic moments, such as the blurry space cowboy songs featuring Lanois's steel guitar. But these are often so exceedingly short in the final cut of the film that they get just as caught up in the weird historical dub aesthetic of the film as everything else. Whether sustained atmosphere or short, detached melodic refrain, Eno's music does in fact create precisely the indifferent "cosmic background" that Chion considers the essential characteristic of anempathetic film sound (2009, 430). Because Eno's sonic cues are never repeated, like Vangelis's varying nonthemes in *Blade Runner*, they function, in this respect, like Guattari's theoretical refrain: they are independent of other song structure (melody, chorus) and play out as microphrases for their own sake within a minimal, self-reflexive cinematic ecology of assemblages that resist precise synchronization of sound and image. The anempathetic assemblage disregards the sympathies between flows of sound and images that Chion attributes to synchronization, whether "predictably or not, variously or monotonously," and which depend on the static or passive receptivity of an image to the added sound, or which comes from a shared rhythmic movement and sensibility of pace (1994, 16). In this way, sound "activates the image," with the range and extent of its activation depending on the variety and veracity of multiple "points of synchronization" (16). The anempathetic music of *For All Mankind* resist sync points even at its most syncopated, as heard on the track "Deep Blue Day," with its slow-motion opiated drift and reverb-drenched shimmer floating over a programmed bass and drum machine sequence.

The highly reverberant ambient spaces of *For All Mankind* recall the fractal reverbs of *Blade Runner*, but not because they tug listeners into "the aural equivalent of the oppressive haze and mist that veil the movie's every scene" (Stiller 1991, 199). Reverb becomes a "unifying element" in *Blade Runner*, with the link between diegetic and nondiegetic sounds making the world bigger than we can perceive, much less comprehend; however, reverb also places that world always at a distance further removed from the point of audition. As the replicated and echoing soundscape turns space itself into a simulation of space, and with increasing sonic saturation and complexity, reverb pushes *Blade Runner* into the chaotic system dynamics of a runaway cybernetic ecology—ultimately the artificial ecology of the city so important to film noir and cyberpunk narratives—built to contain and support replicant consciousness. While Eno's music in *For All Mankind* likewise provides reverberating tonal props instead of specific motific prompts, it does so in order to support a mythic, illusory, and nostalgic longing for an immediate cosmic experience that was never possible in the first place. The cosmos of *Blade Runner* is measured through its highly nuanced sensitivity to diegetic sounds, even those that would normally be inaudible (boiling eggs, heartbeats). The anempathetic character of such noises is particularly pronounced in the case of sounds that persist "as if nothing had happened," such as "the noise of a machine, the hum of a fan, a shower running" (Chion 2009, 9). The world of *Blade Runner,* which I consider an artificial reality used to maintain the programming of replicant constructions, is full of such anempathetic prompts that reinforce our consciousness while reminding us that they could not care less, for we too are merely synthetic props necessary to keep the noir script running. The indifference of Eno's score to Reinert's reverberating nostalgias reaches for something else altogether.

The assemblage of Reinert's film takes advantage of one of the key features of ambient production, which again Eno's 1978 liner notes explain must "accommodate many levels of attention without enforcing one in particular." This observation should begin to unlock Reinert's confrontation of nationalistic power dynamics in the space program that foregrounds instead its mystical and transcendent consequences. *For All Mankind* utilizes the mode of ambient music in service to the manufacture of collective cultural memory. It pushes toward transcendent states of consciousness, those existing outside of the controlling mechanisms of news broadcast to manifest experience outside of history altogether. To get there, we must reconsider Eno's differentiation of ambient music from Muzak. The apparent ability of ambient music to shift fluidly from background to foreground is less an aspect of compositional sensibilities, according to Goodman, than an indication of "a shift in modes of audition within a broader operative logic of power" (2010, 143). The distinction that Eno makes between Muzak and music, background or foreground, is less important than his reliance on an emergent "mode of ubiquitous listening" that perceives the strategically designed mix as evidence of "a parallel process among others in a saturated media environment" (143). According to Goodman, all media in the latter part of the 1980s is acousmatic, with neither clear source nor precise location, and thus truly ubiquitous. What has held over from the Muzak process, Goodman explains—and what distinguishes it from the attention-grabbing leaps of volume in radio, TV, and cinematic advertising—is Muzak's "specific politics of frequency" (143). Muzak's subtraction of the lowest and highest frequencies anticipates the perceptual coding of MP3 format compression; other Muzak techniques feature ways to narrow the sonic experience such that mono was preferred over stereo, centralizing the sound field; vocals were taken out or replaced by lyricless choirs or ensembles, when not simply rendered as instrumental variations; and finally heavily compressed and normalized dynamic ranges reduced variation and surprise. Muzak is an early player in the history of what Goodman calls "ubiquitous music," which points toward "our submersion into a generalized surround sound culture," where it bolsters control, modulates affect, and "smoothes the experience of the ecology of fear" (144). Muzak thus partakes sonically in the larger cultural movement from disciplinary to control societies, which no longer stimulate and manipulate attention but rather modulate affect atmospherically. Rather than altering the intensity or relative mood indicators among different musical selections, Muzak indexes its sonic products according to qualities such as "tempo, color (light or dark), rhythm, popularity and so on to ensure that the *same intensity can be maintained even as the music appears to have changed*. Atmospherics address individuals as they traverse different ambiances through their everyday lives" (144). I believe that a similar form of indexical leveling, which neither stimulates nor manipulates attention in the way that sound-to-visual synchronization in cinema typically does, modulates affect through ambient assemblages in both *Blade Runner* and *For All Mankind*.

432 • SONOROUS OBJECT-ORIENTED ONTOLOGIES

Where *Blade Runner* achieves its distancing effects by creating assemblages across diegetic domains, sonic anempathy in *For All Mankind* comes from the fact that not only are there are so few diegetic sounds in the film, but also the music purposefully fails to fill the void of silence. Most of the footage depicting the astronauts in action is silent, and what sounds we do hear come from telecommunication archives and radio chatter, or from disconnected voice-overs in which the person speaking is not the person we are watching. Reinert's editing style sonically reinforces the indifference of his highly fragmented sources to each other as well as to their visual and historical counterparts through a kind of cut-up. Chion casts this audiovisual indifference in explicitly cosmic terms:

> The indifference of a piece of music is given to the spectator precisely so that he or she takes it as a mirror reflecting his or her own solitude and the insignificance of his or her own fate. This indifference is an emotion—not in the music itself, even though we talk as though it is, but within our poor human state of being that feels this music as the infinite resistance of the real. When poets speak of the indifference of the stars, they do not mean that stars are conscious; on the contrary, they are alluding to the muteness of these distant cold glimmerings to the unanswered messages that we send them. (2009, 432)

Distant-sounding music—quiet music, slow music, minimal or fragmented music, space music, full of echoing and reverberant sounds—all convey not so much the memory, recollection, or nostalgia of experience but rather its absence. Reinert sustains this feeling of absence throughout much of *For All Mankind,* which aims for nothing resembling the vicarious but direct experience of transcendent cosmic consciousness that Stanley Kubrick attains with the extended star gate sequence near the end of *2001.* Reinert instead evokes the cosmic experience as memory, an act of recollection that is also a form of loss.

Both Reinert's film *For All Mankind* and Eno's album *Apollo: Atmospheres & Soundtracks* perform a profound distancing that recasts the Apollo missions as a lost, ambient technomyth, and it is for this reason that I consider them a form of science fiction, and a form of sonic novum, respectively. Both evoke a kind of anempathetic surplus, interspersing concretely asignifying sonic objects among nonreverberant voice-overs, the flatness of which "takes total possession of the diegetic space. It is both completely internal and invading the entire universe" (Chion 2009, 79–80). This also happens in the voice-over theatrical cut of *Blade Runner*, and it happens for the mythic Apollo überastronaut that is created as a composite of multiple, separate experiences and points of view. Both films trigger what Goodman calls *déjà entendu*, the "partial recognition of something heard but corresponding to the inability to attribute cause or location to the source of that sound effect" (2010, 147). This is in fact another kind of acousmatic ambience, an "affective tonality [that] possesses, abducts, or envelops a subject rather than being possessed by one" (189). It screens us from direct, lived experience. As a sonic psychotechnology, *For All Mankind* periodically introduces Eno's music as a momentary enveloping of the listening subject during a disruptive gap, a moment of atmospheric possession and absorption that distances rather than pulls closer, a "short-circuiting of attention and consciousness by mnemonic processes," Goodman describes, "and the sonically induced, temporary, psychoaffective vacation of the present, leaving residues of feeling," but not feeling itself (189).

Situated both against and within Reinert's ambient cosmic cinema, most of Eno's music is profoundly anempathetic, its indifference to the flow of historical scenes so conspicuous that it somehow makes the footage even more cosmic. The music pulls away into the depths of the screen in a way similar to Leith Steven's Sonovox-processed strings retreating from the flat matte lunar landscape. The fragmented nature of Reinert's use of Eno's music only reinforces this underlying disconnect. Rather than just smearing the Eno music across the film as a constant and eventually invisible, if not inconsequential, backdrop that might unify the frequent edits of visual, dialogic, and diegetic sound edits, Reinert rather mixes in the more musical segments during discrete vignettes of isolated space footage. This harkens back to the original version of the film, which consisted only of space music and otherwise silent shots of rockets, outer space, and the moon. The music will occasionally suggest concrete kinds of effects, like the subaquatic creatures that seem to lurk throughout the track "Matta," or the shimmering effects of "Under Stars," which points back to Steven's time-suspension tricks. In fact, many of the shots of photographic stills accompanied by Eno's most processed ambient music recall the blurry strings and phasing wind instruments heard in *Destination Moon*. At once new and familiar, a memory of something that hasn't happened yet, the sonic *déjà entendu* is a future ghost sound, less like affective recall than an audible intention cast backward through time, and which comes upon us out of nowhere, out in space.

• Acknowledgments •

Thanks first and foremost to the creative imagination and ingenuity of all those involved in making the numerous science fiction films that I write about in this book. My life would be too quiet without the out-there sound worlds of Louis and Bebe Barron, Bernard Herrmann, Jerry Goldsmith, Edward Artemiev, Gil Mellé, Wendy Carlos, Walter Murch, John Carpenter, Sun Ra and His Arkestra, Vangelis, and Eno.

Sincerest thanks to Douglas Armato, director of the University of Minnesota Press, for his guidance of this project, as well as to Istvan Csicsery-Ronay Jr., whose readings of this book at multiple stages were insightful and motivating. I would also like to thank the faculty senate and associate provost of the University of Denver for support of the project through faculty research funds as well as professional research opportunities for faculty grants.

I thank my colleagues and students of the Emergent Digital Practices program at the University of Denver, who encouraged me to test-drive my ideas in numerous classes and extracurricular contexts. Particular thanks go out to Justin Eckstein for fine-tuning the sound studies and always keeping me well fed on theory, and especially Adrienne Russell for her expert writing advice and support. I am grateful for the many years of encouragement from Bruno Clarke, Cary Wolfe, tobias c. van veen, Paul Prudence, Arie Altena, and Graham St. John. More broadly, I acknowledge the countless great conversations at the meetings of the Society for Literature, Science, and the Arts, as well as Sonic Acts.

I am fortunate to have more friends than I can thank personally here, but I want to single out Darren Barkett, David Fodel, Darwin Grosse, Cory Metcalf, Noah Phillips, and John Tomasic—thanks for helping me keep it cosmic!

I dedicate this book to my family, Leah, Lucy, and Eli, for living with this book and me for all these years. And to my dad, Glen Reddell, always ready to come to the rescue. And to Mom and my sister, Shasta—I am sad that you aren't here to celebrate this with us, but I know the stars above sang more brilliantly when you joined their chorus.

• Bibliography •

Agel, Jerome. 1970. *The Making of Kubrick's "2001."* New York: Signet.

Albright, Daniel. 2004. *Modernism and Music: An Anthology of Sources.* Chicago: University of Chicago Press.

Aldiss, Brian W. 1969. *Barefoot in the Head: A European Fantasia.* Garden City, N.Y.: Doubleday.

Aldiss, Brian. n.d. Publisher's blurb for *Barefoot in the Head* (1969). http://brian aldiss.co.uk/writing/novels/novels-a-c/barefoot-in-the-head/.

Andriopoulos, Stefan. 2008. *Possessed: Hypnotic Crimes, Corporate Fiction, and the Invention of Cinema.* Chicago: Chicago University Press.

Artemiev, Edward. 1988. "Edward Artemiev: He Has Been and Will Always Remain a Creator." Interview by Tatyana Egorova. *Muzikalnaya Zhizn,* no. 17. http://www.electroshock.ru/eng/edward/interview/egorova/.

Artemiev, Edward. 1993. "Edward Artemiev: I Am Sure that There Will Be a Creative Explosion." Interview by Galina Drubachevskaya. *Musical Academy* 2. http://www.electroshock.ru/eng/edward/interview/drubachevskaya/index.html.

Artemiev, Edward. 2004. "Interview with Edward Artemiev." Interview by Archie Patterson. Electroshock Records. http://www.electroshock.ru/eng/edward/interview/patterson/index.html.

Artemiev, Edward. 2006. "Interview with Edward Artemiev." Interview by Margarita Katunjan. *Music in Russia* 3 (10). http://www.electroshock.ru/eng/edward/interview/katunjan/index.html.

Attali, Jacques. 1985. *Noise: The Political Economy of Music.* Translated by Brian Massumi. Minneapolis: University of Minnesota Press.

Ball, Alan M. 2003. *Imagining America: Influence and Images in Twentieth-Century Russia.* Lanham, Md.: Rowman & Littlefield.

438 • BIBLIOGRAPHY

Ballard, J. G. 1974. *Crash*. New York: Vintage Books.

Barry, Robert. 2011. "Sound on Film: The Sound of Soviet Science Fiction." *Sound and Music*, July 25, 2011. http://www.soundandmusic.org/features/sound-film/sound-soviet-science-fiction.

Barry, Robert. 2013. "The High Pitch of Strangeness: *Ikarie XB-1*." In Electric Sheep: A Deviant View of Cinema, September 27, 2013. http://www.electricsheepmagazine.co.uk/features/2013/09/27/the-high-pitch-of-strangeness-ikarie-xb-1/.

Bar-Sagi, Aitam. 2013. "Gottfried Huppertz Biography." Gottfried Huppertz, October 30, 2013. http://fimumu.com/huppertz/#b.

Bar-Sagi, Aitam, Martin Koerber, and the 78 RPM Records Mailing List. 2001. "Vox 78s: The 2 *Metropolis* Singles." March 5, 2001. https://www.uow.edu.au/~morgan/Metroe2.htm.

Bartkowiak, Mathew J. 2010a. "The Intergalactic Lounge: *Barbarella* and Hearing the Future." In Bartkowiak 2010b.

Bartkowiak, Mathew J., ed. 2010b. *Sounds of the Future: Essays on Music in Science Fiction Film*. Jefferson, N.C.: McFarland.

Bates, Harry. 1940. "Farewell to the Master." *Astounding Science Fiction* 26 (2).

Benjamin, Walter. (1936) 1969. "The Work of Art in the Age of Mechanical Reproduction." In *Illuminations: Essays and Reflections*. Edited by Hannah Arendt. Translated by Harry Zohn. New York: Schocken.

Bereś, Stanisław. 1987. *Rozmowy ze Stanisławem*. Cracow: Wydawnictwo Literackie. English-language translation excerpted at http://english.lem.pl/arround-lem/adaptations/qsolarisq-by-tarkovsky/176-lem-about-the-tarkovskys-adaptation.

Billson, Anne. 1997. *The Thing*. London: BFI.

Bliss, Arthur. 1970. *As I Remember*. London: Faber & Faber.

Bogost, Ian. 2012. *Alien Phenomenology, or, What It's Like to Be a Thing*. Minneapolis: University of Minnesota Press.

Booker, M. Keith. 2006. *Alternate Americas: Science Fiction Film and American Culture*. Westport, Conn.: Praeger.

Boulenger, Gilles. 2003. *John Carpenter: The Prince of Darkness*. Los Angeles, Calif.: Silman-James Press.

Brend, Mark. 2012. *The Sound of Tomorrow: How Electronic Music Was Smuggled into the Mainstream*. New York: Bloomsbury Academic.

Brigden, Charlie. 2017. "The Great Unknown: The Story Behind Jerry Goldsmith's Score for *Alien*." Balder & Dash, May 17, 2017. https://www.roger

ebert.com/balder-and-dash/the-great-unknown-the-story-behind-jerry -goldsmiths-score-for-alien.

Broad, Lisa K. 2010. *"Aelita: Queen of Mars."* Senses of Cinema, April 2010. http://sensesofcinema.com/2010/cteq/aelita-queen-of-mars/.

Buhler, James. 2000. *"Star Wars,* Music, and Myth." In *Music and Cinema,* edited by James Buhler, Caryl Flinn, and David Neumeyer. Middletown, Conn.: Wesleyan University Press.

Bukatman, Scott. 1997. *Blade Runner.* London: BFI.

Burgess, Anthony. (1963) 2012. *A Clockwork Orange.* 50th anniversary edition. New York: Norton.

Burlingame, Jon. 2004a. "Composer Goldsmith Dead at 74." *Variety,* July 22, 2004.

Burlingame, Jon. 2004b. "Jerry Goldsmith: An Appreciation." Film Music Society, August 2, 2004. http://www.filmmusicsociety.org/news_events/features /2004/080204.html.

Burroughs, William S. (1961) 2004. "The Invisible Generation." In Cox and Warner 2004.

Burroughs, William S. (1970) 2001. *The Electronic Revolution.* Bonn: Expanded Media Editions.

Burroughs, William S. 1981. *Nothing Here Now but the Recordings.* LP. London: Industrial Records.

Burroughs, William S. 1986. "Origin and Theory of the Tape Cut-ups." *Break Through in Grey Room.* Sub Rosa.

Cage, John. (1937) 2004. "The Future of Music: Credo." In Cox and Warner 2004.

Cage, John. 1990. *I–VI.* Middleton, Conn.: Wesleyan University Press.

Carlos, Wendy. 2001. "First Report: *TRON* Remastered!" Wendy Carlos, December 2001. http://www.wendycarlos.com/+tron.html.

Chadabe, Joel. 1997. *Electronic Sound: The Past and Promise of Electronic Music.* Upper Saddle River, N.J.: Prentice Hall.

Chion, Michel. 1994. *Audio-Vision: Sound on Screen.* Translated by Claudio Gorbman. New York: Columbia University Press.

Chion, Michel. 2001. *Kubrick's Cinema Odyssey.* Translated by Claudia Gorbman. London: BFI.

Chion, Michel. 2009. *Film: A Sound Art.* Translated by Claudia Gorbman. New York: Columbia University Press.

Chtcheglov, Ivan. (1953) 2006. "Formulary for a New Urbanism." In *Situationist*

440 • BIBLIOGRAPHY

International Anthology, revised and expanded edition, translated by Ken Knabb. Berkeley, Calif.: Bureau of Public Secrets.

Clynes, Manfred E. (1970) 1995. "Cyborg II: Sentic Space Travel." In *The Cyborg Handbook,* edited by Chris Hables Gray, Heidi Figueroa-Sarriera, and Steven Mentor. New York: Routledge.

Clynes, Manfred E., and Nathan S. Kline. (1960) 1995. "Cyborgs and Space." In *The Cyborg Handbook,* edited by Chris Hables Gray, Heidi Figueroa-Sarriera, and Steven Mentor. New York: Routledge.

Conolly, Jez. 2013. *The Thing.* Leighton, U.K.: Auteur.

Corbett, John. 1994. *Extended Play: Sounding Off from John Cage to Dr. Funkenstein.* Durham, N.C.: Duke University Press.

Cormack, Mike. 2006. "The Pleasures of Ambiguity: Using Classical Music in Film." In *Changing Tunes: The Use of Pre-existing Music in Film,* edited by Phil Powrie and Robynn Stilwell. Aldershot, U.K.: Ashgate.

Coupland, Philip. 2000. "H. G. Wells's 'Liberal Fascism.'" *Journal of Contemporary History* 35.

Cowell, Henry. (1919) 1996. *New Musical Resources.* Cambridge: Cambridge University Press.

Cox, Christoph, and Daniel Warner, eds. 2004. *Audio Culture: Readings in Modern Music.* New York: Continuum.

Crab, Simon. n.d. "The 'ANS Synthesiser' Yevgeny Murzin. Russia, 1958." 120 Years of Electronic Music. http://120years.net/the-ans-synthesiser eugeniy-murzinsoviet-union1958-2/.

Csicsery-Ronay Jr., Istvan. 2008. *The Seven Beauties of Science Fiction.* Middletown, Conn.: Wesleyan University Press.

Csicsery-Ronay Jr., Istvan. 2010. "Sound Is the New Light." Review-essay of William Whittington, *Sound Design and Science Fiction* (2007). *Science Fiction Studies* 37. https://www.depauw.edu/sfs/review_essays/icr115.html.

Darke, Chris. 2005. *Alphaville.* Champaign: University of Illinois Press.

De Landa, Manuel. 1991. *War in the Age of Intelligent Machines.* New York: Zone Books.

Debord, Guy. (1955) 2006. "Introduction to a Critique of Urban Geography." In *Situationist International Anthology,* revised and expanded edition, translated by Ken Knabb. Berkeley, Calif.: Bureau of Public Secrets.

Debord, Guy. (1958) 2006. "Theory of the Dérive." In *Situationist International Anthology,* revised and expanded edition, translated by Ken Knabb. Berkeley, Calif.: Bureau of Public Secrets.

Deleon, Cara Marisa. 2010. "A Familiar Sound in a New Place: The Use of the Musical Score within the Science Fiction Film." In Bartkowiak 2010b.

Deleuze, Gilles. 1989. *Cinema 2: The Time-Image.* Translated by Hugh Tomlinson and Robert Galeta. Minneapolis: University of Minnesota Press.

Deleuze, Gilles, and Félix Guattari. 1987. *A Thousand Plateaus.* Translated by Brian Massumi. Minneapolis: University of Minnesota Press.

Deleuze, Gilles, and Félix Guattari. 1994. *What Is Philosophy?* Translated by Hugh Tomlinson and Graham Burchill. London: Verso.

Demers, Joanna. 2010. *Listening through the Noise: The Aesthetics of Experimental Electronic Music.* Oxford: Oxford University Press.

Donnelly, K. J. 2010. "Hearing Deep Seated Fears: John Carpenter's *The Fog* (1980)." In *Music in the Horror Film: Listening to Fear,* edited by Neil Lerner. New York: Routledge.

Doyle, Richard. 2011. *Darwin's Pharmacy: Sex, Plants, and the Evolution of the Noösphere.* Seattle: University of Washington Press.

Driscoll, Robert. (1963) 1995. "Engineering Man for Space: The Cyborg Study." In *The Cyborg Handbook,* edited by Chris Hables Gray, Heidi Figueroa-Sarriera, and Steven Mentor. New York: Routledge.

DuPont, Alexandra. 2004. "*THX-1138*: George Lucas Director's Cut." DVD Journal, 2004. http://www.dvdjournal.com/reviews/t/thx1138.shtml.

Dyson, Frances. 2009. *Sounding New Media: Immersion and Embodiment in the Arts and Culture.* Berkeley: University of California Press.

Elsaesser, Thomas. 2000. "Innocence Restored? Reading and Rereading a 'Classic.'" In Minden and Bachmann 2000.

Eno, Brian. 1996. *A Year with Swollen Appendices.* London: Faber & Faber.

Eno, Brian. 2004a. "Ambient Music." In Cox and Warner 2004.

Eno, Brian. 2004b. "The Studio as Compositional Tool." In Cox and Warner 2004.

Erickson, Glenn. 2000. Review of *First Spaceship on Venus.* DVD Savant. August 19, 2000. https://www.dvdtalk.com/dvdsavant/s138first.html.

Erickson, Glenn. 2002. Review of *Alphaville* (1965). DVD Savant, July 6, 2002. https://www.dvdtalk.com/dvdsavant/s549alpha.html.

Erickson, Glenn. 2010. "*Metropolis* and the Frame Rate Issue." DVD Savant, May 1, 2010. http://www.dvdtalk.com/dvdsavant/s3200frame.html.

Erickson, Glenn. 2011. *Sci-Fi Savant: Classic Sci-Fi Review Reader.* Rockville: Point Blank/Wildside Press.

442 • BIBLIOGRAPHY

Eshun, Kodwo. 1998. *More Brilliant than the Sun: Adventures in Sonic Fiction.* London: Quartet Books.

Fiegel, Todd E. 2003. "Bernard Herrmann as Musical Colorist: A Musicodramatic Analysis of His Score for *The Day the Earth Stood Still.*" *Journal of Film Music* 1 (2/3).

Fischinger, Oskar. 1932. "Klingende Ornamente." *Deutsche Allgemeine Zeitung, Kraft Und Stoff* 30 (July 28, 1932). http://www.centerforvisualmusic.org/Fischinger/SoundOrnaments.htm.

Fox, Jordan. 1980. "Walter Murch: Making Beaches Out of Grains of Sand." *Cinefex* 3 (December 1980).

Franklin, Peter. 2017. "Mystical Intimations, the Scenic Sublime, and the Opening of the Vault: De-classicizing the Late-romantic Revival in the Scoring of 'New Hollywood' Blockbusters c. 1977–1993." In *The Routledge Companion to Screen Music and Sound,* edited by Miguel Mera, Ronald Sadoff, and Ben Winters. New York: Routledge.

Frayling, Christopher. 1995. *Things to Come.* London: British Film Institute.

Freedman, Carl. 2000. *Critical Theory and Science Fiction.* Middletown, Conn.: Wesleyan University Press.

Frith, Simon. 1996. *Performing Rites: On the Value of Popular Music.* Cambridge, Mass.: Harvard University Press.

Frome, Jonathan. 2010. "'I Wasn't Expecting That!': Cognition and Shock in *Alien*'s (1979) Chestburster Scene." In *Film Moments: Criticism, History, Theory,* edited by Tom Brown and James Walters. London: BFI.

Gabbard, Krin and Shailja Sharma. 2003. "Stanley Kubrick and the Art Cinema." In McDougal 2003.

Gengaro, Christine Lee. 2013. *Listening to Stanley Kubrick: The Music in His Films.* Lanham, MD: Scarecrow Press.

Geselowitz, Michael. 2016. "The Masterpiece Behind the Music in *A Clockwork Orange.*" The Institute: The IEEE News Source, December 8, 2016. http://theinstitute.ieee.org/tech-history/technology-history/the-masterpiece-behind-the-music-in-a-clockwork-orange.

Gioia, Ted. 2012. Review of *Babel-17,* by Samuel R. Delany. Conceptual Fiction, March 31, 2012. http://www.conceptualfiction.com/.

Glinsky, Albert. 2005. *Theremin: Ether Music and Espionage.* Champaign: University of Illinois Press.

Golden, Barb. 1995. "Vortex 4, May 1958 (?), Program Notes, Typed by Barb Golden, 4/95 974w." http://www.o-art.org/history/50s&_60s/Vortex/Vortex_4.html.

Goodman, Steve. 2010. *Sonic Warfare: Sound, Affect, and the Ecology of Fear.* Cambridge, Mass.: MIT Press.

Guattari, Félix. 1992. *Chaosmosis: An Ethico-Aesthetic Paradigm.* Translated by Paul Bains and Julian Pefanis. Bloomington: Indiana University Press.

Guattari, Félix. 2011. *The Machinic Unconscious: Essays in Schizoanalysis.* Translated by Taylor Adkins. Los Angeles, Calif.: Semiotext(e).

Gunning, Tom. 1986. "The Cinema of Attraction: Early Film, Its Spectator and the Avant-Garde." *Wide Angle* 8. http://film110.pbworks.com/f/Gunning +Cinema+of+Attractions.pdf.

Hannan, Michael, and Melissa Carey. 2004. "Ambient Soundscapes in *Blade Runner.*" In Hayward 2004c.

Harper, Adam. 2011. *Infinite Music: Imagining the Next Millennium of Human Music-Making.* Tacoma, Wash.: Zero Books.

Harrison, Max, Eric Thacker and Stuart Nicholson. 2000. *The Essential Jazz Recordings, Vol. 2: Modernism to Postmodernism.* London: Mansell.

Harvey, Brian. 2007. *Russian Planetary Exploration: History, Development, Legacy, and Prospects.* Chichester, U.K.: Praxis.

Hayward, Philip. 1997. "Danger Retro-Affectivity! The Cultural Career of the Theremin." *Convergence* 3.

Hayward, Philip. 2004a. "Inter-planetary Soundclash: Music, Technology and Territorialisation in *Mars Attacks!*" In Hayward 2004c.

Hayward, Philip. 2004b. "Sci-Fidelity: Music, Sound and Genre History." In Hayward 2004c.

Hayward, Philip, ed. 2004c. *Off the Planet: Music, Sound, and Science Fiction Cinema.* New Barnet, U.K.: John Libbey.

Herrmann, Bernard. 1971. "The Colour of the Music: An Interview with Bernard Herrmann." Interview by Ted Gilling. *Sight and Sound* 41.

Hilliker, Lee. 2000. "The History of the Future in Paris: Chris Marker and Jean-Luc Godard in the 1960s." *Film Criticism* 24 (3).

Holmes, Thom. 2012. *Electronic and Experimental Music: Technology, Music, and Culture.* 4th ed. New York: Routledge.

Holmes, Thom. 2016. *Electronic and Experimental Music: Technology, Music, and Culture.* 5th ed. New York: Routledge.

Hosokawa, Shuhei. 2004. "Atomic Overtones and Primitive Undertones: Akira Ifukube's Sound Design for *Godzilla.*" In Hayward 2004c.

Husarik, Stephen. 2010. "Suspended Motion in the Title Scene from *The Day the Earth Stood Still.*" In Bartkowiak 2010b.

Jameson, Fredric. 1972. *Marxism and Form: Twentieth-Century Dialectical Theories of Literature*. Princeton, N.J.: Princeton University Press.

Jameson, Fredric. 1992. *Postmodernism, or, The Cultural Logic of Late Capitalism*. Durham, N.C.: Duke University Press.

Jameson, Fredric. 2005. *Archaeologies of the Future: The Desire Called Utopia and Other Science Fictions*. London: Verso.

Kahn, Douglas. 1999. *Noise, Water, Meat: A History of Sound in the Arts*. Cambridge, Mass.: MIT Press.

Kaminskij, Konstantin. 2011. "The Voice of Electricity in Early Soviet and East-European Science Fiction Movies." Paper presented at Electrified Voices: Medial, Socio-historical and Cultural Aspects of Voice Transfer, June 16–18, 2011, Konstanz, Germany.

Kaminskij, Konstantin. 2013. "The Voices of the Cosmos: Electronic Synthesis of Special Sound Effects in Soviet vs. American Science Fiction Movies from *Sputnik 1* to *Apollo 8*." In *Electrified Voices: Medial, Socio-historical and Cultural Aspects of Voice Transfer*, edited by N. Meise and D. Zakharine. Göttingen, Germany: V&R unipress.

Keefer, Cindy. 2008. "Raumlichtmusik—Early 20th Century Abstract Cinema, Immersive Environments." *Leonardo Electronic Almanac* 16 (6–7).

Kember, Sarah, and Joanna Zylinksa. 2012. *Life after New Media: Mediation as a Vital Process*. Cambridge, Mass.: MIT Press.

Kendall, Lukas, comp. 2001. "Vinyl Mail Bag." Film Score Monthly, August 15, 2001. http://filmscoremonthly.com/daily/article.cfm/articleID/3430/Vinyl-Mail-Bag/.

Kittler, Friedrich. 1999. *Gramophone, Film, Typewriter*. Translated by Geoffrey Winthrop-Young and Michael Wutz. Stanford, Calif.: Stanford University Press.

Kobayashi, A. 1998. *Ifukube Akira no Eiga Ongaku* [Akira Ifukube's film music]. Tokyo: Waizu Shuppan.

Konzett, Matthias. 2010. "Sci-Fi Film and Sounds of the Future." In Bartkowiak 2010b.

Kostelanetz, Richard. 2003. *Conversing with Cage*. 2nd ed. New York: Routledge.

Kramer, Peter. 2010. *2001: A Space Odyssey*. London: BFI.

Kreichi, Stanislav. 1997. "The ANS Synthesizer: Composing on a Photoelectronic Instrument." Theremin, November 10, 1997. http://www.theremin.ru/archive/ans.htm.

Kubrick, Stanley. 1972. "Now Kubrick Fights Back." Letter to *New York Times*, February 27, 1972.

BIBLIOGRAPHY • 445

Landon, Brooks. 2002. *Science Fiction after 1900: From the Steam Man to the Stars.* New York: Routledge.

Langdale, Allan. 2002. "Stimulation of Mind: The Film Theory of Hugo Münsterberg." In *Hugo Münsterberg on Film,* edited by Allan Langdale. New York: Routledge.

Langguth, Jerome J. 2010. "Proposing an Alter-Destiny: Science Fiction in the Art and Music of Sun Ra." In Bartkowiak 2010b.

Larson, Randall D. 1985. *Musique Fantastique: A Survey of Film Music in the Fantastic Cinema.* Lanham, Md.: Scarecrow Press..

Larson, Randall D. 2012. *Musique Fantastique.* 2nd ed., bk. 1. Sierra Madre, Calif.: Creature Features.

Latham, Rob. 2011. "A Journey beyond the Stars: *2001: A Space Odyssey* and the Psychedelic Revolution in 1960s Science Fiction." In *Science Fiction and the Prediction of the Future: Essays on Foresight and Fallacy,* edited by Gary Westfahl, Wong Kin Yuen, and Amy Kit-Sze Chan. Jefferson, N.C.: McFarland.

Lerner, Neil. 2004. "Nostalgia, Masculinist Discourse and Authoritarianism in John Williams' Scores for *Star Wars* and *Close Encounters of the Third Kind.*" In Hayward 2004c.

Lessour, Théo. 2013. "Decoder: Einstürzende Neubauten, Genesis P-Orridge and Sonic Terrorism." Red Bull Music Academy Daily, September 4, 2013. http://daily.redbullmusicacademy.com/2013/09/decoder -einsturzende-neubauten-sonic-terrorism.

Leydon, Rebecca. 1999. "Utopias of the Tropics: The Exotic Music of Les Baxter and Yma Sumac." In *Widening the Horizon: Exoticism in Post-war Popular Music,* edited by Philip Hayward. New Barnet, U.K.: John Libbey.

Leydon, Rebecca. 2004a. "*Forbidden Planet*: Effects and Affects in the Electro Avant Garde." In Hayward 2004c.

Leydon, Rebecca. 2004b. "Hooked on Aetherophonics: *The Day the Earth Stood Still.*" In Hayward 2004c.

Lilly, John C. 1966. "The Need for an Adequate Model of the Human End of the Interspecies Communication Program." Paper presented at 1965 IEEE Military Electronics Conference (MIL-E-CON 9), on Communication with Extraterrestrial Intelligence, Washington, D.C. *IEEE Spectrum* 3 (3).

Lilly, John C. 1968. *Programming and Metaprogramming in the Human Biocomputer.* New York: Julian Press.

Lock, Graham. 1999. *Bluetopia: Visions of the Future and Revisions of the Past in the Work of Sun Ra, Duke Ellington, and Anthony Braxton.* Durham, N.C.: Duke University Press.

446 • BIBLIOGRAPHY

Lopate, Phillip. 2011. "*Solaris*: Inner Space." Current (blog), The Criterion Collection. May 24, 2011. https://www.criterion.com/current/posts/239-solaris-inner-space.

Louv, Jason, ed. 2006. *Generation Hex*. New York: Disinformation Books.

Luckhurst, Roger. 2014. *Alien*. London: British Film Institute.

MacDonald, Scott. 1998. *A Critical Cinema 3: Interviews with Independent Filmmakers*. Berkeley: University of California Press.

Maeck, Klaus. 2008. "An Interview with Klaus Maeck." Interview by Jack Sargeant. In *Naked Lens: Beat Cinema*. Berkeley, Calif.: Soft Skull Press.

Maeck, Klaus, and Walter Hartmann, eds. 1984. *Decoder Handbuch*. Duisburg: Trikont Duisburg.

Manvell, Roger, and John Huntley. 1957. *The Technique of Film Music*. London: Focal Press.

Marché, Jordan. 2005. *Theaters of Time and Space: American Planetaria, 1930–1970*. New Brunswick, N.J.: Rutgers University Press.

Margolin, Uri. 2005. "Russian Formalism." In *The John Hopkins Guide to Literary Theory and Criticism*, 2nd ed., edited by Michael Groden, Martin Kreiswirth, and Imre Szeman Baltimore. Baltimore, Md.: John Hopkins University Press.

Martin, Tim. 2014. "Godzilla: Why the Japanese Original Is No Joke." *Telegraph*, May 15, 2014. http://www.telegraph.co.uk/culture/film/10788996/Godzilla-why-the-Japanese-original-is-no-joke.html.

Matthews, Melvin E. 2007. *1950s Science Fiction Films and 9/11: Hostile Aliens, Hollywood, and Today's News*. New York: Algora.

Maynes, Charles. 2003. "Mescherin Blasts Off: The Orchestra of Electro-Musical Instruments Swings the Sputnk Once Again." Transisions Online, January 15, 2003. http://www.tol.org/client/article/8346-mescherin-blasts-off.html.

Maynes, Charles. 2004. "File Under Soviet Bizarre: Vyacheslav Mescherin's Orchestra of Electro-Musical Instruments" (audio file). Third Coast International Audio Festival. https://www.thirdcoastfestival.org/explore/feature/file-under-soviet-bizarre-vyacheslav-mescherins-orchestra-of-electro-musical-instruments.

McDougal, Stuart Y., ed. 2003. *Stanley Kubrick's "A Clockwork Orange."* Cambridge: Cambridge University Press.

McEneany, Chris. 2010. "The *Andromeda Strain* Soundtrack (1971)." Review of *The Andromeda Strain* motion picture soundtrack. AV Forums, March 5, 2010. https://www.avforums.com/review/the-andromeda-strain-motion-picture-soundtrack-soundtrack-review.4122.

McGinney, William L. 2013. "Inside the Underscore for *Planet of the Apes*." In *"Planet of the Apes" and Philosophy: Great Apes Think Alike*, edited by John Huss. Chicago: Open Court.

McKenna, Terence. 1992. *The Archaic Revival*. San Francisco, Calif.: HarperCollins.

McLuhan, Marshall. (1964) 1994. *Understanding Media: The Extensions of Man*. Cambridge, Mass.: MIT Press.

Mellé, Gil. (1983) 2004. "Music à la Mellé." March 1983 interview with Gil Mellé. Interview by Randall D. Larson. Mania Sound Entertainment, November 11, 2004. https://web.archive.org/web/20120928104148/http://www.mania.com/music-la-melle_article_42953.html.

Metzer, David. 2003. *Quotation and Cultural Meaning in Twentieth-century Music*. Cambridge: Cambridge University Press.

Michelson, Annette. 1971. "Film and the Radical Aspiration." In *Film Culture: An Anthology*, edited by P. A. Sitney. London: Secker and Warburg.

Miller, Cynthia. 2010. "Seeing Beyond His Own Time: The Sounds of Jerry Goldsmith." In Bartkowiak 2010b.

Minden, Michael, and Holger Bachmann, eds. 2000. Introduction to *Fritz Lang's "Metropolis": Cinematic Visions of Technology and Fear*. Rochester, N.Y.: Camden House.

MisterScott99. 2007. "Incredible Sonovox—Kay Kyser—1940 film *You'll Find Out*." YouTube, July 30. https://www.youtube.com/watch?v=kH-krlgo2e8.

Moog, Robert. 1982. "Secrets behind the Soundtrack of *TRON*." *Keyboard*, November 1982. http://www.dix-project.net/item/1200/keyboard-magazine-secrets-behind-the-soundtrack-of-tron.

Moog, Robert. 2002. Foreword to *Analog Days: The Invention and Impact of the Moog Synthesizer*, by Trevor Pinch and Frank Trocco. Cambridge, Mass.: Harvard University Press.

Morton, Timothy. 2013. *Hyperobjects: Philosophy and Ecology after the End of the World*. Minneapolis: University of Minnesota Press.

Moylan, Tom. 2001. "'Look into the Dark': On Dystopia and the *Novum*." In *Learning from Other Worlds: Estrangement, Cognition, and the Politics of Science Fiction and Utopia*, edited by Patrick Parrinder. Durham, N.C.: Duke University Press.

Mulhall, Kevin. 1993. *Alex North's "2001": The Legendary Original Score*. VSD-5400. Varèse Sarabande Records.

Münsterberg, Hugo. (1916) 2002a. "Interview with Hugo Münsterberg." In *Hugo Münsterberg on Film*, edited by Allan Langdale. New York: Routledge.

448 • BIBLIOGRAPHY

Münsterberg, Hugo. (1916) 2002b. *The Photoplay: A Psychological Study.* In *Hugo Münsterberg on Film,* edited by Allan Langdale. New York: Routledge.

Nietzsche, Friedrich. 2006. *The Genealogy of Morals.* Edited by K. Ansell-Pearson. Translated by C. Diethe. Cambridge: Cambridge University Press.

O'Donnell, Liam A. 2007. "Preserving the Possibility of the Impossible." Review of Fredric Jameson, *Archaeologies of the Future. The Desire Called Utopia and Other Science Fictions* (2005). *Cosmos and History* 3. http://cosmosand history.org/index.php/journal/article/view/62/124.

Oron, Aryeh. 2012. "Andrzej Markowski (Conductor)." Bach Cantatas, April 2012. http://www.bach-cantatas.com/Bio/Markowski-Andrzej.htm.

Parrinder, Patrick. 2001. "Introduction: Learning from Other Worlds." In *Learning from Other Worlds: Estrangement, Cognition, and the Politics of Science Fiction and Utopia,* edited by Patrick Parrinder. Durham, N.C.: Duke University Press.

Patalas, Enno. 2000. "The City of the Future: A Film of Ruins." In Minden and Bachmann 2000.

Phillips, Gene D. 2016. "Music in *2001: A Space Odyssey.*" In *The Stanley Kubrick Archives,* edited by Alison Castle. Cologne: Taschen.

Pickren, Wade E., and Alexandra Rutherford. 2010. *A History of Modern Psychology in Context.* Hoboken, N.J.: John Wiley & Sons.

Pinch, Trevor, and Frank Trocco. 2002. *Analog Days: The Invention and Impact of the Moog Synthesizer.* Cambridge, Mass.: Harvard University Press.

Pisters, Patricia. 2006. "The Spiritual Dimension of the Brain as Screen Zigzagging from Cosmos to Earth (and Back)." In *Screen Consciousness: Cinema, Mind and World,* edited by Robert Pepperell and Michael Punt. Amsterdam: Rodopi.

Polt, Harriet and Roger Sandall. 1961. "Outside the Frame." *Film Quarterly* 14 (3).

P-Orridge, Genesis. 1983. "Muzak: A Concept in Human Engineering." Oxxiuros, May 1983. http://oxxiuros.tumblr.com/post/53386447201/muzak -a-concept-in-human-engineering-by-genesis.

P-Orridge, Genesis. (1987) 2010. "Behavioural Cut-ups and Magick." In *Thee Psychick Bible: Thee Apocryphal Scriptures Ov Genesis Breyer P-Orridge.* Port Townsend, Wash.: Feral House.

Powell, Anna. 2007. *Deleuze, Altered States, and Film.* Edinburgh: Edinburgh University Press.

Rabinowitz, Peter J. 2003. "'A Bird of Like Rarest Spun Heavenmetal': Music in *A Clockwork Orange.*" In *Stanley Kubrick's* A Clockwork Orange, edited by Stuart Y. McDougal. Cambridge: Cambridge University Press.

Rathford, Ivan. 2014. *Music in Film: The Sound of Godzilla, from 1954 to 2014.* Den of Geek, June 9, 2014. http://www.denofgeek.com/movies/music-in-film/30787/music-in-film-the-sound-of-godzilla-from-1954-to-2014.

Redner, Gregg. 2011. *Deleuze and Film Music: Building a Methodological Bridge between Film Theory and Music.* Bristol, U.K.: Intellect.

Reinert, Al. 1979. "Moon Struck." *Texas Monthly,* July 1979.

Riley, Matthew. 2010. "Music for the Machines of the Future: H. G. Wells, Arthur Bliss, and *Things to Come,* 1936." In *British Music and Modernism, 1895–1960,* edited by Matthew Riley. Burlington, Vt.: Ashgate Publishing.

Rockmore, Clara. 2002. "In Clara's Words: An Interview with Clara Rockmore." Interviewed by Robert Moog. Theremin Vox, October 26, 2002. https://www.thereminvox.com/article/articleview/21.html.

Romney, Jonathan. 2007. "*La Jetée*: Unchained Melody." Current (blog), The Criterion Collection. June 25, 2007. https://www.criterion.com/current/posts/485-la-jetee-unchained-melody.

Rosar, William H. 1994. "Film Music and Heinz Werner's Theory of Physiognomic Perception." *Psychomusicology* 13.

Rosar, William H. 2006. "Music for Martians: Schillinger's Two Tonics and Harmony of Fourths in Leith Stevens' Score for *War of the Worlds* (1953)." *Journal of Film Music* 1.

Ross, Alex. 2007. *The Rest Is Noise: Listening to the Twentieth Century.* New York: Picador.

Roud, Richard. 1966. Introduction to *Alphaville: A Film by Jean-Luc Godard,* by Jean-Luc Godard. Translated by Peter Whitehead. London: Lorrimer.

Roussel, Bertrand. 1989. "Courbes et subversion esthétique: une approche plastique d'Alphaville." *CinémAction* 52.

Rózsa, Miklós. 1983. *Double Life: The Autobiography of Miklós Rózsa.* New York: Hippocrene.

Russian Orthodox Cathedral Choir of Paris, dir. Petr Spassky. 2015. "Tropaire En L'Honneur De La Sainte Croix." *Musique Liturgique Russe.* Philips L 00.402 L.

Russolo, Luigi. (1916) 1986. "The Art of Noises, Futurist Manifesto." In *The Art of Noises.* Translated by Barclay Brown. New York: Pendragon Press.

Ryfle, Steve. 1998. *Japan's Favorite Mon-star: The Unauthorized Biography of "The Big G."* Toronto: ECW Press.

Sadler, Simon. 1998. *The Situationist City.* Cambridge, Mass.: MIT Press.

Schaeffer, Pierre. 1987. "An Interview with Pierre Schaeffer: Pioneer of

450 • BIBLIOGRAPHY

Musique Concrète." Interview by Tim Hodgkinson. *RēR Quarterly* 2 (1). http://timhodgkinson.co.uk/schaeffer.pdf.

Schaeffer, Pierre. 2006. "Acousmatics." In Cox and Warner 2004.

Schaeffer, Pierre. 2017. *Treatise on Musical Objects: An Essay across Disciplines.* Translated by Christine North and John Dack. Berkeley: University of California Press.

Schmidt, Lisa. 2010. "A Popular Avant-Garde: The Paradoxical Tradition of Electronic and Atonal Sound in Sci-Fi Music Scoring." In Bartkowiak 2010b.

Schuller, George. 1986. *Musings: The Musical Worlds of Gunther Schuller.* Oxford: Oxford University Press.

Scorekeeper. 2011. "ScoreKeeper May or May Not Be the thing but BSX Records Latest Release Definitely Is" Ain't It Cool, October 15, 2011. http://www.aintitcool.com/node/51587.

Scott, Ridley. 1979. "Making Alien: Behind the Scenes." Interview by Mark Patrick Carducci. *Cinefantastique* 9 (1).

Shaviro, Steven. 2003. *Connected, or What It Means to Live in the Network Society.* Minneapolis: University of Minnesota Press.

Shaviro, Steven. 2010. *Post-cinematic Affect.* Winchester, U.K.: Zero Books.

Shklovsky, Viktor. (1917) 1998. "Art as Technique." In *Literary Theory: An Anthology,* edited by Julie Rivkin and Michael Ryan. New York: Blackwell.

Siddiqi, Asif A. 2010. *The Red Rockets' Glare: Spaceflight and the Soviet Imagination, 1857–1957.* Cambridge: Cambridge University Press.

Silverman, Kaja, and Harun Farocki. 1998. *Speaking about Godard.* New York: New York University Press.

Smirnov, Andrey. 2013. *Sound in Z: Experiments in Sound and Electronic Music in Early Twentieth Century Russia.* London: Sound and Music/Koenig Books.

Smith, Steven C. 1991. *A Heart at Fire's Center: The Life and Music of Bernard Herrmann.* Berkeley: University of California Press.

Sneyd, Steve. 2010. "Lining Up on the Precipice: The Shape and Role of Poetry in Brian Aldiss' *Barefoot in the Head.*" The Zone, 2010. http://www.zone-sf.com/bithaldiss.html.

Sobchack, Vivian. 1987. *Screening Space: The American Science Fiction Film.* 2nd ed. New Brunswick, N.J.: Rutgers University Press.

Sotiropoulos, Konstantinos. 2010. "Miklós Rózsa: The Midas Touch." International Film Critics Association, November 25, 2010. http://filmmusiccritics.org/ifmca-legends/miklos-rozsa/.

Spring, Katherine. 2010. "*Just Imagine:* The Musical Effacement of Dystopia in an Early Sound Film." In Bartkowiak 2010b.

Stafford, P. G., and B. H. Golightly. 1967. *LSD: The Problem-Solving Psychedelic*. New York: Award Books.

Stanley, Thomas. 2014. *The Execution of Sun Ra*. Shelbyville, Ky.: Wasteland Press.

Steele, Jack. (1960) 1995. "How Do We Get There?" In *The Cyborg Handbook*, edited by Chris Hables Gray, Heidi Figueroa-Sarriera, and Steven Mentor. New York: Routledge.

Steinberg, Aaron. 2002. "Gil Mellé: Instrumental Inventions." *Jazz Times*, December 1, 2002. https://jazztimes.com/departments/overdue-ovation/gil-melle-instrumental-inventions/.

Steinberg, Rick. 2001. "Hexagonal Music: How I Manufactured the *Andromeda Strain* Soundtrack LP." *Film Score Monthly*. August 16, 2001.

Stiller, Andrew. 1991. "The Music in *Blade Runner*." In *Retrofitting Blade Runner*, 2nd ed., edited by Judith Kerman. Madison: University of Wisconsin Press.

Stites, Richard. 1992. *Russian Popular Culture: Entertainment and Society since 1900*. Cambridge: Cambridge University Press.

Stockford, Darren. 2011. "Alan Howarth on Morricone's Score for *The Thing*." Darren Stockford: A Collection of Words and Pictures, September 7, 2011. http://www.darrenstockford.com/2011/09/alan-howarth-on-morricones-score-for-the-thing/.

Stockhausen, Karlheinz. 1995. "Advice to Clever Children." Interview by Dick Witts. *The Wire*, no. 141.

Suvin, Darko. 1979. *Metamorphoses of Science Fiction*. New Haven, Conn.: Yale University Press.

Suvin, Darko. 1988. *Positions and Presuppositions in Science Fiction*. Kent, Ohio: Kent State University Press.

Szwed, John. 1998. *Space Is the Place: The Lives and Times of Sun Ra*. New York: Da Capo Press.

Tarkovsky, Andrei. 1971. Interview conducted with Andreiem Tarkovskim by Nikolai Abramov in Moscow, 1970–71. English-language translation of an anonymous Polish translation excerpted at http://english.lem.pl/arround-lem/adaptations/qsolarisq-by-tarkovsky/178-tarkovsky-about-qsolarisq.

Tarkovsky, Andrei. 1972. "Ziemska moralność w kosmosie, czyli *Solaris* na ekranie." Interview by Zbigniew Podgórzec. *Tygodnik Powszechny* 42. https://people.ucalgary.ca/~tstronds/nostalghia.com/TheTopics/On_Solaris.html.

Tarkovsky, Andrei. 1989. *Sculpting in Time: Reflections on Cinema*. Translated by Kitty Hunter-Blair. Austin: University of Texas Press.

452 • BIBLIOGRAPHY

Tarkovsky, Andrey. 1999. *Collected Screenplays*. London: Faber & Faber.

Taylor, Timothy. 2001. *Strange Sounds: Music, Technology, and Culture*. New York: Routledge.

Telotte, J. P. 1999. *A Distant Technology: Science Fiction Film and the Machine Age*. Middletown, Conn.: Wesleyan University Press.

Tibbetts, John. 2010. "*Rocketship X-M*: The Sounds of a Martian Breeze." In Bartkowiak 2010b.

Tikka, Pia. 2006. "Cinema as Externalization of Consciousness." In *Screen Consciousness: Cinema, Mind, and World*, edited by Robert Pepperell and Michael Punt. Amsterdam: Rodopi.

Toop, David. 1995. *Ocean of Sound: Aether Talk, Ambient Sound and Imaginary Worlds*. London, U.K.: Serpent's Tail.

Underman. n.d. "Andrey Tarkovsky's *Solaris*." Pure Film. http://www .menggang.com/movie/russia/tarkovsky/solaris/e-solaris-g.html.

"Vangelis Scoring Blade Runner." n.d. Nemo Studios. http://www.nemostudios .co.uk/nemo/sections/br/br04.htm.

Vague, Tom. 1985. "*Decoder*: The Sound of Muzak." *ZigZag*, February 1985. http://history-is-made-at-night.blogspot.com/2008/09/decoder-sound -of-muzak.html.

Voegelin, Salomé. 2010. *Listening to Noise and Silence*. London: Continuum.

Volodin, Andrei. 1997. "Ekvodin synthesizer." Theremin, November 10, 1997. http://www.theremin.ru/archive/volodin.htm.

Vuillermoz, Emile. 1928. "Music and the Ether Waves." *Christian Science Monitor*, January 21, 1928.

Waksman, Steve. 1999. *Instruments of Desire: The Electric Guitar and the Shaping of Musical Experience*. Cambridge, Mass.: Harvard University Press.

Walker, Alexander. 1971. *Stanley Kubrick Directs*. New York: Harcourt Brace Jovanovich.

Wells, H. G. 1929. *The King Who Was a King: An Unconventional Novel*. Toronto: Gundy.

Wells, H. G. 1935. *Things to Come: A Film Story Based on the Material Contained in His History of the Future "The Shape of Things to Come."* London: Cresset Press.

West, Phil. 1989. "Decoder." *UW's Blood, Love, and Rhetoric—The Daily of the University of Wisconsin*, October 20, 1989. http://decoder.cultd.net/press .htm#press.

Whittington, William. 2007. *Sound Design and Science Fiction*. Austin: University of Texas Press.

Wiener, Norbert. (1954) 1988. *The Human Use of Human Beings: Cybernetics and Society.* Boston: De Capo Press.

Wierzbicki, James. 2002. "Weird Vibrations: How the Theremin Gave Musical Voice to Hollywood's Extraterrestrial 'Others.'" *Journal of Popular Film and Television* 30 (3).

Wierzbicki, James. 2005. *Louis and Bebe Barron's Forbidden Planet: A Film Score Guide.* Lanham, Md.: Scarecrow Press.

Wierzbicki, James. 2009. *Film Music: A History.* New York: Routledge.

Williams, John. 1998. "An Interview with John Williams." Interview by Laurent Bouzereau. *The Collector's Edition Soundtrack: Close Encounters of the Third Kind.* Arista Records.

Yanow, Scott. n.d. Review of *Gil's Guests,* by the Gil Mellé Quartet/Gil Mellé. https://www.allmusic.com/album/gils-guests-mw0000312424.

Yegorova, Tatiana. 1997. *Soviet Film Music: An Historical Survey.* Amsterdam: Harwood Academic.

Youngblood, Denise J. 1994. "The Return of the Native: Yakov Protazanov and Soviet Cinema." In *Inside the Film Factory: New Approaches to Russian and Soviet Cinema,* edited by Richard Taylor and Ian Christie. London: Routledge.

Youngblood, Gene. 1970. *Expanded Cinema.* New York: Dutton.

Zepke, Stephen. 2012. "Beyond Cognitive Estrangement." *European Journal of Media Studies* (NECSUS), November 22, 2012. https://necsus-ejms.org/beyond-cognitive-estrangement-the-future-of-science-fiction-cinema/.

Zuberi, Nabeel. 2004. "The Transmolecularization of Black Folk: *Space Is the Place,* Sun Ra, and Afrofuturism." In Hayward 2004c.

Index

acid cinematiques, 269–70

"Acid Head Wars" (Aldiss), 195

Aelita: Queen of Mars (film), 44, 46–48, 50, 208

aestheticized politics, 289

After the Gold Rush (album), 305

Agel, Jerome, 263

Age of Electronicus, The (film), 251

Aldiss, Brian, 195–97

Algeria conflict: French new wave cinema and, 225–26

Alien (1979 film), 39, 246, 361–62, 365–83

alien psychogeography: in *Solaris*, 286, 328–30; sonic novums and, 191–92; in *Space is the Place*, 336–43

Aliens (1986 film), 202

Allen, Ioan, 312

Alpert, Herb, 249

Alphaville: A Strange Adventure of Lemmy Caution (film), 6, 39; Lettrist and situationist philos-

ophies in, 120; *Solaris* and, 320; sound design in, 193–94, 225–26, 231–44

"Also sprach Zarathustra" (Strauss), 262, 266–67, 348, 428

"Ambient Music" (Eno), 224–25

American Graffiti (film), 294

American International Pictures (AIP), 192–93, 203–4, 212, 218, 220–25

American Psychological Association, 63

Amok (film), 407

Ampex tape recorder, 164

Anderson, Michael, 369

Andromeda Strain, The (film), 39, 285, 290, 295–304

"Angel Is Love, An" (song), 251, 262

Animalympics (film), 389

animation: in *TRON*, 390–91

Ankrum, Morris, 101

ANS synthesizer, 4, 54, 217; in *Solaris*, 286–87, 319–25, 328, 330

• 455

456 • INDEX

Ant, Adam, 49
Antheil, George, 53, 56
Antonioni, Michelangelo, 250
Apocalypse Now (film), 294
Apollo. See *For All Mankind*
Apollo: Atmospheres & Soundtracks (album), 426
Appollinaire, Guillaume, 44
"Aquarius" (song), 252
Archaeologies of the Future (Jameson), 11–12
Armstrong, Neil, 428
Arness, James, 140
Arnold, Jack, 96, 139–40
ARP 2500 and 2600 modular synthesizer, 354, 369
"Art as Technique" (Shklovsky), 331
Artemiev, Edward, 54, 121, 216–17; *Solaris* score and, 286, 316–17, 319–28, 333–35; *TRON* and, 391
"Art of Noises, The" (Russolo), 56–57
As I Remember (Bliss), 82
Astounding Science Fiction (magazine), 132–33
Astronautics (magazine), 181
Astronauts, The (Lem), 209
Astro-Sounds from Beyond the Year 2000 (album), 251
Atom Heart Mother (album), 305
atonal music, 5; in film, 113–14, 118
Augé, Marc, 237–38
auteur filmmaking, 6
authenticity: in science fiction film, 102–3, 403–7
Autry, Gene, 71–72
avant-garde: electronic music and, 86–87; sound technology and,

52–60; visual effects in science fiction films and, 356–60
Avraamov, Arseny, 53–57

Babel-17 (Delany), 197
Bach, Johann Sebastian, 259, 315, 321–23
Bacharach, Burt, 251
Balázs, Béla, 24–25
Ball, Dave, 414
Ballard, J. G., 194, 244–45, 247–48, 424
Ballet Mécanique (Antheil), 53
Banionis, Donatas, 316
Barbarella (film), 39, 201, 248–62, 270, 290
"Barbarella" (song), 251
Barefoot in the Head (Aldiss), 195–97
Barrandov Studios, 218
Barrett, Syd, 198
Barron, Bebe and Louis, 5, 56, 97–98, 153–59, 164–77, 301, 346
Barry, John, 344
Barry, Robert, 209, 219, 331
Bartkowiak, Mathew J., 7–8, 255–57
Bartók, Bela, 278
Basics of Psychotechnology (Münsterberg), 63
Bates, Harry, 129–35
Battle Beyond the Stars (film), 344, 353
Battle Beyond the Sun (film), 203–4
Battlestar Galactica (film), 344
Bava, Mario, 220
Baxter, Les: *Barbarella* and, 253; pop music and, 89, 251, 428; Soviet films and, 143, 215; *2001* and, 199

Solaris, 315–35; Soviet films and, 201–5, 212–14
Coleman, Ornette, 339
Coltrane, Alice, 339
Coltrane, John, 339
Columbo (television series), 297
Communication with Extraterrestrial Intelligence panel, 168
Comstock, Frank, 252
Coney, John, 120, 335–43
Conolly, Jez, 379
Conquest of Space (film), 201–2, 212
Constantine, Eddy, 232–33
Conversation, The (film), 294
Copland, Aaron, 125
Coppola, Francis, 203–4, 293–95
Corman, Roger, 143, 192, 203–4, 221, 223–25, 344
"Cosmic Capers" (song), 252
Cosmic Man, The (film), 142
Cosmic Music (album), 339
cosmic philosophy: cinema and, 66–72; music and, 34–39; sonic becoming and, 365–67
Cowell, Henry, 116–17
Cozzi, Luigi, 344
credibility: in science fiction film, 102–3
Crewe, Bob, 251, 256–57
critical theory: novum and, 11
Cronenberg, David, 298
Crowley, Aleister, 420
Crown International Pictures, 193, 212, 223
Crumar GDS, 391–98
Cry of Jazz (documentary), 336
Csicsery-Ronay, Istvan, Jr., 12–16, 18–19, 27–29, 197, 319
Cuba Si!, 225

cybernetics: in *Alphaville*, 231–44; in *Blade Runner*, 363; in *Forbidden Planet*, 156–77; music and, 35–36; in *TRON*, 363; Vortex Concerts and, 187–89
Cybernetics, Or Control and Communication in the Animal and the Machine (Weiner), 98–99, 156, 166
cyborg novum, 105
cyborg ritual: Vortex Concerts and, 179–89
"Cyborgs and Space" (Clynes), 180
"Cyborg II" (Clynes), 180–81

Daily News (Los Angeles), 106
Darke, Chris, 237–38, 242
Darwin's Pharmacy (Doyle), 200–201
Daves, Delmer, 127
Davis, Miles, 225
Day the Earth Stood Still, The (film), 5, 39, 93, 95–96; aliens in, 140; nuclear war in, 101, 149, 209; psychotechnology and, 155; sound design in, 110, 123, 127–39, 148, 217, 280; theremin in, 128–39
Debord, Guy, 119–20
Debussy, Claude, 45
Decoder (film), 39–40, 120, 362–65, 407–24
Decoder Handbuch (Maeck), 407
"Deep Blue Day," 429
déjà entendu, 433–34
Delany, Samuel R., 197
Deleon, Cara Marisa, 354, 396
Deleuze, Gilles: cybernetics and, 98–99, 174–75; on deterritorialization, 33, 143, 254, 257–58, 261–62, 303–4; on dystopia, 14; on hallucinogenics, 196; on

460 • INDEX

machinic unconsciousness, 274–75; on music and sound, 25–27; music and work of, 36–37; on noise, 170–71; time-image of, 399

Dell, Monica, 297

Dell'Orso, Edda, 250

Del Val, Jean, 245

Demers, Joanna, 32, 122

Der Geist des Films (Balázs), 25

Derrida, Jacques, 364

Der Schweigende Stern (The Silent Star) (film), 48, 208–15, 219

Deslaw, Eugene, 58

Destination Moon (film), 91–94; influence of, 201–2, 212, 434; sound design in, 99–105, 108–10, 212, 330, 383–84, 427; technological filter in, 118–19, 362

Détective (film), 236

Dick, Philip K., 384, 401–3

Die Arche (film), 43

diegetic soundscapes, 6; in *Alien,* 368–69; in *Alphaville,* 242–44; in *Blade Runner,* 385–88, 400–407; in *For All Mankind,* 428–34; in *Metropolis,* 68–72; psychotechnology and, 97–99; Sonovox processing and, 103–5; in *Things to Come,* 77–84

difference: novum and forms of, 14–17

digital technology: sonic novum and, 40–41

Dinosaurus (film), 222

Disneyland (television series), 201–2

Disney Studios, 244–45, 357, 362–63, 365, 388–98, 400–401

Distant Galaxy (album), 251–52

Do Androids Dream of Electric Sheep? (Dick), 384, 401

Doctor Who (television and radio series), 296

Dodds, Phil, 354

Dolan, Robert E., 123

Dolby sound, 311–13, 358–60, 368, 372–73, 378–79

Dolphy, Eric, 298–99, 339

Donen, Stanley, 344

Donnelly, K. J., 380–83

"Doomsday Machine," 300

Doroga k Zvekdam (The Way to the Stars) (film), 201–2

Downbeat (magazine), 106

Doyle, Richard, 200–201, 258, 267–68, 276

Dreyfus, Richard, 351

Driscoll, Robert W., 180

Dullea, Keir, 271

Duncan, Trevor, 228

DuPont, Alexandra, 291

Dvořák, Anton, 428

Dvorzhetsky, Vladislav, 316

Dylan, Bob, 198

Dyrygent (film), 209

Dyson, Frances, 33, 38, 366–67

dystopian vision: novum and, 14–17

E-actions, 182–83

Eastern bloc films, 46–48, 192–93, 201–8. *See also* Soviet films

East of Eden (film), 246

Echo and Narcissus (Lawrence), 373

Echoplex processor, 276–77, 370, 378

"Effects Generator," 299–300

Eimert, Herbert, 22, 160, 171

Einstürzende Neubauten, 419
Ekvodin synthesizer, 206–7
electric acid rock, 199
electric violin, 142
Electrio (group), 3
Electro-Musical Instruments ensemble, 215
electronic instruments: in *Andromeda Strain*, 295–304; in *Blade Runner*, 386–87; in *Close Encounters*, 354–55; early generations of, 4; emergence of, 5, 58, 107; in *Forbidden Planet*, 156–77; in *Rocketship X-M*, 106; in science fiction cinema, 120–23, 142–43; in Soviet films, 206–8; in *Space is the Place*, 338–43; Vortex Concerts and, 178–89
electronic music: absence of in American science fiction films, 221; in *Barbarella*, 250–62; decline in film of, 193–94; emergence of, 159–63, 252–62; in *Forbidden Planet*, 153; musique concrète and, 242; psychotechnology and, 32–39, 403–7; in science fiction film, 14–17, 88–90, 286; in *Solaris*, 320–25, 332–35; sonic novum and, 17–24; in Soviet films, 206–8; in *Star Wars*, 347–50; Vortex concerts and, 178
"Electronic Revolution, The" (Burroughs), 412, 423–24
elektronische Musik, 22–24, 157–63, 278–83
Electro-Theremin, 143, 157, 252
Elgar, Edward, 76, 308
Elkind, Rachel, 312–13, 389

Ellington, Duke, 296
Ellwood, Robert S., 264
Elsaesser, Thomas, 50
Éluard, Paul, 240
Emge, Charles, 106
Emory, John, 111
Empire Strikes Back, The (film), 388
"Engineering Man for Space" (Driscoll), 180
English Chamber Choir, 386
Eno, Brian, 224–26, 298, 341, 418, 421, 425–34
Eno, Roger, 425
Erickson, Glenn, 212–13, 244
Escape from New York (film), 381–82
Eshun, Kodwo, 421
Essentials of Behavior (Hull), 166
etherphone, 1–2. *See also* theremin
E.T. the Extraterrestrial (film), 344, 353
Evans, Christopher, 196–97
Ewers, Heinz, 326
expressionist movement, 61–72

Fantastic Voyage (film), 39, 244–48, 281, 296
"Farewell to the Master" (Bates), 129–35
fictive novum: in *Aelita*, 46–48; science fiction film and, 8–17
Fifth Symphony (Beethoven), 313
Film Quarterly, 179
fingerboard theremin, 4
First All-Russian Conference on Music, 67–68
First Men in the Moon, The (films), 43
First Spaceship on Venus (film), 212–13

462 • INDEX

Fischinger, Oskar, 54–56
Fleischer, Richard, 245
"Flight of the Bumblebee" (Rimsky-Korsakov), 88
Flying Lotus, 34
Flynn, Errol, 344
Fog, The (film), 377–78, 380–81
Fonda, Jane, 256
For All Mankind (documentary), 40, 184, 362–65, 418, 425–34
Forbidden Planet (film), 5, 39, 97–99, 153–77, 191, 211–12, 298–99, 398
Ford, Harrison, 384
Ford Exposition (New York World's Fair 1939), 107
"Formulary for a New Urbanism" (Chtcheglov), 119–20
Foucault, Michel, 14
"Four Moons" (Mellé), 297
...*4...3...2...1...Morte (Mission Stardust)* (film), 250
Fox, Charles, 251
fox-trots: in *Metropolis,* 67–72
fractals: in *Blade Runner* sound design, 398–400
Frankenstein, Alfred, 179
Freedman, Carl, 327–28
free jazz, 339
Fremer, Michael, 389–98
French new wave cinema, 193–94, 225–26
French Radio Institution, 22
French science fiction films, 225–31. *See also specific films*
Freud (film), 246, 370
Frith, Simon, 125
Frome, Jonathan, 379
Funkadelic (band), 341

Furtseva, Ekaterina, 215
"Future of Music, The" (Cage), 55

Gabbard, Krin, 311–12
Gagarin, Yuri, 208, 216
Gamma One quadrilogy (Marghereti), 250
Gance, Abel, 59–60
"Gayane Ballet Suite (Adagio)" (Khachaturian), 271
gender: in *Barbarella,* 253–54
Geneaology of Morals, The (Nietzsche), 240
Gengaro, Christine Lee, 308–10, 313–14
George, Stefan, 113
Germany Year 90 Nine Zero (film), 233
Gershwin, George, 296
Gertz, Irving, 142
Geselowitz, Michael, 311–12
Gigantis, the Fire Monster (film), 150
Gilman, Lawrence, 1–2
Gil's Guests (album), 296
Gioia, Ted, 197–98
Giombini, Marcello, 250
Giraud, Jean, 390
"Girl, The (Prologue)," 228
"Girl, The (Theme)," 228
Glasser, Albert, 92, 106–7, 110, 114, 121–22
Glinksy, Albert, 87
glissandi (glissando) technique, 113–15; environmental noise studies and, 114–16
Glitterhouse, The (band), 251
Godard, Jean-Luc, 6, 39, 120; and *Alphaville,* 193–94, 225–26, 231–44, 320

Godzilla. See *Gojira*

Godzilla: King of the Monsters! (film), 151

Godzilla Raids Again (film), 150

Gog (film), 212

Gojira (film), 5, 39, 96–98, 146–53, 191, 361–62

Goldsmith, Jerry: *Alien* score by, 361–62, 368–83; *Freud* score by, 246, 370; *Planet of the Apes* and, 273–83, 368; *Star Trek* score by, 344; *2001* and, 265, 267

Golightly, B. H., 269–70

Goodman, Steve: on affective tonality, 359, 372, 433; on audio virology, 193; *déjà entendu* concept of, 359, 433; on Muzak, 431; on predatory capitalism, 223, 304, 359; on sonic warfare, 282–83; on territorialization, 33; on "uneasy listening," 372

"Good Vibrations" (song), 143

Grainger, Percy, 86–87

Gran Concerto Futuristico (Russolo), 57

Grand Canyon Suite (Grofé), 91–92

Grateful Dead (band), 249

Green Hornet, The (radio program), 87–88

Green Woman, The (film), 222

Grimaldi, Hugo, 212–13

Grofé, Ferde, 91–92, 106–7, 114

Groupe de Recherche de Musique Concrète (GRMC), 22–23

Grundzüge der Psychotechnic (Münsterberg), 24

Guattari, Félix: Chaosmosis concept and, 167–68, 399–400; cybernetics and, 98–99; on deterritorialization, 33, 143, 254, 257–58, 261–62, 303–4; on dystopia, 14; "fractal machine" of, 399; on hallucinogenics, 196; on hypersensitivities, 201, 248–49; on the machinic unconscious, 33, 248–49, 274–76, 343; music and work of, 36–37; on noise, 170–71; on sound and music, 429; on subjectivity, 33

Gugusse et l'Automate (film), 43

Gunning, Tom, 356–57

Gysin, Brion, 412, 420

Haggard, Merle, 428

Hair (musical), 252

Hal Hope Orchestra, 90

Halloween (film), 381

Hammond Novachord, 4, 107–8, 117–18, 142, 155–56

Hanich, Davos, 226–27

Hanson, Howard, 370

Hardwicke, Cedric, 80

Harper, Adam, 37, 367

Harrington, Curtis, 222

Hartmann, Walter, 420

Hartstone, Graham, 397–98

Hashimoto, Koji, 344

Hathaway, Robert, 369

Hauer, Rutger, 405

Hawkwind (band), 34, 195, 249

Hayward, Philip, 6, 7–8, 18, 72, 103, 112, 139, 144

Heaven 17 (band), 305

Heinlein, Robert, 102

Helm, Brigette, 51

Helmholtz, Hermann von, 115, 247

Hemmings, David, 255

Hendrix, Jimi, 341, 421

464 • INDEX

Herrmann, Bernard, 5, 96, 110, 125–26, 135–39, 147–49, 280, 301
"Hex" (Mellé), 303
Hilliker, Lee, 226–31
Hills, Gillian, 305
Himmelskibet (film), 43, 46
His Master's Voice (Lem), 197
Hitchcock, Alfred, 123
Hodgkinson, Tim, 278
Hoffman, Samuel J., 89–90, 92, 95, 124, 142–43, 428
Holliman, Earl, 177
Hollywood Reporter, 106
Holm, Ian, 369
Holst, Gustav, 345–47, 369
"Homeward Bound" (Glasser), 121
Honda, Ishirō, 96–98
Honegger, Arthur, 219–20
Hope, Hal, 89–90
Hopkin, Mary, 386
Hopkins, Larry, 383
horror films: science fiction/horror hybrids, 361–83; sound design in, 120–21
Hosokawa, Shuhei, 146–53
Howarth, Alan, 382–83
"How Do We Get There?" (Steele), 181
Hull, Clark, 166
human biocomputer, 169, 185–86, 188
humanism, 70–72
Human Use of Human Beings, The (Weiner), 166
Hunters in the Snow, The (Breugel), 331
Huppertz, Gottfried, 44–45, 48–50, 60–72, 78–79, 82

Husarik, Stephen, 137–38
Huston, John, 246, 370
Hyman, Dick, 251
Hymnen (Stockhausen), 242
hyperobjects, 380–81
hypersensitivites: in *Andromeda Strain,* 303; in *Barbarella,* 262; of the body, 372; in *Clockwork Orange,* 311; in *Close Encounters,* 288, 290; Guattari on, 201, 248–49; of machinic unconscious, 285, 343, 362–63, 368; in *Planet of the Apes,* 273; sonic xenomorph, 375; in *Star Wars,* 288; in *2001,* 265

I Ching, 56
IEEE History Center, 311
IEEE Military Electronics conference (1965), 168
Ifukube, Akira, 5, 96, 146–53, 280
Ikarie XB 1 (film), 202, 218–21
"I Love All the Love in You" (song), 251
imaginary music, 305–10
Indian classical music, 34
"Indian Love Call" (Whitman), 144
industrial music, 407
Infinite Music (Harper), 37
Institute for Industrial Psychotechnology, 61–62
in-studio composition, 225
"Insufficiency of the Means for Musical Expression" (Busoni), 117
Intelligent Dance Music, 303
intermedia works, 187–89
"Internationale, The," 54, 207–8
interspecies communication, 168–69
"In the Summertime" (song), 305

intonarumori, 57–58, 113
"Introduction to a Critique of Urban Geography" (Debord), 119
Introduction to Music (Hosokawa), 152
Invaders from Mars (film), 94, 142–43
Invasion of the Astro-Monster (film), 150
Invasion of the Body Snatchers (film), 154
"Invisible Generation, The" (Burroughs), 412
Ironside (television series), 297
"Iron Works" (Mellé), 297
Island of Doctor Moreau, The (Wells), 72
"Is Sound Recording Like a Language?" (Williams), 373
It Came from Outer Space (film), 94–96, 101, 139–43, 155
It! The Terror from Beyond Space (film), 94, 142

Jacobs, Henry, 40, 99, 177–89, 191–92
Jagger, Mick, 342
James, William, 63, 65
Jameson, Fredric, 11–12, 145, 239–40
Järvet, Jüri, 316
Jaws (film), 353
jazz: electronic versions of, 251–52, 299–304; free jazz, 339; "Third Stream" music and, 296–97
Jazz Electronauts, 299
Jerry, Mungo, 305
Jeter, K. W., 401
Johnny Zhivago and The Humpers (band), 305

John Phillip Law, 259
Johnson, Ray, 336
Jourdain, Robert, 404–5
Journey (band), 392
Just Imagine (film), 70–72

Kacírková, Irena, 218
Kael, Pauline, 256
Kafka, Franz, 232
Kahn, Douglas, 58, 86–87, 115–17
kaiju cinema, 150
Kaminskij, Konstantin, 15, 205, 212, 215, 221–22
Kazantsev, Aleksandr, 214
Karzhukov, Mikhail, 216, 222
Keefer, Cindy, 184–85
Kember, Sarah, 33, 364–65, 375
Kennedy, John F., 425
Kepler, Johannes, 34
Khachaturian, Aram, 271
Khrushchev, Nikita, 204
King Crimson (band), 341
King Kong (1933 film), 87, 123
King Kong vs. Godzilla (film), 150
King Who Was a King, The (film), 77
Kino-gazeta (magazine), 47
Kino International DVD and Blu-Ray, 49
Kinonedelya (newspaper), 47
Kinothek series, 50
Kittler, Friedrich, 25, 325–27
Klein-Rogge, Rudolf, 52
Kline, Nathan S., 180
Klushantsev, Pavel, 201–2, 214–15
Koberidze, Otar, 216, 222
Komsomol—The Patron of Electrification (film), 87
Konzett, Matthias, 355

466 • INDEX

Korda, Alexander, 75, 78–79, 82
Korda, Susan, 425
Korngold, Erich Wolfgang, 344
Kovalskij, Konstantin, 216
Kramer, Stanley, 263–64
Kraushaar, Raoul, 142–43
Krippner, Stanley, 200
Kronos (film), 142
Kruchinin, Valentin, 47
Kubrick, Stanley, 6, 120, 193, 199–202; *Clockwork Orange* and, 305–15; *2001* and, 218, 223, 244, 248–49, 263–73, 285, 316, 348
Kuleshov, Lev, 47
Kyser, Kay, 104

Lacan, Jacques, 328
Lackovic, Otto, 218
Ladbrook Grove, 195
Lady in the Dark (film), 87, 123
La fin du monde (film), 59
L'Age d'Or (film), 58
La Jetée (film), 6, 39, 193–94, 225–31, 235, 243, 270–71
La Marche des Machines (film), 58
Landon, Brooks, 340
Lang, Fritz, 25, 48–52, 60–72, 82; Wells's criticism of, 78–79
language: absence of in *2001,* 263–64, 271; in *Alien,* 373–74; of aliens, 22; in *Alphaville,* 231–32, 237–38; in *Clockwork Orange,* 198–99, 306–10; in *Close Encounters,* 352–54; cybernetics and, 175–76, 186–87; of effects, 15–16; of fantasy and futurism, 119–20; Guattari's discussion of, 248–49, 262; of instrumentality, 178–79;

in *Planet of the Apes,* 274–75; of science, 95; science fiction and, 194–95, 197–98, 213–14; in *Solaris,* 327–29, 332–34; as sonic critique, 7; sonic novum and, 197–98; in *Space is the Place,* 286–87; of stimulus and triggers, 30–31; in *THX-1138,* 291–92
Lanois, Daniel, 425
Larson, Glen, 344
Larson, Randall, 300
Laserium, 99
Lavagnino, Angelo Francesco, 250
"La ville inhumaine" (Misraki), 235
Lawrence, Amy, 373–74
Learning from Other Worlds (Parrinder), 13
Léger, Fernand, 53
leitmotif, 50, 125–26; of the Force in *Star Wars,* 348–50
"leit-timbres," 321
Lem, Stanislaw, 197, 209, 218, 316–19
Lemmy Caution, 232–40
Lenin, Nikolai, 2–3
Leningrad Film Studios for Popular-Scientific Films, 201–2
Leonov, Aleksei, 208
Le Petit soldat (film), 225–26
Lerner, Neil, 351–52
"Le roi David" (Honneger), 219–20
Lessour, Théo, 418
Lettrist movement, 119–20
Lévi-Strauss, Claude, 279
Le Voyage dans la lune (film), 43
Lewis, John, 303–4
Leydon, Rebecca, 32, 94–95, 112, 122–23, 165–66, 171–73, 215

Licht-Raum Modulator (Moholy-Nagy), 78, 84
Ligeti, György, 5, 34, 270, 314, 350–51
Light, Enoch, 251
Lilly, John, 98, 167–70, 185–89
"linguistic science fiction," 197–99
Lippert, Robert, 221
Lippert Pictures, 91, 106–7
Lisberger, Steven, 6, 363, 388–98
Liška, Zdeněk, 219, 221
listening: audience engagement and, 31–32; cosmic philosophy and, 37–39; psychedelic experience and, 200–201; recording technology and, 427–34; science fiction film and, 39–41
Liszt, Franz, 50
"Little Bricks" (Kruchinin), 47
Logan's Run (film), 369
London Symphony Orchestra, 75, 82
Lone Ranger, The (television series), 311
Lopate, Phillip, 315
Lorca (album), 305
Lost Weekend, The (film), 123–28
"Love, Love, Love Drags Me Down" (song), 251
Loverboy (band), 49
LSD: The Problem-Solving Psychedelic (Golightly and Stafford), 269–70
Lucas, George, 6, 202, 285–88, 290–95, 343–44, 368
Lumière brothers, 356
Lunacharsky, Anatoly, 67–68

Macbeth (Shakespeare), 413
MacDonald, Scott, 178–79, 192

Macero, Teo, 224–25
machinic unconscious, 248–49, 275, 362–63
Machowski, Ignacy, 212
Maeck, Klaus, 39–40, 120, 407–24
Maetzig, Kurt, 208–9, 213
Magellanic Cloud, The (film), 218
Magical Mystery Tour (album), 305
Magic Sun (film), 336
"Magnetic Pull, The" (Herrmann), 136–39
magnetic tape manipulation, 5
Making of Kubrick's "2001," The (Agel), 263
Mancini, Henry, 142, 155
Man from Planet X, The (film), 94–95, 101
Man Ray, 53
Mansell, Clint, 298
"Man with the Power, The" (*Outer Limits* episode), 247
Marghereti, Antonio, 250
Marinetti, F. T., 57
Marker, Chris, 6, 39, 193–94, 225–31, 243
Markowski, Andrzej, 208–9
"Mars, the Bringer of War" (Holst), 345–47
Mars Attacks! (film), 144
Martin, Tim, 147
Marxism and Form (Jameson), 11
masculine gaze, 257–61
Massen, Osa, 101
Massey, Raymond, 74
Massine, Léonide, 44
Massumi, Brian, 378–79
Mathieson, Muir, 82
Matrix, The (film), 403

468 • INDEX

matrixed surround track, 375
Mattingly, Ken, 428
Maynes, Charles, 207
McDowell, Malcolm, 305
McGinney, William, 280
McKenna, Terence, 249, 258–59, 274–76
McLuhan, Marshall, 254, 413
Mechte Navstrechu (Toward Meeting a Dream) (film), 48, 54, 202, 216–18, 222
Meitus, Iulii, 205
Méliès, Georges, 43, 356
Mellé, Gil, 295–304
Mellotron keyboard, 341
"Melting Sequence" (Hoffman), 140–41
Menzies, William Cameron, 72–84, 142–43
Mercury, Freddie, 49
Mescherin, Vyacheslav, 206–8, 215–16
Metropolis (film), 25, 39, 44–45; cinematic montage in, 78–80; *Decoder* and, 411; psychotechnology in, 60–72; score of, 52–60, 79–80, 82; sonic novum in, 48–52, 109–10; *Things to Come* and, 79–80; Wells's criticism of, 78–79; Yoshiwara sequence in, 67–72
Metzer, David, 242
Meyer-Eppler, Werner, 22
MGM Studios, 153–54, 160, 165, 250, 264
Mickey Mousing effect, 108, 396
Milland, Ray, 125, 143
Miller, Cynthia, 280–81
Mills, Bart, 399
Minawa, Ichiro, 146

Minkler, Mike, 393–94, 397–98
Minnelli, Vincente, 246
Minstrel Man (documentary), 106
Mirror, The (film), 333
Misraki, Paul, 235
Missile to the Moon (film), 142
mixing desk, 301–4
Moebius, 390
Moholy-Nagy, Laszlo, 78, 84
Monster Maker (film), 106
Montenegro, Hugo, 252
Monterey Pop Festival, 299
Moody Blues (band), 341
Moog, Robert, 35–37, 86, 157, 421–22
MOOG: The Eclectic Electrics of Dick Hyman (album), 251
Moog Machine, 252
Moog Power (album), 252
Moog synthesizer: albums using, 251–52; authenticity and, 403–7; classical music and, 310, 313–14, 324–25; hybrid science fiction/ horror films and, 369; popular music and, 341–42; in *TRON*, 390–98
Moorcock, Michael, 194–95
Morgan, Cindy, 395
Moroder, Giorgio, 49–50
Morricone, Ennio, 382–83
Morrison Planetarium, 99, 178, 187–89, 192
Morrissey, Dick, 386
Morrow, Jeff, 156
Morton, Arthur, 280
Morton, Timothy, 33, 380
Moscow Society for the Study of Interplanetary Communication, 48

INDEX • 469

Moylan, Tom, 12–14
Mulhall, Kevin, 267
multichannel mixing: in *Close Encounters,* 355–56; in hybrid science fiction/horror films, 361–62
Multzvok Group, 54
Münsterberg, Hugo, 24, 30, 33, 45, 60, 63–72, 126–27
Murch, Walter, 6, 285, 291–95, 372
Murphy, Dudley, 53
Murzin, Yevgeny, 54, 217
Muscha (Jürgen Muschalek), 362–64, 407–24
Muschalek, Jürgen. *See* Muscha
Musée de L'homme, 277
Music, the Brain and Ecstasy (Jourdain), 404–5
Musica Futurista (album), 56–57
musical semiotics, 32
Music for Airports (album), 427
Music for Heavenly Bodies (Tanner), 252–53
Music for Peace of Mind (album), 89
Music from Outer Space (Comstock), 252
Music from Out of Space (Revel), 252–53
Music from the Moon (album), 428
music in science fiction films: in *Aelita,* 46–48; in *Clockwork Orange,* 305–15; critical analysis of, 106; in *The Day the Earth Stood Still,* 123–39; in *Destination Moon,* 99–105, 108–10; diegetic representation of, 68–72; in *Gojira,* 146–53; imaginary, 305–15; in *It Came from Outer Space,* 94–96, 101, 139–43; in *Metropolis,* 52–60, 79–80, 82; in *Rocketship X-M,* 106–8, 110–13;

theremin and, 3. *See also specific films*
Music Out of the Moon (album), 89, 143, 215
"Music: The Sick Machine," 179
Music to Watch Birds By (album), 257
Music to Watch Girls By (album), 257
musique concrète, 5, 19–24, 87, 159–65, 178, 242
Muzak: in *Decoder,* 407–24; Eno's discussion of, 427–29
"Muzak: A Concept in Human Engineering" (P-Orridge), 419
My Favorite Martian (television series), 143

Napoleon (film), 59
Naropa Institute, 412
National Physical Laboratory, 196–97
Nebo Zovyot (The Sky is Calling) (film), 48, 202–8, 215–16, 219, 222
Neptune's Daughter (film), 64–65
Neumann, Kurt, 4, 91
New Age music, 34
New Concert Orchestra, 228
Newman, Ernest, 90
New Musical Resources (Cowell), 116–17
New World Ensemble, 107
New Worlds (magazine), 194–95, 245
New World Symphony (Dvořák), 428
New York Dramatic Mirror (newspaper), 66–67
New York Herald Tribune, 2
New York World's Fair (1939), 107
Nielsen, Leslie, 172

470 • INDEX

Nietzsche, Friedrich, 14, 145, 240
Night Gallery (television series), 300
Nijinsky, Vaslav, 44
Ninth Symphony (Beethoven), 308, 311–12, 314–15
Noir (Jeter), 401
noise: in *Decoder,* 418–24; Lilly's research on, 169–70; music as, 68–72; sound technology and, 52–60; Varèse's interest in, 114–16
"None Came Back" (Glasser), 121–22
non-harmonics, 86–87
North, Alexander, 6, 265–73
novum: in critical theory, 11; cyborg, 105; dystopia and, 14–17; in media, 364–65; in science fiction, 8–17; visual effects and, 358–60. *See also* fictive novum; sonic novum
nuclear war: in *Gojira,* 148–53; in science fiction films, 100–101, 121–23; in Soviet and Eastern bloc films, 209–14, 219
Nyby, Christian, 95–96, 140

Oakland Youth Development Program, 338
Oberth, Herman, 102
Ocean of Sound (film), 298–99
Ocora record label, 278
Oda, Motoyoshi, 150
Odna (film), 87
O'Donnell, Liam A., 239–40
Off the Planet (Hayward), 7–8
Ondes Martenot, 4, 142
101 Strings Orchestra, 251
"One More Kiss Dear" (song), 400, 406
"Only Solutions" (song), 392

On the Sensations of Tone as a Physiological Basis for the Theory of Music (Helmholtz), 247
optical music synthesis, 54
Oram, Daphne, 54
Oramics, 54
Orchestra of Electro-Musical Instruments, 206
Orff, Carl, 265
Organization, The (film), 297
Orpheus, myth of, 234–35
O'Shea, Milo, 259
Oswald, Richard, 43
other, the: in *Barbarella,* 253–61; in *Gojira,* 151; in *Solaris,* 328–30; sonic novum and, 14, 144–45, 398–99; in *Space is the Place,* 337–43
Outer Limits, The (television series), 142, 247
"Out in Space" (Stevens), 108–9
Out There (album), 339
Out to Lunch (Dolphy), 298–99
Outward Bound (album), 339
"Over the Rainbow" (song), 252
Owens, Buck, 428

pacifist science fiction films, 101
Pal, George, 91–92, 102, 106, 109, 201–2
Pallenberg, Anita, 259
Parables for the Virtual (Massumi), 378–79
Parade (film), 43–44, 53
Parisian Ballets Russes, 43
Parisian Studio 28, 58
Parliament (band), 341
Parrinder, Patrick, 12–13
Partch, Harry, 154

Patterns in Jazz (album), 296
Peck, Gregory, 123
Pelleas und Melisande (Schoenberg), 113
Penderecki, Krzysztof, 5, 208–9, 351
Percussotron III, 300
Performance (film), 342
Perfume Set to Music (album), 89
Perry, Lee "Scratch," 421
Phantom Empire (serial), 71–72
Phantom from Space (film), 94
Phillips, Gene D., 267
Phillips, Stu, 344
Photoplay, The (Münsterberg), 24, 60–72, 126
Picasso, Pablo, 44
Pinch, Trevor, 35, 341–42
Pink Floyd (band), 34, 195, 249, 305, 341, 421
Pinocchio (film), 351
Pisters, Patricia, 26–27, 30
Planeta Bur (Kazantsev), 214
Planeta Bur (film), 48, 202, 214–18, 222
Planet of Blood (film), 222
Planet of the Apes (film), 201, 249, 273–83, 291, 296, 403
Planet of Vampires (film), 222
Planets, The (Holst), 345–47, 369
Platonic complementarity, 34
Pleasence, Donald, 247
Pochepa, T., 216
Polák, Jindrich, 218
Polish Radio Experimental Studio, 208–9
Polt, Harriet, 179
pop culture: in *A Clockwork Orange,* 305–15; electronic music and, 153–54; science fiction and,

17–18; sound design and, 294–95; theremin in, 4, 89–90
pop music: electronic versions of, 251–52
P-Orridge, Genesis, 414, 418–21
posthumanism, 14
Postmodernism (Jameson), 11
Potlach (journal), 119
Powell, Anna, 30–31, 367
Pratella, Frencesco Balilla, 56–57
Prestige label, 296
Primitive Modern (album), 297
Prisoner, The (television series), 244
Programming and Metaprogramming the Human Biocomputer (Lilly), 168
Project Moonbase (film), 142
Prometheus, 234
Protazanov, Yakov, 46–48
protosynthesizers, 4
pseudo-American aesthetic, 44
psychedelic culture: in *Barbarella,* 250–62; *Planet of the Apes* and, 273–83; sound design and, 178–79, 183–84, 196–201; *2001* and, 263–73
psychogeography: in *Blade Runner,* 401–7; in *Decoder,* 410–24; in *Rocketship X-M,* 330–31; in *Solaris,* 316–17, 330–35; sound design and, 119–23
psychological thrillers: sound design in, 123–28, 136–39
Psychology and Industrial Efficiency (Münsterberg), 63
psychotechnology: cinematic consciousness and, 24–32; in *The Day the Earth Stood Still,* 128–39; in *Forbidden Planet,* 154–77; of

472 • INDEX

memory, 227–31; psonicosmos and, 191–92; in science fiction film, 60–72, 97–99; in *Solaris*, 325–35; sound design and, 31–39, 123–28; in *Star Wars*, 347–50; Vortex Concerts and, 179–89
Pynchon, Thomas, 194
Pythagorean music of the spheres, 34

Quadrama (album), 297
Queen of Blood (film), 222–23

Rabinowitz, Peter J., 306–11
Raiders of the Lost Ark (film), 344
Rank, Otto, 327
Ravel, Maurice, 45
Rawlings, Terry, 369
RCA Corporation, 3
Reagan, Ronald, 423–24
Rebel without a Cause (film), 246
"recording composers," 224–25
Red House, The (film), 87, 127
Redner, Gregg, 74, 262
Reinert, Al, 40, 184, 363–65, 425–34
Rennie, Michael, 93
Resnais, Alain, 225
Return of Jesse James, The, 106
Revel, Harry, 89, 251–53
Revised Boy Scout Manual, The (Burroughs), 412, 422
Rhythmicon, 4
Rice, Bill, 409
Riddle, Nelson, 249
Riley, Matthew, 76–77, 81–82, 84
Rimsky-Korsakov, Nikolai, 87–88
Rip-Off record shop, 407
Rite of Spring, The (Stravinsky), 43, 149, 391

Rocketship X-M (film), 4, 39, 91–92, 94; critical reception of, 105–6; music in, 106–8, 110–14, 148, 321; nuclear disaster in, 121–23, 209, 211–14; psychogeography in, 119, 330–31; sound design in, 99–105, 118–19, 206–7, 383–84
Rockmore, Clara, 3, 86, 88–90, 124
Roddenberry, Gene, 210
Roeg, Nicholas, 342
Romadin, Mikhail, 325
Rosar, William, 109–10
Rose, David, 156
Rosen, Lucie Bigelow, 3, 86, 89–90
Rosenman, Leonard, 245–48, 281
Ross, Alex, 16, 44, 113–14, 247
Rossini, Gioachino, 311, 313
Roussos, Demis, 386
Rózsa, Miklós, 123–28, 136
rumorarmonio, 57–58
Rundfunk Symphony Orchestra, 49
Russian Orthodox Cathedral Choir of Paris, 227–28
Russolo, Luigi, 56–58, 60, 113, 116

Saint-Saën, Camille, 3
Salter, Hans J., 155
Sandall, Roger, 179
Sanderson, William, 399
Satie, Erik, 44, 53
Saturn 3 (film), 344
Saunders, Pharaoh, 339
Sayonara Jupiter (film), 344
Schacht, Roland (Balthasar), 50
Schaeffer, Pierre, 19–23, 33, 38, 157–60, 162–64, 238–39, 278–79, 304, 310; Boulez and, 278–79; on listening, 310; on musique

concrète, 19, 23, 137, 159, 278–79; on "musique habituelle," 279; on sonorous object, 19–24, 33, 38, 159, 162–63, 238–39, 304; on sound and composition, 157–58

Schafer, R. Murray, 271–72

Schaffner, Franklin, 201, 273–83

Schallert, William, 95

Schary, Dore, 154, 159–60, 164–65

Schillinger, Joseph, 4

"schizophonia," 271–72

Schmidt, Lisa, 15, 18, 112, 114, 358, 403–4

Schoenberg, Arnold, 5, 11, 113–14, 118, 160, 247

Schuller, Gunther, 296, 303–4

science fiction film: composers for, 5; internationalization of, 192–201; Lettrist and situationist philosophies and, 119–20; listening to, 39–41; novum and, 8–17; science fiction/horror hybrids, 361–83; sonic novum in, 17–24; sound innovation and, 4–8; theremin in, 4, 84–90; untimeliness in, 145

science fiction writing, 193–95

scientific discovery: science fiction films and, 99–114

Scott, Barbara, 305

Scott, Raymond, 157

Scott, Ridley, 6, 120, 246, 361–63, 367–83, 397

Scriabin, Alexander Nikolayevich, 5, 217, 323–24

Seale, Bobby, 337

Sebastian, John, 222

Sebesky, Dan, 251–52

Second Quartet of 1908 (Schoenberg), 113

Second Viennese School, 5

"Seli" (Garcia Abril), 250

Selznick, David, 123

Serafine, Frank, 393

serialism, 5, 161–62

Serling, Rod, 274, 300

sex: in *Barbarella*, 253–61

"Sex and the Married Frog," 414

Shape of Jazz to Come, The (album), 339

"Shape of Things to Come" (song), 199

Sharma, Shailja, 311–12

Shaviro, Steven, 33, 255, 264, 375–76, 378–79

Shklovsky, Viktor, 331–33

Shore, Howard, 144, 298

Shostakovich, Dmitri, 208

Siddiqi, Asif, 47–48

Siegel, Don, 154

Siemens Studio for Electronic Music, 157

Simon, Günther, 209

"Singin' in the Rain" (song), 308, 314

Siodmak, Robert, 106, 126–27

sirens: theremin compared with, 113; Varèse on, 114–15

situationist psychogeography, 119–20

Six Million Dollar Man, The (television series), 297

Sixties Spiritual Awakening, The (Ellwood), 264

Skerrit, Tom, 379–80

Sketch of a New Esthetic of Music (Busoni), 117

Skotak, Robert, 202

474 • INDEX

Snow Devils (film), 240
Sobchack, Vivian: on authenticity, 102; on *Close Encounters,* 352–53; on *Forbidden Planet,* 158–59, 176; on Soviet film, 221; on *Star Wars,* 345; on technology in films, 118–19; on theremin, 141
Society of Motion Picture and Television Engineeres (SMPTE), 391–92
Solaris (film), 48, 54, 217, 286, 315–35, 384, 398
Solaris (Lem), 316–19
Solntseva, Yuliya, 46
Solonitsyn, Anatoli, 316
"Sonata for Executioner, and Various Young Women" (song), 259
sonic novum, 17–24; in *Alphaville,* 238–44; ambient and alien forms of, 91–99; in *Barbarella,* 249–62; in *Clockwork Orange,* 312–15; in *The Day the Earth Stood Still,* 129–39; in Eastern Bloc films, 208–14; in *Forbidden Planet,* 158–59; hallucinogenics and, 196–97; Lettrist and situationist philosophies and, 119–20; in *Metropolis,* 52; in *Planet of the Apes,* 282–83; in science fiction/horror hybrids, 361, 367–83; in *Solaris,* 319–35; in Soviet films, 201–8; in *Space is the Place,* 336–43; in *2001,* 199–201
sonic objects, 8–17
sonic psychotechnologies, 31–39
sonic regeneration device, 134–35
Sonovox processing, 93, 103–5, 117–19, 330

sound design: Americanization of Soviet films, 143, 192–93, 203–4, 218–25; authenticity in science fiction films and, 102–3; early experiments in, 52–60; film music and, 4–8, 27–31; sound effects in, 345–50; syncretic value of, 117–18; in thrillers, 123–28, 136–39. *See also specific films*
Sound Design and Science Fiction (Whittington), 6–7
Sounds of the Future (Bartkowiak), 7–8
Soviet films: Americanized versions of, 143, 192–93, 203–4, 211–12, 218–225; science fiction, 46–48, 192–93, 201–25, 286, 315–35. *See also specific films*
Sovkino, 47
Sovkino film trust, 46–47
space art, 102
Spaced Out (album), 251
Spaceflight IC-1 (film), 221
Space Is the Place (film), 120, 286–87, 335–43; racial conflict in, 336–43
"Space Station Docking" (North), 266
Spaceways (film), 336
Spartacus (film), 265
Spassky, Piotr V., 228
spectacle, 352–53
Spectator (magazine), 315
Spellbound (film), 123–28
SPFx (magazine), 28
Spielberg, Steven, 220, 286, 343–44, 350–60
Spiral Staircase, The (film), 126–27
spiritualism, 65

Sputnik, 202
Stafford, P. G., 269–70
Starcrash (film), 344, 353
Starlog (magazine), 28
Star Trek (television series), 210, 244, 426
Star Trek: The Motion Picture (film), 344, 353, 369–70
Star Wars (1977 film), 6, 39, 286–91; Dolby Surround mixes in, 358–60; sound design in, 342–50, 365, 368, 388–89, 400, 403
Steele, Jack E., 181
Stein, Herman, 142, 155, 212
Stein, Ronald, 222
Steiner, Max, 123
"Stella by Starlight" (song), 252
Stevens, Leith, 92, 103–4, 108–10, 212, 433–34
Stiller, Andrew, 405–6
Stockhausen, Karlheinz, 22, 34, 160, 171, 242–43, 277–83
Stokowski, Leopold, 2, 4
Strauss, Johann, 199–200, 265
Strauss, Richard, 76, 265, 345, 348
Stravinsky, Igor, 5, 43, 76, 149, 278, 391
"Strobe Crystal Green" (Mellé), 303
Strobel, Frank, 49
Student of Prague (film), 326–27
subjectivity: auditory modes of, 23; cultural constructions of, 310–11, 355–56; Guattari on, 33; information technology and, 25; of listener, 20–21; marketed listening and, 359; of music, 294, 379; objectivity and, 157–58; psychedelics and, 249; sonic psychotechnolo-

gies and, 31–32; sound object and, 304; visual effects and, 357
Sumac, Yma, 215–16
Sun Ra and his Arkestra (band), 34, 286–87, 299, 335–43
Superman (film), 344
Suvin, Darko: on novum, 15–16, 197, 365; on science fiction forms, 9–11, 12, 145
Switched-On Bach (album), 313, 389
Symphonie Fantastique (Berlioz), 428
Symphony for Factory Whistles (Avraamov), 53–54
Symphony No. 2 *"Romantic"* (Hanson), 370
synchresis, 103
synchronized sound: atmospherics and, 431–32; emergence of, 70–72; in *Things to Come,* 76–77, 83–84
Synergy, 298
synthesizers, 157, 251–52, 299; ARP 2500 and 2600 modular synthesizers, 354–55; authenticity in use of, 403–7; in *Space is the Place,* 338–43; in *TRON,* 389–98; in *The Thing,* 377–78
Szwed, John, 343

Tangerine Dream (band), 298, 303, 341
Tanner, Paul, 143, 157, 252–53
tape collage, 56, 96–99, 386–87; Burroughs's discussion of, 412–14; in *Decoder,* 412–24; in *Forbidden Planet,* 164–65, 171–77; in *Gojira,* 147–53; technology, 5–6
Tarkovsky, Andrei, 217, 286, 315–35

476 • INDEX

Tarzan versus IBM. See *Alphaville: A Strange Adventure of Lemmy Caution*
Taylor, Timothy, 160–62, 254
Tchaikovsky, Peter I., 50
Technical Academy of Berlin-Charlottenburg, 61–62
technoacousmatic: cinematic immersion and, 27–31; sonic novum and, 22
technology development: science fiction films and, 99–114, 118–19
television: electronic music in, 17
Telotte, J. P., 71
Tempest, The (Shakespeare), 155
Terkel, Joe, 384
Terminator 2: Judgment Day (film), 202, 357
territorialization of sound, 33, 143, 254, 257–58, 261–62, 265
Terrore Nello Spazio (Planet of the Vampires) (film), 220
"Thème d'amour" (Misraki), 235
theremin: decline in use of, 141–45; in horror film music, 123; impact on music of, 3, 22, 84–90, 114–17; invention of, 1–3; modifications to, 3–4; in pop culture, 4, 89–90; in psychological dramas, 123–28; in science fiction films, 92–99, 106–8, 110–14, 117–23; in Soviet films, 206–8; in Varèse's work, 106
Theremin, Léon: invention of theremin and, 1–3, 85–86; sound research by, 113, 117; theremin modifications, 3–4
Theremin Electrical Symphony Orchestra, 3

Theremin Electro-Ensemble, 3
Thing, The (film), 39, 94–96, 361–62, 367–68, 372, 374, 375–76, 377–79, 381–83
"Thing at the Door, The" (Hoffman), 140–41
Thing from Another World, The (film), 94–96, 110, 118, 140, 361–62
thingness: of sonic novum, 19, 96, 139, 159, 326, 334, 375
Things to Come (film and novel), 39, 44–46, 72–84, 78–80
"*Things to Come* Suite" (Bliss), 75
"Third Stream" music, 296–97
13th Power, 199
This Island Earth (film), 39, 155–56, 212, 288
Thomas, Derek, 222
Thousand Plateaus, A (Deleuze and Guattari), 257–58
Threnody for the Victims of Hiroshima (Penderecki), 351
THX-1138 (film), 6, 285, 290–95, 343, 362
Tibbetts, John, 106
Ticket That Exploded, The (Burroughs), 411–12
Tikka, Pia, 26–27, 30
Time Machine, The (Wells), 72
Time (magazine), 179
Time Out of Mind (film), 106
Tiomkin, Dimitri, 110, 141–43
Titanic (film), 202
"Toccata and Fugue in D Minor" (Bach), 259
Tognazzi, Ugo, 255
Toho Studio, 146–47, 149, 344
Tolstoy, Aleksey Nikolayevich, 46

INDEX • 477

Tome VI (album), 299–301
Toop, David, 298–99
Total Recall (film), 403
Treatise on Musical Objects (Schaeffer), 19–20
"Trip to the Moon" (North), 266
Triumph of the Will (film), 350
Trocco, Frank, 35, 341–42
TRON (film), 6, 40, 357, 362–63, 365, 388–98, 405
"Tropaire En L'Honneur De La Sainte Croix," 228
Troshin, Vladimir, 215
Trumbo, Dalton, 105–6
Tsereteli, Nikolai, 46
twelve-tone music, 5, 160–61, 245–48
20,000 Leagues Under the Sea (film), 245
Twilight Zone, The (television series), 142
2001: A Space Odyssey (film): cybernetics in, 244; influence of, 223; music used in, 6, 199–201, 305, 314, 403; *Solaris* compared with, 315–16, 320; sound design in, 39, 248–49, 262–73, 344; Soviet films and, 218

UFA studios, 49
UFO Club, 195
Ulmer, Edgar G., 95
Ultrachromatic music, 54, 57
Understanding Media (McLuhan), 254, 413
United Kingdom: science fiction films in, 195–201
Universal Studio, 142, 155

untimeliness, 145
"Uranus Unmasked" (song), 252–53
used-future aesthetics, 368–69
U.S.S.R. State Orchestra, 205–6

Vadim, Roger, 201, 248–62
"Valse triste" (Misraki), 235
Van Doren, Mamie, 222
Vangelis, 298, 363, 385–88, 391, 397–407, 429
Varela, Francisco, 167
Varèse, Edgard, 86, 106, 114–16, 137, 265
Variations V (Cage), 86
Variety (magazine), 106, 213, 263–64
"Vastness of Space," 228
Verdens Undergang (film), 43
Verne, Jules, 245
Vernon, Howard, 232
Vers les Robots (film), 58
"Vibrations from Venus" (song), 252
visual effects, 356–60
Voegelin, Salomé, 31–32, 37
Voice of the Xtabay (Baxter), 215
Volodin, Andrei, 206
Vortex Concerts, 40, 99, 177–89, 191–92
Vox label, 49
Voyage to the End of the Universe (film), 218, 220
Voyage to the Planet of Prehistoric Women (film), 222–23
Voyage to the Prehistoric Planet (film), 222

Wagner, Richard, 50, 76–77, 102, 125, 127, 345, 389
Wajda, Andrzej, 209

Walston, Ray, 143

Walter Carlos' A Clockwork Orange (album), 389

War between the Planets (film), 250

Warner Bros. studios, 389

War of the Planets (film), 250

War of the Worlds, The (Wells), 72, 95, 109–10

Warren-Gregory effect, 197

Wassen, Henry, 420

"Wave of a Hand Draws Music from the Air" (Gilman), 1–2

Waxman, Franz, 123

Weaver, Sigourney, 369

Webb, Roy, 126–27

Webern, Anton, 160, 247

Welch, Racquel, 245

Wells, H. G., 43, 72–84

Wesson, Dick, 100

Westdeutscher Rundfunk (WDR) studios, 22–23

"When You Wish Upon a Star" (song), 252, 351, 355

Whitman, Slim, 144

Whittington, William: on *Aliens,* 371–75, 379–80; on *Alphaville,* 230, 241; on *Close Encounters,* 356; on *La Jetée,* 271; on psychotechnology, 97; on sound design, 6–7, 28–29, 357–59, 373–75; on *The Thing,* 378

Wide Angle (magazine), 350

Wiene, Robert, 64

Wiener, Norbert, 98–99, 156, 166–67

Wierzbicki, James, 95, 122, 127

Wilcox, Fred, 97

Wild, Wild Planet (film), 250

Wild Boys, The (Burroughs), 411–12

Wilder, Billy, 123

Wild in the Streets (film), 198–99

Williams, Alan, 373–74

Williams, John, 287–90; *Close Encounters* score by, 350–60, 388; *Star Wars* score by, 344–50, 368–69, 388

Williams, Tony, 350

Williams Mix (Cage), 56

"William Tell Overture" (Rossini), 311

Winters, Shelley, 199

Wise, Robert, 93, 285, 295–304

Wolf Man, The (film), 212

Wollheim, Donald A., 195

workplace regulation: psychotechnology and, 62–72

Work, Wealth, and Happiness of Mankind, The (Wells), 72

X: The Man with the X-ray Eyes (film), 143

Yamaha CS-80, 386

Yardbirds, 250

"You Can't Always Get What You Want" (song), 305

You'll Find Out (film), 104

Young, Neil, 305

Young, Sean, 384

Youngblood, Gene, 178–79, 183–84, 187–89

Your Turn, Darling (film), 234

Zeglio, Primo, 250

Zepke, Stephen, 12–15, 145, 239–41, 289

Zimmer, Hans, 298

Zuberi, Nabeel, 338–40

Zylinska, Joanna, 33, 364–65, 375

Trace Reddell is associate professor of emergent digital practices at the University of Denver.

CPSIA information can be obtained
at www.ICGtesting.com
Printed in the USA
BVHW040033310119
539072BV00008B/31/P